PORTFOLIO MANAGEMENT, ETHICAL AND PROFESSIONAL STANDARDS

CFA® Program Curriculum
2023 • LEVEL 2 • VOLUME 6

WILEY

©2022 by CFA Institute. All rights reserved. This copyright covers material written expressly for this volume by the editor/s as well as the compilation itself. It does not cover the individual selections herein that first appeared elsewhere. Permission to reprint these has been obtained by CFA Institute for this edition only. Further reproductions by any means, electronic or mechanical, including photocopying and recording, or by any information storage or retrieval systems, must be arranged with the individual copyright holders noted.

CFA®, Chartered Financial Analyst®, AIMR-PPS®, and GIPS® are just a few of the trademarks owned by CFA Institute. To view a list of CFA Institute trademarks and the Guide for Use of CFA Institute Marks, please visit our website at www.cfainstitute.org.

This publication is designed to provide accurate and authoritative information in regard to the subject matter covered. It is sold with the understanding that the publisher is not engaged in rendering legal, accounting, or other professional service. If legal advice or other expert assistance is required, the services of a competent professional should be sought.

All trademarks, service marks, registered trademarks, and registered service marks are the property of their respective owners and are used herein for identification purposes only.

ISBN 978-1-953337-10-8 (paper)
ISBN 978-1-953337-34-4 (ebook)

2022

Please visit our website at
www.WileyGlobalFinance.com.

CONTENTS

How to Use the CFA Program Curriculum		**xv**
	Errata	xv
	Designing Your Personal Study Program	xv
	CFA Institute Learning Ecosystem (LES)	xvi
	Feedback	xvi

Portfolio Management

Learning Module 1	**Economics and Investment Markets**	**3**
	Introduction	4
	The Present Value Model	4
	The Present Value Model	4
	Expectations and Asset Values	6
	The Discount Rate on Real Default-Free Bonds: Interest Rates	7
	Real Default-Free Interest Rates	8
	The Discount Rate on Real Default-Free Bonds: Uncertainty and Risk Premiums	11
	The Discount Rate on Real Default-Free Bonds: Risk Premiums on Risky Assets	13
	Default-Free Interest Rates and Economic Growth	17
	Real Default-Free Interest Rates and the Business Cycle	20
	Economic Growth and Real Yields	20
	Real Default-Free Interest Rate Summary	27
	The Yield Curve and the Business Cycle	27
	Short-Term Nominal Interest Rates and the Business Cycle	28
	Treasury Bills and the Business Cycle	29
	Short-Term Interest Rate Summary	34
	Conventional Government Bonds and Break-even Inflation Rates	34
	Break-Even Inflation Rates	34
	The Default-Free Yield Curve and the Business Cycle	38
	The Slope of the Yield Curve and the Term Spread	42
	The Term Spread and the Business Cycle	43
	Evidence on Risk Premiums for Default-Free Bonds	46
	Other Factors	49
	Credit Premiums and the Business Cycle	51
	Credit Spreads and the Credit Risk Premium	53
	Industry- and Company-Specific Credit Quality	57
	Company-Specific Factors	59
	Sovereign Credit Risk	60
	Credit Premium Summary	62
	Equities and the Equity Risk Premium	63
	Equities and Bad Consumption Outcomes	64
	Earnings Growth and the Economic Cycle	66
	How Big is the Equity Risk Premium?	71
	Valuation Multiples	72

◙ indicates an optional segment

	Commercial Real Estate	75
	Regular Cash Flow from Commercial Real Estate Investments	75
	The Pricing Formula for Commercial Real Estate	76
	Commercial Real Estate and the Business Cycle	78
	Summary	*80*
	References	*83*
	Practice Problems	*84*
	Solutions	*90*
Learning Module 2	**Analysis of Active Portfolio Management**	**95**
	Introduction	95
	Active Management and Value Added	96
	Choice of Benchmark	97
	Measuring Value Added	97
	Decomposition of Value Added	99
	The Sharpe Ratio and The Information Ratio	101
	The Sharpe Ratio	101
	The Information Ratio	104
	Constructing Optimal Portfolios	107
	Active Security Returns and The Fundamental Law of Active Management	112
	Active Security Returns	112
	The Basic Fundamental Law	116
	The Full Fundamental Law	118
	Ex Post Performance Measurement	121
	Applications of the Fundamental Law and Global Equity Strategy	123
	Global Equity Strategy	123
	Fixed-Income Strategies	130
	Practical Limitations	136
	Ex Ante Measurement of Skill	136
	Independence of Investment Decisions	137
	Summary	*139*
	References	*141*
	Practice Problems	*142*
	Solutions	*152*
Learning Module 3	**Trading Costs and Electronic Markets**	**159**
	Costs of Trading	159
	Costs of Trading	160
	Effective Spreads and Volume-Weighted Cost Estimates	163
	Implementation Shortfall	164
	VWAP Transaction Cost Estimates	165
	Development of Electronic Markets	167
	Electronic Trading	167
	Advantages of Electronic Trading Systems	168
	Electronification of Bond Markets	168
	Market Fragmentation	169
	Effects on Transaction Costs	170
	Types of Electronic Traders	170
	The Major Types of Electronic Traders	171

◙ indicates an optional segment

Contents

	Electronic Trading System: Characteristics and Uses	173
	Why Speed Matters	174
	Fast Communications	175
	Fast Computations	176
	Advanced Orders, Tactics, and Algorithms	177
	Select Examples of How Electronic Trading Changed Trading Strategies	180
	Electronic Trading Risks	183
	The HFT Arms Race	183
	Systemic Risks of Electronic Trading	183
	Detecting Abusive Trading Practices	188
	Summary	*191*
	Practice Problems	*193*
	Solutions	*198*

Ethical and Professional Standards

Learning Module 1	**Code of Ethics and Standards of Professional Conduct**	**205**
	Preface	205
	Evolution of the CFA Institute Code of Ethics and Standards of Professional Conduct	206
	Standards of Practice Handbook	206
	Summary of Changes in the Eleventh Edition	207
	CFA Institute Professional Conduct Program	209
	Adoption of the Code and Standards	210
	Acknowledgments	210
	Ethics and the Investment Industry	211
	Why Ethics Matters	211
	CFA Institute Code of Ethics and Standards of Professional Conduct	215
	Preamble	215
	The Code of Ethics	216
	Standards of Professional Conduct	216
Learning Module 2	**Guidance for Standards I–VII**	**221**
	Standard I(A): Professionalism - Knowledge of the Law	221
	Standard I(A) Knowledge of the Law	221
	Guidance	221
	Standard I(A): Recommended Procedures	226
	Members and Candidates	226
	Distribution Area Laws	226
	Legal Counsel	226
	Dissociation	226
	Firms	227
	Standard I(A): Application of the Standard	227
	Example 1 (Notification of Known Violations):	227
	Example 2 (Dissociating from a Violation):	228
	Example 3 (Dissociating from a Violation):	228
	Example 4 (Following the Highest Requirements):	228
	Example 5 (Following the Highest Requirements):	229

indicates an optional segment

Example 6 (Laws and Regulations Based on Religious Tenets):	229
Example 7 (Reporting Potential Unethical Actions):	229
Example 8 (Failure to Maintain Knowledge of the Law):	230
Standard I(B): Professionalism - Independence and Objectivity	230
Guidance	230
Standard I(B): Recommended Procedures	236
Standard I(B): Application of the Standard	237
Example 1 (Travel Expenses):	237
Example 2 (Research Independence):	238
Example 3 (Research Independence and Intrafirm Pressure):	238
Example 4 (Research Independence and Issuer Relationship Pressure):	238
Example 5 (Research Independence and Sales Pressure):	239
Example 6 (Research Independence and Prior Coverage):	239
Example 7 (Gifts and Entertainment from Related Party):	239
Example 8 (Gifts and Entertainment from Client):	240
Example 9 (Travel Expenses from External Manager):	240
Example 10 (Research Independence and Compensation Arrangements):	241
Example 11 (Recommendation Objectivity and Service Fees):	241
Example 12 (Recommendation Objectivity):	242
Example 13 (Influencing Manager Selection Decisions):	242
Example 14 (Influencing Manager Selection Decisions):	243
Example 15 (Fund Manager Relationships):	243
Example 16 (Intrafirm Pressure):	243
Standard I(C): Professionalism – Misrepresentation	244
Guidance	244
Standard I(C): Recommended Procedures	248
Factual Presentations	248
Qualification Summary	248
Verify Outside Information	248
Maintain Webpages	249
Plagiarism Policy	249
Standard I(C): Application of the Standard	249
Example 1 (Disclosure of Issuer-Paid Research):	249
Example 2 (Correction of Unintentional Errors):	250
Example 3 (Noncorrection of Known Errors):	250
Example 4 (Plagiarism):	250
Example 5 (Misrepresentation of Information):	251
Example 6 (Potential Information Misrepresentation):	251
Example 7 (Plagiarism):	251
Example 8 (Plagiarism):	252
Example 9 (Plagiarism):	252
Example 10 (Plagiarism):	252
Example 11 (Misrepresentation of Information):	253
Example 12 (Misrepresentation of Information):	253
Example 13 (Avoiding a Misrepresentation):	254
Example 14 (Misrepresenting Composite Construction):	254
Example 15 (Presenting Out-of-Date Information):	254
Example 16 (Overemphasis of Firm Results):	255

◙ indicates an optional segment

Standard I(D): Professionalism – Misconduct	255
Guidance	255
Standard I(D): Recommended Procedures	256
Standard I(D): Application of the Standard	257
Example 1 (Professionalism and Competence):	257
Example 2 (Fraud and Deceit):	257
Example 3 (Fraud and Deceit):	257
Example 4 (Personal Actions and Integrity):	258
Example 5 (Professional Misconduct):	258
Standard II(A): Integrity of Capital Markets - Material Nonpublic Information	258
Standard II(A) Material Nonpublic Information	259
Guidance	259
Standard II(A): Recommended Procedures	263
Achieve Public Dissemination	263
Adopt Compliance Procedures	263
Adopt Disclosure Procedures	263
Issue Press Releases	264
Firewall Elements	264
Appropriate Interdepartmental Communications	264
Physical Separation of Departments	264
Prevention of Personnel Overlap	265
A Reporting System	265
Personal Trading Limitations	265
Record Maintenance	266
Proprietary Trading Procedures	266
Communication to All Employees	266
Standard II(A): Application of the Standard	267
Example 1 (Acting on Nonpublic Information):	267
Example 2 (Controlling Nonpublic Information):	267
Example 3 (Selective Disclosure of Material Information):	267
Example 4 (Determining Materiality):	268
Example 5 (Applying the Mosaic Theory):	268
Example 6 (Applying the Mosaic Theory):	269
Example 7 (Analyst Recommendations as Material Nonpublic Information):	269
Example 8 (Acting on Nonpublic Information):	269
Example 9 (Mosaic Theory):	270
Example 10 (Materiality Determination):	270
Example 11 (Using an Expert Network):	271
Example 12 (Using an Expert Network):	271
Standard II(B): Integrity of Capital Markets - Market Manipulation	271
Guidance	272
Standard II(B): Application of the Standard	273
Example 1 (Independent Analysis and Company Promotion):	273
Example 2 (Personal Trading Practices and Price):	273
Example 3 (Creating Artificial Price Volatility):	274
Example 4 (Personal Trading and Volume):	274
Example 5 ("Pump-Priming" Strategy):	274
Example 6 (Creating Artificial Price Volatility):	275

◙ indicates an optional segment

Example 7 (Pump and Dump Strategy):	276
Example 8 (Manipulating Model Inputs):	276
Example 9 (Information Manipulation):	276
Standard III(A): Duties to Clients - Loyalty, Prudence, and Care	277
Standard III(A) Loyalty, Prudence, and Care	277
Guidance	277
Standard III(A): Recommended Procedures	281
Regular Account Information	281
Client Approval	281
Firm Policies	281
Standard III(A): Application of the Standard	282
Example 1 (Identifying the Client—Plan Participants):	282
Example 2 (Client Commission Practices):	283
Example 3 (Brokerage Arrangements):	283
Example 4 (Brokerage Arrangements):	284
Example 5 (Client Commission Practices):	284
Example 6 (Excessive Trading):	284
Example 7 (Managing Family Accounts):	285
Example 8 (Identifying the Client):	285
Example 9 (Identifying the Client):	285
Example 10 (Client Loyalty):	286
Example 11 (Execution-Only Responsibilities):	286
Standard III(B): Duties to Clients - Fair Dealing	286
Guidance	287
Standard III(B): Recommended Procedures	289
Develop Firm Policies	289
Disclose Trade Allocation Procedures	291
Establish Systematic Account Review	291
Disclose Levels of Service	291
Standard III(B): Application of the Standard	291
Example 1 (Selective Disclosure):	291
Example 2 (Fair Dealing between Funds):	292
Example 3 (Fair Dealing and IPO Distribution):	292
Example 4 (Fair Dealing and Transaction Allocation):	293
Example 5 (Selective Disclosure):	293
Example 6 (Additional Services for Select Clients):	293
Example 7 (Minimum Lot Allocations):	294
Example 8 (Excessive Trading):	294
Example 9 (Limited Social Media Disclosures):	294
Example 10 (Fair Dealing between Clients):	295
Standard III(C): Duties to Clients – Suitability	295
Guidance	296
Standard III(C): Recommended Procedures	299
Investment Policy Statement	299
Regular Updates	299
Suitability Test Policies	299
Standard III(C): Application of the Standard	300
Example 1 (Investment Suitability—Risk Profile):	300
Example 2 (Investment Suitability—Entire Portfolio):	300

◙ indicates an optional segment

Example 3 (IPS Updating):	301
Example 4 (Following an Investment Mandate):	301
Example 5 (IPS Requirements and Limitations):	301
Example 6 (Submanager and IPS Reviews):	302
Example 7 (Investment Suitability—Risk Profile):	302
Example 8 (Investment Suitability):	303
Standard III(D): Duties to Clients - Performance Presentation	303
Guidance	303
Standard III(D): Recommended Procedures	304
Apply the GIPS Standards	304
Compliance without Applying GIPS Standards	304
Standard III(D): Application of the Standard	305
Example 1 (Performance Calculation and Length of Time):	305
Example 2 (Performance Calculation and Asset Weighting):	305
Example 3 (Performance Presentation and Prior Fund/Employer):	305
Example 4 (Performance Presentation and Simulated Results):	306
Example 5 (Performance Calculation and Selected Accounts Only):	306
Example 6 (Performance Attribution Changes):	307
Example 7 (Performance Calculation Methodology Disclosure):	307
Example 8 (Performance Calculation Methodology Disclosure):	307
Standard III(E): Duties to Clients - Preservation of Confidentiality	308
Guidance	308
Standard III(E): Recommended Procedures	309
Communicating with Clients	310
Standard III(E): Application of the Standard	310
Example 1 (Possessing Confidential Information):	310
Example 2 (Disclosing Confidential Information):	311
Example 3 (Disclosing Possible Illegal Activity):	311
Example 4 (Disclosing Possible Illegal Activity):	311
Example 5 (Accidental Disclosure of Confidential Information):	311
Standard IV(A): Duties to Employers – Loyalty	312
Standard IV(A) Loyalty	312
Guidance	312
Standard IV(A): Recommended Procedures	316
Competition Policy	316
Termination Policy	316
Incident-Reporting Procedures	316
Employee Classification	317
Standard IV(A): Application of the Standard	317
Example 1 (Soliciting Former Clients):	317
Example 2 (Former Employer's Documents and Files):	317
Example 3 (Addressing Rumors):	318
Example 4 (Ownership of Completed Prior Work):	318
Example 5 (Ownership of Completed Prior Work):	319
Example 6 (Soliciting Former Clients):	319
Example 7 (Starting a New Firm):	320
Example 8 (Competing with Current Employer):	320
Example 9 (Externally Compensated Assignments):	320
Example 10 (Soliciting Former Clients):	320

◙ indicates an optional segment

Example 11 (Whistleblowing Actions):	321
Example 12 (Soliciting Former Clients):	321
Example 13 (Notification of Code and Standards):	322
Example 14 (Leaving an Employer):	322
Example 15 (Confidential Firm Information):	323
Standard IV(B): Duties to Employers - Additional Compensation Arrangements	323
Guidance	323
Standard IV(B): Recommended Procedures	324
Standard IV(B): Application of the Standard	324
Example 1 (Notification of Client Bonus Compensation):	324
Example 2 (Notification of Outside Compensation):	325
Example 3 (Prior Approval for Outside Compensation):	325
Standard IV(C): Duties to Employers - Responsibilities of Supervisors	326
Guidance	326
Standard IV(C): Recommended Procedures	328
Codes of Ethics or Compliance Procedures	328
Adequate Compliance Procedures	329
Implementation of Compliance Education and Training	330
Establish an Appropriate Incentive Structure	330
Standard IV(C): Application of the Standard	330
Example 1 (Supervising Research Activities):	331
Example 2 (Supervising Research Activities):	331
Example 3 (Supervising Trading Activities):	331
Example 4 (Supervising Trading Activities and Record Keeping):	332
Example 5 (Accepting Responsibility):	332
Example 6 (Inadequate Procedures):	333
Example 7 (Inadequate Supervision):	333
Example 8 (Supervising Research Activities):	334
Example 9 (Supervising Research Activities):	334
Standard V(A): Investment Analysis, Recommendations, and Actions - Diligence and Reasonable Basis	335
Standard V(A) Diligence and Reasonable Basis	335
Guidance	335
Standard V(A): Recommended Procedures	339
Standard V(A): Application of the Standard	340
Example 1 (Sufficient Due Diligence):	340
Example 2 (Sufficient Scenario Testing):	340
Example 3 (Developing a Reasonable Basis):	341
Example 4 (Timely Client Updates):	341
Example 5 (Group Research Opinions):	341
Example 6 (Reliance on Third-Party Research):	342
Example 7 (Due Diligence in Submanager Selection):	342
Example 8 (Sufficient Due Diligence):	343
Example 9 (Sufficient Due Diligence):	343
Example 10 (Sufficient Due Diligence):	343
Example 11 (Use of Quantitatively Oriented Models):	344
Example 12 (Successful Due Diligence/Failed Investment):	344
Example 13 (Quantitative Model Diligence):	345

◙ indicates an optional segment

Contents xi

Example 14 (Selecting a Service Provider):	345
Example 15 (Subadviser Selection):	346
Example 16 (Manager Selection):	346
Example 17 (Technical Model Requirements):	346
Standard V(B): Investment Analysis, Recommendations, and Actions - Communication with Clients and Prospective Clients	347
Guidance	348
Standard V(B): Recommended Procedures	350
Standard V(B): Application of the Standard	351
Example 1 (Sufficient Disclosure of Investment System):	351
Example 2 (Providing Opinions as Facts):	351
Example 3 (Proper Description of a Security):	352
Example 4 (Notification of Fund Mandate Change):	352
Example 5 (Notification of Fund Mandate Change):	353
Example 6 (Notification of Changes to the Investment Process):	353
Example 7 (Notification of Changes to the Investment Process):	353
Example 8 (Notification of Changes to the Investment Process):	353
Example 9 (Sufficient Disclosure of Investment System):	354
Example 10 (Notification of Changes to the Investment Process):	354
Example 11 (Notification of Errors):	354
Example 12 (Notification of Risks and Limitations):	355
Example 13 (Notification of Risks and Limitations):	356
Example 14 (Notification of Risks and Limitations):	356
Standard V(C): Investment Analysis, Recommendations, and Actions - Record Retention	357
Guidance	357
Standard V(C): Recommended Procedures	358
Standard V(C): Application of the Standard	359
Example 1 (Record Retention and IPS Objectives and Recommendations):	359
Example 2 (Record Retention and Research Process):	359
Example 3 (Records as Firm, Not Employee, Property):	359
Standard VI(A): Conflicts of Interest - Disclosure of Conflicts	360
Standard VI(A) Disclosure of Conflicts	360
Guidance	360
Standard VI(A): Recommended Procedures	363
Standard VI(A): Application of the Standard	363
Example 1 (Conflict of Interest and Business Relationships):	363
Example 2 (Conflict of Interest and Business Stock Ownership):	364
Example 3 (Conflict of Interest and Personal Stock Ownership):	364
Example 4 (Conflict of Interest and Personal Stock Ownership):	364
Example 5 (Conflict of Interest and Compensation Arrangements):	365
Example 6 (Conflict of Interest, Options, and Compensation Arrangements):	365
Example 7 (Conflict of Interest and Compensation Arrangements):	366
Example 8 (Conflict of Interest and Directorship):	366
Example 9 (Conflict of Interest and Personal Trading):	366
Example 10 (Conflict of Interest and Requested Favors):	367
Example 11 (Conflict of Interest and Business Relationships):	367

◙ indicates an optional segment

Example 12 (Disclosure of Conflicts to Employers):	368
Standard VI(B): Conflicts of Interest - Priority of Transactions	368
Guidance	369
Standard VI(B): Recommended Procedures	370
Standard VI(B): Application of the Standard	372
Example 1 (Personal Trading):	372
Example 2 (Trading for Family Member Account):	373
Example 3 (Family Accounts as Equals):	373
Example 4 (Personal Trading and Disclosure):	373
Example 5 (Trading Prior to Report Dissemination):	374
Standard VI(C): Conflicts of Interest - Referral Fees	374
Guidance	374
Standard VI(C): Recommended Procedures	375
Standard VI(C): Application of the Standard	375
Example 1 (Disclosure of Referral Arrangements and Outside Parties):	375
Example 2 (Disclosure of Interdepartmental Referral Arrangements):	376
Example 3 (Disclosure of Referral Arrangements and Informing Firm):	376
Example 4 (Disclosure of Referral Arrangements and Outside Organizations):	376
Example 5 (Disclosure of Referral Arrangements and Outside Parties):	377
Standard VII(A): Responsibilities as a CFA Institute Member or CFA Candidate - Conduct as Participants in CFA Institute Programs	378
Standard VII(A) Conduct as Participants in CFA Institute Programs	378
Guidance	378
Standard VII(A): Application of the Standard	380
Example 1 (Sharing Exam Questions):	380
Example 2 (Bringing Written Material into Exam Room):	381
Example 3 (Writing after Exam Period End):	381
Example 4 (Sharing Exam Content):	381
Example 5 (Sharing Exam Content):	382
Example 6 (Sharing Exam Content):	382
Example 7 (Discussion of Exam Grading Guidelines and Results):	382
Example 8 (Compromising CFA Institute Integrity as a Volunteer):	383
Example 9 (Compromising CFA Institute Integrity as a Volunteer):	383
Standard VII(B): Responsibilities as a CFA Institute Member or CFA Candidate - Reference to CFA Institute, the CFA Designation, and the CFA Program	383
Guidance	384
Standard VII(B): Recommended Procedures	386
Standard VII(B): Application of the Standard	387
Example 1 (Passing Exams in Consecutive Years):	387
Example 2 (Right to Use CFA Designation):	387
Example 3 ("Retired" CFA Institute Membership Status):	387
Example 4 (Stating Facts about CFA Designation and Program):	388
Example 5 (Order of Professional and Academic Designations):	388
Example 6 (Use of Fictitious Name):	388
Practice Problems	*389*
Solutions	*408*

◙ indicates an optional segment

Contents

xiii

Learning Module 3	**Application of the Code and Standards: Level II**	**419**
	Introduction	419
	Serengeti Advisory Services	420
	Case Questions	422
	Banco Libertad	432
	Case Questions	435
	QuantHouse	439
	Case Questions	441
	JR and Associates	445
	Case Questions	447
	Magadi Asset Management	452
	Case Questions	454
	Syyark	459
	III. Duties to Clients	461
	IV. Duties to Employers	462
	V. Investment Analysis, Recommendations, and Actions	462
	VI. Conflicts of Interest	463
	Agarway	464
	Professionalism	466
	Conflicts of Interest	467
	Glossary	**G-1**

◙ indicates an optional segment

How to Use the CFA Program Curriculum

The CFA[*] Program exams measure your mastery of the core knowledge, skills, and abilities required to succeed as an investment professional. These core competencies are the basis for the Candidate Body of Knowledge (CBOK™). The CBOK consists of four components:

- A broad outline that lists the major CFA Program topic areas (www. cfainstitute.org/programs/cfa/curriculum/cbok)
- Topic area weights that indicate the relative exam weightings of the top-level topic areas (www.cfainstitute.org/programs/cfa/curriculum)
- Learning outcome statements (LOS) that advise candidates about the specific knowledge, skills, and abilities they should acquire from curriculum content covering a topic area: LOS are provided in candidate study sessions and at the beginning of each block of related content and the specific lesson that covers them. We encourage you to review the information about the LOS on our website (www.cfainstitute.org/programs/cfa/curriculum/study-sessions), including the descriptions of LOS "command words" on the candidate resources page at www.cfainstitute.org.
- The CFA Program curriculum that candidates receive upon exam registration

Therefore, the key to your success on the CFA exams is studying and understanding the CBOK. You can learn more about the CBOK on our website: www.cfainstitute.org/programs/cfa/curriculum/cbok.

The entire curriculum, including the practice questions, is the basis for all exam questions and is selected or developed specifically to teach the knowledge, skills, and abilities reflected in the CBOK.

ERRATA

The curriculum development process is rigorous and includes multiple rounds of reviews by content experts. Despite our efforts to produce a curriculum that is free of errors, there are instances where we must make corrections. Curriculum errata are periodically updated and posted by exam level and test date online on the Curriculum Errata webpage (www.cfainstitute.org/en/programs/submit-errata). If you believe you have found an error in the curriculum, you can submit your concerns through our curriculum errata reporting process found at the bottom of the Curriculum Errata webpage.

DESIGNING YOUR PERSONAL STUDY PROGRAM

An orderly, systematic approach to exam preparation is critical. You should dedicate a consistent block of time every week to reading and studying. Review the LOS both before and after you study curriculum content to ensure that you have mastered the applicable content and can demonstrate the knowledge, skills, and abilities described by the LOS and the assigned reading. Use the LOS self-check to track your progress and highlight areas of weakness for later review.

Successful candidates report an average of more than 300 hours preparing for each exam. Your preparation time will vary based on your prior education and experience, and you will likely spend more time on some study sessions than on others.

CFA INSTITUTE LEARNING ECOSYSTEM (LES)

Your exam registration fee includes access to the CFA Program Learning Ecosystem (LES). This digital learning platform provides access, even offline, to all of the curriculum content and practice questions and is organized as a series of short online lessons with associated practice questions. This tool is your one-stop location for all study materials, including practice questions and mock exams, and the primary method by which CFA Institute delivers your curriculum experience. The LES offers candidates additional practice questions to test their knowledge, and some questions in the LES provide a unique interactive experience.

FEEDBACK

Please send any comments or feedback to info@cfainstitute.org, and we will review your suggestions carefully.

Portfolio Management

LEARNING MODULE

1

Economics and Investment Markets

by Andrew Clare, PhD, and Thomas F. Cosimano, PhD.

Andrew Clare, PhD, is at Cass Business School (United Kingdom). Thomas F. Cosimano, PhD, is Professor Emeritus in Finance at the Mendoza College of Business, University of Notre Dame, and Visiting Scholar, International Monetary Fund (USA).

LEARNING OUTCOMES

Mastery	The candidate should be able to:
☐	explain the notion that to affect market values, economic factors must affect one or more of the following: 1) default-free interest rates across maturities, 2) the timing and/or magnitude of expected cash flows, and 3) risk premiums
☐	explain the role of expectations and changes in expectations in market valuation
☐	explain the relationship between the long-term growth rate of the economy, the volatility of the growth rate, and the average level of real short-term interest rates
☐	explain how the phase of the business cycle affects policy and short-term interest rates, the slope of the term structure of interest rates, and the relative performance of bonds of differing maturities
☐	describe the factors that affect yield spreads between non-inflation-adjusted and inflation-indexed bonds
☐	explain how the phase of the business cycle affects credit spreads and the performance of credit-sensitive fixed-income instruments
☐	explain how the characteristics of the markets for a company's products affect the company's credit quality
☐	explain the relationship between the consumption hedging properties of equity and the equity risk premium
☐	explain how the phase of the business cycle affects short-term and long-term earnings growth expectations
☐	describe cyclical effects on valuation multiples
☐	describe the economic factors affecting investment in commercial real estate

1 INTRODUCTION

The state of the economy and financial market activity are interconnected. Financial markets are the forums where savers are connected with investors. This activity enables savers to defer consumption today for consumption in the future, allows governments to raise the capital necessary to create a secure society, and permits corporations to access capital to exploit profitable investment opportunities, which, in turn, should help to generate future economic growth and employment. Furthermore, all financial instruments essentially represent claims on an underlying economy. There is, therefore, an important and fundamental connection that runs from the decisions of economic agents, as they plan their present and future consumption, to the prices of financial instruments, such as bonds and equities.

The purpose of this reading is to identify and explain the links between the real economy and financial markets and to show how economic analysis can be used to develop ways of valuing both individual financial market securities and aggregations of these securities, such as financial market indexes. We begin by reviewing what we refer to as the fundamental pricing equation for all financial instruments. Using this framework, we then move on to explore the relationship between the economy and real default-free debt. From there, we can extend the analysis to the ways in which the economy can influence the prices of the following: nominal default-free debt; credit risky debt (for example, corporate bonds); publicly traded equities; and commercial real estate.

2 THE PRESENT VALUE MODEL

☐ | explain the notion that to affect market values, economic factors must affect one or more of the following: 1) default-free interest rates across maturities, 2) the timing and/or magnitude of expected cash flows, and 3) risk premiums

The reference point for the analysis of this reading is the present value model of asset valuation. The impact of economic factors on asset values can be studied in the context of that model by examining how economic factors can affect discount rates and future cash flows. These topics are explored in more detail in the following sections.

The Present Value Model

The value of an asset must be related to the benefits that we expect to receive from holding it; for many assets (e.g., financial securities), these benefits are its future cash flows, which may be specified in the security's contract, as is the case with bonds, or be discretionary, as is the case with ordinary shares. Intuitively, a given amount of money received in the future will be valued less by individual investors than the same amount of money received today. Because an investor can use cash for present consumption, he or she needs an incentive to defer it to the future and more so as the future becomes less certain. These considerations provide an economic rationale for valuing an asset by discounting its future cash flows to derive its present value.

Equation 1 presents the fundamental present value formula for the value at time t of any financial asset i, V_t^i, which we assume equals its current market price, P_t^i. In general, we will speak of the time t as "today."

The Present Value Model

$$P_t^i = \sum_{s=1}^{N} \frac{E_t\left[\widetilde{CF}_{t+s}^i\right]}{\left(1 + l_{t,s} + \theta_{t,s} + \rho_{t,s}^i\right)^s},$$

(1)

where

P_t^i = the value of asset i at time t (today)

N = number of cash flows in the life of the asset

$\widetilde{CF}_{t+s}^i$ = the uncertain, nominal cash flow paid s periods in the future

$E_t[\widetilde{CF}]$ = the expectation of the random variable $\widetilde{CF}$ conditional on the information available to investors today (t)

$l_{t,s}$ = yield to maturity on a real default-free investment today (t), which pays one unit of currency s periods in the future

$\theta_{t,s}$ = expected inflation rate between t and $t + s$

$\rho_{t,s}^i$ = the risk premium required today (t) to pay the investor for taking on risk in the cash flow of asset i, s periods in the future

This expression is general enough to be used to value all financial instruments. The present values of all of the instrument's cash flows are summed from 1 to N. Some assets, such as a five-year zero-coupon bond, may have only one cash flow, and so N would equal five in that case, with cash flows in Periods 1–4 equal to zero. At the other extreme, dividend-paying equities produce cash flows in the form of dividends into the indefinite future, in which case N could, technically, be equal to infinity.

According to Equation 1, effects of the economy on asset prices are transmitted through some combination of influences on the numerator—the asset's expected cash flows—and denominator—the discount rate(s) applied to the asset's expected cash flows.

A factor that typically distinguishes one financial asset class from another is the degree of certainty that investors have about future cash flows. At one extreme there may be little uncertainty. For example, despite losing its AAA rating from Standard & Poor's, investors might still attach a relatively low probability to the prospect of the US Treasury not making the scheduled payments on its debts on time and in full. Investors may regard the probability of the German government defaulting on its debts to be very low, too. At the other extreme, investors may be very uncertain about the size and timing of dividend payments from an equity investment and will also have to consider the prospect of receiving no dividends at all in the event that the company declares bankruptcy.

The uncertainty about future cash flows is reflected in the discount rate in Equation 1. We can think of the discount rate as having three distinct components. The first component is $l_{t,s}$ which effectively represents the return that an investor requires on a real default-free fixed-income security at present time t for a cash flow to be paid s periods in the future. For example, readers can think of this return as being analogous to the return expected on an investment in an inflation-linked bond issued by the government of a developed economy.

The second component in the discount rate, $\theta_{t,s}$, represents the additional return required by investors, above that required from investing in a real default-free investment, for investing in a nominal default-free investment. This additional return is required even though an investor may attach a zero probability to not being paid on time and in full, because future nominal payments will be affected by inflation. In essence, this component of the discount rate represents the compensation that investors demand for the inflation that they expect to experience over the investment horizon. Compensation is demanded because investors are concerned about the real purchasing power of their investments in the future rather than in the nominal value of the future cash flows.

The third component of the discount rate in Equation 1, $\rho_{t,s}^i$, represents the additional return that investors expect for investing in financial assets because of uncertainty about the asset's future cash flows. In other words, all securities, even those issued by governments of developed economies and considered risk free in that there is negligible risk that the issuer will default (as we will see later), carry some risks for which risk-averse investors will want to be compensated. Indeed, the size of this risk premium will vary among asset classes, and this variation is largely responsible for the distinction between one asset class and another. We remind the reader of this difference among assets by placing a superscript i to indicate that this premium is specific to the asset under consideration.

As we will show throughout this reading, the size and nature of this addition to expected return, $\rho_{t,s}^i$, will depend on the characteristics of the asset or asset class in question, which, in turn, will be determined by developments and expected developments in the real economy. This means that the discount rates applied to the cash flows of financial assets will almost certainly vary over time as perceptions of expected economic growth, inflation, and cash flow risk change. In particular during recessions, the risk premium that investors demand on financial assets, especially those that are not default-free, may rise because investors in general may be less willing and able to take on heightened default risk during such periods.

The $\rho_{t,s}^i$ component may include more than just the compensation for the uncertainty related to financial cash flows that may be subject to default risk. In particular, $\dot{\rho}_{t,s}$ may also reflect other types of risk—for example, liquidity risk. Liquidity risk refers to the possibility that a financial asset cannot be converted quickly into cash at close to its fair value; it is particularly characteristic of investments in commercial real estate and high-yield corporate bonds/loans. And as many investors learned during the 2008–2009 global financial crisis, some debt instruments, such as mortgage-backed securities, can become very illiquid at just the moment when investors become most risk averse and when they want to be holding cash rather than riskier financial assets.

In summary, the expected cash flows for any financial asset, i, can be discounted using the following general expression for the discount rate (this additive expression is an approximation of the exact multiplicative expression that includes interaction effects between the terms):

$$1 + l_{t,s} + \theta_{t,s} + \rho_{t,s}^i \text{ for } s = 1, \quad \ldots, \quad N. \tag{2}$$

A major purpose of this reading is to identify the relationship between these elements of the discount rate and the underlying economy and also to decompose $\dot{\rho}_{t,s}$ into its component parts for each asset class.

3   EXPECTATIONS AND ASSET VALUES

☐ explain the role of expectations and changes in expectations in market valuation

Examining Equation 1 reveals simple but important observations:

- Asset values depend not on past cash flows but on the expectation of future cash flows.

- These expectations are based on (conditional on) current information (indicated by the time subscript t) that may be relevant to forecasting future cash flows. Any information that may contribute to the accuracy or precision of expectations is relevant.

Because asset values are dependent on expectations of future cash flows, information that changes expectations affects asset values and realized returns. Information that has been anticipated is already reflected in asset prices, but information that is different from what was expected constitutes real news that requires expectations to adjust. The adjustment generates a holding period return that differs from the expected return. This observation about investors' anticipations is important to understanding sometimes seemingly counterintuitive market reactions to economic information releases. Investors judge economic data releases relative to their expectations for the data. Prices may fall (rise) despite "good" ("bad") news if the expectation was for better (worse) news.

Thus, for valuation, one important distinction is information that is "news" or new information and information that has been fully anticipated. Therefore, news is a surprise relative to fully anticipated information.

Although this reading's focus is the effect of economic factors on asset values, investor sentiment (e.g., enthusiasm or despair) can also affect asset values. Economic factors affect asset values through generally direct effects on cash flows and/or discount rates, but investor sentiment affects asset values through direct effects on discount rates via higher or lower risk premiums (and possibly indirect effects on future cash flows).

THE DISCOUNT RATE ON REAL DEFAULT-FREE BONDS: INTEREST RATES

4

☐ explain the notion that to affect market values, economic factors must affect one or more of the following: 1) default-free interest rates across maturities, 2) the timing and/or magnitude of expected cash flows, and 3) risk premiums

Having introduced several fundamental concepts, we can now begin the analysis of economic factors affecting asset values in detail. The first step in understanding the relationship between the economy and investment markets involves noting that the purchase of an investment involves the opportunity cost of lower consumption today. In other words, by buying a financial asset, an investor defers some current consumption. The sum of all of these individual saving and consumption decisions is thus going to have an impact on the price of financial assets.

To explain how investors' concerns for satisfying consumption needs through economic fluctuations affect asset prices, modern finance makes reference to several expressions (Equation 3 through 6) that model how investors evaluate consumption trade-offs. These expressions, and associated (non-testable) calculations, show the analysis behind statements about the relationships between real interest rates, GDP growth, and the volatility of GDP; verbal statements of the intuition behind the relationships are also given that aid in understanding the entire reading.

Real Default-Free Interest Rates

To demonstrate the importance of the aggregation of these individual saving and investment decisions, we can think through how the aggregated consumption and investment decisions of individuals might determine the real default-free interest rate in an economy—that is, $l_{t,s}$ in Equation 1. Consider a single individual who has to choose between using some portion of his or her wealth to consume today (t) or investing that wealth in default-free bonds that will pay investors one dollar when they mature s periods in the future.

Think of this bond as being issued by a highly rated, developed-economy government, so there is only a negligible prospect of default. Also think of this bond as being inflation index-linked so that investors do not need to concern themselves with the impact of future inflation on the bond's future cash flow. An alternative way of conceptualizing the bond is to assume (only for the moment) that it is issued by this government in a world that has no inflation. Later we will re-introduce inflation into the pricing problem.

What sort of return would investors require on a bond that is both default-free and unaffected by future inflation? It is tempting to say that an investor would require no return on such a bond because there is no risk of losing money over the investment period in either nominal or real terms. But the choice to invest today involves the opportunity cost of not consuming today. It is the aggregated opportunity cost of all investors that will determine the price of this asset today and its return over the investment horizon.

Think of the return on the asset as the opportunity cost (price) of consuming today. If the return increases, the investor substitutes away from current consumption to future consumption by purchasing an asset. Consequently, as with any other economic decision, an investor must consider the relative prices of the two alternatives. In this case, the investor can

- pay price $P_{t,s}$ today, t, of a default-free bond paying 1 monetary unit of income s periods in the future or
- buy goods worth $P_{t,s}$ dollars today.

The decision to purchase this bond will be determined by the willingness of individuals to substitute consumption today for consumption in the future. This trade-off is measured by the marginal utility of consumption s periods in the future relative to the marginal utility of consumption today (t). The marginal utility of consumption is the additional satisfaction or utility that a consumer derives from one additional unit of consumption. The ratio of these two marginal utilities—the ratio of the marginal utility of consumption s periods in the future (the numerator) to the marginal utility of consumption today (the denominator)—is known as the **inter-temporal rate of substitution**, denoted $\tilde{m}_{t,s}$.

In "good" economic times, individuals may have relatively high levels of current income so that current consumption is high. In this case, the utility derived from an additional unit of consumption today will be relatively low. Conversely, in "bad" economic times, current income and consumption will tend to be relatively low, which means that the utility derived from an additional unit of consumption today will be relatively high. In addition, the marginal utility of consumption of investors diminishes as their wealth increases because they have already satisfied fundamental needs. Thus, investors would receive a larger benefit (utility) from an asset that pays off more in bad economic times relative to one that pays off in good economic times.

The Discount Rate on Real Default-Free Bonds: Interest Rates

The rate of substitution is a random variable because an investor will not know how much she has available in the future from other sources of income, such as salary from working. This uncertainty is present even for an investment that pays a certain amount in one period because the value of this investment is determined by how much utility the investor receives from this investment.

Given this uncertainty, the investor must make the decision today based on her expectations of future circumstances when she receives the payoff from the investment. This expectation is conditional on the information that the investor has when the decision is made. Thus, if the investor wanted to consider an investment in a zero-coupon bond at time t that is certain to pay off one unit of real consumption in s periods, then

$$P_{t,s} = E_t\left(1\,\tilde{m}_{t,s}\right) = E_t\left(\tilde{m}_{t,s}\right) \tag{3}$$

where $\tilde{m}_{t,s}$ is the investor's marginal willingness to trade consumption at time t for (real) wealth at time $t + s$.[1]

EXAMPLE 1

The Inter-Temporal Rate of Substitution (1 of 3)

1. Suppose the investor's willingness to trade present for future consumption can be represented as

$$\tilde{m}_{t,1} = e^{a+b\tilde{z}}$$

Here, $\tilde{z}$ is a random shock to the economy that affects the cash flows of the marginal investor; $\tilde{z}$ is what makes $\tilde{m}_{t,1}$ a random variable. The exponential form is consistent with assumptions about investor risk aversion and consumption growth often made in finance; a and b are typically negative given those same assumptions.[2] Parameters of the distribution of $\tilde{z}$ consistent with observed market data can also be established. Suppose that $\tilde{z}$, assumed to have a mean of zero, takes on one of two values—a negative value indicating a bad state or a positive value indicating a good state. The probabilities of bad and good states are 0.4 and 0.6, respectively.

Using market-consistent values in the exponent in the expression for $\tilde{m}_{t,1}$, we can calculate the price of a bond promising $1 for sure in one year as the expected value of the investor's willingness to trade present for future consumption:

---

1 The term $\tilde{m}_{t,s}$ is technically defined as $(\delta)[MU(C_{t+s})/MU(C_t)]$, where MU denotes marginal utility of consumption, C, and δ is a discount factor that captures the preference for consumption at t rather than later at t + s. The discount factor applied to MU (C_{t+s}) adjusts it for the time difference of s periods. The tilde on $\tilde{m}_{t,s}$ indicates it is a random (stochastic) variable, and the term may be called the stochastic inter-temporal rate of substitution. As in Example 1, this inter-temporal rate of substitution varies based on the realization of the shock to economic activity, $\tilde{z}$. In the modern theory of asset pricing, the term m is also referred to as the stochastic discount factor or pricing kernel.

2 The negative exponential function expression reflects constant relative risk aversion utility and lognormally distributed consumption growth. In e^{a+bz}, the expected value is a and standard deviation is z. For an explanation of constant relative risk aversion, see an investments text such as Elton, Gruber, Brown, and Goetzmann (2014).

$$E_t\left(\overline{m}_{t,1}\right) = 0.4\,e^{a+b\times(z\text{ for a bad state})} + 0.6\,e^{a+b\times(z\text{ for a good state})}$$
$$= 0.4 \times 0.954676 + 0.6 \times 0.954379 = 0.954498$$

In the calculation, 0.954676 and 0.954379 are the asset's prices in the bad and good states, respectively. Note that the values for the random shock are consistent with the level of the yield curve in the United States from January 1999 to January 2014. The derivation of these numbers is beyond the scope of this reading. Also note the higher value of $1 received in the bad state. Following Equation 3, the investor is willing to buy the risk-free bond today for $0.954498 in exchange for $1 in one year. Also notice that the willingness to invest is smaller for the positive shock (z for a good state), because an investor is willing to pay less for the bond in the case of a good state. Thus, the positive shock is associated with a higher level of consumption today by the investor.[3]

The investor knows that she cannot affect the price of the bond, and so she must decide whether to buy or sell the bond based on this given price, $P_{t,1}$ (0.954498 from Example 1). If this price of the bond was less than the investor's expectation of the inter-temporal rate of substitution (suppose this is 0.9560), then she would prefer to buy more of the bond today. As more bonds are purchased, today's consumption falls and marginal utility of consumption today rises, so expectations conditional on current information of the inter-temporal rate of substitution, $E_t\left(\overline{m}_{t,s}\right)$, fall. This process continues until the rate of substitution is equal to the bond price shown in Equation 3; that is, equivalently, 0.9560 would fall and converge on 0.954498.

It is worthwhile to emphasize this point: All investors are essentially making investment decisions using Equation 3; some will want to sell their bonds to fund additional, current consumption, whereas others will want to buy bonds and defer some additional consumption until the future. To demonstrate the link between the bond price and these consumption/investment decisions, imagine for the moment that the market price of this bond is too "low" for an individual investor. In this case, the investor with a higher initial inter-temporal rate of substitution (higher $\overline{m}_{t,s}$) would buy more of the bond. As a result of this purchase, the investor will consume less today, leading to an increase in today's marginal utility, but he or she would expect to have more consumption and thus lower marginal utility in the future. Consequently, the inter-temporal rate of substitution would fall.

One investor cannot influence the equilibrium price. But if a substantial group of investors responded this way, then the demand and price of the bond would rise; in the illustration earlier, it would mean that it is possible for the price of the bond, 0.954498, to rise at the same time that the individual investor's inter-temporal rate of substitution was falling. This process would continue until all investors' willingness to invest converges on a single equilibrium value so that Equation 3 is true for all individuals and the market price is determined.

Conversely, if the market price of the bond were too "high" for a group of investors, then the investors with a lower inter-temporal rate of substitution would buy less of the bond. They would have more consumption and lower marginal utility today, but they would expect to have less consumption and higher marginal utility in the future. As a result, the inter-temporal rate of substitution would rise and the demand and price of the bond would fall. This process would again continue until Equation 3 is true for all individuals.

---

3 An exponential function, $f(x) = e^x$, is always increasing in the variable x and increases at an increasing rate as x gets large. For example, $f(0) = e^0 = 1$ and $f(0.05) = e^{0.05} = 1.0513$. If x is negative, the more negative x is, the smaller the value of the function. For example, compare $f(-0.05) = e^{-0.05} = 0.9512$ and $f(-0.02) = e^{-0.02} = 0.9802$; the function is still increasing in x.

EXAMPLE 2

The Inter-Temporal Rate of Substitution (2 of 3)

In Example 1, suppose the current market price of the real default-free bond is $9,540 per $10,000, but the investor's inter-temporal rate of substitution is $0.954498 per $1 promised. The investor would then value the guarantee of $10,000 in one period more than the market, so she would purchase it. As she buys more of the bond, her future income will be higher and its marginal utility lower, leading to a fall in her marginal willingness to invest in the risk-free asset. Only if there are many investors with the willingness to trade at $9,544.98 would the market price increase until all investors have the same marginal willingness to invest.

In summary, all investors use Equation 3 to make their investment decisions, so the equilibrium price in the market for these bonds equals the expectation of the inter-temporal rate of substitution of every single investor who participates in the bond market.

If the investment horizon for this bond is one year and the payoff then is $1, the return on this bond can be written as the future payoff minus the current payment relative to the current payment:[4]

$$l_{t,1} = \frac{1 - P_{t,1}}{P_{t,1}} = \frac{1}{E_t\left(\tilde{m}_{t,1}\right)} - 1 \tag{4}$$

Consequently, the return is higher for lower current prices. Equation 4 implies that the one-period real risk-free rate is inversely related to the inter-temporal rate of substitution. That is, the higher the return the investor can earn, the more important current consumption becomes relative to future consumption.

[handwritten: $l_{t,1}$: return on bond]

[handwritten: higher l comes from lower $E_t(\tilde{m}_{t,1})$ i.e. impatience]

[handwritten: $\tilde{m}_{t,1} = \dfrac{u'(C_{t+1})}{u'(C_t)}$]

EXAMPLE 3

The Inter-Temporal Rate of Substitution (3 of 3)

Following the circumstances in Example 1, the one-period real risk-free interest rate is $l_{t,1} = \frac{1 - 0.954498}{0.954498} = 0.047671$, or 4.7671%.

THE DISCOUNT RATE ON REAL DEFAULT-FREE BONDS: UNCERTAINTY AND RISK PREMIUMS

5

☐   explain the notion that to affect market values, economic factors must affect one or more of the following: 1) default-free interest rates across maturities, 2) the timing and/or magnitude of expected cash flows, and 3) risk premiums

[handwritten: — Only changes in default-free real interest rates will affect the price of real, default-free bonds.]

An investor's expected marginal utility associated with a given expected payoff is decreased by any increase in uncertainty of the payoff; thus, the investor must be compensated with a higher expected return. This result follows from decreasing marginal

---

4 The step from the first expression to the second follows from rearranging the first expression, $\frac{1 - P_{t,1}}{P_{t,1}}$, as $\frac{1}{P_{t,1}} - 1$ and then substituting from Equation 3.

utility of wealth or income because the loss of utility from lower wealth is larger than the gain from an equivalent increase in wealth. The risk premium compensates the investor for the loss from this fluctuation in future wealth or income. An individual who requires compensation for this uncertainty is called "risk averse." This property was seen in Example 1, in which the inter-temporal rate of substitution was lower in the good state of the economy compared with the bad state.

For the valuation of cash flows under uncertainty, a second property of most investors' utility is important. In particular, an investor's absolute risk aversion is assumed to fall if he or she has higher wealth or income. Absolute risk aversion relates to the amount held in risky assets at different levels of wealth; under the assumption of decreasing absolute risk aversion made here, an investor invests larger amounts in risky assets as wealth or income increases (note that absolute risk aversion is in contrast to relative risk aversion, which relates to the fraction, not the amount, of wealth held in risky assets at different levels of wealth). Consequently, one's marginal utility is always lower as one's wealth or income increases. In this case, the risk premium for a given risk is lower for wealthier individuals because the average loss of marginal utility (slope of utility) from any risk taking is smaller, which means that relative to poorer individuals, wealthier individuals are more willing to take on a given risk. Consequently, wealthier investors are willing to buy more risky assets because they would value the asset more than poorer investors. But the expected marginal utility for wealthier investors will decline as they buy more of the risky asset. Eventually, both the wealthier and poorer investors would have the same willingness to invest in risky assets when the financial market is in equilibrium.

EXAMPLE 4

The Case of Increasing Wealth

1. This idea can be illustrated by raising the economic shock by a fixed amount regardless of whether the economy is good or bad, which has the effect of increasing the individual's resources and making her wealthier. For example, suppose we add 0.1 to $\tilde{z}$ and thus to the resources of the investor relative to the shock in Example 1. The expected inter-temporal rate of substitution for the investor is now lower for this safe asset (the default-free bond). The expected value of the investor's willingness to trade present for future consumption would then be

$$E_t\left(\widetilde{m}_{t,1}\right) = 0.4 \times 0.954528 + 0.6 \times 0.954231 = 0.954350.$$

Compare this result with Example 1. The inter-temporal rate of substitution is lower under the good and bad shock to the economy. As a result, the expected inter-temporal rate of substitution $E_t\left(\widetilde{m}_{t,1}\right)$ is lower for the wealthier investor by 0.000148 (= 0.954498 – 0.954350). Thus, the wealthier investor will buy the safe bond only at a lower price, and if this lower price is not the equilibrium price, the investor will substitute away from riskless assets to risky assets. Because of decreasing absolute risk aversion with wealth and because their fundamental consumption needs are met, wealthy investors will demand a lower premium than poorer investors for holding risky assets, all else being equal.

An individual with decreasing absolute risk aversion would lower the price of safe assets (see Altug and Labadie [2008] for a derivation of this result). If the rich individuals are a large percentage of the market, then the equilibrium return on the safe asset increases with the lower price. As a result, the poorer individuals would have incentives to increase their savings with the expected higher return on the safe asset. These savings allow all investors to partially compensate for any additional losses during possible bad times. Consequently, all the investors in the financial market would increase their savings when uncertainty about their future income increases. This higher savings means that the expected marginal utility in the future is lower because the investors' future resources are higher. Thus, the equilibrium price based on Equation 3 is lower, meaning that investors are compensated with a higher expected return when uncertainty in income increases.

THE DISCOUNT RATE ON REAL DEFAULT-FREE BONDS: RISK PREMIUMS ON RISKY ASSETS

6

☐ explain the notion that to affect market values, economic factors must affect one or more of the following: 1) default-free interest rates across maturities, 2) the timing and/or magnitude of expected cash flows, and 3) risk premiums

The price of other (non-default-free) financial instruments is established relative to the price of the default-free bond. This relationship can be seen by considering a default-free bond with a maturity of s periods (s is greater than or equal to two). Assume that the investor is holding the security for only one period. Its current price is $P_{t,s}$. In this case, the bond has value $\tilde{P}_{t+1,s-1}$ in one period because the term to maturity of the bond has been reduced by one period relative to its original maturity date. As a result, the investor's decision is now given by

$$P_{t,s} = E_t\left(\tilde{P}_{t+1,s-1}\,\tilde{m}_{t,1}\right) \tag{5}$$

The price in one period is uncertain because the s period bond is sold at the market price before it matures. Also notice that there is no interest payment because the bond promises a payment only at the terminal time. If a coupon is promised at time $t + 1$, then its value would have to be added to the right-hand side of Equation 5.

EXAMPLE 5

Pricing a Two-Period Default-Free Bond

1. In this example, we illustrate how the pricing formula in Equation 5 leads to a risk premium on a two-period default-free bond that is not present in the one-period default-free bond. In these calculations, we use five or six digits to the right of the decimal point because the risk premium is small for a two-period bond relative to a one-period default-free bond.

   Suppose the price at Time 1 of the two-year default-free bond is given by

   $$\tilde{P}_{t+1,2-1} = e^{a'+b'z}$$

   In this case, the future price can be shown to be

   $\tilde{P}_{t+1,2-1} = 0.839181$ for \$1 at Time 2 with probability $p = 0.4$ and

$\tilde{P}_{t+1,2-1} = 0.954840$ for \$1 at Time 2 with probability $p = 0.6$.

The expected price at time $t + 1$ of a \$1 bond maturing at time $t + 2$ is $0.4 \times 0.839181 + 0.6 \times 0.954840 = \$0.908576$. Without considering the investor's willingness to invest, the current value of the two-period bond is the simple present value using the one-period real risk-free interest rate of 4.7671% (from Example 3) as the discount rate. Thus, under the assumption stated, the bond would be worth $\frac{E_t\left(\tilde{P}_{t+1,s-1}\right)}{1 + l_{t,1}} = \frac{0.908576}{1.047671} = \$0.867234$. But the actual price in the financial markets based on Equation 5 is

$$P_{t,s} = E_t\left(\tilde{P}_{t+1,s-1}\tilde{m}_{t,1}\right)$$

$$= 0.4 \times 0.839181 \times 0.954676 + 0.6 \times 0.954840 \times 0.954379$$

$$= 0.867226,$$

where 0.954676 and 0.954379 are the asset's prices in the bad and good states, as determined in Example 1. The price based on Equation 5 is smaller than the present discounted value at the risk-free rate; the difference is 0.000008 per 1 principal value (i.e., $0.867234 - 0.867226 = 0.000008$). Thus, the holder of a two-year bond earns a risk premium. The reason for this result can be seen by calculating

$$E_t\left(\tilde{P}_{t+1,s-1}\right)E_t\left(\tilde{m}_{t,1}\right) = 0.908576(0.4 \times 0.954676 + 0.6 \times 0.954379)$$

$$= 0.867234,$$

where 0.908576 is the Time 1 price of the bond as determined earlier. Consequently, we see that

$$E_t\left(\tilde{P}_{t+1,s-1}\right)E_t\left(\tilde{m}_{t,1}\right) > E_t\left(\tilde{P}_{t+1,s-1}\tilde{m}_{t,1}\right)$$

To summarize, the price uncertainty of the two-period bond at $t = 1$ gives rise to a risk premium, although the bond is default-risk free.

Example 5 showed how future price uncertainty creates a discount for risk. We now derive an alternative expression for the pricing relationship in Equation 5 that explains the nature of that discount and sheds further light on the conclusion of Example 5. In statistics texts, the following relationship between expected values and covariance is proven:

$$E_t(\tilde{x}\tilde{y}) = E_t(\tilde{x})E_t(\tilde{y}) + \text{cov}(\tilde{x},\tilde{y})$$

Here, $\text{cov}_t(\tilde{x},\tilde{y})$ refers to the conditional (on information at time t) covariance of the random variable $\tilde{x}$ with $\tilde{y}$. Thus, from Equation 5,

$$P_{t,s} = E_t\left(\tilde{P}_{t+1,s-1}\tilde{m}_{t,1}\right) = E_t\left(\tilde{P}_{t+1,s-1}\right)E_t\left(\tilde{m}_{t,1}\right) + \text{cov}\left(\tilde{P}_{t+1,s-1},\tilde{m}_{t,1}\right).$$

But from Equation 4, $1 + l_{t,1} = \frac{1}{E_t\left(\tilde{m}_{t,1}\right)}$. So, an alternative way to view the pricing relationship in Equation 5 is

$$P_{t,s} = \frac{E_t\left(\tilde{P}_{t+1,s-1}\right)}{1 + l_{t,1}} + \text{cov}_t\left(\tilde{P}_{t+1,s-1},\tilde{m}_{t,1}\right), \tag{6}$$

where $\text{cov}_t\left(\widetilde{P}_{t+1,s-1}, \overline{m}_{t,1}\right)$ represents the covariance between an investor's inter-temporal rate of substitution, $\overline{m}_{t,1}$, and the random future price of the investment at $t+1$, $\widetilde{P}_{t+1,s-1}$, based on the information available to investors today (t). The subscript is reduced by one because an investment with time to maturity s at time t becomes an investment with time to maturity $s-1$ at time $t+1$ (Cochrane 2005).

Equation 6 expresses the value of a risky asset as the sum of two terms. The first term is the asset's expected future price discounted at the risk-free rate. It may be called the risk-neutral present value because it represents a risky asset's value if investors did not require compensation for bearing risk (notice the parallel with the fundamental pricing equation, Equation 1, if it had one cash flow and no risk premium). In Example 5, this value is 0.867234.

The covariance term is the discount for risk. Note that with a one-period default-free bond, the covariance term is zero because the future price is a known constant ($1) and the covariance of a random quantity with a constant is zero; and intuitively, its value is given by the first term. Consequently, Equation 6 reduces to Equation 3 for the one-period default-free bond. But with the two-period default-free bond, the future price of $1 two periods in the future is known with certainty, but the price one period in the future is not. Consequently, the covariance term is not zero.

In general with risk-averse investors, the covariance term for most risky assets is expected to be negative. That is, when the expected future price of the investment is high, the marginal utility of future consumption relative to that of current consumption is low. Alternatively, during bad economic times, investors expect a smaller labor income in the future, so the marginal utility of future consumption, and hence the inter-temporal rate of substitution, is higher. This relationship leads investors to demand a higher required rate of trade-off of future for current consumption—as in bad economic times when the labor market contracts. Bad economic times also tend to be associated with declining risky asset payouts (declining earnings and dividends for ordinary shares and defaults for bonds), leading to declining asset prices. The result is that the covariance term for risky assets is typically negative, so the price of the asset is lower. This negative covariance term results in a positive risk premium, $\rho_{t,s}^i$ in Equation 1 because a lower price today leads to a higher return over time. Holding all else constant, the risk premium term and the required return for an asset should be higher, and its current market price is lower the larger the magnitude of the negative covariance term.

EXAMPLE 6

An Alternative Method to Evaluate the Price Discount for Risk

1. The covariance between the investor's willingness to invest and the price of the two-year bond next period can also be computed as follows (recall the standard formula for covariance is $\text{cov}(\bar{x}, \bar{y}) = \Sigma p_i[x_i - E(x)][y_i - E(y)]$:

$$\text{cov}_t\left(\overline{m}_{t,1}, \widetilde{P}_{t+1,2-1}\right) = 0.4(0.954676 - 0.954498) \times (0.839181 - 0.908576) + 0.6(0.954379 - 0.954498) \times (0.954840 - 0.908576)$$

$$= -0.000008$$

In the bad state of the economy, the willingness to invest (0.954676) is above its average (0.954498), yet the bond price (0.839181) is below its average (0.908576). The reverse is true in the good state. Thus, the covariance between the inter-temporal rate of substitution and the price of the asset is

> negative. This result means the investor finds this investment inferior to one with a payoff that is independent of her willingness to invest. In particular, we have
>
> $$P_{t,s} = \frac{E_t\left(\widetilde{P}_{t+1,s-1}\right)}{1 + l_{t,1}} = -0.000008.$$
>
> With a lower price, the return on the two-year bond is higher.
>
> In this example, the price discount is not too large because the risk between a one- and two-year US government bond is not that crucial. However, riskier assets, such as equity, will have a higher discount. In addition, the higher risk premium on equity still follows from the covariance between the cash flow and the investor's willingness to invest over the time horizon of the investment. Thus, a higher risk premium for stocks arises from a larger value for this covariance.

The risk premium can be computed as follows: The expected holding period return on the s period bond through time $t + 1$, using the results of Example 5, is given by

$$r_{t,s} = \frac{E_t\left(\widetilde{P}_{t+1,s-1}\right) - P_{t,s}}{P_{t,s}}$$

$$= \frac{0.908576 - 0.867226}{0.867226} = 0.047681, \text{ or } 4.7681\%, \tag{7}$$

so the risk premium $\rho_{t,s}^i = r_{t,s} - l_{t,1} = 0.047681 - 0.047671 = 0.00001$. Alternatively, Equation 7 and 6 can be manipulated so that

$$r_{t,s} - l_{t,1} = \frac{E_t\left(\widetilde{P}_{t+1,s-1}\right)}{P_{t,s}} - \left(1 + l_{t,1}\right) = \frac{\left(1 + l_{t,1}\right)}{P_{t,s}} \text{cov}_t\left(\widetilde{m}_{t,1}, \widetilde{P}_{t+1,s-1}\right)$$

$$= -\left(1 + l_{t,s}\right) \text{cov}_t\left(\widetilde{m}_{t,1}, \frac{\widetilde{P}_{t+1,s-1}}{P_{t,s}}\right) = -\frac{(1 + 0.047671)}{0.867226} \times (-0.000008) \tag{8}$$

$$= 0.00001 = \rho_{t,s}^i,$$

which is the return premium demanded by investors because of the uncertain Time 1 price of the riskless two-period bond.[5]

==This relationship implies that an asset's risk premium, $\rho_{t,s}^i$ in Equation 1, is driven by the covariance of its returns with the inter-temporal rate of substitution for consumption and can exist even for a default-free bond because of the uncertainty of its price before maturity. Most risky assets have returns that tend to be high during good times, when the marginal value of consumption is low, and low during bad times, when the marginal value of consumption is high, and so bear a positive risk premium. Any asset that tended to have relatively high returns when the marginal utility of consumption was high would provide a type of hedge against bad times, bear a negative risk premium, and have a relatively high price and low required rate of return.==

---

5 Notice that simultaneously multiplying Equation 6 by $(1 + l_{t,1})$ and dividing by $P_{t,s}$ gives $(1 + l_{t,1}) =$

$\frac{E_t\left(\widetilde{P}_{t+1,s-1}\right)}{P_{t,s}} + \left(1 + l_{t,1}\right) \text{cov}_t\left(\widetilde{m}_{t,1}, \frac{\widetilde{P}_{t+1,s-1}}{P_{t,s}}\right)$,, wso we can write $\frac{E_t\left(\widetilde{P}_{t+1,s-1}\right)}{P_{t,s}} - \left(1 + l_{t,1}\right)$ in Equation 8 as

$\frac{E_t\left(\widetilde{P}_{t+1,s-1}\right)}{P_{t,s}} - \frac{E_t\left(\widetilde{P}_{t+1,s-1}\right)}{P_{t,s}} - \left(1 + l_{t,1}\right) \text{cov}_t\left(\widetilde{m}_{t,1}, \frac{\widetilde{P}_{t+1,s-1}}{P_{t,s}}\right) = -\left(1 + l_{t,1}\right) \text{cov}_t\left(\widetilde{m}_{t,1}, \frac{\widetilde{P}_{t+1,s-1}}{P_{t,s}}\right).$

DEFAULT-FREE INTEREST RATES AND ECONOMIC GROWTH

7

☐ | explain the relationship between the long-term growth rate of the economy, the volatility of the growth rate, and the average level of real short-term interest rates

From the previous discussion, it is a relatively small conceptual step to understand the relationship between an economy's GDP growth and real default-free interest rates. If there is a known independent change in real GDP growth or a change that can be forecasted perfectly, then an increase in real GDP growth should lead to an increase in the real default-free rate of interest because more goods and services will be available in the future relative to today. The result is that investors' willingness to substitute over time will fall, resulting in less saving and more borrowing, so that the real default-free interest rate increases, as in Equation 4.

$$l_{t,1} = \frac{1}{E_t(\tilde{m}_{t,1})} - 1$$

But GDP growth from one period to the next cannot be perfectly anticipated. Under these uncertain circumstances, interest rates will still be positively related to the expected growth rate of GDP, but additionally they will be positively related to the expected volatility of GDP growth.

EXAMPLE 7

The Effect of Volatility on Prices

1. One can see the effect of volatility by doubling the standard deviation of the random variable $\tilde{z}$ from what was assumed in Example 1. In this case, the price of the one-period bond in Example 1 would be

$$E_t(\tilde{m}_{t,1}) = 0.4 \times 0.954855 + 0.6 \times 0.954260 = 0.954498.$$

Notice that the expected value is the same as in Example 1 but that the prices in each state are more dispersed, reflecting the doubling of the standard deviation. For the two-period default-free bond, continuing with the parameter values (a' and b') from Example 5, we would compute

$$E_t(\overline{P}_{t+1,2-1}) = 0.4 \times 0.776625 + 0.6 \times 1.005451 = 0.913921.$$

Notice that doubling the volatility leads to a somewhat unrealistic price greater than 1 (implying a negative yield) in the good state, even though the expected price is less than 1.

Then,

$$P_{t,s} = E_t\left(\widetilde{P}_{t+1,2-1}\,\overline{m}_{t,1}\right)$$
$$= 0.4 \times 0.776625 \times 0.954855 + 0.6 \times 1.005451 \times 0.954260 = 0.872303.$$

The risk neutral price is $\dfrac{E_t\left(\widetilde{P}_{t+1,2-1}\right)}{1 + l_{t,1}} = \dfrac{0.913921}{1.047671} = 0.872336$. So, from Equation 6, $\text{cov}_t\left(\overline{m}_{t,1}, \widetilde{P}_{t+1,2-1}\right) = 0.872303 - 0.872336 = -0.000033$.

As a result, the holding period return on a two-period bond for one year is higher [i.e., $(0.913921 - 0.872303)/0.872303 = 4.771\%$, compared with 4.768% in Example 6], and because of the higher volatility, investors require a higher premium.

There are two practical implications of this analysis for the values of real default-free interest rates:

- An economy with higher trend real economic growth, other things being equal, should have higher real default-free interest rates than an economy with lower trend growth. We should thus expect to find that real default-free interest rates in fast-growing, developing economies, such as India and China, are higher than in slower-growing, developed economies, such as Western Europe, Japan, and the United States. The higher rate of economic growth occurs for developing economies because a developing economy is typically below its steady state growth, so it grows faster to catch up. During these periods, the marginal product of capital (the additional output resulting from the addition of one unit of capital, holding all else constant) would be expected to be higher, so the real default-free interest rate should also be expected to be higher. Of course, this advantage will dissipate as the economy matures, as in the case of Japan and Western Europe from 1950 to 2000.

- Again, other things being equal, real interest rates are higher in an economy in which GDP growth is more volatile than in an economy in which growth is more stable.

EXAMPLE 8

The Present Value Model and Macroeconomic Factors

1. An asset's risk premium is high when:

    A. there is no relationship between its future payoff and investors' marginal utility from future consumption.

    B. there is a positive relationship between its future payoff and investors' marginal utility from future consumption.

    C. there is a negative relationship between its future payoff and investors' marginal utility from future consumption.

Solution:

C is correct. An asset's risk premium is determined by the relationship between its future payoff and the marginal value of consumption as given by the covariance between the two quantities. When the covariance is negative—that is, payoffs are low and expected utility from consumption is high—or equivalently, when times in the future are expected to be bad and the value of an extra unit of consumption is high, the risk premium will be high. When the covariance term is zero (there is no relationship), the asset is risk free. When the covariance term is positive, the asset is a hedge and will have a rate of return less than the risk-free rate.

2. The relationship between the real risk-free interest rate and real GDP growth is:

    A. negative.

    B. neutral.

    C. positive.

Solution:

C is correct. The real risk-free rate is positively related to real GDP growth. An increase in real GDP growth reduces the need for investors to save for future consumption because more goods and services will be available to them in the future relative to today as a result of higher expected income in the future. A higher real rate of interest is needed to induce individuals to save for future consumption in such circumstances.

3. The relationship between the real risk-free interest rate and the volatility of real GDP growth is:

    A. negative.

    B. neutral.

    C. positive.

Solution:

C is correct. The real risk-free rate is positively related to the volatility of real GDP growth. An increase in volatility of real GDP growth means that there is greater risk that the income available for consumption will be lower than expected. Therefore, risk-averse investors will require a higher real rate of return in compensation.

4. A risky asset offers high positive returns during business downturns. A colleague argues that the nominal required rate of return on the asset may be less than the nominal risk-free rate. Is the colleague correct?

    A. Yes

    B. No, the return must be higher than the nominal risk-free rate.

    C. No, the relationship between the asset's nominal return and the nominal risk-free rate is indeterminate.

Solution:

A is correct. For the required return to be less than the risk-free rate, the asset's risk premium would need to be negative. Because the asset supplies relatively high returns in economic conditions in which the marginal utility of consumption is relatively high, the covariance term in Equation 6 is positive and the asset thus bears a negative risk premium.

5. Suppose you are analyzing the expected impact of an increase in real GDP growth above trend on overall equity market valuation. Assume real growth in income of the corporate sector follows real GDP growth. Assume also that there is no impact of the increase on inflation. On the basis of theory

and holding all else constant, explain why the impact of the assumed increase in real GDP growth on overall equity market valuation is ambiguous.

Solution:

Equation 1 can be applied to the overall equity market, which is the aggregate of individual equity securities. The increase in real GDP growth would be expected to affect both the numerator and denominator of Equation 1 in offsetting ways, so the overall effect on equity market value is ambiguous. The impact of an increase in real GDP growth on expected corporate earnings is positive by assumption, which by itself would suggest an increase in equity market value by a larger numerator value in Equation 1. However, the increase in real GDP should also increase the real risk-free rate, which by itself would suggest a decrease in equity market value by increasing the rate at which expected cash flows are discounted. We cannot infer which effect will dominate from the information given. The overall effect on equity market value is ambiguous, under the assumptions given.

8 REAL DEFAULT-FREE INTEREST RATES AND THE BUSINESS CYCLE

☐ explain how the phase of the business cycle affects policy and short-term interest rates, the slope of the term structure of interest rates, and the relative performance of bonds of differing maturities

One of the crucial insights that macro-finance provides is that there should be a connection between the real risk-free rate of interest available in an economy and the underlying trend rate of economic growth in the same economy. We explored the roots of this relationship earlier. To recap briefly, the willingness of investors to substitute future wealth for current consumption will be inversely related to the change in real GDP growth. In a world where GDP growth could be forecasted perfectly, there will be a positive relationship between the real risk-free rate and real GDP growth. But GDP growth is not perfectly predictable. Because of this unpredictability, we also concluded that the real risk-free rate would not only be positively related to real GDP growth but also positively related to the volatility of real GDP growth.

Equation 1 shows that the real default-free required return, $l_{t,s}$, is a component of the discount rate that we apply to the cash flows generated by all financial instruments.

Economic Growth and Real Yields

For evidence of the relationship between real interest rates and GDP growth, we could focus on the yields available from inflation-linked bonds issued by governments in developed economies. These bonds pay a "real" return (or yield) plus a return that is linked directly to an index of consumer prices. Index-linked bonds are issued by many governments in developed economies, including Canada, France, Germany, Italy, Sweden, the United Kingdom, and the United States, and also by some governments in developing countries, such as Brazil. In some markets—for example, the United Kingdom's index-linked gilt market—both the coupon and principal payments from these bonds are indexed to a measure of consumer prices. In other markets—for example, the US Treasury Inflation-Protected Securities (TIPS) market—the principal payment is indexed and the coupon is a function of the indexed principal. In both cases, any increase in the level of the consumer price index over time (that is, positive inflation) leads to an increase in both the coupon payment and eventual principal payment. Although the details of the indexation vary from bond market to bond market, for all practical purposes, we can think of these bonds as being inflation protected.

Given the earlier discussion in sections on real default-free interest rates and default-free interest rates and economic growth, other things being equal, we would expect the (real) yields on inflation-indexed bonds to be higher for those countries with high growth, such as India and China, relative to those issued by, say, the UK or US governments, where economic growth is much lower. Other things being equal, we should also expect to see real yields on short-dated index-linked bonds issued by governments of economies that are very volatile to be higher than real yields on those issued by governments of economies that are less volatile.

Although many index-linked government bond markets are relatively new, we can examine the cross-sectional relationship between economic growth and real risk-free yields relatively easily. Panel A of Exhibit 1 shows the real yields on a set of short-dated index-linked government bonds in 2007, immediately prior to the 2008–2009 global financial crisis. The real yield on short-dated Japanese government bonds at that time were lower than elsewhere, whereas Panel B shows that Japanese growth had been historically very low and not very volatile up to that point in time. Of the developed-economy bond yields in this exhibit, those issued by the Australian government offered the highest yield, perhaps reflecting the relatively strong Australian economic growth shown in Panel B.

Exhibit 1: Real Yields, GDP Growth, and Volatility for Various Countries

Real Yields, July 2007

Growth and Volatility, 1996–2007

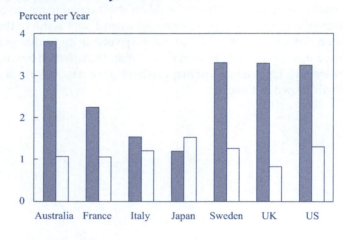

■ Average GDP Growth □ Volatility of GDP Growth

Sources: Based on data from Thomson Reuters and the authors' calculations.

It is difficult to discern a very clear pattern between historical economic growth, the volatility in that growth, and short-term real yields. Nonetheless, it is interesting to note that the correlation between this limited set of bond yields (Panel A of Exhibit 1) and historical growth (gray bars in Panel B of Exhibit 1) is 0.57, but the correlation with historical volatility (white bars in Panel B) is 0.74. So there does appear to be some support for the prediction of macro-theory, although this sample is of course very limited. One of the reasons why there is perhaps not a clearer relationship is that the real yield data are forward looking. The real yield data represent the required real return on these bonds based on expected future growth and volatility in that growth, whereas the GDP-based variables represent historical growth and volatility. If investors use the past as a guide for the future, they might expect a reasonably high correlation between past growth and current real yields. But the past may be a very bad guide for the future, particularly in the case of rapidly developing countries or following the sort of major shock to global economic growth that occurred following the collapse of Lehman Brothers.

EXAMPLE 9

The Evolution of Real Yields

1. We have seen that there is at least tentative evidence to suggest a positive relationship between economic growth and the yields on short-dated real government bonds. But how does the business cycle affect these yields over time?

   The problem in gathering evidence on the drivers of real yields over time is that index-linked government bond markets are a fairly recent financial innovation, especially when compared with conventional government bonds. For example, it was only in 1997 that the first index-linked bond was issued by the US Treasury. The oldest index-linked government bond market is the United Kingdom's. The UK government issued its first index-linked gilt in 1981. To investigate the connections between the macroeconomy and the real risk-free rate over time, we can focus on the UK's index-linked gilt market.

Exhibit 2: Real Yields on UK Index-Linked Gilt and Volatility of UK and OECD GDP Growth

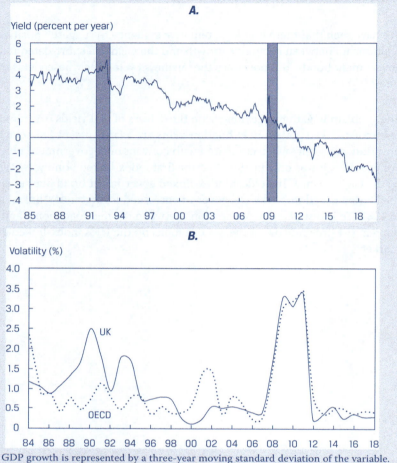

Notes: GDP growth is represented by a three-year moving standard deviation of the variable. Shaded areas in Panel A indicate UK recessions.
Sources: Based on data from OECD.Stat and UK National Statistics Office.

Panel A of Exhibit 2 shows the real yield on a short-dated constant maturity UK index-linked gilt. We will begin by focusing on the period from 1985 to 2007. Although fairly volatile, there is a clear downward trend in this yield from 1985 to 2007. One explanation for this decline could be a commensurate decline in expectations about UK economic growth. However, real economic growth between 1985 and 1999 averaged 2.8%, and between 2000 and 2007 it averaged 2.7%. There was very little change in average growth at a time when real yields were falling, and therefore, it is probably fair to assume that expectations of future growth were relatively stable over this time too. Panel B of Exhibit 2 shows the volatility of UK real GDP growth as represented by a three-year moving standard deviation of this variable. It shows that the volatility of UK economic growth declined quite dramatically from 1995 to 2007. This decline in UK GDP volatility was also experienced elsewhere in the global economy. The same chart shows the decline in GDP volatility for OECD countries. This decline in economic volatility has been called "the great moderation"—that is, a period when the global economy and its financial markets were characterized by relatively low levels of volatility. Therefore, one plausible explanation for the declining level of real interest rates in the United Kingdom is that they were driven down by the moderation in economic volatility between the early 1990s and 2007.

The evidence in Exhibit 2 suggests that declining levels of economic volatility led to declining levels of the real default-free interest rate in the United Kingdom between 1999 and 2007. However, the absence of such markets elsewhere over this sample period does not mean that the same phenomenon was absent or irrelevant in other developed-economy bond markets. The yield on a conventional government bond includes a number of components, one of which is the real default-free rate of return. So, in all likelihood, declining global economic volatility led to declines in the real rates of return required by investors elsewhere, which, in turn, may have contributed to the decline in conventional government bond yields. See Example 10 for an illustration of how the global financial crisis affected real short rates. We will focus on the drivers of conventional government bond yields relative to index-linked government bond yields at a later stage.

EXAMPLE 10

Post–Global Financial Crisis, 2008–2011 Real Default-Free Yields

1. Exhibit 3 shows the yields on short-dated index-linked bonds at the end of 2011. Compared with their pre-crisis levels shown in Exhibit 2, they had all fallen. The collapse of Lehman Brothers and the ensuing liquidity and sovereign debt crisis caused economic and financial market volatility to rise substantially, as shown in Panel B of Exhibit 2. Other things being equal, one would have expected the real yields to rise, not to fall. But other things were not equal. One explanation for the fall in these real yields is that, despite the higher volatility experienced in 2008–2011, investors believed that future real economic growth would be lower and, therefore, that the equilibrium real yield in these economies was deemed to be commensurately lower.

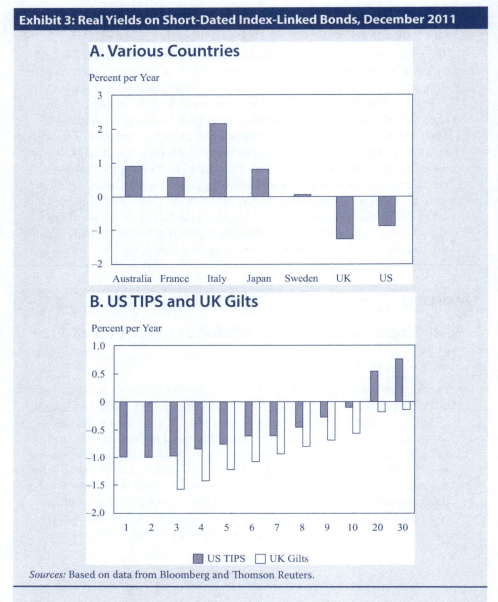

Exhibit 3: Real Yields on Short-Dated Index-Linked Bonds, December 2011

Sources: Based on data from Bloomberg and Thomson Reuters.

Panel A of Exhibit 3 also shows that real short-dated rates in the United Kingdom and United States were not just lower than they were in the immediate pre-crisis period but that they were negative, too. Panel B shows that most inflation-linked bonds issued by the US government (TIPS) and all inflation-linked bonds issued by the UK government (index-linked gilts) at this time were also negative (term structure will be explored in more detail later). One explanation for the lower yields may have been the fear among some investors of very high levels of inflation in the future. Arguably, the easy monetary policy, including both formal (US and UK) and informal (eurozone) quantitative easing programs, implemented because of the collapse of Lehman Brothers along with other events, may have led enough investors to believe that inflation-linked government bonds offered the inflation protection they needed despite the low and even negative historical real yields.

But it is also important to remember that index-linked bonds issued by developed-economy governments not only are quite special, given the credit and inflation protection that they provide, but also are often in very limited supply. These characteristics mean that in times of crisis and of great uncer-

> tainty, investors may see them as a safe haven for their capital, which can, in turn, drive down their yields.

Real Default-Free Interest Rate Summary

The real default-free interest rate, which we have proxied here with the yields on short-term inflation-protected government bonds, has a close connection with the business cycle via the related connection with the saving decisions of individuals. We can put this discussion in the context of the basic pricing shown in Equation 1. For a real default-free bond, Equation 1 simplifies to

$$P_t^i = \sum_{s=1}^{N} \frac{CF_{t+s}^i}{\left(1 + l_{t,s}\right)^s}. \tag{9}$$

Because it is a fixed-interest investment that is default-free, the cash flow at time $t + s$ is certain. Equation 9 implies that it is only changes in $l_{t,s}$ that will affect the price of such a bond. In turn, $l_{t,s}$ will be determined by real economic growth and the volatility in economic growth over time as a result of the aggregation of the consumption and saving decisions of individual investors.

THE YIELD CURVE AND THE BUSINESS CYCLE

9

☐ | explain how the phase of the business cycle affects policy and short-term interest rates, the slope of the term structure of interest rates, and the relative performance of bonds of differing maturities

Earlier, we considered the determination of the price of a real default-free bond (see Equation 9). The analysis demonstrated that the saving and investment decisions of investors mean that the expected return on these bonds will be positively related to both expected real GDP growth and the expected volatility of this growth. We now move on to consider the price of a default-free bond that pays a fixed nominal (currency) amount when it matures. We will consider, for example, a bond issued by a government in a developed economy where the prospect of default is so negligible that it is ignored.

What factors would affect the price of such a bond? First, we consider a world without inflation. In this world, investors would still be giving up current consumption by investing in this bond today, in which case Equation 9 would be appropriate. But of course, deferring consumption at time t in a world with positive inflation will have an impact on the quantity of goods that can be bought at time $t + s$ when the bond matures. Investors will want to be compensated by this bond for the inflation that they expect between t and $t + s$, which we define as $\theta_{t,s}$. If investors could forecast inflation perfectly, they would demand a return given by $l_{t,s} + \theta_{t,s}$ to compensate them for the expected inflation and ensure the real level of consumption. But unless the investment horizon is very short, investors are unlikely to be very confident in their ability to forecast inflation accurately. Because we generally assume that investors are risk averse and thus need to be compensated for taking on risk and because they seek compensation for expected inflation, they will also seek compensation for taking on the uncertainty related to future inflation. We denote this risk premium by $\pi_{t,s}$, which is distinct from the risk premium in Equation 1 ($\rho_{t,s}^i$).[6] We can rewrite our basic pricing formula for a default-free nominal coupon-paying bond from Equation 9 as follows:

$$P_t^i = \sum_{s=1}^{N} \frac{CF_{t+s}^i}{\left(1 + l_{t,s} + \theta_{t,s} + \pi_{t,s}\right)^s}. \tag{10}$$

Note that the bond's payoff is still certain in nominal terms because we are assuming that there is a negligible chance that the issuer (a developed-economy government) will default on its commitments. It is the real value of this payoff that is now uncertain, hence the need for a risk premium, $\pi_{t,s}$, on nominal bonds.

EXAMPLE 11

The Risk Premium for Inflation Uncertainty

1. Suppose that an analyst estimates that the real risk-free rate is 1.25% and that average inflation over the next year will be 2.5%. If the analyst observes the price of a default-free bond with a face value of £100 and one full year to maturity as being equal to £95.92, what would be the implied premium embedded in the bond's price for inflation uncertainty?

Solution

The (approximate) implied premium can be calculated as follows:

$$\pi_{t,s} = 0.504\% = \frac{100}{95.92} - (1 + 0.0125 + 0.025).$$

Having established Equation 10, we will now focus on the relationship between short-term nominal interest rates and the business cycle, in which the nominal bond issued by a government in a developed economy has a very short maturity—for example, a US government Treasury bill.

Short-Term Nominal Interest Rates and the Business Cycle

Treasury bills (T-bills) are very short-dated nominal zero-coupon government bonds. T-bills are issued by most developed-economy governments or by their agents to help smooth the cash flow needs of the government. The short-dated nature of T-bills and the fact that they are often used to implement monetary policy means that their yields are also usually very closely related to the central bank's policy rate. Indeed, because of their short-dated nature, the uncertainty that investors would have about inflation over an investment horizon of, say, s equals three months will usually be relatively low. Therefore, for the purposes of the exposition in this section of the reading, we will assume that $\pi_{t,s}$ is so negligible that we can ignore it. So, we can modify Equation 10 to give Equation 11, which can capture all of the salient features of the pricing dynamics of a T-bill:

$$P_t^i = \frac{CF_{t+s}^i}{\left(1 + l_{t,s} + \theta_{t,s}\right)^s}. \tag{11}$$

Note that the summation term is not needed because there is only one payment from a T-bill.

---

6 Even though it is a risk premium, we have suppressed the superscript i on the inflation uncertainty risk premium because it is not asset specific and applies across all asset classes.

We have already examined the way in which the real default-free rate of interest, $l_{t,s}$, will vary over time with the business cycle and how it may also be affected by its status as a haven in times of economic uncertainty. We now move on to consider how a central bank's policy rate, which is a short-term nominal interest rate, evolves with the business cycle.

TREASURY BILLS AND THE BUSINESS CYCLE

10

☐ explain how the phase of the business cycle affects policy and short-term interest rates, the slope of the term structure of interest rates, and the relative performance of bonds of differing maturities

To summarize briefly, the nominal rate of interest will equal the real interest rate that is required to balance the requirements of savers and investors plus investors' expectations of inflation over the relevant borrowing or lending period. It follows that short-term nominal interest rates will be positively related to short-term real interest rates and to short-term inflation expectations. Other things being equal, we would also expect these interest rates to be higher in economies with higher, more volatile growth and with higher average levels of inflation over time.

Panel A of Exhibit 4 shows the yield on a three-month US T-bill, and Panel B shows the yield on an equivalent T-bill issued by the UK government. In each panel of the exhibit, we also present the inflation rates in these two economies. There is a close correlation between measured inflation and T-bill yields in both economies. Although measured inflation is not the same as expected inflation, it is likely that current inflation plays a big role in the formation of inflation expectations, particularly over the very short investment horizon involved when investing in a T-bill.

Exhibit 4: Treasury Bill Rates and Inflation

United States

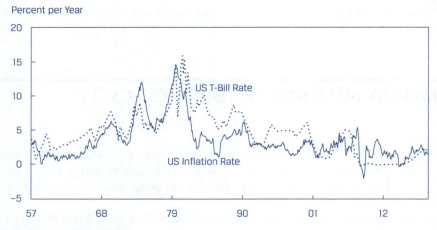

United Kingdom

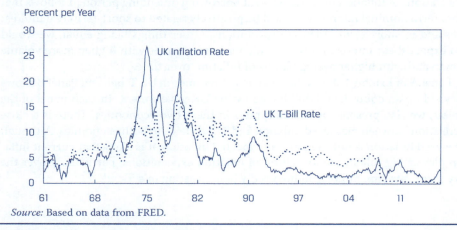

Source: Based on data from FRED.

Exhibit 4 clearly shows that the inflation environment is a key driver of short-term interest rates. The central banks and monetary authorities responsible for setting interest rates in an economy do so in response to the economy's position in the business cycle—cutting their policy rates when activity and/or inflation are judged to be "too low" and raising rates when activity and/or inflation are judged to be "too high." In other words, a responsible central bank or monetary authority will usually set its policy rate with reference to the level of expected economic activity and the expected rate of increase of prices—that is, inflation. Exhibit 5 shows the close relationship between the yields on short-term default-free T-Bills in the United States and United Kingdom and the policy rates of their respective central banks.

Treasury Bills and the Business Cycle

Exhibit 5: Interest Rates and Policy Rates

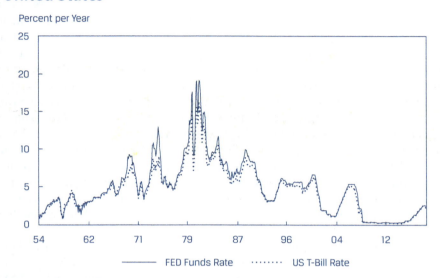

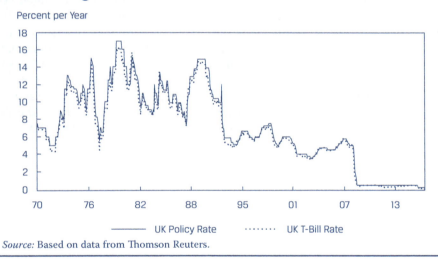

Source: Based on data from Thomson Reuters.

A US economist, John Taylor, devised a rule for setting policy rates, a rule that could help rate setters gauge whether their policy rate is at an "appropriate" level (Taylor 1993). This rule is known as the Taylor rule, and it takes the following form:

$$\begin{aligned} pr_t &= l_t + \iota_t + 0.5\left(\iota_t - \iota_t^*\right) + 0.5\left(Y_t - Y_t^*\right) \\ &= l_t + 1.5\,\iota_t - 0.5\,\iota_t^* + 0.5\left(Y_t - Y_t^*\right), \end{aligned} \qquad (12)$$

where pr_t is the policy rate at time t, l_t is the level of real short-term interest rates that balances long-term savings and borrowing in the economy, ι_t is the rate of inflation, ι_t^* is the target rate of inflation, and Y_t and Y_t^* are, respectively, the logarithmic levels of actual and potential real GDP. The difference between Y_t and Y_t^* is known as the "output gap," which is essentially measured in percentage terms. When the output gap is positive, it implies that the economy is producing beyond its sustainable capacity. This situation is similar to a marathon runner who sets off way too fast at the start of a race; in the end, he will overheat and break down unless he reduces his running pace. Conversely, when the output gap is negative, it implies that the economy is producing below its sustainable capacity. This situation is similar to a marathon runner who sets off too slowly. If he wants to win the race, at some point, he will have to use up conserved energy and speed up. Positive output gaps are usually associated with high and/or rising inflation, whereas negative output gaps are usually accompanied by high levels of unemployment. Generally, the policy rule should have a larger weight on inflation (1.5) relative to the weight on output (0.5). The purpose is to stabilize inflation over the longer term near the targeted inflation rate (note that the reason for the weightings is that the inflation rate appears twice in the equation; see the first line of Equation 12). When inflation is close to the targeted or preferred rate and when the output gap is zero, the appropriate policy rate will be equal to the level of the short-term real interest rate, l_t, that balances long-term savings and borrowing in the economy plus the targeted/preferred rate of inflation. This level of the policy rate is often referred to by economists as the neutral policy rate—that is, the policy rate that neither spurs on nor impedes real economic activity. Other things being equal, when inflation is above (below) the targeted level, the policy rate should be above (below) the neutral rate, and when the output gap is positive (negative), the policy rate should also be above (below) the neutral rate. For example, if l_t is 2.0%, ι_t is 3.0%, ι_t^* is 2.0%, and the output gap is 2.0%, then the "appropriate" policy rate implied in the Taylor rule would be 6.5%.

Using fairly conservative parameters, including inflation targets when they are known, and a measure of the output gap estimated by the OECD, we have calculated policy rates based on the Taylor rule for three developed economies back to 1990, as shown in Exhibit 6. The policy rates based on the Taylor rule for the United States, shown in Panel A, seem to track the Fed's actual policy rates fairly closely until the collapse of the high-tech bubble in the early 2000s. According to the Taylor rule, the Fed kept policy rates "too low for too long" between 2002 and 2005. A similar picture emerges for Canada, as shown in Panel B. There is less evidence that policy rates were kept "too low for too long" after the collapse of the high-tech bubble in the United Kingdom, as shown in Panel C. More recently, in response to the liquidity and credit crisis, all three central banks cut their policy rates sharply. According to the Taylor rule, for all three economies, policy rates were "too low" by the end of 2018.

Exhibit 6: Policy Rates and Taylor Rule Calculations

United States

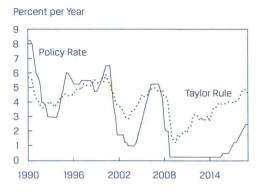

Canada

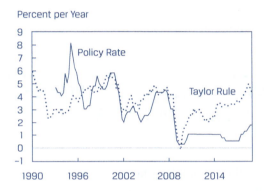

United Kingdom

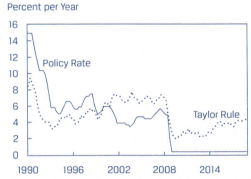

Sources: Based on data from each country's central bank and the authors' calculations.

The notion that short-term interest rates can be at too high or too low a level implies that the relationship between short-term interest rates and the business cycle are interdependent. In other words, instead of moderating the business cycle over time with deft changes to the policy rate, central bankers can exaggerate any cycle by not responding optimally to economic conditions—that is, by committing policy errors. For example, setting rates too low for too long risks creating a credit bubble, whereas setting them too high for too long could lead to recessionary or even depression-like economic conditions.

Short-Term Interest Rate Summary

Short-term default-free interest rates tend to be very heavily influenced by the inflation environment and inflation expectations over time. But they will also be influenced by real economic activity, which, in turn, is influenced by the saving and investment decisions of households. But these interest rates will also be affected by the central bank's policy rate, which, in turn, should fluctuate around the neutral policy rate as central banks respond over time to deviations in inflation from a preferred or target rate and to developments in the output gap. Finally, it is important to remember that the neutral rate will also vary with the level of real economic growth and with the expected volatility of that growth. In addition, the neutral rate might also change if the level of inflation targeted or preferred by the central bank changes. Between 1992 and 1997, the UK inflation target was between 2% and 4%; in 1997, the target became 2.5% with a 1 percentage point allowance around this target. The target was changed in 2003 to 2.0% and to a different definition of inflation, with a 1 percentage point allowance around this target.

In the next section of this reading, we will focus on the relationship between the underlying economy and longer-term nominal default-free government bonds.

11 CONVENTIONAL GOVERNMENT BONDS AND BREAK-EVEN INFLATION RATES

> ☐ | describe the factors that affect yield spreads between
> | non-inflation-adjusted and inflation-indexed bonds

The pricing equation shown in Equation 10 can be used to highlight the key components that go into pricing conventional (coupon-paying) government bonds. We will consider the impact that time to maturity can have on the pricing formula later, but first we will focus on the impact of inflation expectations on conventional bond prices.

Break-Even Inflation Rates

The fundamental difference between the pricing formula as applied to, for example, a three-month T-bill (as in Equation 11) and its application to, for example, a default-free zero-coupon bond (as in Equation 10) relates to their investment horizons. The relative certainty about the real payoff from a three-month T-Bill and thus the relative certainty about the amount of consumption that the investor will be able to undertake with the payoff means that the investment in the T-Bill will be a good hedge against possible bad consumption outcomes. In other words, the payoff, in real terms, from a three-month T-bill is highly unlikely to fall if the investor loses his or her job during the T-bill's three-month investment horizon. The low, probably zero, correlation between the T-bill's payoff with bad consumption outcomes will mean that the risk premium needed to tempt an investor to invest in the T-bill will be close to zero (hence Equation 11).

However, it is unlikely that the same level of certainty would apply, for example, to a 20-year default-free conventional government bond. For such a bond, it would seem reasonable to assume that the risk premium would be higher than that related to a one- or three-month T-bill. Note that the cash flow in Equation 10 is still certain, but only in nominal terms. Because investors will naturally have less confidence in their ability to form views about future inflation over 20 years relative to their ability

Conventional Government Bonds and Break-even Inflation Rates

to form those views over three months, the greater uncertainty about the real value of the bond's payoff will cause investors to demand a premium in compensation for this uncertainty, represented by $\pi_{t,s}$ in Equation 10.

The difference between the yield on, for example, a zero-coupon default-free nominal bond and on a zero-coupon default-free real bond of the same maturity is known as the break-even inflation (BEI) rate. It should be clear from the discussion earlier that this break-even inflation rate will incorporate the inflation expectations of investors over the investment horizon of the two bonds, $\theta_{t,s}$, plus a risk premium that will be required by investors to compensate them predominantly for uncertainty about future inflation, $\pi_{t,s}$. Although the evolution of real zero-coupon default-free yields over time should be driven mainly by the inter-temporal rate of substitution, the evolution of their nominal equivalents will, in addition, be driven by changing expectations about inflation and changing perceptions about the uncertainty of the future inflation environment. We can see this evolution by plotting the constant maturity zero-coupon break-even inflation rates over time.

Panels A, B, and C of Exhibit 7 show the 10-year break-even inflation rates derived from three government bond markets in developed economies where index-linked government bonds have been available for some time now—Australia, the United Kingdom, and the United States—along with the respective inflation rates of each economy. The UK and Australian data, which are available for longer historical periods, show the gradual decline in break-even inflation rates since the mid-1980s. This decline was probably driven by the changing inflation environment in these economies. Between 1985 and 1990, inflation averaged approximately 6.0% and 7.5% in the United Kingdom and Australia, respectively. Between 2000 and 2011, having fallen steadily during the 1990s, inflation averaged 3.0% and 3.2% in the United Kingdom and Australia, respectively. Ten-year break-even rates in the United States were only available starting in 1997, a period when US inflation was relatively low and stable. Panel D of Exhibit 7 highlights the impact of the liquidity and credit crisis of 2008–2009 on break-even rates for a range of economies. It shows that for all of these developed economies, 10-year break-even inflation rates fell in response to the weaker global economic environment and weaker inflationary backdrop. The weaker inflationary pressure arises from the lower demand for resources in an economic downturn, so that cost and prices do not rise as fast. For example, 10-year Italian break-even inflation rates fell from 2.3% to 0.8%, reflecting the effect of the eurozone crisis on the Italian economy at that time.

> nominal yield
> − real yield (i.e., TIPS)
> = BEI rate

Exhibit 7: Break-Even Inflation Rates and Inflation

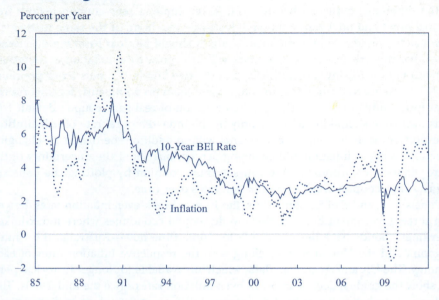

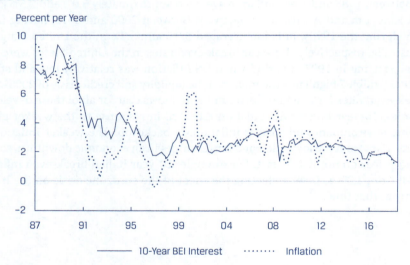

Conventional Government Bonds and Break-even Inflation Rates

United States

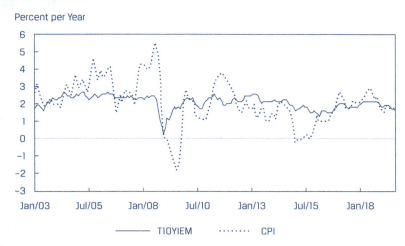

Changes in BEI Rates

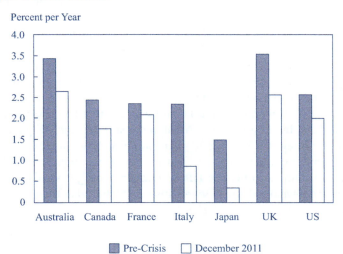

Sources: Based on data from Bloomberg and the authors' calculations.

Being able to measure financial market expectations of future inflation is of great value to central banks. Break-even inflation rates provide an independent view about future inflation that can be compared with the judgment of the central bank; although, of course, this judgment can be interdependent. However, it is important to remember that break-even inflation rates are not simply the markets' best guess of future inflation over the relevant investment horizon. Break-even inflation rates will also include a risk premium to compensate investors for their uncertainty largely about future inflation and, therefore, the uncertainty about the quantity of goods and services that they will be able to consume in the future.

12 THE DEFAULT-FREE YIELD CURVE AND THE BUSINESS CYCLE

☐ explain how the phase of the business cycle affects policy and short-term interest rates, the slope of the term structure of interest rates, and the relative performance of bonds of differing maturities

So far we have discussed the fundamental pricing relationship for default-free real and nominal bonds and short-term nominal interest rates. We now elaborate on these relationships over different investment horizons. We have already indicated that the maturity of a bond will have an impact on the way that investors price it. We now focus on this relationship more specifically. But first consider Panel A in Exhibit 8, which shows the US zero-coupon Treasury curve on three different dates. From July 2007 (just prior to the wider financial crisis) to the end of 2011, the US Treasury curve shifted down by between 3 and 4 percentage points and also became steeper. The short end of the curve was clearly influenced by the reduction in the Fed's policy rate over this period, which fell from 5.25% to virtually 0%. Panel B shows that there was a similar decline in the short end of the gilt curve, as the UK central bank gradually cut its policy rate from 5.75% to 0.50% in response to the same crisis.

Panel A shows that the Treasury curve was upward sloping on each of these dates. Panel B shows that by the end of 2011 the UK government and US government curves looked very similar, but what is interesting is that the UK government curve was downward sloping in July 2007. This slope meant that the UK government could borrow 1-year money at 6.25% but 30-year money at 4.8%. In fact, on the same date, the UK government could borrow 50-year money at just over 3.0%. What economic factors could explain not only the fall in Treasury and gilt yields, as well as those elsewhere in the developed world, over this period but also the very negative slope of the gilt curve in the summer of 2007?

The Default-Free Yield Curve and the Business Cycle

Exhibit 8: US and UK Government Bond Yields and Break-Even Inflation Rates for July 2007, December 2010, and December 2011

US Treasury Curve

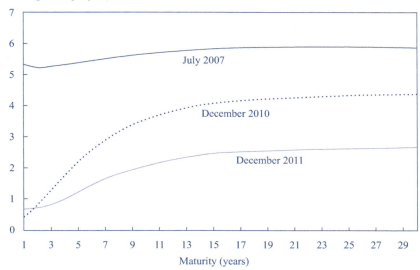

UK Gilt Curve

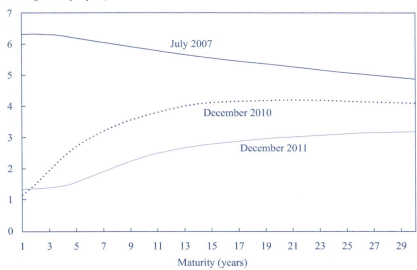

US BEI Rates

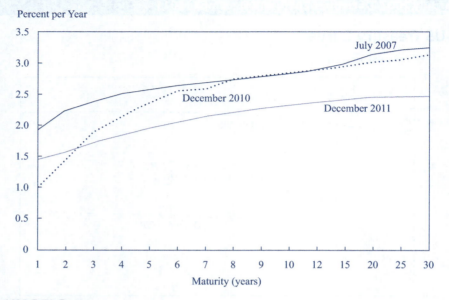

UK BEI Rates

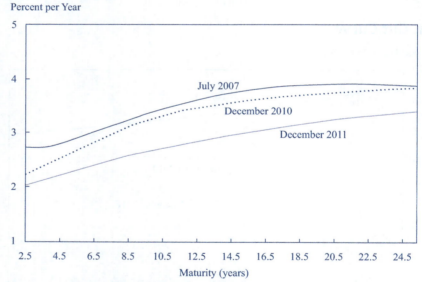

Sources: Based on data from the Bank of England and Thomson Reuters.

Panels A and B of Exhibit 8 show how the shape of the default-free yield curves shifted in response to the financial crisis precipitated by the collapse of Lehman Brothers. Panels C and D of the exhibit show how break-even inflation rates shifted over the same period. When there is a significant shift in the yield curve, it is often very informative to break down the change into the real and inflationary components. Over this period, the US and UK break-even curves both shifted by just less than a full percentage point across the entire maturity spectrum. This fact could be taken to indicate that as the global recession gathered pace, US and UK government bond investors gradually "priced in" lower and lower levels of future inflation. But crucially, Panels A and B show that the nominal curves shifted down by more than 1 percentage point. For example, the US curve fell by as much as 3 percentage points. These facts suggest that market participants saw the financial crisis as potentially having a bigger impact on economic growth than on inflation. Indeed, by December 2011 the US and UK break-even inflation curves were both upward sloping.

The Default-Free Yield Curve and the Business Cycle 41

This dissection of default-free yield curves and the interpretations that are often made by analysts based on the relative movements of the real and break-even components can be very informative, but the analysis presupposes either that there is no risk premium embedded in investors' return expectations or that any risk premium is constant over time. But the risk premium is unlikely to be zero or constant over time.

EXAMPLE 12

Level, Slope, and Curvature of the Yield Curve

1. The yield curves shown in Exhibit 8 all have three distinct characteristics. These characteristics are referred to as *level*, which indicates whether rates are high or low, on average; *slope*, which is an indicator of the steepness of the curve, or how quickly or slowly rates change with maturity; and *curvature*, an indicator of how much the curve is different from a straight line. These characteristics were first noted in rates by Steeley in 1990 and Litterman and Scheinkman in 1991. All three components can change over time. We can calculate how much of the change in any yield curve is attributable to each of these factors over time. We have performed this calculation for the UK and US yield curves using data with maturities ranging from 3 months to 10 years, spanning the period from January 1999 to January 2014. The principal components analysis technique was used to perform the analysis. These results are shown in Exhibit 9. The majority of movement of the US (92.7%) and UK (95.2%) yield curves is in the level—that is, shifts up and down in the yield curve over time. The slope component accounts for a much smaller proportion of the change over time—6.9% for the US curve and 4.5% for the UK curve. Curvature changes account for only 0.3% in each case (note that we have rounded these figures to the nearest decimal point for convenience). Taken together then, changes in these three factors explain the vast majority of changes to these two yield curves over time. These results are typical for government bond yield curves in developed economies.

Exhibit 9: Percentage of Yield Curve Movement Explained by Three Components

	Level	Slope	Curvature
United States	92.7%	6.9%	0.3%
United Kingdom	95.2%	4.5%	0.3%

Sources: Based on data from Bloomberg and the authors' calculations.

Exhibit 10 presents another way of viewing the dynamics of the US yield curve for 15 years starting in 1999. The chart shows the way in which the level, slope, and curvature of the US Treasury curve has changed over time.

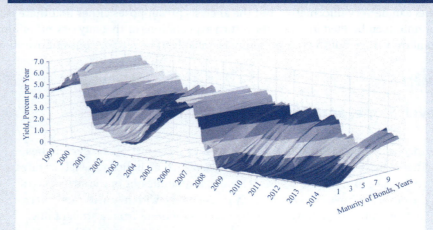

Exhibit 10: The US Yield Curve, 1999–2014

We would expect the level of economic activity to influence yield curve levels. We would also expect that views of future inflation will determine the level of these yield curves because these are nominally dominated bonds. The slope of the yield curve will be influenced by the magnitude of the risk premium in Equation 5 between the price of the bond and the inter-temporal rate of substitution over the investor's time horizon. A positive slope would be a reflection of this risk premium. However, it is not the only variable that affects the slope of the yield curve. The policy rate of the central bank is set based on Taylor rule–like considerations (that is, consideration of the components that make up the rule) so that short rates will tend to be lower during recessions because central banks tend to lower their policy rate in these times. (Note that no suggestion is made that central banks slavishly follow the Taylor rule; the rule just neatly encapsulates two of the key macroeconomic considerations that go into the process of setting the interest rate.) But the impact of monetary policy on longer-term rates will not be as strong because the central bank will usually be expected to bring short-term rates back to normal as the recession recedes and the risk-free rates will increase as economic growth recovers. Thus, the slope of the yield curve will increase during the recession. Finally, if investors anticipate that policy rates as well as short-term risk-free rates will revert back to normal as the recession recedes, then the yield curve will become steeper for the short-term maturities but flatter for the long-term maturities so that the curvature can increase as well. As a result, the shape of the yield curve and its three factors can provide valuable information for both central banks and investors.

13. THE SLOPE OF THE YIELD CURVE AND THE TERM SPREAD

☐ explain how the phase of the business cycle affects policy and short-term interest rates, the slope of the term structure of interest rates, and the relative performance of bonds of differing maturities

The required return on future default-risk-free cash flow was explained as consisting of a real interest rate, a premium for expected inflation, and a risk premium demanded by risk-averse investors for the uncertainty about what inflation will actually be (see Equation 10). Thus, referring to government yield curves, expectations of increasing or decreasing short-term interest rates might be connected to expectations related to future inflation rates and/or the maturity structure of inflation risk premiums.

Expectations of declining short-term interest rates can explain the downward-sloping UK gilt curve in the summer of 2007. If bond market participants expect interest rates to decline, then reinvestment of the principal amounts of maturing short-term bonds at declining interest rates would offset the initial yield advantage of the shorter-dated bonds. These expectations caused the United Kingdom's yield curve to be downward sloping or inverted.

Thus, the variation in short rates over time—in particular, the central bank's policy rate—can influence the shape of the yield curve. These short rates are, in turn, driven by the positive relationship between the real rate of interest that balances investment and saving decisions over time and by the level of and volatility in GDP growth, as well as by the variation of the rate of inflation around the central bank's target, or preferred, level.

The Term Spread and the Business Cycle

Exhibit 11 shows the time variation in the slope of the US and UK government yield curves since 1900. In both cases, the slopes have been calculated as the difference (spread) between a long-dated government bond and the yield on an equivalent one-year bond.

Exhibit 11: US and UK Government Yield Curve Spreads

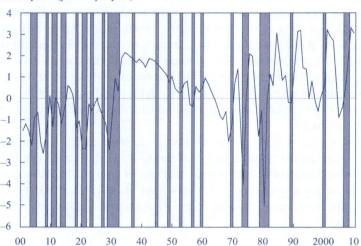

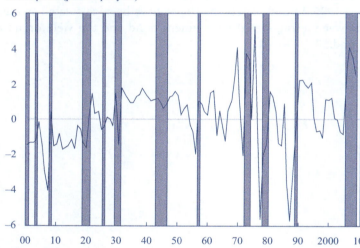

Note: Shaded areas indicate recessions.
Sources: Based on data from NBER and the Bank of England.

In both markets, there are times when the curves were very steep. For example, in the mid-1970s the steep slope implied expectations of a sharp increase in interest rates. This was a time when both inflation and inflation expectations were high, following the first oil shock of 1973.

But there are times when both curves are steeply inverted—for example, in 1979–1980. The inverted curves in these times implied an expectation of sharply falling inflation and future interest rates. In both economies, the nominal policy rates were extremely high: Policy rates peaked at 17.5% in the United States in December 1980 and at 17% in the United Kingdom in November 1979. During this period, the Fed chairman, Paul Volcker, and Margaret Thatcher had raised policy rates in their respective economies in response to the second oil shock of 1979 and administrations on both sides of the Atlantic came to the conclusion that the defeat of inflation should be the number one policy objective. The inverted curves in both markets suggest that investors expected rates to come down once the causes of high current inflation had

The Slope of the Yield Curve and the Term Spread

been removed. Generally speaking, Exhibit 11 also reveals that a recession is often preceded by a flattening, or even an inversion, in the yield curve. In general, the late stages of a business expansion are often characterized by a peak in inflation and thus relatively high short-term interest rates. If longer-maturity yields reflect lower inflation rates and diminished business credit demand, the yield curve would tend to flatten or invert. An inverted yield curve, in particular, is often read as being a predictor of recession.

> *- The slope of the yield curve will typically steepen during a recession.*

EXAMPLE 13

Interest Rates, the Yield Curve, and the Business Cycle

1. What financial instrument is best suited to the study of the relationship of real interest rates with the business cycle?

   A. Default-free nominal bonds
   B. Investment-grade corporate bonds
   C. Default-free inflation-indexed bonds

Solution:

C is correct. These bonds' prices are sensitive to changes in real interest rates because the payments are adjusted for changes in the price of goods.

2. Suppose investors forecast an unanticipated increase in real GDP growth and the volatility of GDP growth for a particular country. The effect of such a forecast would be for the coupon payments of an inflation-indexed bond issued by the government of the country:

   A. to rise.
   B. to fall.
   C. to be indeterminate.

Solution:

A is correct. The coupon payments would be expected to increase, reflecting an increase in the real interest rate.

3. The yield spread between non-inflation-adjusted and inflation-indexed bonds of the same maturity is affected by:

   A. a risk premium for future inflation uncertainty only.
   B. investors' inflation expectations over the remaining maturity of the bonds.
   C. both a risk premium for future inflation uncertainty and investors' inflation expectations over the remaining maturity of the bonds.

Solution:

C is correct. The difference between the yield on a zero-coupon default-free nominal bond (such as a US government STRIP) and on a zero-coupon default-free real bond of the same maturity (such as a US government TIPS) is called the break-even inflation rate. The break-even inflation rate should incorporate investors' inflation expectations over the remaining maturity plus a risk premium for uncertainty about future inflation, as in Equation 10.

4. State an economic reason why inverted yield may predict a recession.

Solution:

The late stages of business cycles are often characterized by relatively high inflation and high short-term interest rates. To the extent that longer-term yields reflect expectations of declining inflation and a slackening in demand for credit, the yield curve would be expected to flatten or invert.

14 EVIDENCE ON RISK PREMIUMS FOR DEFAULT-FREE BONDS

☐ explain how the phase of the business cycle affects policy and short-term interest rates, the slope of the term structure of interest rates, and the relative performance of bonds of differing maturities

If, as seems likely, most investors want to be compensated for taking on risk, then the yield curve, as well as containing information about the interest rate expectations of investors, will also embody a risk premium.

We have already explained why investors would value investments that paid off more in bad times relative to those investments that paid off less in these times or produced negative returns. This preference tends to drive the expected return down and the price of these favored investments up relative to those with prices that are more positively correlated with bad times. The average slopes of the US and UK government curves from 1900 to 2011 were 0.24% and 0.14%, respectively; in the post-1945 period, they were 0.50% and 0.40%, respectively. This difference suggests that, on average, investors have been willing to pay a premium for shorter-dated US and UK government bonds, which, in turn, means that longer-dated bonds may not be such a good hedge against economic bad times. One interpretation of an upward-sloping yield curve is that short-dated bonds are less positively (or more negatively) correlated with bad times than are long-dated bonds.

Exhibit 12 presents information on the relationship of government bonds with a range of maturities from a selection of countries. Panel A shows that the average yield differences (longer minus shorter) between different bond maturities, with one exception, are all positive. This fact suggests that the bond risk premium generally rises with maturity, which is why it is often referred to as the term premium. Panel B presents the total return on these government bonds by maturity. Over the sample periods, the total returns achieved generally rise with maturity in each of the bond markets. But why have government bond investors generally been rewarded for holding longer-dated government bonds relative to shorter-dated bonds?

In Panel C, we present the correlation between (1) the total return on bonds with various maturities and (2) the economic growth of the relevant economy. One thing to notice is that the correlations are predominantly negative. This fact suggests that government bonds in these markets tend to pay off in bad times, which means that investors are willing to pay a relatively high price for them. Therefore, investors should be willing to accept a relatively low return from government bonds because they are at least a partial hedge against "bad" consumption outcomes.

Evidence on Risk Premiums for Default-Free Bonds

Exhibit 12: Government Bond Spreads, Total Returns, and GDP Growth Correlations for Four Markets

Panel A: Spreads

	5 vs. 2	10 vs. 5	30 vs. 10
Canada	0.40	0.40	
France	0.46	0.52	0.60
UK	0.27	0.26	−0.05
US	0.55	0.44	0.39

Panel B: Total Returns

	2	5	10	30
Canada	5.61%	6.70%	8.08%	9.60%
France	4.44%	6.09%	7.80%	10.24%
UK	7.14%	7.82%	10.12%	11.03%
US	5.77%	6.91%	7.72%	9.07%

Panel C: Correlation with GDP

	2	5	10	30
Canada	−4.93%	−5.12%	−0.70%	2.75%
France	4.71%	−9.14%	−10.27%	−2.13%
UK	−4.66%	−2.74%	−5.11%	0.79%
US	−7.30%	−14.33%	−12.31%	−10.35%

Note: The sample period for the United Kingdom and the United States is January 1980 to December 2018. For France and Canada, it is January 1985 to December 2018.
Sources: Thomson Reuters and authors' calculations.

The results shown in Exhibit 12 suggest that government bond risk premiums

- are positive,
- are probably related to the consumption hedging benefits of government bonds, and
- are positively related to bond maturity, which means that the "normal" shape for the yield curve is upward sloping.

The last point also helps to explain why the US Treasury curve was generally upward sloping between the summer of 2007 and the end of 2011: A significant portion of the slope was probably related to the existence of a positive risk premium on US Treasuries that increased with maturity.

However, bond risk premiums ($\pi_{t,s}$), like other risk premiums, will not be constant over time. In times of economic uncertainty, investors will tend to more highly value assets that pay off in bad times—government bonds—which will force their prices up as the risk premium demanded falls. Unfortunately, it is impossible to say how big or small this premium really is or should be or how it evolves with the business cycle. But we can get some idea by performing the following experiment. Suppose we can assume that the real return on an index-linked government bond is a good proxy for the real rate of interest that balances savings and investment in an economy over time. If we subtract the yield on an index-linked government bond from the yield on a conventional government bond with a similar maturity and then subtract from this amount a survey-based measure of inflation expectations, what is left over is the bond risk premium. That is, the extra yield investors require for holding a conventional government bond over and above the real required return and the return in compensation for expected inflation.

Exhibit 13: Bond Risk Premiums (BRPs)

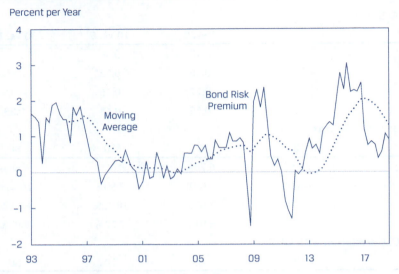

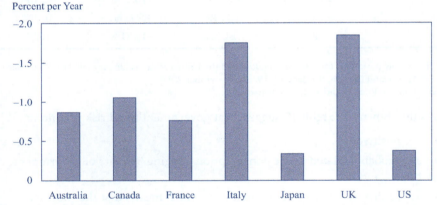

Note: The period 1993–1997 in Panel A was before the inflation-targeting regime.

Panel A of Exhibit 13 presents a calculation of this kind for the UK government bond market. There are a number of points worth noting with respect to this particular representation of the bond risk premium. First, it is certainly imperfect because it shows that the bond risk premium is negative at times. A negative bond risk premium implies that investors are willing to pay for assuming risk, which is inconsistent with risk aversion. Second, putting aside these negative values for the moment, we can see that the bond risk premium varies over time. Between 1993 and mid-1997, the risk premium on UK government bonds averages just less than 1.5%; from mid-1997 to 2005, it averages around 0.25%; and from 2013 to 2018, it averages around 1.42%.

Panel B in Exhibit 13 is based on similar estimates for the bond risk premiums over the global financial crisis for a range of markets and shows the change in the bond risk premiums from July 2007 to December 2011. For all the government bond markets for which we could make these calculations, the bond risk premium fell—in some cases, quite substantially. This fact implies that investors placed greater value on the consumption-hedging properties of government bonds as a result of the financial crisis. Other things being equal, this implies that they were willing to pay a higher price for these bonds compared with the price they were willing to pay before the crisis. This also implies that bond risk premiums will tend to rise in times when investors place less value on the consumption hedging properties of government bonds.

OTHER FACTORS

15

☐ | explain how the phase of the business cycle affects policy and short-term interest rates, the slope of the term structure of interest rates, and the relative performance of bonds of differing maturities

In practice, the shape of the yield curve and the relative performance of bonds with different maturities over the business cycle depend on a complex mixture of interest rate expectations and risk premium considerations. For example, a downward-sloping curve is probably largely the result of investor expectations of future declines in interest rates. The drivers of an upward-sloping curve are more ambiguous. For example, the existence of bond risk premiums that are positively related to maturity means that an upward-sloping curve may not embody expectations of future rate increases. Conversely, it could imply a combination of expected rate increases and risk premiums or even expected rate cuts that are more than offset by the existence of positive risk premiums.

— In the case of an upward sloping yield curve, expectations relating to the future direction of interest rates are indeterminate

We have to acknowledge that there will also be times when other factors play a part in shaping the yield curve. Developed-economy government bonds are technically default-free because these governments can, in principle, always print cash to meet the promised payments. In this sense, they are very special financial instruments. These markets can also be influenced by supply and demand factors that seem to move yields in ways that do not appear to be consistent with the business cycle. Consider the following examples:

- In the late 1990s, fiscal surpluses in the United States led some investors to take the view that the supply of Treasuries would shrink as the US government paid back its debts (leading to the Treasury scare of 2000). This perceived reduction in future supply was said to have been responsible for the decline in yields as investors bought up these bonds in anticipation of their future scarcity.

- In the early 2000s, Treasury yields were apparently being pushed down by Asian central banks that were using their growing trade surpluses to purchase US Treasuries.

- Regulatory factors can also play an important role in determining government bond yields. This influence is particularly clear in the gilt market. In 1997, the UK government passed legislation that effectively compelled UK pension funds to buy long-dated gilts. This legislation appears to have been one of the main drivers of the inversion of the long end of the United Kingdom's yield curve (see Exhibit 8, Panel B). Since that time, new accounting rules for pensions—FRS17, followed by IAS19—forced UK pension schemes to increase their demand for long-dated UK government bonds further still. These actions created a vicious circle because the new accounting rules required the schemes to discount their liabilities using the long-dated yields as the discount rate. Consequently, UK pension funds bought long-dated bonds, forcing their yields down. The decline in yields caused the present value of pension liabilities to rise relative to the value of scheme assets, creating deficits. To achieve a better match between assets and liabilities, schemes tried to buy more long-dated gilts, causing their yields to fall further and liabilities to rise further. A similar phenomenon affected core eurozone bond and swap markets. For more than three years, the yield spread between 10- and 30-year Dutch government bonds (30 minus 10) was negative. It was argued that the negative spread was a direct result of the hedging activities of Dutch pension funds, which had over €1 trillion of pension liabilities. The buying pressure on a government bond market that was only around 60% the size of these liabilities thus caused long-dated Dutch government bond prices to rise.

There is no doubt that supply and demand considerations along with poorly thought out regulatory or accounting rules can have an impact on government bond markets. But determining the extent of these effects is very difficult. Nevertheless, it is difficult to explain the very inverted shape of the long end of the gilt curve, which has persisted for many years now, without reference to such factors.

EXAMPLE 14

The Japanese Yield Curve and Business Cycle, 1990–2018

1. During the 1980s, real Japanese GDP growth averaged more than 4.60% per year. During the 1990s and 2000s, it averaged around 1.5%. The catalyst for the decline in growth was the collapse of Japan's property bubble and the stock crash in the early 1990s. Exhibit 14 shows Japan's real annual GDP growth over the post-bubble period, which incorporates the global financial crisis of 2008–2009. The exhibit also shows how real short-term policy rates fell steadily from a level of 4%–5% in 1990, finally becoming negative by 1997. Since that time, real rates have generally been negative as Japan's central bank, the Bank of Japan, has tried to stimulate its economy by cutting its nominal policy rate to (near) zero.

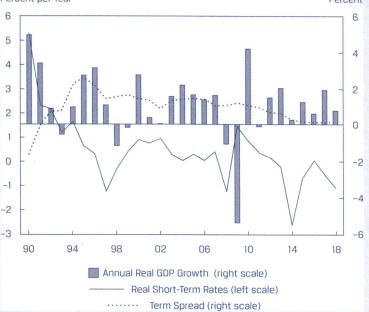

Exhibit 14: Japan's GDP Growth, Real Short-Term Rates, and Term Spread, 1990–2018

Sources: Based on data from Thomson Reuters and the authors' calculations.

Exhibit 14 also shows the term spread over this period—that is, the slope of the yield curve (created by subtracting the policy rate from 10-year Japanese government bonds). At the start of the period, as the Bank of Japan cut its policy rate from just over 8.0% at the end of 1990 to 0.45% by the end of 1995, the curve steepened—from −1.63% at the end of 1990 to 2.59% by the end of 1995. The sharp steepening of the curve in response to the cuts in the policy rate arguably indicated the market's view that the policy stimulus would work; that is, the yields on longer-dated Japanese government bonds embedded some expectation of positive growth and inflation in the future. However, since the mid-1990s, despite cutting its policy rate to zero and enacting programs of quantitative easing, the term spread has fallen steadily. By the end of 2018, it was virtually 0.00%. The weak economic growth and inflation environment in Japan since the collapse of the property bubble is reflected in the fall and flattening of the Japanese yield curve.

CREDIT PREMIUMS AND THE BUSINESS CYCLE

☐ explain how the phase of the business cycle affects credit spreads and the performance of credit-sensitive fixed-income instruments

Earlier we discussed the economic drivers of what we have referred to as default-free interest rates and bond yields. But the financial crisis has caused many to question what "default-free" really means. The bonds issued by many European governments, including those issued by France and Italy as well as those issued by the Greek, Portuguese, Irish, Belgian, and Spanish governments, were all thought to be default-free before the euro financial crisis from 2010 to 2012. Even the default-free status of US Treasuries has now been questioned by both investors and credit rating agencies. Any bond that is perceived to be default-free will, by definition, not have to compensate investors for taking on default, or credit, risk. However, for any corporate or government bond that embodies the non-zero probability that the issuer may default on its obligations, bondholders will demand a risk premium, referred to as the credit premium.

In Equation 1, we emphasized that the discount rate on the cash flows of financial assets will normally include a risk premium, which we defined generically as $\rho_{t,s}^i$. When we considered the pricing formula for default-free government bonds, we emphasized that the risk premium attached to these bonds, $\pi_{t,s}$, is largely a function of uncertainty about future inflation and that this uncertainty is likely to be greater for longer-dated bonds relative to shorter-dated bonds (recall that this risk premium, $\pi_{t,s}$, is distinct from the addition to return that investors require on the basis of their expectations of inflation over the investment horizon, $\theta_{t,s}$, per Equation 1). But it is important to emphasize that these factors will play a role in the pricing of bonds that embody credit risk, too. In other words, the evolution of $\pi_{t,s}$ plays a role in determining the price of credit risky bonds too. We thus need to acknowledge the separate role that credit risk plays in the price of a corporate bond or, indeed, any bond with default risk. We have therefore adapted our basic pricing Equation 1 to augment the discount rate with a credit premium, $\gamma_{t,s}^i$, which is distinct from the inflation-based risk premium attached to default-free bonds, $\pi_{t,s}$, as shown in Equation 13.

$$P_t^i = \sum_{s=1}^{N} \frac{E_t\left[\overline{CF}_{t+s}^i\right]}{\left(1 + l_{t,s} + \theta_{t,s} + \pi_{t,s} + \gamma_{t,s}^i\right)^s} \tag{13}$$

Notice that Equation 13 acknowledges the uncertain nature of the cash flows, $CF_{t,s}$, on credit risky bonds; although the schedule of these payments is known, the existence of credit risk means that there will be uncertainty about whether they will be paid as scheduled. In the event of a default, the amount that the bond investor receives will depend on the recovery rate, which will also be an unknown quantity. The risk premium demanded by investors because of these uncertainties is represented by $\gamma_{t,s}$ in Equation 13.

In this section, we will focus on the credit premium, $\gamma_{t,s}^i$, and in particular on the relationship between the business cycle and the credit premium on corporate bonds.

EXAMPLE 15

The Credit Risk Premium

1. Suppose that an analyst estimates that the real risk-free rate is 1.25%, average inflation over the next year will be 2.5%, and the premium required by investors for inflation uncertainty is 0.50%. If the analyst observes the price of a corporate bond with a face value of £100, with one full year to maturity, as being equal to £94.21, what would be the implied credit premium embedded in the bond's price for inflation uncertainty?

Solution

The (approximate) implied premium can be calculated as follows:

$$\gamma_{t,s}^i = 1.90\% = \frac{100}{94.21} - (1 + 1.25\% + 2.50\% + 0.50\%).$$

Credit Spreads and the Credit Risk Premium

The difference between the yield on a corporate bond and that on a government bond with the same currency denomination and maturity is generally referred to as the credit spread. It is demanded by investors in compensation for the additional credit risk that they bear compared with that embodied in the government bond.

As Equation 13 shows, credit risky bonds share the same risk as default-free bonds, which market participants often refer to as interest rate risk, but they also embody credit risk, $\gamma_{t,s}^i$. Other things being equal, a parallel shift up in the yield curve will have an almost identical proportionate impact on the prices of, say, a five-year government bond and a five-year corporate bond. And over time, again other things being equal, the interest rate component of a corporate bond will be driven by the same factors that drive government bond yields and returns. In other words, they are both subject to interest rate risk.

It is the credit risk component of a corporate bond, $\gamma_{t,s}^i$, and the evolution of bond spreads that will cause corporate and comparable government bond returns to diverge over time. It would seem sensible to assume that the premium demanded would tend to rise in times of economic weakness, when the probability of a corporate default and bankruptcy is highest. Exhibit 15 confirms this view. The exhibit shows a representative spread on both AAA/Aaa and BBB/Baa rated US corporate bonds over US Treasuries. (The AAA rating category in "AAA/Aaa" is the rating category used by both Standard & Poor's and Fitch Ratings; Aaa is the equivalent rating category used by Moody's Investors Service.) First, the Baa spread is always higher than the Aaa spread, reflecting the lower credit quality of Baa rated bonds relative to Aaa rated bonds. Second, the US recession periods shaded grey in the chart indicate that both low- and higher-grade corporate bond spreads do tend to rise in the lead-up to and during a recession and to decline once the economy comes out of recession.

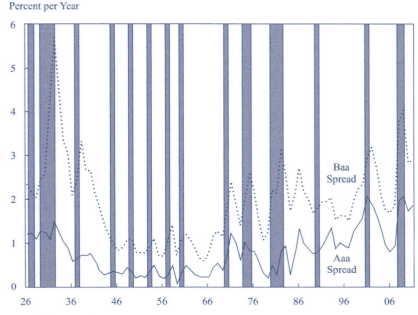

Exhibit 15: Credit Spreads and the Business Cycle

Note: Shaded areas indicate recessions.
Source: Based on data from Moody's Investors Service.

As expected, the business cycle has a profound effect on credit spreads, but what are the basic components of the credit spread? If we assume that investors are risk neutral, then they will simply demand a return (yield) on their corporate bond investments sufficient to compensate them for the possible loss that they could incur from holding a corporate bond. In turn, this expected loss will depend on the probability of default and the expected recovery rate in the event of default, as shown in Equation 14:

$$\text{Expected loss} = \text{Probability of default} \times (1 - \text{Recovery rate}). \tag{14}$$

In the instance where investors are risk neutral, the expected return on, say, a 10-year government bond would be equal to the loss-adjusted expected return on a comparable 10-year corporate bond. In practice, however, investors are risk averse, so the expected return on a corporate bond will be higher than that on a comparable government bond, even if a significant amount of the credit risk can be mitigated by holding a diversified portfolio of corporate bonds. One of the main reasons why investors continue to be exposed to considerable market risk even in a well-diversified portfolio is that defaults tend to cluster around downturns in the business cycle. Panels A and B of Exhibit 16 show this quite clearly. Panel A shows the number of US corporate defaults per year since 1920, and Panel B shows annual default rates over the same period. Both charts show that there are often long periods of time when there are very few defaults. However, the US depression of the 1930s and the recessions in the 1980s, 1990s, and 2000s were all associated with relatively high default levels and rates. The historical default rates on different ratings classes are sometimes used by analysts as a proxy for the probability of default in Equation 14 for expected loss.

Credit Premiums and the Business Cycle

Exhibit 16: US Corporate Defaults, Default Rates, Recovery Rates, and Loss Rates

Number of Defaults

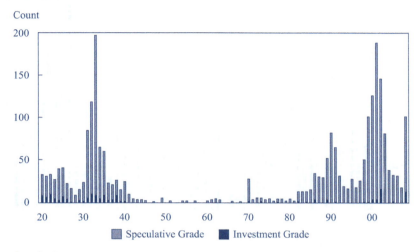

Default Rates

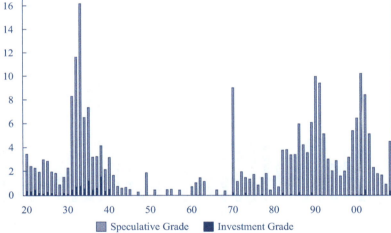

Recovery Rates

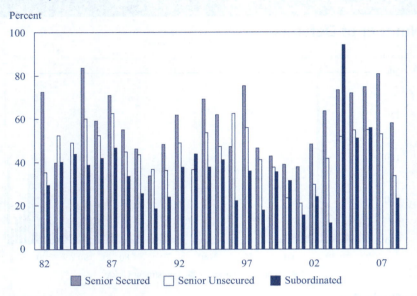

Loss Rates

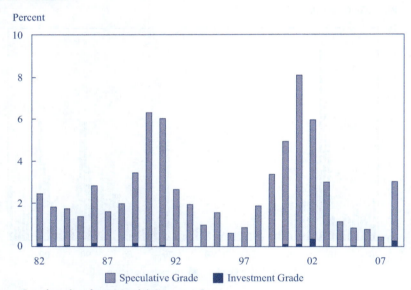

Source: Based on data from Moody's Investors Service.

Panel C of Exhibit 16 shows the evolution of recovery rates on three types of corporate bonds: senior secured, senior unsecured, and subordinated. Senior secured debt, as the name suggests, is secured by a lien or other claim against some or all of the company's assets, whereas senior unsecured debt has no explicit claim to the company's assets in the event of bankruptcy. This explains why recovery rates are generally higher for secured as opposed to unsecured debt holders. Subordinated debt holders, as the name suggests, have an inferior claim on the company's assets compared with senior debt holders, and unsurprisingly, recovery rates are often very low. The recovery rate ranking is interesting, but we can also see from Panel C that recovery rates tend to be higher when the economy is expanding and lower when it is contracting. The reason is that assets that can be sold in order to recover value for bond holders are likely to fetch a higher price in a buoyant economic environment than in a stagnant one. Finally, Panel D shows the loss rates on US corporate debt from 1982 to 2008. These loss rates are the net result of the defaults and recovery rates over time. Unsurprisingly, these loss rates are counter-cyclical with regard to the business cycle, meaning that they tend to rise as economic activity declines.

INDUSTRY- AND COMPANY-SPECIFIC CREDIT QUALITY

17

☐ | explain how the characteristics of the markets for a company's products affect the company's credit quality

Although spreads will evolve with the business cycle, Exhibit 17 illustrates that spreads between corporate bond sectors with different ratings will often have very different sensitivities to the business cycle. Panel A presents a shorter but finer picture of the relative performance of US corporate bonds by Moody's rating category. The graph shows that when spreads are narrowing relative to government bonds, the spreads between higher- and lower-rated bond categories also narrow. In these times, although corporate bonds will generally outperform government bonds, lower-rated corporate bonds will tend to outperform higher-rated bonds. The converse is true as spreads widen, a phenomenon that is illustrated most graphically following the collapse of Lehman Brothers in 2008. The spread on speculative, or high-yield, debt rose from a pre-Lehman Brothers collapse low of around 2.8% to a peak of just more than 20.0%. Over the same period, Baa rated debt spreads rose from around 1.1% to 8.5% and Aaa corporate bond spreads rose from 0.6% to 4.5%.

— The issuers with a good credit rating tend to outperform those with lower ratings as the spread between low-and higher-quality issuers widens.

Exhibit 17: US Credit Spreads and the Business Cycle

Moody's Rating

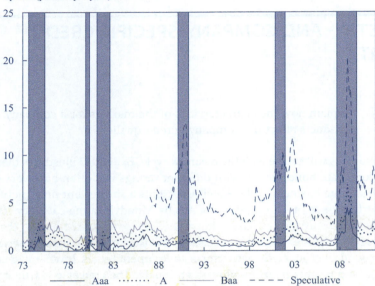

Industrial Sector

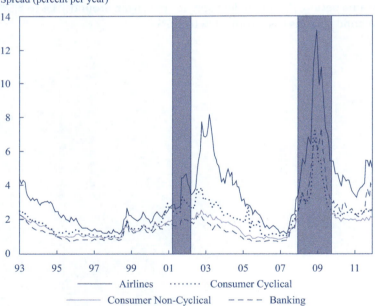

Note: Shaded areas indicate recessions.
Sources: Based on data from Thomson Reuters and the authors' calculations.

Panel B in Exhibit 17 illustrates another determinant of credit spreads: industrial sector. Analysis by industrial sector addresses the question of how the type of goods and services that individual companies produce may be related to credit quality. Some industrial sectors are more sensitive to the business cycle than others. This sensitivity can be related to the types of goods and services that they sell or to the indebtedness of the companies in the sector. Panel B shows evidence of only the divergent performance of corporate bond sectors over a relatively short period, but the performance of the four sectors shown is very different in times of economic stress. First, in both of the recessions that this period covers (indicated by the shaded areas in Panel B), the spread on the consumer cyclical sector rose more dramatically than it did for corporate bonds in the consumer non-cyclical sector. For example, the spread on the consumer cyclical sector peaked at just under 4.0% in 2003, compared with around 2.5% for the consumer non-cyclical sector. Second, the graph shows how sensitive the airline sector's credit spread is to the business cycle. The sharp widening of spreads in this sector as a result of both recessions is probably also a function of the lower credit quality, on average, of companies in the airline sector. Third, the recession of the early 2000s had only a mild impact on the spreads of banks but a much larger impact in the post-Lehman period, when the sector spread peaked at nearly 7.5%. This difference highlights the fact that the last recession and crisis were first and foremost a banking crisis. But perhaps the most interesting feature is the narrowing of sector spreads in the summers of 1998 and 2007. In both of these periods, investors were content to receive virtually the same credit spread, $\gamma_{t,s}^{i}$, on airline company debt as on debt issued by companies in the consumer non-cyclical sector.

Company-Specific Factors

Corporate bond spreads will be driven over time by the business cycle, but the impact of the economic environment on spreads will depend on issuers' industrial sector and rating. When spreads widen, the spreads on bonds issued by corporations with a low credit rating and/or that are part of a cyclical sector will tend to widen the most. Company-specific factors will also play a part in determining the difference in the yield of an individual corporate issuer and that of a government bond with the same maturity. Issuers that are profitable, have low debt interest payments, and are not heavily reliant on debt financing will tend to have a high credit rating because their ability to pay is commensurately high.

Exhibit 18 provides summary statistics on financial statements for companies across a range of Moody's rating categories. Pre-tax interest coverage is calculated by dividing total pre-tax earnings by total debt interest payments. On average, Aaa companies had $17.60 of pre-tax earnings for every $1 of interest payment to which they were committed. By contrast, on average, Baa companies had only $2.50, whereas the average B and Caa rated companies could not cover their interest payments with current-period pre-tax earnings. The ratio of free operating cash flow to total debt gives another indication of the profitability and financial flexibility of a company relative to its outstanding debt. There is again a clear deterioration in this metric as average rating quality declines. Finally, the ratio of total debt to total capital gives an idea of the overall indebtedness of a company. Together these and other ratios allow analysts and credit rating agencies to determine a company's ability to meet its debt obligations as they come due. If this ability declines relative to other issuers in their sector, then the spread demanded on their debt will rise, relative to the sector average, and their rating may be lowered by the rating agency.

Exhibit 18: Ratings and Financial Ratios

	Aaa	Aa	A	Baa	Ba	B	Caa
Pre-tax interest coverage (×)	17.6	7.6	4.1	2.5	1.5	0.9	0.7
Free operating cash flow/Total debt (%)	42.3	28	13.6	6.1	3.2	1.6	0.8
Total debt/Total capital (%)	21.9	32.7	40.3	48.8	66.2	71.5	71.2

Source: Based on data from Moody's Investors Service.

18 SOVEREIGN CREDIT RISK

> explain how the phase of the business cycle affects credit spreads and the performance of credit-sensitive fixed-income instruments

— The fact that countries have both printed money to pay back debt and defaulted on it gives rise to a non-zero credit risk premium

So far we have discussed the risk premium demanded by investors on both default-free and corporate debt. But credit premiums have always been an important component of the expected return on bonds issued by governments in developing or emerging economies. Even though many of these governments can print money to meet their debt obligations *in extremis*, meaning that they could technically avoid defaulting on these debts, many developing-economy governments have defaulted on their debts in the past. For example, the Russian government defaulted on its debt in 1998, and many others, including Argentina, Brazil, and Mexico, have also defaulted. Such defaults are often very country specific in character, but the global economic environment, oil prices, and the evolution of global trade will often play a part in precipitating such sovereign defaults.

The credit risk embodied in bonds issued by governments in emerging markets is normally expressed by comparing the yields on these bonds with the yields on bonds with comparable maturity issued by the US Treasury. Panel A of Exhibit 19 shows the evolution of this spread for three emerging market bond indexes. The impact of the credit crisis is clear; spreads rose in response to the uncertain economic environment globally. But the volatility of the spreads from 1998 to 2003 is a function of the Asian financial crisis in 1997, the Russian debt crisis in 1998, and the recession in developed economies in 2001–2002 following the collapse of the high-tech bubble. What is interesting is the decline in spreads for US Treasuries up to 2007, along with the much narrower spreads between the regions at this time. Strong global economic growth between 2003 and 2007 convinced investors that they did not need such a high reward for emerging market default risk and that they did not need to differentiate much between regions.

Sovereign Credit Risk

Exhibit 19: Sovereign Credit Spreads

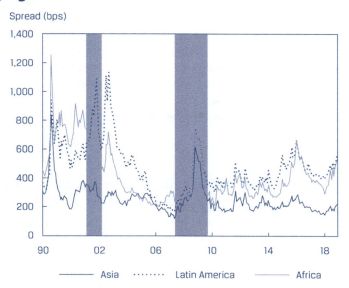

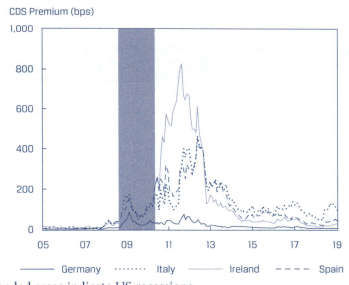

Note: Shaded areas indicate US recessions.
Sources: Based on data from Thomson Reuters and the authors' calculations.

The 2008–2009 global financial crisis caused many investors to question what is meant by the term "default-free." Until that time, there was thought to be a set of developed-economy government issuers for which the likelihood of debt default was so low that it could almost be ignored. In other words, investors did not demand meaningful compensation for assuming this risk. Panel B of Exhibit 19 shows how this perception changed dramatically for the debts of a set of eurozone economies during the crisis. The chart shows the cost that an investor would have to pay for insuring themselves against a sovereign default on German, Italian, Irish, and Spanish government debt over the next five years through the purchase of credit default swaps (CDSs). For example, in January 2006 that cost was 1.8, 8.8, 2.5, and 2.8 bps, respectively. So, to insure oneself against a default on bonds issued by these governments with, say, a notional value of €10 million would have cost €1,800, €8,800, €2,500, and

€2,800, respectively, per year. However, by August 2011, this insurance cost had risen to €59,830, €306,860, €825,390, and €300,610, respectively. Although the causes of this reassessment of sovereign credit risk inherent in developed-economy debt were complex, the basic reason for the increase in the credit risk premium was a reassessment by investors of these sovereign issuers' ability to pay and the likelihood that they might default. The perception of their ability to pay deteriorated dramatically as private-sector debts were absorbed onto sovereign balance sheets. And so, to some extent, the rise in this insurance cost was related to the balance sheets of these sovereign nations in much the same way that a deterioration in the quality of the balance sheet of a corporate borrower would cause its credit spread to widen.

> **EXAMPLE 16**
>
> ### The Credit Premium for the Royal Bank of Scotland
>
> The global financial crisis had an impact on the prices of all financial assets. Exhibits 15 and 17 show the impact of the crisis on credit spreads derived from indexes, whereas Exhibit 19 demonstrates how the same crisis caused the credit spreads on some sovereign issuers to rise dramatically too. In Exhibit 20, we focus on the impact of the crisis on the CDS premium (a close proxy for the credit spread) on five-year Royal Bank of Scotland senior unsecured debt. The exhibit shows the same increase in the perception of credit risk. The eventual decline in the premium was a consequence of the UK government's nationalization of this systemically important global bank.
>
>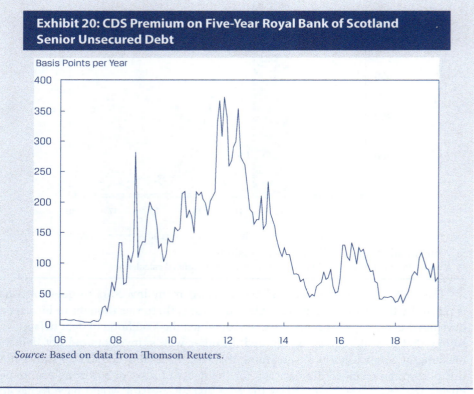
>
> **Exhibit 20: CDS Premium on Five-Year Royal Bank of Scotland Senior Unsecured Debt**
>
> Source: Based on data from Thomson Reuters.

Credit Premium Summary

The credit premium ($\gamma_{t,s}^i$) is the additional yield required by investors over and above the yield required on comparable default-free debt that investors demand for taking on credit risk. It will tend to rise and fall with the business cycle, mainly because

Equities and the Equity Risk Premium

credit risk will tend to rise as an economy turns down and to fall as an economy turns up. However, when credit spreads are generally narrowing, the rate of improvement will tend to be greater for those bonds issued by entities with a relatively weaker ability to pay. At these times too, investors seem to be less discerning among issuers with weak and strong credit credentials. But as the business cycle turns down, those issuers with a good credit rating tend to outperform those with lower ratings as the spread between low- and higher-quality issuers widens. This relationship between the economic cycle and defaults means that credit risky bonds (corporate or sovereign) tend to perform poorly in bad economic times, and because of this tendency, investors demand a credit premium.

EQUITIES AND THE EQUITY RISK PREMIUM

19

☐ | explain the relationship between the consumption hedging properties of equity and the equity risk premium

Earlier we discussed the credit risk embedded in a bond that has been issued by either a corporation or government, which might not honor its promise to pay the coupons and principal payment in full and on time. Investors can thus not be certain that they will receive the future scheduled cash flows from credit risky bonds. However, when investors purchase bonds that embody credit risk, normally they at least know the proposed schedule of payments and how they are to be determined. But there are other financial instruments in which both the size and timing of the cash flows are uncertain and, indeed, where the cash flows may not materialize at all. The best example of a security that has cash flows with these characteristics is equity because the dividend payment is not promised, can rise and fall over time, and in the event that the issuing corporation becomes bankrupt, can cease altogether.

For equities, we can rewrite the generic pricing equation, Equation 1, as follows:

$$P_t^i = \sum_{s=1}^{\infty} \frac{E_t\left[\overline{CF}^i_{t+s}\right]}{\left(1 + l_{t,s} + \theta_{t,s} + \pi_{t,s} + \gamma^i_{t,s} + \kappa^i_{t,s}\right)^s} \qquad (15)$$

Notice that this equation is essentially the same as that for credit risky bonds (Equation 13), but there is no maturity to the cash flows, so investors are essentially buying cash flows (dividends) into perpetuity (∞). In addition, we now have a new term in the discount rate, $\kappa^i_{t,s}$, which is the additional return that investors require for investing in equities, over and above what they require for investing in credit risky bonds $\left(l_{t,s} + \theta_{t,s} + \pi_{t,s} + \gamma^i_{t,s}\right)$.

The term $\kappa^i_{t,s}$ is essentially the equity premium relative to credit risky bonds. This is not the way the equity risk premium is usually expressed. We have expressed it this way for the moment because of the following reasons:

- If a company experiences financial difficulties because the company's debt holders have the senior claim on the company's cash flow, the equity holders will receive the residue, which could be zero, and

- in the event that a company's financial difficulties become so bad that the company is forced into bankruptcy, both bond and equity investors will lose. But depending on the quality of the company, investors in the corporate bond can usually expect to get some of their investment back. The equity investors, however, will normally lose all of their investment. Both debt and equity investors are exposed to risk, but the potential loss is greater for the equity investor.

These are the reasons why investors will require a risk premium, $\kappa_{t,s}^i$, over and above the one that they would require on the corporation's debt, $\gamma_{t,s}^i$. Equation 15 shows that both corporate bond and equity holders face what we might define as corporate risk. It is the combination of this risk that is usually referred to as the equity risk premium. Because the risk associated with equities is normally expressed relative to default-free debt of the same currency, we can rewrite Equation 15 as follows:

$$P_t^i = \sum_{s=1}^{\infty} \frac{E_t\left[\overline{CF}_{t+s}^i\right]}{\left(1 + l_{t,s} + \theta_{t,s} + \pi_{t,s} + \lambda_{t,s}^i\right)^s} \tag{16}$$

where the equity risk premium, $\lambda_{t,s}^i$, is equal to $\gamma_{t,s}^i + \kappa_{t,s}^i$. That is, it is the addition to return required by investors over and above the compensation for risk that they require for holding a default-free government bond of the same currency (technically, a very long-dated, plain-vanilla, coupon-paying, default-free bond).

Equities and Bad Consumption Outcomes

Equity investors will demand an equity risk premium if the consumption hedging properties of equities are poor—that is, if equities tend not to pay off in bad times. Our arguments earlier indicate that the equity risk premium should be positive and therefore, implicitly, that equities are a bad hedge for bad consumption outcomes. However, tying down the exact relationship between equity performance and consumption over time has proved to be very difficult. But we can get some idea of the relationship if we consider a very long history of the real returns produced by equities.

—If investors demand high equity risk premiums, they are likely expecting their future consumption and equity returns to be positively correlated

Equities and the Equity Risk Premium

Exhibit 21: Annual Real Equity Returns, 1900–2010

United States

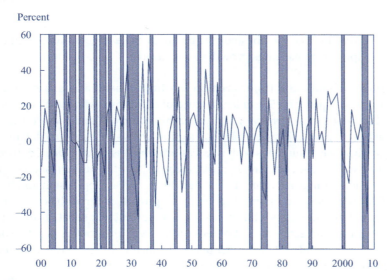

United Kingdom

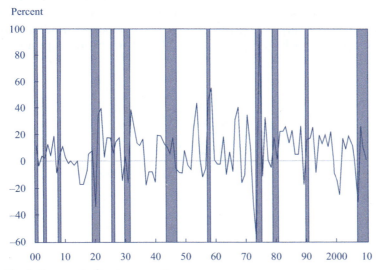

Note: Shaded areas indicate recessions.
Sources: Based on data from Shiller (2000), the Bank of England, and the authors' calculations.

Exhibit 21 shows the annual real (inflation-adjusted) returns generated by both US (Panel A) and UK (Panel B) equities from 1900 to 2010. Generally speaking, sharp falls in equity prices are associated with recessions—bad times. For example, real UK equity prices more than halved as a recession hit the United Kingdom in 1972, and real US equity prices fell by more than 40% during the Great Depression. More recently, real UK and US equity prices fell by 30% and 40%, respectively, in 2009. Given this evidence, it is difficult to argue that equities are a good hedge for bad consumption outcomes. We would thus expect the equity risk premium to be positive, and given the scale of the declines in prices possible in bad times, we might expect it to be quite large.

Before we consider how large the equity premium should be, we will first focus on the cash flow that equities generate. It is the nature of this cash flow that leads investors to demand an equity risk premium in the first place.

20 EARNINGS GROWTH AND THE ECONOMIC CYCLE

☐ explain how the phase of the business cycle affects short-term and long-term earnings growth expectations

The uncertainty about—and time variation in—future dividends, as represented by the numerator in Equation 15, is a key feature of equity investment. Panels A and B of Exhibit 22 show a long history of US real earnings growth and a shorter history of UK real earnings growth, respectively. The exhibit shows that a sharp decline in real earnings nearly always coincides with a recession, which is to be expected; recessions are associated with declines in employment, incomes, output, and, subsequently, profitability. US real earnings fell dramatically during the Great Depression and by nearly 60% in 2009. Conversely, sharp increases in profit growth occur at the end of a period of recession and in some cases while recession conditions still persist. Thus, corporate profitability can lead an economy out of recession as well as into it: A negative demand shock can cause demand and corporate profits to shrink. In response, companies lay off workers, reducing their cost base and thereby adding to the recessionary backdrop. When an upturn in demand occurs, perhaps in response to monetary policy stimulus, demand growth on a lower cost base can lead to a sharp increase in corporate profits, which then leads companies to invest and hire more staff, and so on. Some analysts thus consider corporate profitability to be an important leading indicator of the business cycle and believe it provides useful information about future growth.

Earnings Growth and the Economic Cycle

Exhibit 22: Real Equity Earnings Growth in the United States and the United Kingdom

United States

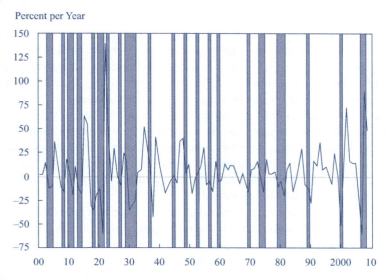

United Kingdom

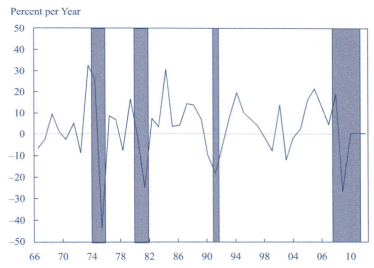

Note: Shaded areas indicate recessions.
Sources: Based on data from Shiller (2000) and the Bank of England.

Equity analysts spend the majority of their time focusing on the numerator in Equation 15—that is, forming views about expected earnings and, therefore, about dividends and free cash flow. Given the close relationship between aggregate earnings, or profits, and the business cycle shown in Exhibit 22, an understanding of the business cycle is crucial for earnings projections, particularly in the short term. However, the business cycle will not affect the corporate profits of every company in the same way. The type of product sold or service provided by the company will have an impact on earnings and consequently on equity performance over the business cycle.

Some companies make products or provide services that are relatively insensitive to general economic conditions. Toothpaste might fall into this category. Because the cost of toothpaste usually only represents a small proportion of the overall household budget, people will generally still want to keep their teeth clean even if the economy is in recession, and because they are unlikely to want to clean their teeth more often simply because the economy is booming, the demand for toothpaste will remain fairly stable over the business cycle. Companies and equity sectors that produce such products are referred to as non-cyclical or defensive investments. By contrast, some companies, such as airlines, will produce goods or provide services that are extremely sensitive to the business cycle. In difficult economic conditions, consumers are much more likely to postpone or cancel their vacations or to vacation at home than to reduce their consumption of toothpaste, and businesses are likely to cut back on airline travel. Generally speaking, an annual family vacation will constitute a large proportion of the household budget, and most people do not need a vacation in the same way that they need toothpaste or soap. Businesses may rely on alternatives to expensive travel for meetings, such as video conferencing. By contrast, in good times when real incomes are rising, people are more likely to take more vacations or more expensive ones, and the increase in business activity may necessitate more meetings in new, often distant markets. Economists and investment strategists may view a rise in the earnings of cyclical companies after a period of decline as an indicator of a likely improvement in wider economic growth in the future.

Exhibit 23 shows the annual growth rates (year over year) of real GDP and of the consumption of both durable and non-durable goods for Canada (Panel A) and the United States (Panel B). Both panels of the exhibit show how sensitive durable goods consumption is to the economic cycle. We can expect then that the profits of companies that produce durable as opposed to non-durable goods to be commensurately more volatile too.

Earnings Growth and the Economic Cycle

Exhibit 23: Year-over-Year Growth Rate of GDP and the Consumption of Durable and Non-Durable Goods, 1996–2012

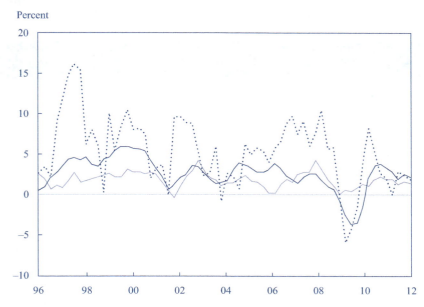

Canada

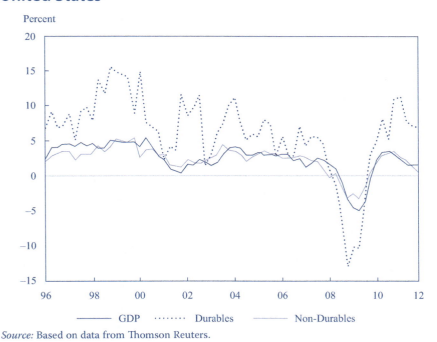

United States

——— GDP ········ Durables ——— Non-Durables

Source: Based on data from Thomson Reuters.

Stock market participants often classify stocks as being cyclical and non-cyclical. Exhibit 24 shows the real earnings growth of the non-cyclical and cyclical goods sectors of both the United States (Panel A) and the United Kingdom (Panel B). The cyclical sectors in this case are represented by companies that produce discretionary consumer goods, whereas the non-cyclical index is represented by an index that includes companies that produce staple (or less discretionary) consumer goods. Panel A shows the clearest evidence of the greater sensitivity to business conditions of the cyclical sector. Real earnings growth rises and falls dramatically over the business cycle. By contrast, although the real earnings of non-cyclical companies vary across the business cycle, the peaks and troughs are less extreme. The time variation in UK real earnings over the business cycle is also evident from the exhibit. However, the difference between the real earnings growth of the UK's cyclical and non-cyclical sectors is less clear, although the cyclical sector tended to experience more significant troughs in real earnings growth over this period.

Exhibit 24: The Real Earnings Growth of Discretionary and Staple Consumer Goods Companies, 1974–2012

United States

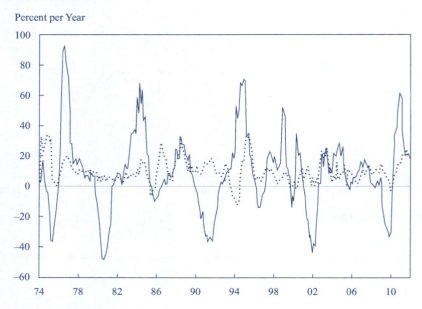

United Kingdom

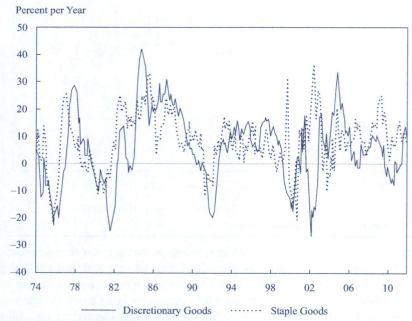

Source: Based on data from Thomson Reuters.

There are, of course, other factors that determine the earnings growth of an equity or equity sector: the financial structure of the company, the quality and experience of its management, and the ease with which new entrants can establish themselves to compete away any abnormal profits. However, the relationship between the business cycle and the nature of the type of good or service sold will remain important. Indeed, in a booming economy, even bad managers of companies with poor financial structures can generate or appear to generate profits—for example, WorldCom and Enron. But tougher, recessionary conditions often expose weak companies as demand turns down and financing becomes harder to access.

HOW BIG IS THE EQUITY RISK PREMIUM? 21

☐ explain the relationship between the consumption hedging properties of equity and the equity risk premium

The real earnings of companies are clearly affected by the underlying economy. This relationship is positive in that when the economy turns down, so (normally) do corporate profits. But it is in these bad times that investors need their investments to offset these worsening earnings. Because of the pro-cyclicality of economies and corporate profits (in aggregate), equities are not a good hedge against bad consumption outcomes, which, in turn, means that investors will require a risk premium. But how big should this premium $\left(\lambda_{t,s}^i\right)$ be?

It is impossible to quantify the equity risk premium *ex ante*. But we can at least look at its *ex post* value using very long runs of data. Exhibit 25 shows the real annual return on equities and government bonds over the period of 1900–2017 for a range of developed-economy equity markets. Over this very long period, equities in each country have outperformed government bonds. The bars representing the *ex post* equity risk premium range from 2.2% per year in Switzerland to 5.1% per year in Australia. US equities, which constitute the world's largest equity market, have outperformed US Treasuries by 4.5% per year on average over the 117 years under measurement, whereas the global equity market has produced an equity risk premium of 3.2% per year (premium versus bonds). Of course, there is no guarantee that a premium earned in the past will be earned in the future, but this long span of data shows that the *ex ante* equity risk premium for developed-economy equity markets could be somewhere between 3% and 5% per year.

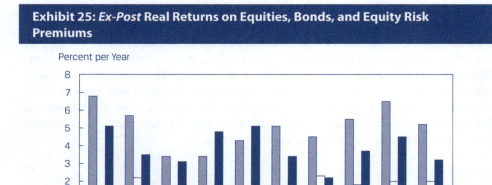

Exhibit 25: *Ex-Post* Real Returns on Equities, Bonds, and Equity Risk Premiums

Source: Based on data from Chapter 1 of Dimson, Marsh, Staunton (2018).

22 VALUATION MULTIPLES

☐ describe cyclical effects on valuation multiples

Analysis of company earnings prospects is usually the central focus of equity analysts and strategists. To help compare equities within and among sectors, they will generally monitor valuation multiples, such as the price-to-earnings ratio (P/E) or the price-to-book ratio (P/B). P/E is calculated as the ratio of the current share price to the earnings per share (EPS) generated by the company. This ratio tells investors the price they are paying for the shares as a multiple of the company's earnings per share. Investors use this ratio to compare the valuations attributed to individual equities, sectors, and markets. For instance, if a stock is trading with a low P/E relative to the rest of the market, it implies that investors are not willing to pay a high price for a dollar's worth of the company's earnings. The reason may be that the market believes the prospect of strong earnings growth in the future is low. Alternatively, a share trading with a very high P/E relative to the rest of the market indicates that investors are willing to pay a higher price for each dollar's worth of the company's earnings. They may be willing to do so because they expect this company's earnings to grow rapidly in the future. When the EPS used to estimate the ratio refers to last year's earnings, the P/E is referred to as being a historical or a trailing P/E. However, when the EPS is based on an estimate of future earnings, it is referred to as the leading or forward P/E. If a company's EPS is expected to grow, then its historical P/E will be greater than its

Valuation Multiples

forward P/E. However, what constitutes a high or low P/E very much depends on the market, sector, or company in question and, in particular, on the economic backdrop. US P/Es between 1900 and 2018 are shown in Exhibit 26.

Another popular valuation multiple is the price-to-book ratio, which measures the ratio of the company's share price to its net assets or its assets minus liabilities attributed to each share. The P/B tells investors the extent to which the value of their shares is "covered" by the company's net assets. Some of these assets, such as office buildings, are tangible, whereas others, such as patents and copyrights, are intangible. Furthermore, some of the assets are actually on the balance sheet and hence part of book value, whereas others are not. It also indicates the strength of investors' expectations about the company's ability to generate a high return on its net assets, adjusted for risk. The higher the ratio, the greater the expectations for growth but the lower the safety margin if things do not turn out as expected. Again, what constitutes a high or low P/B is determined by the market, sector, and stock in question.

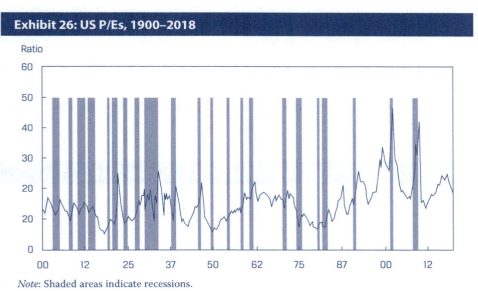

Exhibit 26: US P/Es, 1900–2018

Note: Shaded areas indicate recessions.
Sources: Based on data from Shiller (2000) and www.econ.yale.edu/~shiller/.

One of the problems for equity strategists is to ascertain whether the P/E (or P/B) is high or low. The average trailing US P/E between 1900 and 1990 was 13.5, indicating that investors were willing to pay $13.5 for a dollar's worth of the previous year's earnings; by the late 1990s and early 2000s, they were willing to pay $45. The expansion in the US equity market's P/E during the 1990s was a global phenomenon. Equity strategists justified the rise in the price of earnings with many ad hoc explanations—for example, the end of the cold war, better macro-policy that would ensure that major recessions were a thing of the past, and the internet revolution, to name just a few. However, with regard to the basic pricing relationship, shown in Equation 15, the high P/E could be the result of a number of factors, including

a. an increase in expectation of future real earnings growth $\left(E_t\left[\overline{CF}^i_{t+s}\right]\right)$;

b. falling real interest rates ($l_{t,s}$), possibly associated with falling volatility in real GDP growth;

c. a decrease in inflation expectations ($\theta_{t,s}$);

d. a decline in uncertainty about future inflation ($\pi_{t,s}$); or

   e. a decrease in the equity risk premium $\left(\lambda_{t,s}^i\right)$.

Other things being equal, any one of these changes or all of them combined could justify higher equity prices (P) relative to current earnings (E) and thus higher equilibrium P/Es. There were some investors, however, who were not convinced that such high P/Es relative to historical levels were justifiable, particularly on the grounds of much higher future earnings growth. The US Federal Reserve Board chairman, Alan Greenspan, alarmed by the rise in P/Es, described the valuation of equity markets in 1996 as essentially the result of "irrational exuberance" on the part of equity investors.

Robert Shiller has proposed an alternative valuation multiple—the real cyclically adjusted P/E (CAPE). The CAPE is derived in the same way as the P/E, but the "P" represents the real (or inflation-adjusted) price of the equity market and the "E" is a 10-year moving average of the market's real (or inflation-adjusted) earnings. Deflating the real equity price by a moving average of real earnings irons out the short-term volatility in this indicator over time. Exhibit 27 shows this ratio for the United States from 1900 to 2018. The very high price that equity investors were willing to pay for equities in 1929 and 1999 and, to a lesser extent, in 1965 is still apparent. It is worth noting that the average real return on US equities in the 10 years following the peaks in the CAPE in 1929, 1965, and 1999 were −0.3% per year, −5.4% per year, and −4.1% per year, respectively. Conversely, the average real return over the 10-year period after the two lowest values of the CAPE in 1921 and 1980 were 12.3% per year and 7.3% per year, respectively.

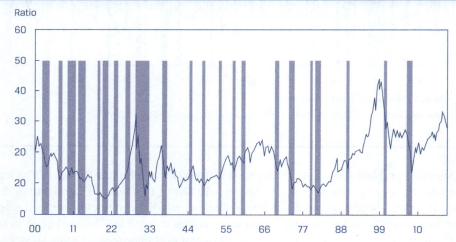

Exhibit 27: Real US Cyclically Adjusted P/E (CAPE), 1900–2018

Note: Shaded areas indicate recessions.

Source: Based on data from Shiller (2000) and www.econ.yale.edu/~shiller/.

COMMERCIAL REAL ESTATE

23

☐ | describe the economic factors affecting investment in commercial real estate

The basic pricing formula can be applied to asset classes besides bonds and equities. To demonstrate how the basic pricing framework presented in Equation 1 can be extended to other asset classes, we will consider commercial real estate.

Regular Cash Flow from Commercial Real Estate Investments

When investors invest in commercial real estate, the cash flow they hope to receive is derived from the rents paid by the tenants. These rents are normally collected net of ownership costs, such as those related to the upkeep of the building, according to a fixed schedule from the businesses that lease the property from the investors who act as landlords. Although practices vary from country to country, the rental agreement will be reviewed regularly and may be reset. In some countries, rents are subjected to "upward only" restrictions, which means that existing tenants will not see their rents fall, only potentially rise. Rents may also be indexed so that they rise in line with a pre-specified index of (usually) consumer prices.

Thus to a large extent, the rental income can be viewed as being analogous to the coupon income derived from a bond. Because a well-diversified portfolio of commercial property could be expected to generate a stream of rental income for investors, they might view such a portfolio as being similar to a well-diversified portfolio of bonds. The credit quality of a commercial property portfolio will be determined by the credit quality of the underlying tenants, in much the same way that the credit quality of a bond portfolio will be determined by the credit ratings of the bond issuers of the constituent bonds. Generally speaking, the lower the credit quality of the tenants, the less likely they will be to pay their rent on time or at all.

The Equity Component of an Investment in Commercial Real Estate

Investors in commercial real estate will receive regular cash flows derived from the rents paid by tenants, but there is another important element to property investment that is less bond-like. When a bond matures, the investor generally receives the face value of the bond along with the final coupon. But when the lease on a property expires, the investors (acting as landlords) will take back possession of the property and will have to decide whether to re-rent it to another tenant, to sell it to another investor, or to redevelop it for a future sale. The determining factor is likely to be the value of the property at the time. Its value may have risen dramatically over time, or it might now be worth much less. The value of the property will arguably be determined by two key factors: the property's location and the state of the underlying economy. If, during the time of the lease, the area in which the property is situated has become more popular, then the property might be sold at a profit or it might be worth redeveloping the property. Similarly, if the lease expires when general economic activity is high and thus there is strong demand for property, then the sale or redevelopment option might be worth pursuing. But if, when the lease expires, the location is deemed to be less desirable or the economy is weak, then redevelopment may not be an option, future rents may have to be lower on the property, and investors may come to the view that the property should be sold, even at a loss.

The potential for profit or loss and the uncertainty related to this profit from redevelopment add an equity-like dimension to investment in commercial real estate. In other words, this potential and uncertainty add either a positive increment to cash flow or a negative one. To this extent, some investors like to think about the cash flow derived from a commercial real estate portfolio as being part bond, part equity.

Illiquidity and Investment in Commercial Real Estate

There is a third aspect to investing in commercial real estate that is also crucial: its illiquidity. Anyone who has sold a home knows that it usually takes a great deal of time and effort to put the property up for sale, to find a buyer, and (if a buyer can be found) to finalize the deal. For similar reasons, it can take months and sometimes years to exit from a commercial property investment, and the high transactions costs often discourage investors further from liquidating holdings. By contrast, it is relatively easy in normal market conditions to transform a holding in developed-economy government bonds, investment-grade corporate debt, or publicly traded equities into cash. Generally speaking, most of the asset classes that we have considered so far in this reading are liquid relative to an investment in commercial property.

The Pricing Formula for Commercial Real Estate

Commercial real estate is a "special" asset class; it can be viewed as being part equity, part bond, and it is usually very illiquid. However, with some minor adaptions of the generic pricing formula in Equation 1, we can still capture all of the salient features of the price of commercial real estate, as follows:

$$P_t^i = \sum_{s=1}^{N} \frac{E_t\left(\overline{CF}_{t+s}^i\right)}{\left(1 + l_{t,s} + \theta_{t,s} + \pi_{t,s} + \gamma_{t,s}^i + \kappa_{t,s}^i + \phi_{t,s}^i\right)^s}. \tag{17}$$

The pricing formula shown in Equation 17 acknowledges that the expected cash flow from an investment in commercial real estate, $E_t\left(\overline{CF}_{t+s}^i\right)$, will be uncertain because tenants may default on the rental agreement. The quality of this rental income will depend on the quality of the tenants, just as the reliability or quality of the coupons from a corporate bond will be dependent on the credit standing of the corporate bond issuer. Furthermore, the property's value in the future cannot be known with certainty.

But what should the discount rate look like? To understand the construction of the discount rate in Equation 17, consider the following tenants and associated rental/leasing agreements:

1. a developed-economy government tenant that agrees to pay rental income that is indexed to inflation $(1 + l_{t,s})$,

2. a developed-economy government tenant that agrees to pay fixed nominal rental income $(1 + l_{t,s} + \theta_{t,s} + \pi_{t,s})$, and

3. a corporate tenant that agrees to pay a fixed nominal rental income $(1 + l_{t,s} + \theta_{t,s} + \pi_{t,s} + \gamma_{t,s}^i)$.

In each case, the expressions in parentheses represent the composition of the discount rate that would be applied to the cash flows of bonds issued by these entities: (1) is analogous to the purchase of a real default-free government bond, (2) is analogous to the purchase of a nominal default-free government bond, and (3) is analogous to the purchase of a credit risky nominal bond. In each case, though, we need to add a risk premium to take into account the uncertainty relating to the value of the property at the end of the lease. This premium is analogous to the equity risk premium, $\kappa_{t,s}^i$.

Finally, we have to take into account the illiquidity of a commercial property investment. Because investors cannot easily convert their property investments into cash, there exists the possibility that they will not be able to liquidate their investment in

Commercial Real Estate

bad economic times. In other words, other things being equal, illiquidity acts to reduce an asset class's usefulness as a hedge against bad consumption outcomes. Because of this, investors will demand a liquidity risk premium, which we have expressed as $\phi^i_{t,s}$ in Equation 17.

The discount rates that investors would apply to an investment in commercial property in each of the three instances previously listed are, therefore,

1. $1 + l_{t,s} + \kappa^i_{t,s} + \phi^i_{t,s}$,
2. $1 + l_{t,s} + \theta_{t,s} + \pi^i_{t,s} + \kappa^i_{t,s} + \phi^i_{t,s}$, and
3. $1 + l_{t,s} + \theta_{t,s} + \pi^i_{t,s} + \gamma^i_{t,s} + \kappa^i_{t,s} + \phi^i_{t,s}$.

The relative sizes of the components listed will vary depending on the length of the lease, the quality of the tenant, and the location of the property.

EXAMPLE 17

A Real Estate Investment Decision

1. An analyst estimates that the real risk-free rate is 1.25%, average inflation over the next year will be 2.5%, and the premium required by investors for inflation uncertainty is 0.50%. He also observes that the yield on a 10-year senior unsecured bond issued by Supermarket plc is 5.75%. From these figures, he deduces that the credit spread on Supermarket plc's 10-year debt is 1.50%.

    The same analyst is asked to review for a client (an investor) the opportunity to buy a site currently occupied by Supermarket plc. Once the investor purchases the property, Supermarket plc will lease it back and pay $500,000 annual rent in arrears to the investor. "Rent in arrears" in this case means that the first annual rental payment is due in 12 months, covering the first year's tenancy, and the second is due in 24 months, and so on. Like the Supermarket bond, the lease on the property has 10 full years to expire. At the end of this period, the property and land will revert to the investor, and the analyst estimates that the resale value of the property after 10 years will be $10 million, net of all transactions costs.

    The investor tells the analyst that it normally expects to receive a risk premium of 0.50% on any cash flow from a commercial property investment to compensate it for the uncertainty of the final value of the property and the uncertainty relating to the receipt of rental income, plus a liquidity premium of 1.0% on these cash flows. The investor's required return on the property is thus 7.25% (= 5.75% + 0.5% + 1.0%). If the purchase price of this piece of commercial property is $8.2 million, should the analyst recommend the purchase to the client?

Discount Rate: 7.25%		
Payment Due (years)	Cash Flow	Present Value
1	$500,000	$466,200
2	500,000	434,686
3	500,000	405,301
4	500,000	377,903
5	500,000	352,357

	Discount Rate: 7.25%	
Payment Due (years)	Cash Flow	Present Value
6	500,000	328,538
7	500,000	306,330
8	500,000	285,622
9	500,000	266,314
10	10,500,000	5,214,543
Implied property value		$8,437,796

The cash flows in the table, along with their associated present values, demonstrate that at a discount rate of 7.25%, the property would be priced at $8,437,796. Any asking price above this value would imply a return of less than the investor's hurdle rate of 7.25%, whereas any price below this price implies a return above this hurdle rate. On the basis of this information, the analyst should recommend that the client go ahead with the investment.

24 COMMERCIAL REAL ESTATE AND THE BUSINESS CYCLE

☐ describe the economic factors affecting investment in commercial real estate

The nature of the cash flows from commercial property and the complex structure of the discount rate will all be influenced by the evolution of the underlying economy. Panel A of Exhibit 28 shows the annual growth rate of UK commercial property income over a 30-year period. It is remarkably stable over this period, averaging 6.5% per year; in other words, UK commercial property rental income has grown by approximately 6.5% annually in nominal terms (or 2.5% in real terms) over the 30-year period. The stability of this income stream, over a number of business cycles, suggests that investors might calculate its present value using a very low discount rate. But as well as showing the annual change in rent from a portfolio of UK commercial property, Panel A also shows the annual percentage change in the capital value of the United Kingdom's commercial property market. Whereas rental income appears to have been relatively stable (in nominal terms) and almost immune to the business cycle, commercial property capital values are much more sensitive to the economic cycle. Between 1990 and 1992, as the UK economy experienced a deep recession, UK commercial property prices fell by a cumulative 30%. Over the course of the United Kingdom's 1990s recession, the capital value of the UK property market fell by 26%. In Panel B of the exhibit, we present the capital value changes in a number of markets around the world between 2008 and 2009. It is clear that the global recession had a significant impact on commercial property prices. For example, in Ireland, one of the developed economies arguably worst hit by the crisis, commercial property prices fell by 55.5%.

Commercial Real Estate and the Business Cycle

Exhibit 28: Commercial Property

UK Commercial Property Returns, 1981–2011

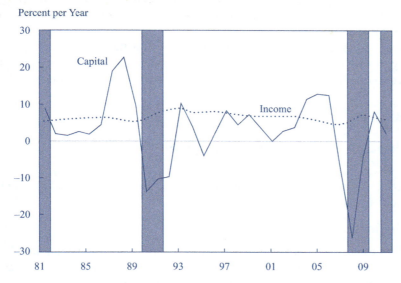

International Comparison of Commercial Property Value Changes, 2008–2009

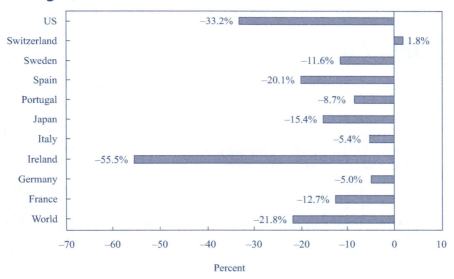

Note: Shaded areas in Panel A indicate recessions.
Source: Based on data from Investment Property Databank (www.ipd.com).

Taken together, the two panels in Exhibit 28 show that even though nominal rental income might be relatively stable, the capital values of commercial property are highly sensitive to the economic environment. A recession will generally cause these values to fall, whereas more robust economic conditions will tend to cause commercial property prices to rise, often dramatically. For example, the recovering and then strong global economy between 2003 and 2006 caused world commercial property prices to rise by nearly 20%. Over the same period, they rose by 41% in the United Kingdom and by a staggering 51% in Ireland.

The pro-cyclical nature of commercial property prices means that investors will generally demand a relatively high risk premium in return for investing in this asset class. The reason is that commercial property does not appear to be a very good hedge against bad economic outcomes. In fact, the sharp declines in capital values in recessionary periods resemble the sort of declines that investors in equity experience, although these occurrences are more frequent with equity investment. Thus, the sort of risk premium that investors will demand from their commercial property investments arguably will be closer to that demanded on equities than on default-free government bonds.

Finally, although it is difficult to derive a value for the property risk premium, it is likely to vary over time with economic conditions and to be relatively highly and positively correlated with the risk premiums on corporate bonds and equities.

EXAMPLE 18

Valuation and the Business Cycle

1. Describe how real estate valuation is distinguished from valuation of public equities.

Solution

Real estate does not trade in public markets (the exception being REITs). Compared with the valuation of public equities, the valuation of real estate should reflect a discount for relative lack of liquidity.

SUMMARY

In this reading, we have sought to explain the fundamental connection between the prices of financial assets and the underlying economy. The connection should be strong because ultimately all financial assets represent a claim on the real economy. Because all financial assets offer a means of deferring consumption, to make the connection tangible we have explored the relationship between these asset prices and the consumption and saving decisions of economic agents.

- At any point in time, the market value of any financial security is simply the sum of discounted values of the cash flows that the security is expected to produce. The timing and magnitude of these expected cash flows will thus be an integral part of the security's market value, as will the discount rate applied to these expected cash flows, which is the sum of a real default-free interest rate, expected inflation, and possibly several risk premiums. Each of these elements will be influenced by the business cycle. It is through these components that the real economy exerts its influence on the market value of financial instruments.

- The average level of real short-term interest rates is positively related to the trend rate of growth of the underlying economy and also to the volatility of economic growth in the economy. Other things being equal, these relationships mean that we should expect to find that the average level of real short-term interest rates is higher in an economy with high and volatile growth and lower in an economy with lower, more stable growth.

- On average, over time, according to the Taylor rule, a central bank's policy rate should comprise the sum of an economy's trend growth plus inflation expectations, which might, in turn, be anchored to an explicit inflation target. This policy rate level is referred to as the neutral rate. Other things being equal, when inflation is above (below) the targeted level, the policy rate should be above (below) the neutral rate, and when the output gap is positive (negative), the policy rate should also be above (below) the neutral rate. The policy rate can thus vary over time with inflation expectations and the economy's output gap.

- Short-term nominal rates will be closely related to a central bank's policy rate of interest and will comprise the real interest rate that is required to balance the requirements of savers and investors plus investors' expectations of inflation over the relevant borrowing or lending period. Short-term nominal interest rates will be positively related to short-term real interest rates and to inflation expectations.

- If bond investors were risk neutral, then the term structure of interest rates would be determined by short-term interest rate expectations. But bond investors are risk averse, which means that they will normally demand a risk premium for investing in even default-free government bonds. This risk premium will generally rise with the maturity of these bonds because longer-dated government bonds tend to be less negatively correlated with consumption and, therefore, represent a less useful consumption hedge for investors. Overall, the shape of the curve will be determined by a combination of short-term interest rates and inflation expectations as well as risk premiums. In turn, these factors will be influenced by the business cycle and policymakers.

- The yield differential between default-free conventional government bonds and index-linked equivalents will be driven by inflation expectations and a risk premium. The risk premium will be largely influenced by investors' uncertainty about future inflation.

- The difference between the yield on a corporate bond and that on a government bond with the same currency denomination and maturity is referred to as the measured credit spread. It is conceptually akin (but not equal) to the risk premium demanded by investors in compensation for the additional credit risk that they bear compared with that embodied in the default-free government bond. It tends to rise in times of economic weakness, as the probability of default rises, and tends to narrow in times of robust economic growth, when defaults are less common.

- The uncertainty about and time variation in future equity cash flows (dividends) is a distinct feature of equity investment, as opposed to corporate bond investment. This feature explains why we would expect the equity premium to be larger than the credit premium. In times of economic weakness or stress, the uncertainty about future dividends will tend to be higher, and we should thus expect the equity risk premium to rise in such an economic environment.

- Given the uncertain nature of the cash flows generated by equities, investors will demand an equity risk premium because the consumption hedging properties of equities are poor. In other words, equities tend not to pay off in bad times. Because in the event of company failure an equity holder will lose all of his or her investment whereas an investor in the company's bonds may recover a significant portion of his or her investment, it would be reasonable to assume that a risk-averse investor would demand a higher premium on an equity holding than on a corporate bond holding. The two premiums will tend to be positively correlated over time and will tend to be influenced by the business cycle in similar ways.

- The P/E tends to rise during periods of economic expansion and to fall during recessions. A "high" P/E could be the result of a number of factors, including the following: falling real interest rates, a decline in the equity risk premium, an increase in the expectation of future real earnings growth, an expectation of lower operating and/or financial risk, or a combination of all of these factors. All of these components will be influenced by the business cycle.

- The market value of an investment in commercial property can be derived in much the same way as the market value of an investment in equity. The cash flows come in the form of rent, which can be enhanced with additional redevelopment values as leases on properties expire. These cash flows are uncertain, and the uncertainty surrounding them will tend to rise when the economy turns down. We might thus expect the risk premium demanded on commercial property investments to rise in these times.

- The pro-cyclical nature of commercial property prices means that investors will generally demand a relatively high risk premium in return for investing in this asset class. The reason is that commercial property is not a very good hedge against bad economic outcomes. In addition, the illiquid nature of property investment means that investors may also demand a liquidity premium for investing in this asset class.

REFERENCES

Altug, Sumru, Pamela Labadie. 2008. Asset Pricing for Dynamic Economies. Cambridge, UK: Cambridge University Press.

Cochrane, John H. 2005. Asset Pricing. Princeton, NJ: Princeton University Press.

Dimson, Elroy, Paul Marsh, Mike Staunton. 2018. Credit Suisse Global Investment Returns Yearbook 2018. Credit Suisse Research Institute.

Elton, Edward J., Martin J. Gruber, Stephen J. Brown, William N. Goetzmann. 2014. Modern Portfolio Theory and Investment Analysis, 9th Ed. New York: John Wiley & Sons.

Shiller, Robert J. 2000. Irrational Exuberance. Princeton, NJ: Princeton University Press.

Taylor, John B. 1993. "Discretion versus Policy Rules in Practice." Carnegie-Rochester Conference Series on Public Policy, vol. 39: 195–214. 10.1016/0167-2231(93)90009-L

PRACTICE PROBLEMS

1. All else equal, which of the following would *most likely* explain the fall in price of a particular company's shares?

   A. The expected inflation rate falls.

   B. The company's future cash flows are expected to increase.

   C. The yield to maturity on real default-free investments rises.

The following information relates to questions 2-8

Julie Carlisle is a financial planner at a large wealth management firm. One of her clients, Esteban Blake, just received a sizable inheritance. He invests a portion of the inheritance in an annuity that will immediately increase his income by a substantial amount. He enlists Carlisle's help to invest the remaining amount of the inheritance.

Blake informs Carlisle that he would like some short-term bonds in his portfolio. Carlisle proposes purchasing a one-year domestic government zero-coupon bond. It has a face value of $100 and is currently priced at $96.37. Carlisle estimates the one-year real risk-free rate at 1.15% and expects inflation over the next year to be 2.25%.

In an effort to provide Blake with some exposure to international markets, Carlisle proposes three countries to look for investment opportunities. Selected data on the three countries are presented in Exhibit 1.

Exhibit 1: Selected Macroeconomic Data					
	Nominal GDP Growth	Inflation Rate	Volatility of Real GDP Growth	Yield Curve Shape	Trailing 12-Month Equity Index P/E
Country #1	6.5%	4.0%	Low	Flat	16.5
Country #2	5.0%	2.5%	High	Upward slope	17.3
Country #3	3.5%	2.0%	Low	Flat	18.2

In her analysis, Carlisle observes that the spread between the three-year default-free nominal bond and the default-free real zero-coupon bond in Country #3 is 2.0%.

Blake expresses concern that stocks may be currently overvalued in Country 3 given its 20-year historical equity index P/E of 16.0. Carlisle comments,

I think the equilibrium P/E in Country #3 has increased because of changes in market conditions.

Carlisle predicts that Country #3 will slip into a recession next quarter. She thinks it will be short-lived, lasting only 12 months or so, and considers the impact of such a recession on the performance of the country's stocks and bonds.

Practice Problems

Exhibit 2: Three-Year Corporate Bonds from Country #3

Corporate Bond	Moody's Investors Service Rating	Spread*
Bond A	Aaa	1.4%
Bond B	Baa1	3.2%
Bond C	B3	5.3%

Spread versus three-year sovereign bond

2. Holding all else constant, the change in Blake's income will *most likely* result in:

   A. an increase in his marginal utility of consumption.

   B. an increase in his inter-temporal rate of substitution.

   C. a decrease in his required risk premium for investing in risky assets.

3. The implied premium for inflation uncertainty for the one-year government zero-coupon bond proposed by Carlisle is *closest* to:

   A. 0.23%.

   B. 0.37%.

   C. 1.10%.

4. Based on the data in Exhibit 1, current real short-term interest rates would *most likely* be highest in:

   A. Country #1.

   B. Country #2.

   C. Country #3.

5. The recent change in Country #3's break-even inflation rate suggests that the expected rate of inflation over the next three years is:

   A. less than 2.0%.

   B. equal to 2.0%.

   C. greater than 2.0%.

6. Which of the following changes in market conditions *best* supports Carlisle's comment regarding the equilibrium P/E for Country #3?

   A. An increase in the equity risk premium

   B. A decrease in uncertainty about future inflation

   C. A decrease in expectation of future real earnings growth

7. If Carlisle's prediction about the economy of Country #3 is realized, the yield curve in Country #3 will *most likely*:

   A. remain flat.

   B. become upward sloping.

C. become downward sloping.

8. Based on Exhibit 2, if Carlisle's prediction for Country #3 is realized, then over the next 12 months:

   A. Bond A would be expected to outperform Bond C.

   B. Bond B would be expected to outperform Bond A.

   C. Bond C would be expected to outperform Bond B.

9. The covariance between a risk-averse investor's inter-temporal rate of substitution and the expected future price of a risky asset is typically:

   A. negative.

   B. zero.

   C. positive.

10. The prices of one-period, real default-free government bonds are likely to be *most* sensitive to changes in:

    A. investors' inflation expectations.

    B. the expected volatility of economic growth.

    C. the covariance between investors' inter-temporal rates of substitution and the expected future prices of the bonds.

11. Default-free real interest rates tend to be relatively high in countries with high expected economic growth because investors:

    A. increase current borrowing.

    B. have high inter-temporal rates of substitution.

    C. have high uncertainty about levels of future consumption.

12. Positive output gaps are usually associated with:

    A. deflation.

    B. high unemployment.

    C. economic growth beyond sustainable capacity.

13. All else equal, an investor expects future inflation to increase, but the uncertainty of future inflation to fall. For such an investor the break-even inflation rate:

    A. is uncertain.

    B. is expected to fall.

    C. is expected to rise.

14. The difference between the yield on a zero-coupon, default-free nominal bond and the yield on a zero-coupon, default-free real bond of the same maturity reflects:

    A. investors' expectations about future inflation only.

Practice Problems

87

    B. a premium for the uncertainty of future inflation only.

    C. both, investors' expectations about future inflation and a premium for the uncertainty of future inflation.

15. During a recession, the slope of the yield curve for default-free government bonds is *most likely* to:

    A. flatten.

    B. steepen.

    C. become inverted.

16. One interpretation of an upward sloping yield curve is that the returns to short-dated bonds are:

    A. uncorrelated with bad times.

    B. more positively correlated with bad times than are returns to long-dated bonds.

    C. more negatively correlated with bad times than are returns to long-dated bonds.

17. An analyst, who measures yield as a combination of interest rates and premiums, observes an upward-sloping, default-free government bond nominal yield curve. Which of the following statements is correct?

    A. Interest rates must be expected to rise in the future.

    B. Bond risk premiums must be expected to rise in the future.

    C. Expectations relating to the future direction of interest rates are indeterminate.

18. A corporate bond has a remaining maturity of 1 year, has a face value of EUR100, and is currently priced at EUR90.90. The real risk-free rate is 3.25%. Inflation is expected to be 2.0% next year, and the premium required by investors for inflation uncertainty is 0.25%.

    The implied credit risk premium embedded in the bond's price is *best* described as:

    A. equal to $(100/90.90) - 1 = 10\%$.

    B. 10% reduced by the real risk-free rate and expected inflation.

    C. 10% reduced by the real risk-free rate, expected inflation, and the premium for inflation uncertainty.

19. A decrease in the prices of AAA-rated corporate bonds during a recession would *most likely* be the result of:

    A. expectations of higher inflation.

    B. increases in credit risk premiums.

    C. increases in short-term, default-free interest rates.

20. During an economic period when spreads between corporate and government

bonds are narrowing, and spreads between higher- and lower-rated corporate bond categories are also narrowing, it can be expected that:

A. government bonds will outperform corporate bonds.

B. lower-rated corporate bonds will outperform higher-rated corporate bonds.

C. higher-rated corporate bonds will outperform lower-rated corporate bonds.

21. The sensitivity of a corporate bond's spread to changes in the business cycle is *most likely* to be:

A. uncorrelated with the level of cyclicality in the company's business.

B. positively correlated with the level of cyclicality in the company's business.

C. negatively correlated with the level of cyclicality of the company's business.

22. The category of bonds whose spreads can be expected to widen the *most* during an economic downturn are bonds from the:

A. cyclical sector with low credit ratings.

B. cyclical sector with high credit ratings.

C. non-cyclical sector with low credit ratings.

23. With regard to the credit risk of the sovereign debt issued by country governments, which of the following statements is correct? The credit risk premium on such debt is:

A. zero because governments can print money to settle their debt.

B. negligibly small because no country has defaulted on sovereign debt.

C. a non-zero and positive quantity that varies depending on a country's creditworthiness.

24. Risk-averse investors demanding a large equity risk premium are *most likely* expecting their future consumption outcomes and equity returns to be:

A. uncorrelated.

B. positively correlated.

C. negatively correlated.

25. Which of the following financial assets is likely to offer the *most* effective hedge against bad consumption outcomes?

A. Equities.

B. Short-dated, default-free government bonds.

C. Long-dated, default-free government bonds.

26. When assessing investment opportunities in equities, investors should:

A. assign higher equity risk premiums to non-cyclical companies, relative to cyclical companies.

Practice Problems

    B. forecast lower volatility in the growth rate of earnings for cyclical companies, relative to non-cyclical companies.

    C. forecast higher growth rates in earnings for cyclical companies coming out of a recession, relative to non-cyclical companies.

27. Other things equal, equilibrium price-to-earnings ratios (P/Es) will *most likely* decrease if:

    A. real interest rates decrease.

    B. inflation is expected to increase.

    C. there is less uncertainty about future inflation.

28. Which of the following statements relating to commercial real estate is correct?

    A. Rental income from commercial real estate is generally unstable across business cycles.

    B. Commercial real estate investments generally offer a good hedge against bad consumption outcomes.

    C. The key difference in the discount rates applied to the cash flows of equity investments and commercial real estate investments relates to liquidity.

SOLUTIONS

1. C is correct. According to the fundamental pricing equation, the market value of an asset is affected by economic factors that influence the asset's expected future cash flows, default-free interest rates, expected inflation rates, or the asset's risk premium. From Equation 1, expected cash flows are in the numerator, while expected inflation and the real risk-free rate are in the denominator. Consequently, a rise in the real risk-free rate (the yield to maturity on a default-free instrument) will lead to a fall in the price of a risky asset, such as stock, by increasing the rate at which its cash flows are discounted.

2. C is correct. The additional annuity payment substantially increases Blake's income and wealth, which decreases his marginal utility of consumption. As a result, the average loss of marginal utility from any risk taking decreases as his wealth increases. Thus, he requires a lower risk premium and is willing to buy more risky assets.

3. B is correct. The pricing equation for a default-free nominal coupon-paying bond is

$$P_t^i = \sum_{s=1}^{N} \frac{CF_{t+s}^i}{\left(1 + l_{t,s} + \theta_{t,s} + \pi_{t,s}\right)^s}.$$

For a one-year bond, the pricing formula reduces to

$$P_t = \frac{CF_{t+1}}{\left(1 + l_{t,1} + \theta_{t,1} + \pi_{t,1}\right)^1}.$$

Thus, the implied premium for inflation uncertainty for the one-year government zero-coupon bond is calculated as

$$\pi_{t,1} = \frac{CF_{t+1}}{P_t} - \left(1 + l_{t,1} + \theta_{t,1}\right)$$

$$= \frac{100}{96.37} - (1 + 0.0115 + 0.0225)$$

$$= 1.0377 - 1.0340$$

$$= 0.0037, \text{ or } 0.37\%.$$

4. B is correct. Real short-term interest rates are positively related to both real GDP growth and the volatility of real GDP growth. Country 1 and Country 2 have the highest real GDP growth, as estimated by the difference between nominal GDP growth and average inflation (6.5% − 4.0% = 2.5% and 5.0% − 2.5% = 2.5%, respectively), while Country 3 has the lowest real GDP growth (3.5% − 2.0% = 1.5%). Looking at the volatility of real GDP growth, Country 2 has high real GDP growth volatility, whereas Country 1 and Country 3 have low real GDP growth volatility. Therefore, Country 2 would most likely have the highest real short-term interest rates.

5. A is correct. The difference, or spread, between the yields on the country's three-year default-free nominal bond and on the default-free real zero-coupon bond is 2.0%. This spread is known as the break-even rate of inflation (BEI), which is composed of the expected rate of inflation plus a risk premium for the uncertainty of future inflation. Because this risk premium component is most likely positive, because investors are unlikely to be very confident in their ability to predict inflation accurately, the expected rate of inflation component would be less than 2.0%.

Solutions 91

6. B is correct. Stock prices are a function of expected cash flows discounted by inflation expectations, the uncertainty of future inflation, and the equity risk premium, among other factors. Holding all else equal, a decline in the uncertainty of future inflation would result in lower discount rates and higher valuations. This result would support a higher equilibrium P/E, thus justifying Country 3's current trailing P/E being higher than its historical average.

7. B is correct. The yield curve in Country 3 is currently flat (Exhibit 1), and Carlisle predicts a recession. During a recession, short-term rates tend to be lower because central banks tend to lower their policy rate in these times. However, the impact of monetary policy on longer-term rates will not be as strong because the central bank will usually be expected to bring short-term rates back to normal as the recession recedes. Thus, the slope of the yield curve will likely become upward sloping during the recession.

8. A is correct. If Country 3 experiences a recession over the next 12 months, the credit spreads for corporate bonds would be expected to widen as investors sell the low-quality debt of issuers with high default risk and trade up to the higher-quality debt of issuers with low default risk. The issuers with a good credit rating (such as Aaa rated Bond A) tend to outperform those with lower ratings (such as B3 rated Bond C) as the spread between low- and higher-quality issuers widens. As a result, Bond A would be expected to outperform Bond C over the next 12 months.

9. A is correct. For risk-averse investors, when the expected future price of the investment is high (low), the marginal utility of future consumption relative to that of current consumption is low (high). Hence, the covariance of the inter-temporal rate of substitution with asset price is expected to be negative for risk-averse investors.

10. B is correct. Only changes in default-free real interest rates will affect the price of real, default-free bonds. The average level of default-free real interest rates is positively related to the volatility of economic growth in the economy; thus, changes in the expected volatility of economic growth would likely lead to changes in default-free real interest rates, which in turn would affect the prices of real, default-free government bonds.

11. A is correct. The average level of default-free real interest rates is positively related to the expected rate of growth of the underlying economy and also to the volatility of economic growth in the economy. During periods of high expected economic growth, investors are less worried about the future and their consumption abilities in the future; that is, their inter-temporal rate of substitution is low, so they borrow more today and save less. Other things being equal, this means that the average level of default-free real interest rates (the reciprocal of the rate of substitution, see Equation 4) should be higher in an economy with high growth and lower in an economy with lower, more stable growth.

12. C is correct. An economy operating with a positive output gap—that is, where the level of actual GDP exceeds potential GDP—is producing beyond its sustainable capacity. Positive output gaps are usually associated with high and/or rising inflation, while high levels of unemployment usually accompany negative output gaps.

13. A is correct. The break-even inflation rate is the difference between the yield on a zero-coupon, default-free nominal bond and on a zero-coupon, default-free real bond of the same maturity. The rate incorporates changing expectations about inflation and changing perceptions about the uncertainty of the future inflation

environment. Consequently, if inflation is expected to rise while the uncertainty about future inflation falls (in Equation 10, $\theta_{t,s}$ rises but $\pi_{t,s}$ falls), it is unclear in which direction break-even inflation rates will move.

14. C is correct. The difference between the yield on a zero-coupon, default-free nominal bond and the yield on a zero-coupon, default-free real bond of the same maturity is known as the break-even inflation rate. This break-even inflation rate will incorporate the inflation expectations of investors over the investment horizon of the two bonds, plus a risk premium to compensate investors for uncertainty about future inflation. Break-even inflation rates are not simply the market's best estimate of future inflation over the relevant investment horizon, because break-even inflation rates also include a risk premium to compensate investors for their uncertainty about future inflation.

15. B is correct. During a recession, short rates are often lower because central banks tend to lower their policy rate in these times because the output gap is likely to be negative. However, the impact of such monetary policy on longer-term rates will not be as strong, so long rates may not fall by as much as short rates. The central bank will usually be expected to bring short-term rates back to normal as the recession recedes, and the risk-free rates will increase as economic growth recovers. Thus, the slope of the yield curve will typically steepen during a recession.

16. C is correct. One interpretation of an upward-sloping yield curve is that returns to short-dated bonds are more negatively correlated with bad times than are returns to long-dated bonds. This interpretation is based on the notion that investors are willing to pay a premium and accept a lower return for short-dated bonds if they believe that long-dated bonds are not a good hedge against economic "bad times."

17. C is correct. An upward-sloping yield curve may be caused by a combination of expected rate increases and positive bond risk premiums. It may also be a combination of expectations that interest rates will be unchanged in the future coupled with positive bond risk premiums. Lastly, an upward-sloping yield curve may actually be a reflection of expected rate cuts that are more than offset by the existence of positive bond risk premiums. So, expectations relating to the future direction of interest rates are indeterminate.

18. C is correct. The implied credit risk premium embedded in the bond's price is the yield (10%) less the default-risk-free nominal interest rate, which includes a premium for inflation uncertainty. See Example 15. The credit risk premium can be calculated as 4.51% in this case:

$$\gamma_{t,s}^i = \frac{100}{90.90} - (1 + 0.0325 + 0.02 + 0.0025).$$
$$\gamma_{t,s}^i = 4.51\%.$$

19. B is correct. During recessions, the risk premium that investors demand on financial assets, particularly those that are not default-free, such as corporate bonds, may rise because investors in general may be less willing and able to take on heightened default risk during such periods. Specifically, the credit risk premium demanded by investors tends to rise in times of economic weakness, when the probability of a corporate default and bankruptcy is highest.

20. B is correct. When spreads are narrowing, investors seem to be less discerning between issues with weak versus strong credit, and the rate of improvement will tend to be greater for those bonds issued by entities with a relatively weaker ability to pay. Thus, during times when corporate bond spreads are narrowing relative to government bonds and the spreads between higher- and lower-rated

Solutions

bond categories are also narrowing, corporate bonds will generally outperform government bonds and lower-rated corporate bonds will tend to outperform higher-rated corporate bonds.

21. B is correct. The sensitivity of a corporate bond's spread to changes in the business cycle and the level of cyclicality tend to be positively correlated. The greater the level of cyclicality, the greater the sensitivity of the bond's spread to changes in the business cycle.

22. A is correct. During an economic downturn, the spreads of corporate bonds can be expected to widen, because the risk premium that investors demand on risky financial assets will increase. When spreads widen, the spreads on bonds issued by corporations with a low credit rating and that are part of the cyclical sector will tend to widen the most.

23. C is correct. Credit premiums have been an important component of the expected return on bonds issued by countries (sovereign debt). The credit premium varies from country to country depending on how creditworthy investors consider it to be. The fact that countries have both printed money to pay back debt and defaulted on it gives rise to a non-zero credit risk premium.

24. B is correct. If investors demand high equity risk premiums, they are likely expecting their future consumption and equity returns to be positively correlated. The positive correlation indicates that equities will exhibit poor hedging properties, because equity returns will be high (i.e., pay off) during "good times" and will be low (i.e., not pay off) during "bad times." In other words, the covariance between risk-averse investors' inter-temporal rates of substitution and the expected future prices of equities is highly negative, resulting in a positive and large equity risk premium. This is the case because in good times, when equity returns are high, the marginal value of consumption is low. Similarly, in bad times, when equity returns are low, the marginal value of consumption is high. Holding all else constant, the larger the magnitude of the negative covariance term, the larger the risk premium.

25. B is correct. The relative certainty about the real payoff from short-dated, default-free government bonds and, therefore, the relative certainty about the amount of consumption that the investor will be able to undertake with the payoff indicate that an investment in such bonds would be a good hedge against bad consumption outcomes.

26. C is correct. During recessions, cyclical companies are likely to experience sharp declines in earnings, more so than non-cyclical companies. In contrast, while coming out of a recession, cyclical companies are likely to generate higher earnings growth relative to non-cyclical companies.

27. B is correct. Other things being equal, an increase in inflation expectations would result in lower equity prices relative to current earnings. This would result in lower equilibrium P/Es.

28. C is correct. To arrive at an appropriate discount rate to be used to discount the cash flows from a commercial real estate investment, a liquidity premium is added to the discount rate applicable to equity investments. The added liquidity premium provides additional compensation for the risk that the real estate investment may be very illiquid in bad economic times.

LEARNING MODULE

2

Analysis of Active Portfolio Management

by Roger G. Clarke, PhD, Harindra de Silva, PhD, CFA, and Steven Thorley, PhD, CFA.

Roger G. Clarke, PhD (USA). Harindra de Silva, PhD, CFA, is at Analytic Investors, Wells Fargo Asset Management (USA). Steven Thorley, PhD, CFA, is Emeritus Faculty at the Marriott School, BYU (USA).

— Difficult
— Memorize circled formulas

LEARNING OUTCOMES	
Mastery	*The candidate should be able to:*
☐	describe how value added by active management is measured
☐	calculate and interpret the information ratio (ex post and ex ante) and contrast it to the Sharpe ratio
☐	describe and interpret the fundamental law of active portfolio management, including its component terms—transfer coefficient, information coefficient, breadth, and active risk (aggressiveness)
☐	explain how the information ratio may be useful in investment manager selection and choosing the level of active portfolio risk
☐	compare active management strategies, including market timing and security selection, and evaluate strategy changes in terms of the fundamental law of active management
☐	describe the practical strengths and limitations of the fundamental law of active management

INTRODUCTION

1

The Markowitz (1952) framework of what was originally called modern portfolio theory (MPT) has now become the prominent paradigm for communicating and applying principles of risk and return in portfolio management. Much of the mathematics and terminology of mean–variance portfolio theory was subsequently combined with the notion of informational efficiency by Sharpe (1964) and other financial economists to develop equilibrium models, such as the traditional capital asset pricing model. Separately, the tools of MPT were applied by Treynor and Black (1973) to guide investors in their selection of securities when prices differ from their equilibrium values. The application of portfolio theory to active management was further developed by Grinold (1989) in "The Fundamental Law of Active Management" and by Black and Litterman (1992).

We summarize the principles of active portfolio management using the terminology and mathematics of the fundamental law introduced by Grinold (1989) and further developed by Clarke, de Silva, and Thorley (2002). Active management theory deals with how an investor should construct a portfolio given an assumed competitive advantage or skill in predicting returns. Thus, active management relies on the assumption that financial markets are not perfectly efficient. Although investors might ultimately care about total risk and return, when asset management is delegated to professional investors in institutional settings (e.g., pension funds) the appropriate perspective is risk and return relative to a benchmark portfolio. In addition to the principal–agent problem in delegated asset management, the availability of passively managed portfolios requires a focus on value added above and beyond the alternative of a low-cost index fund.

We assume an understanding of basic portfolio theory, including the mathematics of expected values, variances, and correlation coefficients, as well as some familiarity with the related disciplines of mean–variance optimization and multi-factor risk models. The following sections introduce the mathematics of value added through active portfolio management, including the concepts of active weights, relative returns, and performance attribution systems. The subsequent section compares the well-known Sharpe ratio for measuring the total risk-adjusted value added with the information ratio for measuring relative risk-adjusted value added. This section also makes a distinction between *ex ante*, or expected, risk and return versus *ex post*, or realized, risk and return and explains that the information ratio is the best criterion for evaluating active investors. We then introduce the fundamental law that describes how relative skill, breadth of application, active management aggressiveness, and the constraints in portfolio construction combine to affect value added. The remaining sections provide examples of active portfolio management strategies in both the equity and fixed-income markets, describe some of the practical limitations of the fundamental law, and provide a summary of the concepts and principles.

2 ACTIVE MANAGEMENT AND VALUE ADDED

☐ | describe how value added by active management is measured

The objective of active management is to add value in the investment process by doing better than a benchmark portfolio. Value added is a relative performance comparison to investing in the benchmark portfolio, often called passive investing. If the investor outperforms the benchmark portfolio, value added is positive. If the investor underperforms the benchmark portfolio, value added is negative. In the latter case, the investor would have been better off during the measurement period by simply holding the benchmark portfolio, particularly net of fees and expenses. Examples of indexes that are used as benchmark portfolios include the MSCI All Country World Index and the Bloomberg Barclays Global Aggregate Bond Index, which represent the performance of global equities and global bonds, respectively.

Choice of Benchmark

A benchmark or passive portfolio should have a number of qualities to serve as a relevant comparison for active management:

- The benchmark is representative of the assets from which the investor will select.
- Positions in the benchmark portfolio can actually be replicated at low cost.
- Benchmark weights are verifiable *ex ante*, and return data are timely *ex post*.

An available security market index is often used as the benchmark portfolio. The most common market indexes weight the individual assets by their market capitalization. Capitalization weighting has played a prominent role in the development of capital market theory because such indexes are generally self-rebalancing and can be simultaneously held by many investors. Float-adjusted market capitalization-weighted indexes represent an incremental improvement over non-float-adjusted indexes by accounting for the percentage of a security or asset that is not privately held and thus available to the general investing public. One important consequence of using a float-adjusted capitalization-weighted market index as the benchmark is that when all relevant assets are included in the market, the value added from active management becomes a zero-sum game with respect to the market. Because the market portfolio represents the average performance across all investors that own securities before costs, active investors as a group cannot outperform the market (i.e., active management is a zero-sum game). For benchmarks that have a narrower definition than the total market, active management is not a zero-sum game because investors can select assets outside the benchmark.

The return on the benchmark portfolio, R_B, is based on the returns to the individual securities and the weights of each security in the portfolio:

$$R_B = \sum_{i=1}^{N} w_{B,i} R_i, \tag{1}$$

where R_i is the return on security i, $w_{B,i}$ is the benchmark weight of security i, and N is the number of securities. Similarly, the return on an actively managed portfolio, R_P, is a function of the weights of the securities, i, held in the portfolio, $w_{P,i}$, and the returns to the individual securities:

$$R_P = \sum_{i=1}^{N} w_{P,i} R_i. \tag{2}$$

The benchmark might include securities that are not part of the actively managed portfolio and thus would have a weight of zero by definition or simply be left out of the calculation in Equation 2. Similarly, an investor could include securities in the active portfolio that are not in the benchmark, and those would have a benchmark weight of zero in Equation 1. Please note that for simplicity, the same notation, N, is used in the summation in the expression for the managed portfolio return and the benchmark return, although fewer or more securities may be in the managed portfolio than in the benchmark.

Measuring Value Added

The value added or "active return" of an actively managed portfolio is typically calculated as the simple difference between the return on that portfolio and the return on the benchmark portfolio,

$$R_A = R_P - R_B,$$

— If a benchmark does not contain many assets that the manager wants to invest in, the benchmark may not be representative of the manager's investment approach.

— Active return is not the same as alpha.

and can thus be either positive or negative. A risk-adjusted calculation of value added, which we will refer to as the managed portfolio's alpha, incorporates some estimate of the managed portfolio's risk relative to the benchmark, often captured by the portfolio's beta, $\alpha_P = R_P - \beta_P R_B$. Unfortunately, the term *alpha* in practice is often used to refer to active return as well, which implicitly assumes that the beta of the managed portfolio relative to the benchmark is 1.

Equations 1 and 2 can be combined to illustrate the important principle that value added is ultimately driven by the differences in managed portfolio weights and benchmark weights: $\Delta w_i = w_{P,i} - w_{B,i}$. These values are called the active weights of the managed portfolio, and the symbol Δ (Greek letter delta) is used to indicate the difference from the benchmark weights. Combining Equations 1 and 2 and employing this definition for active weights yields the conceptually important result that value added is the sum product of the active weights and asset returns:

value added

$$R_A = \sum_{i=1}^{N} \Delta w_i R_i.$$

$\sum w_{P,i} = 1$
$\sum w_{B,i} = 1$

Given that the sum of the active weights is zero, we can also write the value added as the sum product of active weights and active security returns:

value added

$$R_A = \sum_{i=1}^{N} \Delta w_i R_{Ai}, \tag{3}$$

where $R_{Ai} = R_i - R_B$. Equation 3 indicates that positive value added is generated when securities that have returns greater than the benchmark are overweighted and securities that have returns less than the benchmark are underweighted.

Whereas many applications of value added focus on individual securities as the assets, we first illustrate the concept with a simple numerical example of a composite portfolio that has just two assets—a stock portfolio and a bond portfolio. Suppose the benchmark is a 60/40 weighted composite portfolio of stocks and bonds. The investor believes that over the next year stocks will outperform bonds, so the investor holds a portfolio that is weighted 70% stocks and 30% bonds. The managed portfolio is said to be *overweight* stocks by 10 percentage points and *underweight* bonds by 10 percentage points—in other words, an active weight of –10 percentage points on bonds. Assume that *ex post* (i.e., "after the fact"), the return on the stock market turned out to be 14.0% and the return on the bond market turned out to be just 2.0%. In this case, the return on the managed portfolio is 0.70(14.0) + 0.30(2.0) = 10.4% and the return on the benchmark is 0.60(14.0) + 0.40(2.0) = 9.2%.

From these final numbers, one could directly calculate the value added as 10.4 – 9.2 = 1.2%. But using Equation 3, a more informative calculation of value added showing the contributions from each segment is R_A = 0.10(14.0 – 9.2) – 0.10(2.0 – 9.2) = 0.5 + 0.7 = 1.2%. This breakout suggests that a 0.5% return relative to the benchmark was generated by being overweight stocks, and a 0.7% return was generated simultaneously by being underweight bonds—for a total of 1.2%. Of course, the actual returns might have been different—with the stock market return being lower than the bond market return, resulting in negative value added in the managed portfolio. For example, if the stock market had a return of –14.0% instead of +14.0%, the portfolio return and benchmark return would have been –9.2% and –7.6%, respectively. Then the value added from this single overweight/underweight decision would have been R_A = 0.10(–14.0) – 0.10(2.0) = –1.4% – 0.2% = –1.6%.

Active Management and Value Added

EXAMPLE 1

Value Added and Country Equity Markets

Consider the MSCI EAFE Index as the benchmark for an actively managed portfolio that includes allocations to individual countries, as given in the following exhibit. The portfolio (both benchmark and managed) weights are for the beginning of 2018. The portfolio manager actively changes country allocations but does not engage in security selection.

Country	Benchmark Weight	Portfolio Weight	2018 Return
United Kingdom	17%	16%	−7.6%
Japan	25%	14%	−9.0%
France	11%	8%	−3.5%
Germany	9%	24%	−15.8%
Other Countries	38%	38%	−0.1%

Source: Data from MSCI.

1. Which countries have the largest overweight and largest underweight in the managed portfolio compared with the benchmark portfolio? What are the active weights for these two countries?

Solution to 1:

Germany has the largest overweight at 24 − 9 = +15%, and Japan has the largest underweight at 14 − 25 = −11%.

2. Using active weights and total returns, what was the value added of the managed portfolio over the benchmark portfolio in the calendar year 2018?

Solution to 2:

The value added is −0.01(−7.6) − 0.11(−9.0) − 0.03(−3.5) + 0.15(−15.8) = −1.2%. Note that the "Other Countries" active weight is zero, so this asset does not contribute anything to the portfolio's active return. The value added can also be calculated using relative returns in Equation 3 with the same net result.

Decomposition of Value Added

In contrast to the previous simple example, performance attribution systems often attempt to decompose the value added into *multiple* sources. The most common decomposition is between value added due to asset allocation and value added due to security selection. Consider a composite portfolio of stocks and bonds where the asset allocation weights differ from a composite benchmark *and* each asset class is actively managed by selecting individual securities. The total value added is the difference between the actual portfolio return and the benchmark return:

$$R_A = \sum_{j=1}^{M} w_{P,j} R_{P,j} - \sum_{j=1}^{M} w_{B,j} R_{B,j}.$$

Value added from security selection:
Sum of the actual portfolio weights multiplied by each sub-portfolio's value added measure

Value added from asset allocation:
Sum of the differences in the weights between the benchmark allocation and the actual sub-portfolio allocation multiplied by each sub-portfolio's benchmark return

The first summation has both portfolio weights and the returns on actively managed portfolios, designated by the "P" subscript. The second summation has both benchmark weights and benchmark returns, designated by the "B" subscript. The subscript $j = 1$ to M counts the number of asset classes, leaving the notation subscript $i = 1$ to N for use elsewhere to count the securities within each asset class.

We can rewrite the total value added as the sum of the active asset allocation decisions and the weighted sum of the value added from security selection, $R_{A,j} = R_{P,j} - R_{B,j}$, within each asset class:

$$R_A = \underbrace{\sum_{j=1}^{M} \Delta w_j R_{B,j}}_{\text{active asset allocation}} + \underbrace{\sum_{j=1}^{M} w_{P,j} R_{A,j}}_{\text{Security Selection}}, \tag{4}$$

although this formulation arbitrarily assigns an interactive effect to security selection. The performance attribution system in Equation 4 may be easier to conceptualize with just two asset classes, stocks and bonds (in other words, with $M = 2$). Using *stocks* and *bonds* as the subscripts, Equation 4 becomes:

$$R_A = \left(\Delta w_{stocks} R_{B,stocks} + \Delta w_{bonds} R_{B,bonds}\right) + \left(w_{P,stocks} R_{A,stocks} + w_{P,bonds} R_{A,bonds}\right).$$

The first (parenthetical) term is the value added from the asset allocation decision. The second term is the value added from security selection within the stock and bond portfolios. The active weights in the first term refer to differences from the policy portfolio. For example, the long-term policy portfolio might be 60/40 stocks versus bonds, and the investor deviates from this policy portfolio from year to year based on beliefs about the returns to each asset class.

To give a numerical example, consider the fund returns for the calendar year 2018 in the following table.

Fund	Fund Return (%)	Benchmark Return (%)	Value Added (%)
Fidelity Magellan	−5.6	−4.5	−1.1
PIMCO Total Return	−0.3	0.0	−0.3
Portfolio Return	−3.9	−2.7	−1.2

Specifically, the Fidelity Magellan mutual fund had a return of −5.6%, compared with a −4.5% return for its benchmark, the S&P 500 Index. In the same year, the PIMCO Total Return Fund had a return of −0.3%, compared with a 0.0% return for its benchmark, the Bloomberg Barclays US Aggregate Index. Consider an investor who invested in both actively managed funds, with 68% of the total portfolio in Fidelity and 32% in PIMCO. Assume that the investor's policy portfolio (strategic asset allocation) specifies weights of 60% for equities and 40% for bonds.

- As shown in the table, Fidelity Magellan added value of $R_A = R_P - R_B = $ −5.6% − (−4.5)% = −1.1%, and PIMCO Total Return added value of $R_A = R_P - R_B = $ −0.3% − (0.0%) = −0.3%. These value added numbers represent the skill in security selection within each individual fund.

- Using the actual weights of 68% and 32% in the Fidelity and PIMCO funds, the combined value added from security selection was 0.68(−1.1%) + 0.32(−0.3%) = −0.8%.

- The active asset allocation weights in 2018 were 68% − 60% = +8% for equities and −8% for bonds, so the value added by the active asset allocation decision was 0.08(−4.5%) − 0.08(0.0%) = −0.4%. The total value added by the investor's active asset allocation decision *and* by the mutual funds through security selection was −0.8% − 0.4% = −1.2%. To confirm this total value added, note that the return on the investor's portfolio was 0.68(−5.6%) + 0.32(−0.3%) = −3.9% and the return on the policy portfolio was 0.60(−4.5%) + 0.40(0.0%) = −2.7%, for a difference of −3.9% − (−2.7) = −1.2%.

Performance attribution systems can be expanded to include several asset classes—for example, stocks, bonds, real estate, and cash (in other words, with $M = 4$ in Equation 4). For a given asset class, the performance attribution system might also include value added from the selection of industries or sectors relative to the benchmark. For example, an equity portfolio might measure value added from over- and underweighting different industry sectors, as well as individual stock selection within those sectors, and a fixed-income portfolio might decompose value added from the mix of sovereign government bonds versus corporate bonds, as well as individual bond selection.

In summary, deviations from portfolio benchmark weights drive the value added by active portfolio management. If every asset in the managed portfolio is held at its benchmark weight, there would be no value added relative to the benchmark. The total value added can be decomposed into various sources that capture the contribution from different decisions, such as asset allocation and security selection.

THE SHARPE RATIO AND THE INFORMATION RATIO

3

☐ | calculate and interpret the information ratio (ex post and ex ante) and contrast it to the Sharpe ratio

The risk–return trade-off of a portfolio can be represented in either *absolute* or *relative* terms. The Sharpe ratio provides an absolute expected (*ex ante*) or realized (*ex post*) reward-to-risk measure. As we have noted, however, value added is a relative return comparison. The information ratio provides a benchmark relative expected (*ex ante*) or realized (*ex post*) reward-to-risk measure.

The Sharpe Ratio

The Sharpe ratio is used to compare the portfolio return in excess of a riskless rate with the volatility of the portfolio return. The ratio provides a measure of how much the investor is receiving in excess of a riskless rate for assuming the risk of the portfolio. The Sharpe ratio, SR_P, is calculated for any portfolio, either actively managed or a benchmark, using the formula

$$\text{SR}_P = \frac{R_P - R_F}{\sigma_P},\qquad(5)$$

absolute reward-to-risk measure

where R_P is the portfolio return, R_F is the risk-free rate, and σ_P is the standard deviation of the portfolio return. In this context, the standard deviation of the portfolio return is often called either volatility or total risk. The Sharpe ratio can be used as an *ex ante* measure of *expected* return and risk, in which case the general formula in Equation 5 would have the expected portfolio return, $E(R_P)$, minus the risk-free rate in the numerator and a forecast of volatility in the denominator. As subjective forecasts, the expected return and standard deviation of return will likely vary among different investors.

The Sharpe ratio can also be used to measure the *ex post* or *realized* performance of a portfolio over some time period. In that case, when applied to multiple time periods, the numerator in Equation 5 is the difference between the average realized portfolio return, $\overline{R_P}$, and the average risk-free rate, $\overline{R_F}$, and the denominator in Equation 5 is the sample standard deviation. The convention for Sharpe ratios is to annualize both the portfolio average return and the portfolio risk. For example, if the past return data are measured monthly, the average monthly return can be multiplied by 12 and the monthly return volatility can be multiplied by the square root of 12. The logic for multiplying the standard deviation by the *square root* of 12 is that variance (i.e., standard deviation squared), under certain assumptions, increases proportionally with time.

Although this scaling convention is common in practice, multiplying monthly returns by a factor of 12 for averages and the square root of 12 for standard deviations ignores the multiplicative (i.e., compound) nature of returns over time. Simple multiplication factors (e.g., 250 and the square root of 250 for annualizing trading-day returns) are only technically correct if the underlying returns are independent and continuously compounded or logarithmic. Similarly, annualized compound returns for the two values in the numerator of the Sharpe ratio (i.e., the portfolio return and the riskless rate) may be used instead of the annualized difference of arithmetic returns. The various methodologies produce slightly different results but should not be a serious problem as long as comparisons between different portfolios use the same approach.

Exhibit 1: Benchmark Sharpe Ratios for 1994–2018 (based on a risk-free rate of 2.3%)

	MSCI World	S&P 500	Russell 2000	MSCI EAFE	Bloomberg Barclays US Aggregate
Average annual return	7.9%	9.9%	10.3%	6.3%	5.0%
Return standard dev.	14.5%	14.4%	19.1%	15.8%	3.5%
Sharpe ratio	0.38	0.53	0.41	0.25	0.77

Exhibit 1 reports the annualized monthly historical return data (not compounded) in US dollars for several different benchmark portfolios for the 25-year period from 1994 to 2018. Long-term *ex post* Sharpe ratios for equity benchmarks have typically fallen within a range of 0.20–0.60, although over a shorter horizon they will vary over a wider range and can be either negative or positive. The Sharpe ratio for the Bloomberg Barclays US Aggregate fixed-income benchmark in Exhibit 1 is particularly high because of the secular decline in interest rates over this 25-year period that boosted the average return for fixed income. Exhibit 2 reports historical return data and Sharpe ratios from 1994 to 2018 for some well-known actively managed mutual funds over the same period. The Sharpe ratios in both exhibits are based on a risk-free rate of 2.3%, the average annualized US Treasury bill return during this 25-year period. The comparison of Sharpe ratios between funds intentionally uses data from the same measurement period. One should not compare the Sharpe ratio of one fund over one period with that of another fund over a different period.

The Sharpe Ratio and The Information Ratio

Exhibit 2: Active Fund Sharpe Ratios for 1994–2018 (based on a risk-free rate of 2.3%)

	Fidelity Magellan	Growth Fund of America	Templeton World	T. Rowe Price Small Cap	JPMorgan Bond
Average annual return	8.5%	11.1%	7.9%	11.6%	5.2%
Return standard dev.	16.5%	15.7%	15.2%	16.7%	3.6%
Sharpe ratio	0.38	0.56	0.37	0.56	0.80

Note: The selection of funds for illustration was made without any intended implication, positive or negative, concerning their performance relative to other possible choices.

An important property is that the Sharpe ratio is unaffected by the addition of cash or leverage in a portfolio. Consider a combined portfolio with a weight of w_P on the actively managed portfolio and a weight of $(1 - w_P)$ on risk-free cash. The return on the combined portfolio is $R_C = w_P R_P + (1 - w_P)R_F$, and the volatility of the combined portfolio is just $\sigma_C = w_P \sigma_P$ because the $(1 - w_P)R_F$ portion is risk free. Applying these two relationships in Equation 5 gives the Sharpe ratio for the combined portfolio as

$$SR_C = \frac{R_C - R_F}{\sigma_C} = \frac{w_P (R_P - R_F)}{w_P \sigma_P} = SR_P,$$

which is the same as the Sharpe ratio of the actively managed portfolio. Note that the weight in the combined portfolio, w_P, could be greater than 1, so $(1 - w_P)$ could be negative, indicating that leverage created by *borrowing* risk-free cash and investing in risky assets also does not affect the portfolio's Sharpe ratio.

The proposition that independent of preferences investors should form portfolios using two funds—one of which is the risk-free asset and the other the risky asset portfolio with the highest Sharpe ratio—is known as two-fund separation. On the one hand, if the expected volatility of the risky asset portfolio is higher than the investor prefers, the volatility can be reduced by holding more cash and less of the risky portfolio. On the other hand, if the expected volatility of the risky portfolio is lower than the investor allows, the volatility and expected return can be increased by leverage. For example, suppose an investor believes the performance of the Growth Fund of America shown in Exhibit 2 will repeat going forward but only allows a volatility of 10%. The investor might invest 64% of assets in the Growth Fund of America and 36% in cash to reduce overall portfolio risk. The expected return of the combined portfolio is 0.64(11.1%) + 0.36(2.3%) = 7.9%. The volatility of the combined portfolio is 0.64(15.7%) = 10.0%. The Sharpe ratio of the combined portfolio is (7.9% – 2.3%)/10.0% = 0.56, the same as the 0.56 Sharpe ratio of the Growth Fund of America shown in Exhibit 2.

EXAMPLE 2

Adjusting Risk and Return Using the Sharpe Ratio

Consider an investor choosing between two risky portfolios: a large-cap stock portfolio and a small-cap stock portfolio. Although forecasts about the future are subjective, suppose for simplicity that the investor expects that the future statistics will be those in the following table, with a risk-free rate of 2.3%. The forecasted 0.42 Sharpe ratio of the small-cap portfolio is higher than the 0.40 ratio of the large-cap portfolio, but suppose the investor does not want the high 19.2% volatility associated with the small-cap stocks.

	Large Cap	Small Cap
Expected return	8.2%	10.3%
Expected volatility	14.6%	19.2%
Sharpe ratio	0.40	0.42

1. What percentage of the portfolio would an investor need to hold in cash to reduce the risk of a portfolio invested in the small-cap portfolio and cash to the same risk level as that of the large-cap portfolio?

Solution:

We want to reduce the 19.2% volatility to 14.6% by adding cash. The weight of small-cap stocks in the combined portfolio must therefore be 14.6/19.2 = 76%, leaving a 24% weight in risk-free cash. With that amount of cash, the volatility of the combined portfolio will be 0.76(19.2%) = 14.6%, the same as the large-cap portfolio.

2. Based on your answer to 1, calculate the Sharpe ratio of the small-cap plus cash portfolio.

Solution:

The Sharpe ratio of the combined portfolio is unaffected by the amount in cash, so it remains 0.42.

3. Compare the expected return of the small-cap plus cash portfolio with the expected return of the large-cap portfolio.

Solution:

The expected return of the combined portfolio is 0.76(10.3%) + 0.24(2.3%) = 8.4%, 20 basis points (bps) higher than the 8.2% expected return on the large-cap portfolio, but with the same risk as the large-cap portfolio. To reconfirm, the Sharpe ratio of the combined portfolio is (8.4% − 2.3%)/14.6% = 0.42, the same as the original 0.42 value.

The Information Ratio

The simplest definition of the information ratio compares the active return from a portfolio relative to a benchmark with the volatility of the active return, called "active risk" or "benchmark tracking risk." The information ratio can be thought of as a way to measure the consistency of active return, as most investors would prefer a more evenly generated value added (low active risk) rather than a lumpy active return pattern. Like the more formal distinction between active portfolio return and alpha, active risk has a more exact beta-adjusted counterpart, which Grinold and Kahn (1999) called "residual risk." In this discussion, the information ratio is based on the implicit assumption that the beta of the managed portfolio relative to the benchmark is exactly 1.0, although in practice that assumption can be relaxed. For example, Fischer and Wermers (2013) present the information ratio that does not assume beta is 1.

The information ratio tells the investor how much active return has been earned, or is expected to be earned, for incurring the level of active risk. Active return, R_A, is the difference between the managed portfolio return, R_P, and the benchmark portfolio return, R_B. The information ratio of an actively managed portfolio, IR, is calculated by dividing the active return by active risk:

$$IR = \frac{R_P - R_B}{\sigma(R_P - R_B)} = \frac{R_A}{\sigma_A} \qquad R_A = IR \times \sigma_A \qquad (6)$$

where $\sigma(\cdot)$ is the standard deviation function—in this case, the standard deviation of the excess return of the portfolio (R_P) over the return of the benchmark (R_B). As with the Sharpe ratio, the typical convention is to annualize both the active return and the active risk. The information ratio can refer to the investor's *ex ante*, or forecasted, active return. Thus, the numerator in Equation 6 would be replaced by the expected returns—that is, $E(R_A) = E(R_P) - E(R_B)$—and the denominator would be the expected active risk. Alternatively, the calculation of an *ex post*, or historical, information ratio would use realized average active returns and the realized sample standard deviation of the active return.

Two investment strategies and associated terminology can help reinforce the conceptual distinction between the Sharpe ratio and the information ratio. First, a "closet index fund" (a fund that advertises itself as being actively managed but is actually close to being an index fund) will have a Sharpe ratio that is close to the benchmark because the excess return and volatility will be similar to the benchmark. However, the closet index fund will have a small amount of active risk, although positive by definition like any volatility estimate. While there may be little active risk, the information ratio of a closet index fund will likely be close to zero or slightly negative if value added cannot overcome the management fees. If one has the actual holdings of the fund, closet indexing is easy to detect on the basis of a measurement called "active share," a measure of how similar a portfolio is to its benchmark. [Cremers and Petajisto (2009) defined active share as half the sum of the absolute values of the active weights.] As a second example, the Sharpe ratio and the information ratio for a market-neutral long–short equity fund (a fund with offsetting long and short positions that has a beta of zero with respect to the market) would be identical if we consider the benchmark to be the riskless rate because the excess return and active return would be the same calculation, as would be total risk and active risk.

Exhibit 3 shows historical information ratios for the mutual funds in Exhibit 2, with the benchmark portfolio for each calculation shown at the bottom of Exhibit 3. The average active return in the first row of Exhibit 3 can be calculated by subtracting the specified benchmark average return in Exhibit 1 from the average fund return in Exhibit 2. The active risk is the annualized standard deviation of the return differences from 1994 to 2018, which cannot be verified with just the summary data in Exhibit 1 and Exhibit 2.

As shown in Exhibit 3, *ex post* information ratios will be negative if the active return is negative. In fact, under the zero-sum property of active management, the average realized information ratio across investment funds with the same benchmark should be about zero. The realized information ratios in Exhibit 3 are within a range of about −0.30 to +0.30, although the range would be much wider over shorter periods. Of course, *ex ante*, or before the fact, if an investor did not expect the information ratio to be positive, he or she would simply invest in the benchmark. Note that ranking by active risk, a relative measure, does not necessarily equate to ranking by total risk, an absolute measure. For example, the relative risk of Fidelity Magellan in Exhibit 3 is slightly lower than the relative risk of the Growth Fund of America; however, the absolute risk of Fidelity Magellan in Exhibit 2 is slightly higher.

Exhibit 3: Active Fund Information Ratios for 2014–2018

	Fidelity Magellan	Growth Fund of America	Templeton World	T. Rowe Price Small Cap	JPMorgan Bond
Active return	−1.4%	1.2%	0.0%	1.4%	0.2%
Active risk	5.1%	6.2%	5.0%	4.7%	1.0%
Information ratio	−0.27	0.20	0.00	0.29	0.19
Benchmark	S&P 500	S&P 500	MSCI World	Russell 2000	Bloomberg Barclays US Aggregate

Unlike the Sharpe ratio, the information ratio is affected by the addition of cash or the use of leverage. For example, if the investor adds cash to a portfolio of risky assets, the information ratio for the combined portfolio will generally shrink. However, the information ratio of an unconstrained portfolio is unaffected by the aggressiveness of active weights. Specifically, if the active security weights, Δw_i, defined as deviations from the benchmark portfolio weights, are all multiplied by some constant, c, the information ratio of an actively managed portfolio will remain unchanged.

Recall the expression for the active return of a managed portfolio in Equation 3. If each active weight in Equation 3 is multiplied by some constant, c, then the active return on the altered portfolio, R_C, is

$$R_C = \sum_{i=1}^{N} c \Delta w_i R_{Ai} = c \sum_{i=1}^{N} \Delta w_i R_{Ai} = c R_A.$$

Similarly, the active risk of the altered portfolio is $c\sigma_A$, so the information ratio of the altered portfolio is

$$IR_C = \frac{c R_A}{c \sigma_A} = IR,$$

the same as that of the actively managed portfolio with no proportional increase in the active weights. Specifically, if the active weights in a managed portfolio are all doubled, the expected active return (or realized average active return) would be doubled, along with the expected or realized active risk, leaving the information ratio unchanged.

Of course, an outside investor would not be able to adjust the active risk of an existing fund by changing the individual asset active weight positions, but the same objective can be met by taking positions in the benchmark portfolio. For example, if the active risk of a fund is 5.0%, combining that fund in an 80/20 mix with the benchmark portfolio (i.e., a benchmark portfolio weight of 20%) will result in an active risk of the combined portfolio of 0.80(5.0%) = 4.0%, with a proportional reduction in the active return. Similarly, the investor can short sell the benchmark portfolio and use the proceeds to invest in the actively managed fund to increase the active risk and return. Note that in practice, institutional investors might simply reduce the amount they would have otherwise invested in the benchmark portfolio—or, if possible, another actively managed fund—rather than employ an explicit short sell.

CONSTRUCTING OPTIMAL PORTFOLIOS

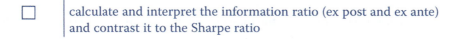

☐ calculate and interpret the information ratio (ex post and ex ante) and contrast it to the Sharpe ratio

An important concept from basic portfolio theory is that with a risk-free asset, the portfolio on the efficient frontier of risky assets that is tangent to a ray extended from the risk-free rate is optimal because it has the highest possible Sharpe ratio. Thus, given the opportunity to adjust absolute risk and return with cash or leverage, the overriding objective is to find the single risky asset portfolio with the maximum Sharpe ratio, whatever the investor's risk aversion. A similarly important property in active management theory is that given the opportunity to adjust active risk and return by investing in both the actively managed and benchmark portfolios, the squared Sharpe ratio of an actively managed portfolio is equal to the squared Sharpe ratio of the benchmark plus the information ratio squared:

$$SR_P^2 = SR_B^2 + IR^2. \qquad (7)$$

Equation 7 implies that the active portfolio with the highest (squared) information ratio will also have the highest (squared) Sharpe ratio. (Note that Equation 7 is not practical for comparisons of investment skill involving negative IR because the sign is lost in squaring.) As a consequence, according to mean–variance theory, the expected information ratio is the single best criterion for assessing active performance among various actively managed funds with the same benchmark (Grinold 1989). For any given asset class, an investor should choose the manager with the highest expected skill as measured by the information ratio, because investing with the highest information-ratio manager will produce the highest Sharpe ratio for the investor's portfolio.

The preceding discussion on adjusting active risk raises the issue of determining the *optimal* amount of active risk, without resorting to utility functions that measure risk aversion. For unconstrained portfolios, the level of active risk that leads to the optimal result in Equation 7 is

$$\sigma(R_A) = \frac{IR}{SR_B}\sigma_B, \qquad (8)$$

where σ_B is the standard deviation of the benchmark return. (Note that the right-hand side of the equation should be multiplied by the benchmark beta of the actively managed portfolio if that value is different from 1.) This Sharpe ratio-maximizing level of active risk or "aggressiveness" comes from the general mean–variance optimality condition that the ratio of expected active return to active return variance of the managed portfolio be set equal to the ratio of expected benchmark excess return to benchmark return variance:

$$\frac{E(R_A)}{\sigma_A^2} = \frac{E(R_B - R_F)}{\sigma_B^2}.$$

For example, if the actively managed portfolio has an information ratio of 0.30 and active risk of 8.0% and the benchmark portfolio has an expected excess return of 6.4% and total risk of 16.0% resulting in a Sharpe ratio of 0.40, then according to Equation 8, the optimal amount of aggressiveness in the actively managed portfolio is (0.30/0.40)16.0% = 12.0%. If the actively managed portfolio is constructed with this amount of active risk, the Sharpe ratio will be $(0.40^2 + 0.30^2)^{1/2} = 0.50$, as shown in Equation 7. To verify this Sharpe ratio, note that the more aggressively managed portfolio in this example has an expected active return of (0.30)12.0% = 3.6% over the benchmark, or a total expected excess return of 6.4% + 3.6% = 10.0%. By definition, the total risk of the actively managed portfolio is the sum of the benchmark return variance and active return variance,

$$\sigma_P^2 = \sigma_B^2 + \sigma_A^2.$$

At the optimal active risk of 12.0%, the total portfolio risk is $(16.0^2 + 12.0^2)^{1/2} = 20.0\%$, verifying the maximum possible Sharpe ratio of 10.0/20.0 = 0.50.

The initial actively managed portfolio has active risk of only 8.0%, whereas the optimal amount required under the assumed information ratio needed to maximize the Sharpe ratio is 12.0%. The actively managed portfolio would thus need to be managed more aggressively to increase the active risk while preserving the same information ratio; alternatively, the investor could short the benchmark and use the proceeds to increase the amount invested in the actively managed fund. The proportion required to be invested in the actively managed fund would be 12.0/8.0 = 1.5 times; shorting the benchmark by 0.5 times would fund the increase.

For readers familiar with risk–return charts in basic portfolio theory, Exhibit 4 will help illustrate these concepts.

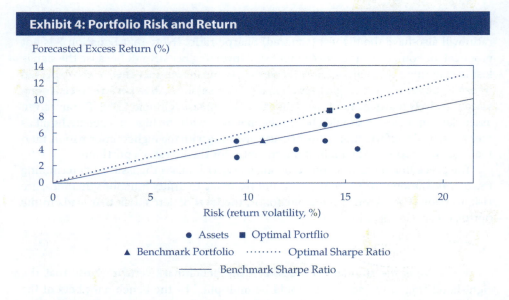

Exhibit 4: Portfolio Risk and Return

Several individual risky assets are plotted in Exhibit 4 in terms of their forecasted return in excess of the risk-free rate ("excess return") on the vertical axis and risk on the horizontal axis. The values for the individual assets are based on subjective assessments supplied by the investor. The theory described here explains how to optimally employ those expectations assuming they are based on reasonable judgment. Using the benchmark portfolio weights (not shown), the risks and expected returns of the individual assets combine into the benchmark portfolio risk and expected return shown in Exhibit 4. Because the expected returns plotted along the vertical axis are in excess of the risk-free rate, the slope of a line that emanates from the origin (zero risk and zero excess return) is the Sharpe ratio of the benchmark portfolio. Specifically, the Sharpe ratio of the benchmark portfolio (i.e., slope of the dark line) in Exhibit 4 is the expected excess return of 5.0% divided by return volatility of 10.8%, or 5.0%/10.8% = 0.46.

Because of diversification, the Sharpe ratio of the benchmark portfolio is higher than those of most of the individual assets; however, the benchmark portfolio does not have the highest possible Sharpe ratio of all portfolios that can be constructed from these assets. In fact, the optimal portfolio (i.e., mean–variance efficient frontier portfolio with the highest possible Sharpe ratio) shown in Exhibit 4 has an expected excess return of 8.7% and return volatility of 14.2%, resulting in a Sharpe ratio of 8.7%/14.2% = 0.61 (i.e., slope of the dotted line). This higher Sharpe ratio could be retained in the portfolio while adjusting the level of risk through the use of cash or leverage. For example, the risk of the optimal portfolio could be reduced along the dotted line to the benchmark portfolio risk of 10.8% with an expected excess return of 0.61(10.8%) = 6.6%, compared with the benchmark expected excess return of 5.0%.

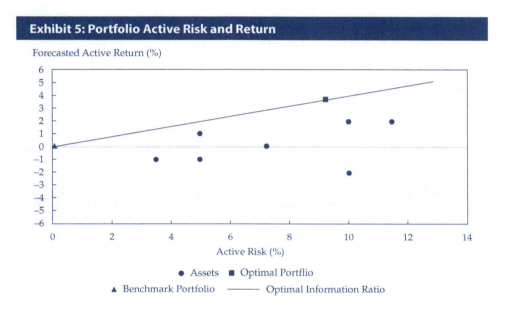

Exhibit 5: Portfolio Active Risk and Return

Exhibit 5 plots the same individual assets, the benchmark portfolio, and the optimal portfolio from Exhibit 4 in terms of their expected *active* return on the vertical axis and *active* risk on the horizontal axis. By definition, the benchmark portfolio is plotted at the origin in Exhibit 5 with zero active return and zero active risk. The individual assets have both positive and negative expected active returns compared with the benchmark portfolio return, whereas the optimal portfolio has a positive active return of 3.8% and active risk of 9.4%. The information ratio of the optimal portfolio is therefore 3.8%/9.4% = 0.40, the slope of the dark line in Exhibit 5. The information ratio of the optimal portfolio is higher than that of any of the individual assets; in fact, it can be shown to be the square root of the sum of the squared values of the individual assets' information ratios, similar to Equation 7, including those assets with negative information ratios. The asset weights required for the construction of this optimal portfolio are the subject of the next section, but here we note they might be negative for negative-IR assets—that is, short sells of individual assets may be required.

Although the information ratio will remain constant at 0.40, various levels of aggressiveness can be applied to the actively managed portfolio in Exhibit 5 by scaling the optimal active weights or, alternatively, taking a position in the benchmark portfolio—leading to portfolios that plot along the dark line. But to construct the *optimal* actively managed portfolio given the assumed information ratio, the active risk must be adjusted to a level of (0.40/0.46)10.8% = 9.4% in accordance with Equation 8. Specifically, this level of aggressiveness is required to construct the optimal portfolio in Exhibit 4, and according to Equation 7, the Sharpe ratio of this optimal portfolio is $(0.46^2 + 0.40^2)^{1/2} = 0.61$.

As we will see later, optimal levels of active risk in equity management practice are typically lower than those shown in this numerical example because the underlying portfolios are constrained to be long only, leading to information ratios that are substantially lower. As the information ratio gets close to zero, either because of constraints or because the manager is judged to be less skilled, the optimal amount of active risk in Equation 8 goes to zero (i.e., the optimal portfolio becomes the passive benchmark portfolio).

EXAMPLE 3

Expected Value Added Based on the Information Ratio

Suppose that the historical performance of the Fidelity Magellan and Growth Fund of America mutual funds from Exhibits 2 and 3 are indicative of the future performance of hypothetical funds, "Fund I" and "Fund II." In addition, suppose that the historical performance of the S&P 500 benchmark portfolio shown in Exhibit 1 is indicative of expected returns and risk going forward, as shown in the following excerpts. We use historical values in this problem for convenience, but in practice the forecasted, or expected, values for both the benchmark portfolio and the active funds would be subjectively determined by the investor.

Excerpted from Exhibits 1 and 2 (based on a risk-free rate of 2.3%)

	S&P 500	Fidelity Magellan (Fund I)	Growth Fund of America (Fund II)
Average annual return	9.9%	8.5%	11.1%
Return standard dev.	14.4%	16.5%	15.7%
Sharpe ratio	0.53	0.38	0.56

Excerpted from Exhibit 3

	Fidelity Magellan (Fund I)	Growth Fund of America (Fund II)
Active return	−1.4%	1.2%
Active risk	5.1%	6.2%
Information ratio	−0.27	0.20
Benchmark	S&P 500	S&P 500

1. State which of the two actively managed funds, Fund I or Fund II, would be better to combine with the passive benchmark portfolio and why.

Solution:

Fund II is better, as measured by the combined Sharpe ratio, because Fund II has the higher expected information ratio: 0.20 compared with −0.27 in Fund I.

Constructing Optimal Portfolios

2. Calculate the possible improvement over the S&P 500 Sharpe ratio from the optimal deployment of Fund II, which has an expected information ratio of 0.20.

Solution:

Properly combined with the S&P 500 benchmark portfolio, Fund II has the potential to increase the expected Sharpe ratio from 0.53 for the passive benchmark portfolio to an expected Sharpe ratio of $(0.53^2 + 0.20^2)^{1/2} = 0.57$.

3. Fund I comes with an active (i.e., benchmark relative) risk of 5.1%, but the investor wants to adjust the active risk to 5.4%. Describe how that adjustment would be made. (No calculations are required; give a qualitative description.)

Solution:

To increase the active risk of Fund I, the investor would need to be more aggressive in managing the portfolio, take a short (i.e., negative) position in the benchmark, or, more simply, invest less than he or she otherwise would have in the benchmark or another actively managed fund.

4. Fund II comes with an active risk of 6.2%. Determine the weight of the benchmark portfolio required to create a combined portfolio with the highest possible expected Sharpe ratio.

Solution:

According to Equation 8, the optimal amount of active risk is $(0.20/0.53)14.4\% = 5.4\%$. A positive position in the benchmark is needed to adjust the active weight down from 6.2%. Specifically, the benchmark portfolio weight needed to adjust the active risk in Fund II is $1 - 5.4\%/6.2\% = 13\%$.

Note that at the 5.4% optimal level of active risk, Fund II has an expected active return of $0.20(5.4\%) = 1.1\%$, a total expected excess return of $7.6\% + 1.1\% = 8.7\%$, and a total risk of $(14.4^2 + 5.4^2)^{1/2} = 15.4\%$. The result is an expected Sharpe ratio of $8.7/15.4 = 0.57$, the same as the value calculated for Question 2.

In summary, the information ratio is active return over active risk (in contrast to the excess return-to-risk measure known as the Sharpe ratio). Information ratios help investors focus on the relative valued added by active management. The information ratio is unaffected by the aggressiveness of the active weights (i.e., deviations from benchmark weights) in the managed portfolio because both the active return and the active risk increase proportionally. The potential improvement in an active portfolio's expected Sharpe ratio compared with the benchmark's Sharpe ratio is a function of the squared information ratio. Thus, the expected information ratio becomes the single best criterion for constructing an actively managed portfolio, and the *ex post* information ratio is the best criterion for evaluating the past performance of various actively managed funds.

5 ACTIVE SECURITY RETURNS AND THE FUNDAMENTAL LAW OF ACTIVE MANAGEMENT

> ☐ describe and interpret the fundamental law of active portfolio management, including its component terms—transfer coefficient, information coefficient, breadth, and active risk (aggressiveness)
>
> ☐ explain how the information ratio may be useful in investment manager selection and choosing the level of active portfolio risk

The fundamental law is a framework for thinking about the potential value added through active portfolio management. The framework can be used to size individual asset active weights, estimate the expected value added of an active management strategy, or measure the realized value added after the fact; however, the most common use is the description and evaluation of active management strategies. The law itself is a mathematical relationship that relates the expected information ratio of an actively managed portfolio to a few key parameters.

Active Security Returns

On the basis of the prior section, we assume that the investor is concerned about maximizing the managed portfolio's active return subject to a limit on active risk (also called "benchmark tracking risk"). To this end, the investor uses forecasts for each security of the active return, R_{Ai}, or thus the benchmark relative return,

$$R_{Ai} = R_i - R_B, \tag{9}$$

for the N individual assets that might be included in the portfolio. Our notation for the investor's forecasts of the active security returns is μ_i (Greek letter mu). The term μ_i can be thought of as the security's expected active return, $\mu_i = E(R_{Ai})$, referring to the investor's subjective expectation, in contrast to an expectation based on a formal equilibrium model.

Although we focus on the simple definition of active security return in Equation 9, there are several possible choices depending on the assumed risk model (i.e., statistical model of returns) and the desired trade-off between a conceptual treatment and more complex but implementable formulas. For example, Equation 9 can be modified to define the active security return as the residual return in a single-factor model, $R_{Ai} = R_i - \beta_i R_B$, where β_i is the sensitivity of the security return to the benchmark return. Although this expression may appear to be related to the CAPM, the benchmark return may or may not be the market return. Moreover, the fundamental law does not require the empirical validity of the CAPM, the multi-factor APT (arbitrage pricing theory), or any other equilibrium theory of required returns. The individual security active return can also be defined as the residual return in a multi-factor model:

$$R_{Ai} = R_i - \sum_{j=1}^{K} \beta_{j,i} R_j,$$

with K market-wide factor returns, R_j, and security sensitivities, $\beta_{j,i}$, to those factors.

Exhibit 6 provides a conceptual diagram in which to think about the various parameters in the fundamental law of active management. At the three corners of the triangle are the sets of forecasted active returns, μ_i, active portfolio weights, Δw_i, and realized active returns, R_{Ai}. The base of the triangle reflects the realized value added through active management, defined as the difference between the realized returns on the actively managed portfolio and the benchmark portfolio. Value added is the sum

Active Security Returns and The Fundamental Law of Active Management

of the products of active weights and active returns for the $i = 1$ to N securities in the portfolio, as shown in Equation 3. The value of this sum is ultimately a function of the correlation coefficient between the active weights, Δw_i, and realized active returns, R_{Ai}.

Exhibit 6: The Correlation Triangle

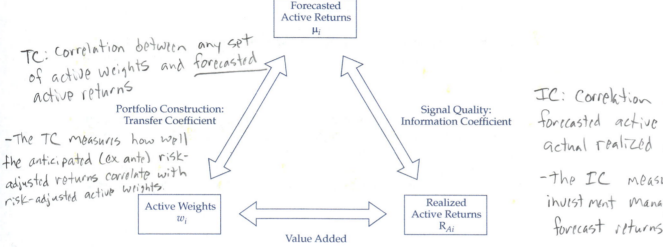

To understand the role of the correlation coefficient, consider the following algebraic expansion of Equation 3 that uses COV, STD (σ), and COR (ρ) to designate the covariance, standard deviation, and correlation coefficient functions, respectively:

$$R_A = \sum_{i=1}^{N} \Delta w_i R_{Ai}$$
$$= \rho(\Delta w_i, R_{Ai}) N$$
$$= \rho(\Delta w_i, R_{Ai}) \sigma(\Delta w_i) \sigma(R_{Ai}) N$$

The exact equalities in this expansion depend on the fact that the cross-sectional means of active weights and active returns are zero. Specifically, the population covariance between two variables, X and Y, is calculated as $COV(X,Y) = \frac{1}{N}\sum_{i=1}^{N}(X_i - \bar{X})(Y_i - \bar{Y})$, or simply $COV(X,Y) = \frac{1}{N}\sum_{i=1}^{N} X_i Y_i$. Similarly, the population variance for a single variable is $VAR(X) = \frac{1}{N}\sum_{i=1}^{N} X_i^2$ if the mean is zero.

In Exhibit 6, the arrows in the legs of the triangle represent the correlation between the quantities at the corners of the triangle to which the arrows point. While the arrow at the base of the triangle reflects value added, a better understanding of the sources and limitations of value added can be obtained by examining the correlations on the two vertical legs. First, there is little hope of adding value if the investor's forecasts of active returns do not correspond at least loosely to the realized active returns. Signal quality is measured by the correlation between the forecasted active returns, μ_i, at the top of the triangle, and the realized active returns, R_{Ai}, at the right corner, commonly called the information coefficient (IC). Investors with higher IC, or ability to forecast returns, will add more value over time but only to the extent that those forecasts are exploited in the construction of the managed portfolio. The correlation between any set of active weights—Δw_i, in the left corner, and forecasted active returns, μ_i, at the top of the triangle—measures the degree to which the investor's forecasts are translated into active weights, called the transfer coefficient (TC).

The mathematics of the fundamental law were introduced by Grinold (1989) and further developed by Clarke, de Silva, and Thorley (2002). The mean–variance-optimal active security weights for uncorrelated active returns, subject to a limit on active portfolio risk, are given by

$$\Delta w_i^* = \frac{\mu_i}{\sigma_i^2} \frac{\sigma_A}{\sqrt{\sum_{i=1}^{N} \frac{\mu_i^2}{\sigma_i^2}}},$$

where σ_A represents active portfolio risk and σ_i is the forecasted volatility of the active return on security i. This formula for active weights makes intuitive sense. The deviation (positive or negative) from the benchmark weight for security i are higher for larger values of the forecasted active return, μ_i, but are reduced by forecasted volatility, σ_i. In addition, the active weights are scaled by the active risk of the portfolio, σ_A, so that the desire for more active portfolio risk requires larger individual active weights.

In addition to employing mean–variance optimization, proofs of the fundamental law generally assume that active return forecasts are scaled prior to optimization using the Grinold (1994) rule:

$$\mu_i = \text{IC}\sigma_i S_i, \tag{10}$$

where IC is the expected information coefficient and S_i represents a set of standardized forecasts of expected returns across securities, sometimes called "scores." Scores with a cross-sectional variance of 1 are used in Equation 10 to ensure that the scaling process using the multipliers σ_i (separate values for individual securities) and IC (one value for all securities) result in expected active returns of the correct magnitude. Specifically, if the assumed IC value is low, then the cross-sectional variation of the expected active returns in Equation 10 will be low. However, the exact process for calculating expected active returns may be more involved than the simple rule indicated in Equation 10 depending on how the investor's views on individual asset returns are originally formulated.

Using the Grinold rule shown in Equation 10, the mean–variance optimal active weights are

$$\Delta w_i^* = \frac{\mu_i}{\sigma_i^2 \text{IC}\sqrt{\text{BR}}} \frac{\sigma_A}{}, \tag{11}$$

where IC stands for information coefficient and BR, which has replaced the symbol N, stands for breadth. We discuss these two key fundamental law parameters next.

As previously stated, IC is the *ex ante* (i.e., anticipated) cross-sectional correlation between the N forecasted active returns, μ_i, and the N realized active returns, R_{Ai}. To be more accurate, IC is the *ex anterisk-weighted* correlation

$$\text{IC} = \rho\left(\frac{R_{Ai}}{\sigma_i}, \frac{\mu_i}{\sigma_i}\right), \tag{12}$$

where $\rho(\cdot)$ indicates correlation. As a correlation coefficient, IC can take on values anywhere from −1.00 to +1.00, although small positive values less than 0.20 are often the norm. The *ex ante*, or anticipated, IC must be positive or the investor would not pursue active management but simply invest in the passive benchmark. Later, we will discuss the realized, or *ex post*, information coefficient in terms of measuring active management performance after the fact—where the realized information coefficient might be either positive or negative, leading to positive or negative value added.

The other important fundamental law parameter in Equation 11 is BR, or breadth, conceptually equal to the number of independent decisions made per year by the investor in constructing the portfolio. The simplest case for the calculation of breadth is a single-factor risk model, where the only source of correlation between the securities is the common market factor and decisions about the active return for any given security are independent from one year to the next. In this case, breadth is equal to the number of securities: Each active return is independent from the other active return forecasts for that period and independent from the forecast for that security in subsequent periods.

Active Security Returns and The Fundamental Law of Active Management

However, most risk models will incorporate other factors—for example, economic sectors or industries. If the risk model includes the assumption that all the securities within a given industry are positively correlated, then part of the forecast that the active returns for securities in that industry will be higher or lower is based on just one perspective the investor has about the industry. In this case, breadth is intuitively lower than the number of securities. Alternatively, breadth can be higher than the number of securities if factors in the risk model suggest that their active returns are negatively correlated. For these more complicated cases, breadth will be a non-integer number, as noted in Clarke, de Silva, and Thorley (2006).

Similarly, if some aspect of a security is fairly constant over time and the investor makes decisions about expected active return based on that characteristic, then breadth over time is lower. Alternatively, if the investor makes quarterly or monthly forecasts about a security that are truly independent over time, then breadth can be as high as the number of securities times the number of rebalancing periods per year.

EXAMPLE 4

Scaling Active Return Forecasts and Sizing Active Weights

Consider the simple case of four individual securities whose active returns are assumed to be uncorrelated with each other and have active return volatilities of 25.0% and 50.0%. After some analysis, an active investor believes the first two securities will outperform the other two over the next year and thus assigns scores of +1 and −1 to the first and second groups, respectively. The scenario is depicted in the following exhibit:

Security	Score	Volatility
#1	1.0	25.0%
#2	1.0	50.0%
#3	−1.0	25.0%
#4	−1.0	50.0%

1. Assume that the anticipated accuracy of the investor's ranking of securities is measured by an information coefficient of IC = 0.20. What are the forecasted active returns for each of the four securities using the scaling rule $\mu_i = IC\sigma_i S_i$?

Solution:

The forecasted active return to Security #1 is 0.20(25.0%)(1.0) = 5.0%. Similar calculations for the other three securities are shown in the following exhibit.

Security	Score	Active Return Volatility	Expected Active Return
#1	1.0	25.0%	5.0%
#2	1.0	50.0%	10.0%
#3	−1.0	25.0%	−5.0%
#4	−1.0	50.0%	−10.0%

2. Given the assumptions that the four securities' active returns are uncorrelated with each other and forecasts are independent from year to year, what is the breadth of the investor's forecasts?

Solution:

If the active returns are uncorrelated with each other and the forecasts are independent from year to year, then the investor has made four separate decisions and breadth is BR = 4, the number of securities.

3. Suppose the investor wants to maximize the expected active return of the portfolio subject to an active risk constraint of 9.0%. Calculate the active weights that should be assigned to each of these securities using the formula $\Delta w_i^* = \frac{\mu_i}{\sigma_i^2} \frac{\sigma_A}{IC \sqrt{BR}}$.

Solution:

The size of the active weight for Security #1 is $\Delta w_i^* = \frac{0.05}{0.25^2} \frac{0.09}{0.20 \sqrt{4}} = 18\%$. Similar calculations for the other four securities are shown in the following exhibit.

Security	Expected Active Return	Active Return Volatility	Active Weight
#1	5.0%	25.0%	18.0%
#2	10.0%	50.0%	9.0%
#3	−5.0%	25.0%	−18.0%
#4	−10.0%	50.0%	−9.0%

The Basic Fundamental Law

On the basis of Equation 3, the anticipated value added for an actively managed portfolio, or expected active portfolio return, is the sum product of active security weights and forecasted active security returns:

$$E(R_A) = \sum_{i=1}^{N} \Delta w_i \mu_i.$$

Using the optimal active weights in Equation 11 and forecasted active security returns in Equation 10, the expected active portfolio return is

$$E(R_A)^* = IC \sqrt{BR} \, \sigma_A, \tag{13}$$

where the * indicates that the actively managed portfolio is constructed from *optimal* active security weights, Δw_i^*. Remember that the algebra for this result assumes that breadth is the number of securities: BR = N. A more general proof where breadth is different from the number of securities is provided in Clarke, de Silva, and Thorley (2006).

The basic fundamental law of active management in Equation 13 states that the optimal expected active return, $E(R_A)^*$, is the product of three key parameters: the assumed information coefficient, IC, the square root of breadth, BR, and portfolio active risk, σ_A. Using Equation 13, we can also express the information ratio of the unconstrained optimal portfolio, $E(R_A)^*/\sigma_A$, as the product of just two terms: IR* = IC $\sqrt{BR}$.

Active Security Returns and The Fundamental Law of Active Management

EXAMPLE 5

The Basic Fundamental Law

Consider the simple case of four individual securities whose active returns are uncorrelated with each other and forecasts are independent from year to year. The active return forecasts, active risks, and the active weights for each security are shown in the following exhibit.

Security	Expected Active Return	Active Return Volatility	Active Weight
#1	5.0%	25.0%	18%
#2	10.0%	50.0%	9%
#3	−5.0%	25.0%	−18%
#4	−10.0%	50.0%	−9%

[handwritten annotations: μ_i's; σ_i's; ΔW_i's]

1. Suppose that the benchmark portfolio for these four securities is equally weighted (i.e., $w_{B,i}$ = 25% for each security) and that the forecasted return on the benchmark portfolio is 10.0%. What are the portfolio weights and the total expected returns for each of the four securities?

[handwritten annotation: expected return for each security in the benchmark portfolio is 10%]

Solution:

The portfolio weight for Security #1 is the benchmark weight plus the active weight, 25% + 18% = 43%. The total expected return for Security #1 is the expected benchmark return plus the expected active return, 10.0% + 5.0% = 15.0%. Similar calculations for the other three securities are shown in the following exhibit.

Security	Total Weight	Total Return Forecast
#1	43%	15.0%
#2	34%	20.0%
#3	7%	5.0%
#4	16%	0.0%
	100%	

2. Calculate the forecasted total return and active return of the managed portfolio.

Solution:

The forecasted total return of the portfolio is the sum of portfolio weights times total returns for each security: 0.43(15.0) + 0.34(20.0) + 0.07(5.0) + 0.16(0.0) = 13.6%. The expected active return of the portfolio is the managed portfolio return minus the benchmark return: 13.6 − 10.0 = 3.6%. Alternatively, the calculation is the sum of active weights times active returns for each security: 0.18(5.0%) + 0.09(10.0%) − 0.18(−5.0%) − 0.09(−10.0%) = 3.6%.

3. Calculate the active risk of the managed portfolio.

Solution:

The active risk of the managed portfolio is the square root of the sum of active weights squared times the active volatility squared for each security, which gives $[0.18^2 \times 25.0^2 + 0.09^2 \times 50.0^2 + (-0.18)^2 \times 25.0^2 + (-0.09)^2 \times 50.0^2]^{1/2} = 9.0\%$.

4. Verify the basic fundamental law of active management using the expected active return and active risk of the managed portfolio. The individual security active return forecasts and active weights were sized using an information coefficient of IC = 0.20, breadth of BR = 4, and active risk of $\sigma_A = 9.0\%$.

Solution:

The basic fundamental law states that the expected active portfolio return is $IC \sqrt{BR}\, \sigma_A = 0.20 \times 4^{1/2} \times 9.0 = 3.6\%$, which is consistent with the calculation in the Solution to 2. Alternatively, the information ratio of $3.6/9.0 = 0.40$ confirms the basic fundamental law that $IR^* = IC \sqrt{BR} = 0.20 \times 4^{1/2} = 0.40$.

6 THE FULL FUNDAMENTAL LAW

☐ describe and interpret the fundamental law of active portfolio management, including its component terms—transfer coefficient, information coefficient, breadth, and active risk (aggressiveness)

☐ explain how the information ratio may be useful in investment manager selection and choosing the level of active portfolio risk

Although we were able to derive an analytic (i.e., formula-based) solution for the set of unconstrained optimal active weights in Equation 11, a number of practical or strategic constraints are often imposed in practice. For example, if the unconstrained active weight of a particular security is negative and large, that might lead to a negative absolute weight or short sell of the security. Many investors are constrained to be long only, either by regulation or by preference because of the extra complexity and costs of short selling. For quantitatively oriented investors, optimal solutions for active weights under long-only constraints, limits on turnover, ESG screens, or other constraints generally require the use of a numerical optimizer. Alternatively, one can use the fundamental law framework to better analyze the active weights that are subjectively determined by less quantitative techniques.

TC: transfer coefficient

Let Δw_i (without an *) represent the *actual* active security weights for a constrained portfolio—in contrast to the optimal active weights, Δw_i^*, specified in Equation 11. As explained previously, the transfer coefficient, TC, is essentially the cross-sectional correlation between the forecasted active security returns and actual active weights. To be more precise, for a single-factor risk model, TC is the following *risk-weighted* correlation:

$$TC = \rho(\mu_i/\sigma_i, \Delta w_i \sigma_i).$$

The Full Fundamental Law 119

Based on the correspondence between optimal active weights and forecasted active returns in Equation 11, the transfer coefficient can also be expressed as the risk-weighted correlation between the optimal active weights and the actual active weights, TC = $\rho\left(\Delta w_i^* \sigma_i, \Delta w_i \sigma_i\right)$.

As a correlation coefficient, TC can take on values anywhere from −1.00 to +1.00, although TC values are typically positive and range from about 0.20 to 0.90. A low TC results from the formal or informal constraints imposed on the structure of the portfolio. In fact, at TC = 0.00, there would be no correspondence between the active return forecasts and active weights taken and thus no expectation of value added from active management. In contrast, TC = 1.00 (no binding constraints) represents a perfect correspondence between active weights taken and forecasted active returns, allowing the full expected value added to be reflected in the portfolio structure. The portfolio TC could even conceivably be negative if relative weights are negatively correlated with current expected returns because the portfolio needs rebalancing.

Including the impact of the transfer coefficient, the expanded fundamental law is expressed in the following equation:

$$E\left(R_A\right) = (TC)(IC)\sqrt{BR}\,\sigma_A, \tag{14}$$

where an * is not used because the managed portfolio is constructed from *constrained* active security weights, Δw_i. The expanded fundamental law of active management shown in Equation 14, which we will refer to simply as the *fundamental law* henceforward, states that the expected active return, $E(R_A)$, is the product of four key parameters: the transfer coefficient, TC, the assumed information coefficient, IC, the square root of breadth, BR, and portfolio active risk, σ_A. Using Equation 14, we can also express the portfolio's information ratio, $E(R_A)/\sigma_A$, as the product of just three terms: IR = (TC)(IC)$\sqrt{BR}$.

The fundamental law as stated in Equation 14, although more practical than Equation 13, is still based on a simple risk model for the individual securities. Specifically, the equations in this section are based on the simplifying assumption of a single-index model; so, the active security returns are residual returns and are uncorrelated with each other. If we go even further in terms of simplicity and assume that the individual securities all have the same residual volatility, then the correlation formulas for IC and TC do not need to be risk weighted. Alternatively, we could move in the direction of more complexity by using the single-factor risk model with factor sensitivity: $R_{Ai} = R_i - \beta_i R_B$. In quantitative portfolio management practice, even more sophisticated multi-factor risk models are used with correspondingly more complex fundamental law parameter values, although the basic form of Equation 14 is preserved.

EXAMPLE 6

The Expanded Fundamental Law

Consider the simple case of four individual securities whose active returns are uncorrelated with each other and forecasts are independent from year to year. The securities have a range of active return forecasts, risks, optimal active weights, and actual active weights as given in the following exhibit. The optimal active weights are based on a formula for maximizing the active return of a managed portfolio for a given level of active risk. The actual active weights are the result of a numerical optimizer with a number of constraints, in addition to the active risk constraint of 9.0%.

Security	Expected Active Return	Active Return Volatility	Optimal Active Weight	Actual Active Weight
#1	5.0%	25.0%	18%	6%

Security	Expected Active Return	Active Return Volatility	Optimal Active Weight	Actual Active Weight
#2	10.0%	50.0%	9%	4%
#3	−5.0%	25.0%	−18%	7%
#4	−10.0%	50.0%	−9%	−17%

1. Calculate the transfer coefficient (TC) as the risk-weighted correlation coefficient between the four active return forecasts and the four actual active weights. Compare this number with the transfer coefficient for the optimal active weights.

Solution:

The transfer coefficient is the correlation between the risk-weighted expected active returns and actual active weights: $TC = \rho(\Delta w_i \sigma_i, \mu_i/\sigma_i)$, where ρ denotes correlation (you can use the Microsoft Excel function CORREL) with four pairs of numbers. The risk-weighted values for Security #1 are $\Delta w_1 \sigma_1 = 0.06(25.0) = 1.5\%$ and $\mu_1/\sigma_1 = 5.0/25.0 = 20.0\%$. The correlation coefficient across all four securities (calculated in Excel) is $TC = 0.58$. The transfer coefficient for the optimal active weights is by definition 1.0 but can be verified by the calculated correlation coefficient. The risk-weighted values for Security #1 are then $\Delta w_1 \sigma_1 = 0.18(25.0) = 4.5\%$ and $\mu_1/\sigma_1 = 5.0/25.0 = 20.0\%$.

2. The forecasted active return of the optimal portfolio is the sum of the active weights times active returns for each security: $0.18(5.0) + 0.09(10.0) + (−0.18)(−5.0) + (−0.09)(−10.0) = 3.6\%$. The active risk of the optimal portfolio is the square root of the sum of active weights squared times the active volatility squared for each security: $[(0.18)^2(25.0)^2 + (0.09)^2 (50.0)^2 + (−0.18)^2 (25.0)^2 + (−0.09)^2 (50.0)^2]^{1/2} = 9.0\%$. Calculate the forecasted active return and active risk of the managed portfolio using the *actual* rather than unconstrained optimal active weights.

Solution:

The forecasted active return of the managed portfolio is $0.06(5.0) + 0.04(10.0) + 0.07(−5.0) + (−0.17)(−10.0) = 2.1\%$. The active risk of the managed portfolio is the square root of the sum of actual active weights squared times the active volatility squared for each security, $[(0.06)^2(25.0)^2 + (0.04)^2 (50.0)^2 + (0.07)^2 (25.0)^2 + (−0.17)^2 (50.0)^2]^{1/2} = 9.0\%$, as specified by the active risk constraint.

3. Verify the expanded fundamental law of active management using the active portfolio return, active portfolio risk, and transfer coefficient calculations in Parts 1 and 2. The individual active return forecasts and optimal active weights were sized using an information coefficient of $IC = 0.20$ and breadth of $BR = 4$.

Solution:

The expanded fundamental law states that the expected portfolio active return will be $E(R_A) = (TC)(IC)\sqrt{BR}\,\sigma_A = 0.58 \times 0.20 \times (4)^{1/2} \times 9.0 = 2.1\%$, consistent with the direct calculation in the Solution to 2.

The Full Fundamental Law

We close this sub-section by noting that the transfer coefficient, TC, also comes into play when calculating the optimal amount of active risk for an actively managed portfolio with constraints. Specifically, with constraints and using notation consistent with expressions in the fundamental law, Equation 8 becomes

$$\sigma_A = TC\frac{IR^*}{SR_B}\sigma_B,$$

where IR* is the information ratio of an otherwise unconstrained portfolio. Employing this optimal level of aggressiveness leads to a maximum possible value of the constrained portfolio's squared Sharpe ratio:

$$SR_P^2 = SR_B^2 + (TC)^2(IR^*)^2.$$

As noted previously, the active risk of an actively managed fund can be adjusted to its optimal level while preserving the information ratio by adding long or short positions in the benchmark portfolio. For further insight, note that with a transfer coefficient of 0.00, the optimal amount of active risk calculated is zero. In other words, the investor should just invest in the benchmark portfolio.

We now illustrate the impact of the transfer coefficient with the following example. If the actively managed portfolio has a transfer coefficient of 0.50 and an unconstrained information ratio of 0.30 and the benchmark portfolio has a Sharpe ratio of 0.40 and risk of 16.0%, then the optimal amount of aggressiveness in the actively managed portfolio is 0.50(0.30/0.40)16.0 = 6.0%. If the actively managed portfolio is constructed with this amount of active risk, the Sharpe ratio will be $(0.40^2 + 0.50^2 \times 0.30^2)^{1/2}$ = 0.43. If the constrained portfolio has an active risk of 8.0%, the active risk can be lowered to the optimal level of 6.0% by mixing 1 – 6.0/8.0 = 25% in the benchmark and 75.0% in the actively managed fund.

Ex Post Performance Measurement

Most of the fundamental law perspectives discussed up to this point relate to the expected value added through active portfolio management. Actual performance in any given period will vary from its expected value in a range determined by the benchmark tracking risk. We now turn our attention to examining actual performance, the *ex post* analysis of the realized value added.

The key determinant of the sign and magnitude of the realized value added in Equation 3 is the degree to which the portfolio has positive active weights on securities that realize positive relative returns and negative active weights on securities that realize negative relative returns. In other words, actual performance is measured by the relationship between relative weights and realized relative returns. Knowing how actual returns match up with realized returns (the *realized* information coefficient, IC_R) allows the investor to examine what realized return to expect given the transfer coefficient. Specifically, expected value added conditional on the realized information coefficient, IC_R, is

$$E\left(R_A|IC_R\right) = (TC)\left(IC_R\right)\sqrt{BR}\,\sigma_A. \tag{15}$$

Equation 15 is similar to the fundamental law, shown in Equation 14, but in Equation 15 the realized information coefficient, IC_R, replaces the *expected* information coefficient, IC.

We can represent any difference between the actual active return of the portfolio and the conditional expected active return with a noise term:

$$R_A = E(R_A \mid IC_R) + Noise. \tag{16}$$

Equation 16 states that the realized value added of an actively managed portfolio can be divided into two parts. The first part comes from the expected value added given the realized skill of the investor that period. The second part represents any noise that results from constraints that impinge on the optimal portfolio structure.

Equation 15 also leads to an *ex post* (i.e., realized) decomposition of the portfolio's active return variance into two parts: variation due to the realized information coefficient and variation due to constraint-induced noise. Clarke, de Silva, and Thorley (2005) showed that the two parts of the realized variance are proportional to TC^2 and $1 - TC^2$. For example, with a TC value of, say, 0.60, only $TC^2 = 36\%$ of the realized variation in performance is attributed to variation in the realized information coefficient, and $1 - TC^2 = 64\%$ comes from constraint-induced noise. Low-TC investors will frequently experience periods when the forecasting process succeeds but actual performance is poor or when actual performance is good even though the return-forecasting process fails.

EXAMPLE 7

Ex Post Performance

Consider an active management strategy that includes BR = 100 investment decisions (e.g., 100 individual stocks, whose active returns are uncorrelated, and annual rebalancing), an expected information coefficient of IC = 0.05, a transfer coefficient of TC = 0.80, and annualized active risk of $\sigma_A = 4.0\%$. Thus, the expected value added according to the fundamental law is

$$E\left(R_A\right) = (TC)(IC)\sqrt{BR}\,\sigma_A = 0.80 \times 0.05 \times \sqrt{100} \times 4.0\% = 1.6\%.$$

---

1. Suppose that the *realized* information coefficient in a given period is −0.10, instead of the expected value of IC = 0.05. In the absence of constraint-induced noise, what would be the value added that period?

Solution:

The value added, without including constraint-induced noise (which has an expected value of zero) is

$$E\left(R_A | IC_R\right) = (TC)\left(IC_R\right)\sqrt{BR}\,\sigma_A = 0.80 \times (-0.10) \times \sqrt{100} \times 4.0\%$$
$$= -3.2\%.$$

In other words, conditional on the actual information coefficient, the investor should expect an active return that is negative because the realized information coefficient is negative.

---

2. Suppose that the actual return on the active portfolio was −2.6%. Given the −0.10 realized information coefficient, how much of the forecasted active return was offset by the noise component?

Solution:

The noise portion of the active return is the difference between the actual active return and the forecasted active return: −2.6 − (−3.2) = 0.6%. In other words, the noise component helped offset the negative value added from poor return forecasting. Of course, the constraint-induced noise component could just as easily have gone the other way, exacerbating the negative value added. Note that the negative realized active return of −2.6% is well within the range associated with the tracking error (active risk) of 4.0% per period.

3. What percentage of the performance variance (i.e., tracking risk squared) in this strategy over time is attributed to variation in the realized information coefficient (i.e., forecasting success), and what percentage of performance variance is attributed to constraint-induced noise?

Solution:

Given the transfer coefficient of TC = 0.80, TC^2 = 64% of the variation in performance over time is attributed to the success of the forecasting process, leaving 36% due to constraint-induced noise.

APPLICATIONS OF THE FUNDAMENTAL LAW AND GLOBAL EQUITY STRATEGY

7

	explain how the information ratio may be useful in investment manager selection and choosing the level of active portfolio risk
	compare active management strategies, including market timing and security selection, and evaluate strategy changes in terms of the fundamental law of active management

In this section, we discuss three specific applications of active portfolio management: one application to a global equity strategy with different sets of active return forecasts and constraints and two applications to US fixed income. These applications will further illustrate how the fundamental law is used to evaluate active portfolio strategies, including security selection and market timing.

Global Equity Strategy

In our first example, we show how the fundamental law can be used to calculate the expected active return for an actively managed portfolio benchmarked to the MSCI All Country World Index (ACWI). This global equity example focuses on the cross-sectional characteristics of the fundamental law, whereas the US fixed-income examples that follow also include time-series implications of the law. The investable assets in this example are the individual MSCI market indexes—including the 21 EAFE (Europe, Australasia, and Far East) markets, the United States, Canada, and the Emerging Markets Index—for a total of 24 assets. "Now" is the beginning of the calendar year 2019. For purposes of illustration, we will assume that the future will be like the past in terms of active risk, and thus we will base our estimates on the US dollar return to the MSCI market indexes from 2009 to 2018. In practice, managerial judgment or a commercial model would be used to forecast risk. The various rankings of the markets' forecasted active returns for the calendar year 2019 are hypothetical.

The *ex ante* expected active risk of each asset is equal to the annualized historical standard deviation of beta-adjusted differences between the individual market return and the ACWI return, as shown in the third column of Exhibit 7. For example, the active risk of the United Kingdom is 6.4% and the active risk of Japan is 9.1%. Note that the risk estimates are for active returns (i.e., the difference between the individual asset and benchmark returns). The total risk of each market would be higher based on the estimated risk of the benchmark and the benchmark beta.

Exhibit 7: Long–Short Global Equity Fund for 2019 (risk statistics based on MSCI returns from 2009 to 2018)

Market	Score	Active Return Volatility	Expected Active Return	Active Weight	ACWI Benchmark Weight	Portfolio Weight
United Kingdom	2.0	6.4%	1.3%	15.7%	5.2%	20.9%
Japan	0.0	9.1%	0.0%	−2.0%	7.6%	5.7%
France	−2.0	8.5%	−1.7%	−12.0%	3.4%	−8.5%
Germany	0.0	8.4%	0.0%	2.8%	2.7%	5.6%
Switzerland	2.0	7.8%	1.6%	9.7%	2.7%	12.3%
Australia	0.0	11.1%	0.0%	−1.0%	2.1%	1.1%
Spain	−2.0	16.0%	−3.2%	−5.3%	1.0%	−4.3%
Sweden	0.0	10.1%	0.0%	−1.2%	0.8%	−0.4%
Hong Kong SAR	1.0	12.0%	1.2%	2.3%	1.2%	3.5%
Netherlands	0.0	7.9%	0.0%	1.8%	1.1%	2.9%
Italy	−1.0	15.1%	−1.5%	−0.8%	0.7%	−0.1%
Singapore	0.0	11.8%	0.0%	−1.8%	0.4%	−1.3%
Belgium	1.0	10.2%	1.0%	4.4%	0.3%	4.7%
Denmark	0.0	12.3%	0.0%	−1.2%	0.5%	−0.7%
Finland	−1.0	13.7%	−1.4%	−2.5%	0.3%	−2.2%
Norway	0.0	13.7%	0.0%	0.1%	0.2%	0.3%
Israel	1.0	15.3%	1.5%	1.4%	0.2%	1.6%
Ireland	0.0	14.9%	0.0%	0.3%	0.2%	0.5%
Austria	−1.0	14.6%	−1.5%	−1.6%	0.1%	−1.6%
Portugal	0.0	15.2%	0.0%	0.9%	0.0%	0.9%
New Zealand	1.0	14.2%	1.4%	1.8%	0.1%	1.8%
United States	0.0	3.8%	0.0%	−5.3%	54.3%	48.9%
Canada	−1.0	9.2%	−0.9%	−6.7%	3.0%	−3.7%
Emerging	0.0	9.0%	0.0%	0.1%	11.9%	12.0%
Total	0.0			0.0%	100.0%	100.0%

Transfer Coefficient	Information Coefficient	Breadth
0.995	0.099	24.5

Active Return	Active Risk	Information Ratio
0.98%	2.00%	0.49

The 24 individual assets in Exhibit 7 are listed approximately by size in the EAFE benchmark, followed by the United States, Canada, and the emerging markets. For example, the United Kingdom has a benchmark weight of 5.2% and Canada has a benchmark weight of 3.0%. Scores representing an active investor's forecasts of the relative performance of each asset during 2019 are assigned to each market. The scores are one of five numerical values that represent a managerial forecast of strong outperformance (2.0), weak outperformance (1.0), neutral performance (0.0), weak underperformance (−1.0), and strong underperformance (−2.0). The number of scores in each of these five categories is based on the requirement that the scores sum to zero and have a cross-sectional standard deviation of 1.

The active return forecasts in the fourth column of Exhibit 7 are based on the Grinold rule in Equation 10 of "IC times volatility times score," where IC is the *ex ante* information coefficient that measures the assumed accuracy of the investor's relative rankings, as illustrated by the right leg of the correlation triangle in Exhibit 6. In this example, we use an assumed information coefficient of 0.10; thus, forecasted and realized active security returns are expected to have a cross-sectional correlation coefficient of 0.10. For example, the active return forecast for the United Kingdom, which has a score of 2.0, is 0.10(6.4)(2.0) = 1.3%. Alternatively, the active return forecast for Japan is 0.0% because the score is 0. As explained later, the information coefficient used in fundamental law accounting will be adjusted down to 0.095, as shown at the bottom of Exhibit 7, to account for the assignment of scores in this particular example.

The active weights for each market are based on the active return forecast and a numerical optimizer (i.e., Excel Solver) with the objective to maximize the expected active return of the portfolio, subject to a 2.00% constraint on active risk. Note that while the active weights for each market are generally correlated with the forecasted active returns in Exhibit 7, they are not perfectly proportional for two reasons. First, the optimizer also takes into account the estimated correlations between each market's active return, based on the MSCI monthly return data from 2009 to 2018. Exhibit 8 reports the estimated active return correlations for the eight largest EAFE countries; the full correlation matrix is not reported to conserve space. For example, the correlation coefficient between the United Kingdom (GB) and Japan (JP) is fairly low at −0.02, while the correlation coefficient between France (FR) and Germany (DE) is higher at 0.30. Note that these correlation coefficients are for *active* returns (i.e., the differences between the individual market and ACWI benchmark returns). The correlations for *total* market returns would all be positive and much higher—for example, values that range from 0.4 to 0.9.

Exhibit 8: Active Return Correlation Coefficients for Eight Countries (based on MSCI returns from 2009 to 2018)

Country	GB	JP	FR	DE	CH	AU	ES	SE	
GB	1.000	−0.02	0.21	0.08	0.13	0.00	0.18	0.14	...
JP	−0.02	1.000	−0.08	−0.03	0.04	−0.08	0.01	−0.07	...
FR	0.21	−0.08	1.000	0.30	0.16	−0.03	0.34	0.15	...
DE	0.08	−0.03	0.30	1.000	0.10	−0.07	0.19	0.15	...
CH	0.13	0.04	0.16	0.10	1.000	0.06	0.11	0.10	...
AU	0.00	−0.08	−0.03	−0.07	0.06	1.000	0.01	0.06	...
ES	0.18	0.01	0.34	0.19	0.11	0.01	1.000	0.11	...
SE	0.14	−0.07	0.15	0.15	0.10	0.06	0.11	1.000	...
	...	...	...	...	...	...	...	...	...

The second reason that the active weights in Exhibit 7 are not perfectly proportional to the forecasted active returns is that the active weights are constrained by the optimizer to sum to zero. For example, the highest active weight in Exhibit 7 is for the United Kingdom, at 15.7%, and the lowest active weight is for France, at −12.0%. These active weights are added to the benchmark weights to give the total portfolio weights in the last column of Exhibit 7. For example, the total weight for the United States is 48.9%, even though the active weight is −5.3%, because the US benchmark weight in the ACWI is 54.3%. In fact, the optimization in Exhibit 7 is for a relatively unconstrained long–short portfolio where the sum of the positive total weights is about 120% and the sum of the negative total weights is about –20%, what might be called a "120/20 long–short" strategy in practice.

Because the optimization is basically unconstrained, the transfer coefficient or risk-weighted correlation between active return forecasts and active weights shown at the bottom of Exhibit 7 is 0.995, almost perfect. The transfer coefficient in this example takes into account all the risk statistics (i.e., forecasted active volatilities *and* forecasted correlations), but it is not exactly 1.0 because of the budget constraint that the active weights sum to zero. Alternatively, if the sum of active weights were allowed to be non-zero, effectively allowing for risk-free cash or leverage in the equity portfolio to meet the budget constraint, the transfer coefficient would be exactly 1.0. The breadth of the strategy shown at the bottom of Exhibit 7 is 24.5, slightly higher than the number of individual assets, 24.0, because the risk model includes active return correlation coefficients that are different from zero. If all the off-diagonal correlations in the extended table in Exhibit 8 were exactly zero, then breadth would be exactly 24.0, instead of 24.5.

The fundamental law in Equation 14 states that the expected active return on the portfolio is $E(R_A) = (TC)(IC)\sqrt{BR}\,\sigma_A = 0.995 \times 0.099 \times (24.5)^{1/2} \times 2.00 = 0.98\%$. Alternatively, the expected active return of 0.98%, shown at the bottom of Exhibit 7, is calculated as the sum of the active weights times active returns. Thus, the accuracy of the fundamental law is quite high. The fundamental law is often expressed in terms of the information ratio, or forecasted active return over active risk. Using this framework, the validation of the fundamental law is $IR = (TC)(IC)\sqrt{BR} = 0.995 \times 0.099 \times (24.5)^{1/2} = 0.49$, equal to actual forecasted active return divided by active risk, $0.98/2.00 = 0.490$. Because the information ratio in this relatively unconstrained portfolio is unaffected by the aggressiveness of the strategy, we would get the same IR value if the active risk were allowed to be higher. For example, if the active risk specified to the optimizer were increased to 3.00%, the forecasted active return would increase to 1.47%, an information ratio of, again, $1.47/3.00 = 0.49$.

Exhibit 9 continues examining the global equity strategy but uses a slightly different assignment of scores than Exhibit 7 to illustrate how this change affects the values in the fundamental law. Specifically, the scores for Germany (DE) and the United Kingdom (UK) have been switched as well as the scores for Switzerland (CH) and Australia (AU). While the breadth in Exhibit 9 is unchanged at 24.5, the information coefficient has increased slightly to 0.105, compared with 0.099 in Exhibit 7. Even though the assumed IC used to create the expected active returns in Exhibit 9 is still 0.10, the IC used in fundamental law accounting has increased because the new assignment of scores represents a slightly more ambitious forecast. For example, the active (i.e., benchmark relative) returns for France and Germany in Exhibit 9 are now forecasted to go strongly in opposite directions, even though they are positively correlated according to the risk model in Exhibit 8. Given the increase in IC and slight change in TC, the fundamental law calculation for Exhibit 9 is now $IR = (TC)(IC)\sqrt{BR} = 0.997 \times 0.105 \times (24.5)^{1/2} = 0.532$, equal to the actual value of 0.52.

Exhibit 9: Long–Short Global Equity Fund with Different Scores for 2019 (risk statistics based on MSCI returns from 2009 to 2018)

Market	Score	Active Return Volatility	Expected Active Return	Active Weight	ACWI Benchmark Weight	Portfolio Weight
United Kingdom	0.0	6.4%	0.0%	1.7%	5.2%	6.9%
Japan	0.0	9.1%	0.0%	–0.3%	7.6%	7.3%

Applications of the Fundamental Law and Global Equity Strategy

Market	Score	Active Return Volatility	Expected Active Return	Active Weight	ACWI Benchmark Weight	Portfolio Weight
France	−2.0	8.5%	−1.7%	−11.4%	3.4%	−8.0%
Germany	2.0	8.4%	1.7%	14.5%	2.7%	17.2%
Switzerland	0.0	7.8%	0.0%	−2.0%	2.7%	0.6%
Australia	2.0	11.1%	2.2%	7.7%	2.1%	9.9%
Spain	−2.0	16.0%	−3.2%	−4.9%	1.0%	−4.0%
Sweden	0.0	10.1%	0.0%	−1.2%	0.8%	−0.4%
Hong Kong SAR	1.0	12.0%	1.2%	2.8%	1.2%	4.0%
Netherlands	0.0	7.9%	0.0%	3.0%	1.1%	4.1%
Italy	−1.0	15.1%	−1.5%	−0.9%	0.7%	−0.2%
Singapore	0.0	11.8%	0.0%	−1.4%	0.4%	−1.0%
Belgium	1.0	10.2%	1.0%	5.8%	0.3%	6.1%
Denmark	0.0	12.3%	0.0%	−0.7%	0.5%	−0.1%
Finland	−1.0	13.7%	−1.4%	−3.2%	0.3%	−2.9%
Norway	0.0	13.7%	0.0%	1.3%	0.2%	1.5%
Israel	1.0	15.3%	1.5%	1.5%	0.2%	1.7%
Ireland	0.0	14.9%	0.0%	0.2%	0.2%	0.4%
Austria	−1.0	14.6%	−1.5%	−1.8%	0.1%	−1.7%
Portugal	0.0	15.2%	0.0%	1.4%	0.0%	1.4%
New Zealand	1.0	14.2%	1.4%	1.4%	0.1%	1.4%
United States	0.0	3.8%	0.0%	−5.0%	54.3%	49.2%
Canada	−1.0	9.2%	−0.9%	−5.3%	3.0%	−2.3%
Emerging	0.0	9.0%	0.0%	−2.9%	11.9%	9.0%
Total	0.0			0.0%	100.0%	100.0%

Transfer Coefficient	Information Coefficient	Breadth
0.997	0.105	24.5

Active Return	Active Risk	Information Ratio
1.04%	2.00%	0.52

We now apply constraints to the global equity strategy to focus on the transfer coefficient. Specifically, Exhibit 10 shows two *constrained* portfolio optimizations using the same score assignments and thus active return forecasts as in Exhibit 7. The first optimization, shown on the left-hand side of Exhibit 10, has two constraints. First, the portfolio is constrained to be long only (i.e., a negative active weight for any given market cannot be bigger than the benchmark weight). For example, France has an active weight of −3.4%, bounded by the benchmark weight of 3.4%, so that the total weight for France in the managed portfolio is zero. Second, the portfolio weights are constrained to not be more than 10.0% over or under the benchmark weight (i.e., the absolute value of any given market active weight cannot be greater than 10.0%). For example, the active weights for the United Kingdom and Switzerland are limited to 10.0% and the active weight for the United States is limited to −10.0%.

Exhibit 10: Constrained Global Equity Funds for 2019 (risk statistics based on MSCI returns from 2009 to 2018)

Market	Active Weight	ACWI Benchmark Weight	Portfolio Weight	Active Weight	ACWI Benchmark Weight	Portfolio Weight
United Kingdom	10.0%	5.2%	15.2%	8.6%	5.2%	15.2%
Japan	−6.6%	7.6%	1.0%	−7.8%	7.76%	0.0%
France	−3.4%	3.4%	0.0%	−3.7%	3.4%	0.0%
Germany	−2.7%	2.7%	0.0%	−3.5%	2.7%	0.0%
Switzerland	10.0%	2.7%	12.7%	10.0%	2.7%	12.7%
Australia	−2.1%	2.1%	0.0%	−2.8%	2.1%	0.0%
Spain	−1.0%	1.0%	0.0%	−1.2%	1.0%	0.0%
Sweden	−0.8%	0.8%	0.0%	−1.2%	0.8%	0.0%
Hong Kong SAR	5.9%	1.2%	7.1%	9.5%	1.2%	5.7%
Netherlands	−1.1%	1.1%	0.0%	−1.0%	1.1%	0.0%
Italy	−0.7%	0.7%	0.0%	−0.8%	0.7%	0.0%
Singapore	−0.4%	0.4%	0.0%	−0.5%	0.4%	0.0%
Belgium	6.1%	0.3%	6.4%	−0.4%	0.3%	0.0%
Denmark	−0.5%	0.5%	0.0%	−0.4%	0.5%	0.0%
Finland	−0.3%	0.3%	0.0%	−0.3%	0.3%	0.0%
Norway	−0.2%	0.2%	0.0%	−0.3%	0.2%	0.0%
Israel	4.2%	0.2%	4.4%	10.0%	0.2%	10.2%
Ireland	−0.2%	0.2%	0.0%	−0.1%	0.2%	0.0%
Austria	−0.1%	0.1%	0.0%	−0.1%	0.1%	0.0%
Portugal	0.0%	0.0%	0.0%	−0.1%	0.0%	0.0%
New Zealand	4.7%	0.1%	4.8%	10.0%	0.1%	10.1%
United States	−10.0%	54.3%	44.3%	−10.0%	54.3%	44.3%
Canada	−3.0%	3.0%	0.0%	−3.7%	3.0%	0.0%
Emerging	−7.7%	11.9%	4.2%	−10.0%	11.9%	1.9%
Total	0.0%	100.0%	100.0%	0.0%	100.0%	100.0%

Transfer Coefficient	Information Coefficient	Breadth	Transfer Coefficient	Information Coefficient	Breadth
0.694	0.099	24.5	0.567	0.099	24.5

Active Return	Active Risk	Information Ratio	Active Return	Active Risk	Information Ratio
0.68%	2.00%	0.34	0.76%	2.74%	0.28

The long-only and maximum over- or underweight constraints substantially reduce the transfer of active return forecasts into active weights, as shown by the transfer coefficient of 0.694 at the bottom of the left side of Exhibit 10, compared with 0.995 for the same scores and active return forecasts in Exhibit 7. The impact of this transfer coefficient on expected active return according to the fundamental law is $\mathrm{E}(R_A) = (\mathrm{TC})(\mathrm{IC})\sqrt{\mathrm{BR}}\,\sigma_A = 0.694 \times 0.099 \times (24.5)^{1/2} \times 2.00 = 0.68\%$, compared with 0.98% for the unconstrained portfolio in Exhibit 7. Similarly, the impact of this transfer coefficient measured by the information ratio is $\mathrm{IR} = (\mathrm{TC})(\mathrm{IC})\sqrt{\mathrm{BR}} = 0.694 \times 0.099 \times$

Applications of the Fundamental Law and Global Equity Strategy

$(24.5)^{1/2} = 0.34$, compared with 0.49 for the unconstrained portfolio. In other words, the expected active return and information ratio are reduced by almost a third because of the constraints imposed in portfolio construction.

As previously mentioned, an increase in the allowed active risk from 2.00% to 3.00% in the unconstrained portfolio in Exhibit 7 proportionally increases the active return, leaving the information ratio at about 0.49. However, an increase in allowed active risk to 3.00% does *not* preserve the information ratio of the constrained portfolio, as shown by the optimization on the right-hand side of Exhibit 10. Specifically, the higher active risk leads to more variation in unconstrained active weights, as shown in Equation 11; thus, the constraints become more binding. For example, the active weight for New Zealand, which is 4.7% on the left-hand side of Exhibit 10, is capped at the maximum possible value of 10.0% on the right-hand side of Exhibit 10. The result is a further reduction in the transfer coefficient from 0.694 to 0.567, leading to a reduction in the information ratio to $IR = (TC)(IC)\sqrt{BR} = 0.567 \times 0.099 \times (24.5)^{1/2} = 0.28$, compared with 0.34 at the lower active portfolio risk of 2.0%.

The key concept is that although an unconstrained IR is invariant to the level of active risk, as shown by the dark line in Exhibit 5, the IR for a *constrained* portfolio generally decreases with the aggressiveness of the strategy. Specifically, the dark line in Exhibit 5 for a constrained portfolio would curve downward from left to right in accordance with an increasingly lower transfer coefficient. Thus, the constraints that are imposed on the portfolio should inform the decision of how aggressively to apply an active management strategy.

EXAMPLE 8

Compare and Contrast Active Management Strategies

Consider two active management strategies: individual stock selection, with a benchmark composed of 100 securities, and industrial sector selection, with a benchmark of nine sectors. The active security returns are defined as residuals in a risk model and thus are essentially uncorrelated, and forecasts are independent from year to year. Suppose the individual stock investor is expected to exhibit skill as measured by an information coefficient of 0.05, while the industrial sector investor has a higher information coefficient of 0.15.

1. Conceptually, what is the breadth (i.e., number of independent decisions per year) of each active management strategy?

Solution:

Given that the active asset returns in each strategy are uncorrelated and forecasts are independent from year to year, the breadth of the security selection strategy is $BR = 100$ and of the sector selection strategy is $BR = 9$.

2. Calculate the expected information ratio for each strategy under the assumption that each investor's forecasts can be implemented without constraints, such as the long-only constraint or a limit on turnover each year.

Solution:

The expected information ratio of the unconstrained security selection strategy is calculated as $IR = (IC)\sqrt{BR} = 0.05 \times \sqrt{100} = 0.50$, while the information ratio of the industrial sector selection strategy is $IR = (IC)\sqrt{BR} = 0.15 \times \sqrt{9} = 0.45$.

3. Suppose the aggressiveness of each active management strategy is established by a portfolio active risk target of 3.0% per year. What is the expected active return to each strategy?

Solution:

The expected active return to the unconstrained security selection strategy is 0.50(3.0) = 1.50%, while the expected active return of the industrial sector selection strategy is 0.45(3.0) = 1.35%.

4. Under the more realistic assumption that the individual security selection strategy is constrained to be long only and has turnover limits, the transfer coefficient has a value of 0.60. Calculate the constrained information ratio and expected active return of the security selection strategy.

Solution:

The information ratio of the constrained security selection strategy is $IR = (TC)(IC)\sqrt{BR} = 0.60 \times 0.05 \times \sqrt{100} = 0.30$, rather than 0.50, and the expected active return is 0.30(3.0) = 0.90%, rather than 1.50%.

5. Suppose the aggressiveness of the constrained individual security selection strategy is increased to a portfolio active risk target of 4.0% per year. Conceptually, what is likely to happen to the information ratio, and why?

Solution:

A more aggressive implementation of the constrained security selection strategy will likely result in larger deviations of constrained weights from unconstrained weights and thus a lower transfer coefficient. For example, the transfer coefficient might drop from 0.60 to 0.50, leading to an information ratio of only $IR = (TC)(IC)\sqrt{BR} = 0.50 \times 0.05 \times \sqrt{100} = 0.25$. Thus, instead of a proportional increase in the expected active return associated with an increase in the active portfolio risk from 3.0% to 4.0%, the expected active return would only increase from 0.9% to 0.25(4.0) = 1.0%.

8 FIXED-INCOME STRATEGIES

☐ explain how the information ratio may be useful in investment manager selection and choosing the level of active portfolio risk

☐ compare active management strategies, including market timing and security selection, and evaluate strategy changes in terms of the fundamental law of active management

Two additional examples of the fundamental law in practice are based on the Bloomberg Barclays US fixed-income index returns. Consider first an active management strategy of over- and underweighting credit exposure once a quarter using corporate investment-grade and high-yield bond portfolios as assets. Let the benchmark portfolio be composed of 70% investment-grade bonds and 30% high-yield bonds. Each quarter, the active investor makes a single dichotomous decision either to overweight the investment-grade asset (and thus underweight the high-yield asset) or to overweight

Fixed-Income Strategies

the high-yield asset (and thus underweight the investment-grade asset). In addition to switching to a fixed-income example, we are also now moving into a time-series application of the fundamental law instead of the purely cross-sectional application.

For example, consider two bond portfolios, an investment-grade portfolio and a high-yield portfolio. The quarterly return volatility of the IG (investment-grade) asset is 2.84%, and the quarterly return volatility of the HY (high-yield) asset is 4.64%, with an estimated correlation between the two of 0.575. The *active* risk of this decision is the volatility of the differential returns between the two bond portfolios, $[(2.84)^2 - 2(2.84)(4.64)(0.575) + (4.64)^2]^{1/2} = 3.80\%$. In effect, the active investor assigns a "score" of either +1.0 or −1.0 on credit exposure each quarter, with an *annualized* active risk of $3.80 \times (4)^{1/2} = 7.60\%$. Suppose the fixed-income investor expects to call the market correctly 55% of the time (i.e., 11 out of 20 quarters). If the investor makes the correct decision 55% of the time and an incorrect decision 45% of the time, then the time-series information coefficient is $0.55 - 0.45 = 0.10$.

If a time series of T predicted dichotomous (i.e., plus or minus 1.0) scores, $S_{P,t}$, and a time series of T realized dichotomous scores, $S_{R,t}$, both have zero means, then the time-series covariance between the two is $COV(S_P, S_R) = \frac{1}{T}\sum_{t=1}^{T} S_{P,t} S_{R,t}$. The product of the two scores at time period t is 1.0 if the scores have the same sign (i.e., the decision is correct) and −1.0 if the scores have different signs (i.e., the decision is incorrect). Because the scores have unit variances, the correlation coefficient is equal to the covariance. Thus, the time-series correlation is equal to the number of correct decisions minus the number of incorrect decisions all over total decisions, or, in other words, the percentage correct minus the percentage incorrect.

Without a limit on active risk, the expected active return can be calculated using a simple probability-weighted average: $0.55(3.80) + 0.45(−3.80) = 38$ bps per quarter. But to illustrate the fundamental law, we use the Grinold rule in Equation 10 of "alpha equals IC times volatility times score": $0.10(3.80)(1.0) = 38$ bps.

The investor decides to limit the annual active risk to 2.00% and thus sets the active weight (i.e., deviation from the 70/30 benchmark weights) at $2.00/7.60 = 26.3\%$. Under the assumption that active returns are uncorrelated over time, the breadth of this strategy is 4.0, the four quarterly rebalancing decisions made each year. Thus, in quarters when the investor believes credit risk will pay off, the managed portfolio is invested $70.0\% - 26.3\% = 43.7\%$ in investment-grade bonds and $30\% + 26.3\% = 56.3\%$ in high-yield bonds. Alternatively, in quarters where the investor believes credit risk will not pay off, the active portfolio has $70.0\% + 26.3\% = 96.3\%$ in investment-grade bonds and only $30\% - 26.3\% = 3.7\%$ in high-yield bonds. According to the simple form of the fundamental law, the expected annualized active return to this strategy is $E(R_A) = (IC)\sqrt{BR}\,\sigma_A = 0.10 \times (4.0)^{1/2} \times 2.00 = 40$ bps a year, or 10 bps per quarter. Alternatively, given the active weight of 26.3% motivated by the desire to limit active risk, the expected quarterly return can be calculated more directly as $0.263 \times 38 = 10$ bps. Given the small breadth of this strategy, the annual information ratio is only $IR = (IC)\sqrt{BR} = 0.10 \times (4.0)^{1/2} = 0.20$.

The key concept in this illustration is that the breadth of the strategy is only 4, meaning four active management decisions per year. The same small-breadth problem also applies to quarterly tactical asset allocation decisions in a simple strategy that switches between equity and cash. There are so few opportunities to make an active decision in these "market-timing" strategies that the investor's accuracy as measured by the information coefficient must be quite high to achieve even a modest information ratio. A full description of the breadth calculation requires relatively complex matrix formulas that take into account the correlations between security returns. However, one "rule of thumb" is that breadth is approximately $BR = N/[1 + (N - 1)\rho]$, where N is the number of securities and ρ is the average correlation between the active security returns. In this fixed-income example, $\rho = 0.0$, so breadth is $BR = 4.0$.

A natural question is whether the expected information ratio can be increased by switching more frequently—say, monthly. Although it is somewhat more complicated to show, the basic answer is yes—*if* the information coefficient of 0.10 can be maintained and *if* the credit exposure decisions in this example are truly independent over time. For example, making monthly decisions that do not change during the quarter (i.e., signals of +1.0, +1.0, and +1.0 in January, February, and March) will *not* increase the information ratio of 0.20. However, if the monthly signals are truly uncorrelated with each other, then the information ratio in this example would be $IR = (IC) \sqrt{BR} = 0.10 \times \sqrt{12} = 0.35$. Although somewhat implausible, if an investor made daily decisions (250 trading days a year) that were truly independent and were *still* correct 55% of the time, the expected information ratio could potentially increase to $IR = (IC) \sqrt{BR} = 0.10 \times \sqrt{250} = 1.58$.

The high 1.58 information ratio indicates that the investor could earn an expected active return of 3.16% with active risk of only 2.00%. With such a high information ratio, the investor might be inclined to increase the aggressiveness of the credit risk strategy—for example, doubling to an expected return of $2 \times 3.16\% = 6.32\%$ and active risk of $2 \times 2.00\% = 4.00\%$. Besides the issue of transaction costs, this more aggressive strategy would likely bump up against various constraints. For example, at the higher 4.00% active risk, the required active weights would be plus and minus $4.00/7.60 = 52.6\%$. In other words, a tilt against credit risk would require a total portfolio weight of $70\% + 52.6\% = 122.6\%$ in investment-grade bonds funded by a -22.6% *short* position in high-yield bonds.

The essential logic of this example is not confined to a dichotomous decision; the same general perspectives would hold if the single credit risk signal were continuous— for example, numbers like -0.57 or 1.32. Then under the more aggressively applied active risk target of 4.0%, a signal of -0.57 would require an active weight of $-0.57(4.0)/7.6 = -30.0\%$. With a benchmark portfolio of 70.0% investment-grade and 30.0% high-yield bonds, this active weight translates into a 100% position in investment-grade bonds and no position in high-yield bonds. Alternatively, for a positive credit risk signal of 1.32, the required active weight would be $1.32(4.00)/7.60 = 69.5\%$ (i.e., 100% in high-yield bonds and almost no position in investment-grade bonds). In other words, for this more aggressive strategy under a long-only constraint, the transfer coefficient would be less than 1 and the expanded fundamental law, $IR = (TC) (IC) \sqrt{BR}$, would come into play. Under a normal distribution for scores, the transfer coefficient of this strategy is 0.62, so the expected information ratio is only $IR = 0.62 \times 0.10 \times \sqrt{250} = 0.98$, not 1.58. For an active risk of 4.00%, the expected active return is thus only $0.98 \times 4.00\% = 3.92\%$, not 6.32%. Please note that the transfer coefficient in this example is based on the calculation $\Phi(1.32) - \Phi(-0.57) = 0.62$, where $\Phi(S)$ is the cumulative standard normal distribution function. Given long-only limits on positions, the actual active risk of the constrained portfolio would be lower than 4.0%. In other words, the actual active weights (determined by a numerical optimizer) would need to be larger than the simple formula $(S)4.0/7.6$ to get back up to an actual active risk of 4.0%.

For our second fixed-income example, consider an active management strategy using the five US Treasury bond portfolios in Exhibit 11 as the individual assets. Let the neutral benchmark be an equally weighted composite portfolio of the five, or 20% invested in each asset, but with annual rebalancing. In other words, we are now moving back into a purely cross-sectional application of the fundamental law.

Fixed-Income Strategies

Exhibit 11: Bloomberg Barclays US Treasury Bond Average Returns and Risk (return statistics from 2009 to 2018)

	Treas. 0–1	Treas. 1–3	Treas. 3–7	Treas. 7–10	Treas. 10–20
Avg. Ret.	0.40%	0.90%	2.21%	3.15%	3.89%
Volatility	0.17%	0.85%	3.20%	5.86%	7.95%

Exhibit 12 shows the volatility of the historical return differences between each asset and the equally weighted benchmark. Note that while the absolute volatility of each asset return goes up with maturity in Exhibit 11, the *active* volatility with respect to the benchmark is highest for the assets with the shortest maturity, at 3.45%, and the longest maturity, at 4.57%. Exhibit 12 also shows the estimated active (i.e., benchmark relative) return correlation matrix, which has both positive and negative values, in contrast to the absolute return correlation matrix (not shown), which would only have large positive values. For example, the correlation between the 0–1-year T-bond active return and the 1–3-year T-bond active return in Exhibit 12 is *positive* 0.49, showing that these shorter-maturity active returns tend to move together. However, the correlation between the 0–1-year active return and the 7–10-year active return is *negative*, at −0.49, showing that these two diverse maturity active returns tend to move apart.

Exhibit 12: US Treasury Bond Estimated Active Return Risk and Correlations (return statistics from 2009 to 2018)

	Treas. 0–1	Treas. 1–3	Treas. 3–7	Treas. 7–10	Treas. 10–20
Active Vol.	3.45%	2.85%	1.05%	2.40%	4.57%

Active Corr.	Treas. 0–1	Treas. 1–3	Treas. 3–7	Treas. 7–10	Treas. 10–20
Treas. 0–1	1.000	0.49	0.21	−0.49	−0.47
Treas. 1–3	0.49	1.000	0.26	−0.49	−0.49
Treas. 3–7	0.21	0.26	1.000	−0.19	−0.33
Treas. 7–10	−0.49	−0.49	−0.19	1.000	0.46
Treas. 10–20	−0.47	−0.49	−0.33	0.46	1.000

The breadth associated with the risk estimates in Exhibit 12 is 9.4, even though there are only 5 assets. The breadth is different from the number of assets because the off-diagonal values in the correlation matrix are substantially different from zero. Exhibit 13 shows the fundamental law calculations for two sets of scores given an active portfolio risk target of 1.0% per year. The first set of scores has positive values for the shorter-maturity bonds and negative scores for the longer-maturity bonds. The associated active returns are calculated using the Grinold rule in Equation 10 and an assumed information coefficient of 0.20; for example, the active return for 10–20-year T-bonds is 0.20 × 4.57% × −1.76 = −1.61%. The active weights in Exhibit 13 are calculated by an optimizer given the constraint on active risk of 1.00%. For example, the active weight for the 10–20-year T-bonds is −19.1%, shown in the upper half of Exhibit 13. Given the benchmark weights of 20% for each asset, this results in a total weight of only 20 − 19.1 = 0.9% in the managed portfolio.

Although the information coefficient used to scale the active returns was 0.20, the first set of scores in Exhibit 13 does not represent a very ambitious forecast, so the information coefficient used in the fundamental law calculation is 0.12. The intuition for the large downward adjustment in the information coefficient is that the positive scores for the shorter-maturity bonds and the negative scores for the longer-maturity bonds are all based on essentially one active decision that interest rates will rise. Specifically, the expected active (i.e., benchmark relative) return for the managed fixed-income portfolio is $E(R_A) = (IC)\sqrt{BR}\,\sigma_A = 0.12 \times (9.4)^{1/2} \times 1.00 = 37$ bps a year.

Exhibit 13: Signals and Weights for a Fixed-Income Portfolio with Breadth of 9.4 and Active Risk of 1.00% (return statistics from 2009 to 2018)

	Treas. 0–1	Treas. 1–3	Treas. 3–7	Treas. 7–10	Treas. 10–20	IC	Active Ret.
Score	0.63	0.67	0.92	−0.46	−1.76	0.12	0.37%
Active Ret.	0.43%	0.38%	0.19%	−0.22%	−1.61%		
Active Wgt.	−1.6%	−2.1%	15.4%	7.4%	−19.1%		
Total Wgt.	18.4%	17.9%	35.4%	27.4%	0.9%		
Score	−0.22	1.20	0.23	0.57	−1.77	0.18	0.55%
Active Ret.	−0.15%	0.68%	0.05%	0.27%	−1.62%		
Active Wgt.	−11.3%	17.0%	−12.8%	24.3%	−17.2%		
Total Wgt.	8.7%	37.0%	7.2%	44.3%	2.8%		

In contrast, the second set of scores in Exhibit 13 is a more ambitious set of active forecasts that specify a modification in the shape of the yield curve. As a result, the information coefficient is 0.18, not much lower than the 0.20 value used to scale the active returns, and the expected active return for the portfolio using the fundamental law is $E(R_A) = (IC)\sqrt{BR}\,\sigma_A = 0.18 \times (9.4)^{1/2} \times 1.00 = 55$ bps a year. The fundamental law in terms of the expected information ratio for the second set of scores in Exhibit 13 is $IR = (IC)\sqrt{BR} = 0.18 \times (9.4)^{1/2} = 0.55$, alternatively calculated as the expected active return over active risk, $55/100 = 0.55$.

At this relatively high information ratio, the investor may be inclined to increase the active risk to, say, 2.00% instead of 1.00%. However, given that the longest-maturity asset has a total weight that is approaching zero (i.e., 2.8%, as shown in the lower right-hand corner of Exhibit 13), such a strategy would likely require shorting; if short sells are not allowed, the transfer coefficient would likely end up being less than 1.00.

EXAMPLE 9

Breadth and Rebalancing in Active Management Strategies

Consider an active portfolio management strategy that involves decisions on overweighting or underweighting four individual assets. For example, the assets might be ETFs for four country equity markets or four different fixed-income ETFs. The active returns to Assets #1 and #2 are positively correlated, as are the active returns to Assets #3 and #4. However, the assumed risk model for active returns has no other non-zero correlations. The correlation structure in this risk model is shown in the following 4-by-4 correlation matrix, and the breadth

Fixed-Income Strategies

calculation is BR = 3.2. For simplicity, we will assume that the portfolio management decisions are dichotomous; thus, each year the investor forecasts two of the assets to outperform the benchmark and the other two assets to underperform.

Correlations	#1	#2	#3	#4
#1	1.00	0.25	0.00	0.00
#2	0.25	1.00	0.00	0.00
#3	0.00	0.00	1.00	0.25
#4	0.00	0.00	0.25	1.00

1. Conceptually speaking (i.e., exact numbers are not necessary), why is the breadth less than the number of assets for this strategy?

Solution:

According to the risk model, the active returns to Assets #1 and #2 tend to move together, with a correlation coefficient of 0.25, as do the active returns for Assets #3 and #4. As a result, the 3.2 breadth of this strategy is lower than the number of assets, $N = 4$.

2. Suppose the investor predicts that Assets #1 and #2 will outperform and that Assets #3 and #4 will underperform. Conceptually speaking (i.e., exact numbers are not necessary), how will these scores affect the information coefficient in the fundamental law compared with a prediction that Assets #1 and #3 will outperform and Assets #2 and #4 will underperform?

Solution:

According to the risk model, the active returns to Assets #1 and #2 tend to move together, so a forecast that both will outperform is not as ambitious as a forecast that one will outperform while the other underperforms. As a result, the information coefficient will be adjusted downward by more under the first set of forecasts than under the second set of forecasts.

3. Suppose the active investor rebalances monthly instead of just once a year. Explain how this would affect the information ratio of this strategy, clearly stating your assumptions.

Solution:

Rebalancing monthly instead of annually could increase the breadth by a factor of 12 but only if the active management decisions for each asset are truly uncorrelated over time. For example, the breadth could increase to as much as $12 \times 3.2 = 38.4$. However, to increase the information ratio, one would have to assume that the information coefficient remains at the same level and that there are no constraints to fully implementing the active management decisions (i.e., a transfer coefficient of 1.00). For example, turnover constraints might limit the degree to which the monthly active management decisions could be fully implemented into new active positions, resulting in a lower transfer coefficient.

In summary, these examples illustrate how the information coefficient, IC, measures the strength of the return-forecasting process, or signal. The information coefficient is the correlation between the forecasted and realized security active returns and is anticipated to be positive or active management is not justified. Breadth, BR, measures the number of independent decisions made by the investor each year and is equal to the number of securities if the active returns are cross-sectionally uncorrelated. Similarly, breadth increases with the number of rebalancing periods but only if the active returns are uncorrelated over time.

Like the information coefficient, the transfer coefficient, TC, is a simple multiplicative factor in the fundamental law. It measures the extent to which constraints reduce the expected value added of the investor's forecasting ability. In the absence of constraints, the transfer coefficient is approximately 1.00, resulting in the basic form of the fundamental law. However, in practice, investors often work under constraints that result in TC values between 0.20 and 0.80. The lower transfer coefficient suggests that average performance in practice is only a fraction (20%–80%) of what would otherwise be predicted by the basic form of the fundamental law.

9 PRACTICAL LIMITATIONS

> describe the practical strengths and limitations of the fundamental law of active management

The limitations of the fundamental law include both practical considerations, such as ignoring transaction costs and taxes, and more conceptual issues, such as dynamic implementation over time. In this section, we focus on two limitations: the *ex ante* measurement of skill using the information coefficient and assumptions of independence in forecasts across assets and over time. The fundamental law extends the mean–variance-optimization approach to relative performance and hence has many of the same limitations of mean–variance optimization. In our discussion, we do not deal with the shortcomings of mean–variance optimization in general (e.g., assumptions of normality in return distributions or the degree of risk aversion) or the technical problems associated with the estimation and use of a risk model (e.g., the correct set of risk factors, nonlinearities, and non-stationary returns). The fundamental law takes as given that mean–variance optimization to balance risk and return against a benchmark is the correct objective function and that the investor has a way to adequately model risk.

Ex Ante Measurement of Skill

A core element of the fundamental law is the information coefficient, generally defined as the correlation between the portfolio investor's forecasts and actual outcomes. Active investors assume that the financial market they are trading in is not perfectly efficient in terms of public information and that they have some differential skill in competing with other active investors; otherwise, active management is generally not justified. Behaviorally, one might argue that investors tend to overestimate their own skills as embedded in the assumed IC, but even if that bias did not exist, questions about assessing an accurate level of skill remain. Furthermore, forecasting ability probably differs among different asset segments and varies over time.

For example, Qian and Hua (2004) expanded the basic form of the fundamental law by including the uncertainty about the level of skill, or the reality that the realized information coefficient can vary over time. Specifically, they showed that realized

Practical Limitations

active portfolio risk, σ_A, is a product of both the benchmark tracking risk predicted by the risk model, denoted σ_{RM}, and the additional risk induced by the uncertainty of the information coefficient, denoted σ_{IC}:

$$\sigma_A = \sigma_{IC}\sqrt{N}\,\sigma_{RM}. \tag{17}$$

Their insight about "strategy risk" is derived under the simplifying assumptions that portfolio positions are unconstrained, TC = 1.00, and that breadth is the number of securities, BR = N, but can be expanded to include both refinements. In other words, they suggest that a more accurate representation of the basic fundamental law using the expression in Equation 17 is

$$E\left(R_A\right) = \frac{IC}{\sigma_{IC}}\sigma_A. \tag{18}$$

The key impact of accounting for the uncertainty of skill is that actual information ratios are substantially lower than predicted by an objective application of the original form of the fundamental law. Specifically, security (i.e., individual stock) selection strategies can be analytically and empirically confirmed to be 45%–91% of original estimates using the fundamental law. Like the refinement for implementation issues associated with constraints as measured by the transfer coefficient, strategy risk reduces expected and average realized information ratios. The higher the uncertainty about forecasting ability, the smaller the likely expected value added.

Independence of Investment Decisions

As we have discussed, the number of individual assets, N, is not an adequate measure of strategy breadth, BR, when the active returns between individual assets are correlated, as defined by the risk model, and forecasts are not independent from period to period. Specifically, decisions to overweight all the stocks in a given industry or all the countries in a given region because they are responding to similar influences cannot be counted as completely independent decisions, so breadth in these contexts is lower than the number of assets. Similarly, when fundamental law concepts are applied to hedging strategies using derivatives or other forms of arbitrage, breadth can increase well beyond the number of securities.

For example, arbitrage of just two securities—say, a country equity market ETF traded on two different exchanges—can have extremely high breadth (i.e., the expected active return on the strategy is large compared with the active risk). To illustrate, Clarke, de Silva, and Thorley (2006) showed that a practical measure of breadth is

$$BR = \frac{N}{1 + (N-1)\rho}, \tag{19}$$

where ρ is the same correlation coefficient in all the off-diagonal elements of the risk model. For just two securities, $N = 2$, and a correlation coefficient associated with near-arbitrage opportunities, $\rho = -0.8$, breadth could be BR = 2/[1 – (2 – 1)0.8] = 10.0 so that information ratios are quite high for even modest values of IC or forecasting skill.

Another example of the limitation of the fundamental law due to the lack of decision independence is the active management of fixed-income portfolios. Most descriptions of the fundamental law are based on individual stock selection strategies where the risk of equity securities is decomposed into systematic and idiosyncratic factors by a risk model. Once the systematic risk factors are removed, the active asset returns (defined as the idiosyncratic returns) are essentially independent, so breadth can be more easily determined. In contrast, almost all bonds represent some form of duration risk, as well as credit risk and optionality, so returns are highly correlated in more subtle ways. In addition, the implicit assumption of normality in the realized return distribution of bonds with default risk and embedded options is clearly unwarranted.

The limitation of independent decisions within the fundamental law also affects time-series implementation. In particular, increasing the rebalancing frequency may increase the realized information ratio but only to the extent that sequential active return forecasts are independent from period to period. Refinements on the concept of breadth—for example, Buckle (2004)—have improved the cross-sectional operationalization of the fundamental law, but more work is needed to provide conceptually useful modifications of the fundamental law in a multi-period, multi-asset setting.

In summary, the fundamental law is a useful conceptual framework in many active management applications and can even produce operational measurements of the essential elements of an active management strategy. But an understanding of the limitations of the law is warranted—particularly the issues of uncertainty in the level of assumed skill and the measurement of breadth in the face of time-dependent rebalancing policies and multi-period optimization.

EXAMPLE 10

Limitations of the Fundamental Law

1. Consider an active portfolio management strategy of selecting individual stocks in the S&P 500 on a monthly basis. The investor does a quick calculation of the fundamental law based on an information coefficient of IC = 0.05 and BR = 12 × 500 = 6,000, giving an astounding information ratio of IR = 3.87. In other words, at an active portfolio risk of 3.0%, the expected active return would be 3.87(3.0) = 11.6%.

Provide at least two different explanations of *why* the information ratio in this example could be too high based on practical limitations of the fundamental law.

Solution:

Potential answers include the following:

1. Cross-sectional dependence: The active returns on the 500 stocks in the S&P 500 are probably correlated, so the number of independent monthly decisions is lower than 500. For example, the investor could be forecasting outperformance of all the stocks in a given industrial sector and underperformance of all the stocks in another sector.

2. Time-series dependence: The decisions on any particular stock may be correlated from month to month. For example, the forecasting process might be based on the earnings yield (reported EPS over price), which changes slowly over time. A stock that is forecasted to outperform in one month is likely to retain the outperformance forecast for several months in a row.

3. Uncertainty: Although an information coefficient of 0.05 appears to be modest, the basic form of the fundamental law does not account for uncertainty in the information coefficient or the likelihood that the information coefficient changes over time and could be different for different sets of stocks.

4. Constraints: An answer that involves accounting for such constraints as long only or turnover limits using a transfer coefficient is a weaker answer because the impact of constraints and the transfer coefficient is a well-known refinement of the fundamental law, even though it does not appear to be used in this example.

SUMMARY

We have covered a number of key concepts and principles associated with active portfolio management. Active management is based on the mathematics and principles of risk and return from basic mean–variance portfolio theory but with a focus on value added compared with a benchmark portfolio. Critical concepts include the following:

- Value added is defined as the difference between the return on the managed portfolio and the return on a passive benchmark portfolio. This difference in returns might be positive or negative after the fact but would be expected to be positive before the fact or active management would not be justified.

- Value added is related to active weights in the portfolio, defined as differences between the various asset weights in the managed portfolio and their weights in the benchmark portfolio. Individual assets can be overweighted (have positive active weights) or underweighted (have negative active weights), but the complete set of active weights sums to zero.

- Positive value added is generated when positive-active-weight assets have larger returns than negative-active-weight assets. By defining individual asset active returns as the difference between the asset total return and the benchmark return, value added is shown to be positive if and only if end-of-period realized active asset returns are positively correlated with the active asset weights established at the beginning of the period.

- Value added can come from a variety of active portfolio management decisions, including security selection, asset class allocation, and even further decompositions into economic sector weightings and geographic or country weights.

- The Sharpe ratio measures reward per unit of risk in absolute returns, whereas the information ratio measures reward per unit of risk in benchmark relative returns. Either ratio can be applied *ex ante* to expected returns or *ex post* to realized returns. The information ratio is a key criterion on which to evaluate actively managed portfolios.

- Higher information ratio portfolios can be used to create higher Sharpe ratio portfolios. The optimal amount of active management that maximizes a portfolio's Sharpe ratio is positively related to the assumed forecasting accuracy or *ex ante* information coefficient of the active strategy.

- The active risk of an actively managed strategy can be adjusted to its desired level by combining it with a position in the benchmark. Furthermore, once an investor has identified the maximum Sharpe ratio portfolio, the total volatility of a portfolio can be adjusted to its desired level by combining it with cash (two-fund separation concept).

- The fundamental law of active portfolio management began as a conceptual framework for evaluating the potential value added of various investment strategies, but it has also emerged as an operational system for measuring the essential components of those active strategies.

- Although the fundamental law provides a framework for analyzing investment strategies, the essential inputs of forecasted asset returns and risks still require judgment in formulating the expected returns.

- The fundamental law separates the expected value added, or portfolio return relative to the benchmark return, into the basic elements of the strategy:

  - *skill* as measured by the information coefficient,
  - *structuring* of the portfolio as measured by the transfer coefficient,
  - *breadth* of the strategy measured by the number of independent decisions per year, and
  - *aggressiveness* measured by the benchmark tracking risk.

  The last three of these four elements may be beyond the control of the investor if they are specified by investment policy or constrained by regulation.

- The fundamental law has been applied in settings that include the selection of country equity markets in a global equity fund and the timing of credit and duration exposures in a fixed-income fund.

- The fundamental law of active management has limitations, including uncertainty about the *ex ante* information coefficient and the conceptual definition of breadth as the number of independent decisions by the investor.

REFERENCES

Black, Fischer, Robert Litterman. 1992. "Global Portfolio Optimization." Financial Analysts Journal48 (5): 28–43. 10.2469/faj.v48.n5.28

Buckle, David. 2004. "How to Calculate Breadth: An Evolution of the Fundamental Law of Active Portfolio Management." Journal of Asset Management4 (6): 393–405. 10.1057/palgrave.jam.2240118

Clarke, Roger, Harindra de Silva, Steven Thorley. 2002. "Portfolio Constraints and the Fundamental Law of Active Management." Financial Analysts Journal58 (5): 48–66. 10.2469/faj.v58.n5.2468

Clarke, Roger, Harindra de Silva, Steven Thorley. 2005. "Performance Attribution and the Fundamental Law." Financial Analysts Journal61 (5): 70–83. 10.2469/faj.v61.n5.2758

Clarke, Roger, Harindra de Silva, Steven Thorley. 2006. "The Fundamental Law of Active Portfolio Management." Journal of Investment Management4 (3): 54–72.

Cremers, K.J. Martijn, Antti Petajisto. 2009. "How Active Is Your Fund Manager?" Review of Financial Studies22 (9): 3329–65. 10.1093/rfs/hhp057

Fischer, Bernd, Russell Wermers. 2013. Performance Evaluation and Attribution of Security Portfolios. Oxford, UK: Elsevier Inc.

Grinold, Richard C. 1989. "The Fundamental Law of Active Management." Journal of Portfolio Management15 (3): 30–37. 10.3905/jpm.1989.409211

Grinold, Richard C. 1994. "Alpha Is Volatility Times IC Times Score, or Real Alphas Don't Get Eaten." Journal of Portfolio Management20 (4): 9–16. 10.3905/jpm.1994.409482

Grinold, Richard C., Ronald N. Kahn. 1999. Active Portfolio Management: A Quantitative Approach for Providing Superior Returns and Controlling Risk. 2nd ed.New York: McGraw-Hill.

Markowitz, Harry M. 1952. "Portfolio Selection." Journal of Finance7 (1): 77–91.

Qian, Edward, Ronald Hua. 2004. "Active Risk and Information Ratio." Journal of Investment Management2 (3): 20–34.

Sharpe, William F. 1964. "Capital Asset Prices: A Theory of Market Equilibrium under Conditions of Risk." Journal of Finance19 (3): 425–42.

Treynor, J., Fischer Black. 1973. "How to Use Security Analysis to Improve Portfolio Selection." Journal of Business46:66–86. 10.1086/295508

PRACTICE PROBLEMS

1. Wei Liu makes two statements about active portfolio management:

   Statement 1   The "active return" of an actively managed portfolio is the difference between the portfolio's return and the return on the benchmark portfolio, and it is equal to the managed portfolio's alpha.

   Statement 2   The active weights are the differences in the managed portfolio's weights and the benchmark's weights.

   Are Liu's statements correct?

   A. Only Statement 1 is correct.

   B. Only Statement 2 is correct.

   C. Both statements are correct.

2. The benchmark weights and returns for each of the five stocks in the Capitol Index are given in the following table. The Tukol Fund uses the Capitol Index as its benchmark, and the fund's portfolio weights are also shown in the table.

Stock	Portfolio Weight (%)	Benchmark Weight (%)	20X2 Return (%)
1	30	24	14
2	30	20	15
3	20	20	12
4	10	18	8
5	10	18	10

   What is the value added (active return) for the Tukol Fund?

   A. 0.00%

   B. 0.90%

   C. 1.92%

3. Consider the following asset class returns for calendar year 20X2:

Asset Class	Portfolio Weight (%)	Benchmark Weight (%)	Portfolio Return (%)	Benchmark Return (%)
Domestic equities	55	40	10	8
International equities	20	30	10	9
Bonds	25	30	5	6

   What is the value added (or active return) for the managed portfolio?

   A. 0.25%

   B. 0.35%

   C. 1.05%

Practice Problems

143

The following information relates to questions 4-10

James Frazee is chief investment officer at H&F Capital Investors. Frazee hires a third-party adviser to develop a custom benchmark for three actively managed balanced funds he oversees: Fund X, Fund Y, and Fund Z. (Balanced funds are funds invested in equities and bonds.) The benchmark needs to be composed of 60% global equities and 40% global bonds. The third-party adviser submits the proposed benchmark to Frazee, who rejects the benchmark based on the following concerns:

Concern 1: Many securities he wants to purchase are not included in the benchmark portfolio.

Concern 2: One position in the benchmark portfolio will be somewhat costly to replicate.

Concern 3: The benchmark portfolio is a float-adjusted, capitalization-weighted portfolio.

After the third-party adviser makes adjustments to the benchmark to alleviate Frazee's concerns, Frazee accepts the benchmark portfolio. He then asks his research staff to develop risk and expected return forecasts for Funds X, Y, and Z as well as for the benchmark. The forecasts are presented in Exhibit 1.

Exhibit 1: Forecasted Portfolio Statistics for Funds X, Y, and Z and the Benchmark

	Fund X	Fund Y	Fund Z	Benchmark
Portfolio weights:				
Global equities (%)	60.0	65.0	68.0	60.0
Global bonds (%)	40.0	35.0	32.0	40.0
Expected return (%)	10.0	11.6	13.2	9.4
Expected volatility (%)	17.1	18.7	22.2	16.3
Active risk (%)	5.2	9.2	15.1	N/A
Sharpe ratio (SR)	0.45	0.50	0.49	0.44

Note: Data are based on a risk-free rate of 2.3%.

Frazee decides to add a fourth offering to his group of funds, Fund W, which will use the same benchmark as in Exhibit 1. Frazee estimates Fund W's information ratio to be 0.35. He is considering adding the following constraint to his portfolio construction model: Fund W would now have maximum over- and underweight constraints of 7% on single-country positions.

Frazee conducts a search to hire a manager for the global equity portion of Fund W and identifies three candidates. He asks the candidates to prepare risk and return forecasts relative to Fund W's benchmark based on their investment strategy, with the only constraint being no short selling. Each candidate develops independent annual forecasts with active return projections that are uncorrelated and constructs a portfolio made up of stocks that are diverse both geographically and across economic sectors. Selected data for the three candidates' portfolios are presented in Exhibit 2.

Exhibit 2: Forecasted Portfolio Data for Equity Portion of Fund W

	Candidate A	Candidate B	Candidate C
Rebalancing	Annually	Annually	Annually
Number of securities	100	64	36
Information ratio (IR)	0.582	0.746	0.723
Transfer coefficient (TC)	0.832	0.777	0.548
Information coefficient*	0.07	0.12	0.22

Information coefficient based on previously managed funds.

Frazee asks Candidate C to re-evaluate portfolio data given the following changes:

Change 1: Fix the number of securities to 50.

Change 2: Rebalance on a semi-annual basis.

Change 3: Add maximum over- or underweight constraints on sector weightings.

4. Which of Frazee's concerns *best* justifies his decision to reject the proposed benchmark?

   A. Concern 1

   B. Concern 2

   C. Concern 3

5. Based on Exhibit 1, the expected active return from asset allocation for Fund X is:

   A. negative.

   B. zero.

   C. positive.

6. Based on Exhibit 1, which fund is expected to produce the greatest consistency of active return?

   A. Fund X

   B. Fund Y

   C. Fund Z

7. Based on Exhibit 1, combining Fund W with a fund that replicates the benchmark would produce a Sharpe ratio *closest* to:

   A. 0.44.

   B. 0.56.

   C. 0.89.

8. If Frazee added the assumption he is considering in Fund W's portfolio construc-

Practice Problems

tion, it would *most likely* result in:

A. a decrease in the optimal aggressiveness of the active strategy.

B. the information ratio becoming invariant to the level of active risk.

C. an increase in the transfer of active return forecasts into active weights.

9. Based on the data presented in Exhibit 2, the candidate with the greatest skill at achieving active returns appears to be:

A. Candidate A.

B. Candidate B.

C. Candidate C.

10. Which proposed change to Fund W would *most likely* decrease Candidate C's information ratio?

A. Change 1

B. Change 2

C. Change 3

The following information relates to questions 11-14

John Martinez is assessing the performance of the actively managed diversified asset portfolio. The diversified asset portfolio is invested in equities, bonds, and real estate, and allocations to these asset classes and to the holdings within them are unconstrained.

Selected return and financial data for the portfolio for 2019 are presented in Exhibit 1.

Exhibit 1: Diversified Asset Portfolio 2019 Portfolio Performance

	Sub-Portfolio Return (%)	Benchmark Return (%)	Portfolio Allocation (%)	Strategic Asset Allocation (%)
Equities sub-portfolio	36.9	31.6	63	60
Bond sub-portfolio	−2.4	−2.6	28	35
Real estate sub-portfolio	33.4	28.3	9	5

Martinez uses several risk-adjusted return metrics to assess the performance of the diversified asset portfolio, including the information ratio and the Sharpe ratio. Selected risk, return, and statistical data for the portfolio are presented in Exhibit 2.

Exhibit 2: Diversified Asset Portfolio Data, 2000-2019

	Transfer Coefficient (TC)	Information Coefficient (IC)	Breadth (BR)
Equities sub-portfolio	0.90	0.091	21
Bond sub-portfolio	0.79	0.087	23
Real estate sub-portfolio	0.86	0.093	19

Martinez has recently hired Kenneth Singh to help him evaluate portfolios. Martinez asks Singh about the possible effects on the portfolio's information ratio if cash were added to the diversified asset portfolio or if the aggressiveness of the portfolio's active weights were increased. Singh responds with two statements:

Statement 1 Adding cash to the portfolio would change the portfolio's information ratio.

Statement 2 Increasing the aggressiveness of active weights would not change the portfolio's information ratio.

11. Based on Exhibit 1, the value added to the diversified asset portfolio attributable to the security selection decision in 2019 was *closest* to:

   A. 2.3%.

   B. 3.9%.

   C. 6.1%.

12. Based on Exhibit 1, the value added of the diversified asset portfolio attributable to the asset allocation decision in 2019 was *closest* to:

   A. 2.3%.

   B. 3.9%.

   C. 6.1%.

13. Based on data in Exhibit 2 and using the information ratio as the criterion for evaluating performance, which sub-portfolio had the best performance in the period 2000–2019?

   A. The bond sub-portfolio.

   B. The equities sub-portfolio.

   C. The real estate sub-portfolio.

14. Which of Singh's statements regarding the information ratio is correct?

   A. Only Statement 1

   B. Only Statement 2

   C. Both Statement 1 and Statement 2

Practice Problems 147

15. Gertrude Fischer mentions two properties of the Sharpe ratio and the information ratio that she says are very useful.

Property 1	The Sharpe ratio is unaffected by the addition of cash or leverage in a portfolio.
Property 2	The information ratio for an unconstrained portfolio is unaffected by the aggressiveness of the active weights.

Are Fischer's two properties correct?

A. Yes.

B. No. Only Property 1 is correct.

C. No. Only Property 2 is correct.

16. An analyst is given the following information about a portfolio and its benchmark. In particular, the analyst is concerned that the portfolio is a closet index fund. The T-bill return chosen to represent the risk-free rate is 0.50%.

	Benchmark	Portfolio
Return	8.75%	8.90%
Risk	17.50%	17.60%
Active return	0.00%	0.15%
Active risk	0.00%	0.79%
Sharpe ratio	0.4714	0.4773
Information ratio	N/A	0.1896

Which of the following three statements *does not* justify your belief that the portfolio is a closet index?

i.   The Sharpe ratio of the portfolio is close to the Sharpe ratio of the benchmark.

ii. The information ratio of the portfolio is relatively small.

iii. The active risk of the portfolio is very low.

A. Statement I

B. Statement II

C. Statement III

17. You have a portfolio 100% allocated to a manager with an *ex post*, active risk at 8.0%. You choose to allocate a 75% position to the active manager and 25% to the benchmark to bring the portfolio back to your target active risk of 6.0%. If the manager's information ratio is 0.50, what happens to the information ratio of the portfolio after the reallocation?

A. The information ratio increases because the lower active risk reduces the denominator of the ratio.

B. The information ratio remains unchanged because allocations between the active portfolio and the benchmark don't affect the information ratio.

C. The information ratio decreases because allocating some of the portfolio to the benchmark means that the external manager generates less active return.

The following information relates to questions 18–19

	S&P 500	Indigo Fund
Expected annual return	9.0%	10.5%
Return standard deviation	18.0%	25.0%
Sharpe ratio	0.333	0.30
Active return		1.2%
Active risk		8.0%
Information ratio		0.15

Note: Data are based on a risk-free rate of 2.3%.

18. What is the maximum Sharpe ratio that a manager can achieve by combining the S&P 500 benchmark portfolio and the Indigo Fund?

   A. 0.333

   B. 0.365

   C. 0.448

19. Which of the following pairs of weights would be used to achieve the highest Sharpe ratio and optimal amount of active risk through combining the Indigo Fund and benchmark portfolio, respectively?

   A. 1.014 on Indigo and −0.014 on the benchmark

   B. 1.450 on Indigo and −0.450 on the benchmark

   C. 1.500 on Indigo and −0.500 on the benchmark

20. The benchmark portfolio is the S&P 500. Which of the following three portfolios can be combined with the benchmark portfolio to produce the highest combined Sharpe ratio?

	S&P 500	Portfolio A	Portfolio B	Portfolio C
Expected annual return	9.0%	10.0%	9.5%	9.0%
Return standard deviation	18.0%	20.0%	20.0%	18.0%
Sharpe ratio	0.333	0.350	0.325	0.333
Active return	0	1.0%	0.5%	0
Active risk	0	10.0%	3.0%	2.0%

Note: Data are based on a risk-free rate of 2.3%.

   A. Portfolio A

   B. Portfolio B

Practice Problems

149

    C. Portfolio C

21. You are considering three managers for a small-cap growth mandate. After careful analysis, you produce the following forward-looking expectations about the managers' active risk and active return:

	Manager A	Manager B	Manager C
Active return	0.7%	0.6%	1.2%
Active risk	3.2%	3.1%	6.3%

If you intend to rely on the information ratio to make your decision, which manager should you choose?

    A. Manager A

    B. Manager B

    C. Manager C

22. Based on the fundamental law of active management, if a portfolio manager has an information ratio of 0.75, an information coefficient of 0.1819, and a transfer coefficient of 1.0, how many securities are in the portfolio manager's fund, making the assumption that the active returns are uncorrelated.

    A. About 2

    B. About 4

    C. About 17

23. Two analysts make the following statements about the transfer coefficient in the expanded fundamental law of active management:

Analyst One says, "The transfer coefficient measures how well the realized returns correlate with the anticipated returns, adjusted for risk."

Analyst Two says, "The transfer coefficient measures how well the realized returns correlate with the active weights, adjusted for risk."

Which, if either, analyst is correct?

    A. Only Analyst One is correct.

    B. Only Analyst Two is correct.

    C. Neither analyst is correct.

24. The expanded fundamental law of active management is stated as follows:

$$E\left(R_A\right) = (TC)\,(IC)\,\sqrt{BR}\,\sigma_A.$$

Which component on the righthand side represents the extent to which the portfolio manager's expectations are realized? The

    A. transfer coefficient, TC.

    B. information coefficient, IC.

    C. breadth, BR.

The following information relates to questions 25-26

You are analyzing three investment managers for a new mandate. The following table provides the managers' ex-ante active return expectations and portfolio weights. The last two columns include the risk and the *ex post*, realized active returns for the four stocks. Use the following data for the following two questions:

	Manager 1		Manager 2		Manager 3			Realized
	Δw	$E(R_A)$	Δw	$E(R_A)$	Δw	$E(R_A)$	Risk	R_A
Security 1	−0.125	0.03	0.2	0.04	−0.05	0.025	0.17	0.06
Security 2	0.025	0.04	0	0.01	0.05	0.015	0.10	0.07
Security 3	0.075	0.05	−0.1	0	0.05	0.005	0.12	0.04
Security 4	0.025	0.06	−0.1	0.02	−0.05	0.015	0.25	0.02

25. Suppose all three managers claim to be good at forecasting returns. According to the expanded fundamental law of active management, which manager is the best at efficiently building portfolios by anticipating future returns?

   A. Manager 1

   B. Manager 2

   C. Manager 3

26. Suppose all three managers claim to be efficient in portfolio construction. According to the expanded fundamental law of active management, which manager is the best at building portfolios to make full use of their ability to correctly anticipate returns?

   A. Manager 1

   B. Manager 2

   C. Manager 3

27. Manager 1 has an information coefficient of 0.15, a transfer coefficient of 1.0, and invests in 50 securities. Manager 2 has a different strategy, investing in more securities; however, he is subject to investment constraints that reduce his transfer coefficient. Manager 2 has an information coefficient of 0.10, a transfer coefficient of 0.8, and invests in 100 securities. The investment selections of each manager are independent decisions. If both managers target an active risk of 5.0%, which manager will have the greater expected active return?

   A. Manager 1

   B. Manager 2

   C. Both managers will have the same active return.

28. Nick Young is concerned that Goudon Partners, one of his money managers, overestimates its expected active return because Goudon overstates its strategy

Practice Problems

breadth. Young makes two notes about his concern:

Note 1   Although Goudon claims that the number of independent asset decisions is high because it uses 200 stocks, many of these stocks cluster in industries where the same general analysis applies to several stocks.

Note 2   Goudon claims that each stock is independent and evaluated each month, or 12 times per year. These analyses are not independent because some of their strategies, such as favoring a particular industry or favoring value stocks, persist beyond one month. For example, a strategy of favoring low-P/E stocks will persist for several months and the investment decisions are not independent.

If his judgments are correct, are Young's notes about the overstatement of breadth correct?

A. Only Note 1 is correct.

B. Only Note 2 is correct.

C. Both Notes 1 and 2 are correct.

29. Caramel Associates uses the fundamental law to estimate its expected active returns. Two things have changed. First, Caramel will lower its estimate of the information coefficient because they felt their prior estimates reflected overconfidence. Second, their major clients have relaxed several constraints on their portfolios—including social screens, prohibitions on short selling, and constraints on turnover. Which of these changes will increase the expected active return?

A. Only the lower information coefficient.

B. Only the relaxation of several portfolio constraints.

C. Both the lower information coefficient and the relaxation of portfolio constraints.

SOLUTIONS

1. B is correct. Although the first part of Statement 1 is correct (active return, or value added, equals the difference between the managed portfolio return and the benchmark return), active return is not the same as alpha. In other words, $R_A = R_P - R_B$, while $\alpha_P = R_P - \beta_P \times R_B$. Statement 2 correctly defines active weights.

2. B is correct. The portfolio active return is equal to the portfolio return minus the benchmark return:

   $R_A = R_P - R_B$.

   The portfolio return is $R_P = \sum_{i=1}^{n} w_{P,i} R_i$;

   $R_P = 0.30(14\%) + 0.30(15\%) + 0.20(12\%) + 0.10(8\%) + 0.10(10\%) = 12.9\%$.

   The benchmark return is $R_B = \sum_{i=1}^{n} w_{B,i} R_i$;

   $R_B = 0.24(14\%) + 0.20(15\%) + 0.20(12\%) + 0.18(8\%) + 0.18(10\%) = 12.0\%$.

   Thus, the active return is

   $R_A = R_P - R_B = 12.9\% - 12.0\% = 0.9\%$.

   Note that this same correct answer can be obtained in two other equivalent ways. The active weights are the differences between the portfolio and benchmark weights, or $\Delta w_i = w_{P,i} - w_{B,i}$. Computing the active weights from the table provided, the active return is

   $R_A = \sum_{i=1}^{N} \Delta w_i R_i$

   $= 0.06(14\%) + 0.10(15\%) + 0(12\%) - 0.08(8\%) - 0.08(10\%)$

   $= 0.9\%$.

   Finally, we could express the active security returns as their differences from the benchmark return, or $R_{Ai} = R_i - R_B$. Computing the active security returns from the table provided, the portfolio active return is the sum product of the active weights and the active security returns:

   $R_A = \sum_{i=1}^{N} \Delta w_i R_{Ai}$

   $= 0.06(2\%) + 0.10(3\%) + 0(0\%) - 0.08(-4\%) - 0.08(-2\%)$

   $= 0.9\%$.

3. C is correct. The active return is equal to the portfolio return minus the benchmark return:

   $R_A = R_P - R_B = \sum_{j=1}^{M} w_{P,j} R_{P,j} - \sum_{j=1}^{M} w_{B,j} R_{B,j}$.

   The portfolio return is $R_P = \sum_{i=1}^{n} w_{P,i} R_i = 0.55(10\%) + 0.20(10\%) + 0.25(5\%) = 8.75\%$.
   The benchmark return is $R_B = \sum_{i=1}^{n} w_{B,i} R_i = 0.40(8\%) + 0.30(9\%) + 0.30(6\%) = 7.70\%$.

   Thus, $R_A = R_P - R_B = 8.75\% - 7.70\% = 1.05\%$.

4. A is correct. Because the benchmark does not contain many assets that Frazee wants to invest in, the benchmark may not be representative of his investment approach. Concern 2, as stated, is less important because it does not imply that

Solutions 153

the cost of replicating the benchmark is a serious concern. Finally, Concern 3 actually states a generally positive feature of the benchmark.

5. B is correct. Active return from asset allocation is derived from differences between the benchmark weight and the portfolio weight across asset classes. For Fund X, the expected active return from asset allocation is calculated as

$$\sum_{j=1}^{M} \Delta w_j R_{B,j} = (60 - 60) R_{B,e} + (40 - 40) R_{B,b} = 0,$$

where Δw_j is the difference in the active portfolio and the benchmark asset weights, $R_{B,e}$ is the benchmark's return from global equities, and $R_{B,b}$ is the benchmark's return from global bonds.

Because Fund X has the same asset weights as the benchmark across the two asset classes (60% global equities, 40% global bonds), the expected active return from asset allocation is zero.

6. C is correct. The IR measures the consistency of active return. The IR is calculated for the three funds as follows:

$$IR = \frac{R_P - R_B}{\sigma(P_P - R_B)} = \frac{R_A}{\sigma_A}.$$

IR for Fund X = $(10.0 - 9.4)/5.2 = 0.6/5.2 = 0.12$.

IR for Fund Y = $(11.6 - 9.4)/9.2 = 2.2/9.2 = 0.24$.

IR for Fund Z = $(13.2 - 9.4)/15.1 = 3.8/15.1 = 0.25$.

Fund Z has the largest IR and thus is expected to produce the greatest consistency of active return.

7. B is correct. Given the IR for Fund W of 0.35 and the benchmark's SR of 0.44, the combination of the benchmark portfolio and Fund W would produce an SR of 0.56, calculated as follows:

$$SR_P^2 = SR_B^2 + IR^2;$$

$$SR_P = (0.44^2 + 0.35^2)^{0.5} = 0.56.$$

8. A is correct. The new assumption adds constraints to Fund W. The IR for a constrained portfolio generally decreases with the aggressiveness of the strategy because portfolio constraints reduce the transfer of active return forecasts into active weights. Furthermore, the optimal active risk is given by the following formula:

$$\sigma_A = TC \frac{IR}{SR_B} \sigma_B.$$

The addition of portfolio constraints reduces the TC, thus also reducing the optimal active risk.

So, having maximum over- and underweight constraints on single-country positions decreases the optimal aggressiveness of the active management strategy.

9. B is correct. The IR measures the consistency of active return generation. A higher ratio generally indicates better managerial skill at achieving active returns on a risk-adjusted basis. The IR for Candidate B (0.746) is higher than the IR for Candidate A (0.582) and Candidate C (0.723).

Thus, Candidate B appears to have the greatest skill, as indicated by the highest IR of 0.746.

10. C is correct. The IR is calculated as IR = (TC) (IC) $\sqrt{BR}$, where BR is breadth. Change 3, establishing new constraints of caps on the over- and underweight of sectors, reduces the correlation of optimal active weights with the actual active weights, which results in a decreased TC and thus a decrease in the IR. Change 1 (increasing portfolio size from 36 to 50) and Change 2 (increasing the frequency of rebalancing from annually to semi-annually) would both likely have the effect of increasing the BR of the portfolio, which would increase the IR.

11. B is correct. Based on the differences in returns for the portfolio and benchmark in Exhibit 1, the value added by each asset class within the portfolio is shown in the following table:

	Sub-Portfolio Return (%)	Benchmark Return (%)	Value Added (%)	Portfolio Allocation (%)
Equities sub-portfolio	36.9	31.6	5.3	63
Bond sub-portfolio	−2.4	−2.6	0.2	28
Real estate sub-portfolio	33.4	28.3	5.1	9

The value added from security selection is calculated as the sum of the actual portfolio weights multiplied by each sub-portfolio's value added measure. Thus, the value added from security selection is calculated as: Value added from security selection = 0.63(5.3%) + 0.28(0.2%) + 0.09(5.1%) = 3.9%.

A is incorrect. It represents the value added from asset allocation (2.3%).

C is incorrect. It represents the total value added (2.3% + 3.9% = 6.1%, with rounding).

12. A is correct. The value added from asset allocation is calculated as the sum of the differences in the weights between the strategic (benchmark) allocation and the actual sub-portfolio allocation multiplied by each sub-portfolio's benchmark return.

	Benchmark Return (%)	Actual Asset Allocation (%)	Strategic Asset Allocation (%)	Actual – Strategic Asset Allocation (%)
Equities sub-portfolio	31.6	63	60	+3
Bond sub-portfolio	−2.6	28	35	−7
Real estate sub-portfolio	28.3	9	5	+4

Thus, the value added by the active asset allocation decision is calculated as

Value added from asset allocation decision = 0.03(31.6%) − 0.07(−2.6%) + 0.04(28.3%)

= 2.3%.

B is incorrect. It is the value added from security selection.

C is incorrect. It is the total value added.

13. B is correct. The information ratio for a portfolio can be expressed as follows:

Solutions 155

$$IR = (TC)(IC)\sqrt{BR}.$$

The information ratios for the three sub-portfolios are calculated as follows:

	Information Ratio
Equities sub-portfolio	$0.90 \times 0.091 \times (21)^{0.5} = 0.38$
Bond sub-portfolio	$0.79 \times 0.087 \times (23)^{0.5} = 0.33$
Real estate sub-portfolio	$0.86 \times 0.093 \times (19)^{0.5} = 0.35$

Based on the information ratio, the equities sub-portfolio outperformed the real estate sub-portfolio. The information ratio for the equities sub-portfolio of 0.38 was higher than the information ratio for the real estate sub-portfolio of 0.35 and the bond sub-portfolio of 0.33.

14. C is correct. The information ratio for a portfolio of risky assets will generally shrink if cash is added to the portfolio. Because the diversified asset portfolio is an unconstrained portfolio, its information ratio would be unaffected by an increase in the aggressiveness of active weights.

15. A is correct. Both properties are correct. For Property 1, if w_P is the weight of an actively managed portfolio and $(1 - w_P)$ is the weight on risk-free cash, changing w_P does not change the Sharpe ratio, as can be seen in this equation:

$$SR_C = \frac{R_C - R_F}{\sigma_C} = \frac{w_P(R_P - R_F)}{w_P \sigma_P} = SR_P.$$

For Property 2, the information ratio of an unconstrained portfolio is unaffected by multiplying the active security weights, Δw_i, by a constant.

16. B is correct. A closet index will have a very low active risk and will also have a Sharpe ratio very close to the benchmark. Therefore, Statements I and III are consistent with a closet index portfolio. A closet index's information ratio can be indeterminate (because the active risk is so low) and is often negative due to management fees.

17. B is correct. The information ratio is unaffected by rebalancing the active portfolio and the benchmark portfolio. In this case, the active return and active risk are both reduced by 25% and the information ratio will be unchanged.

18. B is correct. The highest squared Sharpe ratio of an actively managed portfolio is

$$SR_P^2 = SR_B^2 + IR^2 = 0.333^2 + 0.15^2 = 0.1334.$$

The highest Sharpe ratio is $SR_P = \sqrt{0.1334} = 0.365$.

19. A is correct. The optimal amount of active risk is

$$\sigma_A = \frac{IR}{SR_B}\sigma_B = \frac{0.15}{0.333}18.0\% = 8.11\%.$$

The weight on the active portfolio (Indigo) would be 8.11%/8.0% = 1.014, and the weight on the benchmark portfolio would be 1 − 1.014 = −0.014.

We can demonstrate that these weights achieve the maximum Sharpe ratio (of 0.365). Note that 8.11% is the optimal level of active risk and that Indigo has an expected active return of 1.014(1.2%) = 1.217% over the benchmark and a total excess return of 6.0% + 1.217% = 7.217%. The portfolio total risk is

$$\sigma_P^2 = \sigma_B^2 + \sigma_A^2 = 18.0^2 + 8.111^2 = 389.788.$$

Taking the square root, $\sigma_P = 19.743$, and the optimal Sharpe ratio is indeed 7.217/19.743 = 0.365.

20. B is correct. The optimal active portfolio is the portfolio with the highest information ratio, the ratio of active return to active risk. The IRs for the three active portfolios are as follows:

$$IR_A = 1.0/10.0 = 0.10$$

$$IR_B = 0.5/3.0 = 0.167$$

$$IR_C = 0/2.0 = 0.00$$

Portfolio B has the highest IR and is the best active portfolio; it is therefore the best portfolio to combine with the benchmark.

21. A is correct. Manager A has the highest information ratio. The information ratio is defined as $IR = \frac{\text{active return}}{\text{active risk}}$. The managers in this example have the following information ratios:

	Manager A	Manager B	Manager C
Information ratio	0.7/3.2 = 0.219	0.6/3.1 = 0.194	1.2/6.3 = 0.190

22. C is correct. Using the equation $IR^* = IC \times \sqrt{BR}$ and assuming that breadth can be interpreted as number of securities in the portfolio, solving for breadth in the equation yields $\left(\frac{0.75}{0.1819}\right)^2 = 17.000$.

23. C is correct. The transfer coefficient measures how well the anticipated (*ex ante*), risk-adjusted returns correlate with the risk-adjusted active weights. This is also expressed in the equation for the transfer coefficient: $TC = \rho(\mu_i/\sigma_i, \Delta w_i \sigma_i)$.

24. B is correct. The IC measures an investment manager's ability to forecast returns.

25. C is correct. The proper statistic to calculate is the information coefficient, and it is defined as follows:

$$IC = \rho\left(\frac{R_{Ai}}{\sigma_i}, \frac{\mu_i}{\sigma_i}\right).$$

A manager is a good forecaster if his or her *ex ante*, active return expectations (forecasts) are highly correlated with the realized active returns. The information coefficient requires that these forecasts and realized returns be risk-weighted. When this is done for the three managers, the risk-weighted forecasts and realized returns are:

	Risk-Weighted Forecasts, μ_i/σ_i			R_{Ai}/σ_i
	Manager 1	Manager 2	Manager 3	Realized
Security 1	0.176	0.235	0.147	0.353
Security 2	0.400	0.100	0.150	0.700
Security 3	0.417	0.000	0.042	0.333
Security 4	0.240	0.080	0.060	0.080

The ICs are found by calculating the correlations between each manager's forecasts and the realized risk-weighted returns. The three managers have the following ICs:

Solutions

	Manager 1	Manager 2	Manager 3
Information coefficient	0.5335	0.0966	0.6769

Manager 3 has the highest IC.

26. B is correct. The proper statistic to calculate is the transfer coefficient, and it is defined as follows:

$$TC = \rho(\mu_i/\sigma_i, \Delta w_i \sigma_i)$$

The TC is the cross-sectional correlation between the forecasted active security returns and the actual active weights, adjusted for risk.

	Risk-Weighted Forecasts, μ_i/σ_i			Risk-Adjusted Weights, $\Delta w_i \sigma_i$		
	Manager 1	Manager 2	Manager 3	Manager 1	Manager 2	Manager 3
Security 1	0.1765	0.2353	0.1471	−0.0213	0.0340	−0.0085
Security 2	0.4000	0.1000	0.1500	0.0025	0.0000	0.0050
Security 3	0.4167	0.0000	0.0417	0.0090	−0.0120	0.0060
Security 4	0.2400	0.0800	0.0600	0.0063	−0.0250	−0.0125

The three managers have the following TCs:

	Manager 1	Manager 2	Manager 3
Transfer coefficient	0.7267	0.8504	−0.0020

Manager 2 has the highest TC.

27. A is correct. Manager 1's IR = TC × IC × $\sqrt{BR}$ = 1.0 × 0.15 × $\sqrt{50}$ = 1.06. Manager 2's IR = 0.8 × 0.10 × $\sqrt{100}$ = 0.80. Manager 1's active return is 1.06(5.0) = 5.3%, and Manager 2's expected active return is 0.80(5.0) = 4.0%. Manager 1 has the greater expected active return.

28. C is correct. If the decisions about each of the 200 stocks are not independent, and if the decisions about a stock from one month to the next are not independent, then Goudon Partners is overstating its estimates of its breadth and its expected active returns.

29. B is correct. Although the relaxation of portfolio constraints will increase the transfer coefficient (and expected active returns), the lower information coefficient reduces the information ratio and the expected active return.

LEARNING MODULE

3

Trading Costs and Electronic Markets

by Larry Harris, PhD, CFA.

Larry Harris, PhD, CFA, is at the USC Marshall School of Business (USA).

LEARNING OUTCOMES	
Mastery	*The candidate should be able to:*
☐	explain the components of execution costs, including explicit and implicit costs
☐	calculate and interpret effective spreads and VWAP transaction cost estimates
☐	describe the implementation shortfall approach to transaction cost measurement
☐	describe factors driving the development of electronic trading systems
☐	describe market fragmentation
☐	identify and contrast the types of electronic traders
☐	describe characteristics and uses of electronic trading systems
☐	describe comparative advantages of low-latency traders
☐	describe the risks associated with electronic trading and how regulators mitigate them
☐	describe abusive trading practices that real-time surveillance of markets may detect

COSTS OF TRADING

1

☐ explain the components of execution costs, including explicit and implicit costs

Securities research, portfolio management, and securities trading support the investment process. Of the three, trading is often the least understood and least appreciated function. Among the questions addressed in this reading are the following:

- What are explicit and implicit trading costs, and how are they measured?
- How is a limit order book interpreted?
- How have trading strategies adapted to market fragmentation?
- What types of electronic traders can be distinguished?

This reading is organized as follows: Section 2 discusses the direct and indirect costs of trading.[1] Section 3 discusses developments in electronic trading and the effects they had on transaction costs and market fragmentation. Section 4 identifies the most important types of electronic traders. Section 5 describes electronic trading facilities and some important ways traders use them. Section 6 discusses risks posed by electronic trading and how regulators control them. Finally, Section 7 summarizes the reading.

Costs of Trading

Understanding the costs of trading is critical for ensuring optimal execution and transaction cost management for portfolios. Because trading costs are a significant source of investment performance slippage, investment sponsors and their investment managers pay close attention to trading processes.

The costs of trading include fixed costs and variable costs. For buy-side institutions, fixed trading costs include the costs of employing buy-side traders, the costs of equipping them with proper trading tools (electronic systems and data), and the costs of office space (trading rooms or corners). Small buy-side institutions often avoid these costs by not employing buy-side traders. Their portfolio managers submit their orders directly to their brokers. Variable transaction costs arise from trading activity and consist of explicit and implicit costs.

Explicit costs are the direct costs of trading, such as broker commission costs, transaction taxes, stamp duties, and fees paid to exchanges. They are costs for which a trader could receive a receipt.

Implicit costs, by contrast, are indirect costs caused by the market impact of trading. Buyers often must raise prices to encourage sellers to trade with them, and sellers often must lower prices to encourage buyers. The price concessions that impatient traders make to complete their trades are called the market impacts of their trades. For small orders, market impact often is limited to buying at bid prices and selling at lower ask prices. Small market orders generally have small market impact because these orders often are immediately filled by traders willing to trade at quoted bid and offer prices, or even better prices. Larger orders have greater market impact when traders must move the market to fill their orders. In these cases, traders must accept larger price concessions (less attractive prices) to execute their orders in entirety. Although no receipt can be given for implicit costs, they are real nonetheless.

Implicit costs result from the following issues:

- The **bid–ask spread** is the ask price (the price at which a trader will sell a specified quantity of a security) minus the bid price (the price at which a trader will buy a specified quantity of a security). Traders who want to trade quickly buy at higher prices and sell at lower prices than those willing to wait for others to trade with them.

---

1 CFA Institute would like to thank Ananth Madhavan, PhD, at BlackRock (USA) for his contribution to this section, which includes material first written by him.

Costs of Trading

161

- **Market impact** (or price impact) is the effect of the trade on transaction prices. Traders who want to fill large orders often must move prices to encourage others to trade with them.

- **Delay costs** (also called slippage) arise from the inability to complete the desired trade immediately. Traders fail to profit when they fill their orders after prices move as they expect.

- **Opportunity costs** (or unrealized profit/loss) arise from the failure to execute a trade promptly. Traders fail to profit when their orders fail to trade and price move as they expect.

Dealer Quotes

Dealers provide liquidity to other traders when they allow traders to buy and sell when those traders want to trade. Those traders may be the clients known to the dealers, or they may be unknown traders whose orders exchanges assign to standing dealer orders and quotes.

Unlike brokers, dealers trade for their accounts when filling their customers' orders. When dealers buy or sell, they increase or reduce their inventories. Dealers profit by selling at ask prices that are higher than the bid prices at which they buy. If buying interest is greater than selling interest, dealers raise their ask prices to discourage buyers and raise their bid prices to encourage sellers. Likewise, if selling interest is greater than buying interest, dealers lower their ask prices to encourage buyers and lower their bid prices to discourage sellers.

Dealers help markets function well by being continuously available to take the other side of a trade when other traders want to trade. Dealers thus make markets more continuous. They are especially important in markets for infrequently traded securities in which buyers and sellers rarely are present at the same time. For example, most bond markets are overwhelmingly dealer markets because most bonds rarely trade. If an investor wants to sell a rarely traded bond, the investor might have a long wait before another investor interested in buying that bond arrives. Instead, a dealer generally will buy the bond and then try to market it to potential buyers. Practitioners say that dealers "make market" when they offer to trade.

Bid–Ask Spreads and Order Books

The prices at which dealers will buy or sell specified quantities of a security are, respectively, their **bid prices** and **ask prices**. (Ask prices are also known as offer prices.) The excess of the ask price over the bid price is the dealer's **bid–ask spread**.

When several dealers offer bid prices, the **best bid** is the offer to buy with the highest bid price. The best bid is also known as the **inside bid**. The **best ask**, also known as the **best offer** or **inside ask**, is the offer to sell with the lowest ask price.

The spread between the best bid price and the best ask price in a market is the market bid–ask spread, which is also known as the **inside spread**. It will be smaller (tighter or narrower) than the individual dealer spreads if the dealer with the highest bid price is not also the dealer with the lowest ask price.

For example, suppose that a portfolio manager gives the firm's trading desk an order to buy 1,000 shares of Economical Chemical Systems, Inc. (ECSI). Three dealers (coded A, B, and C) make a market in those shares. When the trader views the market in ECSI at 10:22 a.m. on his computer screen, the three dealers have put in the following limit orders to trade at an exchange market:

- Dealer A: *bid*: 98.85 for 600 shares; *ask*: 100.51 for 1,000 shares
- Dealer B: *bid*: 98.84 for 500 shares; *ask*: 100.55 for 500 shares
- Dealer C: *bid*: 98.82 for 700 shares; *ask*: 100.49 for 200 shares

The bid–ask spreads of Dealers A, B, and C are, respectively,

- 100.51 − 98.85 = 1.66
- 100.55 − 98.84 = 1.71
- 100.49 − 98.82 = 1.67

The best bid price, 98.85 by Dealer A, is lower than the best ask price, 100.49 by Dealer C. The market spread is thus 100.49 − 98.85 = 1.64, which is lower than any of the dealers' spreads.

The trader might see the quote information organized on his screen as shown in Exhibit 1. In this display, called a **limit order book**, the bids and asks are separately ordered from best to worst with the best at the top. The trader also notes that the **midquote price** (halfway between the market bid and ask prices) is (100.49 + 98.85)/2 = 99.67.

Exhibit 1: The Limit Order Book for Economical Chemical Systems, Inc.

	Bids				Asks		
Dealer	Time Entered	Price	Size	Dealer	Time Entered	Price	Size
A	10:21 a.m.	98.85	600	C	10:21 a.m.	100.49	200
B	10:21 a.m.	98.84	500	A	10:21 a.m.	100.51	1,000
C	10:19 a.m.	98.82	700	B	10:19 a.m.	100.55	500

Note: The bids are ordered from highest to lowest, while the asks are ordered from lowest to highest. These orderings are from best bid or ask to worst bid or ask.

If the trader on the firm's trading desk submits a market buy order for 1,000 shares, the trader would purchase 200 shares from Dealer C at 100.49 per share and 800 shares from Dealer A at 100.51 per share.

market impact

Note that filling the second part of the order cost the trader 0.02 per share more than the first part because Dealer C's ask size was insufficient to fill the entire order. Large orders have price impact when they move down the book as they fill. The price impact of an order depends on its size and the available liquidity.

If this market were not an exchange market, the trader might choose to direct the buy order to a specific dealer—for example, to Dealer A. The trader may do so for many reasons. The trader may believe that Dealer A more likely will honor her quote than would Dealer C. Alternatively, the trader may believe that Dealer A more likely will settle the trade than Dealer C. Such considerations are especially important in markets for which no clearinghouse guarantees that all trades will settle—for example, most currency markets. Institutions active in such markets may screen counterparties on credit criteria. Finally, the trader might fear that Dealer A will cancel her quote when she (or a computer managing her quote) sees that a trade took place at 100.49. Sending the order first to Dealer A thus could produce a better average price.

Implicit Transaction Cost Estimates

Investment managers and traders measure transaction costs so that they can better predict the cost of filling orders and so that they can better manage the brokers and dealers who fill their orders. Buyers, of course, want to trade at low prices, while sellers want to trade at high prices. Expensive trades are purchases arranged at high prices or sales arranged at low prices.

To estimate transaction costs, analysts compare trade prices to a benchmark price. Commonly used price benchmarks include the midquote price at the time of the trade, the midquote price at the time of the order submission, and a volume-weighted average price around the time of the trade. These three benchmarks, respectively, correspond to the effective spread, implementation shortfall, and VWAP methods of transaction cost estimation.

EFFECTIVE SPREADS AND VOLUME-WEIGHTED COST ESTIMATES

2

☐ calculate and interpret effective spreads and VWAP transaction cost estimates

☐ describe the implementation shortfall approach to transaction cost measurement

The market spread is a measure of trade execution costs. It is how much traders would lose per quantity traded if they simultaneously submitted buy and sell market orders that respectively execute at the ask and bid prices. The loss is the cost of trading, because this strategy otherwise accomplishes nothing. Given that two trades generated the cost, the cost per trade is one half of the quoted spread.

The prices that traders receive when trading often differ from quoted prices. Smaller orders sometimes fill at better prices; larger orders often fill at worse prices. Standing orders offering liquidity fill at same-side prices (buy at bid, sell at ask), if they fill at all.

The effective spread provides a more general estimate of the cost of trading. It uses the midquote price (the average, or midpoint, of the bid and the ask prices at the time the order was entered) as the benchmark price:

$$\text{Effective spread transaction cost estimate} =$$
$$\text{Trade size} \times \begin{cases} \text{Trade price} - \left(\dfrac{\text{Bid} + \text{Ask}}{2}\right) & \text{for buy orders} \\ \left(\dfrac{\text{Bid} + \text{Ask}}{2}\right) - \text{Trade price} & \text{for sell orders} \end{cases}$$

For a buy order filled at the ask, the estimated implicit cost of trading is half the bid–ask spread, because Ask − [(Bid + Ask)/2] = [(Ask − Bid)/2]. Multiplying this midquote price benchmark transaction cost estimate by 2 produces a statistic called the **effective spread**. It is the spread that traders would have observed if the quoted ask (for a purchase) or the bid (for a sale) were equal to the trade price.

The effective spread is a sensible estimate of transaction costs when orders are filled in single trades. If an order fills at a price better than the quoted price (e.g., a buy order fills at a price below the ask price), the order is said to receive **price improvement** and the spread is effectively lower. Price improvement occurs when trade execution prices are better than quoted prices. An order that fills at a price outside the quoted spread has an effective spread that is larger than the quoted spread. Such results occur when trade execution prices are worse than quoted prices.

The effective spread is a poor estimate of transaction costs when traders split large orders into many parts to fill over time. Such orders often move the market and cause bid and ask prices to rise or fall. The impact of the order on market prices, called **market impact**, makes trading expensive—especially for the last parts to fill—but the effective spread will not fully identify this cost if it is computed separately for each trade.

For example, suppose that a buy order for 10,000 shares fills in two trades. The prices and sizes of these trades and the best bids and offers in the market when the trades occurred appear in the following table:

Trade	Trade Price	Trade Size	Prevailing Bid	Prevailing Offer
#1	10.21	4,000	10.19	10.21
#2	10.22	6,000	10.20	10.22

For this buy order, the effective spread transaction cost per share is 0.01, or [(10.21− 10.19)/2] and [(10.22 − 10.20)/2], for both trades (the effective spreads are both 0.02). Thus, the total transaction cost estimate measured using the midquote price benchmark is 100 = 0.01 × 10,000. This estimate is problematic because it reflects the higher price of the second trade, which was likely caused by the market impact of the trader's first trade.

Effective spreads also do not measure **delay costs** (also called slippage) that arise from the inability to complete the desired trade immediately because of its size in relation to the available market liquidity. Delay costs also arise when portfolio managers or their traders fail to create and route orders quickly to the markets where they will fill most quickly. Analysts often measure delay costs on the portion of the order carried over from one day to the next. Delay is costly when price moves away from an order (up for a buy order, down for a sell order), often because information leaks into the market before or during the execution of the order.

When delays in execution cause a portion of the order to go unfilled, the associated cost is called **opportunity cost**. For example, suppose a futures trader places an order to buy 10 contracts with a limit price of 99.00, good for one day, when the market quote is 99.01 to 99.04. The order does not execute, and the contract closes at 99.80. If the order could have been filled at 99.04, the difference (99.80 − 99.04 = 0.76) reflects the opportunity cost per contract. By trading more aggressively, the trader might have avoided these costs. Opportunity costs are difficult to measure. In the example, the one-day time frame is arbitrary, and the assumption that the order could fill at 99.04 may be suspect. The estimate usually is sensitive to the time frame chosen for measurement and to assumptions about the prices at which orders could trade.

Implementation Shortfall

The implementation shortfall method of measuring trading costs addresses the problems associated with the effective spread method. Implementation shortfall is also attractive because it views trading from an investment management perspective and measures the total cost of implementing an investment decision by capturing all explicit and implicit costs. The implementation shortfall method includes the market impact costs and delay costs as well as opportunity costs, which are often significant for large orders.

Implementation shortfall compares the values of the actual portfolio with that of a paper portfolio constructed on the assumption that trades could be arranged at the prices that prevailed when the decision to trade is made. The prevailing price—also called the decision price, the arrival price, or the strike price—is generally taken to be the midquote price at the time of the trade decision. The excess of the paper value over the actual value is the **implementation shortfall**. The coverage of implementation shortfall is continued at Level III.

VWAP Transaction Cost Estimates

Volume-weighted average price (VWAP) is one of the most widely used benchmark prices that analysts use to estimate transaction costs. Analysts typically compute the VWAP using all trades that occurred from the start of the order until the order was completed, a measure that is often referred to as "interval VWAP." The VWAP is the sum of the total dollar value of the benchmark trades divided by the total quantity of the trades. The VWAP transaction cost estimate formula is as follows:

$$\text{VWAP transaction cost estimate} = \text{Trade size} \times \begin{cases} \text{Trade VWAP} - \text{VWAP benchmark} & \text{for buy orders} \\ \text{VWAP benchmark} - \text{Trade VWAP} & \text{for sell orders} \end{cases}$$

The VWAP transaction cost estimate is popular in part because it is easy to interpret. It answers this question: Did you get a better or worse average price than all traders trading when you were trading?

Interpreting VWAP transaction cost estimates is problematic when the trades being evaluated are a substantial fraction of all trades in the VWAP benchmark, or, more generally, when the trades took place at the same rate as other trades in the market. In both cases, the Trade VWAP and the VWAP benchmark will be nearly equal, which would suggest that the evaluated trades were not costly. But this conclusion would be misleading if the trade had substantial price impact. For example, if a large trader were the only buyer for a given trading period (or interval), the VWAP transaction cost estimate would be zero regardless of the market impact.

This bias toward zero helps explain why the measure is so popular. Investment managers like to show their investment sponsors transaction cost estimates that suggest that trading is not expensive.

EXAMPLE 1

Transaction Cost Analyses for an Illiquid Stock

Arapahoe Tanager, portfolio manager of a Canadian small-cap equity mutual fund, and his firm's chief trader, Lief Schrader, are reviewing the execution of a ticket to sell 12,000 shares of Alpha Company, limit C$9.95. The order was traded over the day.

Schrader split the ticket into three orders that executed that day as follows:

A. A market order to sell 2,000 shares executed at a price of C$10.15. Upon order submission, the market was C$10.12 bid for 3,000 shares, 2,000 shares offered at C$10.24.

B. A market order to sell 3,000 shares executed at a price of C$10.11. Upon order submission, the market was C$10.11 bid for 3,000 shares, 2,000 shares offered at C$10.22.

C. Toward the end of the trading day, Schrader submitted an order to sell the remaining 7,000 shares, limit C$9.95. The order executed in part, with 5,000 shares trading at an average price of C$10.01. Upon order submission, the market was C$10.05 bid for 3,000 shares, 2,000 shares offered at C$10.19. This order exceeded the quoted bid size and "walked down" the limit order book (i.e., after the market bid was filled, the order continued to sell at lower prices). After the market closed, Schrader allowed the order to cancel. Tanager did want to sell the 2,000 unfilled shares on the next trading day.

Only two other trades in Alpha Company occurred on this day: 2,000 shares at C$10.20 and 1,000 shares at C$10.15. The last trade price of the day was C$9.95; it was C$9.50 on the following day.

1. For each of the three fund trades, compute the quoted spread. Also, compute the average quoted spreads prevailing at the times of each trade.

Solution:

The quoted spread is the difference between the ask and bid prices. For the first order, the quoted spread is C\$10.24 – C\$10.12 = C\$0.12. Similarly, the quoted spreads for the second and third orders are C\$0.11 and C\$0.14, respectively. The average quoted spread is (C\$0.12 + C\$0.11 + C\$0.14)/3 = C\$0.1233.

2. For each of the three fund trades, compute the effective spread (use the average fill price for the third trade). Also, compute the average effective spread.

Solution:

The effective spread for a sell order is 2 × (Midpoint of the market at the time of order entry – Trade price). For the first order, the midpoint of the market at the time of order entry is (C\$10.12 + C\$10.24)/2 = C\$10.18, so that the effective spread is 2 × (C\$10.18 – C\$10.15) = C\$0.06.

The effective spread for the second order is 2 × [(C\$10.11 + C\$10.22)/2 – C\$10.11] = C\$0.11.
The effective spread for the third order is 2 × [(C\$10.05 + C\$10.19)/2 – C\$10.01] = C\$0.22.
The average effective spread is (C\$0.06 + C\$0.11 + C\$0.22)/3 = C\$0.13.

3. Explain the relative magnitudes of quoted and effective spreads for each of the three fund trades.

Solution:

The first trade received price improvement because the shares sold at a price above the bid price. Therefore, the effective spread is less than the quoted spread. No price improvement occurred for the second trade because the shares sold at the bid price. Also, the second trade had no price impact beyond trading at the bid; the entire order traded at the quoted bid. Accordingly, the effective and quoted spreads are equal. The effective spread for the third trade is greater than the quoted spread because the large order size, which was greater than the bid size, caused the order to walk down the limit order book. The average sale price was less than the bid so that the effective spread was higher than the quoted spread.

4. Calculate the VWAP for all 13,000 Alpha Company shares that traded that day and for the 10,000 shares sold by the mutual fund. Compute the VWAP transaction cost estimate for the 10,000 shares sold.

Solution:

The VWAP for the day is the total dollar volume divided by the total number of shares traded. The dollar volume is 2,000 shares × C\$10.15 + 3,000 shares × C\$10.11 + 5,000 shares × C\$10.01 + 2,000 shares × C\$10.20 + 1,000 shares at C\$10.15 = C\$131,230. Dividing this by the 13,000-share total volume gives a VWAP of C\$10.0946. A similar calculation using only the sales made by the mutual fund gives a trade VWAP of C\$10.0680. The VWAP transaction cost estimate for the sale is the difference multiplied by the 10,000

> shares sold: C$266.15 = 10,000 shares × (C$10.0946 − C$10.0680) [differences due to rounding].

DEVELOPMENT OF ELECTRONIC MARKETS

3

- ☐ describe factors driving the development of electronic trading systems
- ☐ describe market fragmentation

The application of new information technologies to trading processes produced radical changes in how investment managers trade. Automated trading systems and trading strategies replaced manual processes. New electronic exchanges, alternative trading systems, electronic traders, and securities dramatically changed trading in most markets. The resulting efficiencies generally improved market quality, but electronic trading also produced new regulatory concerns. High levels of fragmentation and electronification now characterize most global trading markets.

Electronic Trading

Trading at organized exchanges now depends critically on automated electronic systems used both by exchanges and by their trader clients. The exchanges use electronic systems to arrange trades by matching orders submitted by buyers with those submitted by sellers. Traders use electronic systems to generate the orders that the exchanges process. The most important electronic traders are dealers, arbitrageurs, and buy-side institutional traders who use algorithmic trading tools provided by their brokers to fill their large orders.

The two types of systems are co-dependent: Traders need high-speed order processing and communication systems to implement their electronic trading strategies, and the exchanges need electronic exchange systems to process the vast numbers of orders that these electronic traders produce. The adoption of electronic exchange systems led to huge growth in automated order creation and submission systems.

The widespread use of electronic trading systems significantly decreased trading costs for buy-side traders. Costs fell as exchanges obtained greater cost efficiencies from using electronic matching systems instead of floor-based, manual trading systems. These technologies also decreased costs and increased efficiencies for the dealers and arbitrageurs, who provide much of the liquidity offered at exchanges. Competition forced them to pass along many of the benefits of their new technologies to buy-side traders in the form of narrower spreads quoted for larger sizes. New electronic buy-side order management systems also decreased buy-side trading costs by allowing a smaller number of buy-side traders to process more orders and to process them more efficiently than manual traders.

Advantages of Electronic Trading Systems

Compared with floor-based trading systems, electronic order-matching systems enjoy many advantages:

- Most obviously, electronic systems are cheap to operate once built. Operating in server rooms, they require less physical space than trading floors. Also, in contrast to floor-based trading systems, electronic trading systems do not require exchange officials to record and report prices.

- Electronic exchange systems do exactly what they are programmed to do. When properly programmed, they precisely enforce the exchange's trading order precedence and pricing rules without error or exception.

- Electronic exchange systems can also keep perfect audit trails so that forensic investigators can determine the exact sequence and timing of events that may interest them.

- Electronic exchange systems that support hidden orders keep those orders perfectly hidden. Unlike floor brokers, they never inadvertently or fraudulently reveal their clients' hidden orders to others.

- In contrast to floor-based brokers and exchange officials, electronic order-matching systems can operate, for the most part, on a continuous, "around-the-clock" basis.

- Finally, electronic exchanges can operate when bad weather or other events would likely prevent workers from convening on a floor.

These efficiencies led to great growth. Electronic trading systems have largely displaced floor-based trading systems in all instruments for which order-driven markets are viable. Order-driven markets—markets in which orders submitted by traders are arranged based on a rules-based, order-matching system run by an exchange, a broker, or an alternative trading system (ATS)—are now organized by most exchanges and electronic communication networks (ECNs).

Additionally, computers have come to dominate the implementation of many trading strategies because they are so efficient and so unlike human traders:

- Computers have infinite attention spans and a very wide attention scope. They can continuously watch and respond to information from many instruments and many markets simultaneously and essentially forever.

- Their responses are extraordinarily fast.

- Computers are perfectly disciplined and do only what they are instructed (programmed) to do.

- Computers do not forget any information that their programmers want to save.

Electronification of Bond Markets

The electronic market structures of equity, futures, and options markets have attracted tremendous attention throughout the world. Much less attention has been given to the market structures of corporate and municipal bond markets, most of which, from the customer's point of view, have changed little since the late 19th century. Despite the efforts of many creative developers of electronic bond trading systems, most public investors in these markets still trade largely over the counter with dealers. The potential for electronic trading systems in these markets—and the attendant growth in electronic trading strategies—is quite large. Such systems undoubtedly will reflect the fact that

Development of Electronic Markets

bond issues—especially municipal bonds—vastly outnumber stock issues. Accordingly, except for the most actively traded bonds, limit order book trading systems will not be successful because buyers and sellers rarely will be present at the same time.

However, systems can be built that would allow public investors to trade with each other when both sides are present in the market. These systems would provide order display facilities, where public investors and proprietary traders could post limit orders so that all traders could see them. Like marketable orders, limit orders seek to obtain the best price immediately available; additionally, they instruct not to accept a price higher than a specified limit price when buying or a price lower than a specified limit price when selling. If these facilities also had automatic execution mechanisms and regulations or legal decisions to prevent dealers from trading through displayed orders when arranging their trades, bond transaction costs would drop substantially and bond trading would become much more active. Many such electronic bond order-matching systems already exist, but they primarily serve dealers and not public investors. Recent empirical research suggests that public investors would greatly benefit if their brokers provided them with direct access to these systems as they presently do in the equity markets. Instead, most broker/dealers commonly interpose themselves.

Market Fragmentation

Markets for many asset classes have become increasingly fragmented throughout the world because venues trading the same instruments have proliferated and trading in any given instrument now occurs in multiple venues. Available liquidity for an instrument on any one exchange now often represents just a small fraction of the aggregate liquidity for that instrument. **Market fragmentation**—trading the same instrument in multiple venues—increases the potential for price and liquidity disparities across venues because buyers and sellers often are not in the same venues at the same time.

For example, in the United States, order flow in exchange-listed equities is now divided among 11 exchanges, 40 alternative trading systems, and numerous dealers. In the late 20th century, however, trading mainly occurred on three primary exchanges, a few minor regional exchanges, and in the offices of some large institutional broker/dealers. Alternative trading systems (ATSs), also known as electronic communication networks (ECNs) or multilateral trading facilities (MTFs), are increasingly important trading venues. They function like exchanges but do not exercise regulatory authority over their subscribers except concerning the conduct of their trading in their trading systems.

With increasing market fragmentation, traders filling large orders now adapt their trading strategies to search for liquidity across multiple venues and across time to control the market impacts of their trades. Electronic algorithmic trading techniques, such as liquidity aggregation and smart order routing, help traders manage the challenges and opportunities presented by fragmentation. Liquidity aggregators create "super books" that present liquidity across markets for a given instrument. These tools offer global views of market depth (available liquidity) for each instrument regardless of which trading venue offers the liquidity. For example, the best bid, or highest price a buyer is willing to pay, for a Eurodollar future may be on the Chicago Mercantile Exchange (CME) and the second best on ELX Markets, a fully electronic futures exchange. Smart order-routing algorithms send orders to the markets that display the best-quoted prices and sizes.

Effects on Transaction Costs

Numerous studies show that transaction costs declined with the growth of electronic trading over time. Some studies also show that at a given point in time, lower transaction costs are found in those markets with the greatest intensity of electronic trading. These time-series and cross-sectional results are not surprising. They result from the greater cost efficiencies associated with electronic trading.

With the growth of electronic trading, bid–ask spreads decreased substantially. These decreases lowered transaction costs for retail traders and institutions trading small orders.

Overall transaction costs also decreased for large orders, many of which are now broken into smaller parts for execution. A study of the execution costs of tens of thousands of equity orders for US stocks involving tens of millions of dollars of principal value shows that the implementation shortfall cost of filling those orders dropped with the growth of electronic trading. This evidence suggests that any profits obtained by parasitic traders from front running orders are smaller than the cost savings obtained by buy-side traders from trading in electronic markets using algorithms.

4   TYPES OF ELECTRONIC TRADERS

☐ | identify and contrast the types of electronic traders

The proliferation of electronic exchange trading systems has led to the adoption of electronic trading by proprietary traders, buy-side traders, and the electronic brokers that serve them. Proprietary traders include dealers, arbitrageurs, and various types of front runners—all of whom are profit-motivated traders. In contrast, buy-side traders trade to fill orders for investment and risk managers who use the markets to establish positions from which they derive various utilitarian and profit-motivated benefits. Electronic brokers serve both types of traders.

Electronic traders differ in how they send orders to markets. Those proprietary traders who are registered as broker/dealers usually send their orders directly to exchanges. Those who are not broker/dealers must send their orders to brokers, who then forward them to exchanges. These brokers are said to provide sponsored access to their proprietary electronic trader clients. Brokers who provide sponsored access have very fast electronic order processing systems that allow them to forward orders to exchanges as quickly as possible while still undertaking the regulatory functions necessary to protect the markets and themselves from various financial and operational risks associated with brokering orders for proprietary electronic traders.

Electronic trading strategies are most profitable or effective when they can act on new information quickly. Accordingly, proprietary traders and electronic brokers build automated trading systems that are extremely fast. These systems often can receive information of interest to the trader, process it, and place a trading instruction at an exchange in less than a few milliseconds—and sometimes much faster.

The events that interest electronic traders include:

- trade reports and quote changes in the securities or contracts that they trade;
- similar data for instruments that are correlated with the securities or contracts that they trade;

Types of Electronic Traders

- indexes that summarize these data across markets and for various instrument classes;

- changes in limit order books; and

- news releases from companies, governments, and other producers and aggregators of information.

Electronic traders typically receive information about these events via high-speed electronic data feeds. Not all electronic traders analyze all these different information sources, but many do.

Electronic proprietary traders include high-frequency traders and low-latency traders. High-frequency and low-latency (i.e., extremely fast) traders must often trade very quickly in response to new information to be profitable. They are distinguished by how often they trade.

High-frequency traders (HFTs) generally complete round trips composed of a purchase followed by a sale (or a sale followed by a purchase) within a minute and often as quickly as a few milliseconds. During a day, they may trade in and out of an actively traded security or contract more than a thousand times—but usually only in small sizes.

Low-latency traders include news traders who trade on electronic news feeds and certain parasitic traders. Parasitic traders are speculators who base their predictions about future prices on information they obtain about orders that other traders intend, or will soon intend, to fill. Parasitic traders include front runners, who trade in front of traders who demand liquidity, and quote matchers, who trade in front of traders who supply liquidity. When trying to open or close positions, low-latency traders often need to send or cancel orders very quickly in response to new information. In contrast to HFTs, low-latency traders may hold their positions for as long as a day and sometimes longer.

The distinction between HFTs and low-latency traders is relatively new. Many commentators do not make any distinction, calling all electronic traders who need to trade quickly HFTs.

The Major Types of Electronic Traders

Electronic news traders subscribe to high-speed electronic news feeds that report news releases made by corporations, governments, and other aggregators of information. They then quickly analyze these releases to determine whether the information they contain will move the markets and, if so, in which direction. They trade on this information by sending marketable orders—instructions to fill the order at the best available price—to wherever they expect they may be filled. News traders profit when they can execute against stale orders—orders that do not yet reflect the new information.

For example, stock prices usually rise when a company announces earnings of 25 pence a share when the consensus forecast is only 10 pence. Electronic news traders who receive the initial press release will use their computers to parse the text of the release to find the earnings number. The computers then will compare that number with the consensus forecast, which they have stored in their memory rather than on disk to reduce access time. If the 15 pence difference is sufficiently large, news traders may send one or more marketable buy orders to exchanges for execution. News traders must be very quick to ensure that they get to the market before others do. If they are too late, the price may have changed already or liquidity suppliers may have canceled their quotes.

Some news traders also process news releases that do not contain quantitative data. Using natural language-processing techniques, they try to identify the importance of the information for market valuations. For example, a report stating that "our main pesticide plant shut down because of the accidental release of poisonous chemicals" might be marked as having strong negative implications for values. Electronic news traders would sell on this information. If they are correct, the market will drop as other, slower traders read, interpret, and act on the information. If they are wrong, the market will not react to the information. In that case, news traders will reverse their position and lose the transaction costs associated with their round-trip trades. (Note that these transaction costs could be high if many news traders made the same wrong inference.) Because round-trip transaction costs usually are lower than the profits that electronic news traders can occasionally make when significant news arrives, news traders often may trade with the expectation of being right only occasionally.

Electronic dealers, like all dealers, make markets by placing bids (prices at which they are willing to buy) and offers (prices at which they are willing to sell) with the expectation that they can profit from round trips at favorable net spreads. Those who trade at the highest frequencies tend to be very wary. On the first indication that prices may move against their inventory positions (i.e., price decreases if they are long or own the asset; price increases if they are short or sold an asset they do not own), they immediately take liquidity by executing on the opposite side to reduce their exposure. They generally will not hold large inventory positions in actively traded stocks. As soon as they reach their inventory limit on one side of the market or the other, they cease bidding or offering on that side. Electronic dealers often monitor electronic news feeds. They may immediately cancel all their orders in any security mentioned in a news report. If the news is material, they do not want to offer liquidity to news traders to whom they would lose. If the news is immaterial, they merely lose whatever opportunity to trade may have come their way while out of the market.

Electronic dealers, like all other dealers, also keep track of scheduled news releases. They cancel their orders just before releases to avoid offering liquidity to traders who can act faster than they can. They also may try to reduce their inventories before a scheduled release to avoid holding a risky position.

Electronic arbitrageurs look across markets for arbitrage opportunities in which they can buy an undervalued instrument and sell a similar overvalued one. The combination of these two positions is called an arbitrage portfolio, and the positions are called legs. Electronic arbitrageurs try to construct their arbitrage portfolios at minimum cost and risk.

Electronic front runners are low-latency traders who use artificial intelligence methods to identify when large traders, or many small traders, are trying to fill orders on the same side of the market. They will purchase when they believe that an imbalance of buy orders over sell orders will push the market up and sell when they believe the opposite. Their order anticipation strategies try to identify predictable patterns in order submission. They may search for patterns in order submissions, trades, or the relations between trades and other events.

In most jurisdictions, dealers and brokers cannot legally front run orders that their clients have submitted. These orders include large orders that they know their clients are breaking up to fill in small pieces. But dealers and brokers can study records of their clients' past orders to identify patterns in their behavior that would allow them to predict orders not yet submitted.

Some front runners also look for patterns in executed trades. For example, suppose that a trader sees that trades of a given size have been occurring at the offer every 10 minutes for an hour. If the trader has seen this pattern of trading before, the trader may suspect that the activity will continue. If so, the trader may buy on the assumption that a trader is in the market filling a large buy order by breaking it into smaller pieces.

Buy-side traders, and the brokers who provide them with algorithms to manage large orders, are aware of the efforts that electronic traders make to detect and front run their orders. Accordingly, they randomize their strategies to make them more difficult to detect. They submit orders at random times instead of at regular intervals, and they submit various sizes instead of the same size. Although these techniques make detection more difficult, hiding large, liquidity-demanding trades is always challenging because sophisticated traders can ultimately identify them by the inevitable relation between prices and volumes that they create. Electronic front runners look for these patterns, often using very advanced, automated data-mining tools.

Finally, some front runners examine the relation between trades and other events to predict future trades. Traders who identify these events quickly may be able to profit by buying ahead of retail or institutional traders. Because many traders initiate trades in response to common stimuli or in response to predictable situations, traders who can identify patterns in the relations between trades and events may profit from trading ahead. When the time between the stimulus and the response is short, electronic traders have a clear advantage.

Electronic quote matchers try to exploit the option values of standing orders. Standing orders are limit orders waiting to be filled. Options to trade are valuable to quote matchers because they allow them to take positions with potentially limited losses. Quote matchers buy when they believe they can rely on standing buy orders to get out of their positions, and they sell when they can do the same with standing sell orders. Traders say that quote matchers lean on these orders. If prices then move in the quote matchers' favor, they profit for as long as they stay in the security or contract. But if the quote matchers conclude that prices are moving against them, they immediately try to exit by trading with the standing orders and thereby limiting their losses.

For example, a fast quote matcher may buy when a slow trader is bidding at 20. If the price subsequently rises, the quote matcher will profit. If the quote matcher believes that the price will fall, the quote matcher will sell the position to the buyer at 20 and thereby limit his losses. The main risk of the quote-matching strategy is that the standing order may be unavailable when the quote matcher needs it. Standing orders disappear when filled by another trader or when canceled.

Most large buy-side traders use electronic order management systems (OMSs) to manage their trading. These systems keep track of the orders that their portfolio managers want to be filled, which orders have been sent out to be filled, and which fills have been obtained. Buy-side OMSs generally allow the buy-side trader to route orders to brokers for further handling, along with instructions for how the orders should be handled. These entities may include exchanges, brokers, dealers, and various alternative trading systems. The OMSs typically have dashboards that allow the buy-side trader to see summaries of all activity of interest so that the trader can better manage the trading process. Finally, the OMSs help the buy-side traders report and confirm the trades to all interested parties.

Buy-side traders often employ electronic brokers to arrange their trades. In addition to supporting standard order instructions, such as limit or market orders, these brokers often provide a full suite of advanced orders, trading tactics, and algorithms. The broker's electronic trading system generally manages these advanced orders, tactics, and algorithms, but in some cases, exchange computers may perform these functions.

ELECTRONIC TRADING SYSTEM: CHARACTERISTICS AND USES

5

☐ | describe characteristics and uses of electronic trading systems

☐ | describe comparative advantages of low-latency traders

Traders value speed because it allows them to act before other traders can act. This section identifies the three situations where speed is valuable, how exchanges and traders build and use fast trading systems, and some select examples of how electronic trading changed trading strategies.

Why Speed Matters

Electronic traders must be fast to trade effectively, regardless of whether they are proprietary traders or buy-side traders. Electronic traders have three needs for speed:

1. **Taking**. Electronic traders sometimes want to take a trading opportunity before others do. A new trading opportunity may attract many traders, and an existing trading opportunity may attract many traders when market events cause it to become more valuable (e.g., a standing limit order to sell becomes much more attractive when the prices of correlated securities rise). Often only the first trader to reach the attractive opportunity will benefit. Thus, electronic traders must be fast so they can beat other traders to attractive trading opportunities.

2. **Making**. Market events often create attractive opportunities to offer liquidity. For example, at most exchanges when prices rise, the first traders to place bids at improved prices acquire time precedence at those prices that may allow them to trade sooner or at better prices than they otherwise would be able to trade. Therefore, electronic traders must be fast so they can acquire priority when they want it and before other traders do.

3. **Canceling**. Frequently, traders must quickly cancel orders they no longer want to fill, often because market events have increased the option values of those orders. For example, if traders have limit buy orders standing at the best bid and large trades take place at other exchanges at the same price, these traders may reasonably conclude that prices may drop and that they may obtain better executions at a lower price. They must cancel their orders as quickly as possible to reduce the probability that they will trade.

Note that electronic traders do not simply need to be fast to trade effectively: They must be faster than their competitors. Little inherent value comes from being fast; the value lies in being faster. The reason electronic trading systems have such low latencies (i.e., are extremely fast) is because electronic traders have been trying for years to be faster than their competitors.

Electronic order-handling systems used by exchanges also have grown faster as exchanges compete for order flows from electronic traders. Electronic traders often will not send orders to exchanges where they cannot quickly cancel them, especially if other exchanges have faster trading systems. Accordingly, exchanges with slow order-handling systems have lost market share.

Latency is the elapsed time between the occurrence of an event and a subsequent action that depends on that event. For example, the event might be a trade at one exchange, and the action might be the receipt by another exchange of an instruction to cancel a standing order that a trader has sent upon learning of the trade. Electronic traders measure these latencies in milliseconds or microseconds (millionths of a second).

The latency of a linear multi-step process is the sum of the latencies of each step in the process. The submission of an order instruction by a trader in response to an event consists of three major steps, each of which involves many smaller steps beyond the scope of this discussion:

1. The trader must learn that the event took place.

Electronic Trading System: Characteristics and Uses

2. The trader must respond to the new information with a new order instruction.

3. The trader must send, and the exchange must receive, the new instruction.

Traders must use very fast communication systems to minimize the latencies associated with steps 1 and 3 (communicating in and out), and they must use very fast computer systems to minimize the latency associated with step 2 (responding).

Fast Communications

Electronic traders and brokers use several strategies to minimize their communication times. These strategies involve minimizing communication distances and maximizing line speeds. Note that the relevant measure of communication distance is the total of two distances that signals must travel. The first distance is from where the event is reported (often an exchange but sometimes another type of news source) to the computer that will process the information. The second distance is from the computer to the exchange trading system where the trader wants to deliver an order instruction.

Electronic traders and brokers locate their computers as close as possible to the exchanges at which they trade to minimize latencies resulting from physics: No message can travel faster than the speed of light. At 300,000 kilometers (186,000 miles) per second in a vacuum, light travels 300 kilometers in a millisecond. Although the speed of light is incredibly fast, a fast computer with a clock speed of 5 GHz (billion cycles per second) can do 5 million operations in a millisecond—which often is more than required to receive information, process it, and send out an order instruction in response.

Communication latencies are particularly important when messages must travel significant distances. For example, the great circle (shortest) distances between Chicago and New York and between New York and London are, respectively, 1,146 kilometers and 5,576 kilometers. Thus, round-trip communications between these two pairs of cities have minimum latencies of approximately 8 and 37 milliseconds simply because of the speed of light. (The actual minimum latencies are longer because the speed of light in standard optical fiber is 31% slower than the speed of light in a vacuum.) Such delays illustrate that no electronic trader located at any significant distance from where information is created or must be delivered can effectively compete with traders who have minimized these combined distances.

Many exchanges allow electronic traders to place their servers in the rooms where the exchange servers operate, a practice called collocation. Exchanges charge substantial fees for collocation space and related services, such as air conditioning and power. Note that even within collocation centers, concerns about fairness dictate that the communication lines connecting proprietary servers to exchange servers all be of the same length for all customers buying the same class of collocation service.

Electronic traders and brokers also use the fastest communication technologies they can obtain to collect and transmit information when any distance separates the places where information events occur from the places where they act on those events. To that end, they use the fastest and most direct communication lines that are available. For example, they prefer line-of-sight microwave channels to fiber-optic and copper channels because of the differences in speed of electromagnetic wave propagation through these materials. (Microwaves travel through air at just slightly below the speed of light, whereas signals travel through fiber-optic channels and copper wires only two-thirds as quickly.) They also ensure that their communications pass through the fewest electronic routers and switches possible because passage through each of these devices adds its latency to the total latency of the line.

Finally, electronic traders and brokers subscribe to special high-speed data feeds directly from exchanges and other data vendors. The vendors charge premium prices for these services, which are delivered over very high-speed communication lines. Some exchanges provide multiple classes of data services that vary by speed to price-discriminate among their clients.

Fast Computations

Once electronic traders receive information about an event of interest, they must decide whether to act on that information and how. Those traders who can make decisions faster than their competitors will trade more profitably. Electronic traders minimize the latencies associated with their decision making by using several strategies.

First and most obviously, they use very fast computers. They overclock their processors (i.e., run them faster than the processor designers intended) and use liquid cooling systems to keep them from melting. They store all information in fast memory to avoid the latencies associated with physical disk drives, which cannot deliver information while their heads are seeking the right track and can only deliver information as fast as their disks spin once the right track is found. They sometimes use specialized processors designed to solve their specific trading problems quickly, and they may even use processors etched on gallium arsenide rather than silicon.

Electronic traders also must run very efficient software. They often use simple and specialized operating systems to avoid the overhead associated with supporting operating system functions they do not use. Remarkably, many electronic trading systems run under variants of the original MS-DOS operating system because of its simplicity.

Electronic traders optimize their computer code for speed. They often write important functions that they repeatedly use in assembler language to ensure that they run quickly. (Code written in high-level languages, such as C++, tends to be slower because their compilers are designed to handle all types of code, not just code written to solve trading problems.) And they avoid using such languages as Python because they are interpreter languages that compile (create executable machine code) as they run, rather than compiling only once when first written.

Some electronic trading problems change so frequently that speed of coding is more important than speed of execution. For example, some problems depend on ever-changing sets of conditions or exceptions that present or constrain profit opportunities. For such problems, traders use high-level languages (e.g., Python), because they can code faster and more accurately in these languages than in lower-level languages, such as C++. If they expect that the software will remain useful, they may later recode their routines in other languages to make them run faster.

Some electronic traders also reduce latency by creating contingency tables that contain prearranged action plans. For example, suppose that a bid rises in a market in which electronic traders are active. In response to the increased bid, traders may want to raise their bids or offers. The decision to do so may depend on their inventory positions and perhaps on many other factors as well. To decide what to do following an increased bid may require substantial analyses, which take time. Traders can reduce their decision latencies by doing these analyses before the bid increases instead of afterward. Seeing the increased bid, they can respond by simply looking up the optimal response in a contingency table stored in memory. To be most useful, the contingency tables must be kept up to date and must include responses for most-likely events. In this example, traders presumably would also have precomputed responses for a decrease in the bid, among many other contingencies.

EXAMPLE 2

Latency

1. Explain why low-latency is important to electronic traders.

Solution:

Electronic traders need a comparative speed advantage to 1) take advantage of market opportunities before others do, 2) receive time precedence that would allow them to trade sooner when offering liquidity to others, and 3) ensure order cancellation when they no longer want to fill the order. To gain a comparative advantage relative to others, electronic traders try to minimize latency—the time between an event occurring and a subsequent action, typically the submission of an order instruction, based upon that event. To minimize latency, electronic traders invest in very fast communication systems and very fast computer systems.

Advanced Orders, Tactics, and Algorithms

Buy-side traders often use electronic brokers and their systems for advanced orders, trading tactics, and algorithms provided by their electronic brokers to search for liquidity.

Advanced order types.

Advanced orders generally are limit orders with limit prices that change as market conditions change. An example would be a pegged limit order for which the trader would like to maintain a bid or an offer at a specified distance relative to some benchmark. Suppose that a trader wants to peg a limit buy order two ticks below the current ask. A broker who supports this instruction may forward it to an exchange that supports the instruction if the probability of the order's filling at that exchange is favorable compared with other exchanges. When the ask rises or falls, the exchange system will immediately cancel the order and replace it with a new limit order to keep the order at two ticks below the current ask. If the exchange does not support this instruction, the broker's computer will manage the order by submitting a limit order priced two ticks below the current ask and adjusting it as necessary to maintain the peg when the market moves. Effective management of a pegged limit order requires an electronic trading system with very low latency. If the order is not adjusted quickly enough, it risks being executed at an unfavorable price (in this example, if prices drop) or being resubmitted after other orders have been placed at the new price so the probability of execution at that price will be lower (if prices rise). Traders sometimes call pegged limit orders floating limit orders.

Trading tactics.

A trading tactic is a plan for executing a simple function that generally involves the submission of multiple orders. Note that the distinction between advanced orders and tactics can be arbitrary, and not all traders will use the same language to describe various trading functions. An example of a trading tactic is an instruction to sweep through every market at a given price to find hidden trading opportunities.

Suppose that the best exposed bid among all trading venues is 20.00 and the best exposed offer is 20.02. Because many trading systems permit traders to hide their orders, hidden buyers or sellers may be willing to trade at the 20.01 midpoint.

Depending on the exchange, at least three types of orders could permit a trade at the midpoint. First, among exchanges that permit hidden orders, one or more exchanges may be holding a hidden limit order at 20.01. Second, among exchanges that permit discretionary limit orders, one or more exchanges may be holding a discretionary limit order that can be filled at the midpoint. For example, suppose that an exchange is holding a limit order to buy at 19.99 with 0.02 discretion. This order can be filled at 20.01 if a suitable sell limit order arrives at that price. Finally, among exchanges and dark pools that permit midspread orders, one or more exchanges or dark pools may be holding such an order. Dark pools are trading venues that do not publish their liquidity and are only available to selected clients. A midspread order is a limit order that is pegged to the midpoint of the quoted bid–ask spread.

To find such hidden liquidity, an electronic trading system may submit an immediate or cancel (IOC) order priced at 20.01 to the exchange that the trader expects will most likely have hidden liquidity on the needed side of the market. If such liquidity exists, the order will execute up to the minimum of the sizes of the two orders. If not, the exchange will immediately cancel the order and report the cancellation. If the order has any remaining unfilled size, the electronic trading system will search for liquidity at another exchange. This process will continue until the order is filled or until the trader decides that further search is probably futile. This sweeping tactic is most effective when the electronic trading system managing it has very low latency. A slow system may lose an opportunity to trade if someone else takes it first. Also, a slow system that obtains one or more partial fills may lose opportunities to trade at other exchanges if the proprietary electronic trading systems managing the standing orders that provide those opportunities cancel their standing orders when they suspect someone is sweeping the market, as they might if they see trade reports inside the quoted spread.

An example of another trading tactic is placing a limit order at some price with the hope that it will fill at that price. If the order does not fill after some time period (which might be random or based on information), the electronic trading system will cancel the order and resubmit it with an improved price (i.e., a higher price for a buy order or a lower price for a sell order). The process is repeated until the order fills.

Algorithms.

Algorithms ("algos" for short) are programmed strategies for filling orders. Algorithms may use combinations or sequences of simple orders, advanced orders, or multiple orders to achieve their objectives. Buy-side traders use algorithms, often provided by brokers, extensively to trade small orders and to reduce the price impacts of large trades. For example, many algorithms break up large orders and submit the pieces to various markets over time. Breaking up orders makes it difficult for other traders to infer that a trader is trying to fill a large order. The algorithms typically submit the orders at random times, in random sizes, and sometimes to randomly selected exchanges to hide their common origin.

The rates at which algorithms try to fill large orders may depend on market volumes or on elapsed time. For example, VWAP algorithms attempt to obtain a volume-weighted average fill price that is close to (or better than) the volume-weighted average price (VWAP) of all trades arranged within a prespecified time interval. To minimize the variation between the actual average fill price and the VWAP over the interval, these algorithms try to participate in an equal fraction of all trading volume throughout the interval. To do so, they forecast volumes based on the historical volume profile and on current volumes. The algorithm trades more during periods of historically high volume (e.g., around market open and close) and when the market has been more active than normal. It trades less during periods of relatively low volume. In practice, the execution rate will vary because volumes will differ from expectations. Buy-side traders use VWAP algorithms when spreading the order over time and when obtaining the average market price within an interval is acceptable to them or their portfolio managers.

Many algorithms use floating limit orders with the hope of obtaining cheap executions. If they fail to fill after some time period, they may switch to more-aggressively priced orders or to marketable orders to ensure that they fill. Large traders who use algorithms to manage their orders are especially concerned about hiding their intentions from front runners. Many electronic traders use artificial intelligence systems to detect when large traders are present in the market. In particular, they look for patterns that large traders may leave. For example, a poorly designed algorithm may submit orders exactly at the same millisecond within a second whenever it submits an order. A clever trader who is aware of this regularity may detect when a large trader is in the market and, equally important, when the trader has completed filling his order. To avoid these problems, algorithm designers often randomize order submission times and sizes to avoid producing patterns that might give them away. They also sometimes try to hide their orders among other orders so that front runners cannot easily identify their intentions.

Developing good algorithms requires extensive research into the origins of transaction costs. Algorithm authors must understand transaction costs well so that they can design algorithms that will trade effectively. To that end, algorithm providers build and estimate models of the costs of trading orders of various sizes, models of the impact trades of a given size or frequency will have on prices, and models of the probabilities that limit orders will fill under a variety of conditions. They must also predict volumes accurately. The most effective algorithms are based on the best research and implemented on the fastest and most capable electronic systems.

Good algorithms generally obtain low-cost executions by knowing when and where to offer liquidity via limit orders, when to use market orders, and how to most effectively keep the market from being aware of their efforts. They reduce the price impacts of large trades and greatly reduce the costs of managing many small trades.

EXAMPLE 3

Use of Electronic Brokers

1. You have recently been hired recently as a junior buy-side analyst. Part of your training (on-boarding) has been to sit with the trading desk to learn how the desk trades through its electronic brokers. In a meeting with your manager, she asks you to explain the use of electronic brokers for advanced orders, trading tactics, and algorithmic trading tools that your electronic brokers provide. What would you say?

Solution:

The use of electronic brokers and their systems is valuable for such advanced order types as pegged or floating limit orders, whose limit prices change as market conditions change. Traders use these order types to supply liquidity at a specified distance from the market. These orders require continuous real-time evaluation to determine if an order cancellation or replacement is needed as market conditions change. The use of electronic brokers relieves the need for the trader to continuously monitor the market to cancel and resubmit orders when prices change. An electronic broker is also valuable for orders placed a few ticks outside the best market that will be among the last orders to supply liquidity to a large trader, hopefully at a good price.

Electronic brokers also allow their clients to access order execution tactics (presented as another complex order type) that involve multiple submissions that may "sweep" through markets to uncover hidden liquidity. These tactics allow traders to submit multiple orders with a single instruction.

Finally, electronic brokers also provide algorithmic trading tools. Algorithms are automated (programmed trading strategies for combinations of simple and single, advanced, or multiple orders and various trading tactics) to fill small orders efficiently based on various criteria. They often break up large orders into smaller pieces to minimize the market impact of filling the order. They may route the orders to multiple venues at the same time or to the same venue at various times. For example, VWAP algorithms attempt to fill orders at the volume-weighted average price (or better) of all trades over a specified interval. The systems running algorithms that place standing limit orders must be very fast to cancel orders in trading. In these cases, low latency is critical to ensure order cancellation before unfavorable executions occur. Fast systems also help ensure that traders are first to respond when market conditions change and to maintain time precedence.

Select Examples of How Electronic Trading Changed Trading Strategies

The growth in electronic trading systems changed how traders interact with the market. Proprietary traders, buy-side traders, and brokers adapted their trading strategies to use new electronic tools and facilities. Select characteristics of electronic trading are described below.

Hidden orders.

Hidden orders are very common in electronic markets. Hidden orders are orders that are exposed (or shown) only to the brokers or exchanges who receive them. Traders—especially large traders—submit them when they do not want to reveal the existence of the trading options that their standing orders provide to the markets. Traders concerned about quote matchers can protect themselves to some extent by submitting hidden limit orders. Note that hidden limit orders are the electronic equivalent of giving orders to floor brokers to fill with the understanding that the floor brokers may expose the orders only if they can arrange trades. Such orders work better at electronic exchanges than at floor-based exchanges because computers never inadvertently or intentionally display these orders improperly. In electronic markets, the most common type of order by far is the immediate or cancel (IOC) limit order. Traders use these orders to discover hidden orders that may stand in the spread between a market's quoted bid and ask prices. Because they cancel immediately if they do not find liquidity, these orders are also hidden and thus do not reveal trade intentions.

Some electronic traders try to discover hidden orders by pinging the market: They submit a small IOC limit order for only a few shares at the price at which they are looking for hidden orders. If the pinging order trades, they know that a hidden order is present at that price; however, they do not know the full size of the order (which they can discover only by trading with it). Traders then may use this information to adjust their trading strategies.

Electronic Trading System: Characteristics and Uses

All traders who subscribe to a complete trade feed that includes odd-lot transactions (substandard transaction sizes) can see the results of a ping that discovers liquidity. At almost all exchanges, however, only the pinger will know on which side of the market the hidden liquidity lies. Nonetheless, the information produced by someone else's successful ping can be useful to various traders. It indicates that someone in the market is concerned enough about liquidity conditions that pinging is worthwhile and that hidden liquidity is available on one side of the market.

Leapfrog.
When bid–ask spreads are wide, dealers often are willing to trade at better prices than they quote. They quote wide spreads because they hope to trade at more favorable prices. When another trader quotes a better price, dealers often immediately quote an even better price. For example, if the market is 20 bid, offered at 28, and a buy-side trader bids at 21, a dealer might instantly bid at 22. (The improved price might also come from a quote matcher.) This behavior frustrates buy-side traders, who then must quote a better price to maintain order precedence. If the spread is sufficiently wide, a game of leapfrog may ensue as the dealer jumps ahead again.

Flickering quotes.
Electronic markets often have flickering quotes, which are exposed limit orders that electronic traders submit and then cancel shortly thereafter, often within a second. Electronic dealers and algorithmic buy-side traders submit and repeatedly cancel and resubmit their orders when they do not want their orders to stand in the market; rather, they want other traders to see that they are willing to trade at the displayed price. Traders who wish to trade with a flickering quote can place a hidden limit order at the price where the quote is flickering. If the flickering order returns, it will hit their hidden limit order, and then they will trade with it.

Electronic arbitrage.
Electronic arbitrageurs use electronic trading systems to implement three types of arbitrage trading strategies:

1. **Take liquidity on both sides**. The costliest and least risky arbitrage trading strategy involves using marketable orders to fill both legs, or positions (i.e., buying an undervalued instrument and selling a similar overvalued instrument), of the arbitrage portfolio. This strategy is profitable only if the arbitrage spread is sufficiently large, but competition among arbitrageurs ensures that such large arbitrage spreads are quite rare. Arbitrageurs can seldom simultaneously take liquidity in two markets for identical instruments and make a profit. To effectively execute this strategy, arbitrageurs must use very fast trading systems so that they can lock in the arbitrage spread before prices in one or both markets change.

2. **Offer liquidity on one side**. In this strategy, arbitrageurs offer liquidity in one or both markets in which they trade. When they obtain a fill in one market, they immediately take liquidity in the other market to complete the construction of their arbitrage portfolio. This strategy produces lower-cost executions, but it is a bit riskier than the first strategy.

   For example, suppose that Markets A and B are both quoting 20 bid, offered at 21 for the same instrument. An arbitrageur may place a bid at 19 in Market A with the hope that a large seller will come along who takes all liquidity at 20 (i.e., fills all bids at 20) in Market A and then proceeds to fill the arbitrageur's order at 19. If so, the arbitrageur will immediately try to sell to the 20 bid in Market B. If the arbitrageur is quick enough, he may be able to fill his order before the bidder at 20 in Market B cancels that bid and before any other trader—particularly the large trader—takes it. If successful, the arbitrageur realizes a profit of 1. Of course, the arbitrageur will immediately cancel his 19 bid in Market A if the 20 bid in Market B disappears.

3. **Offer liquidity on both sides.** The final arbitrage strategy involves offering liquidity in both markets. In this strategy, after the first order to execute fills, the arbitrageur continues to offer liquidity to complete the second trade. This strategy is the riskiest strategy because arbitrageurs are exposed to substantial price risk when one leg is filled and the other is not. Moreover, if prices are moving because well-informed traders are on the same side in both markets—as they might be if the well-informed traders possess information about common risk factors—the leg providing liquidity to the informed traders will fill quickly, whereas the other leg probably will not fill.

Arbitrageurs using this strategy trade much like dealers—switching from offering (supplying) liquidity to taking (demanding) liquidity when they believe that offering liquidity may be too risky. They may also often cancel and resubmit their orders when market conditions change. Thus, they are most effective when they use fast trading systems.

When the arbitrage spread reverts, as the arbitrageurs expect, the arbitrageurs will reverse their trades, often using the same strategy they used to acquire their arbitrage portfolios. Of course, if the spread never reverts, arbitrageurs will lose regardless of how they trade. They will lose less, however, if they can trade their arbitrage portfolio by offering liquidity in one or both legs.

Machine learning.

Machine learning, also known as data mining, uses advanced statistical methods to characterize data structures, particularly relations among variables. These methods include neural nets, genetic algorithms, classifiers, and other methods designed to explain variables of interest using sparse data or data for which the number of potential explanatory variables far exceeds the number of observations.

Machine-learning methods produce models based on observed empirical regularities rather than on theoretical principles identified by analysts. These methods can be powerful when stable processes generate vast amounts of data, such as occurs in active financial markets.

Many trading problems are ideally suited for machine-learning analyses because the problems repeat regularly and often. For such problems, machine-based learning systems can be extraordinarily powerful.

However, these systems are often useless—or worse—when trading becomes extraordinary (e.g., when volatilities shoot up). Machine-learning systems frequently do not produce useful information during volatility episodes because these episodes have few precedents from which the machines can learn. Thus, traders often instruct their electronic trading systems to stop trading—and sometimes to close out their positions—whenever they recognize that they are entering uncharted territory. Many traders shut down when volatility spikes, both because high-volatility episodes are uncommon and thus not well understood and because even if such episodes were well understood, they represent periods of exceptionally high risk.

ELECTRONIC TRADING RISKS

6

☐ | describe the risks associated with electronic trading and how regulators mitigate them

The advent of electronic trading affected securities markets in many ways. Investors now benefit from greater trade process efficiencies and reduced transaction costs, but electronic trading also creates new systemic risks for market participants.

The HFT Arms Race

The competition among high-frequency traders (HFTs) has created an "arms race" in which each trader tries to be faster than the next. Consequently, the state-of-the-art, high-frequency trading technologies necessary to compete successfully are now very expensive, making entry quite costly. These costs form barriers to entry that can create natural monopolies. Although substantial evidence suggests that electronic trading benefits the markets, these benefits may erode if only a few HFTs survive and can exploit their unique positions. Already, many HFTs are quitting the markets because they cannot compete effectively.

More generally, many commentators have observed that most of the costly technologies that high-frequency traders acquire do little to promote better or more-liquid markets. HFTs primarily incur these costs so they can beat their competitors. The utilitarian traders who demand liquidity ultimately pay these costs. Concerns about the costs of the HFT arms race have led to calls for changes in market structure that would diminish the advantages of being faster. Some commentators suggest that markets be slowed by running call markets once a second or more often instead of trading continuously. Others suggest that the order processing be delayed by random intervals to reduce the benefits of being fast and thus the incentives to invest in speed.

Systemic Risks of Electronic Trading

Electronic trading created new systemic risks that concern regulators and practitioners. A systemic risk is a risk that some failure will hurt more than just the entity responsible for the failure. Systemic risks are particularly problematic when the responsible entity is not required or is unable to compensate others for the costs its failure imposes on them. When people do not bear the full costs of their behaviors, they tend not to be as careful in avoiding damaging behaviors as they otherwise would be.

Systemic risks associated with fast trading may be caused by electronic exchange trading system failures or excessive orders submitted by electronic traders. Electronic exchange trading system failures occur when programmers make mistakes, exchange servers have insufficient capacity to handle traffic, or computer hardware or communication lines fail.

The 18 May 2012 Facebook IPO at NASDAQ is an example of a trading system failure caused by a programming error that unexpectedly high demands on capacity revealed. In this case, two software processes locked into an infinite loop as they took turns responding to each other.

Examples of systemic risks caused by excessive orders submitted by electronic traders include the following:

- *Runaway algorithms* produce streams of unintended orders that result from programming mistakes. The problems sometimes occur when programmers do not anticipate some contingency. The Knight Capital trading failure on

1 August 2012 may be the most extreme example of a runaway algorithm incident. Owing to a software programming mistake, Knight sent millions of orders to the markets over a 45-minute period when it intended only to fill 212 orders, some of which normally might have been broken up but none of which would have generated so many orders. These orders produced 4 million executions involving 397 stocks. Knight lost $400 million in the incident.

- *Fat finger errors* occur when a manual trader submits a larger order than intended. They are called fat finger errors because they sometimes occur when a trader hits the wrong key or hits a key more often than intended. These types of errors are not unique to electronic trading systems, but their consequences are often greater in electronic systems because of the speed at which they operate and because clerks often catch these errors in manual trading systems before they cause problems.

- *Overlarge orders* demand more liquidity than the market can provide. In these events, a trader—often inexperienced—will try to execute a marketable order that is too large for the market to handle without severely disrupting prices in the time given to fill the order. The 6 May 2010 Flash Crash occurred as a result of such an order. The crash was triggered when a large institutional trader tried to sell $4.1 billion in E-mini S&P 500 futures contracts using an algorithm over a short period. The algorithm was designed to participate in a fixed fraction of the market volume. When the initial trades depressed S&P 500 futures prices, trading volumes increased substantially as arbitrageurs and others started to trade. The increase in trading volumes caused the algorithm to increase the rate of its order submissions, which exacerbated the problem. The market reverted to its former levels after the Chicago Mercantile Exchange briefly halted trading in the E-mini S&P 500 futures contract, and the large order eventually was filled.

- *Malevolent order streams* are created deliberately to disrupt the markets. The perpetrators may be market manipulators; aggrieved employees, such as traders or software engineers; or terrorists. Traders conducting denial-of-service attacks designed to overwhelm their competitors' electronic trading systems with excessive quotes also may create malevolent order streams.

The solutions to the systemic risk problems associated with electronic trading systems are multifold:

- Most obviously, traders must test software thoroughly before using it in live trading. Exchanges often conduct mock trading sessions to allow developers to test their software.

- Rigorous market access controls must ensure that only those orders coming from approved sources enter electronic order-matching systems.

- Rigorous access controls on software developers must ensure that only authorized developers can change software. Best practice mandates that these controls also include the requirement that all software be read, understood, and vouched for by at least one developer besides its author.

- The electronic traders who generate orders and the electronic exchanges that receive orders must surveil their order flow in real time to ensure that it conforms to preset parameters that characterize its expected volume, size, and other characteristics. When the order flow is different than expected, automatic controls must shut it off immediately.

Electronic Trading Risks

- Brokers must surveil all client orders that clients introduce into electronic trading systems to ensure that their clients' trading is appropriate. Brokers must not allow their clients to enter orders directly into exchange trading systems—a process called sponsored naked access—because it would allow clients to avoid broker oversight.

- Some exchanges have adopted price limits and trade halts to stop trading when prices move too quickly. These rules stop trading when excess demands for liquidity occur. They also prevent the extreme price changes that can occur in electronic markets when market orders arrive and no liquidity is present. Most brokers now automatically convert market orders into marketable limit orders to ensure that they do not trade at unreasonable prices.

HISTORICAL EVENT: THE FLASH CRASH

The 6 May 2010 Flash Crash was the most notable market structure event in recent memory. During the crash, which started at about 2:42 p.m. ET, the E-mini S&P 500 futures contract dropped approximately 5% in 5 minutes and then recovered nearly fully in the next 10 minutes. The price volatility spilled from the equity futures market into the stock market, where some stocks traded down more than 99% or up more than 1,000%. In the immediate aftermath of the crash, regulators decided that more than 20,000 trades in more than 300 securities that occurred more than 60% away from earlier prices would be broken (canceled).

This extraordinary event raised many concerns about security market structure—in particular, how the adoption of electronic trading may have increased potential systemic risks. This subsection describes the events that led up to the crash, what happened during the crash, and the regulatory responses to the crash.

The Event and Its Causes

On Thursday, 6 May 2010, the stock market traded down throughout the day at an accelerating rate. By 2:30 p.m., it had lost about 4% from its previous close. Contemporaneous commentators attributed the fall to concerns about Greek sovereign debt and the implications of a Greek default for other markets. During the day, many traders who had been providing liquidity to the market were accumulating substantial long positions as people demanded to sell. As the day wore on, their willingness to continue to accumulate additional inventory decreased. Moreover, day traders, who do not normally carry inventory overnight, also were considering how and when they would sell their losing positions.

Presumably, in response to the European concerns and perhaps other concerns, portfolio managers at Waddell & Reed Financial Inc. (W&R) decided to reduce US equity exposure in their $27 billion Asset Strategy Fund by selling 75,000 June 2010 E-mini S&P 500 futures contracts with a nominal value of approximately $4.1 billion. They gave this order to their buy-side trader, who proceeded to fill it using an algorithm that split the order into small pieces for execution. Although the order was the largest single order submitted to the E-mini futures market that year, it was not without precedent. Two earlier orders in the previous year were of similar size or larger, one of which had been submitted by W&R. Those orders had been filled in more stable markets and over longer periods of time than W&R's 6 May order. The order started to execute at 2:32 p.m.

W&R's head trader, who normally would have handled such a large order, was out of the office that day. Instead, a less-senior trader in his office handled the order.

The trader set parameters on the algorithm to target an execution rate of 9% of the trading volume calculated over the previous minute without regard to price or time. This trading strategy was more aggressive than the one W&R had used to fill its large order from the previous year. The trader probably set an aggressive rate because he feared that the firm would obtain a worse execution if prices continued to fall. The more aggressive strategy contributed to the crash.

When the initial trades depressed S&P 500 futures prices, trading volumes increased substantially as arbitrageurs and others started to trade, many of them trading with each other as they normally did. The arbitrageurs bought the futures and sold equities and equity ETFs (exchange-traded funds), such as the SPDR S&P 500 Trust (ticker SPY). Some arbitrageurs also sold call option contracts and bought put option contracts. The increase in trading volumes caused the algorithm to increase the rate of its order submissions as it tried to keep up with its mandate to participate in 9% of the market volume. The increasing order submission rate exacerbated the problem.

Initially, high-frequency traders and other liquidity suppliers in the E-mini futures markets supplied liquidity to W&R's order and accumulated long positions. Between 2:41 p.m. and 2:44 p.m., these short-term traders sold these positions as the algorithm continued to pump more orders into the market. During this 4-minute period, the E-mini dropped 3%. By the end of this period, buy-side depth (total size of standing buy orders) in the E-mini contract dropped to only 1% of the average depth observed earlier in the day. The E-mini contract then dropped 1.7% in the next 15 seconds.

The arbitrage trades caused the equity markets to drop. In many securities— especially the ETFs—falling prices triggered stock loss market orders, which further depressed prices. The levered ETFs were particularly affected because their high volatilities make them popular with technical traders and retail traders, many of whom routinely place stop orders to protect their positions.

As the prices changed quickly, many traders who were providing liquidity in the futures and equity markets dropped out because they were unwilling to trade in the face of such extreme volatility. Many also had already accumulated large inventory positions from earlier in the day and did not want to buy more. Interestingly, researchers later discovered that the largest and most active high-frequency trading firms did not withdraw. Nonetheless, limit order books thinned out—especially on the buy side—as traders canceled standing orders and as sellers filled those buy orders still standing.

In some stocks, all standing buy orders were exhausted and trading stopped. In other stocks, all buy orders except those placed with a limit price of only a cent or two were exhausted. In these stocks, exchange trading systems blindly filled market sell orders at extraordinarily low prices. In a few other stocks, the withdrawal of liquidity suppliers from the market also removed essentially all liquidity from the sell side of the market. Some stocks then traded at prices as high as $100,000 when market buy orders were filled against sell orders placed at extraordinarily high prices.

The slide stopped at 2:45:28 p.m. when a Chicago Mercantile Exchange trading rule called Stop Logic Functionality caused the exchange's computers to halt trading briefly in the E-mini S&P 500 futures contract and to clear the limit order book of all standing limit orders. The rule is triggered when it becomes apparent that pending order executions would cause prices to jump too far. The futures contract dropped about 5% from when the algorithm started to trade at 2:32 p.m. to the market halt at 2:45 p.m. The algorithm sold about 35,000 contracts during this period.

When trading resumed 5 seconds later, the buy-side algorithm continued to trade, but many liquidity suppliers were now willing to provide liquidity. Prices rose quickly in orderly markets.

The episode largely ended when the big W&R order completed filling at around 2:51 p.m., about 20 minutes after it started. However, the market remained quite volatile during the remainder of the day as traders adjusted their positions and responded to the extreme volatility.

Following the crash, regulators broke all trades that had occurred more than 60% away from the previous close.

Implications for Traders

The Flash Crash provided three important lessons for observant traders:

- First, market orders are incompatible with electronic order-matching systems that do not curb trading when prices move too quickly. Had traders priced all their orders, no trades would have taken place at unreasonably high or low prices. Following the crash, many retail brokers adopted a policy of converting all customer market orders into marketable limit orders with limit prices set about 10% above the current ask for buy orders and 10% below the current bid for sell orders.

- Second, institutional traders using algorithms must be careful not to demand more liquidity than orderly markets can provide. Most buy-side investors probably immediately recognized that W&R lost a substantial amount of its clients' money owing to the extraordinarily high transaction costs associated with the trade. To obtain a crude estimate of this loss, assume that the algorithm traded all $4.1 billion of its order at a uniform rate throughout the 5% price reversal. The average market impact of the trade would have been 2.5%, which implies total transaction costs of about $100 million, or 0.37% of the $27 billion in assets of the W&R Asset Strategy Fund. Such significant losses attract attention. Within a week, many algorithm writers probably coded limits into their algorithms to help prevent them from being used irresponsibly.

- Finally, algorithm writers and the traders who use algorithms must pay much more attention to the dangers of using algorithms that can create destructive feedback loops. They particularly must understand how algorithms respond to market conditions that they may create themselves.

Regulatory Responses

Following the Flash Crash, regulators adopted new rules to prevent a similar crash from happening again. They placed curbs that halt trades in a stock for 5 minutes if prices move up or down by more than 10% for large stocks and 20% for smaller stocks. This rule ensures that prices cannot move too quickly, but it does not prevent traders from behaving foolishly. Had it been in effect during the Flash Crash, the rule would have stopped trades from occurring at ridiculously low or high prices, but it would not have stopped the W&R trader from submitting an unrealistically aggressive order.

Regulators also adopted rules to establish when and which trades will be broken in the event of another extreme price change. Such rules should help ensure that liquidity suppliers who are afraid that their trades may be broken do not withdraw from the market prematurely.

EXAMPLE 4

Electronic Trading and Transaction Costs

1. Describe the impact of electronic trading on transaction costs.

Solution:

Growth in electronic trading has resulted in greater trade process efficiencies and reduced transaction costs for investors. Electronic systems are much cheaper to operate than floor-based systems (requiring less physical space and fewer exchange personnel). These systems can operate on a close-to-continuous basis at far greater scale and scope and at much faster speeds than humans. Process efficiencies from electronic trading have led to significant decreases in bid–ask spreads, which have lowered transaction costs for investors.

7 DETECTING ABUSIVE TRADING PRACTICES

☐ describe abusive trading practices that real-time surveillance of markets may detect

Regulators around the world recognize that real-time market monitoring and surveillance systems allow faster responses to potential crises and market abuses with the potential for rapid intervention to prevent or minimize damages. Many trading venues have long used real-time surveillance technologies, but their use is not consistent across all markets. The goal of real-time market surveillance is to detect potential market abuse while it is happening. Real-time surveillance often can detect the following damaging behaviors:

Front running.
Front running involves buying in front of anticipated purchases and selling in front of anticipated sales. In most jurisdictions, front running is illegal if the front runners acquire their information about orders improperly—for example, by a tip from a broker handling a large order.

Some traders use electronic artificial intelligence systems to identify when traders are filling large orders over time by breaking them up into small pieces. When these traders suspect that buyers or sellers are working large orders, they will trade ahead on the same side with the hope of benefiting when the large traders move prices as they fill their orders. This front-running strategy is legal if the information on which it is based is properly obtained— for example, by watching a market data feed.

Front running increases transaction costs for the traders whose orders are front run because the front runners take liquidity that the front-run traders otherwise would have taken for themselves.

Market manipulation.
In general, market manipulation consists of any trading strategy whose purpose is to produce misleading or false market prices, quotes, or fundamental information to profit from distorting the normal operation of markets. Market manipulators are parasitic traders who attempt to fool or force others into making disadvantageous trades. Many market manipulation strategies exist—including bluffing, squeezing, cornering, and gunning.

In most jurisdictions, market manipulation strategies are illegal. Enforcement is often difficult, however, because the exact infractions can be hard to define and because prosecutors generally must prove scienter (a legal term meaning intent or knowledge of wrongdoing), which can be difficult when defendants suggest alternative explanations for their behavior.

Market manipulation strategies usually involve one or more of the following improper market activities:

- *Trading for market impact* involves trading to raise or lower prices deliberately. A market manipulator often is willing to incur substantial transaction costs to raise or lower the price of a security to influence other traders' perceptions of value.

- *Rumormongering* is the dissemination of false information about fundamental values or about other traders' trading intentions to alter investors' value assessments. Financial analysts must be careful to ensure that they base their analyses on valid information and not on false information designed to fool them into making poor decisions. Note that although rumormongering

Detecting Abusive Trading Practices 189

is illegal in most jurisdictions, simply reporting one side of an issue is not illegal. Financial analysts, therefore, must also be careful to ensure that they base their analyses on balanced information and not on information that is true but selectively presented to them with the purpose of distorting their analyses.

- *Wash trading* consists of trades arranged among commonly controlled accounts to create the impression of market activity at a particular price. The purpose of wash trading is to fool investors into believing that a market is more liquid than it truly is and to thereby increase investors' confidence both in their ability to exit positions without substantial cost and in their assessments of security values. Manipulators also can achieve these purposes by falsely reporting trades that never occurred, which is essentially what happens when they arrange trades among commonly controlled accounts.

- *Spoofing*, also known as *layering*, is a trading practice in which traders place exposed standing limit orders to convey an impression to other traders that the market is more liquid than it is or to suggest to other traders that the security is under- or overvalued. For example, suppose that a spoofer wants to buy stock cheaply or quickly. The spoofer might place a hidden buy order in the market. The spoofer then places one or more exposed sell limit orders in the market to convey the impression that prices may soon fall. Seeing the spoofing sell orders, one or more traders may conclude that values may be lower than market prices suggest. On that basis, they may sell into the spoofer's buy order, enabling the spoofer to obtain a quick and possibly cheaper purchase than the spoofer otherwise would have obtained had the spoofer not placed the spoofing sell orders. Of course, immediately following the execution of the buy order, the spoofer will cancel the sell orders.

  Spoofing is risky because the spoofing orders that spoofers submit might execute before their intended orders execute. Spoofers can manage this risk by keeping track of the orders in the limit order book ahead of their spoofing orders. If these orders fill before the spoofers' intended orders fill, spoofers will cancel their spoofing orders to prevent them from executing. To effectively manage these processes, spoofers use electronic systems to monitor trading and to ensure that they can quickly cancel their orders as soon as they no longer want them to stand.

Market manipulators often use these improper market activities singly or in combination when they try to fool or force other traders into trades that will ultimately prove to be disadvantageous to them. Market manipulation strategies include:

- **Bluffing**. Bluffing involves submitting orders and arranging trades to influence other traders' perceptions of value. Bluffers often prey on momentum traders, who buy when prices are rising and sell when prices are falling. For example, consider typical "pump-and-dump" schemes in which bluffers buy stock to raise its price and thereby encourage momentum traders to buy. The bluffers then sell the stock to the momentum traders at higher prices. To further the scheme, bluffers may engage in such activities as rumormongering or wash trading. Note also that bluffers may time their purchases to immediately follow the release of valid positive information about the security and thereby fool traders into overvaluing the material significance of the new information.

In a pump-and-dump manipulation, the bluffer tries to raise prices. Similar manipulations can occur on the short side, though they are less common. In such manipulations, manipulators take short positions and then try to repurchase shares at lower prices. These manipulations are often called "short and distorts."

To avoid falling into these traps, financial analysts must ensure that they base their analyses on independent assessments of value. Their analyses must have a proper foundation as required by Standard V(A): Diligence and Reasonable Basis, of the CFA Institute Code of Ethics and Standards of Professional Conduct.

- **Gunning the market**. Gunning the market is a strategy used by market manipulators to force traders to do disadvantageous trades. A manipulator generally guns the market by selling quickly to push prices down with the hope of triggering stop-loss sell orders. A stop-loss (or stop) sell order becomes valid for execution once the specified stop price condition is met by a trade occurring at or below the stop price. For example, suppose that a market manipulator believes that traders have placed many stop-loss sell orders at 50. These sell orders would become valid upon a trade occurring at 50 or below. The manipulator may sell aggressively to push prices down from 51 to 50 and thereby trigger the stop-loss sell orders. The manipulator then may be able to profit by repurchasing at lower prices.

- **Squeezing and cornering**. Squeezing, cornering, and gunning the market are all schemes that market manipulators use to force traders to do disadvantageous trades. In a squeeze or corner, the manipulator obtains control over resources necessary to settle trading contracts. The manipulator then unexpectedly withdraws those resources from the market, which causes traders to default on their contracts, some of which the manipulator may hold. The manipulator profits by providing the resources at high prices or by closing the contracts at exceptionally high prices.

For example, in short squeezes, manipulators obtain control of a substantial fraction of all available lendable stock shares or bonds. If the securities are overvalued, as they might be if the manipulators are also engaging in a pump and dump, many speculators may be short selling the securities by unknowingly borrowing them from the manipulators. The manipulators then will recall the security loans. If the short sellers ("shorts") cannot borrow the securities from others, they will be forced to buy securities in the market to cover their stock loans. Their purchases will raise prices and allow the manipulators to sell their securities at overvalued prices. Manipulators also may profit by raising the rates they charge to lend their securities. To avoid being caught in a short squeeze, short sellers must be sure that the market for lendable securities has many participants and is not concentrated in the hands of one or more entities acting in concert.

In commodity market corners, manipulators buy many futures contracts while simultaneously buying in the spot markets much of the deliverable supply of the commodity. When the contract approaches expiration, the manipulators then demand delivery from the shorts, most of whom will not own the deliverable commodity. The shorts then must buy the deliverable

Detecting Abusive Trading Practices 191

supply from the manipulators at exceptionally high prices. Alternatively, they may repurchase their contracts from the manipulators, again at very high prices.

Corners can occur in commodity markets because most participants in commodity futures contracts do not demand to receive or make delivery when the contract expires. Instead, they close their positions by arranging offsetting trades in the futures market, either because they are simultaneously accepting or making delivery elsewhere or because they are rolling their positions into future contract months. Accordingly, most short sellers neither expect nor intend to make delivery. When forced to make delivery, they are caught short.

Corners are illegal in most jurisdictions, and they always violate the rules of the exchanges on which futures contracts trade. In general, long holders cannot demand delivery if they do not have a valid business reason for doing so. However, enforcement is complicated by the fact that manipulators may offer plausible reasons for requesting unexpected deliveries. Note also that sometimes, unexpected supply shortages coupled with unexpected legitimate demands for delivery can result in inadvertent short squeezes. Thus, short sellers who do not intend to make delivery should try to close their positions early to ensure that they are not caught in an intentional corner or an inadvertent squeeze.

SUMMARY

This reading explains the implicit and explicit costs of trading as well as widely used methods for estimating transaction costs. The reading also describes developments in electronic trading, the main types of electronic traders, their needs for speed and ways in which they trade. Electronic trading benefits investors through lower transaction costs and greater efficiencies but also introduces systemic risks and the need to closely monitor markets for abusive trading practices. Appropriate market governance and regulatory policies will help reduce the likelihood of events such as the 2010 Flash Crash. The reading's main points include:

- Dealers provide liquidity to buyers and sellers when they take the other side of a trade if no other willing traders are present.

- The bid–ask spread is the difference between the bid and the ask prices. The effective spread is two times the difference between the trade price and the midquote price before the trade occurred. The effective spread is a poor estimate of actual transaction costs when large orders have been filled in many parts over time or when small orders receive price improvement.

- Transaction costs include explicit costs and implicit costs. Explicit costs are the direct costs of trading. They include broker commissions, transaction taxes, stamp duties, and exchange fees. Implicit costs include indirect costs, such as the impact of the trade on the price received. The bid–ask spread, market impact, delay, and unfilled trades all contribute to implicit trading costs.

- The implementation shortfall method measures the total cost of implementing an investment decision by capturing all explicit and implicit trading costs. It includes the market impact costs, delay costs, as well as opportunity costs.

- The VWAP method of estimating transaction costs compares average fill prices to average market prices during a period surrounding the trade. It tends to produce lower transaction cost estimates than does implementation shortfall because it often does not measure the market impact of an order well.
- Markets have become increasingly fragmented as venues trading the same instruments have proliferated. Trading in any given instrument now occurs in multiple venues.
- The advantages of electronic trading systems include cost and operational efficiencies, lack of human bias, extraordinarily fast speed, and infinite span and scope of attention.
- Latency is the elapsed time between the occurrence of an event and a subsequent action that depends on that event. Traders use fast communication systems and fast computer systems to minimize latency to execute their strategies faster than others.
- Hidden orders, quote leapfrogging, flickering quotes, and the use of machine learning to support trading strategies commonly are found in electronic markets.
- Traders commonly use advanced order types, trading tactics, and algorithms in electronic markets.
- Electronic trading has benefited investors through greater trade process efficiencies and reduced transaction costs. At the same time, electronic trading has increased systemic risks.
- Examples of systemic risks posed by electronic traders include: runaway algorithms that produce streams of unintended orders caused by programming mistakes, fat finger errors that occur when a manual trader submits a larger order than intended, overlarge orders that demand more liquidity than the market can provide, and malevolent order streams created deliberately to disrupt the markets.
- Real-time surveillance of markets often can detect order front running and various market manipulation strategies.
- Market manipulators use such improper activities as trading for market impact, rumormongering, wash trading, and spoofing to further their schemes.
- Market manipulation strategies include bluffing, squeezing, cornering, and gunning.

Practice Problems

193

PRACTICE PROBLEMS

The following information relates to questions 1-10

Brian Johnson is a senior manager at Star Asset Management (SAMN), a large asset management firm in the United States. Tim Martin has just earned his advanced degree in statistics and was hired to support the trading team at SAMN. Martin meets with Johnson to undergo a training relating to SAMN's trading activities.

Johnson begins the training with a review of the limit order book for Light Systems, Inc., which is presented in Exhibit 1. Three dealers make market for the shares of Light Systems. Based on these prices, SAMN's trading desk executes a market sell order for 1,100 shares of Light Systems.

Exhibit 1: Limit Order Book for Light Systems, Inc.

	Bid				Ask		
Dealer	Time Entered	Price	Size	Dealer	Time Entered	Price	Size
B	10.10 a.m.	$17.15	900	C	10.11 a.m.	$17.19	1,200
C	10.11 a.m.	$17.14	1,500	B	10.10 a.m.	$17.20	800
A	10.11 a.m.	$17.12	1,100	A	10.12 a.m.	$17.22	1,100

Johnson then discusses a market buy order for 5,000 shares of an illiquid stock. The order was filled in three trades, and details about the three trades are presented in Exhibit 2.

Exhibit 2: Buy Trade Order Details

Trade #	Time	Trade Price	Trade Size	Bid Price	Ask Price
1	9.45 a.m.	$25.20	1,200	$25.17	$25.20
2	9.55 a.m.	$25.22	1,300	$25.19	$25.22
3	11.30 a.m.	$25.27	2,500	$25.22	$25.26

Johnson explains to Martin that the number of venues trading the same instruments has proliferated in recent years, and trading in any given instrument has now been distributed across these multiple venues. As a result, the available liquidity on any one of those exchanges represents just a small portion of the aggregate liquidity for that security. As a result, SAMN has had to adapt its trading strategies, particularly for large trades.

Johnson asks Martin about his views on how the introduction of electronic trading might have impacted SAMN. Martin tells Johnson:

Statement 1	Once built, electronic trading systems are more efficient and cheaper to operate than floor-based trading systems.
Statement 2	Electronic trading systems have attracted a lot of new buy-side traders, and the increased competition has resulted in narrower bid–ask spreads.
Statement 3	The introduction of electronic markets has had a much greater impact on the trading of corporate and municipal bonds than on the trading of equities.

Johnson tells Martin that communication speed is SAMN's current highest priority. All of SAMN's competitors have increased their communication speeds in recent months, and Johnson says management wants SAMN to be faster than its competitors. SAMN's trading desk is located in a residential area far from downtown where the exchanges it works with are located. SAMN's trading team is relatively large with experienced investment professionals, and the firm recently invested in fast computers with the latest algorithms.

At the end of the training, Johnson gives Martin his first assignment. The assignment is for Martin to use the vast amount of data that SAMN has collected to design a machine learning (ML) model using advanced statistical methods to characterize data structures and relations. Then he has to build a trading algorithm based on the same model. Since electronic trading has added systemic risk to the market, Johnson asks Martin to suggest ways to minimize the systemic risk introduced by his algorithm. Martin offers two suggestions:

| Suggestion 1 | Perform extensive testing of the algorithm before its launch. |
| Suggestion 2 | Impose mandatory trading halts if prices change outside a threshold range. |

A month into the job, Johnson sends Martin to an investment conference focused on abusive trading practices. Based on what he learned at the conference, Martin recommends to Johnson that SAMN incorporate a new rule that news be validated before a trade triggered by news is executed.

1. Based on Exhibit 1, the inside bid–ask spread for the limit order book for Light Systems is *closest* to:

   A. $0.04.

   B. $0.07.

   C. $0.10.

2. Based on Exhibit 1, the total amount that SAMN will receive, on a per share basis, for executing the market sell order is *closest* to:

   A. $17.14.

   B. $17.15.

   C. $17.22.

3. Based on Exhibit 2, the market impact relating to Trade 2, on a per share basis, is *closest* to:

   A. $0.02.

   B. $0.03.

Practice Problems

C. $0.07.

4. Based on Exhibit 2, the average effective spread of the three trades is *closest to*:

A. $0.0333.

B. $0.0367.

C. $0.0400.

5. The reason for SAMN having to adapt its trading strategies is a result of:

A. latency.

B. market fragmentation.

C. high frequency trading.

6. Which of Martin's statements relating to the introduction of electronic markets is correct?

A. Statement 1

B. Statement 2

C. Statement 3

7. Which of the following changes should SAMN make to address its key priority?

A. Hire more investment professionals

B. Upgrade to more complex operating systems

C. Move the trading desk physically closer to the exchanges it works with

8. The model that Martin is tasked with designing will likely be *most* effective:

A. for testing new markets.

B. in a well-understood market environment.

C. during periods of higher than normal market volatility.

9. Which of Martin's suggestions will *most likely* be effective in limiting the systemic risk introduced by his algorithm?

A. Only Suggestion 1

B. Only Suggestion 2

C. Both Suggestion 1 and Suggestion 2

10. Which market manipulation strategy is *most likely* the target of the new rule suggested by Martin?

A. Rumormongering

B. Gunning the market

C. Trading for market impact

The following information relates to questions 11-16

Michael Bloomfield is a trader at 2Fast Trading, a proprietary trading company that uses machine learning and algorithms to execute trades. He works with Amy Riley, a junior trader at the company. Bloomfield and Riley meet to review the company's trading systems and several trades in Bloomfield's trading account.

They discuss the increasing impact of market fragmentation on available liquidity for the company's trading strategies. Riley makes the following comments regarding market fragmentation:

Comment 1	Liquidity aggregation and smart order routing help traders manage the challenges and opportunities presented by fragmentation.
Comment 2	With increasing market fragmentation, traders who fill large orders now search for liquidity across multiple venues and across time to control market impact.

Bloomfield tells Riley that he noticed trades of 500 shares of BYYP stock were executed every 20 minutes for an hour. Bloomfield saw the same pattern of trading in the stock during the previous trading day. He instructs Riley to submit an order to purchase BYYP shares on the assumption that a trader seeks liquidity and is executing a large buy order by breaking it into pieces. The prices of these trades and the best bids and offers in the market when the BYYP trades occurred are presented in Exhibit 1.

Exhibit 1: BYYP Trade Details

Trade	Trade Price	Prevailing Bid	Prevailing Offer
1	41.50	41.45	41.50
2	41.75	41.73	41.75

Bloomfield shifts the conversation to AXZ Corp. Bloomfield notes that AXZ's bid–ask spread is narrow, even though AXZ's share price has been experiencing a period of high volatility. After extensive research, Bloomfield will purchase AXZ shares using a trading strategy that does not include standing orders.

Bloomfield then assesses the risks that 2Fast's electronic trading strategies introduce into the market. He is concerned that these risks may bring on more regulation. Bloomfield claims that the risks can be reduced by changing the structure of the market, and those structural changes can maintain 2Fast's primary competitive advantage, which is trading faster than competitors.

Bloomfield mentions that a regulatory body is investigating a competitor's trading practices. The investigation involves a tip that the competitor is manipulating markets by submitting orders and arranging trades to influence other traders' perceptions of value. Specifically, regulators were informed that the competitor has been buying stock to raise its price, thereby encouraging momentum traders to buy, and then selling the stock to them at higher prices. The regulator confirmed that the competitor did not use standing limit orders or commonly controlled accounts for the trades under investigation.

11. Which of Riley's comments related to market fragmentation is accurate?

A. Only Comment 1

Practice Problems 197

    B. Only Comment 2

    C. Both Comment 1 and Comment 2

12. Bloomfield's strategy to purchase BYYP shares is *best* classified as electronic:

    A. arbitrage.

    B. front running.

    C. quote matching.

13. Based on Exhibit 1, the average effective spread of the BYYP trades is *closest* to:

    A. $0.018.

    B. $0.035.

    C. $0.070.

14. Bloomfield's trading strategy for the purchase of AXZ shares *most likely* includes the use of:

    A. flickering quotes.

    B. machine learning.

    C. leapfrogging quotes.

15. Which structural change for the market associated with electronic trading systems is *most* consistent with Bloomfield's claim?

    A. Delaying order processing by random intervals

    B. Exchanges using trade halts when prices move too quickly

    C. Slowing markets by running call markets once a second or more often instead of trading continuously

16. The competitor company's trading is *best* described as:

    A. bluffing.

    B. spoofing.

    C. wash trading.

SOLUTIONS

1. A is correct. The inside bid–ask spread, or market bid–ask spread, is the difference between the highest bid price and the lowest ask price. The highest bid price for Light Systems is $17.15, and the lowest ask price is $17.19. Therefore, the inside bid–ask spread = $17.19 – $17.15 = $0.04.

2. B is correct. SAMN's trading desk executes a market sell order for 1,100 shares. Based on the limit order book, the trader would first sell 900 shares at $17.15 (highest bid, Dealer B) and then sell the remaining 200 shares at $17.14 (second highest bid, Dealer C). Therefore, the approximate price per share received by SAMN for selling the 1,100 shares is equal to [(900 × $17.15) + (200 × $17.14)] / 1,100 = $17.1482 per share ($17.15 rounded).

3. A is correct. Market impact, or price impact, is the effect of a trade on transaction prices. After the first trade (Trade 1) was executed at $25.20, Trade 2 was executed at $25.22, which is $0.02 per share higher than the trade price of Trade 1. So, the execution of Trade 1 led to a price impact of $0.02 per share on Trade 2.

4. C is correct. The effective bid–ask spread for buy orders is calculated as:

   Effective bid–ask spread (buy order) = 2 × {Trade price − [(Ask price + Bid price) / 2)]} or

   = 2 × (Trade price − Midpoint of the market at the time an order is entered).

   So, the effective bid–ask spreads for the three buy trades are calculated as:

   Effective spread of Trade 1 = 2 × {$25.20 − [($25.20 + $25.17)/2]} = $0.0300.

   Effective spread of Trade 2 = 2 × {$25.22 − [($25.22 + 25.19)/2]} = $0.0300.

   Effective spread of Trade 3 = 2 × {$25.27 − [($25.26 + $25.22)/2]} = $0.0600.

   The resulting average effective spread is then calculated as:

   Average effective spread

   = (Effective spread of Trade 1 + Effective spread of Trade 2 + Effective spread of Trade 3)/3.

   Average effective spread = ($0.0300 + $0.0300 + $0.0600)/3 = $0.0400.

5. B is correct. According to Johnson, markets have become increasingly fragmented as the number of venues trading the same instruments has proliferated and trading in any given instrument has been split (or fragmented) across these multiple venues. As a result, the available liquidity on any one exchange represents just a small portion of the aggregate liquidity for that instrument. This phenomenon is known as market fragmentation and creates the potential for price and liquidity disparities across venues. As a result, SAMN has had to adapt its trading strategies to this fragmented liquidity to avoid intensifying the market impact of a large trade.

6. A is correct. Once built, electronic systems are indeed cheaper to operate than floor-based trading systems. They require less physical space than do trading floors, and in contrast to floor-based trading systems, they do not require exchange officials to record and report prices. Furthermore, the widespread use of electronic trading systems significantly decreased trading costs for buy-side

Solutions

199

traders. Costs fell as exchanges obtained greater cost efficiencies from using electronic matching systems instead of floor-based manual trading systems. These technologies also decreased costs and increased efficiencies for the dealers and arbitrageurs who provide much of the liquidity offered at exchanges. Competition forced them to pass along much of the benefits of their new technologies to buy-side traders in the form of narrower spreads quoted for larger sizes. New electronic buy-side order management systems also decreased buy-side trading costs by allowing a smaller number of buy-side traders to process more orders and to process them more efficiently than manual traders.

While electronic trading has had a significant effect on equity markets, it has not had as much of an effect on the markets for corporate and municipal bonds. The market structures of corporate and municipal bond markets have hardly changed since the late 19th century. Despite the efforts of many creative developers of electronic bond trading systems, most public investors in these markets still trade largely over the counter with dealers.

7. C is correct. The speed required by electronic traders is affected by fast communication and fast computations. The shorter the distance between the trader and the exchange, the faster the communication. Many exchanges allow electronic traders to place their servers in the rooms where the exchange servers operate, a practice called collocation.

8. B is correct. Many trading problems are ideally suited for machine learning analyses because the problems repeat regularly and often. For such problems, machine-based learning systems can be extraordinarily powerful. However, these systems are often useless—or worse—when trading becomes extraordinary, as when volatilities shoot up. Machine learning systems frequently do not produce useful information during volatility episodes because they have few precedents from which the machines can learn. Thus, traders often instruct their electronic trading systems to stop trading—and sometimes to close out their positions— whenever they recognize that they are entering uncharted territory. Many traders shut down when volatility spikes—both because high-volatility episodes are uncommon and thus not well understood and because even if such episodes were well understood, they represent periods of exceptionally high risk.

9. C is correct. Both suggestions will likely be effective in minimizing the systemic risk introduced by electronic trading. First, exhaustive testing of the algorithm prior to its launch can minimize risk relating to programming errors, which could result in an extreme market reaction that could trigger an even more extreme market reaction. Second, imposing mandatory trade halts in case of large price changes (outside a given threshold) would limit potential undesired results and help minimize systemic risk.

10. A is correct. Rumormongering is the dissemination of false information about fundamental values or about other traders' trading intentions in an attempt to alter investors' value assessments. Martin's suggested news validation rule would reduce the likelihood that SAMN would be adversely affected by this market manipulation strategy.

11. C is correct. Both of Riley's comments are correct. Electronic algorithmic trading techniques, such as liquidity aggregation and smart order routing, help traders manage the challenges and opportunities presented by fragmentation. Liquidity aggregators create "super books" that present liquidity across markets for a given instrument. These tools offer global views of market depth (available liquidity) for each instrument regardless of the trading venue that offers the liquidity. Smart order-routing algorithms send orders to the markets that display the best quoted prices and sizes. Additionally, with increasing market fragmentation, traders

filling large orders adapt their trading strategies to search for liquidity across multiple venues and across time to control the market impacts of their trades.

12. B is correct. Bloomfield noticed a pattern of trading in BYYP and decided to front run shares on the assumption that a trader is in the market filling a large buy order by breaking it into pieces. Electronic front runners trade in front of traders who demand liquidity. They identify when large traders or many small traders are trying to fill orders on the same side of the market. The order anticipation strategies of electronic front runners try to identify predictable patterns in order submission. They may search for patterns in order submissions, trades, or the relations between trades and other events.

A is incorrect because electronic arbitrageurs look across markets for arbitrage opportunities in which they can buy an undervalued instrument and sell a similar overvalued one. His decision to purchase BYYP shares is based on the pattern of trading that Bloomfield observed.

C is incorrect because quote matchers trade in front of traders who supply (not demand) liquidity. Bloomfield decides to purchase BYYP shares on the assumption that a trader is in the market seeking (not supplying) liquidity, which is consistent with front running (not quote matching). Quote matchers trade in front of traders who supply liquidity and try to exploit the option values of standing orders. Quote matchers buy when they believe they can rely on standing buy orders to get out of their positions, and they sell when they can do the same with standing sell orders.

13. B is correct. The effective spread is calculated as follows:

$$\text{Effective spread} = 2 \times (\text{Trade price} - \text{Midpoint of market at time of order entry})$$

$$\text{Effective spread of Trade } 1 = 2 \times (\$41.50 - \$41.475) = \$0.05$$

$$\text{Effective spread of Trade } 2 = 2 \times (\$41.75 - \$41.74) = \$0.02$$

$$\text{Average Effective Spread} = (\$0.05 + \$0.02)/2 = \$0.035$$

14. A is correct. Flickering quotes are exposed limit orders that electronic traders submit and then cancel shortly thereafter, often within a second. Electronic dealers and algorithmic buy-side traders submit and repeatedly cancel and resubmit their orders when they do not want their orders to stand in the market; rather, they want other traders to see that they are willing to trade at the displayed price. Bloomfield does not want his orders to stand in the market; using flickering quotes to purchase AXZ shares would satisfy that objective.

B is incorrect because AXZ shares are currently in a period of high volatility, so Bloomfield would not likely use machine learning to execute his trades. Machine-learning systems frequently do not produce useful information during volatility episodes because these episodes have few precedents from which the machines can learn. Machine-learning methods produce models based on observed empirical regularities rather than on theoretical principles identified by analysts. Many traders shut down when volatility spikes, both because high-volatility episodes are uncommon and thus not well understood and because even if such episodes were well understood, they represent periods of exceptionally high risk.

C is incorrect because market participants use leapfrogging quotes when spreads are wide (not narrow), and Bloomfield noted that the bid–ask spread for AXZ shares is narrow. When bid–ask spreads are wide, dealers often are willing to trade at better prices than they quote. They quote wide spreads because they hope to trade at more favorable prices. When another trader quotes a better

Solutions 201

price, dealers often immediately quote an even better price. If the spread is sufficiently wide, a game of leapfrog may ensue as the dealer jumps ahead again.

15. B is correct. To reduce the systemic risks associated with fast trading, some exchanges have adopted trade halts when prices move too quickly. These rules stop trading when excess demand for liquidity occurs. They also prevent the extreme price changes that can occur in electronic markets when market orders arrive and no liquidity is present. 2Fast Trading's competitive advantage will be maintained despite exchange trading halts because the company will be free to trade faster than its competitors once trading resumes. Therefore, exchanges using trade halts to stop trading is the risk reduction strategy that most likely maintains 2Fast Trading's competitive advantage and is consistent with Bloomfield's claim that risks can be reduced by changing the structure of the market.

A is incorrect because delaying order processing by random intervals reduces the benefits of high-frequency traders being faster than their competitors and investing in speed. Therefore, delaying order processing by random order intervals does not maintain 2Fast Trading's primary competitive advantage, which is trading faster than competitors, because that advantage will be reduced.

C is incorrect because slowing markets by running call markets once a second or more often instead of trading continuously diminishes the benefits of high-frequency traders being faster than their competitors and investing with speed. Therefore, slowing markets once a second or more often instead of trading continuously does not maintain 2Fast Trading's primary competitive advantage, which is trading faster than competitors, because that advantage will be reduced.

16. A is correct. Bluffing involves submitting orders and arranging trades to influence other traders' perceptions of value. Bluffers often prey on momentum traders, who buy when prices are rising and sell when prices are falling. Similarly, Bloomfield mentioned that regulators were informed that 2Fast's competitor has been submitting orders and arranging trades to influence other traders' perceptions of value; regulators were informed the competitor has been buying stock to raise its price, thereby encouraging momentum traders to buy, and then selling the stock to them at higher prices.

B is incorrect because the competitor did not use standing limit orders—those orders that are used in a spoofing strategy—for the trades the regulator is investigating. Spoofing is a trading practice in which traders place exposed standing limit orders to convey an impression to other traders that the market is more liquid than it is or to suggest to other traders that the security is under- or overvalued.

C is incorrect because the competitor did not use commonly controlled accounts—those accounts that are used in a wash trading strategy—for the trades that regulators are investigating. Wash trading consists of trades arranged among commonly controlled accounts to create the impression of market activity at a particular price. The purpose of wash trading is to fool investors into believing that a market is more liquid than it truly is and to thereby increase investors' confidence both in their ability to exit positions without substantial cost and in their assessments of security values.

Ethical and Professional Standards

LEARNING MODULE

1

Code of Ethics and Standards of Professional Conduct

LEARNING OUTCOMES

Mastery	The candidate should be able to:
☐	describe the six components of the Code of Ethics and the seven Standards of Professional Conduct
☐	explain the ethical responsibilities required of CFA Institute members and candidates in the CFA Program by the Code and Standards

PREFACE

1

☐	describe the six components of the Code of Ethics and the seven Standards of Professional Conduct
☐	explain the ethical responsibilities required of CFA Institute members and candidates in the CFA Program by the Code and Standards

The *Standards of Practice Handbook* (*Handbook*) provides guidance to the people who grapple with real ethical dilemmas in the investment profession on a daily basis; the *Handbook* addresses the professional intersection where theory meets practice and where the concept of ethical behavior crosses from the abstract to the concrete. The *Handbook* is intended for a diverse and global audience: CFA Institute members navigating ambiguous ethical situations; supervisors and direct/indirect reports determining the nature of their responsibilities to each other, to existing and potential clients, and to the broader financial markets; and candidates preparing for the Chartered Financial Analyst (CFA) examinations.

Recent events in the global financial markets have tested the ethical mettle of financial market participants, including CFA Institute members. The standards taught in the CFA Program and by which CFA Institute members and candidates must abide represent timeless ethical principles and professional conduct for all market conditions. Through adherence to these standards, which continue to serve as the model for ethical behavior in the investment professional globally, each market participant does his or her part to improve the integrity and efficient operations of the financial markets.

The *Handbook* provides guidance in understanding the interconnectedness of the aspirational and practical principles and provisions of the Code of Ethics and Standards of Professional Conduct (Code and Standards). The Code contains high-level aspirational ethical principles that drive members and candidates to create a positive and reputable investment profession. The Standards contain practical ethical principles of conduct that members and candidates must follow to achieve the broader industry expectations. However, applying the principles individually may not capture the complexity of ethical requirements related to the investment industry. The Code and Standards should be viewed and interpreted as an interwoven tapestry of ethical requirements. Through members' and candidates' adherence to these principles as a whole, the integrity of and trust in the capital markets are improved.

Evolution of the CFA Institute Code of Ethics and Standards of Professional Conduct

Generally, changes to the Code and Standards over the years have been minor. CFA Institute has revised the language of the Code and Standards and occasionally added a new standard to address a prominent issue of the day. For instance, in 1992, CFA Institute added the standard addressing performance presentation to the existing list of standards.

Major changes came in 2005 with the ninth edition of the *Handbook*. CFA Institute adopted new standards, revised some existing standards, and reorganized the standards. The revisions were intended to clarify the requirements of the Code and Standards and effectively convey to its global membership what constitutes "best practice" in a number of areas relating to the investment profession.

The Code and Standards must be regularly reviewed and updated if they are to remain effective and continue to represent the highest ethical standards in the global investment industry. CFA Institute strongly believes that revisions of the Code and Standards are not undertaken for cosmetic purposes but to add value by addressing legitimate concerns and improving comprehension.

Changes to the Code and Standards have far-reaching implications for the CFA Institute membership, the CFA Program, and the investment industry as a whole. CFA Institute members and candidates are *required* to adhere to the Code and Standards. In addition, the Code and Standards are increasingly being adopted, in whole or in part, by firms and regulatory authorities. Their relevance goes well beyond CFA Institute members and candidates.

Standards of Practice Handbook

The periodic revisions of the Code and Standards have come in conjunction with updates of the *Standards of Practice Handbook*. The *Handbook* is the fundamental element of the ethics education effort of CFA Institute and the primary resource for guidance in interpreting and implementing the Code and Standards. The *Handbook* seeks to educate members and candidates on how to apply the Code and Standards to their professional lives and thereby benefit their clients, employers, and the investing public in general. The *Handbook* explains the purpose of the Code and Standards and how they apply in a variety of situations. The sections discuss and amplify each standard and suggest procedures to prevent violations.

Examples in the "Application of the Standard" sections are meant to illustrate how the standard applies to hypothetical but factual situations. The names contained in the examples are fictional and are not meant to refer to any actual person or entity. Unless otherwise stated (e.g., one or more people specifically identified), individuals in each example are CFA Institute members and holders of the CFA designation. Because

Preface

factual circumstances vary so widely and often involve gray areas, the explanatory material and examples are not intended to be all inclusive. Many examples set forth in the application sections involve standards that have legal counterparts; ***members are strongly urged to discuss with their supervisors and legal and compliance departments the content of the Code and Standards and the members' general obligations under the Code and Standards***.

CFA Institute recognizes that the presence of any set of ethical standards may create a false sense of security unless the documents are fully understood, enforced, and made a meaningful part of everyday professional activities. The *Handbook* is intended to provide a useful frame of reference that suggests ethical professional behavior in the investment decision-making process. This book cannot cover every contingency or circumstance, however, and it does not attempt to do so. The development and interpretation of the Code and Standards are evolving processes; the Code and Standards will be subject to continuing refinement.

Summary of Changes in the Eleventh Edition

The comprehensive review of the Code and Standards in 2005 resulted in principle requirements that remain applicable today. The review carried out for the eleventh edition focused on market practices that have evolved since the tenth edition. Along with updates to the guidance and examples within the *Handbook*, the eleventh edition includes an update to the Code of Ethics that embraces the members' role of maintaining the social contract between the industry and investors. Additionally, there are three changes to the Standards of Professional Conduct, which recognize the importance of proper supervision, clear communications with clients, and the expanding educational programs of CFA Institute.

Inclusion of Updated CFA Institute Mission

The CFA Institute Board of Governors approved an updated mission for the organization that is included in the Preamble to the Code and Standards. The new mission conveys the organization's conviction in the investment industry's role in the betterment of society at large.

> #### Mission:
>
> To lead the investment profession globally by promoting the highest standards of ethics, education, and professional excellence for the ultimate benefit of society.

Updated Code of Ethics Principle

One of the bullets in the Code of Ethics was updated to reflect the role that the capital markets have in the greater society. As members work to promote and maintain the integrity of the markets, their actions should also help maintain the social contract with investors.

> #### Old:
>
> Promote the integrity of and uphold the rules governing capital markets.

> #### New:
>
> Promote the integrity and viability of the global capital markets for the ultimate benefit of society.

New Standard Regarding Responsibilities of Supervisors [IV(C)]

The standard for members and candidates with supervision or authority over others within their firms was updated to bring about improvements in preventing illegal and unethical actions from occurring. The prior version of Standard IV(C) focused on the detection and prevention of violations. The updated version stresses broader compliance expectations, which include the detection and prevention aspects of the original version.

Old:

Members and Candidates must make reasonable efforts to detect and prevent violations of applicable laws, rules, regulations, and the Code and Standards by anyone subject to their supervision or authority.

New:

Members and Candidates must make reasonable efforts to ensure that anyone subject to their supervision or authority complies with applicable laws, rules, regulations, and the Code and Standards.

Additional Requirement under the Standard for Communication with Clients and Prospective Clients [V(B)]

Given the constant development of new and exotic financial instruments and strategies, the standard regarding communicating with clients now includes an implicit requirement to discuss the risks and limitations of recommendations being made to clients. The new principle and related guidance take into account the fact that levels of disclosure will differ between products and services. Members and candidates, along with their firms, must determine the specific disclosures their clients should receive while ensuring appropriate transparency of the individual firms' investment processes.

Addition:

Disclose to clients and prospective clients significant limitations and risks associated with the investment process.

Modification to Standard VII(A)

Since this standard was developed, CFA Institute has launched additional educational programs. The updated standard not only maintains the integrity of the CFA Program but also expands the same ethical considerations when members or candidates participate in such programs as the CIPM Program and the CFA Institute Investment Foundations certificate program. Whether participating as a member assisting with the curriculum or an examination or as a sitting candidate within a program, we expect them to engage in these programs as they would participate in the CFA Program.

Old:

Conduct as Members and Candidates in the CFA Program

Members and Candidates must not engage in any conduct that compromises the reputation or integrity of CFA Institute or the CFA designation or the integrity, validity, or security of the CFA examinations.

New:

Conduct as Participants in CFA Institute Programs

Preface

Members and Candidates must not engage in any conduct that compromises the reputation or integrity of CFA Institute or the CFA designation or the integrity, validity, or security of CFA Institute programs.

General Guidance and Example Revision

The guidance and examples were updated to reflect practices and scenarios applicable to today's investment industry. Two concepts that appear frequently in the updates in this edition relate to the increased use of social media for business communications and the use of and reliance on the output of quantitative models. The use of social media platforms has increased significantly since the publication of the tenth edition. And although financial modeling is not new to the industry, this update reflects upon actions that are viewed as possible contributing factors to the financial crises of the past decade.

CFA Institute Professional Conduct Program

All CFA Institute members and candidates enrolled in the CFA Program are required to comply with the Code and Standards. The CFA Institute Board of Governors maintains oversight and responsibility for the Professional Conduct Program (PCP), which, in conjunction with the Disciplinary Review Committee (DRC), is responsible for enforcement of the Code and Standards. The DRC is a volunteer committee of CFA charterholders who serve on panels to review conduct and partner with Professional Conduct staff to establish and review professional conduct policies. The CFA Institute Bylaws and Rules of Procedure for Professional Conduct (Rules of Procedure) form the basic structure for enforcing the Code and Standards. The Professional Conduct division is also responsible for enforcing testing policies of other CFA Institute education programs as well as the professional conduct of Certificate in Investment Performance Measurement (CIPM) certificants.

Professional Conduct inquiries come from a number of sources. First, members and candidates must self-disclose on the annual Professional Conduct Statement all matters that question their professional conduct, such as involvement in civil litigation or a criminal investigation or being the subject of a written complaint. Second, written complaints received by Professional Conduct staff can bring about an investigation. Third, CFA Institute staff may become aware of questionable conduct by a member or candidate through the media, regulatory notices, or another public source. Fourth, candidate conduct is monitored by proctors who complete reports on candidates suspected to have violated testing rules on exam day. Lastly, CFA Institute may also conduct analyses of scores and exam materials after the exam, as well as monitor online and social media to detect disclosure of confidential exam information.

When an inquiry is initiated, the Professional Conduct staff conducts an investigation that may include requesting a written explanation from the member or candidate; interviewing the member or candidate, complaining parties, and third parties; and collecting documents and records relevant to the investigation. Upon reviewing the material obtained during the investigation, the Professional Conduct staff may conclude the inquiry with no disciplinary sanction, issue a cautionary letter, or continue proceedings to discipline the member or candidate. If the Professional Conduct staff believes a violation of the Code and Standards or testing policies has occurred, the member or candidate has the opportunity to reject or accept any charges and the proposed sanctions.

If the member or candidate does not accept the charges and proposed sanction, the matter is referred to a panel composed of DRC members. Panels review materials and presentations from Professional Conduct staff and from the member or candidate. The panel's task is to determine whether a violation of the Code and Standards or testing policies occurred and, if so, what sanction should be imposed.

Sanctions imposed by CFA Institute may have significant consequences; they include public censure, suspension of membership and use of the CFA designation, and revocation of the CFA charter. Candidates enrolled in the CFA Program who have violated the Code and Standards or testing policies may be suspended or prohibited from further participation in the CFA Program.

Adoption of the Code and Standards

The Code and Standards apply to individual members of CFA Institute and candidates in the CFA Program. CFA Institute does encourage firms to adopt the Code and Standards, however, as part of their code of ethics. Those who claim compliance should fully understand the requirements of each of the principles of the Code and Standards.

Once a party—nonmember or firm—ensures its code of ethics meets the principles of the Code and Standards, that party should make the following statement whenever claiming compliance:

> "[Insert name of party] claims compliance with the CFA Institute Code of Ethics and Standards of Professional Conduct. This claim has not been verified by CFA Institute."

CFA Institute welcomes public acknowledgement, when appropriate, that firms are complying with the CFA Institute Code of Ethics and Standards of Professional Conduct and encourages firms to notify us of the adoption plans. For firms that would like to distribute the Code and Standards to clients and potential clients, attractive one-page copies of the Code and Standards, including translations, are available on the CFA Institute website (www.cfainstitute.org).

CFA Institute has also published the Asset Manager Code of Professional Conduct, which is designed, in part, to help asset managers comply with the regulations mandating codes of ethics for investment advisers. Whereas the Code and Standards are aimed at individual investment professionals who are members of CFA Institute or candidates in the CFA Program, the Asset Manager Code was drafted specifically for firms. The Asset Manager Code provides specific, practical guidelines for asset managers in six areas: loyalty to clients, the investment process, trading, compliance, performance evaluation, and disclosure. The Asset Manager Code and the appropriate steps to acknowledge adoption or compliance can be found on the CFA Institute website (www.cfainstitute.org).

Acknowledgments

CFA Institute is a not-for-profit organization that is heavily dependent on the expertise and intellectual contributions of member volunteers. Members devote their time because they share a mutual interest in the organization's mission to promote and achieve ethical practice in the investment profession. CFA Institute owes much to the volunteers' abundant generosity and energy in extending ethical integrity.

The CFA Institute Standards of Practice Council (SPC), a group consisting of CFA charterholder volunteers from many different countries, is charged with maintaining and interpreting the Code and Standards and ensuring that they are effective. The SPC draws its membership from a broad spectrum of organizations in the securities field, including brokers, investment advisers, banks, and insurance companies. In most instances, the SPC members have important supervisory responsibilities within their firms.

The SPC continually evaluates the Code and Standards, as well as the guidance in the *Handbook*, to ensure that they are

- representative of high standards of professional conduct,
- relevant to the changing nature of the investment profession,
- globally applicable,
- sufficiently comprehensive, practical, and specific,
- enforceable, and
- testable for the CFA Program.

The SPC has spent countless hours reviewing and discussing revisions to the Code and Standards and updates to the guidance that make up the eleventh edition of the *Handbook*. Following is a list of the current and former members of the SPC who generously donated their time and energy to this effort.

James E. Hollis III, CFA, Chair

Rik Albrecht, CFA

Terence E. Burns, CFA

Laura Dagan, CFA

Samuel B. Jones, Jr., CFA

Ulrike Kaiser-Boeing, CFA

Jinliang (Jack) Li, CFA

Christopher C. Loop, CFA,

James M. Meeth, CFA

Guy G. Rutherfurd, Jr., CFA

Edouard Senechal, CFA

Wenliang (Richard) Wang, CFA

Peng Lian Wee, CFA

ETHICS AND THE INVESTMENT INDUSTRY

2

Society ultimately benefits from efficient markets where capital can freely flow to the most productive or innovative destination. Well-functioning capital markets efficiently match those needing capital with those seeking to invest their assets in revenue-generating ventures. In order for capital markets to be efficient, investors must be able to trust that the markets are fair and transparent and offer them the opportunity to be rewarded for the risk they choose to take. Laws, regulations, and enforcement play a vital role but are insufficient alone to guarantee fair and transparent markets. The markets depend on an ethical foundation to guide participants' judgment and behavior. CFA Institute maintains and promotes the Code of Ethics and Standards of Professional Conduct in order to create a culture of ethics for the ultimate benefit of society.

Why Ethics Matters

Ethics can be defined as a set of moral principles or rules of conduct that provide guidance for our behavior when it affects others. Widely acknowledged fundamental ethical principles include honesty, fairness, diligence, and care and respect for others. Ethical conduct follows those principles and balances self-interest with both the direct and the indirect consequences of that behavior for other people.

Not only does unethical behavior by individuals have serious personal consequences—ranging from job loss and reputational damage to fines and even jail—but unethical conduct from market participants, investment professionals, and those who service investors can damage investor trust and thereby impair the sustainability of the global capital markets as a whole. Unfortunately, there seems to be an unending parade of stories bringing to light accounting frauds and manipulations, Ponzi schemes, insider-trading scandals, and other misdeeds. Not surprisingly, this has led to erosion in public confidence in investment professionals. Empirical evidence from numerous surveys documents the low standing in the eyes of the investing public of banks and financial services firms—the very institutions that are entrusted with the economic well-being and retirement security of society.

Governments and regulators have historically tried to combat misconduct in the industry through regulatory reform, with various levels of success. Global capital markets are highly regulated to protect investors and other market participants. However, compliance with regulation alone is insufficient to fully earn investor trust. Individuals and firms must develop a "culture of integrity" that permeates all levels of operations and promotes the ethical principles of stewardship of investor assets and working in the best interests of clients, above and beyond strict compliance with the law. A strong ethical culture that helps honest, ethical people engage in ethical behavior will foster the trust of investors, lead to robust global capital markets, and ultimately benefit society. That is why ethics matters.

Ethics, Society, and the Capital Markets

CFA Institute recently added the concept "for the ultimate benefit of society" to its mission. The premise is that we want to live in a socially, politically, and financially stable society that fosters individual well-being and welfare of the public. A key ingredient for this goal is global capital markets that facilitate the efficient allocation of resources so that the available capital finds its way to places where it most benefits that society. These investments are then used to produce goods and services, to fund innovation and jobs, and to promote improvements in standards of living. Indeed, such a function serves the interests of the society. Efficient capital markets, in turn, provide a host of benefits to those providing the investment capital. Investors are provided the opportunity to transfer and transform risk because the capital markets serve as an information exchange, create investment products, provide liquidity, and limit transaction costs.

However, a well-functioning and efficient capital market system is dependent on trust of the participants. If investors believe that capital market participants—investment professionals and firms—cannot be trusted with their financial assets or that the capital markets are unfair such that only insiders can be successful, they will be unlikely to invest or, at the very least, will require a higher risk premium. Decreased investment capital can reduce innovation and job creation and hurt the economy and society as a whole. Reduced trust in capital markets can also result in a less vibrant, if not smaller, investment industry.

Ethics for a global investment industry should be universal and ultimately support trust and integrity above acceptable local or regional customs and culture. Universal ethics for a global industry strongly supports the efficiency, values, and mission of the industry as a whole. Different countries may be at different stages of development in establishing standards of practice, but the end goal must be to achieve rules, regulations, and standards that support and promote fundamental ethical principles on a global basis.

Capital Market Sustainability and the Actions of One

Individuals and firms also have to look at the indirect impacts of their actions on the broader investment community. The increasingly interconnected nature of global finance brings to the fore an added consideration of market sustainability that was,

Ethics and the Investment Industry

perhaps, less appreciated in years past. In addition to committing to the highest levels of ethical behavior, today's investment professionals and their employers should consider the long-term health of the market as a whole.

As recent events have demonstrated, apparently isolated and unrelated decisions, however innocuous when considered on an individual basis, in aggregate can precipitate a market crisis. In an interconnected global economy and marketplace, each participant should strive to be aware of how his or her actions or the products he or she distributes may have an impact on capital market participants in other regions or countries.

Investment professionals should consider how their investment decision-making processes affect the global financial markets in the broader context of how they apply their ethical and professional obligations. Those in positions of authority have a special responsibility to consider the broader context of market sustainability in their development and approval of corporate policies, particularly those involving risk management and product development. In addition, corporate compensation strategies should not encourage otherwise ethically sound individuals to engage in unethical or questionable conduct for financial gain. Ethics, sustainability, and properly functioning capital markets are components of the same concept of protecting the best interests of all. To always place the interests of clients ahead of both investment professionals' own interests and those of their employer remains a key ethos.

The Relationship between Ethics and Regulations

Some equate ethical behavior with legal behavior: If you are following the law, you must be acting appropriately. Ethical principles, like laws and regulations, prescribe appropriate constraints on our natural tendency to pursue self-interest that could harm the interests of others. Laws and regulations often attempt to guide people toward ethical behavior, but they do not cover all unethical behavior. Ethical behavior is often distinguished from legal conduct by describing legal behavior as what is required and ethical behavior as conduct that is morally correct. Ethical principles go beyond that which is legally sufficient and encompass what is the right thing to do.

Given many regulators' lack of sufficient resources to enforce well-conceived rules and regulations, relying on a regulatory framework to lead the charge in establishing ethical behavior has its challenges. Therefore, reliance on compliance with laws and regulation alone is insufficient to ensure ethical behavior of investment professionals or to create a truly ethical culture in the industry.

The recent past has shown us that some individuals will succeed at circumventing the regulatory rules for their personal gain. Only the application of strong ethical principles, at both the individual level and the firm level, will limit abuses. Knowing the rules or regulations to apply in a particular situation, although important, may not be sufficient to ensure ethical conduct. Individuals must be able both to recognize areas that are prone to ethical pitfalls and to identify and process those circumstances and influences that can impair ethical judgment.

Applying an Ethical Framework

Laws, regulations, professional standards, and codes of ethics can guide ethical behavior, but individual judgment is a critical ingredient in making principled choices and engaging in appropriate conduct. When faced with an ethical dilemma, individuals must have a well-developed set of principles; otherwise, their thought processes can lead to, at best, equivocation and indecision and, at worst, fraudulent conduct and destruction of the public trust. Establishing an ethical framework for an internal thought process prior to deciding to act is a crucial step in engaging in ethical conduct.

Most investment professionals are used to making decisions from a business (profit/loss) outlook. But given the importance of ethical behavior in carrying out professional responsibilities, it is critical to also analyze decisions and potential conduct from an ethical perspective. Utilizing a framework for ethical decision making will help investment professionals effectively examine their conduct in the context of conflicting interests common to their professional obligations (e.g., researching and gathering information, developing investment recommendations, and managing money for others). Such a framework will allow investment professionals to analyze their conduct in a way that meets high standards of ethical behavior.

An ethical decision-making framework can come in many forms but should provide investment professionals with a tool for following the principles of the firm's code of ethics. Through analyzing the particular circumstances of each decision, investment professionals are able to determine the best course of action to fulfill their responsibilities in an ethical manner.

Commitment to Ethics by Firms

A firm's code of ethics risks becoming a largely ignored, dusty compilation if it is not truly integrated into the fabric of the business. The ability to relate an ethical decision-making framework to a firm's code of ethics allows investment professionals to bring the aspirations and principles of the code of ethics to life—transforming it from a compliance exercise to something that is at the heart of a firm's culture.

An investment professional's natural desire to "do the right thing" must be reinforced by building a culture of integrity in the workplace. Development, maintenance, and demonstration of a strong culture of integrity within the firm by senior management may be the single most important factor in promoting ethical behavior among the firm's employees. Adopting a code that clearly lays out the ethical principles that guide the thought processes and conduct the firm expects from its employees is a critical first step. But a code of ethics, while necessary, is insufficient.

Simply nurturing an inclination to do right is no match for the multitude of daily decisions that investment managers make. We need to exercise ethical decision-making skills to develop the muscle memory necessary for fundamentally ethical people to make good decisions despite the reality of agent conflicts. Just as coaching and practice transform our natural ability to run across a field into the technique and endurance required to run a race, teaching, reinforcing, and practicing ethical decision-making skills prepare us to confront the hard issues effectively. It is good for business, individuals, firms, the industry, and the markets, as well as society as a whole, to engage in the investment management profession in a highly ethical manner.

Ethical Commitment of CFA Institute

An important goal of CFA Institute is to ensure that the organization and its members and candidates develop, promote, and follow the highest ethical standards in the investment industry. The CFA Institute Code of Ethics (Code) and Standards of Professional Conduct (Standards) are the foundation supporting the organization's quest to uphold the industry's highest standards of individual and corporate practice and to help serve the greater good. The Code is a set of principles that define the overarching conduct CFA Institute expects from its members and CFA Program candidates. The Code works in tandem with the Standards, which outline professional conduct that constitutes fair and ethical business practices.

For more than 50 years, CFA Institute members and candidates have been required to abide by the organization's Code and Standards. Periodically, CFA Institute has revised and updated its Code and Standards to ensure that they remain relevant to the changing nature of the investment profession and representative of the highest standard of professional conduct. Within this *Handbook*, CFA Institute addresses ethical principles for the profession, including individual professionalism; responsibilities to capital markets, clients, and employers; ethics involved in investment analysis, recommendations, and actions; and possible conflicts of interest. Although

CFA Institute Code of Ethics and Standards of Professional Conduct

the investment world has become a far more complex place since the first publication of the *Standard of Practice Handbook*, distinguishing right from wrong remains the paramount principle of the Code and Standards.

New challenges will continually arise for members and candidates in applying the Code and Standards because many decisions are not unambiguously right or wrong. The dilemma exists because the choice between right and wrong is not always clear. Even well-intentioned investment professionals can find themselves in circumstances that may tempt them to cut corners. Situational influences can overpower the best of intentions.

CFA Institute has made a significant commitment to providing members and candidates with the resources to extend and deepen their understanding of how to appropriately apply the principles of the Code and Standards. The product offerings from CFA Institute offer a wealth of material. Through publications, conferences, webcasts, and podcasts, the ethical challenges of investment professionals are brought to light. Archived issues of these items are available on the CFA Institute website (www.cfainstitute.org).

By reviewing these resources and discussing with their peers, market participants can further enhance their abilities to apply an effective ethical decision-making framework. In time, this should help restore some of the trust recently lost by investors.

Markets function to an important extent on trust. Recent events have shown the fragility of this foundation and the devastating consequences that can ensue when it is fundamentally questioned. Investment professionals should remain mindful of the long-term health of financial markets and incorporate this concern for the market's sustainability in their investment decision making. CFA Institute and the Standards of Practice Council hope this edition of the *Handbook* will assist and guide investment professionals in meeting the ethical demands of the highly interconnected global capital markets for the ultimate benefit of society.

CFA INSTITUTE CODE OF ETHICS AND STANDARDS OF PROFESSIONAL CONDUCT

3

Preamble

The CFA Institute Code of Ethics and Standards of Professional Conduct are fundamental to the values of CFA Institute and essential to achieving its mission to lead the investment profession globally by promoting the highest standards of ethics, education, and professional excellence for the ultimate benefit of society. High ethical standards are critical to maintaining the public's trust in financial markets and in the investment profession. Since their creation in the 1960s, the Code and Standards have promoted the integrity of CFA Institute members and served as a model for measuring the ethics of investment professionals globally, regardless of job function, cultural differences, or local laws and regulations. All CFA Institute members (including holders of the Chartered Financial Analyst [CFA] designation) and CFA candidates have the personal responsibility to embrace and uphold the provisions of the Code and Standards and are encouraged to notify their employer of this responsibility. Violations may result in disciplinary sanctions by CFA Institute. Sanctions can include revocation of membership, revocation of candidacy in the CFA Program, and revocation of the right to use the CFA designation.

The Code of Ethics

Members of CFA Institute (including CFA charterholders) and candidates for the CFA designation ("Members and Candidates") must:

- Act with integrity, competence, diligence, and respect and in an ethical manner with the public, clients, prospective clients, employers, employees, colleagues in the investment profession, and other participants in the global capital markets.
- Place the integrity of the investment profession and the interests of clients above their own personal interests.
- Use reasonable care and exercise independent professional judgment when conducting investment analysis, making investment recommendations, taking investment actions, and engaging in other professional activities.
- Practice and encourage others to practice in a professional and ethical manner that will reflect credit on themselves and the profession.
- Promote the integrity and viability of the global capital markets for the ultimate benefit of society.
- Maintain and improve their professional competence and strive to maintain and improve the competence of other investment professionals.

Standards of Professional Conduct

i.   PROFESSIONALISM

A. Knowledge of the Law

Members and Candidates must understand and comply with all applicable laws, rules, and regulations (including the CFA Institute Code of Ethics and Standards of Professional Conduct) of any government, regulatory organization, licensing agency, or professional association governing their professional activities. In the event of conflict, Members and Candidates must comply with the more strict law, rule, or regulation. Members and Candidates must not knowingly participate or assist in and must dissociate from any violation of such laws, rules, or regulations.

B. Independence and Objectivity

Members and Candidates must use reasonable care and judgment to achieve and maintain independence and objectivity in their professional activities. Members and Candidates must not offer, solicit, or accept any gift, benefit, compensation, or consideration that reasonably could be expected to compromise their own or another's independence and objectivity.

C. Misrepresentation

Members and Candidates must not knowingly make any misrepresentations relating to investment analysis, recommendations, actions, or other professional activities.

D. Misconduct

Members and Candidates must not engage in any professional conduct involving dishonesty, fraud, or deceit or commit any act that reflects adversely on their professional reputation, integrity, or competence.

CFA Institute Code of Ethics and Standards of Professional Conduct

ii. INTEGRITY OF CAPITAL MARKETS

A. Material Nonpublic Information

Members and Candidates who possess material nonpublic information that could affect the value of an investment must not act or cause others to act on the information.

B. Market Manipulation

Members and Candidates must not engage in practices that distort prices or artificially inflate trading volume with the intent to mislead market participants.

iii. DUTIES TO CLIENTS

A. Loyalty, Prudence, and Care

Members and Candidates have a duty of loyalty to their clients and must act with reasonable care and exercise prudent judgment. Members and Candidates must act for the benefit of their clients and place their clients' interests before their employer's or their own interests.

B. Fair Dealing

Members and Candidates must deal fairly and objectively with all clients when providing investment analysis, making investment recommendations, taking investment action, or engaging in other professional activities.

C. Suitability

1. When Members and Candidates are in an advisory relationship with a client, they must:

a. Make a reasonable inquiry into a client's or prospective client's investment experience, risk and return objectives, and financial constraints prior to making any investment recommendation or taking investment action and must reassess and update this information regularly.

b. Determine that an investment is suitable to the client's financial situation and consistent with the client's written objectives, mandates, and constraints before making an investment recommendation or taking investment action.

c. Judge the suitability of investments in the context of the client's total portfolio.

2. When Members and Candidates are responsible for managing a portfolio to a specific mandate, strategy, or style, they must make only investment recommendations or take only investment actions that are consistent with the stated objectives and constraints of the portfolio.

D. Performance Presentation

When communicating investment performance information, Members and Candidates must make reasonable efforts to ensure that it is fair, accurate, and complete.

E. Preservation of Confidentiality

Members and Candidates must keep information about current, former, and prospective clients confidential unless:

1. The information concerns illegal activities on the part of the client or prospective client,

2. Disclosure is required by law, or

3. The client or prospective client permits disclosure of the information.

iv. DUTIES TO EMPLOYERS

A. Loyalty

In matters related to their employment, Members and Candidates must act for the benefit of their employer and not deprive their employer of the advantage of their skills and abilities, divulge confidential information, or otherwise cause harm to their employer.

B. Additional Compensation Arrangements

Members and Candidates must not accept gifts, benefits, compensation, or consideration that competes with or might reasonably be expected to create a conflict of interest with their employer's interest unless they obtain written consent from all parties involved.

C. Responsibilities of Supervisors

Members and Candidates must make reasonable efforts to ensure that anyone subject to their supervision or authority complies with applicable laws, rules, regulations, and the Code and Standards.

v. INVESTMENT ANALYSIS, RECOMMENDATIONS, AND ACTIONS

A. Diligence and Reasonable Basis

Members and Candidates must:

1. Exercise diligence, independence, and thoroughness in analyzing investments, making investment recommendations, and taking investment actions.

2. Have a reasonable and adequate basis, supported by appropriate research and investigation, for any investment analysis, recommendation, or action.

B. Communication with Clients and Prospective Clients

Members and Candidates must:

1. Disclose to clients and prospective clients the basic format and general principles of the investment processes they use to analyze investments, select securities, and construct portfolios and must promptly disclose any changes that might materially affect those processes.

2. Disclose to clients and prospective clients significant limitations and risks associated with the investment process.

3. Use reasonable judgment in identifying which factors are important to their investment analyses, recommendations, or actions and include those factors in communications with clients and prospective clients.

CFA Institute Code of Ethics and Standards of Professional Conduct

    4. Distinguish between fact and opinion in the presentation of investment analysis and recommendations.

  C. Record Retention

Members and Candidates must develop and maintain appropriate records to support their investment analyses, recommendations, actions, and other investment-related communications with clients and prospective clients.

vi. CONFLICTS OF INTEREST

  A. Disclosure of Conflicts

Members and Candidates must make full and fair disclosure of all matters that could reasonably be expected to impair their independence and objectivity or interfere with respective duties to their clients, prospective clients, and employer. Members and Candidates must ensure that such disclosures are prominent, are delivered in plain language, and communicate the relevant information effectively.

  B. Priority of Transactions

Investment transactions for clients and employers must have priority over investment transactions in which a Member or Candidate is the beneficial owner.

  C. Referral Fees

Members and Candidates must disclose to their employer, clients, and prospective clients, as appropriate, any compensation, consideration, or benefit received from or paid to others for the recommendation of products or services.

vii. RESPONSIBILITIES AS A CFA INSTITUTE MEMBER OR CFA CANDIDATE

  A. Conduct as Participants in CFA Institute Programs

Members and Candidates must not engage in any conduct that compromises the reputation or integrity of CFA Institute or the CFA designation or the integrity, validity, or security of CFA Institute programs.

  B. Reference to CFA Institute, the CFA Designation, and the CFA Program

When referring to CFA Institute, CFA Institute membership, the CFA designation, or candidacy in the CFA Program, Members and Candidates must not misrepresent or exaggerate the meaning or implications of membership in CFA Institute, holding the CFA designation, or candidacy in the CFA Program.

LEARNING MODULE

2

Guidance for Standards I–VII

LEARNING OUTCOMES

Mastery	The candidate should be able to:
☐	demonstrate a thorough knowledge of the CFA Institute Code of Ethics and Standards of Professional Conduct by applying the Code and Standards to specific situations
☐	recommend practices and procedures designed to prevent violations of the Code of Ethics and Standards of Professional Conduct

STANDARD I(A): PROFESSIONALISM - KNOWLEDGE OF THE LAW

1

☐	demonstrate a thorough knowledge of the CFA Institute Code of Ethics and Standards of Professional Conduct by applying the Code and Standards to specific situations

Standard I(A) Knowledge of the Law

Members and Candidates must understand and comply with all applicable laws, rules, and regulations (including the CFA Institute Code of Ethics and Standards of Professional Conduct) of any government, regulatory organization, licensing agency, or professional association governing their professional activities. In the event of conflict, Members and Candidates must comply with the more strict law, rule, or regulation. Members and Candidates must not knowingly participate or assist in and must dissociate from any violation of such laws, rules, or regulations.

Guidance

Highlights:

- *Relationship between the Code and Standards and Applicable Law*

- *Participation in or Association with Violations by Others*
- *Investment Products and Applicable Laws*

Members and candidates must understand the applicable laws and regulations of the countries and jurisdictions where they engage in professional activities. These activities may include, but are not limited to, trading of securities or other financial instruments, providing investment advice, conducting research, or performing other investment services. On the basis of their reasonable and good faith understanding, members and candidates must comply with the laws and regulations that directly govern their professional activities and resulting outcomes and that protect the interests of the clients.

When questions arise, members and candidates should know their firm's policies and procedures for accessing compliance guidance. This standard does not require members and candidates to become experts, however, in compliance. Additionally, members and candidates are not required to have detailed knowledge of or be experts on all the laws that could potentially govern their activities.

During times of changing regulations, members and candidates must remain vigilant in maintaining their knowledge of the requirements for their professional activities. New financial products and processes, along with uncovered ethical missteps, create an environment for recurring and potentially wide-ranging regulatory changes. Members and candidates are also continually provided improved and enhanced methods of communicating with both clients and potential clients, such as mobile applications and web-based social networking platforms. As new local, regional, and global requirements are updated to address these and other changes, members, candidates, and their firms must adjust their procedures and practices to remain in compliance.

Relationship between the Code and Standards and Applicable Law

Some members or candidates may live, work, or provide investment services to clients living in a country that has no law or regulation governing a particular action or that has laws or regulations that differ from the requirements of the Code and Standards. When applicable law and the Code and Standards require different conduct, members and candidates must follow the more strict of the applicable law or the Code and Standards.

"Applicable law" is the law that governs the member's or candidate's conduct. Which law applies will depend on the particular facts and circumstances of each case. The "more strict" law or regulation is the law or regulation that imposes greater restrictions on the action of the member or candidate or calls for the member or candidate to exert a greater degree of action that protects the interests of investors. For example, applicable law or regulation may not require members and candidates to disclose referral fees received from or paid to others for the recommendation of investment products or services. Because the Code and Standards impose this obligation, however, members and candidates must disclose the existence of such fees.

Members and candidates must adhere to the following principles:

- Members and candidates must comply with applicable laws or regulations related to their professional activities.
- Members and candidates must not engage in conduct that constitutes a violation of the Code and Standards, even though it may otherwise be legal.
- In the absence of any applicable law or regulation or when the Code and Standards impose a higher degree of responsibility than applicable laws and regulations, members and candidates must adhere to the Code and Standards. Applications of these principles are outlined in Exhibit 1.

Standard I(A): Professionalism - Knowledge of the Law

The applicable laws governing the responsibilities of a member or candidate should be viewed as the minimal threshold of acceptable actions. When members and candidates take actions that exceed the minimal requirements, they further support the conduct required of Standard I(A).

CFA Institute members are obligated to abide by the CFA Institute Articles of Incorporation, Bylaws, Code of Ethics, Standards of Professional Conduct, Rules of Procedure, Membership Agreement, and other applicable rules promulgated by CFA Institute, all as amended periodically. CFA candidates who are not members must also abide by these documents (except for the Membership Agreement) as well as rules and regulations related to the administration of the CFA examination, the Candidate Responsibility Statement, and the Candidate Pledge.

Participation in or Association with Violations by Others

Members and candidates are responsible for violations in which they *knowingly* participate or assist. Although members and candidates are presumed to have knowledge of all applicable laws, rules, and regulations, CFA Institute acknowledges that members may not recognize violations if they are not aware of all the facts giving rise to the violations. Standard I(A) applies when members and candidates know or should know that their conduct may contribute to a violation of applicable laws, rules, or regulations or the Code and Standards.

If a member or candidate has reasonable grounds to believe that imminent or ongoing client or employer activities are illegal or unethical, the member or candidate must dissociate, or separate, from the activity. In extreme cases, dissociation may require a member or candidate to leave his or her employment. Members and candidates may take the following intermediate steps to dissociate from ethical violations of others when direct discussions with the person or persons committing the violation are unsuccessful. The first step should be to attempt to stop the behavior by bringing it to the attention of the employer through a supervisor or the firm's compliance department. If this attempt is unsuccessful, then members and candidates have a responsibility to step away and dissociate from the activity. Dissociation practices will differ on the basis of the member's or candidate's role in the investment industry. It may include removing one's name from written reports or recommendations, asking for a different assignment, or refusing to accept a new client or continue to advise a current client. Inaction combined with continuing association with those involved in illegal or unethical conduct may be construed as participation or assistance in the illegal or unethical conduct.

CFA Institute strongly encourages members and candidates to report potential violations of the Code and Standards committed by fellow members and candidates. Although a failure to report is less likely to be construed as a violation than a failure to dissociate from unethical conduct, the impact of inactivity on the integrity of capital markets can be significant. Although the Code and Standards do not compel members and candidates to report violations to their governmental or regulatory organizations unless such disclosure is mandatory under applicable law (voluntary reporting is often referred to as whistleblowing), such disclosure may be prudent under certain circumstances. Members and candidates should consult their legal and compliance advisers for guidance.

Additionally, CFA Institute encourages members, nonmembers, clients, and the investing public to report violations of the Code and Standards by CFA Institute members or CFA candidates by submitting a complaint in writing to the CFA Institute Professional Conduct Program via e-mail (pcprogram@cfainstitute.org) or the CFA Institute website (www.cfainstitute.org).

Investment Products and Applicable Laws

Members and candidates involved in creating or maintaining investment services or investment products or packages of securities and/or derivatives should be mindful of where these products or packages will be sold as well as their places of origination. The applicable laws and regulations of the countries or regions of origination and expected sale should be understood by those responsible for the supervision of the services or creation and maintenance of the products or packages. Members or candidates should make reasonable efforts to review whether associated firms that are distributing products or services developed by their employing firm also abide by the laws and regulations of the countries and regions of distribution. Members and candidates should undertake the necessary due diligence when transacting cross-border business to understand the multiple applicable laws and regulations in order to protect the reputation of their firm and themselves.

Given the complexity that can arise with business transactions in today's market, there may be some uncertainty surrounding which laws or regulations are considered applicable when activities are being conducted in multiple jurisdictions. Members and candidates should seek the appropriate guidance, potentially including the firm's compliance or legal departments and legal counsel outside the organization, to gain a reasonable understanding of their responsibilities and how to implement them appropriately.

Exhibit 1: Global Application of the Code and Standards

Members and candidates who practice in multiple jurisdictions may be subject to varied securities laws and regulations. If applicable law is stricter than the requirements of the Code and Standards, members and candidates must adhere to applicable law; otherwise, they must adhere to the Code and Standards. The following chart provides illustrations involving a member who may be subject to the securities laws and regulations of three different types of countries:

NS: country with no securities laws or regulations

LS: country with *less* strict securities laws and regulations than the Code and Standards

MS: country with *more* strict securities laws and regulations than the Code and Standards

Applicable Law	Duties	Explanation
Member resides in NS country, does business in LS country; LS law applies.	Member must adhere to the Code and Standards.	Because applicable law is less strict than the Code and Standards, the member must adhere to the Code and Standards.
Member resides in NS country, does business in MS country; MS law applies.	Member must adhere to the law of MS country.	Because applicable law is stricter than the Code and Standards, member must adhere to the more strict applicable law.
Member resides in LS country, does business in NS country; LS law applies.	Member must adhere to the Code and Standards.	Because applicable law is less strict than the Code and Standards, member must adhere to the Code and Standards.

Standard I(A): Professionalism - Knowledge of the Law

Applicable Law	Duties	Explanation
Member resides in LS country, does business in MS country; MS law applies.	Member must adhere to the law of MS country.	Because applicable law is stricter than the Code and Standards, member must adhere to the more strict applicable law.
Member resides in LS country, does business in NS country; LS law applies, but it states that law of locality where business is conducted governs.	Member must adhere to the Code and Standards.	Because applicable law states that the law of the locality where the business is conducted governs and there is no local law, the member must adhere to the Code and Standards.
Member resides in LS country, does business in MS country; LS law applies, but it states that law of locality where business is conducted governs.	Member must adhere to the law of MS country.	Because applicable law of the locality where the business is conducted governs and local law is stricter than the Code and Standards, member must adhere to the more strict applicable law.
Member resides in MS country, does business in LS country; MS law applies.	Member must adhere to the law of MS country.	Because applicable law is stricter than the Code and Standards, member must adhere to the more strict applicable law.
Member resides in MS country, does business in LS country; MS law applies, but it states that law of locality where business is conducted governs.	Member must adhere to the Code and Standards.	Because applicable law states that the law of the locality where the business is conducted governs and local law is less strict than the Code and Standards, member must adhere to the Code and Standards.
Member resides in MS country, does business in LS country with a client who is a citizen of LS country; MS law applies, but it states that the law of the client's home country governs.	Member must adhere to the Code and Standards.	Because applicable law states that the law of the client's home country governs (which is less strict than the Code and Standards), member must adhere to the Code and Standards.
Member resides in MS country, does business in LS country with a client who is a citizen of MS country; MS law applies, but it states that the law of the client's home country governs.	Member must adhere to the law of MS country.	Because applicable law states that the law of the client's home country governs and the law of the client's home country is stricter than the Code and Standards, the member must adhere to the more strict applicable law.

STANDARD I(A): RECOMMENDED PROCEDURES

☐ demonstrate a thorough knowledge of the CFA Institute Code of Ethics and Standards of Professional Conduct by applying the Code and Standards to specific situations

Members and Candidates

Suggested methods by which members and candidates can acquire and maintain understanding of applicable laws, rules, and regulations include the following:

- *Stay informed*: Members and candidates should establish or encourage their employers to establish a procedure by which employees are regularly informed about changes in applicable laws, rules, regulations, and case law. In many instances, the employer's compliance department or legal counsel can provide such information in the form of memorandums distributed to employees in the organization. Also, participation in an internal or external continuing education program is a practical method of staying current.

- *Review procedures*: Members and candidates should review, or encourage their employers to review, the firm's written compliance procedures on a regular basis to ensure that the procedures reflect current law and provide adequate guidance to employees about what is permissible conduct under the law and/or the Code and Standards. Recommended compliance procedures for specific items of the Code and Standards are discussed in this *Handbook* in the "Guidance" sections associated with each standard.

- *Maintain current files*: Members and candidates should maintain or encourage their employers to maintain readily accessible current reference copies of applicable statutes, rules, regulations, and important cases.

Distribution Area Laws

Members and candidates should make reasonable efforts to understand the applicable laws—both country and regional—for the countries and regions where their investment products are developed and are most likely to be distributed to clients.

Legal Counsel

When in doubt about the appropriate action to undertake, it is recommended that a member or candidate seek the advice of compliance personnel or legal counsel concerning legal requirements. If a potential violation is being committed by a fellow employee, it may also be prudent for the member or candidate to seek the advice of the firm's compliance department or legal counsel.

Dissociation

When dissociating from an activity that violates the Code and Standards, members and candidates should document the violation and urge their firms to attempt to persuade the perpetrator(s) to cease such conduct. To dissociate from the conduct, a member or candidate may have to resign his or her employment.

Firms

The formality and complexity of compliance procedures for firms depend on the nature and size of the organization and the nature of its investment operations. Members and candidates should encourage their firms to consider the following policies and procedures to support the principles of Standard I(A):

- *Develop and/or adopt a code of ethics*: The ethical culture of an organization starts at the top. Members and candidates should encourage their supervisors or managers to adopt a code of ethics. Adhering to a code of ethics facilitates solutions when people face ethical dilemmas and can prevent the need for employees to resort to a "whistleblowing" solution publicly alleging concealed misconduct. CFA Institute has published the *Asset Manager Code of Professional Conduct*, which firms may adopt or use as the basis for their codes (visit www.cfainstitute.org).

- *Provide information on applicable laws*: Pertinent information that highlights applicable laws and regulations might be distributed to employees or made available in a central location. Information sources might include primary information developed by the relevant government, governmental agencies, regulatory organizations, licensing agencies, and professional associations (e.g., from their websites); law firm memorandums or newsletters; and association memorandums or publications (e.g., *CFA Institute Magazine*).

- *Establish procedures for reporting violations*: Firms might provide written protocols for reporting suspected violations of laws, regulations, or company policies.

STANDARD I(A): APPLICATION OF THE STANDARD

3

☐ | demonstrate a thorough knowledge of the CFA Institute Code of Ethics and Standards of Professional Conduct by applying the Code and Standards to specific situations

Example 1 (Notification of Known Violations):

Michael Allen works for a brokerage firm and is responsible for an underwriting of securities. A company official gives Allen information indicating that the financial statements Allen filed with the regulator overstate the issuer's earnings. Allen seeks the advice of the brokerage firm's general counsel, who states that it would be difficult for the regulator to prove that Allen has been involved in any wrongdoing.

> *Comment*: Although it is recommended that members and candidates seek the advice of legal counsel, the reliance on such advice does not absolve a member or candidate from the requirement to comply with the law or regulation. Allen should report this situation to his supervisor, seek an independent legal opinion, and determine whether the regulator should be notified of the error.

Example 2 (Dissociating from a Violation):

Lawrence Brown's employer, an investment banking firm, is the principal underwriter for an issue of convertible debentures by the Courtney Company. Brown discovers that the Courtney Company has concealed severe third-quarter losses in its foreign operations. The preliminary prospectus has already been distributed.

> *Comment*: Knowing that the preliminary prospectus is misleading, Brown should report his findings to the appropriate supervisory persons in his firm. If the matter is not remedied and Brown's employer does not dissociate from the underwriting, Brown should sever all his connections with the underwriting. Brown should also seek legal advice to determine whether additional reporting or other action should be taken.

Example 3 (Dissociating from a Violation):

Kamisha Washington's firm advertises its past performance record by showing the 10-year return of a composite of its client accounts. Washington discovers, however, that the composite omits the performance of accounts that have left the firm during the 10-year period, whereas the description of the composite indicates the inclusion of all firm accounts. This omission has led to an inflated performance figure. Washington is asked to use promotional material that includes the erroneous performance number when soliciting business for the firm.

> *Comment*: Misrepresenting performance is a violation of the Code and Standards. Although she did not calculate the performance herself, Washington would be assisting in violating Standard I(A) if she were to use the inflated performance number when soliciting clients. She must dissociate herself from the activity. If discussing the misleading number with the person responsible is not an option for correcting the problem, she can bring the situation to the attention of her supervisor or the compliance department at her firm. If her firm is unwilling to recalculate performance, she must refrain from using the misleading promotional material and should notify the firm of her reasons. If the firm insists that she use the material, she should consider whether her obligation to dissociate from the activity requires her to seek other employment.

Example 4 (Following the Highest Requirements):

James Collins is an investment analyst for a major Wall Street brokerage firm. He works in a developing country with a rapidly modernizing economy and a growing capital market. Local securities laws are minimal—in form and content—and include no punitive prohibitions against insider trading.

> *Comment*: Collins must abide by the requirements of the Code and Standards, which might be more strict than the rules of the developing country. He should be aware of the risks that a small market and the absence of a fairly regulated flow of information to the market represent to his ability to obtain information and make timely judgments. He should include this factor in formulating his advice to clients. In handling material nonpublic information that accidentally comes into his possession, he must follow Standard II(A)–Material Nonpublic Information.

Standard I(A): Application of the Standard

Example 5 (Following the Highest Requirements):

Laura Jameson works for a multinational investment adviser based in the United States. Jameson lives and works as a registered investment adviser in the tiny, but wealthy, island nation of Karramba. Karramba's securities laws state that no investment adviser registered and working in that country can participate in initial public offerings (IPOs) for the adviser's personal account. Jameson, believing that, as a US citizen working for a US-based company, she should comply only with US law, has ignored this Karrambian law. In addition, Jameson believes that as a charterholder, as long as she adheres to the Code and Standards requirement that she disclose her participation in any IPO to her employer and clients when such ownership creates a conflict of interest, she is meeting the highest ethical requirements.

> *Comment*: Jameson is in violation of Standard I(A). As a registered investment adviser in Karramba, Jameson is prevented by Karrambian securities law from participating in IPOs regardless of the law of her home country. In addition, because the law of the country where she is working is stricter than the Code and Standards, she must follow the stricter requirements of the local law rather than the requirements of the Code and Standards.

Example 6 (Laws and Regulations Based on Religious Tenets):

Amanda Janney is employed as a fixed-income portfolio manager for a large international firm. She is on a team within her firm that is responsible for creating and managing a fixed-income hedge fund to be sold throughout the firm's distribution centers to high-net-worth clients. Her firm receives expressions of interest from potential clients from the Middle East who are seeking investments that comply with Islamic law. The marketing and promotional materials for the fixed-income hedge fund do not specify whether or not the fund is a suitable investment for an investor seeking compliance with Islamic law. Because the fund is being distributed globally, Janney is concerned about the reputation of the fund and the firm and believes disclosure of whether or not the fund complies with Islamic law could help minimize potential mistakes with placing this investment.

> *Comment*: As the financial market continues to become globalized, members and candidates will need to be aware of the differences between cultural and religious laws and requirements as well as the different governmental laws and regulations. Janney and the firm could be proactive in their efforts to acknowledge areas where the new fund may not be suitable for clients.

Example 7 (Reporting Potential Unethical Actions):

Krista Blume is a junior portfolio manager for high-net-worth portfolios at a large global investment manager. She observes a number of new portfolios and relationships coming from a country in Europe where the firm did not have previous business and is told that a broker in that country is responsible for this new business. At a meeting on allocation of research resources to third-party research firms, Blume notes that this broker has been added to the list and is allocated payments for research. However, she knows the portfolios do not invest in securities in the broker's country, and she has not seen any research come from this broker. Blume asks her supervisor about the name being on the list and is told that someone in marketing is receiving the research and that the name being on the list is OK. She believes that what may be going on is that the broker is being paid for new business through the inappropriate research payments, and she wishes to dissociate from the misconduct.

Comment: Blume should follow the firm's policies and procedures for reporting potential unethical activity, which may include discussions with her supervisor or someone in a designated compliance department. She should communicate her concerns appropriately while advocating for disclosure between the new broker relationship and the research payments.

Example 8 (Failure to Maintain Knowledge of the Law):

Colleen White is excited to use new technology to communicate with clients and potential clients. She recently began posting investment information, including performance reports and investment opinions and recommendations, to her Facebook page. In addition, she sends out brief announcements, opinions, and thoughts via her Twitter account (for example, "Prospects for future growth of XYZ company look good! #makingmoney4U"). Prior to White's use of these social media platforms, the local regulator had issued new requirements and guidance governing online electronic communication. White's communications appear to conflict with the recent regulatory announcements.

Comment: White is in violation of Standard I(A) because her communications do not comply with the existing guidance and regulation governing use of social media. White must be aware of the evolving legal requirements pertaining to new and dynamic areas of the financial services industry that are applicable to her. She should seek guidance from appropriate, knowledgeable, and reliable sources, such as her firm's compliance department, external service providers, or outside counsel, unless she diligently follows legal and regulatory trends affecting her professional responsibilities.

4 STANDARD I(B): PROFESSIONALISM - INDEPENDENCE AND OBJECTIVITY

☐ demonstrate a thorough knowledge of the CFA Institute Code of Ethics and Standards of Professional Conduct by applying the Code and Standards to specific situations

> Members and Candidates must use reasonable care and judgment to achieve and maintain independence and objectivity in their professional activities. Members and Candidates must not offer, solicit, or accept any gift, benefit, compensation, or consideration that reasonably could be expected to compromise their own or another's independence and objectivity.

Guidance

Highlights:

- *Buy-Side Clients*
- *Fund Manager and Custodial Relationships*
- *Investment Banking Relationships*

Standard I(B): Professionalism - Independence and Objectivity

- *Performance Measurement and Attribution*
- *Public Companies*
- *Credit Rating Agency Opinions*
- *Influence during the Manager Selection/Procurement Process*
- *Issuer-Paid Research*
- *Travel Funding*

Standard I(B) states the responsibility of CFA Institute members and candidates in the CFA Program to maintain independence and objectivity so that their clients will have the benefit of their work and opinions unaffected by any potential conflict of interest or other circumstance adversely affecting their judgment. Every member and candidate should endeavor to avoid situations that could cause or be perceived to cause a loss of independence or objectivity in recommending investments or taking investment action.

External sources may try to influence the investment process by offering analysts and portfolio managers a variety of benefits. Corporations may seek expanded research coverage, issuers and underwriters may wish to promote new securities offerings, brokers may want to increase commission business, and independent rating agencies may be influenced by the company requesting the rating. Benefits may include gifts, invitations to lavish functions, tickets, favors, or job referrals. One type of benefit is the allocation of shares in oversubscribed IPOs to investment managers for their personal accounts. This practice affords managers the opportunity to make quick profits that may not be available to their clients. Such a practice is prohibited under Standard I(B). Modest gifts and entertainment are acceptable, but special care must be taken by members and candidates to resist subtle and not-so-subtle pressures to act in conflict with the interests of their clients. Best practice dictates that members and candidates reject any offer of gift or entertainment that could be expected to threaten their independence and objectivity.

Receiving a gift, benefit, or consideration from a *client* can be distinguished from gifts given by entities seeking to influence a member or candidate to the detriment of other clients. In a client relationship, the client has already entered some type of compensation arrangement with the member, candidate, or his or her firm. A gift from a client could be considered supplementary compensation. The potential for obtaining influence to the detriment of other clients, although present, is not as great as in situations where no compensation arrangement exists. When possible, prior to accepting "bonuses" or gifts from clients, members and candidates should disclose to their employers such benefits offered by clients. If notification is not possible prior to acceptance, members and candidates must disclose to their employer benefits previously accepted from clients. Disclosure allows the employer of a member or candidate to make an independent determination about the extent to which the gift may affect the member's or candidate's independence and objectivity.

Members and candidates may also come under pressure from their own firms to, for example, issue favorable research reports or recommendations for certain companies with potential or continuing business relationships with the firm. The situation may be aggravated if an executive of the company sits on the bank or investment firm's board and attempts to interfere in investment decision making. Members and candidates acting in a sales or marketing capacity must be especially mindful of their objectivity in promoting appropriate investments for their clients.

Left unmanaged, pressures that threaten independence place research analysts in a difficult position and may jeopardize their ability to act independently and objectively. One of the ways that research analysts have coped with these pressures in the past is to use subtle and ambiguous language in their recommendations or to temper the tone of their research reports. Such subtleties are lost on some investors, however, who reasonably expect research reports and recommendations to be straightforward and transparent and to communicate clearly an analyst's views based on unbiased analysis and independent judgment.

Members and candidates are personally responsible for maintaining independence and objectivity when preparing research reports, making investment recommendations, and taking investment action on behalf of clients. Recommendations must convey the member's or candidate's true opinions, free of bias from internal or external pressures, and be stated in clear and unambiguous language.

Members and candidates also should be aware that some of their professional or social activities within CFA Institute or its member societies may subtly threaten their independence or objectivity. When seeking corporate financial support for conventions, seminars, or even weekly society luncheons, the members or candidates responsible for the activities should evaluate both the actual effect of such solicitations on their independence and whether their objectivity might be perceived to be compromised in the eyes of their clients.

Buy-Side Clients

One source of pressure on sell-side analysts is buy-side clients. Institutional clients are traditionally the primary users of sell-side research, either directly or with soft dollar brokerage. Portfolio managers may have significant positions in the security of a company under review. A rating downgrade may adversely affect the portfolio's performance, particularly in the short term, because the sensitivity of stock prices to ratings changes has increased in recent years. A downgrade may also affect the manager's compensation, which is usually tied to portfolio performance. Moreover, portfolio performance is subject to media and public scrutiny, which may affect the manager's professional reputation. Consequently, some portfolio managers implicitly or explicitly support sell-side ratings inflation.

Portfolio managers have a responsibility to respect and foster the intellectual honesty of sell-side research. Therefore, it is improper for portfolio managers to threaten or engage in retaliatory practices, such as reporting sell-side analysts to the covered company in order to instigate negative corporate reactions. Although most portfolio managers do not engage in such practices, the perception by the research analyst that a reprisal is possible may cause concern and make it difficult for the analyst to maintain independence and objectivity.

Fund Manager and Custodial Relationships

Research analysts are not the only people who must be concerned with maintaining their independence. Members and candidates who are responsible for hiring and retaining outside managers and third-party custodians should not accepts gifts, entertainment, or travel funding that may be perceived as impairing their decisions. The use of secondary fund managers has evolved into a common practice to manage specific asset allocations. The use of third-party custodians is common practice for independent investment advisory firms and helps them with trading capabilities and reporting requirements. Primary and secondary fund managers, as well as third-party custodians, often arrange educational and marketing events to inform others about their business strategies, investment process, or custodial services. Members and candidates must review the merits of each offer individually in determining whether they may attend yet maintain their independence.

Investment Banking Relationships

Some sell-side firms may exert pressure on their analysts to issue favorable research reports on current or prospective investment banking clients. For many of these firms, income from investment banking has become increasingly important to overall firm

Standard I(B): Professionalism - Independence and Objectivity

profitability because brokerage income has declined as a result of price competition. Consequently, firms offering investment banking services work hard to develop and maintain relationships with investment banking clients and prospects. These companies are often covered by the firm's research analysts because companies often select their investment banks on the basis of the reputation of their research analysts, the quality of their work, and their standing in the industry.

In some countries, research analysts frequently work closely with their investment banking colleagues to help evaluate prospective investment banking clients. In other countries, because of past abuses in managing the obvious conflicts of interest, regulators have established clear rules prohibiting the interaction of these groups. Although collaboration between research analysts and investment banking colleagues may benefit the firm and enhance market efficiency (e.g., by allowing firms to assess risks more accurately and make better pricing assumptions), it requires firms to carefully balance the conflicts of interest inherent in the collaboration. Having analysts work with investment bankers is appropriate only when the conflicts are adequately and effectively managed and disclosed. Firm managers have a responsibility to provide an environment in which analysts are neither coerced nor enticed into issuing research that does not reflect their true opinions. Firms should require public disclosure of actual conflicts of interest to investors.

Members, candidates, and their firms must adopt and follow perceived best practices in maintaining independence and objectivity in the corporate culture and protecting analysts from undue pressure by their investment banking colleagues. The "firewalls" traditionally built between these two functions must be managed to minimize conflicts of interest; indeed, enhanced firewall policies may go as far as prohibiting all communications between these groups. A key element of an enhanced firewall is separate reporting structures for personnel on the research side and personnel on the investment banking side. For example, investment banking personnel should not have any authority to approve, disapprove, or make changes to research reports or recommendations. Another element should be a compensation arrangement that minimizes the pressures on research analysts and rewards objectivity and accuracy. Compensation arrangements should not link analyst remuneration directly to investment banking assignments in which the analyst may participate as a team member. Firms should also regularly review their policies and procedures to determine whether analysts are adequately safeguarded and to improve the transparency of disclosures relating to conflicts of interest. The highest level of transparency is achieved when disclosures are prominent and specific rather than marginalized and generic.

Performance Measurement and Attribution

Members and candidates working within a firm's investment performance measurement department may also be presented with situations that challenge their independence and objectivity. As performance analysts, their analyses may reveal instances where managers may appear to have strayed from their mandate. Additionally, the performance analyst may receive requests to alter the construction of composite indexes owing to negative results for a selected account or fund. The member or candidate must not allow internal or external influences to affect their independence and objectivity as they faithfully complete their performance calculation and analysis-related responsibilities.

Public Companies

Analysts may be pressured to issue favorable reports and recommendations by the companies they follow. Not every stock is a "buy," and not every research report is favorable—for many reasons, including the cyclical nature of many business activities and market fluctuations. For instance, a "good company" does not always translate into a "good stock" rating if the current stock price is fully valued. In making an investment recommendation, the analyst is responsible for anticipating, interpreting, and assessing a company's prospects and stock price performance in a factual manner. Many company managers, however, believe that their company's stock is undervalued, and these managers may find it difficult to accept critical research reports or ratings downgrades. Company managers' compensation may also be dependent on stock performance.

Due diligence in financial research and analysis involves gathering information from a wide variety of sources, including public disclosure documents (such as proxy statements, annual reports, and other regulatory filings) and also company management and investor-relations personnel, suppliers, customers, competitors, and other relevant sources. Research analysts may justifiably fear that companies will limit their ability to conduct thorough research by denying analysts who have "negative" views direct access to company managers and/or barring them from conference calls and other communication venues. Retaliatory practices include companies bringing legal action against analysts personally and/or their firms to seek monetary damages for the economic effects of negative reports and recommendations. Although few companies engage in such behavior, the perception that a reprisal is possible is a reasonable concern for analysts. This concern may make it difficult for them to conduct the comprehensive research needed to make objective recommendations. For further information and guidance, members and candidates should refer to the CFA Institute publication *Best Practice Guidelines Governing Analyst/Corporate Issuer Relations* (www.cfainstitute.org).

Credit Rating Agency Opinions

Credit rating agencies provide a service by grading the fixed-income products offered by companies. Analysts face challenges related to incentives and compensation schemes that may be tied to the final rating and successful placement of the product. Members and candidates employed at rating agencies should ensure that procedures and processes at the agencies prevent undue influences from a sponsoring company during the analysis. Members and candidates should abide by their agencies' and the industry's standards of conduct regarding the analytical process and the distribution of their reports.

The work of credit rating agencies also raises concerns similar to those inherent in investment banking relationships. Analysts may face pressure to issue ratings at a specific level because of other services the agency offers companies—namely, advising on the development of structured products. The rating agencies need to develop the necessary firewalls and protections to allow the independent operations of their different business lines.

When using information provided by credit rating agencies, members and candidates should be mindful of the potential conflicts of interest. And because of the potential conflicts, members and candidates may need to independently validate the rating granted.

Influence during the Manager Selection/Procurement Process

Members and candidates may find themselves on either side of the manager selection process. An individual may be on the hiring side as a representative of a pension organization or an investment committee member of an endowment or a charitable organization. Additionally, other members may be representing their organizations in attempts to earn new investment allocation mandates. The responsibility of members and candidates to maintain their independence and objectivity extends to the hiring or firing of those who provide business services beyond investment management.

When serving in a hiring capacity, members and candidates should not solicit gifts, contributions, or other compensation that may affect their independence and objectivity. Solicitations do not have to benefit members and candidates personally to

Standard I(B): Professionalism - Independence and Objectivity

conflict with Standard I(B). Requesting contributions to a favorite charity or political organization may also be perceived as an attempt to influence the decision-making process. Additionally, members and candidates serving in a hiring capacity should refuse gifts, donations, and other offered compensation that may be perceived to influence their decision-making process.

When working to earn a new investment allocation, members and candidates should not offer gifts, contributions, or other compensation to influence the decision of the hiring representative. The offering of these items with the intent to impair the independence and objectivity of another person would not comply with Standard I(B). Such prohibited actions may include offering donations to a charitable organization or political candidate referred by the hiring representative.

A clear example of improperly influencing hiring representatives was displayed in the "pay-to-play" scandal involving government-sponsored pension funds in the United States. Managers looking to gain lucrative allocations from the large funds made requested donations to the political campaigns of individuals directly responsible for the hiring decisions. This scandal and other similar events have led to new laws requiring additional reporting concerning political contributions and bans on hiring—or hiring delays for—managers that made campaign contributions to representatives associated with the decision-making process.

Issuer-Paid Research

In light of the recent reduction of sell-side research coverage, many companies, seeking to increase visibility both in the financial markets and with potential investors, have hired analysts to produce research reports analyzing their companies. These reports bridge the gap created by the lack of coverage and can be an effective method of communicating with investors.

Issuer-paid research conducted by independent analysts, however, is fraught with potential conflicts. Depending on how the research is written and distributed, investors may be misled into believing that the research is from an independent source when, in reality, it has been paid for by the subject company.

Members and candidates must adhere to strict standards of conduct that govern how the research is to be conducted and what disclosures must be made in the report. Analysts must engage in thorough, independent, and unbiased analysis and must fully disclose potential conflicts of interest, including the nature of their compensation. Otherwise, analysts risk misleading investors.

Investors need clear, credible, and thorough information about companies, and they need research based on independent thought. At a minimum, issuer-paid research should include a thorough analysis of the company's financial statements based on publicly disclosed information, benchmarking within a peer group, and industry analysis. Analysts must exercise diligence, independence, and thoroughness in conducting their research in an objective manner. Analysts must distinguish between fact and opinion in their reports. Conclusions must have a reasonable and adequate basis and must be supported by appropriate research.

Independent analysts must also strictly limit the type of compensation that they accept for conducting issuer-paid research. Otherwise, the content and conclusions of the reports could reasonably be expected to be determined or affected by compensation from the sponsoring companies. Compensation that might influence the research report could be direct, such as payment based on the conclusions of the report, or indirect, such as stock warrants or other equity instruments that could increase in value on the basis of positive coverage in the report. In such instances, the independent analyst has an incentive to avoid including negative information or making negative conclusions. Best practice is for independent analysts, prior to writing their reports, to negotiate only a flat fee for their work that is not linked to their conclusions or recommendations.

Travel Funding

The benefits related to accepting paid travel extend beyond the cost savings to the member or candidate and his firm, such as the chance to talk exclusively with the executives of a company or learning more about the investment options provided by an investment organization. Acceptance also comes with potential concerns; for example, members and candidates may be influenced by these discussions when flying on a corporate or chartered jet or attending sponsored conferences where many expenses, including airfare and lodging, are covered. To avoid the appearance of compromising their independence and objectivity, best practice dictates that members and candidates always use commercial transportation at their expense or at the expense of their firm rather than accept paid travel arrangements from an outside company. Should commercial transportation be unavailable, members and candidates may accept modestly arranged travel to participate in appropriate information-gathering events, such as a property tour.

5 STANDARD I(B): RECOMMENDED PROCEDURES

☐ demonstrate a thorough knowledge of the CFA Institute Code of Ethics and Standards of Professional Conduct by applying the Code and Standards to specific situations

Members and candidates should adhere to the following practices and should encourage their firms to establish procedures to avoid violations of Standard I(B):

- *Protect the integrity of opinions*: Members, candidates, and their firms should establish policies stating that every research report concerning the securities of a corporate client should reflect the unbiased opinion of the analyst. Firms should also design compensation systems that protect the integrity of the investment decision process by maintaining the independence and objectivity of analysts.

- *Create a restricted list*: If the firm is unwilling to permit dissemination of adverse opinions about a corporate client, members and candidates should encourage the firm to remove the controversial company from the research universe and put it on a restricted list so that the firm disseminates only factual information about the company.

- *Restrict special cost arrangements*: When attending meetings at an issuer's headquarters, members and candidates should pay for commercial transportation and hotel charges. No corporate issuer should reimburse members or candidates for air transportation. Members and candidates should encourage issuers to limit the use of corporate aircraft to situations in which commercial transportation is not available or in which efficient movement could not otherwise be arranged. Members and candidates should take particular care that when frequent meetings are held between an individual issuer and an individual member or candidate, the issuer should not always host the member or candidate.

- *Limit gifts*: Members and candidates must limit the acceptance of gratuities and/or gifts to token items. Standard I(B) does not preclude customary, ordinary business-related entertainment as long as its purpose is not to influence or reward members or candidates. Firms should consider a strict

Standard I(B): Application of the Standard

value limit for acceptable gifts that is based on the local or regional customs and should address whether the limit is per gift or an aggregate annual value.

- *Restrict investments*: Members and candidates should encourage their investment firms to develop formal policies related to employee purchases of equity or equity-related IPOs. Firms should require prior approval for employee participation in IPOs, with prompt disclosure of investment actions taken following the offering. Strict limits should be imposed on investment personnel acquiring securities in private placements.

- *Review procedures*: Members and candidates should encourage their firms to implement effective supervisory and review procedures to ensure that analysts and portfolio managers comply with policies relating to their personal investment activities.

- *Independence policy*: Members, candidates, and their firms should establish a formal written policy on the independence and objectivity of research and implement reporting structures and review procedures to ensure that research analysts do not report to and are not supervised or controlled by any department of the firm that could compromise the independence of the analyst. More detailed recommendations related to a firm's policies regarding research objectivity are set forth in the CFA Institute statement *Research Objectivity Standards* (www.cfainstitute.org).

- *Appointed officer*: Firms should appoint a senior officer with oversight responsibilities for compliance with the firm's code of ethics and all regulations concerning its business. Firms should provide every employee with the procedures and policies for reporting potentially unethical behavior, violations of regulations, or other activities that may harm the firm's reputation.

STANDARD I(B): APPLICATION OF THE STANDARD 6

☐ demonstrate a thorough knowledge of the CFA Institute Code of Ethics and Standards of Professional Conduct by applying the Code and Standards to specific situations

☐ recommend practices and procedures designed to prevent violations of the Code of Ethics and Standards of Professional Conduct

Example 1 (Travel Expenses):

Steven Taylor, a mining analyst with Bronson Brokers, is invited by Precision Metals to join a group of his peers in a tour of mining facilities in several western US states. The company arranges for chartered group flights from site to site and for accommodations in Spartan Motels, the only chain with accommodations near the mines, for three nights. Taylor allows Precision Metals to pick up his tab, as do the other analysts, with one exception—John Adams, an employee of a large trust company who insists on following his company's policy and paying for his hotel room himself.

> *Comment*: The policy of the company where Adams works complies closely with Standard I(B) by avoiding even the appearance of a conflict of interest, but Taylor and the other analysts were not necessarily violating Standard

I(B). In general, when allowing companies to pay for travel and/or accommodations in these circumstances, members and candidates must use their judgment. They must be on guard that such arrangements not impinge on a member's or candidate's independence and objectivity. In this example, the trip was strictly for business and Taylor was not accepting irrelevant or lavish hospitality. The itinerary required chartered flights, for which analysts were not expected to pay. The accommodations were modest. These arrangements are not unusual and did not violate Standard I(B) as long as Taylor's independence and objectivity were not compromised. In the final analysis, members and candidates should consider both whether they can remain objective and whether their integrity might be perceived by their clients to have been compromised.

Example 2 (Research Independence):

Susan Dillon, an analyst in the corporate finance department of an investment services firm, is making a presentation to a potential new business client that includes the promise that her firm will provide full research coverage of the potential client.

Comment: Dillon may agree to provide research coverage, but she must not commit her firm's research department to providing a favorable recommendation. The firm's recommendation (favorable, neutral, or unfavorable) must be based on an independent and objective investigation and analysis of the company and its securities.

Example 3 (Research Independence and Intrafirm Pressure):

Walter Fritz is an equity analyst with Hilton Brokerage who covers the mining industry. He has concluded that the stock of Metals & Mining is overpriced at its current level, but he is concerned that a negative research report will hurt the good relationship between Metals & Mining and the investment banking division of his firm. In fact, a senior manager of Hilton Brokerage has just sent him a copy of a proposal his firm has made to Metals & Mining to underwrite a debt offering. Fritz needs to produce a report right away and is concerned about issuing a less-than-favorable rating.

Comment: Fritz's analysis of Metals & Mining must be objective and based solely on consideration of company fundamentals. Any pressure from other divisions of his firm is inappropriate. This conflict could have been eliminated if, in anticipation of the offering, Hilton Brokerage had placed Metals & Mining on a restricted list for its sales force.

Example 4 (Research Independence and Issuer Relationship Pressure):

As in Example 3, Walter Fritz has concluded that Metals & Mining stock is overvalued at its current level, but he is concerned that a negative research report might jeopardize a close rapport that he has nurtured over the years with Metals & Mining's CEO, chief finance officer, and investment relations officer. Fritz is concerned that a negative report might result also in management retaliation—for instance, cutting him off from participating in conference calls when a quarterly earnings release is made, denying him the ability to ask questions on such calls, and/or denying him access to top management for arranging group meetings between Hilton Brokerage clients and top Metals & Mining managers.

Standard I(B): Application of the Standard

Comment: As in Example 3, Fritz's analysis must be objective and based solely on consideration of company fundamentals. Any pressure from Metals & Mining is inappropriate. Fritz should reinforce the integrity of his conclusions by stressing that his investment recommendation is based on relative valuation, which may include qualitative issues with respect to Metals & Mining's management.

Example 5 (Research Independence and Sales Pressure):

As support for the sales effort of her corporate bond department, Lindsey Warner offers credit guidance to purchasers of fixed-income securities. Her compensation is closely linked to the performance of the corporate bond department. Near the quarter's end, Warner's firm has a large inventory position in the bonds of Milton, Ltd., and has been unable to sell the bonds because of Milton's recent announcement of an operating problem. Salespeople have asked her to contact large clients to push the bonds.

Comment: Unethical sales practices create significant potential violations of the Code and Standards. Warner's opinion of the Milton bonds must not be affected by internal pressure or compensation. In this case, Warner must refuse to push the Milton bonds unless she is able to justify that the market price has already adjusted for the operating problem.

Example 6 (Research Independence and Prior Coverage):

Jill Jorund is a securities analyst following airline stocks and a rising star at her firm. Her boss has been carrying a "buy" recommendation on International Airlines and asks Jorund to take over coverage of that airline. He tells Jorund that under no circumstances should the prevailing buy recommendation be changed.

Comment: Jorund must be independent and objective in her analysis of International Airlines. If she believes that her boss's instructions have compromised her, she has two options: She can tell her boss that she cannot cover the company under these constraints, or she can take over coverage of the company, reach her own independent conclusions, and if they conflict with her boss's opinion, share the conclusions with her boss or other supervisors in the firm so that they can make appropriate recommendations. Jorund must issue only recommendations that reflect her independent and objective opinion.

Example 7 (Gifts and Entertainment from Related Party):

Edward Grant directs a large amount of his commission business to a New York–based brokerage house. In appreciation for all the business, the brokerage house gives Grant two tickets to the World Cup in South Africa, two nights at a nearby resort, several meals, and transportation via limousine to the game. Grant fails to disclose receiving this package to his supervisor.

Comment: Grant has violated Standard I(B) because accepting these substantial gifts may impede his independence and objectivity. Every member and candidate should endeavor to avoid situations that might cause or be perceived to cause a loss of independence or objectivity in recommending investments or taking investment action. By accepting the trip, Grant has opened himself up to the accusation that he may give the broker favored treatment in return.

Example 8 (Gifts and Entertainment from Client):

Theresa Green manages the portfolio of Ian Knowlden, a client of Tisbury Investments. Green achieves an annual return for Knowlden that is consistently better than that of the benchmark she and the client previously agreed to. As a reward, Knowlden offers Green two tickets to Wimbledon and the use of Knowlden's flat in London for a week. Green discloses this gift to her supervisor at Tisbury.

> *Comment*: Green is in compliance with Standard I(B) because she disclosed the gift from one of her clients in accordance with the firm's policies. Members and candidates may accept bonuses or gifts from clients as long as they disclose them to their employer because gifts in a client relationship are deemed less likely to affect a member's or candidate's objectivity and independence than gifts in other situations. Disclosure is required, however, so that supervisors can monitor such situations to guard against employees favoring a gift-giving client to the detriment of other fee-paying clients (such as by allocating a greater proportion of IPO stock to the gift-giving client's portfolio).
>
> Best practices for monitoring include comparing the transaction costs of the Knowlden account with the costs of other accounts managed by Green and other similar accounts within Tisbury. The supervisor could also compare the performance returns with the returns of other clients with the same mandate. This comparison will assist in determining whether a pattern of favoritism by Green is disadvantaging other Tisbury clients or the possibility that this favoritism could affect her future behavior.

Example 9 (Travel Expenses from External Manager):

Tom Wayne is the investment manager of the Franklin City Employees Pension Plan. He recently completed a successful search for a firm to manage the foreign equity allocation of the plan's diversified portfolio. He followed the plan's standard procedure of seeking presentations from a number of qualified firms and recommended that his board select Penguin Advisors because of its experience, well-defined investment strategy, and performance record. The firm claims compliance with the Global Investment Performance Standards (GIPS) and has been verified. Following the selection of Penguin, a reporter from the *Franklin City Record* calls to ask if there was any connection between this action and the fact that Penguin was one of the sponsors of an "investment fact-finding trip to Asia" that Wayne made earlier in the year. The trip was one of several conducted by the Pension Investment Academy, which had arranged the itinerary of meetings with economic, government, and corporate officials in major cities in several Asian countries. The Pension Investment Academy obtains support for the cost of these trips from a number of investment managers, including Penguin Advisors; the Academy then pays the travel expenses of the various pension plan managers on the trip and provides all meals and accommodations. The president of Penguin Advisors was also one of the travelers on the trip.

> *Comment*: Although Wayne can probably put to good use the knowledge he gained from the trip in selecting portfolio managers and in other areas of managing the pension plan, his recommendation of Penguin Advisors may be tainted by the possible conflict incurred when he participated in

Standard I(B): Application of the Standard

a trip partly paid for by Penguin Advisors and when he was in the daily company of the president of Penguin Advisors. To avoid violating Standard I(B), Wayne's basic expenses for travel and accommodations should have been paid by his employer or the pension plan; contact with the president of Penguin Advisors should have been limited to informational or educational events only; and the trip, the organizer, and the sponsor should have been made a matter of public record. Even if his actions were not in violation of Standard I(B), Wayne should have been sensitive to the public perception of the trip when reported in the newspaper and the extent to which the subjective elements of his decision might have been affected by the familiarity that the daily contact of such a trip would encourage. This advantage would probably not be shared by firms competing with Penguin Advisors.

Example 10 (Research Independence and Compensation Arrangements):

Javier Herrero recently left his job as a research analyst for a large investment adviser. While looking for a new position, he was hired by an investor-relations firm to write a research report on one of its clients, a small educational software company. The investor-relations firm hopes to generate investor interest in the technology company. The firm will pay Herrero a flat fee plus a bonus if any new investors buy stock in the company as a result of Herrero's report.

> *Comment*: If Herrero accepts this payment arrangement, he will be in violation of Standard I(B) because the compensation arrangement can reasonably be expected to compromise his independence and objectivity. Herrero will receive a bonus for attracting investors, which provides an incentive to draft a positive report regardless of the facts and to ignore or play down any negative information about the company. Herrero should accept only a flat fee that is not tied to the conclusions or recommendations of the report. Issuer-paid research that is objective and unbiased can be done under the right circumstances as long as the analyst takes steps to maintain his or her objectivity and includes in the report proper disclosures regarding potential conflicts of interest.

Example 11 (Recommendation Objectivity and Service Fees):

Two years ago, Bob Wade, trust manager for Central Midas Bank, was approached by Western Funds about promoting its family of funds, with special interest in the service-fee class of funds. To entice Central to promote this class, Western Funds offered to pay the bank a service fee of 0.25%. Without disclosing the fee being offered to the bank, Wade asked one of the investment managers to review Western's funds to determine whether they were suitable for clients of Central Midas Bank. The manager completed the normal due diligence review and determined that the new funds were fairly valued in the market with fee structures on a par with competitors. Wade decided to accept Western's offer and instructed the team of portfolio managers to exclusively promote these funds and the service-fee class to clients seeking to invest new funds or transfer from their current investments.

Now, two years later, the funds managed by Western begin to underperform their peers. Wade is counting on the fees to reach his profitability targets and continues to push these funds as acceptable investments for Central's clients.

> *Comment*: Wade is violating Standard I(B) because the fee arrangement has affected the objectivity of his recommendations. Wade is relying on the fee as a component of the department's profitability and is unwilling to offer other products that may affect the fees received.
>
> See also Standard VI(A)–Disclosure of Conflicts.

Example 12 (Recommendation Objectivity):

Bob Thompson has been doing research for the portfolio manager of the fixed-income department. His assignment is to do sensitivity analysis on securitized subprime mortgages. He has discussed with the manager possible scenarios to use to calculate expected returns. A key assumption in such calculations is housing price appreciation (HPA) because it drives "prepays" (prepayments of mortgages) and losses. Thompson is concerned with the significant appreciation experienced over the previous five years as a result of the increased availability of funds from subprime mortgages. Thompson insists that the analysis should include a scenario run with –10% for Year 1, –5% for Year 2, and then (to project a worst-case scenario) 0% for Years 3 through 5. The manager replies that these assumptions are too dire because there has never been a time in their available database when HPA was negative.

Thompson conducts his research to better understand the risks inherent in these securities and evaluates these securities in the worst-case scenario, an unlikely but possible environment. Based on the results of the enhanced scenarios, Thompson does not recommend the purchase of the securitization. Against the general market trends, the manager follows Thompson's recommendation and does not invest. The following year, the housing market collapses. In avoiding the subprime investments, the manager's portfolio outperforms its peer group that year.

> *Comment*: Thompson's actions in running the worst-case scenario against the protests of the portfolio manager are in alignment with the principles of Standard I(B). Thompson did not allow his research to be pressured by the general trends of the market or the manager's desire to limit the research to historical norms.
>
> See also Standard V(A)–Diligence and Reasonable Basis.

Example 13 (Influencing Manager Selection Decisions):

Adrian Mandel, CFA, is a senior portfolio manager for ZZYY Capital Management who oversees a team of investment professionals who manage labor union pension funds. A few years ago, ZZYY sought to win a competitive asset manager search to manage a significant allocation of the pension fund of the United Doughnut and Pretzel Bakers Union (UDPBU). UDPBU's investment board is chaired by a recognized key decision maker and long-time leader of the union, Ernesto Gomez. To improve ZZYY's chances of winning the competition, Mandel made significant monetary contributions to Gomez's union reelection campaign fund. Even after ZZYY was hired as a primary manager of the pension, Mandel believed that his firm's position was not secure. Mandel continued to contribute to Gomez's reelection campaign chest as well as to entertain lavishly the union leader and his family at top restaurants on a regular basis. All of Mandel's outlays were routinely handled as marketing expenses reimbursed by ZZYY's expense accounts and were disclosed to his senior management as being instrumental in maintaining a strong close relationship with an important client.

> *Comment*: Mandel not only offered but actually gave monetary gifts, benefits, and other considerations that reasonably could be expected to compromise Gomez's objectivity. Therefore, Mandel was in violation of Standard I(B).

Standard I(B): Application of the Standard

Example 14 (Influencing Manager Selection Decisions):

Adrian Mandel, CFA, had heard about the manager search competition for the UDPBU Pension Fund through a broker/dealer contact. The contact told him that a well-known retired professional golfer, Bobby "The Bear" Finlay, who had become a licensed broker/dealer serving as a pension consultant, was orchestrating the UDPBU manager search. Finlay had gained celebrity status with several labor union pension fund boards by entertaining their respective board members and regaling them with colorful stories of fellow pro golfers' antics in clubhouses around the world. Mandel decided to improve ZZYY's chances of being invited to participate in the search competition by befriending Finlay to curry his favor. Knowing Finlay's love of entertainment, Mandel wined and dined Finlay at high-profile bistros where Finlay could glow in the fan recognition lavished on him by all the other patrons. Mandel's endeavors paid off handsomely when Finlay recommended to the UDPBU board that ZZYY be entered as one of three finalist asset management firms in its search.

> *Comment*: Similar to Example 13, Mandel lavished gifts, benefits, and other considerations in the form of expensive entertainment that could reasonably be expected to influence the consultant to recommend the hiring of his firm. Therefore, Mandel was in violation of Standard I(B).

Example 15 (Fund Manager Relationships):

Amie Scott is a performance analyst within her firm with responsibilities for analyzing the performance of external managers. While completing her quarterly analysis, Scott notices a change in one manager's reported composite construction. The change concealed the bad performance of a particularly large account by placing that account into a new residual composite. This change allowed the manager to remain at the top of the list of manager performance. Scott knows her firm has a large allocation to this manager, and the fund's manager is a close personal friend of the CEO. She needs to deliver her final report but is concerned with pointing out the composite change.

> *Comment*: Scott would be in violation of Standard I(B) if she did not disclose the change in her final report. The analysis of managers' performance should not be influenced by personal relationships or the size of the allocation to the outside managers. By not including the change, Scott would not be providing an independent analysis of the performance metrics for her firm.

Example 16 (Intrafirm Pressure):

Jill Stein is head of performance measurement for her firm. During the last quarter, many members of the organization's research department were removed because of the poor quality of their recommendations. The subpar research caused one larger account holder to experience significant underperformance, which resulted in the client withdrawing his money after the end of the quarter. The head of sales requests that Stein remove this account from the firm's performance composite because the performance decline can be attributed to the departed research team and not the client's adviser.

> *Comment*: Pressure from other internal departments can create situations that cause a member or candidate to violate the Code and Standards. Stein must maintain her independence and objectivity and refuse to exclude specific accounts from the firm's performance composites to which they

belong. As long as the client invested under a strategy similar to that of the defined composite, it cannot be excluded because of the poor stock selections that led to the underperformance and asset withdrawal.

7 STANDARD I(C): PROFESSIONALISM – MISREPRESENTATION

☐ demonstrate a thorough knowledge of the CFA Institute Code of Ethics and Standards of Professional Conduct by applying the Code and Standards to specific situations

Members and Candidates must not knowingly make any misrepresentations relating to investment analysis, recommendations, actions, or other professional activities.

Guidance

Highlights:

- *Impact on Investment Practice*
- *Performance Reporting*
- *Social Media*
- *Omissions*
- *Plagiarism*
- *Work Completed for Employer*

Trust is the foundation of the investment profession. Investors must be able to rely on the statements and information provided to them by those with whom the investors have trusted their financial well-being. Investment professionals who make false or misleading statements not only harm investors but also reduce the level of investor confidence in the investment profession and threaten the integrity of capital markets as a whole.

A misrepresentation is any untrue statement or omission of a fact or any statement that is otherwise false or misleading. A member or candidate must not knowingly omit or misrepresent information or give a false impression of a firm, organization, or security in the member's or candidate's oral representations, advertising (whether in the press or through brochures), electronic communications, or written materials (whether publicly disseminated or not). In this context, "knowingly" means that the member or candidate either knows or should have known that the misrepresentation was being made or that omitted information could alter the investment decision-making process.

Written materials include, but are not limited to, research reports, underwriting documents, company financial reports, market letters, newspaper columns, and books. Electronic communications include, but are not limited to, internet communications, webpages, mobile applications, and e-mails. Members and candidates who use webpages should regularly monitor materials posted on these sites to ensure that they contain

Standard I(C): Professionalism – Misrepresentation

current information. Members and candidates should also ensure that all reasonable precautions have been taken to protect the site's integrity and security and that the site does not misrepresent any information and does provide full disclosure.

Standard I(C) prohibits members and candidates from guaranteeing clients any specific return on volatile investments. Most investments contain some element of risk that makes their return inherently unpredictable. For such investments, guaranteeing either a particular rate of return or a guaranteed preservation of investment capital (e.g., "I can guarantee that you will earn 8% on equities this year" or "I can guarantee that you will not lose money on this investment") is misleading to investors. Standard I(C) does not prohibit members and candidates from providing clients with information on investment products that have guarantees built into the structure of the products themselves or for which an institution has agreed to cover any losses.

Impact on Investment Practice

Members and candidates must not misrepresent any aspect of their practice, including (but not limited to) their qualifications or credentials, the qualifications or services provided by their firm, their performance record and the record of their firm, and the characteristics of an investment. Any misrepresentation made by a member or candidate relating to the member's or candidate's professional activities is a breach of this standard.

Members and candidates should exercise care and diligence when incorporating third-party information. Misrepresentations resulting from the use of the credit ratings, research, testimonials, or marketing materials of outside parties become the responsibility of the investment professional when it affects that professional's business practices.

Investing through outside managers continues to expand as an acceptable method of investing in areas outside a firm's core competencies. Members and candidates must disclose their intended use of external managers and must not represent those managers' investment practices as their own. Although the level of involvement of outside managers may change over time, appropriate disclosures by members and candidates are important in avoiding misrepresentations, especially if the primary activity is to invest directly with a single external manager. Standard V(B)–Communication with Clients and Prospective Clients discusses in further detail communicating the firm's investment practices.

Performance Reporting

The performance benchmark selection process is another area where misrepresentations may occur. Members and candidates may misrepresent the success of their performance record through presenting benchmarks that are not comparable to their strategies. Further, clients can be misled if the benchmark's results are not reported on a basis comparable to that of the fund's or client's results. Best practice is selecting the most appropriate available benchmark from a universe of available options. The transparent presentation of appropriate performance benchmarks is an important aspect in providing clients with information that is useful in making investment decisions.

However, Standard I(C) does not require that a benchmark always be provided in order to comply. Some investment strategies may not lend themselves to displaying an appropriate benchmark because of the complexity or diversity of the investments included. Furthermore, some investment strategies may use reference indexes that do not reflect the opportunity set of the invested assets—for example, a hedge fund comparing its performance with a "cash plus" basis. When such a benchmark is used, members and candidates should make reasonable efforts to ensure that they disclose the reasons behind the use of this reference index to avoid misrepresentations of their performance. Members and candidates should discuss with clients on a continuous basis the appropriate benchmark to be used for performance evaluations and related fee calculations.

Reporting misrepresentations may also occur when valuations for illiquid or non-traded securities are available from more than one source. When different options are available, members and candidates may be tempted to switch providers to obtain higher security valuations. The process of shopping for values may misrepresent a security's worth, lead to misinformed decisions to sell or hold an investment, and result in overcharging clients advisory fees.

Members and candidates should take reasonable steps to provide accurate and reliable security pricing information to clients on a consistent basis. Changing pricing providers should not be based solely on the justification that the new provider reports a higher current value of a security. Consistency in the reported information will improve the perception of the valuation process for illiquid securities. Clients will likely have additional confidence that they were able to make an informed decision about continuing to hold these securities in their portfolios.

Social Media

The advancement of online discussion forums and communication platforms, commonly referred to as "social media," is placing additional responsibilities on members and candidates. When communicating through social media channels, members and candidates should provide only the same information they are allowed to distribute to clients and potential clients through other traditional forms of communication. The online or interactive aspects of social media do not remove the need to be open and honest about the information being distributed.

Along with understanding and following existing and newly developing rules and regulations regarding the allowed use of social media, members and candidates should also ensure that all communications in this format adhere to the requirements of the Code and Standards. The perceived anonymity granted through these platforms may entice individuals to misrepresent their qualifications or abilities or those of their employer. Actions undertaken through social media that knowingly misrepresent investment recommendations or professional activities are considered a violation of Standard I(C).

Omissions

The omission of a fact or outcome can be misleading, especially given the growing use of models and technical analysis processes. Many members and candidates rely on such models and processes to scan for new investment opportunities, to develop investment vehicles, and to produce investment recommendations and ratings. When inputs are knowingly omitted, the resulting outcomes may provide misleading information to those who rely on it for making investment decisions. Additionally, the outcomes from models shall not be presented as fact because they represent the expected results based on the inputs and analysis process incorporated.

Omissions in the performance measurement and attribution process can also misrepresent a manager's performance and skill. Members and candidates should encourage their firms to develop strict policies for composite development to prevent cherry picking—situations in which selected accounts are presented as representative of the firm's abilities. The omission of any accounts appropriate for the defined composite may misrepresent to clients the success of the manager's implementation of its strategy.

Standard I(C): Professionalism – Misrepresentation

Plagiarism

Standard I(C) also prohibits plagiarism in the preparation of material for distribution to employers, associates, clients, prospects, or the general public. Plagiarism is defined as copying or using in substantially the same form materials prepared by others without acknowledging the source of the material or identifying the author and publisher of such material. Members and candidates must not copy (or represent as their own) original ideas or material without permission and must acknowledge and identify the source of ideas or material that is not their own.

The investment profession uses a myriad of financial, economic, and statistical data in the investment decision-making process. Through various publications and presentations, the investment professional is constantly exposed to the work of others and to the temptation to use that work without proper acknowledgment.

Misrepresentation through plagiarism in investment management can take various forms. The simplest and most flagrant example is to take a research report or study done by another firm or person, change the names, and release the material as one's own original analysis. This action is a clear violation of Standard I(C). Other practices include (1) using excerpts from articles or reports prepared by others either verbatim or with only slight changes in wording without acknowledgment, (2) citing specific quotations as attributable to "leading analysts" and "investment experts" without naming the specific references, (3) presenting statistical estimates of forecasts prepared by others and identifying the sources but without including the qualifying statements or caveats that may have been used, (4) using charts and graphs without stating their sources, and (5) copying proprietary computerized spreadsheets or algorithms without seeking the cooperation or authorization of their creators.

In the case of distributing third-party, outsourced research, members and candidates may use and distribute such reports as long as they do not represent themselves as the report's authors. Indeed, the member or candidate may add value for the client by sifting through research and repackaging it for clients. In such cases, clients should be fully informed that they are paying for the ability of the member or candidate to find the best research from a wide variety of sources. Members and candidates must not misrepresent their abilities, the extent of their expertise, or the extent of their work in a way that would mislead their clients or prospective clients. Members and candidates should disclose whether the research being presented to clients comes from another source—from either within or outside the member's or candidate's firm. This allows clients to understand who has the expertise behind the report or whether the work is being done by the analyst, other members of the firm, or an outside party.

Standard I(C) also applies to plagiarism in oral communications, such as through group meetings; visits with associates, clients, and customers; use of audio/video media (which is rapidly increasing); and telecommunications, including electronic data transfer and the outright copying of electronic media.

One of the most egregious practices in violation of this standard is the preparation of research reports based on multiple sources of information without acknowledging the sources. Examples of information from such sources include ideas, statistical compilations, and forecasts combined to give the appearance of original work. Although there is no monopoly on ideas, members and candidates must give credit where it is clearly due. Analysts should not use undocumented forecasts, earnings projections, asset values, and so on. Sources must be revealed to bring the responsibility directly back to the author of the report or the firm involved.

Work Completed for Employer

The preceding paragraphs address actions that would constitute a violation of Standard I(C). In some situations, however, members or candidates may use research conducted or models developed by others within the same firm without committing a violation.

The most common example relates to the situation in which one (or more) of the original analysts is no longer with the firm. Research and models developed while employed by a firm are the property of the firm. The firm retains the right to continue using the work completed after a member or candidate has left the organization. The firm may issue future reports without providing attribution to the prior analysts. A member or candidate cannot, however, reissue a previously released report solely under his or her name.

8 STANDARD I(C): RECOMMENDED PROCEDURES

☐ demonstrate a thorough knowledge of the CFA Institute Code of Ethics and Standards of Professional Conduct by applying the Code and Standards to specific situations

Factual Presentations

Members and candidates can prevent unintentional misrepresentations of their qualifications or the services they or their firms provide if each member and candidate understands the limit of the firm's or individual's capabilities and the need to be accurate and complete in presentations. Firms can provide guidance for employees who make written or oral presentations to clients or potential clients by providing a written list of the firm's available services and a description of the firm's qualifications. This list should suggest ways of describing the firm's services, qualifications, and compensation that are both accurate and suitable for client or customer presentations. Firms can also help prevent misrepresentation by specifically designating which employees are authorized to speak on behalf of the firm. Regardless of whether the firm provides guidance, members and candidates should make certain that they understand the services the firm can perform and its qualifications.

Qualification Summary

In addition, to ensure accurate presentations to clients, each member and candidate should prepare a summary of his or her own qualifications and experience and a list of the services the member or candidate is capable of performing. Firms can assist member and candidate compliance by periodically reviewing employee correspondence and documents that contain representations of individual or firm qualifications.

Verify Outside Information

When providing information to clients from a third party, members and candidates share a responsibility for the accuracy of the marketing and distribution materials that pertain to the third party's capabilities, services, and products. Misrepresentation by third parties can damage the member's or candidate's reputation, the reputation of the firm, and the integrity of the capital markets. Members and candidates should encourage their employers to develop procedures for verifying information of third-party firms.

Maintain Webpages

Members and candidates who publish a webpage should regularly monitor materials posted on the site to ensure that the site contains current information. Members and candidates should also ensure that all reasonable precautions have been taken to protect the site's integrity, confidentiality, and security and that the site does not misrepresent any information and provides full disclosure.

Plagiarism Policy

To avoid plagiarism in preparing research reports or conclusions of analysis, members and candidates should take the following steps:

- *Maintain copies*: Keep copies of all research reports, articles containing research ideas, material with new statistical methodologies, and other materials that were relied on in preparing the research report.

- *Attribute quotations*: Attribute to their sources any direct quotations, including projections, tables, statistics, model/product ideas, and new methodologies prepared by persons other than recognized financial and statistical reporting services or similar sources.

- *Attribute summaries*: Attribute to their sources any paraphrases or summaries of material prepared by others. For example, to support his analysis of Brown Company's competitive position, the author of a research report on Brown might summarize another analyst's report on Brown's chief competitor, but the author of the Brown report must acknowledge in his own report the reliance on the other analyst's report.

STANDARD I(C): APPLICATION OF THE STANDARD

9

☐ demonstrate a thorough knowledge of the CFA Institute Code of Ethics and Standards of Professional Conduct by applying the Code and Standards to specific situations

☐ recommend practices and procedures designed to prevent violations of the Code of Ethics and Standards of Professional Conduct

Example 1 (Disclosure of Issuer-Paid Research):

Anthony McGuire is an issuer-paid analyst hired by publicly traded companies to electronically promote their stocks. McGuire creates a website that promotes his research efforts as a seemingly independent analyst. McGuire posts a profile and a strong buy recommendation for each company on the website indicating that the stock is expected to increase in value. He does not disclose the contractual relationships with the companies he covers on his website, in the research reports he issues, or in the statements he makes about the companies in internet chat rooms.

> *Comment*: McGuire has violated Standard I(C) because the website is misleading to potential investors. Even if the recommendations are valid and supported with thorough research, his omissions regarding the true relationship between himself and the companies he covers constitute a

misrepresentation. McGuire has also violated Standard VI(A)–Disclosure of Conflicts by not disclosing the existence of an arrangement with the companies through which he receives compensation in exchange for his services.

Example 2 (Correction of Unintentional Errors):

Hijan Yao is responsible for the creation and distribution of the marketing materials for his firm, which claims compliance with the GIPS standards. Yao creates and distributes a presentation of performance by the firm's Asian equity composite that states the composite has ¥350 billion in assets. In fact, the composite has only ¥35 billion in assets, and the higher figure on the presentation is a result of a typographical error. Nevertheless, the erroneous material is distributed to a number of clients before Yao catches the mistake.

> *Comment*: Once the error is discovered, Yao must take steps to cease distribution of the incorrect material and correct the error by informing those who have received the erroneous information. Because Yao did not knowingly make the misrepresentation, however, he did not violate Standard I(C). Because his firm claims compliance with the GIPS standards, it must also comply with the GIPS Guidance Statement on Error Correction in relation to the error.

Example 3 (Noncorrection of Known Errors):

Syed Muhammad is the president of an investment management firm. The promotional material for the firm, created by the firm's marketing department, incorrectly claims that Muhammad has an advanced degree in finance from a prestigious business school in addition to the CFA designation. Although Muhammad attended the school for a short period of time, he did not receive a degree. Over the years, Muhammad and others in the firm have distributed this material to numerous prospective clients and consultants.

> *Comment*: Even though Muhammad may not have been directly responsible for the misrepresentation of his credentials in the firm's promotional material, he used this material numerous times over an extended period and should have known of the misrepresentation. Thus, Muhammad has violated Standard I(C).

Example 4 (Plagiarism):

Cindy Grant, a research analyst for a Canadian brokerage firm, has specialized in the Canadian mining industry for the past 10 years. She recently read an extensive research report on Jefferson Mining, Ltd., by Jeremy Barton, another analyst. Barton provided extensive statistics on the mineral reserves, production capacity, selling rates, and marketing factors affecting Jefferson's operations. He also noted that initial drilling results on a new ore body, which had not been made public, might show the existence of mineral zones that could increase the life of Jefferson's main mines, but Barton cited no specific data as to the initial drilling results. Grant called an officer of Jefferson, who gave her the initial drilling results over the telephone. The data indicated that the expected life of the main mines would be tripled. Grant added these statistics to Barton's report and circulated it within her firm as her own report.

Standard I(C): Application of the Standard

Comment: Grant plagiarized Barton's report by reproducing large parts of it in her own report without acknowledgment.

Example 5 (Misrepresentation of Information):

When Ricki Marks sells mortgage-backed derivatives called "interest-only strips" (IOs) to public pension plan clients, she describes them as "guaranteed by the US government." Purchasers of the IOs are entitled only to the interest stream generated by the mortgages, however, not the notional principal itself. One particular municipality's investment policies and local law require that securities purchased by its public pension plans be guaranteed by the US government. Although the underlying mortgages are guaranteed, neither the investor's investment nor the interest stream on the IOs is guaranteed. When interest rates decline, causing an increase in prepayment of mortgages, interest payments to the IOs' investors decline, and these investors lose a portion of their investment.

Comment: Marks violated Standard I(C) by misrepresenting the terms and character of the investment.

Example 6 (Potential Information Misrepresentation):

Khalouck Abdrabbo manages the investments of several high-net-worth individuals in the United States who are approaching retirement. Abdrabbo advises these individuals that a portion of their investments be moved from equity to bank-sponsored certificates of deposit and money market accounts so that the principal will be "guaranteed" up to a certain amount. The interest is not guaranteed.

Comment: Although there is risk that the institution offering the certificates of deposits and money market accounts could go bankrupt, in the United States, these accounts are insured by the US government through the Federal Deposit Insurance Corporation. Therefore, using the term "guaranteed" in this context is not inappropriate as long as the amount is within the government-insured limit. Abdrabbo should explain these facts to the clients.

Example 7 (Plagiarism):

Steve Swanson is a senior analyst in the investment research department of Ballard and Company. Apex Corporation has asked Ballard to assist in acquiring the majority ownership of stock in the Campbell Company, a financial consulting firm, and to prepare a report recommending that stockholders of Campbell agree to the acquisition. Another investment firm, Davis and Company, had already prepared a report for Apex analyzing both Apex and Campbell and recommending an exchange ratio. Apex has given the Davis report to Ballard officers, who have passed it on to Swanson. Swanson reviews the Davis report and other available material on Apex and Campbell. From his analysis, he concludes that the common stocks of Campbell and Apex represent good value at their current prices; he believes, however, that the Davis report does not consider all the factors a Campbell stockholder would need to know to make a decision. Swanson reports his conclusions to the partner in charge, who tells him to "use the Davis report, change a few words, sign your name, and get it out."

Comment: If Swanson does as requested, he will violate Standard I(C). He could refer to those portions of the Davis report that he agrees with if he identifies Davis as the source; he could then add his own analysis and conclusions to the report before signing and distributing it.

Example 8 (Plagiarism):

Claude Browning, a quantitative analyst for Double Alpha, Inc., returns from a seminar in great excitement. At that seminar, Jack Jorrely, a well-known quantitative analyst at a national brokerage firm, discussed one of his new models in great detail, and Browning is intrigued by the new concepts. He proceeds to test the model, making some minor mechanical changes but retaining the concepts, until he produces some very positive results. Browning quickly announces to his supervisors at Double Alpha that he has discovered a new model and that clients and prospective clients should be informed of this positive finding as ongoing proof of Double Alpha's continuing innovation and ability to add value.

Comment: Although Browning tested Jorrely's model on his own and even slightly modified it, he must still acknowledge the original source of the idea. Browning can certainly take credit for the final, practical results; he can also support his conclusions with his own test. The credit for the innovative thinking, however, must be awarded to Jorrely.

Example 9 (Plagiarism):

Fernando Zubia would like to include in his firm's marketing materials some "plain-language" descriptions of various concepts, such as the price-to-earnings (P/E) multiple and why standard deviation is used as a measure of risk. The descriptions come from other sources, but Zubia wishes to use them without reference to the original authors. Would this use of material be a violation of Standard I(C)?

Comment: Copying verbatim any material without acknowledgement, including plain-language descriptions of the P/E multiple and standard deviation, violates Standard I(C). Even though these concepts are general, best practice would be for Zubia to describe them in his own words or cite the sources from which the descriptions are quoted. Members and candidates would be violating Standard I(C) if they either were responsible for creating marketing materials without attribution or knowingly use plagiarized materials.

Example 10 (Plagiarism):

Through a mainstream media outlet, Erika Schneider learns about a study that she would like to cite in her research. Should she cite both the mainstream intermediary source as well as the author of the study itself when using that information?

Comment: In all instances, a member or candidate must cite the actual source of the information. Best practice for Schneider would be to obtain the information directly from the author and review it before citing it in a report. In that case, Schneider would not need to report how she found out about the information. For example, suppose Schneider read in the *Financial Times* about a study issued by CFA Institute; best practice for Schneider would be to obtain a copy of the study from CFA Institute, review it, and then cite it in her report. If she does not use any interpretation of the report from the *Financial Times* and the newspaper does not add value to the report itself, the newspaper is merely a conduit of the original information and does not need to be cited. If she does not obtain the report and review the information, Schneider runs the risk of relying on second-hand information that may misstate facts. If, for example, the *Financial Times* erroneously reported some information from the original CFA Institute study and Schneider copied that erroneous information without acknowledging CFA Institute, she could be the object of complaints. Best practice would be either to obtain the complete study from its original author and cite only that author or to use the information provided by the intermediary and cite both sources.

Example 11 (Misrepresentation of Information):

Paul Ostrowski runs a two-person investment management firm. Ostrowski's firm subscribes to a service from a large investment research firm that provides research reports that can be repackaged by smaller firms for those firms' clients. Ostrowski's firm distributes these reports to clients as its own work.

> *Comment*: Ostrowski can rely on third-party research that has a reasonable and adequate basis, but he cannot imply that he is the author of such research. If he does, Ostrowski is misrepresenting the extent of his work in a way that misleads the firm's clients or prospective clients.

Example 12 (Misrepresentation of Information):

Tom Stafford is part of a team within Appleton Investment Management responsible for managing a pool of assets for Open Air Bank, which distributes structured securities to offshore clients. He becomes aware that Open Air is promoting the structured securities as a much less risky investment than the investment management policy followed by him and the team to manage the original pool of assets. Also, Open Air has procured an independent rating for the pool that significantly overstates the quality of the investments. Stafford communicates his concerns to his supervisor, who responds that Open Air owns the product and is responsible for all marketing and distribution. Stafford's supervisor goes on to say that the product is outside of the US regulatory regime that Appleton follows and that all risks of the product are disclosed at the bottom of page 184 of the prospectus.

> *Comment*: As a member of the investment team, Stafford is qualified to recognize the degree of accuracy of the materials that characterize the portfolio, and he is correct to be worried about Appleton's responsibility for a misrepresentation of the risks. Thus, he should continue to pursue the issue of Open Air's inaccurate promotion of the portfolio according to the firm's policies and procedures.
>
> The Code and Standards stress protecting the reputation of the firm and the sustainability and integrity of the capital markets. Misrepresenting the quality and risks associated with the investment pool may lead to negative consequences for others well beyond the direct investors.

Example 13 (Avoiding a Misrepresentation):

Trina Smith is a fixed-income portfolio manager at a pension fund. She has observed that the market for highly structured mortgages is the focus of salespeople she meets and that these products represent a significant number of trading opportunities. In discussions about this topic with her team, Smith learns that calculating yields on changing cash flows within the deal structure requires very specialized vendor software. After more research, they find out that each deal is unique and that deals can have more than a dozen layers and changing cash flow priorities. Smith comes to the conclusion that, because of the complexity of these securities, the team cannot effectively distinguish between potentially good and bad investment options. To avoid misrepresenting their understanding, the team decides that the highly structured mortgage segment of the securitized market should not become part of the core of the fund's portfolio; they will allow some of the less complex securities to be part of the core.

> *Comment*: Smith is in compliance with Standard I(C) by not investing in securities that she and her team cannot effectively understand. Because she is not able to describe the risk and return profile of the securities to the pension fund beneficiaries and trustees, she appropriately limits the fund's exposure to this sector.

Example 14 (Misrepresenting Composite Construction):

Robert Palmer is head of performance for a fund manager. When asked to provide performance numbers to fund rating agencies, he avoids mentioning that the fund manager is quite liberal in composite construction. The reason accounts are included/excluded is not fully explained. The performance values reported to the rating agencies for the composites, although accurate for the accounts shown each period, may not present a true representation of the fund manager's ability.

> *Comment*: "Cherry picking" accounts to include in either published reports or information provided to rating agencies conflicts with Standard I(C). Moving accounts into or out of a composite to influence the overall performance results materially misrepresents the reported values over time. Palmer should work with his firm to strengthen its reporting practices concerning composite construction to avoid misrepresenting the firm's track record or the quality of the information being provided.

Example 15 (Presenting Out-of-Date Information):

David Finch is a sales director at a commercial bank, where he directs the bank's client advisers in the sale of third-party mutual funds. Each quarter, he holds a division-wide training session where he provides fact sheets on investment funds the bank is allowed to offer to clients. These fact sheets, which can be redistributed to potential clients, are created by the fund firms and contain information about the funds, including investment strategy and target distribution rates.

Finch knows that some of the fact sheets are out of date; for example, one long-only fund approved the use of significant leverage last quarter as a method to enhance returns. He continues to provide the sheets to the sales team without updates because the bank has no control over the marketing material released by the mutual fund firms.

> *Comment*: Finch is violating Standard I(C) by providing information that misrepresents aspects of the funds. By not providing the sales team and, ultimately, the clients with the updated information, he is misrepresenting

Standard I(D): Professionalism – Misconduct

the potential risks associated with the funds with outdated fact sheets. Finch can instruct the sales team to clarify the deficiencies in the fact sheets with clients and ensure they have the most recent fund prospectus document before accepting orders for investing in any fund.

Example 16 (Overemphasis of Firm Results):

Bob Anderson is chief compliance officer for Optima Asset Management Company, a firm currently offering eight funds to clients. Seven of the eight had 10-year returns below the median for their respective sectors. Anderson approves a recent advertisement, which includes this statement: "Optima Asset Management is achieving excellent returns for its investors. The Optima Emerging Markets Equity fund, for example, has 10-year returns that exceed the sector median by more than 10%."

> *Comment*: From the information provided it is difficult to determine whether a violation has occurred as long as the sector outperformance is correct. Anderson may be attempting to mislead potential clients by citing the performance of the sole fund that achieved such results. Past performance is often used to demonstrate a firm's skill and abilities in comparison to funds in the same sectors.
>
> However, if all the funds outperformed their respective benchmarks, then Anderson's assertion that the company "is achieving excellent returns" may be factual. Funds may exhibit positive returns for investors, exceed benchmarks, and yet have returns below the median in their sectors.
>
> Members and candidates need to ensure that their marketing efforts do not include statements that misrepresent their skills and abilities to remain compliant with Standard I(C). Unless the returns of a single fund reflect the performance of a firm as a whole, the use of a singular fund for performance comparisons should be avoided.

STANDARD I(D): PROFESSIONALISM – MISCONDUCT

10

☐ | demonstrate a thorough knowledge of the CFA Institute Code of Ethics and Standards of Professional Conduct by applying the Code and Standards to specific situations

> Members and Candidates must not engage in any professional conduct involving dishonesty, fraud, or deceit or commit any act that reflects adversely on their professional reputation, integrity, or competence.

Guidance

Whereas Standard I(A) addresses the obligation of members and candidates to comply with applicable law that governs their professional activities, Standard I(D) addresses *all* conduct that reflects poorly on the professional integrity, good reputation, or competence of members and candidates. Any act that involves lying, cheating, stealing, or other dishonest conduct is a violation of this standard if the offense reflects adversely on a member's or candidate's professional activities. Although CFA Institute discourages any sort of unethical behavior by members and candidates, the Code and Standards are primarily aimed at conduct and actions related to a member's or candidate's professional life.

Conduct that damages trustworthiness or competence may include behavior that, although not illegal, nevertheless negatively affects a member's or candidate's ability to perform his or her responsibilities. For example, abusing alcohol during business hours might constitute a violation of this standard because it could have a detrimental effect on the member's or candidate's ability to fulfill his or her professional responsibilities. Personal bankruptcy may not reflect on the integrity or trustworthiness of the person declaring bankruptcy, but if the circumstances of the bankruptcy involve fraudulent or deceitful business conduct, the bankruptcy may be a violation of this standard.

In some cases, the absence of appropriate conduct or the lack of sufficient effort may be a violation of Standard I(D). The integrity of the investment profession is built on trust. A member or candidate—whether an investment banker, rating or research analyst, or portfolio manager—is expected to conduct the necessary due diligence to properly understand the nature and risks of an investment before making an investment recommendation. By not taking these steps and, instead, relying on someone else in the process to perform them, members or candidates may violate the trust their clients have placed in them. This loss of trust may have a significant impact on the reputation of the member or candidate and the operations of the financial market as a whole.

Individuals may attempt to abuse the CFA Institute Professional Conduct Program by actively seeking CFA Institute enforcement of the Code and Standards, and Standard I(D) in particular, as a method of settling personal, political, or other disputes unrelated to professional ethics. CFA Institute is aware of this issue, and appropriate disciplinary policies, procedures, and enforcement mechanisms are in place to address misuse of the Code and Standards and the Professional Conduct Program in this way.

11 STANDARD I(D): RECOMMENDED PROCEDURES

☐ demonstrate a thorough knowledge of the CFA Institute Code of Ethics and Standards of Professional Conduct by applying the Code and Standards to specific situations

In addition to ensuring that their own behavior is consistent with Standard I(D), to prevent general misconduct, members and candidates should encourage their firms to adopt the following policies and procedures to support the principles of Standard I(D):

- *Code of ethics*: Develop and/or adopt a code of ethics to which every employee must subscribe, and make clear that any personal behavior that reflects poorly on the individual involved, the institution as a whole, or the investment industry will not be tolerated.

- *List of violations*: Disseminate to all employees a list of potential violations and associated disciplinary sanctions, up to and including dismissal from the firm.

- *Employee references*: Check references of potential employees to ensure that they are of good character and not ineligible to work in the investment industry because of past infractions of the law.

STANDARD I(D): APPLICATION OF THE STANDARD

12

☐　demonstrate a thorough knowledge of the CFA Institute Code of Ethics and Standards of Professional Conduct by applying the Code and Standards to specific situations

☐　recommend practices and procedures designed to prevent violations of the Code of Ethics and Standards of Professional Conduct

Example 1 (Professionalism and Competence):

Simon Sasserman is a trust investment officer at a bank in a small affluent town. He enjoys lunching every day with friends at the country club, where his clients have observed him having numerous drinks. Back at work after lunch, he clearly is intoxicated while making investment decisions. His colleagues make a point of handling any business with Sasserman in the morning because they distrust his judgment after lunch.

> *Comment*: Sasserman's excessive drinking at lunch and subsequent intoxication at work constitute a violation of Standard I(D) because this conduct has raised questions about his professionalism and competence. His behavior reflects poorly on him, his employer, and the investment industry.

Example 2 (Fraud and Deceit):

Howard Hoffman, a security analyst at ATZ Brothers, Inc., a large brokerage house, submits reimbursement forms over a two-year period to ATZ's self-funded health insurance program for more than two dozen bills, most of which have been altered to increase the amount due. An investigation by the firm's director of employee benefits uncovers the inappropriate conduct. ATZ subsequently terminates Hoffman's employment and notifies CFA Institute.

> *Comment*: Hoffman violated Standard I(D) because he engaged in intentional conduct involving fraud and deceit in the workplace that adversely reflected on his integrity.

Example 3 (Fraud and Deceit):

Jody Brink, an analyst covering the automotive industry, volunteers much of her spare time to local charities. The board of one of the charitable institutions decides to buy five new vans to deliver hot lunches to low-income elderly people. Brink offers to donate her time to handle purchasing agreements. To pay a long-standing debt to a friend who operates an automobile dealership—and to compensate herself for her trouble—she agrees to a price 20% higher than normal and splits the surcharge with her friend. The director of the charity ultimately discovers the scheme and tells Brink that her services, donated or otherwise, are no longer required.

> *Comment*: Brink engaged in conduct involving dishonesty, fraud, and misrepresentation and has violated Standard I(D).

Example 4 (Personal Actions and Integrity):

Carmen Garcia manages a mutual fund dedicated to socially responsible investing. She is also an environmental activist. As the result of her participation in nonviolent protests, Garcia has been arrested on numerous occasions for trespassing on the property of a large petrochemical plant that is accused of damaging the environment.

> *Comment*: Generally, Standard I(D) is not meant to cover legal transgressions resulting from acts of civil disobedience in support of personal beliefs because such conduct does not reflect poorly on the member's or candidate's professional reputation, integrity, or competence.

Example 5 (Professional Misconduct):

Meredith Rasmussen works on a buy-side trading desk of an investment management firm and concentrates on in-house trades for a hedge fund subsidiary managed by a team at the investment management firm. The hedge fund has been very successful and is marketed globally by the firm. From her experience as the trader for much of the activity of the fund, Rasmussen has become quite knowledgeable about the hedge fund's strategy, tactics, and performance. When a distinct break in the market occurs and many of the securities involved in the hedge fund's strategy decline markedly in value, Rasmussen observes that the reported performance of the hedge fund does not reflect this decline. In her experience, the lack of effect is a very unlikely occurrence. She approaches the head of trading about her concern and is told that she should not ask any questions and that the fund is big and successful and is not her concern. She is fairly sure something is not right, so she contacts the compliance officer, who also tells her to stay away from the issue of the hedge fund's reporting.

> *Comment*: Rasmussen has clearly come across an error in policies, procedures, and compliance practices within the firm's operations. According to the firm's procedures for reporting potentially unethical activity, she should pursue the issue by gathering some proof of her reason for doubt. Should all internal communications within the firm not satisfy her concerns, Rasmussen should consider reporting the potential unethical activity to the appropriate regulator.
>
> See also Standard IV(A) for guidance on whistleblowing and Standard IV(C) for the duties of a supervisor.

13 STANDARD II(A): INTEGRITY OF CAPITAL MARKETS - MATERIAL NONPUBLIC INFORMATION

☐ demonstrate a thorough knowledge of the CFA Institute Code of Ethics and Standards of Professional Conduct by applying the Code and Standards to specific situations

Standard II(A) Material Nonpublic Information

> Members and Candidates who possess material nonpublic information that could affect the value of an investment must not act or cause others to act on the information.

(handwritten note, right margin) − Blogs and company websites are in the public domain and thus do not constitute inside information.

Guidance

Highlights:

- *What Is "Material" Information?*
- *What Constitutes "Nonpublic" Information?*
- *Mosaic Theory*
- *Social Media*
- *Using Industry Experts*
- *Investment Research Reports*

Trading or inducing others to trade on material nonpublic information erodes confidence in capital markets, institutions, and investment professionals by supporting the idea that those with inside information and special access can take unfair advantage of the general investing public. Although trading on inside information may lead to short-term profits, in the long run, individuals and the profession as a whole suffer from such trading. These actions have caused and will continue to cause investors to avoid capital markets because the markets are perceived to be "rigged" in favor of the knowledgeable insider. When the investing public avoids capital markets, the markets and capital allocation become less efficient and less supportive of strong and vibrant economies. Standard II(A) promotes and maintains a high level of confidence in market integrity, which is one of the foundations of the investment profession.

The prohibition on using this information goes beyond the direct buying and selling of individual securities or bonds. Members and candidates must not use material nonpublic information to influence their investment actions related to derivatives (e.g., swaps or option contracts), mutual funds, or other alternative investments. *Any trading based on material nonpublic information constitutes a violation of Standard II(A).* The expansion of financial products and the increasing interconnectivity of financial markets globally have resulted in new potential opportunities for trading on material nonpublic information.

What Is "Material" Information?

Information is "material" if its disclosure would probably have an impact on the price of a security or if reasonable investors would want to know the information before making an investment decision. In other words, information is material if it would significantly alter the total mix of information currently available about a security in such a way that the price of the security would be affected.

The specificity of the information, the extent of its difference from public information, its nature, and its reliability are key factors in determining whether a particular piece of information fits the definition of material. For example, material information may include, but is not limited to, information on the following:

- earnings;
- mergers, acquisitions, tender offers, or joint ventures;
- changes in assets or asset quality;

- innovative products, processes, or discoveries (e.g., new product trials or research efforts);
- new licenses, patents, registered trademarks, or regulatory approval/rejection of a product;
- developments regarding customers or suppliers (e.g., the acquisition or loss of a contract);
- changes in management;
- change in auditor notification or the fact that the issuer may no longer rely on an auditor's report or qualified opinion;
- events regarding the issuer's securities (e.g., defaults on senior securities, calls of securities for redemption, repurchase plans, stock splits, changes in dividends, changes to the rights of security holders, and public or private sales of additional securities);
- bankruptcies;
- significant legal disputes;
- government reports of economic trends (employment, housing starts, currency information, etc.);
- orders for large trades before they are executed; and
- new or changing equity or debt ratings issued by a third party (e.g., sell-side recommendations and credit ratings).

In addition to the substance and specificity of the information, the source or relative reliability of the information also determines materiality. The less reliable a source, the less likely the information provided would be considered material. For example, factual information from a corporate insider regarding a significant new contract for a company is likely to be material, whereas an assumption based on speculation by a competitor about the same contract is likely to be less reliable and, therefore, not material. Additionally, information about trials of a new drug, product, or service under development from qualified personnel involved in the trials is likely to be material, whereas educated conjecture by subject experts not connected to the trials is unlikely to be material.

Also, the more ambiguous the effect of the information on price, the less material that information is considered. If it is unclear whether and to what extent the information will affect the price of a security, the information may not be considered material. The passage of time may also render information that was once important immaterial.

What Constitutes "Nonpublic" Information?

Information is "nonpublic" until it has been disseminated or is available to the marketplace in general (as opposed to a select group of investors). "Disseminated" can be defined as "made known." For example, a company report of profits that is posted on the internet and distributed widely through a press release or accompanied by a filing has been effectively disseminated to the marketplace. Members and candidates must have a reasonable expectation that people have received the information before it can be considered public. It is not necessary, however, to wait for the slowest method of delivery. Once the information is disseminated to the market, it is public information that is no longer covered by this standard.

Members and candidates must be particularly aware of information that is selectively disclosed by corporations to a small group of investors, analysts, or other market participants. Information that is made available to analysts remains nonpublic until it is made available to investors in general. Corporations that disclose information on a limited basis create the potential for insider-trading violations.

Standard II(A): Integrity of Capital Markets - Material Nonpublic Information

Issues of selective disclosure often arise when a corporate insider provides material information to analysts in a briefing or conference call before that information is released to the public. Analysts must be aware that a disclosure made to a room full of analysts does not necessarily make the disclosed information "public." Analysts should also be alert to the possibility that they are selectively receiving material nonpublic information when a company provides them with guidance or interpretation of such publicly available information as financial statements or regulatory filings.

A member or candidate may use insider information provided legitimately by the source company for the specific purpose of conducting due diligence according to the business agreement between the parties for such activities as mergers, loan underwriting, credit ratings, and offering engagements. In such instances, the investment professional would not be considered in violation of Standard II(A) by using the material information. However, the use of insider information provided by the source company for other purposes, especially to trade or entice others to trade the securities of the firm, conflicts with this standard.

Mosaic Theory

A financial analyst gathers and interprets large quantities of information from many sources. The analyst may use significant conclusions derived from the analysis of public and nonmaterial nonpublic information as the basis for investment recommendations and decisions even if those conclusions would have been material inside information had they been communicated directly to the analyst by a company. Under the "mosaic theory," financial analysts are free to act on this collection, or mosaic, of information without risking violation.

The practice of financial analysis depends on the free flow of information. For the fair and efficient operation of the capital markets, analysts and investors must have the greatest amount of information possible to facilitate making well-informed investment decisions about how and where to invest capital. Accurate, timely, and intelligible communication is essential if analysts and investors are to obtain the data needed to make informed decisions about how and where to invest capital. These disclosures must go beyond the information mandated by the reporting requirements of the securities laws and should include specific business information about items used to guide a company's future growth, such as new products, capital projects, and the competitive environment. Analysts seek and use such information to compare and contrast investment alternatives.

Much of the information used by analysts comes directly from companies. Analysts often receive such information through contacts with corporate insiders, especially investor-relations staff and financial officers. Information may be disseminated in the form of press releases, through oral presentations by company executives in analysts' meetings or conference calls, or during analysts' visits to company premises. In seeking to develop the most accurate and complete picture of a company, analysts should also reach beyond contacts with companies themselves and collect information from other sources, such as customers, contractors, suppliers, and the companies' competitors.

Analysts are in the business of formulating opinions and insights that are not obvious to the general investing public about the attractiveness of particular securities. In the course of their work, analysts actively seek out corporate information not generally known to the market for the express purpose of analyzing that information, forming an opinion on its significance, and informing their clients, who can be expected to trade on the basis of the recommendation. Analysts' initiatives to discover and analyze information and communicate their findings to their clients significantly enhance market efficiency, thus benefiting all investors (see *Dirks v. Securities and Exchange Commission*). Accordingly, violations of Standard II(A) will *not* result when a perceptive analyst reaches a conclusion about a corporate action or event through an analysis of public information and items of nonmaterial nonpublic information.

Investment professionals should note, however, that although analysts are free to use mosaic information in their research reports, they should save and document all their research [see Standard V(C)–Record Retention]. Evidence of the analyst's knowledge of public and nonmaterial nonpublic information about a corporation strengthens the assertion that the analyst reached his or her conclusions solely through appropriate methods rather than through the use of material nonpublic information.

Social Media

The continuing advancement in technology allows members, candidates, and the industry at large to exchange information at rates not previously available. It is important for investment professionals to understand the implications of using information from the internet and social media platforms because all such information may not actually be considered public.

Some social media platforms require membership in specific groups in order to access the published content. Members and candidates participating in groups with membership limitations should verify that material information obtained from these sources can also be accessed from a source that would be considered available to the public (e.g., company filings, webpages, and press releases).

Members and candidates may use social media platforms to communicate with clients or investors without conflicting with this standard. As long as the information reaches all clients or is open to the investing public, the use of these platforms would be comparable with other traditional forms of communications, such as e-mails and press releases. Members and candidates, as required by Standard I(A), should also complete all appropriate regulatory filings related to information distributed through social media platforms.

Using Industry Experts

The increased demand for insights for understanding the complexities of some industries has led to an expansion of engagement with outside experts. As the level of engagement increased, new businesses formed to connect analysts and investors with individuals who have specialized knowledge of their industry (e.g., technology or pharmaceuticals). These networks offer investors the opportunity to reach beyond their usual business circles to speak with experts regarding economic conditions, industry trends, and technical issues relating to specific products and services.

Members and candidates may provide compensation to individuals for their insights without violating this standard. However, members and candidates are ultimately responsible for ensuring that they are not requesting or acting on confidential information received from external experts, which is in violation of security regulations and laws or duties to others. As the recent string of insider-trading cases displayed, some experts are willing to provide confidential and protected information for the right incentive.

Firms connecting experts with members or candidates often require both parties to sign agreements concerning the disclosure of material nonpublic information. Even with the protections from such compliance practices, if an expert provides material nonpublic information, members and candidates would be prohibited from taking investment actions on the associated firm until the information became publicly known to the market.

Investment Research Reports

When a particularly well-known or respected analyst issues a report or makes changes to his or her recommendation, that information alone may have an effect on the market and thus may be considered material. Theoretically, under Standard II(A), such a report would have to be made public at the time it was distributed to clients. The analyst

Standard II(A): Recommended Procedures

is not a company insider, however, and does not have access to inside information. Presumably, the analyst created the report from information available to the public (mosaic theory) and by using his or her expertise to interpret the information. The analyst's hard work, paid for by the client, generated the conclusions.

Simply because the public in general would find the conclusions material does not require that the analyst make his or her work public. Investors who are not clients of the analyst can either do the work themselves or become clients of the analyst to gain access to the analyst's expertise.

STANDARD II(A): RECOMMENDED PROCEDURES

14

☐ demonstrate a thorough knowledge of the CFA Institute Code of Ethics and Standards of Professional Conduct by applying the Code and Standards to specific situations

Achieve Public Dissemination

If a member or candidate determines that information is material, the member or candidate should make reasonable efforts to achieve public dissemination of the information. These efforts usually entail encouraging the issuing company to make the information public. If public dissemination is not possible, the member or candidate must communicate the information only to the designated supervisory and compliance personnel within the member's or candidate's firm and must not take investment action or alter current investment recommendations on the basis of the information. Moreover, members and candidates must not knowingly engage in any conduct that may induce company insiders to privately disclose material nonpublic information.

Adopt Compliance Procedures

Members and candidates should encourage their firms to adopt compliance procedures to prevent the misuse of material nonpublic information. Particularly important is improving compliance in such areas as the review of employee and proprietary trading, the review of investment recommendations, documentation of firm procedures, and the supervision of interdepartmental communications in multiservice firms. Compliance procedures should suit the particular characteristics of a firm, including its size and the nature of its business.

Members and candidates are encouraged to inform their supervisor and compliance personnel of suspected inappropriate use of material nonpublic information as the basis for security trading activities or recommendations being made within their firm.

Adopt Disclosure Procedures

Members and candidates should encourage their firms to develop and follow disclosure policies designed to ensure that information is disseminated to the marketplace in an equitable manner. For example, analysts from small firms should receive the same information and attention from a company as analysts from large firms receive. Similarly, companies should not provide certain information to buy-side analysts but not to sell-side analysts, or vice versa. Furthermore, a company should not discriminate among analysts in the provision of information or "blackball" particular analysts who have given negative reports on the company in the past.

Within investment and research firms, members and candidates should encourage the development of and compliance with procedures for distributing new and updated investment opinions to clients. Recommendations of this nature may represent material market-moving information that needs to be communicated to all clients fairly.

Issue Press Releases

Companies should consider issuing press releases prior to analyst meetings and conference calls and scripting those meetings and calls to decrease the chance that further information will be disclosed. If material nonpublic information is disclosed for the first time in an analyst meeting or call, the company should promptly issue a press release or otherwise make the information publicly available.

Firewall Elements

An information barrier commonly referred to as a "firewall" is the most widely used approach for preventing the communication of material nonpublic information within firms. It restricts the flow of confidential information to those who need to know the information to perform their jobs effectively. The minimum elements of such a system include, but are not limited to, the following:

- substantial control of relevant interdepartmental communications, preferably through a clearance area within the firm in either the compliance or legal department;

- review of employee trading through the maintenance of "watch," "restricted," and "rumor" lists;

- documentation of the procedures designed to limit the flow of information between departments and of the actions taken to enforce those procedures; and

- heightened review or restriction of proprietary trading while a firm is in possession of material nonpublic information.

Appropriate Interdepartmental Communications

Although documentation requirements must, for practical reasons, take into account the differences between the activities of small firms and those of large, multiservice firms, firms of all sizes and types benefit by improving the documentation of their internal enforcement of firewall procedures. Therefore, even at small firms, procedures concerning interdepartmental communication, the review of trading activity, and the investigation of possible violations should be compiled and formalized.

Physical Separation of Departments

As a practical matter, to the greatest extent possible, firms should consider the physical separation of departments and files to prevent the communication of sensitive information that should not be shared. For example, the investment banking and corporate finance areas of a brokerage firm should be separated from the sales and research departments, and a bank's commercial lending department should be segregated from its trust and research departments.

Prevention of Personnel Overlap

There should be no overlap of personnel between the investment banking and corporate finance areas of a brokerage firm and the sales and research departments or between a bank's commercial lending department and its trust and research departments. For a firewall to be effective in a multiservice firm, an employee should be on only one side of the firewall at any time. Inside knowledge may not be limited to information about a specific offering or the current financial condition of a company. Analysts may be exposed to much information about the company, including new product developments or future budget projections that clearly constitute inside knowledge and thus preclude the analyst from returning to his or her research function. For example, an analyst who follows a particular company may provide limited assistance to the investment bankers under carefully controlled circumstances when the firm's investment banking department is involved in a deal with the company. That analyst must then be treated as though he or she were an investment banker; the analyst must remain on the investment banking side of the wall until any information he or she learns is publicly disclosed. In short, the analyst cannot use any information learned in the course of the project for research purposes and cannot share that information with colleagues in the research department.

A Reporting System

A primary objective of an effective firewall procedure is to establish a reporting system in which authorized people review and approve communications between departments. If an employee behind a firewall believes that he or she needs to share confidential information with someone on the other side of the wall, the employee should consult a designated compliance officer to determine whether sharing the information is necessary and how much information should be shared. If the sharing is necessary, the compliance officer should coordinate the process of "looking over the wall" so that the necessary information will be shared and the integrity of the procedure will be maintained.

A single supervisor or compliance officer should have the specific authority and responsibility of deciding whether information is material and whether it is sufficiently public to be used as the basis for investment decisions. Ideally, the supervisor or compliance officer responsible for communicating information to a firm's research or brokerage area would not be a member of that area.

Personal Trading Limitations

Firms should consider restrictions or prohibitions on personal trading by employees and should carefully monitor both proprietary trading and personal trading by employees. Firms should require employees to make periodic reports (to the extent that such reporting is not already required by securities laws) of their own transactions and transactions made for the benefit of family members. Securities should be placed on a restricted list when a firm has or may have material nonpublic information. The broad distribution of a restricted list often triggers the sort of trading the list was developed to avoid. Therefore, a watch list shown to only the few people responsible for compliance should be used to monitor transactions in specified securities. The use of a watch list in combination with a restricted list is an increasingly common means of ensuring effective control of personal trading.

Record Maintenance

Multiservice firms should maintain written records of the communications between various departments. Firms should place a high priority on training and should consider instituting comprehensive training programs, particularly for employees in sensitive areas.

Proprietary Trading Procedures

Procedures concerning the restriction or review of a firm's proprietary trading while the firm possesses material nonpublic information will necessarily depend on the types of proprietary trading in which the firm may engage. A prohibition on all types of proprietary activity when a firm comes into possession of material nonpublic information is *not* appropriate. For example, when a firm acts as a market maker, a prohibition on proprietary trading may be counterproductive to the goals of maintaining the confidentiality of information and market liquidity. This concern is particularly important in the relationships between small, regional broker/dealers and small issuers. In many situations, a firm will take a small issuer public with the understanding that the firm will continue to be a market maker in the stock. In such instances, a withdrawal by the firm from market-making activities would be a clear tip to outsiders. Firms that continue market-making activity while in the possession of material nonpublic information should, however, instruct their market makers to remain passive with respect to the market—that is, to take only the contra side of unsolicited customer trades.

In risk-arbitrage trading, the case for a trading prohibition is more compelling than it is in the case of market making. The impetus for arbitrage trading is neither passive nor reactive, and the potential for illegal profits is greater than in market making. The most prudent course for firms is to suspend arbitrage activity when a security is placed on the watch list. Those firms that continue arbitrage activity face a high hurdle in proving the adequacy of their internal procedures for preventing trading on material nonpublic information and must demonstrate a stringent review and documentation of firm trades.

Communication to All Employees

Members and candidates should encourage their employers to circulate written compliance policies and guidelines to all employees. Policies and guidelines should be used in conjunction with training programs aimed at enabling employees to recognize material nonpublic information. Such information is not always clearly identifiable.

Employees must be given sufficient training to either make an informed decision or to realize they need to consult a supervisor or compliance officer before engaging in questionable transactions. Appropriate policies reinforce that using material nonpublic information is illegal in many countries. Such trading activities based on material nonpublic information undermine the integrity of the individual, the firm, and the capital markets.

Standard II(A): Application of the Standard 267

STANDARD II(A): APPLICATION OF THE STANDARD

15

☐ demonstrate a thorough knowledge of the CFA Institute Code of Ethics and Standards of Professional Conduct by applying the Code and Standards to specific situations

☐ recommend practices and procedures designed to prevent violations of the Code of Ethics and Standards of Professional Conduct

Example 1 (Acting on Nonpublic Information):

Frank Barnes, the president and controlling shareholder of the SmartTown clothing chain, decides to accept a tender offer and sell the family business at a price almost double the market price of its shares. He describes this decision to his sister (SmartTown's treasurer), who conveys it to her daughter (who owns no stock in the family company at present), who tells her husband, Staple. Staple, however, tells his stockbroker, Alex Halsey, who immediately buys SmartTown stock for himself.

Comment: The information regarding the pending sale is both material and nonpublic. Staple has violated Standard II(A) by communicating the inside information to his broker. Halsey also has violated the standard by buying the shares on the basis of material nonpublic information.

Example 2 (Controlling Nonpublic Information):

Samuel Peter, an analyst with Scotland and Pierce Incorporated, is assisting his firm with a secondary offering for Bright Ideas Lamp Company. Peter participates, via telephone conference call, in a meeting with Scotland and Pierce investment banking employees and Bright Ideas' CEO. Peter is advised that the company's earnings projections for the next year have significantly dropped. Throughout the telephone conference call, several Scotland and Pierce salespeople and portfolio managers walk in and out of Peter's office, where the telephone call is taking place. As a result, they are aware of the drop in projected earnings for Bright Ideas. Before the conference call is concluded, the salespeople trade the stock of the company on behalf of the firm's clients and other firm personnel trade the stock in a firm proprietary account and in employees' personal accounts.

Comment: Peter has violated Standard II(A) because he failed to prevent the transfer and misuse of material nonpublic information to others in his firm. Peter's firm should have adopted information barriers to prevent the communication of nonpublic information between departments of the firm. The salespeople and portfolio managers who traded on the information have also violated Standard II(A) by trading on inside information.

Example 3 (Selective Disclosure of Material Information):

Elizabeth Levenson is based in Hanoi and covers the Vietnamese market for her firm, which is based in Singapore. She is invited, together with the other 10 largest shareholders of a manufacturing company, to meet the finance director of that company.

During the meeting, the finance director states that the company expects its workforce to strike next Friday, which will cripple productivity and distribution. Can Levenson use this information as a basis to change her rating on the company from "buy" to "sell"?

> *Comment*: Levenson must first determine whether the material information is public. According to Standard II(A), if the company has not made this information public (a small group forum does not qualify as a method of public dissemination), she cannot use the information.

Example 4 (Determining Materiality):

Leah Fechtman is trying to decide whether to hold or sell shares of an oil-and-gas exploration company that she owns in several of the funds she manages. Although the company has underperformed the index for some time already, the trends in the industry sector signal that companies of this type might become takeover targets. While she is considering her decision, her doctor, who casually follows the markets, mentions that she thinks that the company in question will soon be bought out by a large multinational conglomerate and that it would be a good idea to buy the stock right now. After talking to various investment professionals and checking their opinions on the company as well as checking industry trends, Fechtman decides the next day to accumulate more stock in the oil-and-gas exploration company.

> *Comment*: Although information on an expected takeover bid may be of the type that is generally material and nonpublic, in this case, the source of information is unreliable, so the information cannot be considered material. Therefore, Fechtman is not prohibited from trading the stock on the basis of this information.

Example 5 (Applying the Mosaic Theory):

Jagdish Teja is a buy-side analyst covering the furniture industry. Looking for an attractive company to recommend as a buy, he analyzes several furniture makers by studying their financial reports and visiting their operations. He also talks to some designers and retailers to find out which furniture styles are trendy and popular. Although none of the companies that he analyzes are a clear buy, he discovers that one of them, Swan Furniture Company (SFC), may be in financial trouble. SFC's extravagant new designs have been introduced at substantial cost. Even though these designs initially attracted attention, the public is now buying more conservative furniture from other makers. Based on this information and on a profit-and-loss analysis, Teja believes that SFC's next quarter earnings will drop substantially. He issues a sell recommendation for SFC. Immediately after receiving that recommendation, investment managers start reducing the SFC stock in their portfolios.

> *Comment*: Information on quarterly earnings data is material and nonpublic. Teja arrived at his conclusion about the earnings drop on the basis of public information and on pieces of nonmaterial nonpublic information (such as opinions of designers and retailers). Therefore, trading based on Teja's correct conclusion is not prohibited by Standard II(A).

Example 6 (Applying the Mosaic Theory):

Roger Clement is a senior financial analyst who specializes in the European automobile sector at Rivoli Capital. Because he has been repeatedly nominated by many leading industry magazines and newsletters as a "best analyst" for the automobile industry, he is widely regarded as an authority on the sector. After speaking with representatives of Turgot Chariots—a European auto manufacturer with sales primarily in South Korea—and after conducting interviews with salespeople, labor leaders, his firm's Korean currency analysts, and banking officials, Clement analyzed Turgot Chariots and concluded that (1) its newly introduced model will probably not meet sales expectations, (2) its corporate restructuring strategy may well face serious opposition from unions, (3) the depreciation of the Korean won should lead to pressure on margins for the industry in general and Turgot's market segment in particular, and (4) banks could take a tougher-than-expected stance in the upcoming round of credit renegotiations with the company. For these reasons, he changes his conclusion about the company from "market outperform" to "market underperform." Clement retains the support material used to reach his conclusion in case questions later arise.

> *Comment*: To reach a conclusion about the value of the company, Clement has pieced together a number of nonmaterial or public bits of information that affect Turgot Chariots. Therefore, under the mosaic theory, Clement has not violated Standard II(A) in drafting the report.

Example 7 (Analyst Recommendations as Material Nonpublic Information):

The next day, Clement is preparing to be interviewed on a global financial news television program where he will discuss his changed recommendation on Turgot Chariots for the first time in public. While preparing for the program, he mentions to the show's producers and Mary Zito, the journalist who will be interviewing him, the information he will be discussing. Just prior to going on the air, Zito sells her holdings in Turgot Chariots. She also phones her father with the information because she knows that he and other family members have investments in Turgot Chariots.

> *Comment*: When Zito receives advance notice of Clement's change of opinion, she knows it will have a material impact on the stock price, even if she is not totally aware of Clement's underlying reasoning. She is not a client of Clement but obtains early access to the material nonpublic information prior to publication. Her trades are thus based on material nonpublic information and violate Standard II(A).
>
> Zito further violates the Standard by relaying the information to her father. It would not matter if he or any other family member traded; the act of providing the information violates Standard II(A). The fact that the information is provided to a family member does not absolve someone of the prohibition of using or communicating material nonpublic information.

Example 8 (Acting on Nonpublic Information):

Ashton Kellogg is a retired investment professional who manages his own portfolio. He owns shares in National Savings, a large local bank. A close friend and golfing buddy, John Mayfield, is a senior executive at National. National has seen its stock price drop considerably, and the news and outlook are not good. In a conversation about the economy and the banking industry on the golf course, Mayfield relays the information that National will surprise the investment community in a few days when it announces excellent earnings for the quarter. Kellogg is pleasantly surprised by this information, and thinking that Mayfield, as a senior executive, knows the law and would not disclose inside information, he doubles his position in the bank. Subsequently, National announces that it had good operating earnings but had to set aside reserves for anticipated significant losses on its loan portfolio. The combined news causes the stock to go down 60%.

> *Comment*: Even though Kellogg believes that Mayfield would not break the law by disclosing inside information and money was lost on the purchase, Kellogg should not have purchased additional shares of National. It is the member's or candidate's responsibility to make sure, before executing investment actions, that comments about earnings are not material nonpublic information. Kellogg has violated Standard II(A).

Example 9 (Mosaic Theory):

John Doll is a research analyst for a hedge fund that also sells its research to a select group of paying client investment firms. Doll's focus is medical technology companies and products, and he has been in the business long enough and has been successful enough to build up a very credible network of friends and experts in the business. Doll has been working on a major research report recommending Boyce Health, a medical device manufacturer. He recently ran into an old acquaintance at a wedding who is a senior executive at Boyce, and Doll asked about the business. Doll was drawn to a statement that the executive, who has responsibilities in the new products area, made about a product: "I would not get too excited about the medium-term prospects; we have a lot of work to do first." Doll incorporated this and other information about the new Boyce product in his long-term recommendation of Boyce.

> *Comment*: Doll's conversation with the senior executive is part of the mosaic of information used in recommending Boyce. When holding discussions with a firm executive, Doll would need to guard against soliciting or obtaining material nonpublic information. Before issuing the report, the executive's statement about the continuing development of the product would need to be weighed against the other known public facts to determine whether it would be considered material.

Example 10 (Materiality Determination):

Larry Nadler, a trader for a mutual fund, gets a text message from another firm's trader, whom he has known for years. The message indicates a software company is going to report strong earnings when the firm publicly announces in two days. Nadler has a buy order from a portfolio manager within his firm to purchase several hundred thousand shares of the stock. Nadler is aggressive in placing the portfolio manager's order and completes the purchases by the following morning, a day ahead of the firm's planned earnings announcement.

> *Comment*: There are often rumors and whisper numbers before a release of any kind. The text message from the other trader would most likely be considered market noise. Unless Nadler knew that the trader had an ongoing business relationship with the public firm, he had no reason to suspect he was receiving material nonpublic information that would prevent him from completing the trading request of the portfolio manager.

Example 11 (Using an Expert Network):

Mary McCoy is the senior drug analyst at a mutual fund. Her firm hires a service that connects her to experts in the treatment of cancer. Through various phone conversations, McCoy enhances her understanding of the latest therapies for successful treatment. This information is critical to Mary making informed recommendations of the companies producing these drugs.

> *Comment*: McCoy is appropriately using the expert networks to enhance her evaluation process. She has neither asked for nor received information that may be considered material and nonpublic, such as preliminary trial results. McCoy is allowed to seek advice from professionals within the industry that she follows.

Example 12 (Using an Expert Network):

Tom Watson is a research analyst working for a hedge fund. To stay informed, Watson relies on outside experts for information on such industries as technology and pharmaceuticals, where new advancements occur frequently. The meetings with the industry experts often are arranged through networks or placement agents that have specific policies and procedures in place to deter the exchange of material nonpublic information.

Watson arranges a call to discuss future prospects for one of the fund's existing technology company holdings, a company that was testing a new semiconductor product. The scientist leading the tests indicates his disappointment with the performance of the new semiconductor. Following the call, Watson relays the insights he received to others at the fund. The fund sells its current position in the company and buys many put options because the market is anticipating the success of the new semiconductor and the share price reflects the market's optimism.

> *Comment*: Watson has violated Standard II(A) by passing along material nonpublic information concerning the ongoing product tests, which the fund used to trade in the securities and options of the related company. Watson cannot simply rely on the agreements signed by individuals who participate in expert networks that state that he has not received information that would prohibit his trading activity. He must make his own determination whether information he received through these arrangements reaches a materiality threshold that would affect his trading abilities.

STANDARD II(B): INTEGRITY OF CAPITAL MARKETS - MARKET MANIPULATION

16

☐ | demonstrate a thorough knowledge of the CFA Institute Code of Ethics and Standards of Professional Conduct by applying the Code and Standards to specific situations

Members and Candidates must not engage in practices that distort prices or artificially inflate trading volume with the intent to mislead market participants.

Guidance

Highlights:

- *Information-Based Manipulation*
- *Transaction-Based Manipulation*

Standard II(B) requires that members and candidates uphold market integrity by prohibiting market manipulation. Market manipulation includes practices that distort security prices or trading volume with the intent to deceive people or entities that rely on information in the market. Market manipulation damages the interests of all investors by disrupting the smooth functioning of financial markets and lowering investor confidence.

Market manipulation may lead to a lack of trust in the fairness of the capital markets, resulting in higher risk premiums and reduced investor participation. A reduction in the efficiency of a local capital market may negatively affect the growth and economic health of the country and may also influence the operations of the globally interconnected capital markets. Although market manipulation may be less likely to occur in mature financial markets than in emerging markets, cross-border investing increasingly exposes all global investors to the potential for such practices.

Market manipulation includes (1) the dissemination of false or misleading information and (2) transactions that deceive or would be likely to mislead market participants by distorting the price-setting mechanism of financial instruments. The development of new products and technologies increases the incentives, means, and opportunities for market manipulation. Additionally, the increasing complexity and sophistication of the technologies used for communicating with market participants have created new avenues for manipulation.

Information-Based Manipulation

Information-based manipulation includes, but is not limited to, spreading false rumors to induce trading by others. For example, members and candidates must refrain from "pumping up" the price of an investment by issuing misleading positive information or overly optimistic projections of a security's worth only to later "dump" the investment (i.e., sell it) once the price, fueled by the misleading information's effect on other market participants, reaches an artificially high level.

Transaction-Based Manipulation

Transaction-based manipulation involves instances where a member or candidate knew or should have known that his or her actions could affect the pricing of a security. This type of manipulation includes, but is not limited to, the following:

- transactions that artificially affect prices or volume to give the impression of activity or price movement in a financial instrument, which represent a diversion from the expectations of a fair and efficient market, and
- securing a controlling, dominant position in a financial instrument to exploit and manipulate the price of a related derivative and/or the underlying asset.

Standard II(B) is not intended to preclude transactions undertaken on legitimate trading strategies based on perceived market inefficiencies. The intent of the action is critical to determining whether it is a violation of this standard.

STANDARD II(B): APPLICATION OF THE STANDARD 17

☐ demonstrate a thorough knowledge of the CFA Institute Code of Ethics and Standards of Professional Conduct by applying the Code and Standards to specific situations

☐ recommend practices and procedures designed to prevent violations of the Code of Ethics and Standards of Professional Conduct

Example 1 (Independent Analysis and Company Promotion):

The principal owner of Financial Information Services (FIS) entered into an agreement with two microcap companies to promote the companies' stock in exchange for stock and cash compensation. The principal owner caused FIS to disseminate e-mails, design and maintain several websites, and distribute an online investment newsletter—all of which recommended investment in the two companies. The systematic publication of purportedly independent analyses and recommendations containing inaccurate and highly promotional and speculative statements increased public investment in the companies and led to dramatically higher stock prices.

> *Comment*: The principal owner of FIS violated Standard II(B) by using inaccurate reporting and misleading information under the guise of independent analysis to artificially increase the stock price of the companies. Furthermore, the principal owner violated Standard V(A)–Diligence and Reasonable Basis by not having a reasonable and adequate basis for recommending the two companies and violated Standard VI(A)–Disclosure of Conflicts by not disclosing to investors the compensation agreements (which constituted a conflict of interest).

Example 2 (Personal Trading Practices and Price):

John Gray is a private investor in Belgium who bought a large position several years ago in Fame Pharmaceuticals, a German small-cap security with limited average trading volume. He has now decided to significantly reduce his holdings owing to the poor price performance. Gray is worried that the low trading volume for the stock may cause the price to decline further as he attempts to sell his large position.

Gray devises a plan to divide his holdings into multiple accounts in different brokerage firms and private banks in the names of family members, friends, and even a private religious institution. He then creates a rumor campaign on various blogs and social media outlets promoting the company.

Gray begins to buy and sell the stock using the accounts in hopes of raising the trading volume and the price. He conducts the trades through multiple brokers, selling slightly larger positions than he bought on a tactical schedule, and over time, he is able to reduce his holding as desired without negatively affecting the sale price.

> *Comment*: John violated Standard II(B) by fraudulently creating the appearance that there was a greater investor interest in the stock through the online rumors. Additionally, through his trading strategy, he created the appearance that there was greater liquidity in the stock than actually existed. He was able to manipulate the price through both misinformation and trading practices.

Example 3 (Creating Artificial Price Volatility):

Matthew Murphy is an analyst at Divisadero Securities & Co., which has a significant number of hedge funds among its most important brokerage clients. Some of the hedge funds hold short positions on Wirewolf Semiconductor. Two trading days before the publication of a quarter-end report, Murphy alerts his sales force that he is about to issue a research report on Wirewolf that will include the following opinions:

- quarterly revenues are likely to fall short of management's guidance,
- earnings will be as much as 5 cents per share (or more than 10%) below consensus, and
- Wirewolf's highly respected chief financial officer may be about to join another company.

Knowing that Wirewolf has already entered its declared quarter-end "quiet period" before reporting earnings (and thus would be reluctant to respond to rumors), Murphy times the release of his research report specifically to sensationalize the negative aspects of the message in order to create significant downward pressure on Wirewolf's stock—to the distinct advantage of Divisadero's hedge fund clients. The report's conclusions are based on speculation, not on fact. The next day, the research report is broadcast to all of Divisadero's clients and to the usual newswire services.

Before Wirewolf's investor-relations department can assess the damage on the final trading day of the quarter and refute Murphy's report, its stock opens trading sharply lower, allowing Divisadero's clients to cover their short positions at substantial gains.

> *Comment*: Murphy violated Standard II(B) by aiming to create artificial price volatility designed to have a material impact on the price of an issuer's stock. Moreover, by lacking an adequate basis for the recommendation, Murphy also violated Standard V(A)–Diligence and Reasonable Basis.

Example 4 (Personal Trading and Volume):

Rajesh Sekar manages two funds—an equity fund and a balanced fund—whose equity components are supposed to be managed in accordance with the same model. According to that model, the funds' holdings in stock of Digital Design Inc. (DD) are excessive. Reduction of the DD holdings would not be easy, however, because the stock has low liquidity in the stock market. Sekar decides to start trading larger portions of DD stock back and forth between his two funds to slowly increase the price; he believes market participants will see growing volume and increasing price and become interested in the stock. If other investors are willing to buy the DD stock because of such interest, then Sekar will be able to get rid of at least some of his overweight position without inducing price decreases. In this way, the whole transaction will be for the benefit of fund participants, even if additional brokers' commissions are incurred.

> *Comment*: Sekar's plan would be beneficial for his funds' participants but is based on artificial distortion of both trading volume and the price of the DD stock and thus constitutes a violation of Standard II(B).

Example 5 ("Pump-Priming" Strategy):

ACME Futures Exchange is launching a new bond futures contract. To convince investors, traders, arbitrageurs, hedgers, and so on, to use its contract, the exchange attempts to demonstrate that it has the best liquidity. To do so, it enters into agreements

Standard II(B): Application of the Standard

with members in which they commit to a substantial minimum trading volume on the new contract over a specific period in exchange for substantial reductions of their regular commissions.

> *Comment*: The formal liquidity of a market is determined by the obligations set on market makers, but the actual liquidity of a market is better estimated by the actual trading volume and bid–ask spreads. Attempts to mislead participants about the actual liquidity of the market constitute a violation of Standard II(B). In this example, investors have been intentionally misled to believe they chose the most liquid instrument for some specific purpose, but they could eventually see the actual liquidity of the contract significantly reduced after the term of the agreement expires. If the ACME Futures Exchange fully discloses its agreement with members to boost transactions over some initial launch period, it will not violate Standard II(B). ACME's intent is not to harm investors but, on the contrary, to give them a better service. For that purpose, it may engage in a liquidity-pumping strategy, but the strategy must be disclosed.

Example 6 (Creating Artificial Price Volatility):

Emily Gordon, an analyst of household products companies, is employed by a research boutique, Picador & Co. Based on information that she has gathered during a trip through Latin America, she believes that Hygene, Inc., a major marketer of personal care products, has generated better-than-expected sales from its new product initiatives in South America. After modestly boosting her projections for revenue and for gross profit margin in her worksheet models for Hygene, Gordon estimates that her earnings projection of US$2.00 per diluted share for the current year may be as much as 5% too low. She contacts the chief financial officer (CFO) of Hygene to try to gain confirmation of her findings from her trip and to get some feedback regarding her revised models. The CFO declines to comment and reiterates management's most recent guidance of US$1.95–US$2.05 for the year.

Gordon decides to try to force a comment from the company by telling Picador & Co. clients who follow a momentum investment style that consensus earnings projections for Hygene are much too low; she explains that she is considering raising her published estimate by an ambitious US$0.15 to US$2.15 per share. She believes that when word of an unrealistically high earnings projection filters back to Hygene's investor-relations department, the company will feel compelled to update its earnings guidance. Meanwhile, Gordon hopes that she is at least correct with respect to the earnings direction and that she will help clients who act on her insights to profit from a quick gain by trading on her advice.

> *Comment*: By exaggerating her earnings projections in order to try to fuel a quick gain in Hygene's stock price, Gordon is in violation of Standard II(B). Furthermore, by virtue of previewing her intentions of revising upward her earnings projections to only a select group of clients, she is in violation of Standard III(B)–Fair Dealing. However, it would have been acceptable for Gordon to write a report that
>
> - framed her earnings projection in a range of possible outcomes,
> - outlined clearly the assumptions used in her Hygene models that took into consideration the findings from her trip through Latin America, and
> - was distributed to all Picador & Co. clients in an equitable manner.

Example 7 (Pump and Dump Strategy):

In an effort to pump up the price of his holdings in Moosehead & Belfast Railroad Company, Steve Weinberg logs on to several investor chat rooms on the internet to start rumors that the company is about to expand its rail network in anticipation of receiving a large contract for shipping lumber.

> *Comment*: Weinberg has violated Standard II(B) by disseminating false information about Moosehead & Belfast with the intent to mislead market participants.

Example 8 (Manipulating Model Inputs):

Bill Mandeville supervises a structured financing team for Superior Investment Bank. His responsibilities include packaging new structured investment products and managing Superior's relationship with relevant rating agencies. To achieve the best rating possible, Mandeville uses mostly positive scenarios as model inputs—scenarios that reflect minimal downside risk in the assets underlying the structured products. The resulting output statistics in the rating request and underwriting prospectus support the idea that the new structured products have minimal potential downside risk. Additionally, Mandeville's compensation from Superior is partially based on both the level of the rating assigned and the successful sale of new structured investment products but does not have a link to the long-term performance of the instruments.

Mandeville is extremely successful and leads Superior as the top originator of structured investment products for the next two years. In the third year, the economy experiences difficulties and the values of the assets underlying structured products significantly decline. The subsequent defaults lead to major turmoil in the capital markets, the demise of Superior Investment Bank, and the loss of Mandeville's employment.

> *Comment*: Mandeville manipulates the inputs of a model to minimize associated risk to achieve higher ratings. His understanding of structured products allows him to skillfully decide which inputs to include in support of the desired rating and price. This information manipulation for short-term gain, which is in violation of Standard II(B), ultimately causes significant damage to many parties and the capital markets as a whole. Mandeville should have realized that promoting a rating and price with inaccurate information could cause not only a loss of price confidence in the particular structured product but also a loss of investor trust in the system. Such loss of confidence affects the ability of the capital markets to operate efficiently.

Example 9 (Information Manipulation):

Allen King is a performance analyst for Torrey Investment Funds. King believes that the portfolio manager for the firm's small- and microcap equity fund dislikes him because the manager never offers him tickets to the local baseball team's games but does offer tickets to other employees. To incite a potential regulatory review of the manager, King creates user profiles on several online forums under the portfolio manager's name and starts rumors about potential mergers for several of the smaller companies in the portfolio. As the prices of these companies' stocks increase, the portfolio manager sells the position, which leads to an investigation by the regulator as King desired.

Standard III(A): Duties to Clients - Loyalty, Prudence, and Care

Comment: King has violated Standard II(B) even though he did not personally profit from the market's reaction to the rumor. In posting the false information, King misleads others into believing the companies were likely to be acquired. Although his intent was to create trouble for the portfolio manager, his actions clearly manipulated the factual information that was available to the market.

STANDARD III(A): DUTIES TO CLIENTS - LOYALTY, PRUDENCE, AND CARE

18

☐ demonstrate a thorough knowledge of the CFA Institute Code of Ethics and Standards of Professional Conduct by applying the Code and Standards to specific situations

Standard III(A) Loyalty, Prudence, and Care

> Members and Candidates have a duty of loyalty to their clients and must act with reasonable care and exercise prudent judgment. Members and Candidates must act for the benefit of their clients and place their clients' interests before their employer's or their own interests.

Guidance

Highlights:

- *Understanding the Application of Loyalty, Prudence, and Care*
- *Identifying the Actual Investment Client*
- *Developing the Client's Portfolio*
- *Soft Commission Policies*
- *Proxy Voting Policies*

Standard III(A) clarifies that client interests are paramount. A member's or candidate's responsibility to a client includes a duty of loyalty and a duty to exercise reasonable care. Investment actions must be carried out for the sole benefit of the client and in a manner the member or candidate believes, given the known facts and circumstances, to be in the best interest of the client. Members and candidates must exercise the same level of prudence, judgment, and care that they would apply in the management and disposition of their own interests in similar circumstances.

Prudence requires caution and discretion. The exercise of prudence by investment professionals requires that they act with the care, skill, and diligence that a reasonable person acting in a like capacity and familiar with such matters would use. In the context of managing a client's portfolio, prudence requires following the investment parameters set forth by the client and balancing risk and return. Acting with care requires members and candidates to act in a prudent and judicious manner in avoiding harm to clients.

Standard III(A) sets minimum expectations for members and candidates when fulfilling their responsibilities to their clients. Regulatory and legal requirements for such duties can vary across the investment industry depending on a variety of factors, including job function of the investment professional, the existence of an adviser/client relationship, and the nature of the recommendations being offered. From the perspective of the end user of financial services, these different standards can be arcane and confusing, leaving investors unsure of what level of service to expect from investment professionals they employ. The single standard of conduct described in Standard III(A) benefits investors by establishing a benchmark for the duties of loyalty, prudence, and care and clarifies that all CFA Institute members and candidates, regardless of job title, local laws, or cultural differences, are required to comply with these fundamental responsibilities. Investors hiring members or candidates who must adhere to the duty of loyalty, prudence, and care set forth in this standard can be confident that these responsibilities are a requirement regardless of any legally imposed fiduciary duties.

Standard III(A), however, is not a substitute for a member's or candidate's legal or regulatory obligations. As stated in Standard I(A), members and candidates must abide by the most strict requirements imposed on them by regulators or the Code and Standards, including any legally imposed fiduciary duty. Members and candidates must also be aware of whether they have "custody" or effective control of client assets. If so, a heightened level of responsibility arises. Members and candidates are considered to have custody if they have any direct or indirect access to client funds. Members and candidates must manage any pool of assets in their control in accordance with the terms of the governing documents (such as trust documents and investment management agreements), which are the primary determinant of the manager's powers and duties. Whenever their actions are contrary to provisions of those instruments or applicable law, members and candidates are at risk of violating Standard III(A).

Understanding the Application of Loyalty, Prudence, and Care

Standard III(A) establishes a minimum benchmark for the duties of loyalty, prudence, and care that are required of all members and candidates regardless of whether a legal fiduciary duty applies. Although fiduciary duty often encompasses the principles of loyalty, prudence, and care, Standard III(A) does not render all members and candidates fiduciaries. The responsibilities of members and candidates for fulfilling their obligations under this standard depend greatly on the nature of their professional responsibilities and the relationships they have with clients. The conduct of members and candidates may or may not rise to the level of being a fiduciary, depending on the type of client, whether the member or candidate is giving investment advice, and the many facts and circumstances surrounding a particular transaction or client relationship.

Fiduciary duties are often imposed by law or regulation when an individual or institution is charged with the duty of acting for the benefit of another party, such as managing investment assets. The duty required in fiduciary relationships exceeds what is acceptable in many other business relationships because a fiduciary is in an enhanced position of trust. Although members and candidates must comply with any legally imposed fiduciary duty, the Code and Standards neither impose such a legal responsibility nor require all members or candidates to act as fiduciaries. However, Standard III(A) requires members and candidates to work in the client's best interest no matter what the job function.

A member or candidate who does not provide advisory services to a client but who acts only as a trade execution professional must prudently work in the client's interest when completing requested trades. Acting in the client's best interest requires these professionals to use their skills and diligence to execute trades in the most favorable terms that can be achieved. Members and candidates operating in such positions must use care to operate within the parameters set by the client's trading instructions.

Standard III(A): Duties to Clients - Loyalty, Prudence, and Care

Members and candidates may also operate in a blended environment where they execute client trades and offer advice on a limited set of investment options. The extent of the advisory arrangement and limitations should be outlined in the agreement with the client at the outset of the relationship. For instance, members and candidates should inform clients that the advice provided will be limited to the propriety products of the firm and not include other products available on the market. Clients who want access to a wider range of investment products would have the information necessary to decide not to engage with members or candidates working under these restrictions.

Members and candidates operating in this blended context would comply with their obligations by recommending the allowable products that are consistent with the client's objectives and risk tolerance. They would exercise care through diligently aligning the client's needs with the attributes of the products being recommended. Members and candidates should place the client's interests first by disregarding any firm or personal interest in motivating a recommended transaction.

There is a large variety of professional relationships that members and candidates have with their clients. Standard III(A) requires them to fulfill the obligations outlined explicitly or implicitly in the client agreements to the best of their abilities and with loyalty, prudence, and care. Whether a member or candidate is structuring a new securitization transaction, completing a credit rating analysis, or leading a public company, he or she must work with prudence and care in delivering the agreed-on services.

Identifying the Actual Investment Client

The first step for members and candidates in fulfilling their duty of loyalty to clients is to determine the identity of the "client" to whom the duty of loyalty is owed. In the context of an investment manager managing the personal assets of an individual, the client is easily identified. When the manager is responsible for the portfolios of pension plans or trusts, however, the client is not the person or entity who hires the manager but, rather, the beneficiaries of the plan or trust. The duty of loyalty is owed to the ultimate beneficiaries.

In some situations, an actual client or group of beneficiaries may not exist. Members and candidates managing a fund to an index or an expected mandate owe the duty of loyalty, prudence, and care to invest in a manner consistent with the stated mandate. The decisions of a fund's manager, although benefiting all fund investors, do not have to be based on an individual investor's requirements and risk profile. Client loyalty and care for those investing in the fund are the responsibility of members and candidates who have an advisory relationship with those individuals.

Situations involving potential conflicts of interest with respect to responsibilities to clients may be extremely complex because they may involve a number of competing interests. The duty of loyalty, prudence, and care applies to a large number of persons in varying capacities, but the exact duties may differ in many respects in accord with the relationship with each client or each type of account in which the assets are managed. Members and candidates must not only put their obligations to clients first in all dealings but also endeavor to avoid all real or potential conflicts of interest.

Members and candidates with positions whose responsibilities do not include direct investment management also have "clients" that must be considered. Just as there are various types of advisory relationships, members and candidates must look at their roles and responsibilities when making a determination of who their clients are. Sometimes the client is easily identifiable; such is the case in the relationship between a company executive and the firm's public shareholders. At other times, the client may be the investing public as a whole, in which case the goals of independence and objectivity of research surpass the goal of loyalty to a single organization.

Developing the Client's Portfolio

The duty of loyalty, prudence, and care owed to the individual client is especially important because the professional investment manager typically possesses greater knowledge in the investment arena than the client does. This disparity places the individual client in a vulnerable position; the client must trust the manager. The manager in these situations should ensure that the client's objectives and expectations for the performance of the account are realistic and suitable to the client's circumstances and that the risks involved are appropriate. In most circumstances, recommended investment strategies should relate to the long-term objectives and circumstances of the client.

Particular care must be taken to detect whether the goals of the investment manager or the firm in conducting business, selling products, and executing security transactions potentially conflict with the best interests and objectives of the client. When members and candidates cannot avoid potential conflicts between their firm and clients' interests, they must provide clear and factual disclosures of the circumstances to the clients.

Members and candidates must follow any guidelines set by their clients for the management of their assets. Some clients, such as charitable organizations and pension plans, have strict investment policies that limit investment options to certain types or classes of investment or prohibit investment in certain securities. Other organizations have aggressive policies that do not prohibit investments by type but, instead, set criteria on the basis of the portfolio's total risk and return.

Investment decisions must be judged in the context of the total portfolio rather than by individual investment within the portfolio. The member's or candidate's duty is satisfied with respect to a particular investment if the individual has thoroughly considered the investment's place in the overall portfolio, the risk of loss and opportunity for gains, tax implications, and the diversification, liquidity, cash flow, and overall return requirements of the assets or the portion of the assets for which the manager is responsible.

Soft Commission Policies

An investment manager often has discretion over the selection of brokers executing transactions. Conflicts may arise when an investment manager uses client brokerage to purchase research services, a practice commonly called "soft dollars" or "soft commissions." A member or candidate who pays a higher brokerage commission than he or she would normally pay to allow for the purchase of goods or services, without corresponding benefit to the client, violates the duty of loyalty to the client.

From time to time, a client will direct a manager to use the client's brokerage to purchase goods or services for the client, a practice that is commonly called "directed brokerage." Because brokerage commission is an asset of the client and is used to benefit that client, not the manager, such a practice does not violate any duty of loyalty. However, a member or candidate is obligated to seek "best price" and "best execution" and be assured by the client that the goods or services purchased from the brokerage will benefit the account beneficiaries. "Best execution" refers to a trading process that seeks to maximize the value of the client's portfolio within the client's stated investment objectives and constraints. In addition, the member or candidate should disclose to the client that the client may not be getting best execution from the directed brokerage.

Proxy Voting Policies

The duty of loyalty, prudence, and care may apply in a number of situations facing the investment professional besides those related directly to investing assets.

Part of a member's or candidate's duty of loyalty includes voting proxies in an informed and responsible manner. Proxies have economic value to a client, and members and candidates must ensure that they properly safeguard and maximize this value. An investment manager who fails to vote, casts a vote without considering the impact of the question, or votes blindly with management on nonroutine governance issues (e.g., a change in company capitalization) may violate this standard. Voting of proxies is an integral part of the management of investments.

A cost–benefit analysis may show that voting all proxies may not benefit the client, so voting proxies may not be necessary in all instances. Members and candidates should disclose to clients their proxy voting policies.

STANDARD III(A): RECOMMENDED PROCEDURES

19

☐ | demonstrate a thorough knowledge of the CFA Institute Code of Ethics and Standards of Professional Conduct by applying the Code and Standards to specific situations

Regular Account Information

Members and candidates with control of client assets (1) should submit to each client, at least quarterly, an itemized statement showing the funds and securities in the custody or possession of the member or candidate plus all debits, credits, and transactions that occurred during the period, (2) should disclose to the client where the assets are to be maintained, as well as where or when they are moved, and (3) should separate the client's assets from any other party's assets, including the member's or candidate's own assets.

Client Approval

If a member or candidate is uncertain about the appropriate course of action with respect to a client, the member or candidate should consider what he or she would expect or demand if the member or candidate were the client. If in doubt, a member or candidate should disclose the questionable matter in writing to the client and obtain client approval.

Firm Policies

Members and candidates should address and encourage their firms to address the following topics when drafting the statements or manuals containing their policies and procedures regarding responsibilities to clients:

- *Follow all applicable rules and laws*: Members and candidates must follow all legal requirements and applicable provisions of the Code and Standards.

- *Establish the investment objectives of the client*: Make a reasonable inquiry into a client's investment experience, risk and return objectives, and financial constraints prior to making investment recommendations or taking investment actions.

- *Consider all the information when taking actions*: When taking investment actions, members and candidates must consider the appropriateness and suitability of the investment relative to (1) the client's needs and circumstances, (2) the investment's basic characteristics, and (3) the basic characteristics of the total portfolio.
- *Diversify*: Members and candidates should diversify investments to reduce the risk of loss, unless diversification is not consistent with plan guidelines or is contrary to the account objectives.
- *Carry out regular reviews*: Members and candidates should establish regular review schedules to ensure that the investments held in the account adhere to the terms of the governing documents.
- *Deal fairly with all clients with respect to investment actions*: Members and candidates must not favor some clients over others and should establish policies for allocating trades and disseminating investment recommendations.
- *Disclose conflicts of interest*: Members and candidates must disclose all actual and potential conflicts of interest so that clients can evaluate those conflicts.
- *Disclose compensation arrangements*: Members and candidates should make their clients aware of all forms of manager compensation.
- *Vote proxies*: In most cases, members and candidates should determine who is authorized to vote shares and vote proxies in the best interests of the clients and ultimate beneficiaries.
- *Maintain confidentiality*: Members and candidates must preserve the confidentiality of client information.
- *Seek best execution*: Unless directed by the client as ultimate beneficiary, members and candidates must seek best execution for their clients. (Best execution is defined in the preceding text.)
- *Place client interests first*: Members and candidates must serve the best interests of clients.

20 STANDARD III(A): APPLICATION OF THE STANDARD

☐ demonstrate a thorough knowledge of the CFA Institute Code of Ethics and Standards of Professional Conduct by applying the Code and Standards to specific situations

☐ recommend practices and procedures designed to prevent violations of the Code of Ethics and Standards of Professional Conduct

Example 1 (Identifying the Client—Plan Participants):

First Country Bank serves as trustee for the Miller Company's pension plan. Miller is the target of a hostile takeover attempt by Newton, Inc. In attempting to ward off Newton, Miller's managers persuade Julian Wiley, an investment manager at First Country Bank, to purchase Miller common stock in the open market for the employee pension plan. Miller's officials indicate that such action would be favorably received and would probably result in other accounts being placed with the bank. Although

Standard III(A): Application of the Standard

283

Wiley believes the stock is overvalued and would not ordinarily buy it, he purchases the stock to support Miller's managers, to maintain Miller's good favor toward the bank, and to realize additional new business. The heavy stock purchases cause Miller's market price to rise to such a level that Newton retracts its takeover bid.

> *Comment*: Standard III(A) requires that a member or candidate, in evaluating a takeover bid, act prudently and solely in the interests of plan participants and beneficiaries. To meet this requirement, a member or candidate must carefully evaluate the long-term prospects of the company against the short-term prospects presented by the takeover offer and by the ability to invest elsewhere. In this instance, Wiley, acting on behalf of his employer, which was the trustee for a pension plan, clearly violated Standard III(A). He used the pension plan to perpetuate existing management, perhaps to the detriment of plan participants and the company's shareholders, and to benefit himself. Wiley's responsibilities to the plan participants and beneficiaries should have taken precedence over any ties of his bank to corporate managers and over his self-interest. Wiley had a duty to examine the takeover offer on its own merits and to make an independent decision. The guiding principle is the appropriateness of the investment decision to the pension plan, not whether the decision benefited Wiley or the company that hired him.

Example 2 (Client Commission Practices):

JNI, a successful investment counseling firm, serves as investment manager for the pension plans of several large regionally based companies. Its trading activities generate a significant amount of commission-related business. JNI uses the brokerage and research services of many firms, but most of its trading activity is handled through a large brokerage company, Thompson, Inc., because the executives of the two firms have a close friendship. Thompson's commission structure is high in comparison with charges for similar brokerage services from other firms. JNI considers Thompson's research services and execution capabilities average. In exchange for JNI directing its brokerage to Thompson, Thompson absorbs a number of JNI overhead expenses, including those for rent.

> *Comment*: JNI executives are breaching their responsibilities by using client brokerage for services that do not benefit JNI clients and by not obtaining best price and best execution for their clients. Because JNI executives are not upholding their duty of loyalty, they are violating Standard III(A).

Example 3 (Brokerage Arrangements):

Charlotte Everett, a struggling independent investment adviser, serves as investment manager for the pension plans of several companies. One of her brokers, Scott Company, is close to consummating management agreements with prospective new clients whereby Everett would manage the new client accounts and trade the accounts exclusively through Scott. One of Everett's existing clients, Crayton Corporation, has directed Everett to place securities transactions for Crayton's account exclusively through Scott. But to induce Scott to exert efforts to send more new accounts to her, Everett also directs transactions to Scott from other clients without their knowledge.

> *Comment*: Everett has an obligation at all times to seek best price and best execution on all trades. Everett may direct new client trades exclusively through Scott Company as long as Everett receives best price and execution

on the trades or receives a written statement from new clients that she is *not* to seek best price and execution and that they are aware of the consequence for their accounts. Everett may trade other accounts through Scott as a reward for directing clients to Everett only if the accounts receive best price and execution and the practice is disclosed to the accounts. Because Everett does not disclose the directed trading, Everett has violated Standard III(A).

Example 4 (Brokerage Arrangements):

Emilie Rome is a trust officer for Paget Trust Company. Rome's supervisor is responsible for reviewing Rome's trust account transactions and her monthly reports of personal stock transactions. Rome has been using Nathan Gray, a broker, almost exclusively for trust account brokerage transactions. When Gray makes a market in stocks, he has been giving Rome a lower price for personal purchases and a higher price for sales than he gives to Rome's trust accounts and other investors.

Comment: Rome is violating her duty of loyalty to the bank's trust accounts by using Gray for brokerage transactions simply because Gray trades Rome's personal account on favorable terms. Rome is placing her own interests before those of her clients.

Example 5 (Client Commission Practices):

Lauren Parker, an analyst with Provo Advisors, covers South American equities for her firm. She likes to travel to the markets for which she is responsible and decides to go on a trip to Chile, Argentina, and Brazil. The trip is sponsored by SouthAM, Inc., a research firm with a small broker/dealer affiliate that uses the clearing facilities of a larger New York brokerage house. SouthAM specializes in arranging South American trips for analysts during which they can meet with central bank officials, government ministers, local economists, and senior executives of corporations. SouthAM accepts commission dollars at a ratio of 2 to 1 against the hard-dollar costs of the research fee for the trip. Parker is not sure that SouthAM's execution is competitive, but without informing her supervisor, she directs the trading desk at Provo to start giving commission business to SouthAM so she can take the trip. SouthAM has conveniently timed the briefing trip to coincide with the beginning of Carnival season, so Parker also decides to spend five days of vacation in Rio de Janeiro at the end of the trip. Parker uses commission dollars to pay for the five days of hotel expenses.

Comment: Parker is violating Standard III(A) by not exercising her duty of loyalty to her clients. She should have determined whether the commissions charged by SouthAM are reasonable in relation to the benefit of the research provided by the trip. She also should have determined whether best execution and prices could be received from SouthAM. In addition, the five extra days are not part of the research effort because they do not assist in the investment decision making. Thus, the hotel expenses for the five days should not be paid for with client assets.

Example 6 (Excessive Trading):

Vida Knauss manages the portfolios of a number of high-net-worth individuals. A major part of her investment management fee is based on trading commissions. Knauss engages in extensive trading for each of her clients to ensure that she attains the minimum commission level set by her firm. Although the securities purchased

Standard III(A): Application of the Standard 285

and sold for the clients are appropriate and fall within the acceptable asset classes for the clients, the amount of trading for each account exceeds what is necessary to accomplish the client's investment objectives.

> *Comment*: Knauss has violated Standard III(A) because she is using the assets of her clients to benefit her firm and herself.

Example 7 (Managing Family Accounts):

Adam Dill recently joined New Investments Asset Managers. To assist Dill in building a book of clients, both his father and brother opened new fee-paying accounts. Dill followed all the firm's procedures in noting his relationships with these clients and in developing their investment policy statements.

After several years, the number of Dill's clients has grown, but he still manages the original accounts of his family members. An IPO is coming to market that is a suitable investment for many of his clients, including his brother. Dill does not receive the amount of stock he requested, so to avoid any appearance of a conflict of interest, he does not allocate any shares to his brother's account.

> *Comment*: Dill has violated Standard III(A) because he is not acting for the benefit of his brother's account as well as his other accounts. The brother's account is a regular fee-paying account comparable to the accounts of his other clients. By not allocating the shares proportionately across *all* accounts for which he thought the IPO was suitable, Dill is disadvantaging specific clients.
>
> Dill would have been correct in not allocating shares to his brother's account if that account was being managed outside the normal fee structure of the firm.

Example 8 (Identifying the Client):

Donna Hensley has been hired by a law firm to testify as an expert witness. Although the testimony is intended to represent impartial advice, she is concerned that her work may have negative consequences for the law firm. If the law firm is Hensley's client, how does she ensure that her testimony will not violate the required duty of loyalty, prudence, and care to one's client?

> *Comment*: In this situation, the law firm represents Hensley's employer and the aspect of "who is the client" is not well defined. When acting as an expert witness, Hensley is bound by the standard of independence and objectivity in the same manner as an independent research analyst would be bound. Hensley must not let the law firm influence the testimony she provides in the legal proceedings.

Example 9 (Identifying the Client):

Jon Miller is a mutual fund portfolio manager. The fund is focused on the global financial services sector. Wanda Spears is a private wealth manager in the same city as Miller and is a friend of Miller. At a local CFA Institute society meeting, Spears mentions to Miller that her new client is an investor in Miller's fund. She states that the two of them now share a responsibility to this client.

Comment: Spears' statement is not totally correct. Because she provides the advisory services to her new client, she alone is bound by the duty of loyalty to this client. Miller's responsibility is to manage the fund according to the investment policy statement of the fund. His actions should not be influenced by the needs of any particular fund investor.

Example 10 (Client Loyalty):

After providing client account investment performance to the external-facing departments but prior to it being finalized for release to clients, Teresa Nguyen, an investment performance analyst, notices the reporting system missed a trade. Correcting the omission resulted in a large loss for a client that had previously placed the firm on "watch" for potential termination owing to underperformance in prior periods. Nguyen knows this news is unpleasant but informs the appropriate individuals that the report needs to be updated before releasing it to the client.

Comment: Nguyen's actions align with the requirements of Standard III(A). Even though the correction may lead to the firm's termination by the client, withholding information on errors would not be in the best interest of the client.

Example 11 (Execution-Only Responsibilities):

Baftija Sulejman recently became a candidate in the CFA Program. He is a broker who executes client-directed trades for several high-net-worth individuals. Sulejman does not provide any investment advice and only executes the trading decisions made by clients. He is concerned that the Code and Standards impose a fiduciary duty on him in his dealing with clients and sends an e-mail to the CFA Ethics Helpdesk (ethics@ cfainstitute.org) to seek guidance on this issue.

Comment: In this instance, Sulejman serves in an execution-only capacity and his duty of loyalty, prudence, and care is centered on the skill and diligence used when executing trades—namely, by seeking best execution and making trades within the parameters set by the clients (instructions on quantity, price, timing, etc.). Acting in the best interests of the client dictates that trades are executed on the most favorable terms that can be achieved for the client. Given this job function, the requirements of the Code and Standards for loyalty, prudence, and care clearly do not impose a fiduciary duty.

21 STANDARD III(B): DUTIES TO CLIENTS - FAIR DEALING

> *— Standard III(B) states that members must deal fairly and objectively with all clients whether they are discretionary or non-discretionary accounts.*

☐ demonstrate a thorough knowledge of the CFA Institute Code of Ethics and Standards of Professional Conduct by applying the Code and Standards to specific situations

> Members and Candidates must deal fairly and objectively with all clients when providing investment analysis, making investment recommendations, taking investment action, or engaging in other professional activities.

Standard III(B): Duties to Clients - Fair Dealing

Guidance

Highlights:

- *Investment Recommendations*
- *Investment Action*

Standard III(B) requires members and candidates to treat all clients fairly when disseminating investment recommendations or making material changes to prior investment recommendations or when taking investment action with regard to general purchases, new issues, or secondary offerings. Only through the fair treatment of all parties can the investment management profession maintain the confidence of the investing public.

When an investment adviser has multiple clients, the potential exists for the adviser to favor one client over another. This favoritism may take various forms—from the quality and timing of services provided to the allocation of investment opportunities.

The term "fairly" implies that the member or candidate must take care not to discriminate against any clients when disseminating investment recommendations or taking investment action. Standard III(B) does not state "equally" because members and candidates could not possibly reach all clients at exactly the same time—whether by printed mail, telephone (including text messaging), computer (including internet updates and e-mail distribution), facsimile (fax), or wire. Each client has unique needs, investment criteria, and investment objectives, so not all investment opportunities are suitable for all clients. In addition, members and candidates may provide more personal, specialized, or in-depth service to clients who are willing to pay for premium services through higher management fees or higher levels of brokerage. Members and candidates may differentiate their services to clients, but different levels of service must not disadvantage or negatively affect clients. In addition, the different service levels should be disclosed to clients and prospective clients and should be available to everyone (i.e., different service levels should not be offered selectively).

Standard III(B) covers conduct in two broadly defined categories—investment recommendations and investment action.

Investment Recommendations

The first category of conduct involves members and candidates whose primary function is the preparation of investment recommendations to be disseminated either to the public or within a firm for the use of others in making investment decisions. This group includes members and candidates employed by investment counseling, advisory, or consulting firms as well as banks, brokerage firms, and insurance companies. The criterion is that the member's or candidate's primary responsibility is the preparation of recommendations to be acted on by others, including those in the member's or candidate's organization.

An investment recommendation is any opinion expressed by a member or candidate in regard to purchasing, selling, or holding a given security or other investment. The opinion may be disseminated to customers or clients through an initial detailed research report, through a brief update report, by addition to or deletion from a list of recommended securities, or simply by oral communication. A recommendation that is distributed to anyone outside the organization is considered a communication for general distribution under Standard III(B).

Standard III(B) addresses the manner in which investment recommendations or changes in prior recommendations are disseminated to clients. Each member or candidate is obligated to ensure that information is disseminated in such a manner that all clients have a fair opportunity to act on every recommendation. Communicating with all clients on a uniform basis presents practical problems for members and candidates because of differences in timing and methods of communication with various types of customers and clients. Members and candidates should encourage their firms to design an equitable system to prevent selective or discriminatory disclosure and should inform clients about what kind of communications they will receive.

The duty to clients imposed by Standard III(B) may be more critical when members or candidates change their recommendations than when they make initial recommendations. Material changes in a member's or candidate's prior investment recommendations because of subsequent research should be communicated to all current clients; particular care should be taken that the information reaches those clients who the member or candidate knows have acted on or been affected by the earlier advice. Clients who do not know that the member or candidate has changed a recommendation and who, therefore, place orders contrary to a current recommendation should be advised of the changed recommendation before the order is accepted.

Investment Action

The second category of conduct includes those members and candidates whose primary function is taking investment action (portfolio management) on the basis of recommendations prepared internally or received from external sources. Investment action, like investment recommendations, can affect market value. Consequently, Standard III(B) requires that members or candidates treat all clients fairly in light of their investment objectives and circumstances. For example, when making investments in new offerings or in secondary financings, members and candidates should distribute the issues to all customers for whom the investments are appropriate in a manner consistent with the policies of the firm for allocating blocks of stock. If the issue is oversubscribed, then the issue should be prorated to all subscribers. This action should be taken on a round-lot basis to avoid odd-lot distributions. In addition, if the issue is oversubscribed, members and candidates should forgo any sales to themselves or their immediate families in order to free up additional shares for clients. If the investment professional's family-member accounts are managed similarly to the accounts of other clients of the firm, however, the family-member accounts should not be excluded from buying such shares.

Members and candidates must make every effort to treat all individual and institutional clients in a fair and impartial manner. A member or candidate may have multiple relationships with an institution; for example, the member or candidate may be a corporate trustee, pension fund manager, manager of funds for individuals employed by the customer, loan originator, or creditor. A member or candidate must exercise care to treat all clients fairly.

Members and candidates should disclose to clients and prospective clients the documented allocation procedures they or their firms have in place and how the procedures would affect the client or prospect. The disclosure should be clear and complete so that the client can make an informed investment decision. Even when complete disclosure is made, however, members and candidates must put client interests ahead of their own. A member's or candidate's duty of fairness and loyalty to clients can never be overridden by client consent to patently unfair allocation procedures.

Treating clients fairly also means that members and candidates should not take advantage of their position in the industry to the detriment of clients. For instance, in the context of IPOs, members and candidates must make bona fide public distributions of "hot issue" securities (defined as securities of a public offering that are trading at a premium in the secondary market whenever such trading commences because of the great demand for the securities). Members and candidates are prohibited from withholding such securities for their own benefit and must not use such securities as a reward or incentive to gain benefit.

STANDARD III(B): RECOMMENDED PROCEDURES

22

☐ demonstrate a thorough knowledge of the CFA Institute Code of Ethics and Standards of Professional Conduct by applying the Code and Standards to specific situations

Develop Firm Policies

Although Standard III(B) refers to a member's or candidate's responsibility to deal fairly and objectively with clients, members and candidates should also encourage their firms to establish compliance procedures requiring all employees who disseminate investment recommendations or take investment actions to treat customers and clients fairly. At the very least, a member or candidate should recommend appropriate procedures to management if none are in place. And the member or candidate should make management aware of possible violations of fair-dealing practices within the firm when they come to the attention of the member or candidate.

The extent of the formality and complexity of such compliance procedures depends on the nature and size of the organization and the type of securities involved. An investment adviser who is a sole proprietor and handles only discretionary accounts might not disseminate recommendations to the public, but that adviser should have formal written procedures to ensure that all clients receive fair investment action.

Good business practice dictates that initial recommendations be made available to all customers who indicate an interest. Although a member or candidate need not communicate a recommendation to all customers, the selection process by which customers receive information should be based on suitability and known interest, not on any preferred or favored status. A common practice to assure fair dealing is to communicate recommendations simultaneously within the firm and to customers.

Members and candidates should consider the following points when establishing fair-dealing compliance procedures:

- *Limit the number of people involved*: Members and candidates should make reasonable efforts to limit the number of people who are privy to the fact that a recommendation is going to be disseminated.

- *Shorten the time frame between decision and dissemination*: Members and candidates should make reasonable efforts to limit the amount of time that elapses between the decision to make an investment recommendation and the time the actual recommendation is disseminated. If a detailed institutional recommendation that might take two or three weeks to publish is in preparation, a short summary report including the conclusion might be published in advance. In an organization where both a research committee and an investment policy committee must approve a recommendation, the meetings should be held on the same day if possible. The process of reviewing reports and printing and mailing them, faxing them, or distributing them by e-mail necessarily involves the passage of time, sometimes long periods of time. In large firms with extensive review processes, the time factor is usually not within the control of the analyst who prepares the report. Thus, many firms and their analysts communicate to customers and firm personnel the new or changed recommendations by an update or "flash" report. The communication technique might be fax, e-mail, wire, or short written report.

- *Publish guidelines for pre-dissemination behavior*: Members and candidates should encourage firms to develop guidelines that prohibit personnel who have prior knowledge of an investment recommendation from discussing or taking any action on the pending recommendation.

- *Simultaneous dissemination*: Members and candidates should establish procedures for the timing of dissemination of investment recommendations so that all clients are treated fairly—that is, are informed at approximately the same time. For example, if a firm is going to announce a new recommendation, supervisory personnel should time the announcement to avoid placing any client or group of clients at an unfair advantage relative to other clients. A communication to all branch offices should be sent at the time of the general announcement. (When appropriate, the firm should accompany the announcement of a new recommendation with a statement that trading restrictions for the firm's employees are now in effect. The trading restrictions should stay in effect until the recommendation is widely distributed to all relevant clients.) Once this distribution has occurred, the member or candidate may follow up separately with individual clients, but members and candidates should not give favored clients advance information when such advance notification may disadvantage other clients.

- *Maintain a list of clients and their holdings*: Members and candidates should maintain a list of all clients and the securities or other investments each client holds in order to facilitate notification of customers or clients of a change in an investment recommendation. If a particular security or other investment is to be sold, such a list can be used to ensure that all holders are treated fairly in the liquidation of that particular investment.

- *Develop and document trade allocation procedures*: When formulating procedures for allocating trades, members and candidates should develop a set of guiding principles that ensure

  - fairness to advisory clients, both in priority of execution of orders and in the allocation of the price obtained in execution of block orders or trades,

  - timeliness and efficiency in the execution of orders, and

  - accuracy of the member's or candidate's records as to trade orders and client account positions.

With these principles in mind, members and candidates should develop or encourage their firm to develop written allocation procedures, with particular attention to procedures for block trades and new issues. Procedures to consider are as follows:

- requiring orders and modifications or cancellations of orders to be documented and time stamped;

- processing and executing orders on a first-in, first-out basis with consideration of bundling orders for efficiency as appropriate for the asset class or the security;

- developing a policy to address such issues as calculating execution prices and "partial fills" when trades are grouped, or in a block, for efficiency;

- giving all client accounts participating in a block trade the same execution price and charging the same commission;

- when the full amount of the block order is not executed, allocating partially executed orders among the participating client accounts pro rata on the basis of order size while not going below an established minimum lot size for some securities (e.g., bonds); and

Standard III(B): Application of the Standard

- when allocating trades for new issues, obtaining advance indications of interest, allocating securities by client (rather than portfolio manager), and providing a method for calculating allocations.

Disclose Trade Allocation Procedures

Members and candidates should disclose to clients and prospective clients how they select accounts to participate in an order and how they determine the amount of securities each account will buy or sell. Trade allocation procedures must be fair and equitable, and disclosure of inequitable allocation methods does not relieve the member or candidate of this obligation.

Establish Systematic Account Review

Member and candidate supervisors should review each account on a regular basis to ensure that no client or customer is being given preferential treatment and that the investment actions taken for each account are suitable for each account's objectives. Because investments should be based on individual needs and circumstances, an investment manager may have good reasons for placing a given security or other investment in one account while selling it from another account and should fully document the reasons behind both sides of the transaction. Members and candidates should encourage firms to establish review procedures, however, to detect whether trading in one account is being used to benefit a favored client.

Disclose Levels of Service

Members and candidates should disclose to all clients whether the organization offers different levels of service to clients for the same fee or different fees. Different levels of service should not be offered to clients selectively.

STANDARD III(B): APPLICATION OF THE STANDARD   23

☐ | demonstrate a thorough knowledge of the CFA Institute Code of Ethics and Standards of Professional Conduct by applying the Code and Standards to specific situations

Example 1 (Selective Disclosure):

Bradley Ames, a well-known and respected analyst, follows the computer industry. In the course of his research, he finds that a small, relatively unknown company whose shares are traded over the counter has just signed significant contracts with some of the companies he follows. After a considerable amount of investigation, Ames decides to write a research report on the small company and recommend purchase of its shares. While the report is being reviewed by the company for factual accuracy, Ames schedules a luncheon with several of his best clients to discuss the company. At the luncheon, he mentions the purchase recommendation scheduled to be sent early the following week to all the firm's clients.

> *Comment*: Ames has violated Standard III(B) by disseminating the purchase recommendation to the clients with whom he has lunch a week before the recommendation is sent to all clients.

Example 2 (Fair Dealing between Funds):

Spencer Rivers, president of XYZ Corporation, moves his company's growth-oriented pension fund to a particular bank primarily because of the excellent investment performance achieved by the bank's commingled fund for the prior five-year period. Later, Rivers compares the results of his pension fund with those of the bank's commingled fund. He is startled to learn that, even though the two accounts have the same investment objectives and similar portfolios, his company's pension fund has significantly underperformed the bank's commingled fund. Questioning this result at his next meeting with the pension fund's manager, Rivers is told that, as a matter of policy, when a new security is placed on the recommended list, Morgan Jackson, the pension fund manager, first purchases the security for the commingled account and then purchases it on a pro rata basis for all other pension fund accounts. Similarly, when a sale is recommended, the security is sold first from the commingled account and then sold on a pro rata basis from all other accounts. Rivers also learns that if the bank cannot get enough shares (especially of hot issues) to be meaningful to all the accounts, its policy is to place the new issues only in the commingled account.

Seeing that Rivers is neither satisfied nor pleased by the explanation, Jackson quickly adds that nondiscretionary pension accounts and personal trust accounts have a lower priority on purchase and sale recommendations than discretionary pension fund accounts. Furthermore, Jackson states, the company's pension fund had the opportunity to invest up to 5% in the commingled fund.

> *Comment*: The bank's policy does not treat all customers fairly, and Jackson has violated her duty to her clients by giving priority to the growth-oriented commingled fund over all other funds and to discretionary accounts over nondiscretionary accounts. Jackson must execute orders on a systematic basis that is fair to all clients. In addition, trade allocation procedures should be disclosed to all clients when they become clients. Of course, in this case, disclosure of the bank's policy would not change the fact that the policy is unfair.

Example 3 (Fair Dealing and IPO Distribution):

Dominic Morris works for a small regional securities firm. His work consists of corporate finance activities and investing for institutional clients. Arena, Ltd., is planning to go public. The partners have secured rights to buy an arena football league franchise and are planning to use the funds from the issue to complete the purchase. Because arena football is the current rage, Morris believes he has a hot issue on his hands. He has quietly negotiated some options for himself for helping convince Arena to do the financing through his securities firm. When he seeks expressions of interest, the institutional buyers oversubscribe the issue. Morris, assuming that the institutions have the financial clout to drive the stock up, then fills all orders (including his own) and decreases the institutional blocks.

> *Comment*: Morris has violated Standard III(B) by not treating all customers fairly. He should not have taken any shares himself and should have prorated the shares offered among all clients. In addition, he should have disclosed to his firm and to his clients that he received options as part of the deal [see Standard VI(A)–Disclosure of Conflicts].

Example 4 (Fair Dealing and Transaction Allocation):

Eleanor Preston, the chief investment officer of Porter Williams Investments (PWI), a medium-size money management firm, has been trying to retain a client, Colby Company. Management at Colby, which accounts for almost half of PWI's revenues, recently told Preston that if the performance of its account did not improve, it would find a new money manager. Shortly after this threat, Preston purchases mortgage-backed securities (MBSs) for several accounts, including Colby's. Preston is busy with a number of transactions that day, so she fails to allocate the trades immediately or write up the trade tickets. A few days later, when Preston is allocating trades, she notes that some of the MBSs have significantly increased in price and some have dropped. Preston decides to allocate the profitable trades to Colby and spread the losing trades among several other PWI accounts.

> *Comment*: Preston has violated Standard III(B) by failing to deal fairly with her clients in taking these investment actions. Preston should have allocated the trades prior to executing the orders, or she should have had a systematic approach to allocating the trades, such as pro rata, as soon as practical after they were executed. Among other things, Preston must disclose to the client that the adviser may act as broker for, receive commissions from, and have a potential conflict of interest regarding both parties in agency cross-transactions. After the disclosure, she should obtain from the client consent authorizing such transactions in advance.

Example 5 (Selective Disclosure):

Saunders Industrial Waste Management (SIWM) publicly indicates to analysts that it is comfortable with the somewhat disappointing earnings-per-share projection of US$1.16 for the quarter. Bernard Roberts, an analyst at Coffey Investments, is confident that SIWM management has understated the forecasted earnings so that the real announcement will cause an "upside surprise" and boost the price of SIWM stock. The "whisper number" (rumored) estimate based on extensive research and discussed among knowledgeable analysts is higher than US$1.16. Roberts repeats the US$1.16 figure in his research report to all Coffey clients but informally tells his large clients that he expects the earnings per share to be higher, making SIWM a good buy.

> *Comment*: By not sharing his opinion regarding the potential for a significant upside earnings surprise with all clients, Roberts is not treating all clients fairly and has violated Standard III(B).

Example 6 (Additional Services for Select Clients):

Jenpin Weng uses e-mail to issue a new recommendation to all his clients. He then calls his three largest institutional clients to discuss the recommendation in detail.

> *Comment*: Weng has not violated Standard III(B) because he widely disseminated the recommendation and provided the information to all his clients prior to discussing it with a select few. Weng's largest clients received additional personal service because they presumably pay higher fees or because they have a large amount of assets under Weng's management. If Weng had discussed the report with a select group of clients prior to distributing it to all his clients, he would have violated Standard III(B).

Example 7 (Minimum Lot Allocations):

Lynn Hampton is a well-respected private wealth manager in her community with a diversified client base. She determines that a new 10-year bond being offered by Healthy Pharmaceuticals is appropriate for five of her clients. Three clients request to purchase US$10,000 each, and the other two request US$50,000 each. The minimum lot size is established at US$5,000, and the issue is oversubscribed at the time of placement. Her firm's policy is that odd-lot allocations, especially those below the minimum, should be avoided because they may affect the liquidity of the security at the time of sale.

Hampton is informed she will receive only US$55,000 of the offering for all accounts. Hampton distributes the bond investments as follows: The three accounts that requested US$10,000 are allocated US$5,000 each, and the two accounts that requested US$50,000 are allocated US$20,000 each.

> *Comment*: Hampton has not violated Standard III(B), even though the distribution is not on a completely pro rata basis because of the required minimum lot size. With the total allocation being significantly below the amount requested, Hampton ensured that each client received at least the minimum lot size of the issue. This approach allowed the clients to efficiently sell the bond later if necessary.

Example 8 (Excessive Trading):

Ling Chan manages the accounts for many pension plans, including the plan of his father's employer. Chan developed similar but not identical investment policies for each client, so the investment portfolios are rarely the same. To minimize the cost to his father's pension plan, he intentionally trades more frequently in the accounts of other clients to ensure the required brokerage is incurred to continue receiving free research for use by all the pensions.

> *Comment*: Chan is violating Standard III(B) because his trading actions are disadvantaging his clients to enhance a relationship with a preferred client. All clients are benefiting from the research being provided and should incur their fair portion of the costs. This does not mean that additional trading should occur if a client has not paid an equal portion of the commission; trading should occur only as required by the strategy.

Example 9 (Limited Social Media Disclosures):

Mary Burdette was recently hired by Fundamental Investment Management (FIM) as a junior auto industry analyst. Burdette is expected to expand the social media presence of the firm because she is active with various networks, including Facebook, LinkedIn, and Twitter. Although Burdette's supervisor, Joe Graf, has never used social media, he encourages Burdette to explore opportunities to increase FIM's online presence and ability to share content, communicate, and broadcast information to clients. In response to Graf's encouragement, Burdette is working on a proposal detailing the advantages of getting FIM onto Twitter in addition to launching a company Facebook page.

As part of her auto industry research for FIM, Burdette is completing a report on the financial impact of Sun Drive Auto Ltd.'s new solar technology for compact automobiles. This research report will be her first for FIM, and she believes Sun Drive's technology could revolutionize the auto industry. In her excitement, Burdette sends a quick tweet to FIM Twitter followers summarizing her "buy" recommendation for Sun Drive Auto stock.

Standard III(C): Duties to Clients – Suitability

Comment: Burdette has violated Standard III(B) by sending an investment recommendation to a select group of contacts prior to distributing it to all clients. Burdette must make sure she has received the appropriate training about FIM's policies and procedures, including the appropriate business use of personal social media networks before engaging in such activities.

See Standard IV(C) for guidance related to the duties of the supervisor.

Example 10 (Fair Dealing between Clients):

Paul Rove, performance analyst for Alpha-Beta Investment Management, is describing to the firm's chief investment officer (CIO) two new reports he would like to develop to assist the firm in meeting its obligations to treat clients fairly. Because many of the firm's clients have similar investment objectives and portfolios, Rove suggests a report detailing securities owned across several clients and the percentage of the portfolio the security represents. The second report would compare the monthly performance of portfolios with similar strategies. The outliers within each report would be submitted to the CIO for review.

Comment: As a performance analyst, Rove likely has little direct contact with clients and thus has limited opportunity to treat clients differently. The recommended reports comply with Standard III(B) while helping the firm conduct after-the-fact reviews of how effectively the firm's advisers are dealing with their clients' portfolios. Reports that monitor the fair treatment of clients are an important oversight tool to ensure that clients are treated fairly.

STANDARD III(C): DUTIES TO CLIENTS – SUITABILITY

24

☐ | demonstrate a thorough knowledge of the CFA Institute Code of Ethics and Standards of Professional Conduct by applying the Code and Standards to specific situations

1. When Members and Candidates are in an advisory relationship with a client, they must:

a. Make a reasonable inquiry into a client's or prospective client's investment experience, risk and return objectives, and financial constraints prior to making any investment recommendation or taking investment action and must reassess and update this information regularly.

b. Determine that an investment is suitable to the client's financial situation and consistent with the client's written objectives, mandates, and constraints before making an investment recommendation or taking investment action.

c. Judge the suitability of investments in the context of the client's total portfolio.

> **2.** When Members and Candidates are responsible for managing a portfolio to a specific mandate, strategy, or style, they must make only investment recommendations or take only investment actions that are consistent with the stated objectives and constraints of the portfolio.

Guidance

Highlights:

- *Developing an Investment Policy*
- *Understanding the Client's Risk Profile*
- *Updating an Investment Policy*
- *The Need for Diversification*
- *Addressing Unsolicited Trading Requests*
- *Managing to an Index or Mandate*

Standard III(C) requires that members and candidates who are in an investment advisory relationship with clients consider carefully the needs, circumstances, and objectives of the clients when determining the appropriateness and suitability of a given investment or course of investment action. An appropriate suitability determination will not, however, prevent some investments or investment actions from losing value.

In judging the suitability of a potential investment, the member or candidate should review many aspects of the client's knowledge, experience related to investing, and financial situation. These aspects include, but are not limited to, the risk profile of the investment as compared with the constraints of the client, the impact of the investment on the diversity of the portfolio, and whether the client has the means or net worth to assume the associated risk. The investment professional's determination of suitability should reflect only the investment recommendations or actions that a prudent person would be willing to undertake. Not every investment opportunity will be suitable for every portfolio, regardless of the potential return being offered.

The responsibilities of members and candidates to gather information and make a suitability analysis prior to making a recommendation or taking investment action fall on those members and candidates who provide investment advice in the course of an advisory relationship with a client. Other members and candidates may be simply executing specific instructions for retail clients when buying or selling securities, such as shares in mutual funds. These members and candidates and some others, such as sell-side analysts, may not have the opportunity to judge the suitability of a particular investment for the ultimate client.

Developing an Investment Policy

When an advisory relationship exists, members and candidates must gather client information at the inception of the relationship. Such information includes the client's financial circumstances, personal data (such as age and occupation) that are relevant to investment decisions, attitudes toward risk, and objectives in investing. This information should be incorporated into a written investment policy statement (IPS) that addresses the client's risk tolerance, return requirements, and all investment constraints (including time horizon, liquidity needs, tax concerns, legal and regulatory factors, and unique circumstances). Without identifying such client factors, members and candidates cannot judge whether a particular investment or strategy is suitable for a particular client. The IPS also should identify and describe the roles and responsibilities of the parties to the advisory relationship and investment process, as well as

Standard III(C): Duties to Clients – Suitability

schedules for review and evaluation of the IPS. After formulating long-term capital market expectations, members and candidates can assist in developing an appropriate strategic asset allocation and investment program for the client, whether these are presented in separate documents or incorporated in the IPS or in appendices to the IPS.

Understanding the Client's Risk Profile

One of the most important factors to be considered in matching appropriateness and suitability of an investment with a client's needs and circumstances is measuring that client's tolerance for risk. The investment professional must consider the possibilities of rapidly changing investment environments and their likely impact on a client's holdings, both individual securities and the collective portfolio. The risk of many investment strategies can and should be analyzed and quantified in advance.

The use of synthetic investment vehicles and derivative investment products has introduced particular issues of risk. Members and candidates should pay careful attention to the leverage inherent in many of these vehicles or products when considering them for use in a client's investment program. Such leverage and limited liquidity, depending on the degree to which they are hedged, bear directly on the issue of suitability for the client.

Updating an Investment Policy

Updating the IPS should be repeated at least annually and also prior to material changes to any specific investment recommendations or decisions on behalf of the client. The effort to determine the needs and circumstances of each client is not a one-time occurrence. Investment recommendations or decisions are usually part of an ongoing process that takes into account the diversity and changing nature of portfolio and client characteristics. The passage of time is bound to produce changes that are important with respect to investment objectives.

For an individual client, important changes might include the number of dependents, personal tax status, health, liquidity needs, risk tolerance, amount of wealth beyond that represented in the portfolio, and extent to which compensation and other income provide for current income needs. With respect to an institutional client, such changes might relate to the magnitude of unfunded liabilities in a pension fund, the withdrawal privileges in an employee savings plan, or the distribution requirements of a charitable foundation. Without efforts to update information concerning client factors, one or more factors could change without the investment manager's knowledge.

Suitability review can be done most effectively when the client fully discloses his or her complete financial portfolio, including those portions not managed by the member or candidate. If clients withhold information about their financial portfolios, the suitability analysis conducted by members and candidates cannot be expected to be complete; it must be based on the information provided.

The Need for Diversification

The investment profession has long recognized that combining several different investments is likely to provide a more acceptable level of risk exposure than having all assets in a single investment. The unique characteristics (or risks) of an individual investment may become partially or entirely neutralized when it is combined with other individual investments within a portfolio. Some reasonable amount of diversification is thus the norm for many portfolios, especially those managed by individuals or institutions that have some degree of legal fiduciary responsibility.

An investment with high relative risk on its own may be a suitable investment in the context of the entire portfolio or when the client's stated objectives contemplate speculative or risky investments. The manager may be responsible for only a portion of the client's total portfolio, or the client may not have provided a full financial picture. Members and candidates can be responsible for assessing the suitability of an investment only on the basis of the information and criteria actually provided by the client.

Addressing Unsolicited Trading Requests

Members and candidates may receive requests from a client for trades that do not properly align with the risk and return objectives outlined in the client's investment policy statement. These transaction requests may be based on the client's individual biases or professional experience. Members and candidates will need to make reasonable efforts to balance their clients' trading requests with their responsibilities to follow the agreed-on investment policy statement.

In cases of unsolicited trade requests that a member or candidate knows are unsuitable for a client, the member or candidate should refrain from making the trade until he or she discusses the concerns with the client. The discussions and resulting actions may encompass a variety of scenarios depending on how the requested unsuitable investment relates to the client's full portfolio.

Many times, an unsolicited request may be expected to have only a minimum impact on the entire portfolio because the size of the requested trade is small or the trade would result in a limited change to the portfolio's risk profile. In discussing the trade, the member or candidate should focus on educating the investor on how the request deviates from the current policy statement. Following the discussion, the member or candidate may follow his or her firm's policies regarding the necessary client approval for executing unsuitable trades. At a minimum, the client should acknowledge the discussion and accept the conditions that make the recommendation unsuitable.

Should the unsolicited request be expected to have a material impact on the portfolio, the member or candidate should use this opportunity to update the investment policy statement. Doing so would allow the client to fully understand the potential effect of the requested trade on his or her current goals or risk levels.

Members and candidates may have some clients who decline to modify their policy statements while insisting an unsolicited trade be made. In such instances, members or candidates will need to evaluate the effectiveness of their services to the client. The options available to the members or candidates will depend on the services provided by their employer. Some firms may allow for the trade to be executed in a new unmanaged account. If alternative options are not available, members and candidates ultimately will need to determine whether they should continue the advisory arrangement with the client.

Managing to an Index or Mandate

Some members and candidates do not manage money for individuals but are responsible for managing a fund to an index or an expected mandate. The responsibility of these members and candidates is to invest in a manner consistent with the stated mandate. For example, a member or candidate who serves as the fund manager for a large-cap income fund would not be following the fund mandate by investing heavily in small-cap or start-up companies whose stock is speculative in nature. Members and candidates who manage pooled assets to a specific mandate are not responsible for determining the suitability of the *fund* as an investment for investors who may be purchasing shares in the fund. The responsibility for determining the suitability of an investment for clients can be conferred only on members and candidates who have an advisory relationship with clients.

- Suitability requires members and candidates to judge the suitability of investments in the context of the client's total portfolio.

STANDARD III(C): RECOMMENDED PROCEDURES

25

☐ | demonstrate a thorough knowledge of the CFA Institute Code of Ethics and Standards of Professional Conduct by applying the Code and Standards to specific situations

Investment Policy Statement

To fulfill the basic provisions of Standard III(C), a member or candidate should put the needs and circumstances of each client and the client's investment objectives into a written investment policy statement. In formulating an investment policy for the client, the member or candidate should take the following into consideration:

- client identification—(1) type and nature of client, (2) the existence of separate beneficiaries, and (3) approximate portion of total client assets that the member or candidate is managing;
- investor objectives—(1) return objectives (income, growth in principal, maintenance of purchasing power) and (2) risk tolerance (suitability, stability of values);
- investor constraints—(1) liquidity needs, (2) expected cash flows (patterns of additions and/or withdrawals), (3) investable funds (assets and liabilities or other commitments), (4) time horizon, (5) tax considerations, (6) regulatory and legal circumstances, (7) investor preferences, prohibitions, circumstances, and unique needs, and (8) proxy voting responsibilities and guidance; and
- performance measurement benchmarks.

Regular Updates

The investor's objectives and constraints should be maintained and reviewed periodically to reflect any changes in the client's circumstances. Members and candidates should regularly compare client constraints with capital market expectations to arrive at an appropriate asset allocation. Changes in either factor may result in a fundamental change in asset allocation. Annual review is reasonable unless business or other reasons, such as a major change in market conditions, dictate more frequent review. Members and candidates should document attempts to carry out such a review if circumstances prevent it.

Suitability Test Policies

With the increase in regulatory required suitability tests, members and candidates should encourage their firms to develop related policies and procedures. The procedures will differ according to the size of the firm and the scope of the services offered to its clients.

The test procedures should require the investment professional to look beyond the potential return of the investment and include the following:

- an analysis of the impact on the portfolio's diversification,
- a comparison of the investment risks with the client's assessed risk tolerance, and

26

STANDARD III(C): APPLICATION OF THE STANDARD

☐ demonstrate a thorough knowledge of the CFA Institute Code of Ethics and Standards of Professional Conduct by applying the Code and Standards to specific situations

☐ recommend practices and procedures designed to prevent violations of the Code of Ethics and Standards of Professional Conduct

Example 1 (Investment Suitability—Risk Profile):

Caleb Smith, an investment adviser, has two clients: Larry Robertson, 60 years old, and Gabriel Lanai, 40 years old. Both clients earn roughly the same salary, but Robertson has a much higher risk tolerance because he has a large asset base. Robertson is willing to invest part of his assets very aggressively; Lanai wants only to achieve a steady rate of return with low volatility to pay for his children's education. Smith recommends investing 20% of both portfolios in zero-yield, small-cap, high-technology equity issues.

> *Comment*: In Robertson's case, the investment may be appropriate because of his financial circumstances and aggressive investment position, but this investment is not suitable for Lanai. Smith is violating Standard III(C) by applying Robertson's investment strategy to Lanai because the two clients' financial circumstances and objectives differ.

Example 2 (Investment Suitability—Entire Portfolio):

Jessica McDowell, an investment adviser, suggests to Brian Crosby, a risk-averse client, that covered call options be used in his equity portfolio. The purpose would be to enhance Crosby's income and partially offset any untimely depreciation in the portfolio's value should the stock market or other circumstances affect his holdings unfavorably. McDowell educates Crosby about all possible outcomes, including the risk of incurring an added tax liability if a stock rises in price and is called away and, conversely, the risk of his holdings losing protection on the downside if prices drop sharply.

> *Comment*: When determining suitability of an investment, the primary focus should be the characteristics of the client's entire portfolio, not the characteristics of single securities on an issue-by-issue basis. The basic characteristics of the entire portfolio will largely determine whether investment recommendations are taking client factors into account. Therefore, the most important aspects of a particular investment are those that will affect the characteristics of the total portfolio. In this case, McDowell properly considers the investment in the context of the entire portfolio and thoroughly explains the investment to the client.

Standard III(C): Application of the Standard

Example 3 (IPS Updating):

In a regular meeting with client Seth Jones, the portfolio managers at Blue Chip Investment Advisors are careful to allow some time to review his current needs and circumstances. In doing so, they learn that some significant changes have recently taken place in his life. A wealthy uncle left Jones an inheritance that increased his net worth fourfold, to US$1 million.

> *Comment*: The inheritance has significantly increased Jones's ability (and possibly his willingness) to assume risk and has diminished the average yield required to meet his current income needs. Jones's financial circumstances have definitely changed, so Blue Chip managers must update Jones's investment policy statement to reflect how his investment objectives have changed. Accordingly, the Blue Chip portfolio managers should consider a somewhat higher equity ratio for his portfolio than was called for by the previous circumstances, and the managers' specific common stock recommendations might be heavily tilted toward low-yield, growth-oriented issues.

Example 4 (Following an Investment Mandate):

Louis Perkowski manages a high-income mutual fund. He purchases zero-dividend stock in a financial services company because he believes the stock is undervalued and is in a potential growth industry, which makes it an attractive investment.

> *Comment*: A zero-dividend stock does not seem to fit the mandate of the fund that Perkowski is managing. Unless Perkowski's investment fits within the mandate or is within the realm of allowable investments the fund has made clear in its disclosures, Perkowski has violated Standard III(C).

Example 5 (IPS Requirements and Limitations):

Max Gubler, chief investment officer of a property/casualty insurance subsidiary of a large financial conglomerate, wants to improve the diversification of the subsidiary's investment portfolio and increase its returns. The subsidiary's investment policy statement provides for highly liquid investments, such as large-cap equities and government, supranational, and corporate bonds with a minimum credit rating of AA and maturity of no more than five years. In a recent presentation, a venture capital group offered very attractive prospective returns on some of its private equity funds that provide seed capital to ventures. An exit strategy was already contemplated, but investors would have to observe a minimum three-year lockup period and a subsequent laddered exit option for a maximum of one-third of their shares per year. Gubler does not want to miss this opportunity. After extensive analysis, with the intent to optimize the return on the equity assets within the subsidiary's current portfolio, he invests 4% in this seed fund, leaving the portfolio's total equity exposure still well below its upper limit.

> *Comment*: Gubler is violating Standard III(A)—Loyalty, Prudence, and Care as well as Standard III(C). His new investment locks up part of the subsidiary's assets for at least three years and up to as many as five years and possibly beyond. The IPS requires investments in highly liquid investments and describes accepted asset classes; private equity investments with a lockup period certainly do not qualify. Even without a lockup period, an asset class with only an occasional, and thus implicitly illiquid, market may not be suitable for the portfolio. Although an IPS typically describes objectives and constraints in great detail, the manager must also make

every effort to understand the client's business and circumstances. Doing so should enable the manager to recognize, understand, and discuss with the client other factors that may be or may become material in the investment management process.

Example 6 (Submanager and IPS Reviews):

Paul Ostrowski's investment management business has grown significantly over the past couple of years, and some clients want to diversify internationally. Ostrowski decides to find a submanager to handle the expected international investments. Because this will be his first subadviser, Ostrowski uses the CFA Institute model "request for proposal" to design a questionnaire for his search. By his deadline, he receives seven completed questionnaires from a variety of domestic and international firms trying to gain his business. Ostrowski reviews all the applications in detail and decides to select the firm that charges the lowest fees because doing so will have the least impact on his firm's bottom line.

> *Comment*: When selecting an external manager or subadviser, Ostrowski needs to ensure that the new manager's services are appropriate for his clients. This due diligence includes comparing the risk profile of the clients with the investment strategy of the manager. In basing the decision on the fee structure alone, Ostrowski may be violating Standard III(C).
>
> When clients ask to diversify into international products, it is an appropriate time to review and update the clients' IPSs. Ostrowski's review may determine that the risk of international investments modifies the risk profiles of the clients or does not represent an appropriate investment.
>
> See also Standard V(A)–Diligence and Reasonable Basis for further discussion of the review process needed in selecting appropriate submanagers.

Example 7 (Investment Suitability—Risk Profile):

Samantha Snead, a portfolio manager for Thomas Investment Counsel, Inc., specializes in managing public retirement funds and defined benefit pension plan accounts, all of which have long-term investment objectives. A year ago, Snead's employer, in an attempt to motivate and retain key investment professionals, introduced a bonus compensation system that rewards portfolio managers on the basis of quarterly performance relative to their peers and to certain benchmark indexes. In an attempt to improve the short-term performance of her accounts, Snead changes her investment strategy and purchases several high-beta stocks for client portfolios. These purchases are seemingly contrary to the clients' investment policy statements. Following their purchase, an officer of Griffin Corporation, one of Snead's pension fund clients, asks why Griffin Corporation's portfolio seems to be dominated by high-beta stocks of companies that often appear among the most actively traded issues. No change in objective or strategy has been recommended by Snead during the year.

> *Comment*: Snead violated Standard III(C) by investing the clients' assets in high-beta stocks. These high-risk investments are contrary to the long-term risk profile established in the clients' IPSs. Snead has changed the investment strategy of the clients in an attempt to reap short-term rewards offered by her firm's new compensation arrangement, not in response to changes in clients' investment policy statements.
>
> See also Standard VI(A)–Disclosure of Conflicts.

Standard III(D): Duties to Clients - Performance Presentation

303

Example 8 (Investment Suitability):

Andre Shrub owns and operates Conduit, an investment advisory firm. Prior to opening Conduit, Shrub was an account manager with Elite Investment, a hedge fund managed by his good friend Adam Reed. To attract clients to a new Conduit fund, Shrub offers lower-than-normal management fees. He can do so because the fund consists of two top-performing funds managed by Reed. Given his personal friendship with Reed and the prior performance record of these two funds, Shrub believes this new fund is a winning combination for all parties. Clients quickly invest with Conduit to gain access to the Elite funds. No one is turned away because Conduit is seeking to expand its assets under management.

> *Comment*: Shrub has violated Standard III(C) because the risk profile of the new fund may not be suitable for every client. As an investment adviser, Shrub needs to establish an investment policy statement for each client and recommend only investments that match each client's risk and return profile in the IPS. Shrub is required to act as more than a simple sales agent for Elite.
>
> Although Shrub cannot disobey the direct request of a client to purchase a specific security, he should fully discuss the risks of a planned purchase and provide reasons why it might not be suitable for a client. This requirement may lead members and candidates to decline new customers if those customers' requested investment decisions are significantly out of line with their stated requirements.
>
> See also Standard V(A)–Diligence and Reasonable Basis.

STANDARD III(D): DUTIES TO CLIENTS - PERFORMANCE PRESENTATION

27

☐ | demonstrate a thorough knowledge of the CFA Institute Code of Ethics and Standards of Professional Conduct by applying the Code and Standards to specific situations

> When communicating investment performance information, Members and Candidates must make reasonable efforts to ensure that it is fair, accurate, and complete.

Guidance

Standard III(D) requires members and candidates to provide credible performance information to clients and prospective clients and to avoid misstating performance or misleading clients and prospective clients about the investment performance of members or candidates or their firms. This standard encourages full disclosure of investment performance data to clients and prospective clients.

Standard III(D) covers any practice that would lead to misrepresentation of a member's or candidate's performance record, whether the practice involves performance presentation or performance measurement. This standard prohibits misrepresentations of past performance or reasonably expected performance. A member or candidate must give a fair and complete presentation of performance information whenever communicating data with respect to the performance history of individual accounts, composites or groups of accounts, or composites of an analyst's or firm's performance results. Furthermore, members and candidates should not state or imply that clients will obtain or benefit from a rate of return that was generated in the past.

The requirements of this standard are not limited to members and candidates managing separate accounts. Whenever a member or candidate provides performance information for which the manager is claiming responsibility, such as for pooled funds, the history must be accurate. Research analysts promoting the success or accuracy of their recommendations must ensure that their claims are fair, accurate, and complete.

If the presentation is brief, the member or candidate must make available to clients and prospects, on request, the detailed information supporting that communication. Best practice dictates that brief presentations include a reference to the limited nature of the information provided.

28 STANDARD III(D): RECOMMENDED PROCEDURES

☐ demonstrate a thorough knowledge of the CFA Institute Code of Ethics and Standards of Professional Conduct by applying the Code and Standards to specific situations

☐ recommend practices and procedures designed to prevent violations of the Code of Ethics and Standards of Professional Conduct

Apply the GIPS Standards

For members and candidates who are showing the performance history of the assets they manage, compliance with the GIPS standards is the best method to meet their obligations under Standard III(D). Members and candidates should encourage their firms to comply with the GIPS standards.

Compliance without Applying GIPS Standards

Members and candidates can also meet their obligations under Standard III(D) by

- considering the knowledge and sophistication of the audience to whom a performance presentation is addressed,
- presenting the performance of the weighted composite of similar portfolios rather than using a single representative account,
- including terminated accounts as part of performance history with a clear indication of when the accounts were terminated,
- including disclosures that fully explain the performance results being reported (for example, stating, when appropriate, that results are simulated when model results are used, clearly indicating when the performance record is that of a prior entity, or disclosing whether the performance is gross of fees, net of fees, or after tax), and
- maintaining the data and records used to calculate the performance being presented.

STANDARD III(D): APPLICATION OF THE STANDARD

29

☐ demonstrate a thorough knowledge of the CFA Institute Code of Ethics and Standards of Professional Conduct by applying the Code and Standards to specific situations

Example 1 (Performance Calculation and Length of Time):

Kyle Taylor of Taylor Trust Company, noting the performance of Taylor's common trust fund for the past two years, states in a brochure sent to his potential clients, "You can expect steady 25% annual compound growth of the value of your investments over the year." Taylor Trust's common trust fund did increase at the rate of 25% per year for the past year, which mirrored the increase of the entire market. The fund has never averaged that growth for more than one year, however, and the average rate of growth of all of its trust accounts for five years is 5% per year.

> *Comment*: Taylor's brochure is in violation of Standard III(D). Taylor should have disclosed that the 25% growth occurred only in one year. Additionally, Taylor did not include client accounts other than those in the firm's common trust fund. A general claim of firm performance should take into account the performance of all categories of accounts. Finally, by stating that clients can expect a steady 25% annual compound growth rate, Taylor is also violating Standard I(C)–Misrepresentation, which prohibits assurances or guarantees regarding an investment.

Example 2 (Performance Calculation and Asset Weighting):

Anna Judd, a senior partner of Alexander Capital Management, circulates a performance report for the capital appreciation accounts for the years 1988 through 2004. The firm claims compliance with the GIPS standards. Returns are not calculated in accordance with the requirements of the GIPS standards, however, because the composites are not asset weighted.

> *Comment*: Judd is in violation of Standard III(D). When claiming compliance with the GIPS standards, firms must meet *all* of the requirements, make mandatory disclosures, and meet any other requirements that apply to that firm's specific situation. Judd's violation is not from any misuse of the data but from a false claim of GIPS compliance.

Example 3 (Performance Presentation and Prior Fund/Employer):

Aaron McCoy is vice president and managing partner of the equity investment group of Mastermind Financial Advisors, a new business. Mastermind recruited McCoy because he had a proven six-year track record with G&P Financial. In developing Mastermind's advertising and marketing campaign, McCoy prepares an advertisement that includes the equity investment performance he achieved at G&P Financial. The advertisement for Mastermind does not identify the equity performance as being earned while at G&P. The advertisement is distributed to existing clients and prospective clients of Mastermind.

Comment: McCoy has violated Standard III(D) by distributing an advertisement that contains material misrepresentations about the historical performance of Mastermind. Standard III(D) requires that members and candidates make every reasonable effort to ensure that performance information is a fair, accurate, and complete representation of an individual's or firm's performance. As a general matter, this standard does not prohibit showing past performance of funds managed at a prior firm as part of a performance track record as long as showing that record is accompanied by appropriate disclosures about where the performance took place and the person's specific role in achieving that performance. If McCoy chooses to use his past performance from G&P in Mastermind's advertising, he should make full disclosure of the source of the historical performance.

Example 4 (Performance Presentation and Simulated Results):

Jed Davis has developed a mutual fund selection product based on historical information from the 1990–95 period. Davis tested his methodology by applying it retroactively to data from the 1996–2003 period, thus producing simulated performance results for those years. In January 2004, Davis's employer decided to offer the product and Davis began promoting it through trade journal advertisements and direct dissemination to clients. The advertisements included the performance results for the 1996–2003 period but did not indicate that the results were simulated.

Comment: Davis violated Standard III(D) by failing to clearly identify simulated performance results. Standard III(D) prohibits members and candidates from making any statements that misrepresent the performance achieved by them or their firms and requires members and candidates to make every reasonable effort to ensure that performance information presented to clients is fair, accurate, and complete. Use of simulated results should be accompanied by full disclosure as to the source of the performance data, including the fact that the results from 1995 through 2003 were the result of applying the model retroactively to that time period.

Example 5 (Performance Calculation and Selected Accounts Only):

In a presentation prepared for prospective clients, William Kilmer shows the rates of return realized over a five-year period by a "composite" of his firm's discretionary accounts that have a "balanced" objective. This composite, however, consisted of only a few of the accounts that met the balanced criterion set by the firm, excluded accounts under a certain asset level without disclosing the fact of their exclusion, and included accounts that did not have the balanced mandate because those accounts would boost the investment results. In addition, to achieve better results, Kilmer manipulated the narrow range of accounts included in the composite by changing the accounts that made up the composite over time.

Comment: Kilmer violated Standard III(D) by misrepresenting the facts in the promotional material sent to prospective clients, distorting his firm's performance record, and failing to include disclosures that would have clarified the presentation.

Example 6 (Performance Attribution Changes):

Art Purell is reviewing the quarterly performance attribution reports for distribution to clients. Purell works for an investment management firm with a bottom-up, fundamentals-driven investment process that seeks to add value through stock selection. The attribution methodology currently compares each stock with its sector. The attribution report indicates that the value added this quarter came from asset allocation and that stock selection contributed negatively to the calculated return.

Through running several different scenarios, Purell discovers that calculating attribution by comparing each stock with its industry and then rolling the effect to the sector level improves the appearance of the manager's stock selection activities. Because the firm defines the attribution terms and the results better reflect the stated strategy, Purell recommends that the client reports should use the revised methodology.

> *Comment*: Modifying the attribution methodology without proper notifications to clients would fail to meet the requirements of Standard III(D). Purrell's recommendation is being done solely for the interest of the firm to improve its perceived ability to meet the stated investment strategy. Such changes are unfair to clients and obscure the facts regarding the firm's abilities.
>
> Had Purell believed the new methodology offered improvements to the original model, then he would have needed to report the results of both calculations to the client. The report should also include the reasons why the new methodology is preferred, which would allow the client to make a meaningful comparison to prior results and provide a basis for comparing future attributions.

Example 7 (Performance Calculation Methodology Disclosure):

While developing a new reporting package for existing clients, Alisha Singh, a performance analyst, discovers that her company's new system automatically calculates both time-weighted and money-weighted returns. She asks the head of client services and retention which value would be preferred given that the firm has various investment strategies that include bonds, equities, securities without leverage, and alternatives. Singh is told not to label the return value so that the firm may show whichever value is greatest for the period.

> *Comment*: Following these instructions would lead to Singh violating Standard III(D). In reporting inconsistent return values, Singh would not be providing complete information to the firm's clients. Full information is provided when clients have sufficient information to judge the performance generated by the firm.

Example 8 (Performance Calculation Methodology Disclosure):

Richmond Equity Investors manages a long–short equity fund in which clients can trade once a week (on Fridays). For transparency reasons, a daily net asset value of the fund is calculated by Richmond. The monthly fact sheets of the fund report month-to-date and year-to-date performance. Richmond publishes the performance based on the higher of the last trading day of the month (typically, not the last business day) or the last business day of the month as determined by Richmond. The fact sheet mentions only that the data are as of the end of the month, without giving the exact date. Maggie Clark, the investment performance analyst in charge of the calculations, is concerned about the frequent changes and asks her supervisor whether they are appropriate.

Comment: Clark's actions in questioning the changing performance metric comply with Standard III(D). She has shown concern that these changes are not presenting an accurate and complete picture of the performance generated.

30 STANDARD III(E): DUTIES TO CLIENTS - PRESERVATION OF CONFIDENTIALITY

Members and Candidates must keep information about current, former, and prospective clients confidential unless:

1. The information concerns illegal activities on the part of the client;
2. Disclosure is required by law; or
3. The client or prospective client permits disclosure of the information.

Guidance

Highlights:

- *Status of Client*
- *Compliance with Laws*
- *Electronic Information and Security*
- *Professional Conduct Investigations by CFA Institute*

Standard III(E) requires that members and candidates preserve the confidentiality of information communicated to them by their clients, prospective clients, and former clients. This standard is applicable when (1) the member or candidate receives information because of his or her special ability to conduct a portion of the client's business or personal affairs and (2) the member or candidate receives information that arises from or is relevant to that portion of the client's business that is the subject of the special or confidential relationship. If disclosure of the information is required by law or the information concerns illegal activities by the client, however, the member or candidate may have an obligation to report the activities to the appropriate authorities.

Status of Client

This standard protects the confidentiality of client information even if the person or entity is no longer a client of the member or candidate. Therefore, members and candidates must continue to maintain the confidentiality of client records even after the client relationship has ended. If a client or former client expressly authorizes the member or candidate to disclose information, however, the member or candidate may follow the terms of the authorization and provide the information.

Compliance with Laws

As a general matter, members and candidates must comply with applicable law. If applicable law requires disclosure of client information in certain circumstances, members and candidates must comply with the law. Similarly, if applicable law requires members and candidates to maintain confidentiality, even if the information concerns illegal activities on the part of the client, members and candidates should not disclose such

Standard III(E): Recommended Procedures

309

information. Additionally, applicable laws, such as inter-departmental communication restrictions within financial institutions, can impose limitations on information flow about a client within an entity that may lead to a violation of confidentiality. When in doubt, members and candidates should consult with their employer's compliance personnel or legal counsel before disclosing confidential information about clients.

Electronic Information and Security

Because of the ever-increasing volume of electronically stored information, members and candidates need to be particularly aware of possible accidental disclosures. Many employers have strict policies about how to electronically communicate sensitive client information and store client information on personal laptops, mobile devices, or portable disk/flash drives. In recent years, regulatory authorities have imposed stricter data security laws applying to the use of mobile remote digital communication, including the use of social media, that must be considered. Standard III(E) does not require members or candidates to become experts in information security technology, but they should have a thorough understanding of the policies of their employer. The size and operations of the firm will lead to differing policies for ensuring the security of confidential information maintained within the firm. Members and candidates should encourage their firm to conduct regular periodic training on confidentiality procedures for all firm personnel, including portfolio associates, receptionists, and other non-investment staff who have routine direct contact with clients and their records.

Professional Conduct Investigations by CFA Institute

The requirements of Standard III(E) are not intended to prevent members and candidates from cooperating with an investigation by the CFA Institute Professional Conduct Program (PCP). When permissible under applicable law, members and candidates shall consider the PCP an extension of themselves when requested to provide information about a client in support of a PCP investigation into their own conduct. Members and candidates are encouraged to cooperate with investigations into the conduct of others. Any information turned over to the PCP is kept in the strictest confidence. Members and candidates will not be considered in violation of this standard by forwarding confidential information to the PCP.

STANDARD III(E): RECOMMENDED PROCEDURES

31

☐ | demonstrate a thorough knowledge of the CFA Institute Code of Ethics and Standards of Professional Conduct by applying the Code and Standards to specific situations

The simplest, most conservative, and most effective way to comply with Standard III(E) is to avoid disclosing any information received from a client except to authorized fellow employees who are also working for the client. In some instances, however, a member or candidate may want to disclose information received from clients that is outside the scope of the confidential relationship and does not involve illegal activities. Before making such a disclosure, a member or candidate should ask the following:

- In what context was the information disclosed? If disclosed in a discussion of work being performed for the client, is the information relevant to the work?

- Is the information background material that, if disclosed, will enable the member or candidate to improve service to the client?

Members and candidates need to understand and follow their firm's electronic information communication and storage procedures. If the firm does not have procedures in place, members and candidates should encourage the development of procedures that appropriately reflect the firm's size and business operations.

Communicating with Clients

Technological changes are constantly enhancing the methods that are used to communicate with clients and prospective clients. Members and candidates should make reasonable efforts to ensure that firm-supported communication methods and compliance procedures follow practices designed for preventing accidental distribution of confidential information. Given the rate at which technology changes, a regular review of privacy protection measures is encouraged.

Members and candidates should be diligent in discussing with clients the appropriate methods for providing confidential information. It is important to convey to clients that not all firm-sponsored resources may be appropriate for such communications.

32 STANDARD III(E): APPLICATION OF THE STANDARD

- [ ] demonstrate a thorough knowledge of the CFA Institute Code of Ethics and Standards of Professional Conduct by applying the Code and Standards to specific situations
- [ ] recommend practices and procedures designed to prevent violations of the Code of Ethics and Standards of Professional Conduct

Example 1 (Possessing Confidential Information):

Sarah Connor, a financial analyst employed by Johnson Investment Counselors, Inc., provides investment advice to the trustees of City Medical Center. The trustees have given her a number of internal reports concerning City Medical's needs for physical plant renovation and expansion. They have asked Connor to recommend investments that would generate capital appreciation in endowment funds to meet projected capital expenditures. Connor is approached by a local businessman, Thomas Kasey, who is considering a substantial contribution either to City Medical Center or to another local hospital. Kasey wants to find out the building plans of both institutions before making a decision, but he does not want to speak to the trustees.

> *Comment*: The trustees gave Connor the internal reports so she could advise them on how to manage their endowment funds. Because the information in the reports is clearly both confidential and within the scope of the confidential relationship, Standard III(E) requires that Connor refuse to divulge information to Kasey.

Example 2 (Disclosing Confidential Information):

Lynn Moody is an investment officer at the Lester Trust Company. She has an advisory customer who has talked to her about giving approximately US$50,000 to charity to reduce her income taxes. Moody is also treasurer of the Home for Indigent Widows (HIW), which is planning its annual giving campaign. HIW hopes to expand its list of prospects, particularly those capable of substantial gifts. Moody recommends that HIW's vice president for corporate gifts call on her customer and ask for a donation in the US$50,000 range.

> *Comment*: Even though the attempt to help the Home for Indigent Widows was well intended, Moody violated Standard III(E) by revealing confidential information about her client.

Example 3 (Disclosing Possible Illegal Activity):

Government officials approach Casey Samuel, the portfolio manager for Garcia Company's pension plan, to examine pension fund records. They tell her that Garcia's corporate tax returns are being audited and the pension fund is being reviewed. Two days earlier, Samuel had learned in a regular investment review with Garcia officers that potentially excessive and improper charges were being made to the pension plan by Garcia. Samuel consults her employer's general counsel and is advised that Garcia has probably violated tax and fiduciary regulations and laws.

> *Comment*: Samuel should inform her supervisor of these activities, and her employer should take steps, with Garcia, to remedy the violations. If that approach is not successful, Samuel and her employer should seek advice of legal counsel to determine the appropriate steps to be taken. Samuel may well have a duty to disclose the evidence she has of the continuing legal violations and to resign as asset manager for Garcia.

Example 4 (Disclosing Possible Illegal Activity):

David Bradford manages money for a family-owned real estate development corporation. He also manages the individual portfolios of several of the family members and officers of the corporation, including the chief financial officer (CFO). Based on the financial records of the corporation and some questionable practices of the CFO that Bradford has observed, Bradford believes that the CFO is embezzling money from the corporation and putting it into his personal investment account.

> *Comment*: Bradford should check with his firm's compliance department or appropriate legal counsel to determine whether applicable securities regulations require reporting the CFO's financial records.

Example 5 (Accidental Disclosure of Confidential Information):

Lynn Moody is an investment officer at the Lester Trust Company (LTC). She has stewardship of a significant number of individually managed taxable accounts. In addition to receiving quarterly written reports, about a dozen high-net-worth individuals have indicated to Moody a willingness to receive communications about overall economic and financial market outlooks directly from her by way of a social media platform. Under the direction of her firm's technology and compliance departments, she established a new group page on an existing social media platform specifically for her clients. In the instructions provided to clients, Moody asked them to "join" the group so they may be granted access to the posted content. The instructions also advised clients that all comments posted would be available to the public and thus the platform was not an appropriate method for communicating personal or confidential information.

Six months later, in early January, Moody posted LTC's year-end "Market Outlook." The report outlined a new asset allocation strategy that the firm is adding to its recommendations in the new year. Moody introduced the publication with a note informing her clients that she would be discussing the changes with them individually in their upcoming meetings.

One of Moody's clients responded directly on the group page that his family recently experienced a major change in their financial profile. The client described highly personal and confidential details of the event. Unfortunately, all clients that were part of the group were also able to read the detailed posting until Moody was able to have the comment removed.

> *Comment*: Moody has taken reasonable steps for protecting the confidentiality of client information while using the social media platform. She provided instructions clarifying that all information posted to the site would be publically viewable to all group members and warned against using this method for communicating confidential information. The accidental disclosure of confidential information by a client is not under Moody's control. Her actions to remove the information promptly once she became aware further align with Standard III(E).
>
> In understanding the potential sensitivity clients express surrounding the confidentiality of personal information, this event highlights a need for further training. Moody might advocate for additional warnings or controls for clients when they consider using social media platforms for two-way communications.

33 STANDARD IV(A): DUTIES TO EMPLOYERS – LOYALTY

☐ | demonstrate a thorough knowledge of the CFA Institute Code of Ethics and Standards of Professional Conduct by applying the Code and Standards to specific situations

Standard IV(A) Loyalty

In matters related to their employment, Members and Candidates must act for the benefit of their employer and not deprive their employer of the advantage of their skills and abilities, divulge confidential information, or otherwise cause harm to their employer.

Guidance

Highlights:

- *Employer Responsibilities*
- *Independent Practice*

Standard IV(A): Duties to Employers – Loyalty

- *Leaving an Employer*
- *Use of Social Media*
- *Whistleblowing*
- *Nature of Employment*

Standard IV(A) requires members and candidates to protect the interests of their firm by refraining from any conduct that would injure the firm, deprive it of profit, or deprive it of the member's or candidate's skills and ability. Members and candidates must always place the interests of clients above the interests of their employer but should also consider the effects of their conduct on the sustainability and integrity of the employer firm. In matters related to their employment, members and candidates must not engage in conduct that harms the interests of their employer. Implicit in this standard is the obligation of members and candidates to comply with the policies and procedures established by their employers that govern the employer–employee relationship—to the extent that such policies and procedures do not conflict with applicable laws, rules, or regulations or the Code and Standards.

This standard is not meant to be a blanket requirement to place employer interests ahead of personal interests in all matters. The standard does not require members and candidates to subordinate important personal and family obligations to their work. Members and candidates should enter into a dialogue with their employer about balancing personal and employment obligations when personal matters may interfere with their work on a regular or significant basis.

Employer Responsibilities

The employer–employee relationship imposes duties and responsibilities on both parties. Employers must recognize the duties and responsibilities that they owe to their employees if they expect to have content and productive employees.

Members and candidates are encouraged to provide their employer with a copy of the Code and Standards. These materials will inform the employer of the responsibilities of a CFA Institute member or a candidate in the CFA Program. The Code and Standards also serve as a basis for questioning employer policies and practices that conflict with these responsibilities.

Employers are not obligated to adhere to the Code and Standards. In expecting to retain competent employees who are members and candidates, however, they should not develop conflicting policies and procedures. The employer is responsible for a positive working environment, which includes an ethical workplace. Senior management has the additional responsibility to devise compensation structures and incentive arrangements that do not encourage unethical behavior.

Independent Practice

Included in Standard IV(A) is the requirement that members and candidates abstain from independent competitive activity that could conflict with the interests of their employer. Although Standard IV(A) does not preclude members or candidates from entering into an independent business while still employed, members and candidates who plan to engage in independent practice for compensation must notify their employer and describe the types of services they will render to prospective independent clients, the expected duration of the services, and the compensation for the services. Members and candidates should not render services until they receive consent from their employer to all of the terms of the arrangement. "Practice" means any service that the employer currently makes available for remuneration. "Undertaking independent practice" means engaging in competitive business, as opposed to making preparations to begin such practice.

Leaving an Employer

When members and candidates are planning to leave their current employer, they must continue to act in the employer's best interest. They must not engage in any activities that would conflict with this duty until their resignation becomes effective. It is difficult to define specific guidelines for those members and candidates who are planning to compete with their employer as part of a new venture. The circumstances of each situation must be reviewed to distinguish permissible preparations from violations of duty. Activities that might constitute a violation, especially in combination, include the following:

- misappropriation of trade secrets,
- misuse of confidential information,
- solicitation of the employer's clients prior to cessation of employment,
- self-dealing (appropriating for one's own property a business opportunity or information belonging to one's employer), and
- misappropriation of clients or client lists.

A departing employee is generally free to make arrangements or preparations to go into a competitive business before terminating the relationship with his or her employer as long as such preparations do not breach the employee's duty of loyalty. A member or candidate who is contemplating seeking other employment must not contact existing clients or potential clients prior to leaving his or her employer for purposes of soliciting their business for the new employer. Once notice is provided to the employer of the intent to resign, the member or candidate must follow the employer's policies and procedures related to notifying clients of his or her planned departure. In addition, the member or candidate must not take records or files to a new employer without the written permission of the previous employer.

Once an employee has left the firm, the skills and experience that an employee obtained while employed are not "confidential" or "privileged" information. Similarly, simple knowledge of the names and existence of former clients is generally not confidential information unless deemed such by an agreement or by law. Standard IV(A) does not prohibit experience or knowledge gained at one employer from being used at another employer. Firm records or work performed on behalf of the firm that is stored in paper copy or electronically for the member's or candidate's convenience while employed, however, should be erased or returned to the employer unless the firm gives permission to keep those records after employment ends.

The standard does not prohibit former employees from contacting clients of their previous firm as long as the contact information does not come from the records of the former employer or violate an applicable "noncompete agreement." Members and candidates are free to use public information after departing to contact former clients without violating Standard IV(A) as long as there is no specific agreement not to do so.

Employers often require employees to sign noncompete agreements that preclude a departing employee from engaging in certain conduct. Members and candidates should take care to review the terms of any such agreement when leaving their employer to determine what, if any, conduct those agreements may prohibit.

In some markets, there are agreements between employers within an industry that outline information that departing employees are permitted to take upon resignation, such as the "Protocol for Broker Recruiting" in the United States. These agreements ease individuals' transition between firms that have agreed to follow the outlined procedures. Members and candidates who move between firms that sign such agreements may rely on the protections provided as long as they faithfully adhere to all the procedures outlined.

Standard IV(A): Duties to Employers – Loyalty

For example, under the agreement between many US brokers, individuals are allowed to take some general client contact information when departing. To be protected, a copy of the information the individual is taking must be provided to the local management team for review. Additionally, the specific client information may only be used by the departing employee and not others employed by the new firm.

Use of Social Media

The growth in various online networking platforms, such as LinkedIn, Twitter, and Facebook (commonly referred to as social media platforms), is providing new opportunities and challenges for businesses. Members and candidates should understand and abide by all applicable firm policies and regulations as to the acceptable use of social media platforms to interact with clients and prospective clients. This is especially important when a member or candidate is planning to leave an employer.

Social media use makes determining how and when departure notification is delivered to clients more complex. Members and candidates may have developed profiles on these platforms that include connections with individuals who are clients of the firm, as well as individuals unrelated to their employer. Communications through social media platforms that potentially reach current clients should adhere to the employer's policies and procedures regarding notification of departing employees.

Social media connections with clients are also raising questions concerning the differences between public information and firm property. Specific accounts and user profiles of members and candidates may be created for solely professional reasons, including firm-approved accounts for client engagements. Such firm-approved business-related accounts would be considered part of the firm's assets, thus requiring members and candidates to transfer or delete the accounts as directed by their firm's policies and procedures. Best practice for members and candidates is to maintain separate accounts for their personal and professional social media activities. Members and candidates should discuss with their employers how profiles should be treated when a single account includes personal connections and also is used to conduct aspects of their professional activities.

Whistleblowing

A member's or candidate's personal interests, as well as the interests of his or her employer, are secondary to protecting the integrity of capital markets and the interests of clients. Therefore, circumstances may arise (e.g., when an employer is engaged in illegal or unethical activity) in which members and candidates must act contrary to their employer's interests in order to comply with their duties to the market and clients. In such instances, activities that would normally violate a member's or candidate's duty to his or her employer (such as contradicting employer instructions, violating certain policies and procedures, or preserving a record by copying employer records) may be justified. Such action would be permitted only if the intent is clearly aimed at protecting clients or the integrity of the market, not for personal gain.

Nature of Employment

A wide variety of business relationships exists within the investment industry. For instance, a member or candidate may be an employee or an independent contractor. Members and candidates must determine whether they are employees or independent contractors in order to determine the applicability of Standard IV(A). This issue will be decided largely by the degree of control exercised by the employing entity over the member or candidate. Factors determining control include whether the member's or candidate's hours, work location, and other parameters of the job are set; whether facilities are provided to the member or candidate; whether the member's or candidate's expenses are reimbursed; whether the member or candidate seeks work from other employers; and the number of clients or employers the member or candidate works for.

A member's or candidate's duties within an independent contractor relationship are governed by the oral or written agreement between the member and the client. Members and candidates should take care to define clearly the scope of their responsibilities and the expectations of each client within the context of each relationship. Once a member or candidate establishes a relationship with a client, the member or candidate has a duty to abide by the terms of the agreement.

34 STANDARD IV(A): RECOMMENDED PROCEDURES

☐ demonstrate a thorough knowledge of the CFA Institute Code of Ethics and Standards of Professional Conduct by applying the Code and Standards to specific situations

Employers may establish codes of conduct and operating procedures for their employees to follow. Members and candidates should fully understand the policies to ensure that they are not in conflict with the Code and Standards. The following topics identify policies that members and candidates should encourage their firms to adopt if the policies are not currently in place.

Competition Policy

A member or candidate must understand any restrictions placed by the employer on offering similar services outside the firm while employed by the firm. The policy may outline the procedures for requesting approval to undertake the outside service or may be a strict prohibition of such service. If a member's or candidate's employer elects to have its employees sign a noncompete agreement as part of the employment agreement, the member or candidate should ensure that the details are clear and fully explained prior to signing the agreement.

Termination Policy

Members and candidates should clearly understand the termination policies of their employer. Termination policies should establish clear procedures regarding the resignation process, including addressing how the termination will be disclosed to clients and staff and whether updates posted through social media platforms will be allowed. The firm's policy may also outline the procedures for transferring ongoing research and account management responsibilities. Finally, the procedures should address agreements that allow departing employees to remove specific client-related information upon resignation.

Incident-Reporting Procedures

report potentially unethical and illegal activities in the firm.

Standard IV(A): Application of the Standard

Employee Classification

Members and candidates should understand their status within their employer firm. Firms are encouraged to adopt a standardized classification structure (e.g., part time, full time, outside contractor) for their employees and indicate how each of the firm's policies applies to each employee class.

STANDARD IV(A): APPLICATION OF THE STANDARD

35

☐ demonstrate a thorough knowledge of the CFA Institute Code of Ethics and Standards of Professional Conduct by applying the Code and Standards to specific situations

☐ recommend practices and procedures designed to prevent violations of the Code of Ethics and Standards of Professional Conduct

Example 1 (Soliciting Former Clients):

Samuel Magee manages pension accounts for Trust Assets, Inc., but has become frustrated with the working environment and has been offered a position with Fiduciary Management. Before resigning from Trust Assets, Magee asks four big accounts to leave that firm and open accounts with Fiduciary. Magee also persuades several prospective clients to sign agreements with Fiduciary Management. Magee had previously made presentations to these prospects on behalf of Trust Assets.

> *Comment*: Magee violated the employee–employer principle requiring him to act solely for his employer's benefit. Magee's duty is to Trust Assets as long as he is employed there. The solicitation of Trust Assets' current clients and prospective clients is unethical and violates Standard IV(A).

Example 2 (Former Employer's Documents and Files):

James Hightower has been employed by Jason Investment Management Corporation for 15 years. He began as an analyst but assumed increasing responsibilities and is now a senior portfolio manager and a member of the firm's investment policy committee. Hightower has decided to leave Jason Investment and start his own investment management business. He has been careful not to tell any of Jason's clients that he is leaving; he does not want to be accused of breaching his duty to Jason by soliciting Jason's clients before his departure. Hightower is planning to copy and take with him the following documents and information he developed or worked on while at Jason: (1) the client list, with addresses, telephone numbers, and other pertinent client information; (2) client account statements; (3) sample marketing presentations to prospective clients containing Jason's performance record; (4) Jason's recommended list of securities; (5) computer models to determine asset allocations for accounts with various objectives; (6) computer models for stock selection; and (7) personal computer spreadsheets for Hightower's major corporate recommendations, which he developed when he was an analyst.

> *Comment*: Except with the consent of their employer, departing members and candidates may not take employer property, which includes books, records, reports, and other materials, because taking such materials may interfere with their employer's business opportunities. Taking any employer records, even those the member or candidate prepared, violates Standard IV(A). Employer records include items stored in hard copy or any other medium (e.g., home computers, portable storage devices, cell phones).

Example 3 (Addressing Rumors):

Reuben Winston manages all-equity portfolios at Target Asset Management (TAM), a large, established investment counselor. Ten years previously, Philpott & Company, which manages a family of global bond mutual funds, acquired TAM in a diversification move. After the merger, the combined operations prospered in the fixed-income business but the equity management business at TAM languished. Lately, a few of the equity pension accounts that had been with TAM before the merger have terminated their relationships with TAM. One day, Winston finds on his voice mail the following message from a concerned client: "Hey! I just heard that Philpott is close to announcing the sale of your firm's equity management business to Rugged Life. What is going on?" Not being aware of any such deal, Winston and his associates are stunned. Their internal inquiries are met with denials from Philpott management, but the rumors persist. Feeling left in the dark, Winston contemplates leading an employee buyout of TAM's equity management business.

> *Comment*: An employee-led buyout of TAM's equity asset management business would be consistent with Standard IV(A) because it would rest on the permission of the employer and, ultimately, the clients. In this case, however, in which employees suspect the senior managers or principals are not truthful or forthcoming, Winston should consult legal counsel to determine appropriate action.

Example 4 (Ownership of Completed Prior Work):

Laura Clay, who is unemployed, wants part-time consulting work while seeking a full-time analyst position. During an interview at Bradley Associates, a large institutional asset manager, Clay is told that the firm has no immediate research openings but would be willing to pay her a flat fee to complete a study of the wireless communications industry within a given period of time. Clay would be allowed unlimited access to Bradley's research files and would be welcome to come to the offices and use whatever support facilities are available during normal working hours. Bradley's research director does not seek any exclusivity for Clay's output, and the two agree to the arrangement on a handshake. As Clay nears completion of the study, she is offered an analyst job in the research department of Winston & Company, a brokerage firm, and she is pondering submitting the draft of her wireless study for publication by Winston.

> *Comment*: Although she is under no written contractual obligation to Bradley, Clay has an obligation to let Bradley act on the output of her study before Winston & Company or Clay uses the information to their advantage. That is, unless Bradley gives permission to Clay and waives its rights to her wireless report, Clay would be in violation of Standard IV(A) if she were to immediately recommend to Winston the same transactions recommended in the report to Bradley. Furthermore, Clay must not take from Bradley any research file material or other property that she may have used.

Example 5 (Ownership of Completed Prior Work):

Emma Madeline, a recent college graduate and a candidate in the CFA Program, spends her summer as an unpaid intern at Murdoch and Lowell. The senior managers at Murdoch are attempting to bring the firm into compliance with the GIPS standards, and Madeline is assigned to assist in its efforts. Two months into her internship, Madeline applies for a job at McMillan & Company, which has plans to become GIPS compliant. Madeline accepts the job with McMillan. Before leaving Murdoch, she copies the firm's software that she helped develop because she believes this software will assist her in her new position.

> *Comment*: Even though Madeline does not receive monetary compensation for her services at Murdoch, she has used firm resources in creating the software and is considered an employee because she receives compensation and benefits in the form of work experience and knowledge. By copying the software, Madeline violated Standard IV(A) because she misappropriated Murdoch's property without permission.

Example 6 (Soliciting Former Clients):

Dennis Elliot has hired Sam Chisolm, who previously worked for a competing firm. Chisolm left his former firm after 18 years of employment. When Chisolm begins working for Elliot, he wants to contact his former clients because he knows them well and is certain that many will follow him to his new employer. Is Chisolm in violation of Standard IV(A) if he contacts his former clients?

> *Comment*: Because client records are the property of the firm, contacting former clients for any reason through the use of client lists or other information taken from a former employer without permission would be a violation of Standard IV(A). In addition, the nature and extent of the contact with former clients may be governed by the terms of any noncompete agreement signed by the employee and the former employer that covers contact with former clients after employment.
>
> Simple knowledge of the names and existence of former clients is not confidential information, just as skills or experience that an employee obtains while employed are not "confidential" or "privileged" information. The Code and Standards do not impose a prohibition on the use of experience or knowledge gained at one employer from being used at another employer. The Code and Standards also do not prohibit former employees from contacting clients of their previous firm, in the absence of a noncompete agreement. Members and candidates are free to use public information about their former firm after departing to contact former clients without violating Standard IV(A).
>
> In the absence of a noncompete agreement, as long as Chisolm maintains his duty of loyalty to his employer before joining Elliot's firm, does not take steps to solicit clients until he has left his former firm, and does not use material from his former employer without its permission after he has left, he is not in violation of the Code and Standards.

Example 7 (Starting a New Firm):

Geraldine Allen currently works at a registered investment company as an equity analyst. Without notice to her employer, she registers with government authorities to start an investment company that will compete with her employer, but she does not actively seek clients. Does registration of this competing company with the appropriate regulatory authorities constitute a violation of Standard IV(A)?

> *Comment*: Allen's preparation for the new business by registering with the regulatory authorities does not conflict with the work for her employer if the preparations have been done on Allen's own time outside the office and if Allen will not be soliciting clients for the business or otherwise operating the new company until she has left her current employer.

Example 8 (Competing with Current Employer):

Several employees are planning to depart their current employer within a few weeks and have been careful to not engage in any activities that would conflict with their duty to their current employer. They have just learned that one of their employer's clients has undertaken a request for proposal (RFP) to review and possibly hire a new investment consultant. The RFP has been sent to the employer and all of its competitors. The group believes that the new entity to be formed would be qualified to respond to the RFP and be eligible for the business. The RFP submission period is likely to conclude before the employees' resignations are effective. Is it permissible for the group of departing employees to respond to the RFP for their anticipated new firm?

> *Comment*: A group of employees responding to an RFP that their employer is also responding to would lead to direct competition between the employees and the employer. Such conduct violates Standard IV(A) unless the group of employees receives permission from their employer as well as the entity sending out the RFP.

Example 9 (Externally Compensated Assignments):

Alfonso Mota is a research analyst with Tyson Investments. He works part time as a mayor for his hometown, a position for which he receives compensation. Must Mota seek permission from Tyson to serve as mayor?

> *Comment*: If Mota's mayoral duties are so extensive and time-consuming that they might detract from his ability to fulfill his responsibilities at Tyson, he should discuss his outside activities with his employer and come to a mutual agreement regarding how to manage his personal commitments with his responsibilities to his employer.

Example 10 (Soliciting Former Clients):

After leaving her employer, Shawna McQuillen establishes her own money management business. While with her former employer, she did not sign a noncompete agreement that would have prevented her from soliciting former clients. Upon her departure, she does not take any of her client lists or contact information and she clears her personal computer of any employer records, including client contact information. She obtains the phone numbers of her former clients through public records and contacts them to solicit their business.

Standard IV(A): Application of the Standard

> *Comment*: McQuillen is not in violation of Standard IV(A) because she has not used information or records from her former employer and is not prevented by an agreement with her former employer from soliciting her former clients.

Example 11 (Whistleblowing Actions):

Meredith Rasmussen works on a buy-side trading desk and concentrates on in-house trades for a hedge fund subsidiary managed by a team at the investment management firm. The hedge fund has been very successful and is marketed globally by the firm. From her experience as the trader for much of the activity of the fund, Rasmussen has become quite knowledgeable about the hedge fund's strategy, tactics, and performance. When a distinct break in the market occurs, however, and many of the securities involved in the hedge fund's strategy decline markedly in value, Rasmussen observes that the reported performance of the hedge fund does not reflect this decline. In her experience, the lack of any effect is a very unlikely occurrence. She approaches the head of trading about her concern and is told that she should not ask any questions and that the fund is big and successful and is not her concern. She is fairly sure something is not right, so she contacts the compliance officer, who also tells her to stay away from the issue of this hedge fund's reporting.

> *Comment*: Rasmussen has clearly come upon an error in policies, procedures, and compliance practices in the firm's operations. Having been unsuccessful in finding a resolution with her supervisor and the compliance officer, Rasmussen should consult the firm's whistleblowing policy to determine the appropriate next step toward informing management of her concerns. The potentially unethical actions of the investment management division are appropriate grounds for further disclosure, so Rasmussen's whistleblowing would not represent a violation of Standard IV(A).
>
> See also Standard I(D)–Misconduct and Standard IV(C)–Responsibilities of Supervisors.

Example 12 (Soliciting Former Clients):

Angel Crome has been a private banker for YBSafe Bank for the past eight years. She has been very successful and built a considerable client portfolio during that time but is extremely frustrated by the recent loss of reputation by her current employer and subsequent client insecurity. A locally renowned headhunter contacted Crome a few days ago and offered her an interesting job with a competing private bank. This bank offers a substantial signing bonus for advisers with their own client portfolios. Crome figures that she can solicit at least 70% of her clients to follow her and gladly enters into the new employment contract.

> *Comment*: Crome may contact former clients upon termination of her employment with YBSafe Bank, but she is prohibited from using client records built by and kept with her in her capacity as an employee of YBSafe Bank. Client lists are proprietary information of her former employer and must not be used for her or her new employer's benefit. The use of written, electronic, or any other form of records other than publicly available information to contact her former clients at YBSafe Bank will be a violation of Standard IV(A).

Example 13 (Notification of Code and Standards):

Krista Smith is a relatively new assistant trader for the fixed-income desk of a major investment bank. She is on a team responsible for structuring collateralized debt obligations (CDOs) made up of securities in the inventory of the trading desk. At a meeting of the team, senior executives explain the opportunity to eventually separate the CDO into various risk-rated tranches to be sold to the clients of the firm. After the senior executives leave the meeting, the head trader announces various responsibilities of each member of the team and then says, "This is a good time to unload some of the junk we have been stuck with for a while and disguise it with ratings and a thick, unreadable prospectus, so don't be shy in putting this CDO together. Just kidding." Smith is worried by this remark and asks some of her colleagues what the head trader meant. They all respond that he was just kidding but that there is some truth in the remark because the CDO is seen by management as an opportunity to improve the quality of the securities in the firm's inventory.

Concerned about the ethical environment of the workplace, Smith decides to talk to her supervisor about her concerns and provides the head trader with a copy of the Code and Standards. Smith discusses the principle of placing the client above the interest of the firm and the possibility that the development of the new CDO will not adhere to this responsibility. The head trader assures Smith that the appropriate analysis will be conducted when determining the appropriate securities for collateral. Furthermore, the ratings are assigned by an independent firm and the prospectus will include full and factual disclosures. Smith is reassured by the meeting, but she also reviews the company's procedures and requirements for reporting potential violations of company policy and securities laws.

> *Comment*: Smith's review of the company policies and procedures for reporting violations allows her to be prepared to report through the appropriate whistleblower process if she decides that the CDO development process involves unethical actions by others. Smith's actions comply with the Code and Standards principles of placing the client's interests first and being loyal to her employer. In providing her supervisor with a copy of the Code and Standards, Smith is highlighting the high level of ethical conduct she is required to adhere to in her professional activities.

Example 14 (Leaving an Employer):

Laura Webb just left her position as portfolio analyst at Research Systems, Inc. (RSI). Her employment contract included a non-solicitation agreement that requires her to wait two years before soliciting RSI clients for any investment-related services. Upon leaving, Webb was informed that RSI would contact clients immediately about her departure and introduce her replacement.

While working at RSI, Webb connected with clients, other industry associates, and friends through her LinkedIn network. Her business and personal relationships were intermingled because she considered many of her clients to be personal friends. Realizing that her LinkedIn network would be a valuable resource for new employment opportunities, she updated her profile several days following her departure from RSI. LinkedIn automatically sent a notification to Webb's entire network that her employment status had been changed in her profile.

> *Comment*: Prior to her departure, Webb should have discussed any client information contained in her social media networks. By updating her LinkedIn profile after RSI notified clients and after her employment ended, she has appropriately placed her employer's interests ahead of her own

personal interests. In addition, she has not violated the non-solicitation agreement with RSI, unless it prohibited any contact with clients during the two-year period.

Example 15 (Confidential Firm Information):

Sanjay Gupta is a research analyst at Naram Investment Management (NIM). NIM uses a team-based research process to develop recommendations on investment opportunities covered by the team members. Gupta, like others, provides commentary for NIM's clients through the company blog, which is posted weekly on the NIM password-protected website. According to NIM's policy, every contribution to the website must be approved by the company's compliance department before posting. Any opinions expressed on the website are disclosed as representing the perspective of NIM.

Gupta also writes a personal blog to share his experiences with friends and family. As with most blogs, Gupta's personal blog is widely available to interested readers through various internet search engines. Occasionally, when he disagrees with the team-based research opinions of NIM, Gupta uses his personal blog to express his own opinions as a counterpoint to the commentary posted on the NIM website. Gupta believes this provides his readers with a more complete perspective on these investment opportunities.

> *Comment*: Gupta is in violation of Standard IV(A) for disclosing confidential firm information through his personal blog. The recommendations on the firm's blog to clients are not freely available across the internet, but his personal blog post indirectly provides the firm's recommendations.
>
> Additionally, by posting research commentary on his personal blog, Gupta is using firm resources for his personal advantage. To comply with Standard IV(A), members and candidates must receive consent from their employer prior to using company resources.

STANDARD IV(B): DUTIES TO EMPLOYERS - ADDITIONAL COMPENSATION ARRANGEMENTS

36

☐ demonstrate a thorough knowledge of the CFA Institute Code of Ethics and Standards of Professional Conduct by applying the Code and Standards to specific situations

Members and Candidates must not accept gifts, benefits, compensation, or consideration that competes with or might reasonably be expected to create a conflict of interest with their employer's interest unless they obtain written consent from all parties involved.

Guidance

Standard IV(B) requires members and candidates to obtain permission from their employer before accepting compensation or other benefits from third parties for the services rendered to the employer or for any services that might create a conflict with their employer's interest. Compensation and benefits include direct compensation by the client and any indirect compensation or other benefits received from third parties. "Written consent" includes any form of communication that can be documented (for example, communication via e-mail that can be retrieved and documented).

Members and candidates must obtain permission for additional compensation/benefits because such arrangements may affect loyalties and objectivity and create potential conflicts of interest. Disclosure allows an employer to consider the outside arrangements when evaluating the actions and motivations of members and candidates. Moreover, the employer is entitled to have full knowledge of all compensation/benefit arrangements so as to be able to assess the true cost of the services members or candidates are providing.

There may be instances in which a member or candidate is hired by an employer on a "part-time" basis. "Part-time" status applies to employees who do not commit the full number of hours required for a normal work week. Members and candidates should discuss possible limitations to their abilities to provide services that may be competitive with their employer during the negotiation and hiring process. The requirements of Standard IV(B) would be applicable to limitations identified at that time.

37 STANDARD IV(B): RECOMMENDED PROCEDURES

☐ demonstrate a thorough knowledge of the CFA Institute Code of Ethics and Standards of Professional Conduct by applying the Code and Standards to specific situations

Members and candidates should make an immediate written report to their supervisor and compliance officer specifying any compensation they propose to receive for services in addition to the compensation or benefits received from their employer. The details of the report should be confirmed by the party offering the additional compensation, including performance incentives offered by clients. This written report should state the terms of any agreement under which a member or candidate will receive additional compensation; "terms" include the nature of the compensation, the approximate amount of compensation, and the duration of the agreement.

38 STANDARD IV(B): APPLICATION OF THE STANDARD

☐ demonstrate a thorough knowledge of the CFA Institute Code of Ethics and Standards of Professional Conduct by applying the Code and Standards to specific situations

☐ recommend practices and procedures designed to prevent violations of the Code of Ethics and Standards of Professional Conduct

Example 1 (Notification of Client Bonus Compensation):

Geoff Whitman, a portfolio analyst for Adams Trust Company, manages the account of Carol Cochran, a client. Whitman is paid a salary by his employer, and Cochran pays the trust company a standard fee based on the market value of assets in her

Standard IV(B): Application of the Standard

portfolio. Cochran proposes to Whitman that "any year that my portfolio achieves at least a 15% return before taxes, you and your wife can fly to Monaco at my expense and use my condominium during the third week of January." Whitman does not inform his employer of the arrangement and vacations in Monaco the following January as Cochran's guest.

> *Comment*: Whitman violated Standard IV(B) by failing to inform his employer in writing of this supplemental, contingent compensation arrangement. The nature of the arrangement could have resulted in partiality to Cochran's account, which could have detracted from Whitman's performance with respect to other accounts he handles for Adams Trust. Whitman must obtain the consent of his employer to accept such a supplemental benefit.

Example 2 (Notification of Outside Compensation):

Terry Jones sits on the board of directors of Exercise Unlimited, Inc. In return for his services on the board, Jones receives unlimited membership privileges for his family at all Exercise Unlimited facilities. Jones purchases Exercise Unlimited stock for the client accounts for which it is appropriate. Jones does not disclose this arrangement to his employer because he does not receive monetary compensation for his services to the board.

> *Comment*: Jones has violated Standard IV(B) by failing to disclose to his employer benefits received in exchange for his services on the board of directors. The nonmonetary compensation may create a conflict of interest in the same manner as being paid to serve as a director.

Example 3 (Prior Approval for Outside Compensation):

Jonathan Hollis is an analyst of oil-and-gas companies for Specialty Investment Management. He is currently recommending the purchase of ABC Oil Company shares and has published a long, well-thought-out research report to substantiate his recommendation. Several weeks after publishing the report, Hollis receives a call from the investor-relations office of ABC Oil saying that Thomas Andrews, CEO of the company, saw the report and really liked the analyst's grasp of the business and his company. The investor-relations officer invites Hollis to visit ABC Oil to discuss the industry further. ABC Oil offers to send a company plane to pick Hollis up and arrange for his accommodations while visiting. Hollis, after gaining the appropriate approvals, accepts the meeting with the CEO but declines the offered travel arrangements.

Several weeks later, Andrews and Hollis meet to discuss the oil business and Hollis's report. Following the meeting, Hollis joins Andrews and the investment relations officer for dinner at an upscale restaurant near ABC Oil's headquarters.

Upon returning to Specialty Investment Management, Hollis provides a full review of the meeting to the director of research, including a disclosure of the dinner attended.

> *Comment*: Hollis's actions did not violate Standard IV(B). Through gaining approval before accepting the meeting and declining the offered travel arrangements, Hollis sought to avoid any potential conflicts of interest between his company and ABC Oil. Because the location of the dinner was not available prior to arrival and Hollis notified his company of the dinner upon his return, accepting the dinner should not impair his objectivity. By

disclosing the dinner, Hollis has enabled Specialty Investment Management to assess whether it has any impact on future reports and recommendations by Hollis related to ABC Oil.

39 STANDARD IV(C): DUTIES TO EMPLOYERS - RESPONSIBILITIES OF SUPERVISORS

☐ demonstrate a thorough knowledge of the CFA Institute Code of Ethics and Standards of Professional Conduct by applying the Code and Standards to specific situations

Members and Candidates must make reasonable efforts to ensure that anyone subject to their supervision or authority complies with applicable laws, rules, regulations, and the Code and Standards.

Guidance

Highlights:

- *System for Supervision*
- *Supervision Includes Detection*

Standard IV(C) states that members and candidates must promote actions by all employees under their supervision and authority to comply with applicable laws, rules, regulations, and firm policies and the Code and Standards.

Any investment professional who has employees subject to her or his control or influence—whether or not the employees are CFA Institute members, CFA charterholders, or candidates in the CFA Program—exercises supervisory responsibility. Members and candidates acting as supervisors must also have in-depth knowledge of the Code and Standards so that they can apply this knowledge in discharging their supervisory responsibilities.

The conduct that constitutes reasonable supervision in a particular case depends on the number of employees supervised and the work performed by those employees. Members and candidates with oversight responsibilities for large numbers of employees may not be able to personally evaluate the conduct of these employees on a continuing basis. These members and candidates may delegate supervisory duties to subordinates who directly oversee the other employees. A member's or candidate's responsibilities under Standard IV(C) include instructing those subordinates to whom supervision is delegated about methods to promote compliance, including preventing and detecting violations of laws, rules, regulations, firm policies, and the Code and Standards.

At a minimum, Standard IV(C) requires that members and candidates with supervisory responsibility make reasonable efforts to prevent and detect violations by ensuring the establishment of effective compliance systems. However, an effective compliance system goes beyond enacting a code of ethics, establishing policies and procedures to achieve compliance with the code and applicable law, and reviewing employee actions to determine whether they are following the rules.

Standard IV(C): Duties to Employers - Responsibilities of Supervisors

To be effective supervisors, members and candidates should implement education and training programs on a recurring or regular basis for employees under their supervision. Such programs will assist the employees with meeting their professional obligations to practice in an ethical manner within the applicable legal system. Further, establishing incentives—monetary or otherwise—for employees not only to meet business goals but also to reward ethical behavior offers supervisors another way to assist employees in complying with their legal and ethical obligations.

Often, especially in large organizations, members and candidates may have supervisory responsibility but not the authority to establish or modify firm-wide compliance policies and procedures or incentive structures. Such limitations should not prevent a member or candidate from working with his or her own superiors and within the firm structure to develop and implement effective compliance tools, including but not limited to:

- a code of ethics,
- compliance policies and procedures,
- education and training programs,
- an incentive structure that rewards ethical conduct, and
- adoption of firm-wide best practice standards (e.g., the GIPS standards, the CFA Institute Asset Manager Code of Professional Conduct).

A member or candidate with supervisory responsibility should bring an inadequate compliance system to the attention of the firm's senior managers and recommend corrective action. If the member or candidate clearly cannot discharge supervisory responsibilities because of the absence of a compliance system or because of an inadequate compliance system, the member or candidate should decline in writing to accept supervisory responsibility until the firm adopts reasonable procedures to allow adequate exercise of supervisory responsibility.

System for Supervision

Members and candidates with supervisory responsibility must understand what constitutes an adequate compliance system for their firms and make reasonable efforts to see that appropriate compliance procedures are established, documented, communicated to covered personnel, and followed. "Adequate" procedures are those designed to meet industry standards, regulatory requirements, the requirements of the Code and Standards, and the circumstances of the firm. Once compliance procedures are established, the supervisor must also make reasonable efforts to ensure that the procedures are monitored and enforced.

To be effective, compliance procedures must be in place prior to the occurrence of a violation of the law or the Code and Standards. Although compliance procedures cannot be designed to anticipate every potential violation, they should be designed to anticipate the activities most likely to result in misconduct. Compliance programs must be appropriate for the size and nature of the organization. The member or candidate should review model compliance procedures or other industry programs to ensure that the firm's procedures meet the minimum industry standards.

Once a supervisor learns that an employee has violated or may have violated the law or the Code and Standards, the supervisor must promptly initiate an assessment to determine the extent of the wrongdoing. Relying on an employee's statements about the extent of the violation or assurances that the wrongdoing will not reoccur is not enough. Reporting the misconduct up the chain of command and warning the employee to cease the activity are also not enough. Pending the outcome of the investigation, a supervisor should take steps to ensure that the violation will not be repeated, such as placing limits on the employee's activities or increasing the monitoring of the employee's activities.

Supervision Includes Detection

Members and candidates with supervisory responsibility must also make reasonable efforts to detect violations of laws, rules, regulations, firm policies, and the Code and Standards. The supervisors exercise reasonable supervision by establishing and implementing written compliance procedures and ensuring that those procedures are followed through periodic review. If a member or candidate has adopted reasonable procedures and taken steps to institute an effective compliance program, then the member or candidate may not be in violation of Standard IV(C) if he or she does not detect violations that occur despite these efforts. The fact that violations do occur may indicate, however, that the compliance procedures are inadequate. In addition, in some cases, merely enacting such procedures may not be sufficient to fulfill the duty required by Standard IV(C). A member or candidate may be in violation of Standard IV(C) if he or she knows or should know that the procedures designed to promote compliance, including detecting and preventing violations, are not being followed.

40 STANDARD IV(C): RECOMMENDED PROCEDURES

> ☐ demonstrate a thorough knowledge of the CFA Institute Code of Ethics and Standards of Professional Conduct by applying the Code and Standards to specific situations

Codes of Ethics or Compliance Procedures

Members and candidates are encouraged to recommend that their employers adopt a code of ethics. Adoption of a code of ethics is critical to establishing a strong ethical foundation for investment advisory firms and their employees. Codes of ethics formally emphasize and reinforce the client loyalty responsibilities of investment firm personnel, protect investing clients by deterring misconduct, and protect the firm's reputation for integrity.

There is a distinction, however, between codes of ethics and the specific policies and procedures needed to ensure compliance with the codes and with securities laws and regulations. Although both are important, codes of ethics should consist of fundamental, principle-based ethical and fiduciary concepts that are applicable to all of the firm's employees. In this way, firms can best convey to employees and clients the ethical ideals that investment advisers strive to achieve. These concepts need to be implemented, however, by detailed, firm-wide compliance policies and procedures. Compliance procedures assist the firm's personnel in fulfilling the responsibilities enumerated in the code of ethics and make probable that the ideals expressed in the code of ethics will be adhered to in the day-to-day operation of the firm.

Stand-alone codes of ethics should be written in plain language and should address general fiduciary concepts. They should be unencumbered by numerous detailed procedures. Codes presented in this way are the most effective in stressing to employees that they are in positions of trust and must act with integrity at all times. Mingling compliance procedures in the firm's code of ethics goes against the goal of reinforcing the ethical obligations of employees.

Separating the code of ethics from compliance procedures will also reduce, if not eliminate, the legal terminology and "boilerplate" language that can make the underlying ethical principles incomprehensible to the average person. Above all, to ensure

Standard IV(C): Recommended Procedures

the creation of a culture of ethics and integrity rather than one that merely focuses on following the rules, the principles in the code of ethics must be stated in a way that is accessible and understandable to everyone in the firm.

Members and candidates should encourage their employers to provide their codes of ethics to clients. In this case also, a simple, straightforward code of ethics will be best understood by clients. Unencumbered by the compliance procedures, the code of ethics will be effective in conveying that the firm is committed to conducting business in an ethical manner and in the best interests of the clients.

Adequate Compliance Procedures

A supervisor complies with Standard IV(C) by identifying situations in which legal violations or violations of the Code and Standards are likely to occur and by establishing and enforcing compliance procedures to prevent such violations. Adequate compliance procedures should

- be contained in a clearly written and accessible manual that is tailored to the firm's operations,
- be drafted so that the procedures are easy to understand,
- designate a compliance officer whose authority and responsibility are clearly defined and who has the necessary resources and authority to implement the firm's compliance procedures,
- describe the hierarchy of supervision and assign duties among supervisors,
- implement a system of checks and balances,
- outline the scope of the procedures,
- outline procedures to document the monitoring and testing of compliance procedures,
- outline permissible conduct, and
- delineate procedures for reporting violations and sanctions.

Once a compliance program is in place, a supervisor should

- disseminate the contents of the program to appropriate personnel,
- periodically update procedures to ensure that the measures are adequate under the law,
- continually educate personnel regarding the compliance procedures,
- issue periodic reminders of the procedures to appropriate personnel,
- incorporate a professional conduct evaluation as part of an employee's performance review,
- review the actions of employees to ensure compliance and identify violators, and
- take the necessary steps to enforce the procedures once a violation has occurred.

Once a violation is discovered, a supervisor should

- respond promptly,
- conduct a thorough investigation of the activities to determine the scope of the wrongdoing,
- increase supervision or place appropriate limitations on the wrongdoer pending the outcome of the investigation, and

Implementation of Compliance Education and Training

No amount of ethics education and awareness will deter someone determined to commit fraud for personal enrichment. But the vast majority of investment professionals strive to achieve personal success with dedicated service to their clients and employers.

Regular ethics and compliance training, in conjunction with adoption of a code of ethics, is critical to investment firms seeking to establish a strong culture of integrity and to provide an environment in which employees routinely engage in ethical conduct in compliance with the law. Training and education assist individuals in both recognizing areas that are prone to ethical and legal pitfalls and identifying those circumstances and influences that can impair ethical judgment.

By implementing educational programs, supervisors can train their subordinates to put into practice what the firm's code of ethics requires. Education helps employees make the link between legal and ethical conduct and the long-term success of the business; a strong culture of compliance signals to clients and potential clients that the firm has truly embraced ethical conduct as fundamental to the firm's mission to serve its clients.

Establish an Appropriate Incentive Structure

Even if individuals want to make the right choices and follow an ethical course of conduct and are aware of the obstacles that may trip them up, they can still be influenced to act improperly by a corporate culture that embraces a "succeed at all costs" mentality, stresses results regardless of the methods used to achieve those results, and does not reward ethical behavior. Supervisors can reinforce an individual's natural desire to "do the right thing" by building a culture of integrity in the workplace.

Supervisors and firms must look closely at their incentive structure to determine whether the structure encourages profits and returns at the expense of ethically appropriate conduct. Reward structures may turn a blind eye to how desired outcomes are achieved and encourage dysfunctional or counterproductive behavior. Only when compensation and incentives are firmly tied to client interests and *how* outcomes are achieved, rather than *how much* is generated for the firm, will employees work to achieve a culture of integrity.

---

41   STANDARD IV(C): APPLICATION OF THE STANDARD

- [ ] demonstrate a thorough knowledge of the CFA Institute Code of Ethics and Standards of Professional Conduct by applying the Code and Standards to specific situations
- [ ] recommend practices and procedures designed to prevent violations of the Code of Ethics and Standards of Professional Conduct

Example 1 (Supervising Research Activities):

Jane Mattock, senior vice president and head of the research department of H&V, Inc., a regional brokerage firm, has decided to change her recommendation for Timber Products from buy to sell. In line with H&V's procedures, she orally advises certain other H&V executives of her proposed actions before the report is prepared for publication. As a result of Mattock's conversation with Dieter Frampton, one of the H&V executives accountable to Mattock, Frampton immediately sells Timber's stock from his own account and from certain discretionary client accounts. In addition, other personnel inform certain institutional customers of the changed recommendation before it is printed and disseminated to all H&V customers who have received previous Timber reports.

> *Comment*: Mattock has violated Standard IV(C) by failing to reasonably and adequately supervise the actions of those accountable to her. She did not prevent or establish reasonable procedures designed to prevent dissemination of or trading on the information by those who knew of her changed recommendation. She must ensure that her firm has procedures for reviewing or recording any trading in the stock of a corporation that has been the subject of an unpublished change in recommendation. Adequate procedures would have informed the subordinates of their duties and detected sales by Frampton and selected customers.

Example 2 (Supervising Research Activities):

Deion Miller is the research director for Jamestown Investment Programs. The portfolio managers have become critical of Miller and his staff because the Jamestown portfolios do not include any stock that has been the subject of a merger or tender offer. Georgia Ginn, a member of Miller's staff, tells Miller that she has been studying a local company, Excelsior, Inc., and recommends its purchase. Ginn adds that the company has been widely rumored to be the subject of a merger study by a well-known conglomerate and discussions between them are under way. At Miller's request, Ginn prepares a memo recommending the stock. Miller passes along Ginn's memo to the portfolio managers prior to leaving for vacation, and he notes that he has not reviewed the memo. As a result of the memo, the portfolio managers buy Excelsior stock immediately. The day Miller returns to the office, he learns that Ginn's only sources for the report were her brother, who is an acquisitions analyst with Acme Industries, the "well-known conglomerate," and that the merger discussions were planned but not held.

> *Comment*: Miller violated Standard IV(C) by not exercising reasonable supervision when he disseminated the memo without checking to ensure that Ginn had a reasonable and adequate basis for her recommendations and that Ginn was not relying on material nonpublic information.

Example 3 (Supervising Trading Activities):

David Edwards, a trainee trader at Wheeler & Company, a major national brokerage firm, assists a customer in paying for the securities of Highland, Inc., by using anticipated profits from the immediate sale of the same securities. Despite the fact that Highland is not on Wheeler's recommended list, a large volume of its stock is traded through Wheeler in this manner. Roberta Ann Mason is a Wheeler vice president responsible for supervising compliance with the securities laws in the trading department. Part of her compensation from Wheeler is based on commission revenues from the trading department. Although she notices the increased trading activity, she does nothing to investigate or halt it.

> *Comment*: Mason's failure to adequately review and investigate purchase orders in Highland stock executed by Edwards and her failure to supervise the trainee's activities violate Standard IV(C). Supervisors should be especially sensitive to actual or potential conflicts between their own self-interests and their supervisory responsibilities.

Example 4 (Supervising Trading Activities and Record Keeping):

Samantha Tabbing is senior vice president and portfolio manager for Crozet, Inc., a registered investment advisory and registered broker/dealer firm. She reports to Charles Henry, the president of Crozet. Crozet serves as the investment adviser and principal underwriter for ABC and XYZ public mutual funds. The two funds' prospectuses allow Crozet to trade financial futures for the funds for the limited purpose of hedging against market risks. Henry, extremely impressed by Tabbing's performance in the past two years, directs Tabbing to act as portfolio manager for the funds. For the benefit of its employees, Crozet has also organized the Crozet Employee Profit-Sharing Plan (CEPSP), a defined contribution retirement plan. Henry assigns Tabbing to manage 20% of the assets of CEPSP. Tabbing's investment objective for her portion of CEPSP's assets is aggressive growth. Unbeknownst to Henry, Tabbing frequently places S&P 500 Index purchase and sale orders for the funds and the CEPSP without providing the futures commission merchants (FCMs) who take the orders with any prior or simultaneous designation of the account for which the trade has been placed. Frequently, neither Tabbing nor anyone else at Crozet completes an internal trade ticket to record the time an order was placed or the specific account for which the order was intended. FCMs often designate a specific account only after the trade, when Tabbing provides such designation. Crozet has no written operating procedures or compliance manual concerning its futures trading, and its compliance department does not review such trading. After observing the market's movement, Tabbing assigns to CEPSP the S&P 500 positions with more favorable execution prices and assigns positions with less favorable execution prices to the funds.

> *Comment*: Henry violated Standard IV(C) by failing to adequately supervise Tabbing with respect to her S&P 500 trading. Henry further violated Standard IV(C) by failing to establish record-keeping and reporting procedures to prevent or detect Tabbing's violations. Henry must make a reasonable effort to determine that adequate compliance procedures covering all employee trading activity are established, documented, communicated, and followed.

Example 5 (Accepting Responsibility):

Meredith Rasmussen works on a buy-side trading desk and concentrates on in-house trades for a hedge fund subsidiary managed by a team at the investment management firm. The hedge fund has been very successful and is marketed globally by the firm. From her experience as the trader for much of the activity of the fund, Rasmussen has become quite knowledgeable about the hedge fund's strategy, tactics, and performance. When a distinct break in the market occurs and many of the securities involved in the hedge fund's strategy decline markedly in value, however, Rasmussen observes that the reported performance of the hedge fund does not at all reflect this decline. From her experience, this lack of an effect is a very unlikely occurrence. She approaches the

Standard IV(C): Application of the Standard

head of trading about her concern and is told that she should not ask any questions and that the fund is too big and successful and is not her concern. She is fairly sure something is not right, so she contacts the compliance officer and is again told to stay away from the hedge fund reporting issue.

> *Comment*: Rasmussen has clearly come upon an error in policies, procedures, and compliance practices within the firm's operations. According to Standard IV(C), the supervisor and the compliance officer have the responsibility to review the concerns brought forth by Rasmussen. Supervisors have the responsibility of establishing and encouraging an ethical culture in the firm. The dismissal of Rasmussen's question violates Standard IV(C) and undermines the firm's ethical operations.
>
> See also Standard I(D)–Misconduct and, for guidance on whistleblowing, Standard IV(A)–Loyalty.

Example 6 (Inadequate Procedures):

Brendan Witt, a former junior sell-side technology analyst, decided to return to school to earn an MBA. To keep his research skills and industry knowledge sharp, Witt accepted a position with On-line and Informed, an independent internet-based research company. The position requires the publication of a recommendation and report on a different company every month. Initially, Witt is a regular contributor of new research and a participant in the associated discussion boards that generally have positive comments on the technology sector. Over time, his ability to manage his educational requirements and his work requirements begin to conflict with one another. Knowing a recommendation is due the next day for On-line, Witt creates a report based on a few news articles and what the conventional wisdom of the markets has deemed the "hot" security of the day.

> *Comment*: Allowing the report submitted by Witt to be posted highlights a lack of compliance procedures by the research firm. Witt's supervisor needs to work with the management of On-line to develop an appropriate review process to ensure that all contracted analysts comply with the requirements.
>
> See also Standard V(A)–Diligence and Reasonable Basis because it relates to Witt's responsibility for substantiating a recommendation.

Example 7 (Inadequate Supervision):

Michael Papis is the chief investment officer of his state's retirement fund. The fund has always used outside advisers for the real estate allocation, and this information is clearly presented in all fund communications. Thomas Nagle, a recognized sell-side research analyst and Papis's business school classmate, recently left the investment bank he worked for to start his own asset management firm, Accessible Real Estate. Nagle is trying to build his assets under management and contacts Papis about gaining some of the retirement fund's allocation. In the previous few years, the performance of the retirement fund's real estate investments was in line with the fund's benchmark but was not extraordinary. Papis decides to help out his old friend and also to seek better returns by moving the real estate allocation to Accessible. The only notice of the change in adviser appears in the next annual report in the listing of associated advisers.

> *Comment*: Papis's actions highlight the need for supervision and review at all levels in an organization. His responsibilities may include the selection of external advisers, but the decision to change advisers appears arbitrary.

Members and candidates should ensure that their firm has appropriate policies and procedures in place to detect inappropriate actions, such as the action taken by Papis.

See also Standard V(A)–Diligence and Reasonable Basis, Standard V(B)–Communication with Clients and Prospective Clients, and Standard VI(A)–Disclosure of Conflicts.

Example 8 (Supervising Research Activities):

Mary Burdette was recently hired by Fundamental Investment Management (FIM) as a junior auto industry analyst. Burdette is expected to expand the social media presence of the firm because she is active with various networks, including Facebook, LinkedIn, and Twitter. Although Burdette's supervisor, Joe Graf, has never used social media, he encourages Burdette to explore opportunities to increase FIM's online presence and ability to share content, communicate, and broadcast information to clients. In response to Graf's encouragement, Burdette is working on a proposal detailing the advantages of getting FIM onto Twitter in addition to launching a company Facebook page.

As part of her auto industry research for FIM, Burdette is completing a report on the financial impact of Sun Drive Auto Ltd.'s new solar technology for compact automobiles. This research report will be her first for FIM, and she believes Sun Drive's technology could revolutionize the auto industry. In her excitement, Burdette sends a quick tweet to FIM Twitter followers summarizing her "buy" recommendation for Sun Drive Auto stock.

> *Comment*: Graf has violated Standard IV(C) by failing to reasonably supervise Burdette with respect to the contents of her tweet. He did not establish reasonable procedures to prevent the unauthorized dissemination of company research through social media networks. Graf must make sure all employees receive regular training about FIM's policies and procedures, including the appropriate business use of personal social media networks.
> See Standard III(B) for additional guidance.

Example 9 (Supervising Research Activities):

Chen Wang leads the research department at YYRA Retirement Planning Specialists. Chen supervises a team of 10 analysts in a fast-paced and understaffed organization. He is responsible for coordinating the firm's approved process to review all reports before they are provided to the portfolio management team for use in rebalancing client portfolios.

One of Chen's direct reports, Huang Mei, covers the banking industry. Chen must submit the latest updates to the portfolio management team tomorrow morning. Huang has yet to submit her research report on ZYX Bank because she is uncomfortable providing a "buy" or "sell" opinion of ZYX on the basis of the completed analysis. Pressed for time and concerned that Chen will reject a "hold" recommendation, she researches various websites and blogs on the banking sector for whatever she can find on ZYX. One independent blogger provides a new interpretation of the recently reported data Huang has analyzed and concludes with a strong "sell" recommendation for ZYX. She is impressed by the originality and resourcefulness of this blogger's report.

Very late in the evening, Huang submits her report and "sell" recommendation to Chen without any reference to the independent blogger's report. Given the late time of the submission and the competence of Huang's prior work, Chen compiles this report with the recommendations from each of the other analysts and meets with the portfolio managers to discuss implementation.

Comment: Chen has violated Standard IV(C) by neglecting to reasonably and adequately follow the firm's approved review process for Huang's research report. The delayed submission and the quality of prior work do not remove Chen's requirement to uphold the designated review process. A member or candidate with supervisory responsibility must make reasonable efforts to see that appropriate procedures are established, documented, communicated to covered personnel, and followed.

STANDARD V(A): INVESTMENT ANALYSIS, RECOMMENDATIONS, AND ACTIONS - DILIGENCE AND REASONABLE BASIS

42

☐ | demonstrate a thorough knowledge of the CFA Institute Code of Ethics and Standards of Professional Conduct by applying the Code and Standards to specific situations

Standard V(A) Diligence and Reasonable Basis

Members and Candidates must:

1. Exercise diligence, independence, and thoroughness in analyzing investments, making investment recommendations, and taking investment actions.

2. Have a reasonable and adequate basis, supported by appropriate research and investigation, for any investment analysis, recommendation, or action.

Guidance

Highlights:

- *Defining Diligence and Reasonable Basis*
- *Using Secondary or Third-Party Research*
- *Using Quantitatively Oriented Research*
- *Developing Quantitatively Oriented Techniques*
- *Selecting External Advisers and Subadvisers*
- *Group Research and Decision Making*

The application of Standard V(A) depends on the investment philosophy the member, candidate, or firm is following, the role of the member or candidate in the investment decision-making process, and the support and resources provided by the member's or candidate's employer. These factors will dictate the nature of the diligence and thoroughness of the research and the level of investigation required by Standard V(A).

The requirements for issuing conclusions based on research will vary in relation to the member's or candidate's role in the investment decision-making process, but the member or candidate must make reasonable efforts to cover all pertinent issues when arriving at a recommendation. Members and candidates enhance transparency by providing or offering to provide supporting information to clients when recommending a purchase or sale or when changing a recommendation.

Defining Diligence and Reasonable Basis

Every investment decision is based on a set of facts known and understood at the time. Clients turn to members and candidates for advice and expect these advisers to have more information and knowledge than they do. This information and knowledge is the basis from which members and candidates apply their professional judgment in taking investment actions and making recommendations.

At a basic level, clients want assurance that members and candidates are putting forth the necessary effort to support the recommendations they are making. Communicating the level and thoroughness of the information reviewed before the member or candidate makes a judgment allows clients to understand the reasonableness of the recommended investment actions.

As with determining the suitability of an investment for the client, the necessary level of research and analysis will differ with the product, security, or service being offered. In providing an investment service, members and candidates typically use a variety of resources, including company reports, third-party research, and results from quantitative models. A reasonable basis is formed through a balance of these resources appropriate for the security or decision being analyzed.

The following list provides some, but definitely not all, examples of attributes to consider while forming the basis for a recommendation:

- global, regional, and country macroeconomic conditions,
- a company's operating and financial history,
- the industry's and sector's current conditions and the stage of the business cycle,
- a mutual fund's fee structure and management history,
- the output and potential limitations of quantitative models,
- the quality of the assets included in a securitization, and
- the appropriateness of selected peer-group comparisons.

Even though an investment recommendation may be well informed, downside risk remains for any investment. Members and candidates can base their decisions only on the information available at the time decisions are made. The steps taken in developing a diligent and reasonable recommendation should minimize unexpected downside events.

Using Secondary or Third-Party Research

If members and candidates rely on secondary or third-party research, they must make reasonable and diligent efforts to determine whether such research is sound. Secondary research is defined as research conducted by someone else in the member's or candidate's firm. Third-party research is research conducted by entities outside the member's or candidate's firm, such as a brokerage firm, bank, or research firm. If a member or candidate has reason to suspect that either secondary or third-party research or information comes from a source that lacks a sound basis, the member or candidate must not rely on that information.

Members and candidates should make reasonable enquiries into the source and accuracy of all data used in completing their investment analysis and recommendations. The sources of the information and data will influence the level of the review a member or candidate must undertake. Information and data taken from internet sources, such as personal blogs, independent research aggregation websites, or social media websites, likely require a greater level of review than information from more established research organizations.

Criteria that a member or candidate can use in forming an opinion on whether research is sound include the following:

- assumptions used,
- rigor of the analysis performed,
- date/timeliness of the research, and
- evaluation of the objectivity and independence of the recommendations.

A member or candidate may rely on others in his or her firm to determine whether secondary or third-party research is sound and use the information in good faith unless the member or candidate has reason to question its validity or the processes and procedures used by those responsible for the research. For example, a portfolio manager may not have a choice of a data source because the firm's senior managers conducted due diligence to determine which vendor would provide services; the member or candidate can use the information in good faith assuming the due diligence process was deemed adequate.

A member or candidate should verify that the firm has a policy about the timely and consistent review of approved research providers to ensure that the quality of the research continues to meet the necessary standards. If such a policy is not in place at the firm, the member or candidate should encourage the development and adoption of a formal review practice.

Using Quantitatively Oriented Research

Standard V(A) applies to the rapidly expanding use of quantitatively oriented research models and processes, such as computer-generated modeling, screening, and ranking of investment securities; the creation or valuation of derivative instruments; and quantitative portfolio construction techniques. These models and processes are being used for much more than the back testing of investment strategies, especially with continually advancing technology and techniques. The continued broad development of quantitative methods and models is an important part of capital market developments.

Members and candidates need to have an understanding of the parameters used in models and quantitative research that are incorporated into their investment recommendations. Although they are not required to become experts in every technical aspect of the models, they must understand the assumptions and limitations inherent in any model and how the results were used in the decision-making process.

The reliance on and potential limitations of financial models became clear through the investment crisis that unfolded in 2007 and 2008. In some cases, the financial models used to value specific securities and related derivative products did not adequately demonstrate the level of associated risks. Members and candidates should make reasonable efforts to test the output of investment models and other pre-programed analytical tools they use. Such validation should occur before incorporating the process into their methods, models, or analyses.

Although not every model can test for every factor or outcome, members and candidates should ensure that their analyses incorporate a broad range of assumptions sufficient to capture the underlying characteristics of investments. The omission from the analysis of potentially negative outcomes or of levels of risk outside the norm may misrepresent the true economic value of an investment. The possible scenarios for analysis should include factors that are likely to have a substantial influence on the investment value and may include extremely positive and negative scenarios.

Developing Quantitatively Oriented Techniques

Individuals who create new quantitative models and services must exhibit a higher level of diligence in reviewing new products than the individuals who ultimately use the analytical output. Members and candidates involved in the development and oversight of quantitatively oriented models, methods, and algorithms must understand the technical aspects of the products they provide to clients. A thorough testing of the model and resulting analysis should be completed prior to product distribution.

Members and candidates need to consider the source and time horizon of the data used as inputs in financial models. The information from many commercially available databases may not effectively incorporate both positive and negative market cycles. In the development of a recommendation, the member or candidate may need to test the models by using volatility and performance expectations that represent scenarios outside the observable databases. In reviewing the computer models or the resulting output, members and candidates need to pay particular attention to the assumptions used in the analysis and the rigor of the analysis to ensure that the model incorporates a wide range of possible input expectations, including negative market events.

Selecting External Advisers and Subadvisers

Financial instruments and asset allocation techniques continue to develop and evolve. This progression has led to the use of specialized managers to invest in specific asset classes or diversification strategies that complement a firm's in-house expertise. Standard V(A) applies to the level of review necessary in selecting an external adviser or subadviser to manage a specifically mandated allocation. Members and candidates must review managers as diligently as they review individual funds and securities.

Members and candidates who are directly involved with the use of external advisers need to ensure that their firms have standardized criteria for reviewing these selected external advisers and managers. Such criteria would include, but would not be limited to, the following:

- reviewing the adviser's established code of ethics,
- understanding the adviser's compliance and internal control procedures,
- assessing the quality of the published return information, and
- reviewing the adviser's investment process and adherence to its stated strategy.

Codes, standards, and guides to best practice published by CFA Institute provide members and candidates with examples of acceptable practices for external advisers and advice in selecting a new adviser. The following guides are available at the CFA Institute website (www.cfainstitute.org): Asset Manager Code of Professional Conduct, Global Investment Performance Standards, and Model Request for Proposal (for equity, credit, or real estate managers).

Group Research and Decision Making

Commonly, members and candidates are part of a group or team that is collectively responsible for producing investment analysis or research. The conclusions or recommendations of the group report represent the consensus of the group and are not necessarily the views of the member or candidate, even though the name of the member or candidate is included on the report. In some instances, a member or candidate will not agree with the view of the group. If, however, the member or candidate believes that the consensus opinion has a reasonable and adequate basis and is independent and

Standard V(A): Recommended Procedures

objective, the member or candidate need not decline to be identified with the report. If the member or candidate is confident in the process, the member or candidate does not need to dissociate from the report even if it does not reflect his or her opinion.

STANDARD V(A): RECOMMENDED PROCEDURES

43

☐ | demonstrate a thorough knowledge of the CFA Institute Code of Ethics and Standards of Professional Conduct by applying the Code and Standards to specific situations

Members and candidates should encourage their firms to consider the following policies and procedures to support the principles of Standard V(A):

- Establish a policy requiring that research reports, credit ratings, and investment recommendations have a basis that can be substantiated as reasonable and adequate. An individual employee (a supervisory analyst) or a group of employees (a review committee) should be appointed to review and approve such items prior to external circulation to determine whether the criteria established in the policy have been met.

- Develop detailed, written guidance for analysts (research, investment, or credit), supervisory analysts, and review committees that establishes the due diligence procedures for judging whether a particular recommendation has a reasonable and adequate basis.

- Develop measurable criteria for assessing the quality of research, the reasonableness and adequacy of the basis for any recommendation or rating, and the accuracy of recommendations over time. In some cases, firms may consider implementing compensation arrangements that depend on these measurable criteria and that are applied consistently to all related analysts.

- Develop detailed, written guidance that establishes minimum levels of scenario testing of all computer-based models used in developing, rating, and evaluating financial instruments. The policy should contain criteria related to the breadth of the scenarios tested, the accuracy of the output over time, and the analysis of cash flow sensitivity to inputs.

- Develop measurable criteria for assessing outside providers, including the quality of information being provided, the reasonableness and adequacy of the provider's collection practices, and the accuracy of the information over time. The established policy should outline how often the provider's products are reviewed.

- Adopt a standardized set of criteria for evaluating the adequacy of external advisers. The policy should include how often and on what basis the allocation of funds to the adviser will be reviewed.

STANDARD V(A): APPLICATION OF THE STANDARD

☐ demonstrate a thorough knowledge of the CFA Institute Code of Ethics and Standards of Professional Conduct by applying the Code and Standards to specific situations

☐ recommend practices and procedures designed to prevent violations of the Code of Ethics and Standards of Professional Conduct

Example 1 (Sufficient Due Diligence):

Helen Hawke manages the corporate finance department of Sarkozi Securities, Ltd. The firm is anticipating that the government will soon close a tax loophole that currently allows oil-and-gas exploration companies to pass on drilling expenses to holders of a certain class of shares. Because market demand for this tax-advantaged class of stock is currently high, Sarkozi convinces several companies to undertake new equity financings at once, before the loophole closes. Time is of the essence, but Sarkozi lacks sufficient resources to conduct adequate research on all the prospective issuing companies. Hawke decides to estimate the IPO prices on the basis of the relative size of each company and to justify the pricing later when her staff has time.

> *Comment*: Sarkozi should have taken on only the work that it could adequately handle. By categorizing the issuers by general size, Hawke has bypassed researching all the other relevant aspects that should be considered when pricing new issues and thus has not performed sufficient due diligence. Such an omission can result in investors purchasing shares at prices that have no actual basis. Hawke has violated Standard V(A).

Example 2 (Sufficient Scenario Testing):

Babu Dhaliwal works for Heinrich Brokerage in the corporate finance group. He has just persuaded Feggans Resources, Ltd., to allow his firm to do a secondary equity financing at Feggans Resources' current stock price. Because the stock has been trading at higher multiples than similar companies with equivalent production, Dhaliwal presses the Feggans Resources managers to project what would be the maximum production they could achieve in an optimal scenario. Based on these numbers, he is able to justify the price his firm will be asking for the secondary issue. During a sales pitch to the brokers, Dhaliwal then uses these numbers as the base-case production levels that Feggans Resources will achieve.

> *Comment*: When presenting information to the brokers, Dhaliwal should have given a range of production scenarios and the probability of Feggans Resources achieving each level. By giving the maximum production level as the likely level of production, he has misrepresented the chances of achieving that production level and seriously misled the brokers. Dhaliwal has violated Standard V(A).

Standard V(A): Application of the Standard

Example 3 (Developing a Reasonable Basis):

Brendan Witt, a former junior sell-side technology analyst, decided to return to school to earn an MBA. To keep his research skills and industry knowledge sharp, Witt accepted a position with On-line and Informed, an independent internet-based research company. The position requires the publication of a recommendation and report on a different company every month. Initially, Witt is a regular contributor of new research and a participant in the associated discussion boards that generally have positive comments on the technology sector. Over time, his ability to manage his educational requirements and his work requirements begin to conflict with one another. Knowing a recommendation is due the next day for On-line, Witt creates a report based on a few news articles and what the conventional wisdom of the markets has deemed the "hot" security of the day.

> *Comment*: Witt's knowledge of and exuberance for technology stocks, a few news articles, and the conventional wisdom of the markets do not constitute, without more information, a reasonable and adequate basis for a stock recommendation that is supported by appropriate research and investigation. Therefore, Witt has violated Standard V(A).
>
> See also Standard IV(C)–Responsibilities of Supervisors because it relates to the firm's inadequate procedures.

Example 4 (Timely Client Updates):

Kristen Chandler is an investment consultant in the London office of Dalton Securities, a major global investment consultant firm. One of her UK pension funds has decided to appoint a specialist US equity manager. Dalton's global manager of research relies on local consultants to cover managers within their regions and, after conducting thorough due diligence, puts their views and ratings in Dalton's manager database. Chandler accesses Dalton's global manager research database and conducts a screen of all US equity managers on the basis of a match with the client's desired philosophy/style, performance, and tracking-error targets. She selects the five managers that meet these criteria and puts them in a briefing report that is delivered to the client 10 days later. Between the time of Chandler's database search and the delivery of the report to the client, Chandler is told that Dalton has updated the database with the information that one of the firms that Chandler has recommended for consideration lost its chief investment officer, the head of its US equity research, and the majority of its portfolio managers on the US equity product—all of whom have left to establish their own firm. Chandler does not revise her report with this updated information.

> *Comment*: Chandler has failed to satisfy the requirement of Standard V(A). Although Dalton updated the manager ratings to reflect the personnel turnover at one of the firms, Chandler did not update her report to reflect the new information.

Example 5 (Group Research Opinions):

Evelyn Mastakis is a junior analyst who has been asked by her firm to write a research report predicting the expected interest rate for residential mortgages over the next six months. Mastakis submits her report to the fixed-income investment committee of her firm for review, as required by firm procedures. Although some committee members support Mastakis's conclusion, the majority of the committee disagrees with her conclusion, and the report is significantly changed to indicate that interest rates are likely to increase more than originally predicted by Mastakis. Should Mastakis ask that her name be taken off the report when it is disseminated?

Comment: The results of research are not always clear, and different people may have different opinions based on the same factual evidence. In this case, the committee may have valid reasons for issuing a report that differs from the analyst's original research. The firm can issue a report that is different from the original report of an analyst as long as there is a reasonable and adequate basis for its conclusions.

Generally, analysts must write research reports that reflect their own opinion and can ask the firm not to put their name on reports that ultimately differ from that opinion. When the work is a group effort, however, not all members of the team may agree with all aspects of the report. Ultimately, members and candidates can ask to have their names removed from the report, but if they are satisfied that the process has produced results or conclusions that have a reasonable and adequate basis, members and candidates do not have to dissociate from the report even when they do not agree with its contents. If Mastakis is confident in the process, she does not need to dissociate from the report even if it does not reflect her opinion.

Example 6 (Reliance on Third-Party Research):

Gary McDermott runs a two-person investment management firm. McDermott's firm subscribes to a service from a large investment research firm that provides research reports. McDermott's firm makes investment recommendations on the basis of these reports.

Comment: Members and candidates can rely on third-party research but must make reasonable and diligent efforts to determine that such research is sound. If McDermott undertakes due diligence efforts on a regular basis to ensure that the research produced by the large firm is objective and reasonably based, McDermott can rely on that research when making investment recommendations to clients.

Example 7 (Due Diligence in Submanager Selection):

Paul Ostrowski's business has grown significantly over the past couple of years, and some clients want to diversify internationally. Ostrowski decides to find a submanager to handle the expected international investments. Because this will be his first subadviser, Ostrowski uses the CFA Institute model "request for proposal" to design a questionnaire for his search. By his deadline, he receives seven completed questionnaires from a variety of domestic and international firms trying to gain his business. Ostrowski reviews all the applications in detail and decides to select the firm that charges the lowest fees because doing so will have the least impact on his firm's bottom line.

Comment: The selection of an external adviser or subadviser should be based on a full and complete review of the adviser's services, performance history, and cost structure. In basing the decision on the fee structure alone, Ostrowski may be violating Standard V(A).

See also Standard III(C)–Suitability because it relates to the ability of the selected adviser to meet the needs of the clients.

Example 8 (Sufficient Due Diligence):

Michael Papis is the chief investment officer of his state's retirement fund. The fund has always used outside advisers for the real estate allocation, and this information is clearly presented in all fund communications. Thomas Nagle, a recognized sell-side research analyst and Papis's business school classmate, recently left the investment bank he worked for to start his own asset management firm, Accessible Real Estate. Nagle is trying to build his assets under management and contacts Papis about gaining some of the retirement fund's allocation. In the previous few years, the performance of the retirement fund's real estate investments was in line with the fund's benchmark but was not extraordinary. Papis decides to help out his old friend and also to seek better returns by moving the real estate allocation to Accessible. The only notice of the change in adviser appears in the next annual report in the listing of associated advisers.

> *Comment*: Papis violated Standard V(A). His responsibilities may include the selection of the external advisers, but the decision to change advisers appears to have been arbitrary. If Papis was dissatisfied with the current real estate adviser, he should have conducted a proper solicitation to select the most appropriate adviser.
>
> See also Standard IV(C)–Responsibilities of Supervisors, Standard V(B)–Communication with Clients and Prospective Clients, and Standard VI(A)–Disclosure of Conflicts.

Example 9 (Sufficient Due Diligence):

Andre Shrub owns and operates Conduit, an investment advisory firm. Prior to opening Conduit, Shrub was an account manager with Elite Investment, a hedge fund managed by his good friend Adam Reed. To attract clients to a new Conduit fund, Shrub offers lower-than-normal management fees. He can do so because the fund consists of two top-performing funds managed by Reed. Given his personal friendship with Reed and the prior performance record of these two funds, Shrub believes this new fund is a winning combination for all parties. Clients quickly invest with Conduit to gain access to the Elite funds. No one is turned away because Conduit is seeking to expand its assets under management.

> *Comment*: Shrub violated Standard V(A) by not conducting a thorough analysis of the funds managed by Reed before developing the new Conduit fund. Shrub's reliance on his personal relationship with Reed and his prior knowledge of Elite are insufficient justification for the investments. The funds may be appropriately considered, but a full review of their operating procedures, reporting practices, and transparency are some elements of the necessary due diligence.
>
> See also Standard III(C)–Suitability.

Example 10 (Sufficient Due Diligence):

Bob Thompson has been doing research for the portfolio manager of the fixed-income department. His assignment is to do sensitivity analysis on securitized subprime mortgages. He has discussed with the manager possible scenarios to use to calculate expected returns. A key assumption in such calculations is housing price appreciation (HPA) because it drives "prepays" (prepayments of mortgages) and losses. Thompson is concerned with the significant appreciation experienced over the previous five years as a result of the increased availability of funds from subprime mortgages. Thompson insists that the analysis should include a scenario run with −10% for Year 1, −5% for

Year 2, and then (to project a worst-case scenario) 0% for Years 3 through 5. The manager replies that these assumptions are too dire because there has never been a time in their available database when HPA was negative.

Thompson conducts his research to better understand the risks inherent in these securities and evaluates these securities in the worst-case scenario, a less likely but possible environment. Based on the results of the enhanced scenarios, Thompson does not recommend the purchase of the securitization. Against the general market trends, the manager follows Thompson's recommendation and does not invest. The following year, the housing market collapses. In avoiding the subprime investments, the manager's portfolio outperforms its peer group that year.

> *Comment*: Thompson's actions in running the scenario test with inputs beyond the historical trends available in the firm's databases adhere to the principles of Standard V(A). His concerns over recent trends provide a sound basis for further analysis. Thompson understands the limitations of his model, when combined with the limited available historical information, to accurately predict the performance of the funds if market conditions change negatively.
>
> See also Standard I(B)–Independence and Objectivity.

Example 11 (Use of Quantitatively Oriented Models):

Espacia Liakos works in sales for Hellenica Securities, a firm specializing in developing intricate derivative strategies to profit from particular views on market expectations. One of her clients is Eugenie Carapalis, who has become convinced that commodity prices will become more volatile over the coming months. Carapalis asks Liakos to quickly engineer a strategy that will benefit from this expectation. Liakos turns to Hellenica's modeling group to fulfill this request. Because of the tight deadline, the modeling group outsources parts of the work to several trusted third parties. Liakos implements the disparate components of the strategy as the firms complete them.

Within a month, Carapalis is proven correct: Volatility across a range of commodities increases sharply. But her derivatives position with Hellenica returns huge losses, and the losses increase daily. Liakos investigates and realizes that although each of the various components of the strategy had been validated, they had never been evaluated as an integrated whole. In extreme conditions, portions of the model worked at cross-purposes with other portions, causing the overall strategy to fail dramatically.

> *Comment*: Liakos violated Standard V(A). Members and candidates must understand the statistical significance of the results of the models they recommend and must be able to explain them to clients. Liakos did not take adequate care to ensure a thorough review of the whole model; its components were evaluated only individually. Because Carapalis clearly intended to implement the strategy as a whole rather than as separate parts, Liakos should have tested how the components of the strategy interacted as well as how they performed individually.

Example 12 (Successful Due Diligence/Failed Investment):

Alton Newbury is an investment adviser to high-net-worth clients. A client with an aggressive risk profile in his investment policy statement asks about investing in the Top Shelf hedge fund. This fund, based in Calgary, Alberta, Canada, has reported 20% returns for the first three years. The fund prospectus states that its strategy involves long and short positions in the energy sector and extensive leverage. Based on his analysis of the fund's track record, the principals involved in managing the fund, the

Standard V(A): Application of the Standard

fees charged, and the fund's risk profile, Newbury recommends the fund to the client and secures a position in it. The next week, the fund announces that it has suffered a loss of 60% of its value and is suspending operations and redemptions until after a regulatory review. Newbury's client calls him in a panic and asks for an explanation.

>*Comment*: Newbury's actions were consistent with Standard V(A). Analysis of an investment that results in a reasonable basis for recommendation does not guarantee that the investment has no downside risk. Newbury should discuss the analysis process with the client while reminding him or her that past performance does not lead to guaranteed future gains and that losses in an aggressive investment portfolio should be expected.

Example 13 (Quantitative Model Diligence):

Barry Cannon is the lead quantitative analyst at CityCenter Hedge Fund. He is responsible for the development, maintenance, and enhancement of the proprietary models the fund uses to manage its investors' assets. Cannon reads several high-level mathematical publications and blogs to stay informed of current developments. One blog, run by Expert CFA, presents some intriguing research that may benefit one of CityCenter's current models. Cannon is under pressure from firm executives to improve the model's predictive abilities, and he incorporates the factors discussed in the online research. The updated output recommends several new investments to the fund's portfolio managers.

>*Comment*: Cannon has violated Standard V(A) by failing to have a reasonable basis for the new recommendations made to the portfolio managers. He needed to diligently research the effect of incorporating the new factors before offering the output recommendations. Cannon may use the blog for ideas, but it is his responsibility to determine the effect on the firm's proprietary models.
>
>See Standard VII(B) regarding the violation by "Expert CFA" in the use of the CFA designation.

Example 14 (Selecting a Service Provider):

Ellen Smith is a performance analyst at Artic Global Advisors, a firm that manages global equity mandates for institutional clients. She was asked by her supervisor to review five new performance attribution systems and recommend one that would more appropriately explain the firm's investment strategy to clients. On the list was a system she recalled learning about when visiting an exhibitor booth at a recent conference. The system is highly quantitative and something of a "black box" in how it calculates the attribution values. Smith recommended this option without researching the others because the sheer complexity of the process was sure to impress the clients.

>*Comment*: Smith's actions do not demonstrate a sufficient level of diligence in reviewing this product to make a recommendation for selecting the service. Besides not reviewing or considering the other four potential systems, she did not determine whether the "black box" attribution process aligns with the investment practices of the firm, including its investments in different countries and currencies. Smith must review and understand the process of any software or system before recommending its use as the firm's attribution system.

Example 15 (Subadviser Selection):

Craig Jackson is working for Adams Partners, Inc., and has been assigned to select a hedge fund subadviser to improve the diversification of the firm's large fund-of-funds product. The allocation must be in place before the start of the next quarter. Jackson uses a consultant database to find a list of suitable firms that claim compliance with the GIPS standards. He calls more than 20 firms on the list to confirm their potential interest and to determine their most recent quarterly and annual total return values. Because of the short turnaround, Jackson recommends the firm with the greatest total return values for selection.

> *Comment*: By considering only performance and GIPS compliance, Jackson has not conducted sufficient review of potential firms to satisfy the requirements of Standard V(A). A thorough investigation of the firms and their operations should be conducted to ensure that their addition would increase the diversity of clients' portfolios and that they are suitable for the fund-of-funds product.

Example 16 (Manager Selection):

Timothy Green works for Peach Asset Management, where he creates proprietary models that analyze data from the firm request for proposal questionnaires to identify managers for possible inclusion in the firm's fund-of-funds investment platform. Various criteria must be met to be accepted to the platform. Because of the number of respondents to the questionnaires, Green uses only the data submitted to make a recommendation for adding a new manager.

> *Comment*: By failing to conduct any additional outside review of the information to verify what was submitted through the request for proposal, Green has likely not satisfied the requirements of Standard V(A). The amount of information requested from outside managers varies among firms. Although the requested information may be comprehensive, Green should ensure sufficient effort is undertaken to verify the submitted information before recommending a firm for inclusion. This requires that he goes beyond the information provided by the manager on the request for proposal questionnaire and may include interviews with interested managers, reviews of regulatory filings, and discussions with the managers' custodian or auditor.

Example 17 (Technical Model Requirements):

Jérôme Dupont works for the credit research group of XYZ Asset Management, where he is in charge of developing and updating credit risk models. In order to perform accurately, his models need to be regularly updated with the latest market data.

Dupont does not interact with or manage money for any of the firm's clients. He is in contact with the firm's US corporate bond fund manager, John Smith, who has only very superficial knowledge of the model and who from time to time asks very basic questions regarding the output recommendations. Smith does not consult Dupont with respect to finalizing his clients' investment strategies.

Dupont's recently assigned objective is to develop a new emerging market corporate credit risk model. The firm is planning to expand into emerging credit, and the development of such a model is a critical step in this process. Because Smith seems to follow the model's recommendations without much concern for its quality as he develops his clients' investment strategies, Dupont decides to focus his time on the development of the new emerging market model and neglects to update the US model.

Standard V(B): Investment Analysis, Recommendations, and Actions - Communication with Clients and Prospective Clients

After several months without regular updates, Dupont's diagnostic statistics start to show alarming signs with respect to the quality of the US credit model. Instead of conducting the long and complicated data update, Dupont introduces new codes into his model with some limited new data as a quick "fix." He thinks this change will address the issue without needing to complete the full data update, so he continues working on the new emerging market model.

Several months following the quick "fix," another set of diagnostic statistics reveals nonsensical results and Dupont realizes that his earlier change contained an error. He quickly corrects the error and alerts Smith. Smith realizes that some of the prior trades he performed were due to erroneous model results. Smith rebalances the portfolio to remove the securities purchased on the basis of the questionable results without reporting the issue to anyone else.

> *Comment*: Smith violated standard V(A) because exercising "diligence, independence, and thoroughness in analyzing investments, making investment recommendations, and taking investment actions" means that members and candidates must understand the technical aspects of the products they provide to clients. Smith does not understand the model he is relying on to manage money. Members and candidates should also make reasonable enquiries into the source and accuracy of all data used in completing their investment analysis and recommendations.
>
> Dupont violated V(A) even if he does not trade securities or make investment decisions. Dupont's models give investment recommendations, and Dupont is accountable for the quality of those recommendations. Members and candidates should make reasonable efforts to test the output of pre-programed analytical tools they use. Such validation should occur before incorporating the tools into their decision-making process.
>
> See also Standard V(B)–Communication with Clients and Prospective Clients.

STANDARD V(B): INVESTMENT ANALYSIS, RECOMMENDATIONS, AND ACTIONS - COMMUNICATION WITH CLIENTS AND PROSPECTIVE CLIENTS

45

☐ | demonstrate a thorough knowledge of the CFA Institute Code of Ethics and Standards of Professional Conduct by applying the Code and Standards to specific situations

Members and Candidates must:

1. Disclose to clients and prospective clients the basic format and general principles of the investment processes they use to analyze investments, select securities, and construct portfolios and must promptly disclose any changes that might materially affect those processes.

2. Disclose to clients and prospective clients significant limitations and risks associated with the investment process.

3. Use reasonable judgment in identifying which factors are important to their investment analyses, recommendations, or actions and include those factors in communications with clients and prospective clients.

4. Distinguish between fact and opinion in the presentation of investment analyses and recommendations.

Guidance

Highlights:

- *Informing Clients of the Investment Process*
- *Different Forms of Communication*
- *Identifying Risk and Limitations*
- *Report Presentation*
- *Distinction between Facts and Opinions in Reports*

Standard V(B) addresses member and candidate conduct with respect to communicating with clients. Developing and maintaining clear, frequent, and thorough communication practices is critical to providing high-quality financial services to clients. When clients understand the information communicated to them, they also can understand exactly how members and candidates are acting on their behalf, which gives clients the opportunity to make well-informed decisions about their investments. Such understanding can be accomplished only through clear communication.

Standard V(B) states that members and candidates should communicate in a recommendation the factors that were instrumental in making the investment recommendation. A critical part of this requirement is to distinguish clearly between opinions and facts. In preparing a research report, the member or candidate must present the basic characteristics of the security(ies) being analyzed, which will allow the reader to evaluate the report and incorporate information the reader deems relevant to his or her investment decision-making process.

Similarly, in preparing a recommendation about, for example, an asset allocation strategy, alternative investment vehicle, or structured investment product, the member or candidate should include factors that are relevant to the asset classes that are being discussed. Follow-up communication of significant changes in the risk characteristics of a security or asset strategy is required. Providing regular updates to any changes in the risk characteristics is recommended.

Informing Clients of the Investment Process

Members and candidates must adequately describe to clients and prospective clients the manner in which they conduct the investment decision-making process. Such disclosure should address factors that have positive and negative influences on the recommendations, including significant risks and limitations of the investment process used. The member or candidate must keep clients and other interested parties informed on an ongoing basis about changes to the investment process, especially newly identified significant risks and limitations. Only by thoroughly understanding the nature of the investment product or service can a client determine whether changes to that product or service could materially affect his or her investment objectives.

Understanding the basic characteristics of an investment is of great importance in judging the suitability of that investment on a standalone basis, but it is especially important in determining the impact each investment will have on the characteristics of a portfolio. Although the risk and return characteristics of a common stock might seem to be essentially the same for any investor when the stock is viewed in isolation, the effects of those characteristics greatly depend on the other investments held. For instance, if the particular stock will represent 90% of an individual's investments, the stock's importance in the portfolio is vastly different from what it would be to an investor with a highly diversified portfolio for whom the stock will represent only 2% of the holdings.

A firm's investment policy may include the use of outside advisers to manage various portions of clients' assets under management. Members and candidates should inform the clients about the specialization or diversification expertise provided by the external adviser(s). This information allows clients to understand the full mix of products and strategies being applied that may affect their investment objectives.

Different Forms of Communication

For purposes of Standard V(B), communication is not confined to a written report of the type traditionally generated by an analyst researching a security, company, or industry. A presentation of information can be made via any means of communication, including in-person recommendation or description, telephone conversation, media broadcast, or transmission by computer (e.g., on the internet).

Computer and mobile device communications have rapidly evolved over the past few years. Members and candidates using any social media service to communicate business information must be diligent in their efforts to avoid unintended problems because these services may not be available to all clients. When providing information to clients through new technologies, members and candidates should take reasonable steps to ensure that such delivery would treat all clients fairly and, if necessary, be considered publicly disseminated.

The nature of client communications is highly diverse—from one word ("buy" or "sell") to in-depth reports of more than 100 pages. A communication may contain a general recommendation about the market, asset allocations, or classes of investments (e.g., stocks, bonds, real estate) or may relate to a specific security. If recommendations are contained in capsule form (such as a recommended stock list), members and candidates should notify clients that additional information and analyses are available from the producer of the report.

Identifying Risks and Limitations

Members and candidates must outline to clients and prospective clients significant risks and limitations of the analysis contained in their investment products or recommendations. The type and nature of significant risks will depend on the investment process that members and candidates are following and on the personal circumstances of the client. In general, the use of leverage constitutes a significant risk and should be disclosed.

Members and candidates must adequately disclose the general market-related risks and the risks associated with the use of complex financial instruments that are deemed significant. Other types of risks that members and candidates may consider disclosing include, but are not limited to, counterparty risk, country risk, sector or industry risk, security-specific risk, and credit risk.

Investment securities and vehicles may have limiting factors that influence a client's or potential client's investment decision. Members and candidates must report to clients and prospective clients the existence of limitations significant to the decision-making process. Examples of such factors and attributes include, but are not limited to, investment liquidity and capacity. Liquidity is the ability to liquidate an investment on a timely basis at a reasonable cost. Capacity is the investment amount beyond which returns will be negatively affected by new investments.

The appropriateness of risk disclosure should be assessed on the basis of what was known at the time the investment action was taken (often called an *ex ante* basis). Members and candidates must disclose significant risks known to them at the time of the disclosure. Members and candidates cannot be expected to disclose risks they are unaware of at the time recommendations or investment actions are made. In assessing compliance with Standard V(B), it is important to establish knowledge of a purported significant risk or limitation. A one-time investment loss that occurs after the disclosure does not constitute a pertinent factor in assessing whether significant risks and limitations were properly disclosed. Having no knowledge of a risk or limitation that subsequently triggers a loss may reveal a deficiency in the diligence and reasonable basis of the research of the member or candidate but may not reveal a breach of Standard V(B).

Report Presentation

Once the analytical process has been completed, the member or candidate who prepares the report must include those elements that are important to the analysis and conclusions of the report so that the reader can follow and challenge the report's reasoning. A report writer who has done adequate investigation may emphasize certain areas, touch briefly on others, and omit certain aspects deemed unimportant. For instance, a report may dwell on a quarterly earnings release or new-product introduction and omit other matters as long as the analyst clearly stipulates the limits to the scope of the report.

Investment advice based on quantitative research and analysis must be supported by readily available reference material and should be applied in a manner consistent with previously applied methodology. If changes in methodology are made, they should be highlighted.

Distinction between Facts and Opinions in Reports

Standard V(B) requires that opinion be separated from fact. Violations often occur when reports fail to separate the past from the future by not indicating that earnings estimates, changes in the outlook for dividends, or future market price information are *opinions* subject to future circumstances.

In the case of complex quantitative analyses, members and candidates must clearly separate fact from statistical conjecture and should identify the known limitations of an analysis. Members and candidates may violate Standard V(B) by failing to identify the limits of statistically developed projections because such omission leaves readers unaware of the limits of the published projections.

Members and candidates should explicitly discuss with clients and prospective clients the assumptions used in the investment models and processes to generate the analysis. Caution should be used in promoting the perceived accuracy of any model or process to clients because the ultimate output is merely an estimate of future results and not a certainty.

46 STANDARD V(B): RECOMMENDED PROCEDURES

☐ demonstrate a thorough knowledge of the CFA Institute Code of Ethics and Standards of Professional Conduct by applying the Code and Standards to specific situations

Standard V(B): Application of the Standard

Because the selection of relevant factors is an analytical skill, determination of whether a member or candidate has used reasonable judgment in excluding and including information in research reports depends heavily on case-by-case review rather than a specific checklist. Members and candidates should encourage their firms to have a rigorous methodology for reviewing research that is created for publication and dissemination to clients.

To assist in the after-the-fact review of a report, the member or candidate must maintain records indicating the nature of the research and should, if asked, be able to supply additional information to the client (or any user of the report) covering factors not included in the report.

STANDARD V(B): APPLICATION OF THE STANDARD

47

- [ ] demonstrate a thorough knowledge of the CFA Institute Code of Ethics and Standards of Professional Conduct by applying the Code and Standards to specific situations
- [ ] recommend practices and procedures designed to prevent violations of the Code of Ethics and Standards of Professional Conduct

Example 1 (Sufficient Disclosure of Investment System):

Sarah Williamson, director of marketing for Country Technicians, Inc., is convinced that she has found the perfect formula for increasing Country Technicians' income and diversifying its product base. Williamson plans to build on Country Technicians' reputation as a leading money manager by marketing an exclusive and expensive investment advice letter to high-net-worth individuals. One hitch in the plan is the complexity of Country Technicians' investment system—a combination of technical trading rules (based on historical price and volume fluctuations) and portfolio construction rules designed to minimize risk. To simplify the newsletter, she decides to include only each week's top five "buy" and "sell" recommendations and to leave out details of the valuation models and the portfolio structuring scheme.

> *Comment*: Williamson's plans for the newsletter violate Standard V(B). Williamson need not describe the investment system in detail in order to implement the advice effectively, but she must inform clients of Country Technicians' basic process and logic. Without understanding the basis for a recommendation, clients cannot possibly understand its limitations or its inherent risks.

Example 2 (Providing Opinions as Facts):

Richard Dox is a mining analyst for East Bank Securities. He has just finished his report on Boisy Bay Minerals. Included in his report is his own assessment of the geological extent of mineral reserves likely to be found on the company's land. Dox completed this calculation on the basis of the core samples from the company's latest drilling. According to Dox's calculations, the company has more than 500,000 ounces of gold on the property. Dox concludes his research report as follows: "Based on the fact that the company has 500,000 ounces of gold to be mined, I recommend a strong BUY."

Comment: If Dox issues the report as written, he will violate Standard V(B). His calculation of the total gold reserves for the property based on the company's recent sample drilling is a quantitative opinion, not a fact. Opinion must be distinguished from fact in research reports.

Example 3 (Proper Description of a Security):

Olivia Thomas, an analyst at Government Brokers, Inc., which is a brokerage firm specializing in government bond trading, has produced a report that describes an investment strategy designed to benefit from an expected decline in US interest rates. The firm's derivative products group has designed a structured product that will allow the firm's clients to benefit from this strategy. Thomas's report describing the strategy indicates that high returns are possible if various scenarios for declining interest rates are assumed. Citing the proprietary nature of the structured product underlying the strategy, the report does not describe in detail how the firm is able to offer such returns or the related risks in the scenarios, nor does the report address the likely returns of the strategy if, contrary to expectations, interest rates rise.

Comment: Thomas has violated Standard V(B) because her report fails to describe properly the basic characteristics of the actual and implied risks of the investment strategy, including how the structure was created and the degree to which leverage was embedded in the structure. The report should include a balanced discussion of how the strategy would perform in the case of rising as well as falling interest rates, preferably illustrating how the strategies might be expected to perform in the event of a reasonable variety of interest rate and credit risk–spread scenarios. If liquidity issues are relevant with regard to the valuation of either the derivatives or the underlying securities, provisions the firm has made to address those risks should also be disclosed.

Example 4 (Notification of Fund Mandate Change):

May & Associates is an aggressive growth manager that has represented itself since its inception as a specialist at investing in small-cap US stocks. One of May's selection criteria is a maximum capitalization of US$250 million for any given company. After a string of successful years of superior performance relative to its peers, May has expanded its client base significantly, to the point at which assets under management now exceed US$3 billion. For liquidity purposes, May's chief investment officer (CIO) decides to lift the maximum permissible market-cap ceiling to US$500 million and change the firm's sales and marketing literature accordingly to inform prospective clients and third-party consultants.

Comment: Although May's CIO is correct about informing potentially interested parties as to the change in investment process, he must also notify May's existing clients. Among the latter group might be a number of clients who not only retained May as a small-cap manager but also retained mid-cap and large-cap specialists in a multiple-manager approach. Such clients could regard May's change of criteria as a style change that distorts their overall asset allocations.

Standard V(B): Application of the Standard

Example 5 (Notification of Fund Mandate Change):

Rather than lifting the ceiling for its universe from US$250 million to US$500 million, May & Associates extends its small-cap universe to include a number of non-US companies.

> *Comment*: Standard V(B) requires that May's CIO advise May's clients of this change because the firm may have been retained by some clients specifically for its prowess at investing in US small-cap stocks. Other changes that require client notification are introducing derivatives to emulate a certain market sector or relaxing various other constraints, such as portfolio beta. In all such cases, members and candidates must disclose changes to all interested parties.

Example 6 (Notification of Changes to the Investment Process):

RJZ Capital Management is an active value-style equity manager that selects stocks by using a combination of four multifactor models. The firm has found favorable results when back testing the most recent 10 years of available market data in a new dividend discount model (DDM) designed by the firm. This model is based on projected inflation rates, earnings growth rates, and interest rates. The president of RJZ decides to replace its simple model that uses price to trailing 12-month earnings with the new DDM.

> *Comment*: Because the introduction of a new and different valuation model represents a material change in the investment process, RJZ's president must communicate the change to the firm's clients. RJZ is moving away from a model based on hard data toward a new model that is at least partly dependent on the firm's forecasting skills. Clients would likely view such a model as a significant change rather than a mere refinement of RJZ's process.

Example 7 (Notification of Changes to the Investment Process):

RJZ Capital Management loses the chief architect of its multifactor valuation system. Without informing its clients, the president of RJZ decides to redirect the firm's talents and resources toward developing a product for passive equity management—a product that will emulate the performance of a major market index.

> *Comment*: By failing to disclose to clients a substantial change to its investment process, the president of RJZ has violated Standard V(B).

Example 8 (Notification of Changes to the Investment Process):

At Fundamental Asset Management, Inc., the responsibility for selecting stocks for addition to the firm's "approved" list has just shifted from individual security analysts to a committee consisting of the research director and three senior portfolio managers. Eleanor Morales, a portfolio manager with Fundamental Asset Management, thinks this change is not important enough to communicate to her clients.

> *Comment*: Morales must disclose the process change to all her clients. Some of Fundamental's clients might be concerned about the morale and motivation among the firm's best research analysts after such a change. Moreover, clients might challenge the stock-picking track record of the portfolio managers and might even want to monitor the situation closely.

Example 9 (Sufficient Disclosure of Investment System):

Amanda Chinn is the investment director for Diversified Asset Management, which manages the endowment of a charitable organization. Because of recent staff departures, Diversified has decided to limit its direct investment focus to large-cap securities and supplement the needs for small-cap and mid-cap management by hiring outside fund managers. In describing the planned strategy change to the charity, Chinn's update letter states, "As investment director, I will directly oversee the investment team managing the endowment's large-capitalization allocation. I will coordinate the selection and ongoing review of external managers responsible for allocations to other classes." The letter also describes the reasons for the change and the characteristics external managers must have to be considered.

> *Comment*: Standard V(B) requires the disclosure of the investment process used to construct the portfolio of the fund. Changing the investment process from managing all classes of investments within the firm to the use of external managers is one example of information that needs to be communicated to clients. Chinn and her firm have embraced the principles of Standard V(B) by providing their client with relevant information. The charity can now make a reasonable decision about whether Diversified Asset Management remains the appropriate manager for its fund.

Example 10 (Notification of Changes to the Investment Process):

Michael Papis is the chief investment officer of his state's retirement fund. The fund has always used outside advisers for the real estate allocation, and this information is clearly presented in all fund communications. Thomas Nagle, a recognized sell-side research analyst and Papis's business school classmate, recently left the investment bank he worked for to start his own asset management firm, Accessible Real Estate. Nagle is trying to build his assets under management and contacts Papis about gaining some of the retirement fund's allocation. In the previous few years, the performance of the retirement fund's real estate investments was in line with the fund's benchmark but was not extraordinary. Papis decides to help out his old friend and also to seek better returns by moving the real estate allocation to Accessible. The only notice of the change in adviser appears in the next annual report in the listing of associated advisers.

> *Comment*: Papis has violated Standard V(B). He attempted to hide the nature of his decision to change external managers by making only a limited disclosure. The plan recipients and the fund's trustees need to be aware when changes are made to ensure that operational procedures are being followed.
>
> See also Standard IV(C)–Responsibilities of Supervisors, Standard V(A)–Diligence and Reasonable Basis, and Standard VI(A)–Disclosure of Conflicts.

Example 11 (Notification of Errors):

Jérôme Dupont works for the credit research group of XYZ Asset Management, where he is in charge of developing and updating credit risk models. In order to perform accurately, his models need to be regularly updated with the latest market data.

Standard V(B): Application of the Standard

Dupont does not interact with or manage money for any of the firm's clients. He is in contact with the firm's US corporate bond fund manager, John Smith, who has only very superficial knowledge of the model and who from time to time asks very basic questions regarding the output recommendations. Smith does not consult Dupont with respect to finalizing his clients' investment strategies.

Dupont's recently assigned objective is to develop a new emerging market corporate credit risk model. The firm is planning to expand into emerging credit, and the development of such a model is a critical step in this process. Because Smith seems to follow the model's recommendations without much concern for its quality as he develops his clients' investment strategies, Dupont decides to focus his time on the development of the new emerging market model and neglects to update the US model.

After several months without regular updates, Dupont's diagnostic statistics start to show alarming signs with respect to the quality of the US credit model. Instead of conducting the long and complicated data update, Dupont introduces new codes into his model with some limited new data as a quick "fix." He thinks this change will address the issue without needing to complete the full data update, so he continues working on the new emerging market model.

Several months following the quick "fix," another set of diagnostic statistics reveals nonsensical results and Dupont realizes that his earlier change contained an error. He quickly corrects the error and alerts Smith. Smith realizes that some of the prior trades he performed were due to erroneous model results. Smith rebalances the portfolio to remove the securities purchased on the basis of the questionable results without reporting the issue to anyone else.

> *Comment*: Smith violated V(B) by not disclosing a material error in the investment process. Clients should have been informed about the error and the corrective actions the firm was undertaking on their behalf.
>
> See also Standard V(A)–Diligence and Reasonable Basis.

Example 12 (Notification of Risks and Limitations):

Quantitative analyst Yuri Yakovlev has developed an investment strategy that selects small-cap stocks on the basis of quantitative signals. Yakovlev's strategy typically identifies only a small number of stocks (10–20) that tend to be illiquid, but according to his backtests, the strategy generates significant risk-adjusted returns. The partners at Yakovlev's firm, QSC Capital, are impressed by these results. After a thorough examination of the strategy's risks, stress testing, historical back testing, and scenario analysis, QSC decides to seed the strategy with US$10 million of internal capital in order for Yakovlev to create a track record for the strategy.

After two years, the strategy has generated performance returns greater than the appropriate benchmark and the Sharpe ratio of the fund is close to 1.0. On the basis of these results, QSC decides to actively market the fund to large institutional investors. While creating the offering materials, Yakovlev informs the marketing team that the capacity of the strategy is limited. The extent of the limitation is difficult to ascertain with precision; it depends on market liquidity and other factors in his model that can evolve over time. Yakovlev indicates that given the current market conditions, investments in the fund beyond US$100 million of capital could become more difficult and negatively affect expected fund returns.

Alan Wellard, the manager of the marketing team, is a partner with 30 years of marketing experience and explains to Yakovlev that these are complex technical issues that will muddy the marketing message. According to Wellard, the offering material should focus solely on the great track record of the fund. Yakovlev does not object because the fund has only US$12 million of capital, very far from the US$100 million threshold.

Comment: Yakovlev and Wellard have not appropriately disclosed a significant limitation associated with the investment product. Yakovlev believes this limitation, once reached, will materially affect the returns of the fund. Although the fund is currently far from the US$100 million mark, current and prospective investors must be made aware of this capacity issue. If significant limitations are complicated to grasp and clients do not have the technical background required to understand them, Yakovlev and Wellard should either educate the clients or ascertain whether the fund is suitable for each client.

Example 13 (Notification of Risks and Limitations):

Brickell Advisers offers investment advisory services mainly to South American clients. Julietta Ramon, a risk analyst at Brickell, describes to clients how the firm uses value at risk (VaR) analysis to track the risk of its strategies. Ramon assures clients that calculating a VaR at a 99% confidence level, using a 20-day holding period, and applying a methodology based on an *ex ante* Monte Carlo simulation is extremely effective. The firm has never had losses greater than those predicted by this VaR analysis.

Comment: Ramon has not sufficiently communicated the risks associated with the investment process to satisfy the requirements of Standard V(B). The losses predicted by a VaR analysis depend greatly on the inputs used in the model. The size and probability of losses can differ significantly from what an individual model predicts. Ramon must disclose how the inputs were selected and the potential limitations and risks associated with the investment strategy.

Example 14 (Notification of Risks and Limitations):

Lily Smith attended an industry conference and noticed that John Baker, an investment manager with Baker Associates, attracted a great deal of attention from the conference participants. On the basis of her knowledge of Baker's reputation and the interest he received at the conference, Smith recommends adding Baker Associates to the approved manager platform. Her recommendation to the approval committee included the statement "John Baker is well respected in the industry, and his insights are consistently sought after by investors. Our clients are sure to benefit from investing with Baker Associates."

Comment: Smith is not appropriately separating facts from opinions in her recommendation to include the manager within the platform. Her actions conflict with the requirements of Standard V(B). Smith is relying on her opinions about Baker's reputation and the fact that many attendees were talking with him at the conference. Smith should also review the requirements of Standard V(A) regarding reasonable basis to determine the level of review necessary to recommend Baker Associates.

STANDARD V(C): INVESTMENT ANALYSIS, RECOMMENDATIONS, AND ACTIONS - RECORD RETENTION

48

> ☐ demonstrate a thorough knowledge of the CFA Institute Code of Ethics and Standards of Professional Conduct by applying the Code and Standards to specific situations

Members and Candidates must develop and maintain appropriate records to support their investment analyses, recommendations, actions, and other investment-related communications with clients and prospective clients.

Guidance

Highlights:

- *New Media Records*
- *Records Are Property of the Firm*
- *Local Requirements*

Members and candidates must retain records that substantiate the scope of their research and reasons for their actions or conclusions. The retention requirement applies to decisions to buy or sell a security as well as reviews undertaken that do not lead to a change in position. Which records are required to support recommendations or investment actions depends on the role of the member or candidate in the investment decision-making process. Records may be maintained either in hard copy or electronic form.

Some examples of supporting documentation that assists the member or candidate in meeting the requirements for retention are as follows:

- personal notes from meetings with the covered company,
- press releases or presentations issued by the covered company,
- computer-based model outputs and analyses,
- computer-based model input parameters,
- risk analyses of securities' impacts on a portfolio,
- selection criteria for external advisers,
- notes from clients from meetings to review investment policy statements, and
- outside research reports.

New Media Records

The increased use of new and evolving technological formats (e.g., social media) for gathering and sharing information creates new challenges in maintaining the appropriate records and files. The nature or format of the information does not remove a member's or candidate's responsibility to maintain a record of information used in his or her analysis or communicated to clients.

Members and candidates should understand that although employers and local regulators are developing digital media retention policies, these policies may lag behind the advent of new communication channels. Such lag places greater responsibility on the individual for ensuring that all relevant information is retained. Examples of non-print media formats that should be retained include, but are not limited to,

- e-mails,
- text messages,
- blog posts, and
- Twitter posts.

Records Are Property of the Firm

As a general matter, records created as part of a member's or candidate's professional activity on behalf of his or her employer are the property of the firm. When a member or candidate leaves a firm to seek other employment, the member or candidate cannot take the property of the firm, including original forms or copies of supporting records of the member's or candidate's work, to the new employer without the express consent of the previous employer. The member or candidate cannot use historical recommendations or research reports created at the previous firm because the supporting documentation is unavailable. For future use, the member or candidate must re-create the supporting records at the new firm with information gathered through public sources or directly from the covered company and not from memory or sources obtained at the previous employer.

Local Requirements

Local regulators often impose requirements on members, candidates, and their firms related to record retention that must be followed. Firms may also implement policies detailing the applicable time frame for retaining research and client communication records. Fulfilling such regulatory and firm requirements satisfies the requirements of Standard V(C). In the absence of regulatory guidance or firm policies, CFA Institute recommends maintaining records for at least seven years.

49 STANDARD V(C): RECOMMENDED PROCEDURES

☐ | demonstrate a thorough knowledge of the CFA Institute Code of Ethics and Standards of Professional Conduct by applying the Code and Standards to specific situations

The responsibility to maintain records that support investment action generally falls with the firm rather than individuals. Members and candidates must, however, archive research notes and other documents, either electronically or in hard copy, that support their current investment-related communications. Doing so will assist their firms in complying with requirements for preservation of internal or external records.

STANDARD V(C): APPLICATION OF THE STANDARD

50

☐ demonstrate a thorough knowledge of the CFA Institute Code of Ethics and Standards of Professional Conduct by applying the Code and Standards to specific situations

☐ recommend practices and procedures designed to prevent violations of the Code of Ethics and Standards of Professional Conduct

Example 1 (Record Retention and IPS Objectives and Recommendations):

One of Nikolas Lindstrom's clients is upset by the negative investment returns of his equity portfolio. The investment policy statement for the client requires that the portfolio manager follow a benchmark-oriented approach. The benchmark for the client includes a 35% investment allocation in the technology sector. The client acknowledges that this allocation was appropriate, but over the past three years, technology stocks have suffered severe losses. The client complains to the investment manager for allocating so much money to this sector.

> *Comment*: For Lindstrom, having appropriate records is important to show that over the past three years, the portion of technology stocks in the benchmark index was 35%, as called for in the IPS. Lindstrom should also have the client's IPS stating that the benchmark was appropriate for the client's investment objectives. He should also have records indicating that the investment has been explained appropriately to the client and that the IPS was updated on a regular basis. Taking these actions, Lindstrom would be in compliance with Standard V(C).

Example 2 (Record Retention and Research Process):

Malcolm Young is a research analyst who writes numerous reports rating companies in the luxury retail industry. His reports are based on a variety of sources, including interviews with company managers, manufacturers, and economists; on-site company visits; customer surveys; and secondary research from analysts covering related industries.

> *Comment*: Young must carefully document and keep copies of all the information that goes into his reports, including the secondary or third-party research of other analysts. Failure to maintain such files would violate Standard V(C).

Example 3 (Records as Firm, Not Employee, Property):

Martin Blank develops an analytical model while he is employed by Green Partners Investment Management, LLP (GPIM). While at the firm, he systematically documents the assumptions that make up the model as well as his reasoning behind the assumptions. As a result of the success of his model, Blank is hired to be the head of the research department of one of GPIM's competitors. Blank takes copies of the records supporting his model to his new firm.

Comment: The records created by Blank supporting the research model he developed at GPIM are the records of GPIM. Taking the documents with him to his new employer without GPIM's permission violates Standard V(C). To use the model in the future, Blank must re-create the records supporting his model at the new firm.

51 STANDARD VI(A): CONFLICTS OF INTEREST - DISCLOSURE OF CONFLICTS

☐ demonstrate a thorough knowledge of the CFA Institute Code of Ethics and Standards of Professional Conduct by applying the Code and Standards to specific situations

Standard VI(A) Disclosure of Conflicts

> Members and Candidates must make full and fair disclosure of all matters that could reasonably be expected to impair their independence and objectivity or interfere with respective duties to their clients, prospective clients, and employer. Members and Candidates must ensure that such disclosures are prominent, are delivered in plain language, and communicate the relevant information effectively.

Guidance

Highlights:

- *Disclosure of Conflicts to Employers*
- *Disclosure to Clients*
- *Cross-Departmental Conflicts*
- *Conflicts with Stock Ownership*
- *Conflicts as a Director*

Best practice is to avoid actual conflicts or the appearance of conflicts of interest when possible. Conflicts of interest often arise in the investment profession. Conflicts can occur between the interests of clients, the interests of employers, and the member's or candidate's own personal interests. Common sources for conflict are compensation structures, especially incentive and bonus structures that provide immediate returns for members and candidates with little or no consideration of long-term value creation.

Identifying and managing these conflicts is a critical part of working in the investment industry and can take many forms. When conflicts cannot be reasonably avoided, clear and complete disclosure of their existence is necessary.

Standard VI(A) protects investors and employers by requiring members and candidates to fully disclose to clients, potential clients, and employers all actual and potential conflicts of interest. Once a member or candidate has made full disclosure, the member's or candidate's employer, clients, and prospective clients will have the information needed to evaluate the objectivity of the investment advice or action taken on their behalf.

Standard VI(A): Conflicts of Interest - Disclosure of Conflicts

To be effective, disclosures must be prominent and must be made in plain language and in a manner designed to effectively communicate the information. Members and candidates have the responsibility of determining how often, in what manner, and in what particular circumstances the disclosure of conflicts must be made. Best practices dictate updating disclosures when the nature of a conflict of interest changes materially—for example, if the nature of a conflict of interest worsens through the introduction of bonuses based on each quarter's profits as to opposed annual profits. In making and updating disclosures of conflicts of interest, members and candidates should err on the side of caution to ensure that conflicts are effectively communicated.

Disclosure of Conflicts to Employers

Disclosure of conflicts to employers may be appropriate in many instances. When reporting conflicts of interest to employers, members and candidates must give their employers enough information to assess the impact of the conflict. By complying with employer guidelines, members and candidates allow their employers to avoid potentially embarrassing and costly ethical or regulatory violations.

Reportable situations include conflicts that would interfere with rendering unbiased investment advice and conflicts that would cause a member or candidate to act not in the employer's best interest. The same circumstances that generate conflicts to be reported to clients and prospective clients also would dictate reporting to employers. Ownership of stocks analyzed or recommended, participation on outside boards, and financial or other pressures that could influence a decision are to be promptly reported to the employer so that their impact can be assessed and a decision on how to resolve the conflict can be made.

The mere appearance of a conflict of interest may create problems for members, candidates, and their employers. Therefore, many of the conflicts previously mentioned could be explicitly prohibited by an employer. For example, many employers restrict personal trading, outside board membership, and related activities to prevent situations that might not normally be considered problematic from a conflict-of-interest point of view but that could give the appearance of a conflict of interest. Members and candidates must comply with these restrictions. Members and candidates must take reasonable steps to avoid conflicts and, if they occur inadvertently, must report them promptly so that the employer and the member or candidate can resolve them as quickly and effectively as possible.

Standard VI(A) also deals with a member's or candidate's conflicts of interest that might be detrimental to the employer's business. Any potential conflict situation that could prevent clear judgment about or full commitment to the execution of a member's or candidate's duties to the employer should be reported to the member's or candidate's employer and promptly resolved.

Disclosure to Clients

Members and candidates must maintain their objectivity when rendering investment advice or taking investment action. Investment advice or actions may be perceived to be tainted in numerous situations. Can a member or candidate remain objective if, on behalf of the firm, the member or candidate obtains or assists in obtaining fees for services? Can a member or candidate give objective advice if he or she owns stock in the company that is the subject of an investment recommendation or if the member or candidate has a close personal relationship with the company managers? Requiring members and candidates to disclose all matters that reasonably could be expected to impair the member's or candidate's objectivity allows clients and prospective clients to judge motives and possible biases for themselves.

Often in the investment industry, a conflict, or the perception of a conflict, cannot be avoided. The most obvious conflicts of interest, which should always be disclosed, are relationships between an issuer and the member, the candidate, or his or her firm (such as a directorship or consultancy by a member; investment banking, underwriting, and financial relationships; broker/dealer market-making activities; and material beneficial ownership of stock). For the purposes of Standard VI(A), members and candidates beneficially own securities or other investments if they have a direct or indirect pecuniary interest in the securities, have the power to vote or direct the voting of the shares of the securities or investments, or have the power to dispose or direct the disposition of the security or investment.

A member or candidate must take reasonable steps to determine whether a conflict of interest exists and disclose to clients any known conflicts of the member's or candidate's firm. Disclosure of broker/dealer market-making activities alerts clients that a purchase or sale might be made from or to the firm's principal account and that the firm has a special interest in the price of the stock.

Additionally, disclosures should be made to clients regarding fee arrangements, subadvisory agreements, or other situations involving nonstandard fee structures. Equally important is the disclosure of arrangements in which the firm benefits directly from investment recommendations. An obvious conflict of interest is the rebate of a portion of the service fee some classes of mutual funds charge to investors. Members and candidates should ensure that their firms disclose such relationships so clients can fully understand the costs of their investments and the benefits received by their investment manager's employer.

Cross-Departmental Conflicts

Other circumstances can give rise to actual or potential conflicts of interest. For instance, a sell-side analyst working for a broker/dealer may be encouraged, not only by members of her or his own firm but by corporate issuers themselves, to write research reports about particular companies. The buy-side analyst is likely to be faced with similar conflicts as banks exercise their underwriting and security-dealing powers. The marketing division may ask an analyst to recommend the stock of a certain company in order to obtain business from that company.

The potential for conflicts of interest also exists with broker-sponsored limited partnerships formed to invest venture capital. Increasingly, members and candidates are expected not only to follow issues from these partnerships once they are offered to the public but also to promote the issues in the secondary market after public offerings. Members, candidates, and their firms should attempt to resolve situations presenting potential conflicts of interest or disclose them in accordance with the principles set forth in Standard VI(A).

Conflicts with Stock Ownership

The most prevalent conflict requiring disclosure under Standard VI(A) is a member's or candidate's ownership of stock in companies that he or she recommends to clients or that clients hold. Clearly, the easiest method for preventing a conflict is to prohibit members and candidates from owning any such securities, but this approach is overly burdensome and discriminates against members and candidates.

Therefore, sell-side members and candidates should disclose any materially beneficial ownership interest in a security or other investment that the member or candidate is recommending. Buy-side members and candidates should disclose their procedures for reporting requirements for personal transactions. Conflicts arising from personal investing are discussed more fully in the guidance for Standard VI(B).

Conflicts as a Director

Service as a director poses three basic conflicts of interest. First, a conflict may exist between the duties owed to clients and the duties owed to shareholders of the company. Second, investment personnel who serve as directors may receive the securities

Standard VI(A): Application of the Standard

363

or options to purchase securities of the company as compensation for serving on the board, which could raise questions about trading actions that might increase the value of those securities. Third, board service creates the opportunity to receive material nonpublic information involving the company. Even though the information is confidential, the perception could be that information not available to the public is being communicated to a director's firm—whether a broker, investment adviser, or other type of organization. When members or candidates providing investment services also serve as directors, they should be isolated from those making investment decisions by the use of firewalls or similar restrictions.

STANDARD VI(A): RECOMMENDED PROCEDURES　52

- [ ] demonstrate a thorough knowledge of the CFA Institute Code of Ethics and Standards of Professional Conduct by applying the Code and Standards to specific situations

Members or candidates should disclose special compensation arrangements with the employer that might conflict with client interests, such as bonuses based on short-term performance criteria, commissions, incentive fees, performance fees, and referral fees. If the member's or candidate's firm does not permit such disclosure, the member or candidate should document the request and may consider dissociating from the activity.

Members' and candidates' firms are encouraged to include information on compensation packages in firms' promotional literature. If a member or candidate manages a portfolio for which the fee is based on capital gains or capital appreciation (a performance fee), this information should be disclosed to clients. If a member, a candidate, or a member's or candidate's firm has outstanding agent options to buy stock as part of the compensation package for corporate financing activities, the amount and expiration date of these options should be disclosed as a footnote to any research report published by the member's or candidate's firm.

STANDARD VI(A): APPLICATION OF THE STANDARD　53

- [ ] demonstrate a thorough knowledge of the CFA Institute Code of Ethics and Standards of Professional Conduct by applying the Code and Standards to specific situations
- [ ] recommend practices and procedures designed to prevent violations of the Code of Ethics and Standards of Professional Conduct

Example 1 (Conflict of Interest and Business Relationships):

Hunter Weiss is a research analyst with Farmington Company, a broker and investment banking firm. Farmington's merger and acquisition department has represented Vimco, a conglomerate, in all of Vimco's acquisitions for 20 years. From time to time, Farmington officers sit on the boards of directors of various Vimco subsidiaries. Weiss is writing a research report on Vimco.

Comment: Weiss must disclose in his research report Farmington's special relationship with Vimco. Broker/dealer management of and participation in public offerings must be disclosed in research reports. Because the position of underwriter to a company entails a special past and potential future relationship with a company that is the subject of investment advice, it threatens the independence and objectivity of the report writer and must be disclosed.

Example 2 (Conflict of Interest and Business Stock Ownership):

The investment management firm of Dover & Roe sells a 25% interest in its partnership to a multinational bank holding company, First of New York. Immediately after the sale, Margaret Hobbs, president of Dover & Roe, changes her recommendation for First of New York's common stock from "sell" to "buy" and adds First of New York's commercial paper to Dover & Roe's approved list for purchase.

Comment: Hobbs must disclose the new relationship with First of New York to all Dover & Roe clients. This relationship must also be disclosed to clients by the firm's portfolio managers when they make specific investment recommendations or take investment actions with respect to First of New York's securities.

Example 3 (Conflict of Interest and Personal Stock Ownership):

Carl Fargmon, a research analyst who follows firms producing office equipment, has been recommending purchase of Kincaid Printing because of its innovative new line of copiers. After his initial report on the company, Fargmon's wife inherits from a distant relative US$3 million of Kincaid stock. He has been asked to write a follow-up report on Kincaid.

Comment: Fargmon must disclose his wife's ownership of the Kincaid stock to his employer and in his follow-up report. Best practice would be to avoid the conflict by asking his employer to assign another analyst to draft the follow-up report.

Example 4 (Conflict of Interest and Personal Stock Ownership):

Betty Roberts is speculating in penny stocks for her own account and purchases 100,000 shares of Drew Mining, Inc., for US$0.30 a share. She intends to sell these shares at the sign of any substantial upward price movement of the stock. A week later, her employer asks her to write a report on penny stocks in the mining industry to be published in two weeks. Even without owning the Drew stock, Roberts would recommend it in her report as a "buy." A surge in the price of the stock to the US$2 range is likely to result once the report is issued.

Comment: Although this holding may not be material, Roberts must disclose it in the report and to her employer before writing the report because the gain for her will be substantial if the market responds strongly to her recommendation. The fact that she has only recently purchased the stock adds to the appearance that she is not entirely objective.

Standard VI(A): Application of the Standard

Example 5 (Conflict of Interest and Compensation Arrangements):

Samantha Snead, a portfolio manager for Thomas Investment Counsel, Inc., specializes in managing public retirement funds and defined benefit pension plan accounts, all of which have long-term investment objectives. A year ago, Snead's employer, in an attempt to motivate and retain key investment professionals, introduced a bonus compensation system that rewards portfolio managers on the basis of quarterly performance relative to their peers and to certain benchmark indexes. In an attempt to improve the short-term performance of her accounts, Snead changes her investment strategy and purchases several high-beta stocks for client portfolios. These purchases are seemingly contrary to the clients' investment policy statements. Following their purchase, an officer of Griffin Corporation, one of Snead's pension fund clients, asks why Griffin Corporation's portfolio seems to be dominated by high-beta stocks of companies that often appear among the most actively traded issues. No change in objective or strategy has been recommended by Snead during the year.

> *Comment*: Snead has violated Standard VI(A) by failing to inform her clients of the changes in her compensation arrangement with her employer, which created a conflict of interest between her compensation and her clients' IPSs. Firms may pay employees on the basis of performance, but pressure by Thomas Investment Counsel to achieve short-term performance goals is in basic conflict with the objectives of Snead's accounts.
>
> See also Standard III(C)–Suitability.

Example 6 (Conflict of Interest, Options, and Compensation Arrangements):

Wayland Securities works with small companies doing IPOs or secondary offerings. Typically, these deals are in the US$10 million to US$50 million range, and as a result, the corporate finance fees are quite small. To compensate for the small fees, Wayland Securities usually takes "agent options"—that is, rights (exercisable within a two-year time frame) to acquire up to an additional 10% of the current offering. Following an IPO performed by Wayland for Falk Resources, Ltd., Darcy Hunter, the head of corporate finance at Wayland, is concerned about receiving value for her Falk Resources options. The options are due to expire in one month, and the stock is not doing well. She contacts John Fitzpatrick in the research department of Wayland Securities, reminds him that he is eligible for 30% of these options, and indicates that now would be a good time to give some additional coverage to Falk Resources. Fitzpatrick agrees and immediately issues a favorable report.

> *Comment*: For Fitzpatrick to avoid being in violation of Standard VI(A), he must indicate in the report the volume and expiration date of agent options outstanding. Furthermore, because he is personally eligible for some of the options, Fitzpatrick must disclose the extent of this compensation. He also must be careful to not violate his duty of independence and objectivity under Standard I(B).

Example 7 (Conflict of Interest and Compensation Arrangements):

Gary Carter is a representative with Bengal International, a registered broker/dealer. Carter is approached by a stock promoter for Badger Company, who offers to pay Carter additional compensation for sales of Badger Company's stock to Carter's clients. Carter accepts the stock promoter's offer but does not disclose the arrangements to his clients or to his employer. Carter sells shares of the stock to his clients.

> *Comment*: Carter has violated Standard VI(A) by failing to disclose to clients that he is receiving additional compensation for recommending and selling Badger stock. Because he did not disclose the arrangement with Badger to his clients, the clients were unable to evaluate whether Carter's recommendations to buy Badger were affected by this arrangement. Carter's conduct also violated Standard VI(A) by failing to disclose to his employer monetary compensation received in addition to the compensation and benefits conferred by his employer. Carter was required by Standard VI(A) to disclose the arrangement with Badger to his employer so that his employer could evaluate whether the arrangement affected Carter's objectivity and loyalty.

Example 8 (Conflict of Interest and Directorship):

Carol Corky, a senior portfolio manager for Universal Management, recently became involved as a trustee with the Chelsea Foundation, a large not-for-profit foundation in her hometown. Universal is a small money manager (with assets under management of approximately US$100 million) that caters to individual investors. Chelsea has assets in excess of US$2 billion. Corky does not believe informing Universal of her involvement with Chelsea is necessary.

> *Comment*: By failing to inform Universal of her involvement with Chelsea, Corky violated Standard VI(A). Given the large size of the endowment at Chelsea, Corky's new role as a trustee can reasonably be expected to be time consuming, to the possible detriment of Corky's portfolio responsibilities with Universal. Also, as a trustee, Corky may become involved in the investment decisions at Chelsea. Therefore, Standard VI(A) obligates Corky to discuss becoming a trustee at Chelsea with her compliance officer or supervisor at Universal before accepting the position, and she should have disclosed the degree to which she would be involved in investment decisions at Chelsea.

Example 9 (Conflict of Interest and Personal Trading):

Bruce Smith covers eastern European equities for Marlborough Investments, an investment management firm with a strong presence in emerging markets. While on a business trip to Russia, Smith learns that investing in Russian equities directly is difficult but that equity-linked notes that replicate the performance of underlying Russian equities can be purchased from a New York–based investment bank. Believing that his firm would not be interested in such a security, Smith purchases a note linked to a Russian telecommunications company for his own account without informing Marlborough. A month later, Smith decides that the firm should consider investing in Russian equities by way of the equity-linked notes. He prepares a write-up on the market that concludes with a recommendation to purchase several of the notes. One note he recommends is linked to the same Russian telecom company that Smith holds in his personal account.

Standard VI(A): Application of the Standard

> *Comment*: Smith has violated Standard VI(A) by failing to disclose his purchase and ownership of the note linked to the Russian telecom company. Smith is required by the standard to disclose the investment opportunity to his employer and look to his company's policies on personal trading to determine whether it was proper for him to purchase the note for his own account. By purchasing the note, Smith may or may not have impaired his ability to make an unbiased and objective assessment of the appropriateness of the derivative instrument for his firm, but Smith's failure to disclose the purchase to his employer impaired his employer's ability to decide whether his ownership of the security is a conflict of interest that might affect Smith's future recommendations. Then, when he recommended the particular telecom notes to his firm, Smith compounded his problems by not disclosing that he owned the notes in his personal account—a clear conflict of interest.

Example 10 (Conflict of Interest and Requested Favors):

Michael Papis is the chief investment officer of his state's retirement fund. The fund has always used outside advisers for the real estate allocation, and this information is clearly presented in all fund communications. Thomas Nagle, a recognized sell-side research analyst and Papis's business school classmate, recently left the investment bank he worked for to start his own asset management firm, Accessible Real Estate. Nagle is trying to build his assets under management and contacts Papis about gaining some of the retirement fund's allocation. In the previous few years, the performance of the retirement fund's real estate investments was in line with the fund's benchmark but was not extraordinary. Papis decides to help out his old friend and also to seek better returns by moving the real estate allocation to Accessible. The only notice of the change in adviser appears in the next annual report in the listing of associated advisers.

> *Comment*: Papis has violated Standard VI(A) by not disclosing to his employer his personal relationship with Nagle. Disclosure of his past history with Nagle would allow his firm to determine whether the conflict may have impaired Papis's independence in deciding to change managers.
>
> See also Standard IV(C)–Responsibilities of Supervisors, Standard V(A)–Diligence and Reasonable Basis, and Standard V(B)–Communication with Clients and Prospective Clients.

Example 11 (Conflict of Interest and Business Relationships):

Bob Wade, trust manager for Central Midas Bank, was approached by Western Funds about promoting its family of funds, with special interest in the service-fee class. To entice Central to promote this class, Western Funds offered to pay the bank a service fee of 0.25%. Without disclosing the fee being offered to the bank, Wade asked one of the investment managers to review the Western Funds family of funds to determine whether they were suitable for clients of Central. The manager completed the normal due diligence review and determined that the funds were fairly valued in the market with fee structures on a par with their competitors. Wade decided to accept Western's offer and instructed the team of portfolio managers to exclusively promote these funds and the service-fee class to clients seeking to invest new funds or transfer from their current investments. So as to not influence the investment managers, Wade did not disclose the fee offer and allowed that income to flow directly to the bank.

Comment: Wade is violating Standard VI(A) by not disclosing the portion of the service fee being paid to Central. Although the investment managers may not be influenced by the fee, neither they nor the client have the proper information about Wade's decision to exclusively market this fund family and class of investments. Central may come to rely on the new fee as a component of the firm's profitability and may be unwilling to offer other products in the future that could affect the fees received.

See also Standard I(B)–Independence and Objectivity.

Example 12 (Disclosure of Conflicts to Employers):

Yehudit Dagan is a portfolio manager for Risk Management Bank (RMB), whose clients include retirement plans and corporations. RMB provides a defined contribution retirement plan for its employees that offers 20 large diversified mutual fund investment options, including a mutual fund managed by Dagan's RMB colleagues. After being employed for six months, Dagan became eligible to participate in the retirement plan, and she intends to allocate her retirement plan assets in six of the investment options, including the fund managed by her RMB colleagues. Dagan is concerned that joining the plan will lead to a potentially significant amount of paperwork for her (e.g., disclosure of her retirement account holdings and needing preclearance for her transactions), especially with her investing in the in-house fund.

Comment: Standard VI(A) would not require Dagan to disclose her personal or retirement investments in large diversified mutual funds, unless specifically required by her employer. For practical reasons, the standard does not require Dagan to gain preclearance for ongoing payroll deduction contributions to retirement plan account investment options.

Dagan should ensure that her firm does not have a specific policy regarding investment—whether personal or in the retirement account—for funds managed by the company's employees. These mutual funds may be subject to the company's disclosure, preclearance, and trading restriction procedures to identify possible conflicts prior to the execution of trades.

54 STANDARD VI(B): CONFLICTS OF INTEREST - PRIORITY OF TRANSACTIONS

☐ demonstrate a thorough knowledge of the CFA Institute Code of Ethics and Standards of Professional Conduct by applying the Code and Standards to specific situations

> Investment transactions for clients and employers must have priority over investment transactions in which a Member or Candidate is the beneficial owner.

Standard VI(B): Conflicts of Interest - Priority of Transactions

Guidance

Highlights:

- *Avoiding Potential Conflicts*
- *Personal Trading Secondary to Trading for Clients*
- *Standards for Nonpublic Information*
- *Impact on All Accounts with Beneficial Ownership*

Standard VI(B) reinforces the responsibility of members and candidates to give the interests of their clients and employers priority over their personal financial interests. This standard is designed to prevent any potential conflict of interest or the appearance of a conflict of interest with respect to personal transactions. Client interests have priority. Client transactions must take precedence over transactions made on behalf of the member's or candidate's firm or personal transactions.

Avoiding Potential Conflicts

Conflicts between the client's interest and an investment professional's personal interest may occur. Although conflicts of interest exist, nothing is inherently unethical about individual managers, advisers, or mutual fund employees making money from personal investments as long as (1) the client is not disadvantaged by the trade, (2) the investment professional does not benefit personally from trades undertaken for clients, and (3) the investment professional complies with applicable regulatory requirements.

Some situations occur where a member or candidate may need to enter a personal transaction that runs counter to current recommendations or what the portfolio manager is doing for client portfolios. For example, a member or candidate may be required at some point to sell an asset to make a college tuition payment or a down payment on a home, to meet a margin call, or so on. The sale may be contrary to the long-term advice the member or candidate is currently providing to clients. In these situations, the same three criteria given in the preceding paragraph should be applied in the transaction so as to not violate Standard VI(B).

Personal Trading Secondary to Trading for Clients

Standard VI(B) states that transactions for clients and employers must have priority over transactions in securities or other investments for which a member or candidate is the beneficial owner. The objective of the standard is to prevent personal transactions from adversely affecting the interests of clients or employers. A member or candidate having the same investment positions or being co-invested with clients does not always create a conflict. Some clients in certain investment situations require members or candidates to have aligned interests. Personal investment positions or transactions of members or candidates or their firm should never, however, adversely affect client investments.

Standards for Nonpublic Information

Standard VI(B) covers the activities of members and candidates who have knowledge of pending transactions that may be made on behalf of their clients or employers, who have access to nonpublic information during the normal preparation of research recommendations, or who take investment actions. Members and candidates are prohibited from conveying nonpublic information to any person whose relationship to the member or candidate makes the member or candidate a beneficial owner of the person's securities. Members and candidates must not convey this information to any other person if the nonpublic information can be deemed material.

Impact on All Accounts with Beneficial Ownership

Members or candidates may undertake transactions in accounts for which they are a beneficial owner only after their clients and employers have had adequate opportunity to act on a recommendation. Personal transactions include those made for the member's or candidate's own account, for family (including spouse, children, and other immediate family members) accounts, and for accounts in which the member or candidate has a direct or indirect pecuniary interest, such as a trust or retirement account. Family accounts that are client accounts should be treated like any other firm account and should neither be given special treatment nor be disadvantaged because of the family relationship. If a member or candidate has a beneficial ownership in the account, however, the member or candidate may be subject to preclearance or reporting requirements of the employer or applicable law.

55 STANDARD VI(B): RECOMMENDED PROCEDURES

> ☐ demonstrate a thorough knowledge of the CFA Institute Code of Ethics and Standards of Professional Conduct by applying the Code and Standards to specific situations

Policies and procedures designed to prevent potential conflicts of interest, and even the appearance of a conflict of interest, with respect to personal transactions are critical to establishing investor confidence in the securities industry. Therefore, members and candidates should urge their firms to establish such policies and procedures. Because investment firms vary greatly in assets under management, types of clients, number of employees, and so on, each firm should have policies regarding personal investing that are best suited to the firm. Members and candidates should then prominently disclose these policies to clients and prospective clients.

The specific provisions of each firm's standards will vary, but all firms should adopt certain basic procedures to address the conflict areas created by personal investing. These procedures include the following:

- *Limited participation in equity IPOs*: Some eagerly awaited IPOs rise significantly in value shortly after the issue is brought to market. Because the new issue may be highly attractive and sought after, the opportunity to participate in the IPO may be limited. Therefore, purchases of IPOs by investment personnel create conflicts of interest in two principal ways. First, participation in an IPO may have the appearance of taking away an attractive investment opportunity from clients for personal gain—a clear breach of the duty of loyalty to clients. Second, personal purchases in IPOs may have the appearance that the investment opportunity is being bestowed as an incentive to make future investment decisions for the benefit of the party providing the opportunity. Members and candidates can avoid these conflicts or appearances of conflicts of interest by not participating in IPOs.

  Reliable and systematic review procedures should be established to ensure that conflicts relating to IPOs are identified and appropriately dealt with by supervisors. Members and candidates should preclear their participation in IPOs, even in situations without any conflict of interest between a member's or candidate's participation in an IPO and the client's interests. Members

Standard VI(B): Recommended Procedures

and candidates should not benefit from the position that their clients occupy in the marketplace—through preferred trading, the allocation of limited offerings, or oversubscription.

- *Restrictions on private placements*: Strict limits should be placed on investment personnel acquiring securities in private placements, and appropriate supervisory and review procedures should be established to prevent noncompliance.

  Firms do not routinely use private placements for clients (e.g., venture capital deals) because of the high risk associated with them. Conflicts related to private placements are more significant to members and candidates who manage large pools of assets or act as plan sponsors because these managers may be offered special opportunities, such as private placements, as a reward or an enticement for continuing to do business with a particular broker.

  Participation in private placements raises conflict-of-interest issues that are similar to issues surrounding IPOs. Investment personnel should not be involved in transactions, including (but not limited to) private placements, that could be perceived as favors or gifts that seem designed to influence future judgment or to reward past business deals.

  Whether the venture eventually proves to be good or bad, managers have an immediate conflict concerning private placement opportunities. If and when the investments go public, participants in private placements have an incentive to recommend the investments to clients regardless of the suitability of the investments for their clients. Doing so increases the value of the participants' personal portfolios.

- *Establish blackout/restricted periods*: Investment personnel involved in the investment decision-making process should establish blackout periods prior to trades for clients so that managers cannot take advantage of their knowledge of client activity by "front-running" client trades (trading for one's personal account before trading for client accounts).

  Individual firms must decide who within the firm should be required to comply with the trading restrictions. At a minimum, all individuals who are involved in the investment decision-making process should be subject to the same restricted period. Each firm must determine specific requirements related to blackout and restricted periods that are most relevant to the firm while ensuring that the procedures are governed by the guiding principles set forth in the Code and Standards. Size of firm and type of securities purchased are relevant factors. For example, in a large firm, a blackout requirement is, in effect, a total trading ban because the firm is continually trading in most securities. In a small firm, the blackout period is more likely to prevent the investment manager from front-running.

- *Reporting requirements*: Supervisors should establish reporting procedures for investment personnel, including disclosure of personal holdings/beneficial ownerships, confirmations of trades to the firm and the employee, and preclearance procedures. Once trading restrictions are in place, they must be enforced. The best method for monitoring and enforcing procedures to eliminate conflicts of interest in personal trading is through reporting requirements, including the following:

- **Disclosure of holdings in which the employee has a beneficial interest**. Disclosure by investment personnel to the firm should be made upon commencement of the employment relationship and at least annually thereafter. To address privacy considerations, disclosure of personal holdings should be handled in a confidential manner by the firm.

- **Providing duplicate confirmations of transactions**. Investment personnel should be required to direct their brokers to supply to firms duplicate copies or confirmations of all their personal securities transactions and copies of periodic statements for all securities accounts. The duplicate confirmation requirement has two purposes: (1) The requirement sends a message that there is independent verification, which reduces the likelihood of unethical behavior, and (2) it enables verification of the accounting of the flow of personal investments that cannot be determined from merely looking at holdings.

- **Preclearance procedures**. Investment personnel should examine all planned personal trades to identify possible conflicts prior to the execution of the trades. Preclearance procedures are designed to identify possible conflicts before a problem arises.

- *Disclosure of policies*: Members and candidates should fully disclose to investors their firm's policies regarding personal investing. The information about employees' personal investment activities and policies will foster an atmosphere of full and complete disclosure and calm the public's legitimate concerns about the conflicts of interest posed by investment personnel's personal trading. The disclosure must provide helpful information to investors; it should not be simply boilerplate language, such as "investment personnel are subject to policies and procedures regarding their personal trading."

56 STANDARD VI(B): APPLICATION OF THE STANDARD

☐ demonstrate a thorough knowledge of the CFA Institute Code of Ethics and Standards of Professional Conduct by applying the Code and Standards to specific situations

☐ recommend practices and procedures designed to prevent violations of the Code of Ethics and Standards of Professional Conduct

Example 1 (Personal Trading):

Research analyst Marlon Long does not recommend purchase of a common stock for his employer's account because he wants to purchase the stock personally and does not want to wait until the recommendation is approved and the stock is purchased by his employer.

> *Comment*: Long has violated Standard VI(B) by taking advantage of his knowledge of the stock's value before allowing his employer to benefit from that information.

Example 2 (Trading for Family Member Account):

Carol Baker, the portfolio manager of an aggressive growth mutual fund, maintains an account in her husband's name at several brokerage firms with which the fund and a number of Baker's other individual clients do a substantial amount of business. Whenever a hot issue becomes available, she instructs the brokers to buy it for her husband's account. Because such issues normally are scarce, Baker often acquires shares in hot issues but her clients are not able to participate in them.

> *Comment*: To avoid violating Standard VI(B), Baker must acquire shares for her mutual fund first and acquire them for her husband's account only after doing so, even though she might miss out on participating in new issues via her husband's account. She also must disclose the trading for her husband's account to her employer because this activity creates a conflict between her personal interests and her employer's interests.

Example 3 (Family Accounts as Equals):

Erin Toffler, a portfolio manager at Esposito Investments, manages the retirement account established with the firm by her parents. Whenever IPOs become available, she first allocates shares to all her other clients for whom the investment is appropriate; only then does she place any remaining portion in her parents' account, if the issue is appropriate for them. She has adopted this procedure so that no one can accuse her of favoring her parents.

> *Comment*: Toffler has violated Standard VI(B) by breaching her duty to her parents by treating them differently from her other accounts simply because of the family relationship. As fee-paying clients of Esposito Investments, Toffler's parents are entitled to the same treatment as any other client of the firm. If Toffler has beneficial ownership in the account, however, and Esposito Investments has preclearance and reporting requirements for personal transactions, she may have to preclear the trades and report the transactions to Esposito.

Example 4 (Personal Trading and Disclosure):

Gary Michaels is an entry-level employee who holds a low-paying job serving both the research department and the investment management department of an active investment management firm. He purchases a sports car and begins to wear expensive clothes after only a year of employment with the firm. The director of the investment management department, who has responsibility for monitoring the personal stock transactions of all employees, investigates and discovers that Michaels has made substantial investment gains by purchasing stocks just before they were put on the firm's recommended "buy" list. Michaels was regularly given the firm's quarterly personal transaction form but declined to complete it.

> *Comment*: Michaels violated Standard VI(B) by placing personal transactions ahead of client transactions. In addition, his supervisor violated Standard IV(C)–Responsibilities of Supervisors by permitting Michaels to continue to perform his assigned tasks without having signed the quarterly personal transaction form. Note also that if Michaels had communicated information about the firm's recommendations to a person who traded the security, that action would be a misappropriation of the information and a violation of Standard II(A)–Material Nonpublic Information.

Example 5 (Trading Prior to Report Dissemination):

A brokerage's insurance analyst, Denise Wilson, makes a closed-circuit TV report to her firm's branches around the country. During the broadcast, she includes negative comments about a major company in the insurance industry. The following day, Wilson's report is printed and distributed to the sales force and public customers. The report recommends that both short-term traders and intermediate investors take profits by selling that insurance company's stock. Seven minutes after the broadcast, however, Ellen Riley, head of the firm's trading department, had closed out a long "call" position in the stock. Shortly thereafter, Riley established a sizable "put" position in the stock. When asked about her activities, Riley claimed she took the actions to facilitate anticipated sales by institutional clients.

> *Comment*: Riley did not give customers an opportunity to buy or sell in the options market before the firm itself did. By taking action before the report was disseminated, Riley's firm may have depressed the price of the calls and increased the price of the puts. The firm could have avoided a conflict of interest if it had waited to trade for its own account until its clients had an opportunity to receive and assimilate Wilson's recommendations. As it is, Riley's actions violated Standard VI(B).

57 STANDARD VI(C): CONFLICTS OF INTEREST - REFERRAL FEES

☐ | demonstrate a thorough knowledge of the CFA Institute Code of Ethics and Standards of Professional Conduct by applying the Code and Standards to specific situations

> Members and Candidates must disclose to their employer, clients, and prospective clients, as appropriate, any compensation, consideration, or benefit received from or paid to others for the recommendation of products or services.

Guidance

Standard VI(C) states the responsibility of members and candidates to inform their employer, clients, and prospective clients of any benefit received for referrals of customers and clients. Such disclosures allow clients or employers to evaluate (1) any partiality shown in any recommendation of services and (2) the full cost of the services. Members and candidates must disclose when they pay a fee or provide compensation to others who have referred prospective clients to the member or candidate.

Appropriate disclosure means that members and candidates must advise the client or prospective client, before entry into any formal agreement for services, of any benefit given or received for the recommendation of any services provided by the member or candidate. In addition, the member or candidate must disclose the nature of the consideration or benefit—for example, flat fee or percentage basis, one-time or continuing benefit, based on performance, benefit in the form of provision of research or other noncash benefit—together with the estimated dollar value. Consideration includes all fees, whether paid in cash, in soft dollars, or in kind.

[Handwritten margin note: —Disclosure should be made in writing]

STANDARD VI(C): RECOMMENDED PROCEDURES

58

☐ demonstrate a thorough knowledge of the CFA Institute Code of Ethics and Standards of Professional Conduct by applying the Code and Standards to specific situations

Members and candidates should encourage their employers to develop procedures related to referral fees. The firm may completely restrict such fees. If the firm does not adopt a strict prohibition of such fees, the procedures should indicate the appropriate steps for requesting approval.

Employers should have investment professionals provide to the clients notification of approved referral fee programs and provide the employer regular (at least quarterly) updates on the amount and nature of compensation received.

STANDARD VI(C): APPLICATION OF THE STANDARD

59

☐ demonstrate a thorough knowledge of the CFA Institute Code of Ethics and Standards of Professional Conduct by applying the Code and Standards to specific situations

☐ recommend practices and procedures designed to prevent violations of the Code of Ethics and Standards of Professional Conduct

Example 1 (Disclosure of Referral Arrangements and Outside Parties):

Brady Securities, Inc., a broker/dealer, has established a referral arrangement with Lewis Brothers, Ltd., an investment counseling firm. In this arrangement, Brady Securities refers all prospective tax-exempt accounts, including pension, profit-sharing, and endowment accounts, to Lewis Brothers. In return, Lewis Brothers makes available to Brady Securities on a regular basis the security recommendations and reports of its research staff, which registered representatives of Brady Securities use in serving customers. In addition, Lewis Brothers conducts monthly economic and market reviews for Brady Securities personnel and directs all stock commission business generated by referral accounts to Brady Securities.

Willard White, a partner in Lewis Brothers, calculates that the incremental costs involved in functioning as the research department of Brady Securities are US$20,000 annually.

Referrals from Brady Securities last year resulted in fee income of US$200,000 for Lewis Brothers, and directing all stock trades through Brady Securities resulted in additional costs to Lewis Brothers' clients of US$10,000.

Diane Branch, the chief financial officer of Maxwell Inc., contacts White and says that she is seeking an investment manager for Maxwell's profit-sharing plan. She adds, "My friend Harold Hill at Brady Securities recommended your firm without qualification, and that's good enough for me. Do we have a deal?" White accepts the new account but does not disclose his firm's referral arrangement with Brady Securities.

> *Comment*: White has violated Standard VI(C) by failing to inform the prospective customer of the referral fee payable in services and commissions for an indefinite period to Brady Securities. Such disclosure could have caused Branch to reassess Hill's recommendation and make a more critical evaluation of Lewis Brothers' services.

Example 2 (Disclosure of Interdepartmental Referral Arrangements):

James Handley works for the trust department of Central Trust Bank. He receives compensation for each referral he makes to Central Trust's brokerage department and personal financial management department that results in a sale. He refers several of his clients to the personal financial management department but does not disclose the arrangement within Central Trust to his clients.

> *Comment*: Handley has violated Standard VI(C) by not disclosing the referral arrangement at Central Trust Bank to his clients. Standard VI(C) does not distinguish between referral payments paid by a third party for referring clients to the third party and internal payments paid within the firm to attract new business to a subsidiary. Members and candidates must disclose all such referral fees. Therefore, Handley is required to disclose, at the time of referral, any referral fee agreement in place among Central Trust Bank's departments. The disclosure should include the nature and the value of the benefit and should be made in writing.

Example 3 (Disclosure of Referral Arrangements and Informing Firm):

Katherine Roberts is a portfolio manager at Katama Investments, an advisory firm specializing in managing assets for high-net-worth individuals. Katama's trading desk uses a variety of brokerage houses to execute trades on behalf of its clients. Roberts asks the trading desk to direct a large portion of its commissions to Naushon, Inc., a small broker/dealer run by one of Roberts' business school classmates. Katama's traders have found that Naushon is not very competitive on pricing, and although Naushon generates some research for its trading clients, Katama's other analysts have found most of Naushon's research to be not especially useful. Nevertheless, the traders do as Roberts asks, and in return for receiving a large portion of Katama's business, Naushon recommends the investment services of Roberts and Katama to its wealthiest clients. This arrangement is not disclosed to either Katama or the clients referred by Naushon.

> *Comment*: Roberts is violating Standard VI(C) by failing to inform her employer of the referral arrangement.

Example 4 (Disclosure of Referral Arrangements and Outside Organizations):

Alex Burl is a portfolio manager at Helpful Investments, a local investment advisory firm. Burl is on the advisory board of his child's school, which is looking for ways to raise money to purchase new playground equipment for the school. Burl discusses a plan with his supervisor in which he will donate to the school a portion of his service fee from new clients referred by the parents of students at the school. Upon getting the approval from Helpful, Burl presents the idea to the school's advisory board and

Standard VI(C): Application of the Standard

directors. The school agrees to announce the program at the next parent event and asks Burl to provide the appropriate written materials to be distributed. A week following the distribution of the flyers, Burl receives the first school-related referral. In establishing the client's investment policy statement, Burl clearly discusses the school's referral and outlines the plans for distributing the donation back to the school.

> *Comment*: Burl has not violated Standard VI(C) because he secured the permission of his employer, Helpful Investments, and the school prior to beginning the program and because he discussed the arrangement with the client at the time the investment policy statement was designed.

Example 5 (Disclosure of Referral Arrangements and Outside Parties):

The sponsor of a state employee pension is seeking to hire a firm to manage the pension plan's emerging market allocation. To assist in the review process, the sponsor has hired Thomas Arrow as a consultant to solicit proposals from various advisers. Arrow is contracted by the sponsor to represent its best interest in selecting the most appropriate new manager. The process runs smoothly, and Overseas Investments is selected as the new manager.

The following year, news breaks that Arrow is under investigation by the local regulator for accepting kickbacks from investment managers after they are awarded new pension allocations. Overseas Investments is included in the list of firms allegedly making these payments. Although the sponsor is happy with the performance of Overseas since it has been managing the pension plan's emerging market funds, the sponsor still decides to have an independent review of the proposals and the selection process to ensure that Overseas was the appropriate firm for its needs. This review confirms that, even though Arrow was being paid by both parties, the recommendation of Overseas appeared to be objective and appropriate.

> *Comment*: Arrow has violated Standard VI(C) because he did not disclose the fee being paid by Overseas. Withholding this information raises the question of a potential lack of objectivity in the recommendation of Overseas by Arrow; this aspect is in addition to questions about the legality of having firms pay to be considered for an allocation.
>
> Regulators and governmental agencies may adopt requirements concerning allowable consultant activities. Local regulations sometimes include having a consultant register with the regulatory agency's ethics board. Regulator policies may include a prohibition on acceptance of payments from investment managers receiving allocations and require regular reporting of contributions made to political organizations and candidates. Arrow would have to adhere to these requirements as well as the Code and Standards.

60

STANDARD VII(A): RESPONSIBILITIES AS A CFA INSTITUTE MEMBER OR CFA CANDIDATE - CONDUCT AS PARTICIPANTS IN CFA INSTITUTE PROGRAMS

☐ demonstrate a thorough knowledge of the CFA Institute Code of Ethics and Standards of Professional Conduct by applying the Code and Standards to specific situations

Standard VII(A) Conduct as Participants in CFA Institute Programs

> Members and Candidates must not engage in any conduct that compromises the reputation or integrity of CFA Institute or the CFA designation or the integrity, validity, or security of CFA Institute programs.

Guidance

Highlights:

- *Confidential Program Information*
- *Additional CFA Program Restrictions*
- *Expressing an Opinion*

Standard VII(A) covers the conduct of CFA Institute members and candidates involved with the CFA Program and prohibits any conduct that undermines the public's confidence that the CFA charter represents a level of achievement based on merit and ethical conduct. There is an array of CFA Institute programs beyond the CFA Program that provide additional educational and credentialing opportunities, including the Certificate in Investment Performance Measurement (CIPM) Program and the CFA Institute Investment Foundations™ Program. The standard's function is to hold members and candidates to a high ethical criterion while they are participating in or involved with any CFA Institute program. Conduct covered includes but is not limited to

- giving or receiving assistance (cheating) on any CFA Institute examinations;
- violating the rules, regulations, and testing policies of CFA Institute programs;
- providing confidential program or exam information to candidates or the public;
- disregarding or attempting to circumvent security measures established for any CFA Institute examinations;
- improperly using an association with CFA Institute to further personal or professional goals; and
- misrepresenting information on the Professional Conduct Statement or in the CFA Institute Continuing Education Program.

Standard VII(A): Responsibilities as a CFA Institute Member or CFA Candidate

Confidential Program Information

CFA Institute is vigilant about protecting the integrity of CFA Institute programs' content and examination processes. CFA Institute program rules, regulations, and policies prohibit candidates from disclosing confidential material gained during the exam process.

Examples of information that cannot be disclosed by candidates sitting for an exam include but are not limited to

- specific details of questions appearing on the exam and
- broad topical areas and formulas tested or not tested on the exam.

All aspects of the exam, including questions, broad topical areas, and formulas, tested or not tested, are considered confidential until such time as CFA Institute elects to release them publicly. This confidentiality requirement allows CFA Institute to maintain the integrity and rigor of exams for future candidates. Standard VII(A) does not prohibit candidates from discussing nonconfidential information or curriculum material with others or in study groups in preparation for the exam.

Candidates increasingly use online forums and new technology as part of their exam preparations. CFA Institute actively polices blogs, forums, and related social networking groups for information considered confidential. The organization works with both individual candidates and the sponsors of online or offline services to promptly remove any and all violations. As noted in the discussion of Standard I(A)–Knowledge of the Law, candidates, members, and the public are encouraged to report suspected violations to CFA Institute.

Additional CFA Program Restrictions

The CFA Program rules, regulations, and policies define additional allowed and disallowed actions concerning the exams. Violating any of the testing policies, such as the calculator policy, personal belongings policy, or the Candidate Pledge, constitutes a violation of Standard VII(A). Candidates will find all of these policies on the CFA Program portion of the CFA Institute website (www.cfainstitute.org). Exhibit 2 provides the Candidate Pledge, which highlights the respect candidates must have for the integrity, validity, and security of the CFA exam.

Members may participate as volunteers in various aspects of the CFA Program. Standard VII(A) prohibits members from disclosing and/or soliciting confidential material gained prior to or during the exam and grading processes with those outside the CFA exam development process.

Examples of information that cannot be shared by members involved in developing, administering, or grading the exams include but are not limited to

- questions appearing on the exam or under consideration,
- deliberation related to the exam process, and
- information related to the scoring of questions.

Members may also be asked to offer assistance with other CFA Institute programs, including but not limited to the CIPM and Investment Foundations programs. Members participating in any CFA Institute program should do so with the same level of integrity and confidentiality as is required of participation in the CFA Program.

Expressing an Opinion

Standard VII(A) does *not* cover expressing opinions regarding CFA Institute, the CFA Program, or other CFA Institute programs. Members and candidates are free to disagree and express their disagreement with CFA Institute on its policies, its procedures, or any advocacy positions taken by the organization. When expressing a personal opinion, a candidate is prohibited from disclosing content-specific information, including any actual exam question and the information as to subject matter covered or not covered in the exam.

Exhibit 2: Sample of CFA Program Testing Policies

Candidate Pledge	As a candidate in the CFA Program, I am obligated to follow Standard VII(A) of the CFA Institute Standards of Professional Conduct, which states that members and candidates must not engage in any conduct that compromises the reputation or integrity of CFA Institute or the CFA designation or the integrity, validity, or security of the CFA exam.

- Prior to this exam, I have not given or received information regarding the content of this exam. During this exam, I will not give or receive any information regarding the content of this exam.

- After this exam, I will not disclose **ANY** portion of this exam and I will not remove **ANY** exam materials from the testing room in original or copied form. I understand that all exam materials, including my answers, are the property of CFA Institute and will not be returned to me in any form.

- I will follow **ALL** rules of the CFA Program as stated on the CFA Institute website and the back cover of the exam book. My violation of any rules of the CFA Program will result in CFA Institute voiding my exam results and may lead to suspension or termination of my candidacy in the CFA Program.

61 STANDARD VII(A): APPLICATION OF THE STANDARD

☐ demonstrate a thorough knowledge of the CFA Institute Code of Ethics and Standards of Professional Conduct by applying the Code and Standards to specific situations

☐ recommend practices and procedures designed to prevent violations of the Code of Ethics and Standards of Professional Conduct

Example 1 (Sharing Exam Questions):

Travis Nero serves as a proctor for the administration of the CFA examination in his city. In the course of his service, he reviews a copy of the Level II exam on the evening prior to the exam's administration and provides information concerning the exam questions to two candidates who use it to prepare for the exam.

> *Comment*: Nero and the two candidates have violated Standard VII(A). By giving information about the exam questions to two candidates, Nero provided an unfair advantage to the two candidates and undermined the integrity and validity of the Level II exam as an accurate measure of the knowledge, skills, and abilities necessary to earn the right to use the CFA

Standard VII(A): Application of the Standard

designation. By accepting the information, the candidates also compromised the integrity and validity of the Level II exam and undermined the ethical framework that is a key part of the designation.

Example 2 (Bringing Written Material into Exam Room):

Loren Sullivan is enrolled to take the Level II CFA examination. He has been having difficulty remembering a particular formula, so prior to entering the exam room, he writes the formula on the palm of his hand. During the afternoon section of the exam, a proctor notices Sullivan looking at the palm of his hand. She asks to see his hand and finds the formula.

> *Comment*: Because Sullivan wrote down information from the Candidate Body of Knowledge (CBOK) and took that written information into the exam room, his conduct compromised the validity of his exam performance and violated Standard VII(A). Sullivan's conduct was also in direct contradiction with the rules and regulations of the CFA Program, the Candidate Pledge, and the CFA Institute Code and Standards.

Example 3 (Writing after Exam Period End):

At the conclusion of the morning section of the Level I CFA examination, the proctors announce, "Stop writing now." John Davis has not completed the exam, so he continues to randomly fill in ovals on his answer sheet. A proctor approaches Davis's desk and reminds him that he should stop writing immediately. Davis, however, continues to complete the answer sheet. After the proctor asks him to stop writing two additional times, Davis finally puts down his pencil.

> *Comment*: By continuing to complete his exam after time was called, Davis has violated Standard VII(A). By continuing to write, Davis took an unfair advantage over other candidates, and his conduct compromised the validity of his exam performance. Additionally, by not heeding the proctor's repeated instructions, Davis violated the rules and regulations of the CFA Program.

Example 4 (Sharing Exam Content):

After completing Level II of the CFA exam, Annabelle Rossi posts on her blog about her experience. She posts the following: "Level II is complete! I think I did fairly well on the exam. It was really difficult, but fair. I think I did especially well on the derivatives questions. And there were tons of them! I think I counted 18! The ethics questions were really hard. I'm glad I spent so much time on the Code and Standards. I was surprised to see there were no questions at all about IPO allocations. I expected there to be a couple. Well, off to celebrate getting through it. See you tonight?"

> *Comment*: Rossi did not violate Standard VII(A) when she wrote about how difficult she found the exam or how well she thinks she may have done. By revealing portions of the CBOK covered on the exam and areas not covered, however, she did violate Standard VII(A) and the Candidate Pledge. Depending on the time frame in which the comments were posted, Rossi not only may have assisted future candidates but also may have provided an unfair advantage to candidates yet to sit for the same exam, thereby undermining the integrity and validity of the Level II exam.

Example 5 (Sharing Exam Content):

Level I candidate Etienne Gagne has been a frequent visitor to an internet forum designed specifically for CFA Program candidates. The week after completing the Level I examination, Gagne and several others begin a discussion thread on the forum about the most challenging questions and attempt to determine the correct answers.

> *Comment*: Gagne has violated Standard VII(A) by providing and soliciting confidential exam information, which compromises the integrity of the exam process and violates the Candidate Pledge. In trying to determine correct answers to specific questions, the group's discussion included question-specific details considered to be confidential to the CFA Program.

Example 6 (Sharing Exam Content):

CFA4Sure is a company that produces test-preparation materials for CFA Program candidates. Many candidates register for and use the company's products. The day after the CFA examination, CFA4Sure sends an e-mail to all its customers asking them to share with the company the hardest questions from the exam so that CFA4Sure can better prepare its customers for the next exam administration. Marisol Pena e-mails a summary of the questions she found most difficult on the exam.

> *Comment*: Pena has violated Standard VII(A) by disclosing a portion of the exam questions. The information provided is considered confidential until publicly released by CFA Institute. CFA4Sure is likely to use such feedback to refine its review materials for future candidates. Pena's sharing of the specific questions undermines the integrity of the exam while potentially making the exam easier for future candidates.
>
> If the CFA4Sure employees who participated in the solicitation of confidential CFA Program information are CFA Institute members or candidates, they also have violated Standard VII(A).

Example 7 (Discussion of Exam Grading Guidelines and Results):

Prior to participating in grading CFA examinations, Wesley Whitcomb is required to sign a CFA Institute Grader Agreement. As part of the Grader Agreement, Whitcomb agrees not to reveal or discuss the exam materials with anyone except CFA Institute staff or other graders. Several weeks after the conclusion of the CFA exam grading, Whitcomb tells several colleagues who are candidates in the CFA Program which question he graded. He also discusses the guideline answer and adds that few candidates scored well on the question.

> *Comment*: Whitcomb violated Standard VII(A) by breaking the Grader Agreement and disclosing information related to a specific question on the exam, which compromised the integrity of the exam process.

Standard VII(B): Responsibilities as a CFA Institute Member or CFA Candidate

Example 8 (Compromising CFA Institute Integrity as a Volunteer):

Jose Ramirez is an investor-relations consultant for several small companies that are seeking greater exposure to investors. He is also the program chair for the CFA Institute society in the city where he works. Ramirez schedules only companies that are his clients to make presentations to the society and excludes other companies.

> *Comment*: Ramirez, by using his volunteer position at CFA Institute to benefit himself and his clients, compromises the reputation and integrity of CFA Institute and thus violates Standard VII(A).

Example 9 (Compromising CFA Institute Integrity as a Volunteer):

Marguerite Warrenski is a member of the CFA Institute GIPS Executive Committee, which oversees the creation, implementation, and revision of the GIPS standards. As a member of the Executive Committee, she has advance knowledge of confidential information regarding the GIPS standards, including any new or revised standards the committee is considering. She tells her clients that her Executive Committee membership will allow her to better assist her clients in keeping up with changes to the Standards and facilitating their compliance with the changes.

> *Comment*: Warrenski is using her association with the GIPS Executive Committee to promote her firm's services to clients and potential clients. In defining her volunteer position at CFA Institute as a strategic business advantage over competing firms and implying to clients that she would use confidential information to further their interests, Warrenski is compromising the reputation and integrity of CFA Institute and thus violating Standard VII(A). She may factually state her involvement with the Executive Committee but cannot infer any special advantage to her clients from such participation.

STANDARD VII(B): RESPONSIBILITIES AS A CFA INSTITUTE MEMBER OR CFA CANDIDATE - REFERENCE TO CFA INSTITUTE, THE CFA DESIGNATION, AND THE CFA PROGRAM

62

☐ | demonstrate a thorough knowledge of the CFA Institute Code of Ethics and Standards of Professional Conduct by applying the Code and Standards to specific situations

> When referring to CFA Institute, CFA Institute membership, the CFA designation, or candidacy in the CFA Program, Members and Candidates must not misrepresent or exaggerate the meaning or implications of membership in CFA Institute, holding the CFA designation, or candidacy in the CFA Program.

Guidance

Highlights:

- *CFA Institute Membership*
- *Using the CFA Designation*
- *Referring to Candidacy in the CFA Program*

Standard VII(B) is intended to prevent promotional efforts that make promises or guarantees that are tied to the CFA designation. Individuals must not exaggerate the meaning or implications of membership in CFA Institute, holding the CFA designation, or candidacy in the CFA Program.

Standard VII(B) is not intended to prohibit factual statements related to the positive benefit of earning the CFA designation. However, statements referring to CFA Institute, the CFA designation, or the CFA Program that overstate the competency of an individual or imply, either directly or indirectly, that superior performance can be expected from someone with the CFA designation are not allowed under the standard.

Statements that highlight or emphasize the commitment of CFA Institute members, CFA charterholders, and CFA candidates to ethical and professional conduct or mention the thoroughness and rigor of the CFA Program are appropriate. Members and candidates may make claims about the relative merits of CFA Institute, the CFA Program, or the Code and Standards as long as those statements are implicitly or explicitly stated as the opinion of the speaker. Statements that do not express opinions have to be supported by facts.

Standard VII(B) applies to any form of communication, including but not limited to communications made in electronic or written form (such as on firm letterhead, business cards, professional biographies, directory listings, printed advertising, firm brochures, or personal resumes) and oral statements made to the public, clients, or prospects.

CFA Institute Membership

The term "CFA Institute member" refers to "regular" and "affiliate" members of CFA Institute who have met the membership requirements as defined in the CFA Institute Bylaws. Once accepted as a CFA Institute member, the member must satisfy the following requirements to maintain his or her status:

- remit annually to CFA Institute a completed Professional Conduct Statement, which renews the commitment to abide by the requirements of the Code and Standards and the CFA Institute Professional Conduct Program, and

- pay applicable CFA Institute membership dues on an annual basis.

If a CFA Institute member fails to meet any of these requirements, the individual is no longer considered an active member. Until membership is reactivated, individuals must not present themselves to others as active members. They may state, however, that they were CFA Institute members in the past or refer to the years when their membership was active.

Using the CFA Designation

Those who have earned the right to use the Chartered Financial Analyst designation are encouraged to do so but only in a manner that does not misrepresent or exaggerate the meaning or implications of the designation. The use of the designation may be accompanied by an accurate explanation of the requirements that have been met to earn the right to use the designation.

Standard VII(B): Responsibilities as a CFA Institute Member or CFA Candidate

"CFA charterholders" are those individuals who have earned the right to use the CFA designation granted by CFA Institute. These people have satisfied certain requirements, including completion of the CFA Program and required years of acceptable work experience. Once granted the right to use the designation, individuals must also satisfy the CFA Institute membership requirements (see above) to maintain their right to use the designation.

If a CFA charterholder fails to meet any of the membership requirements, he or she forfeits the right to use the CFA designation. Until membership is reactivated, individuals must not present themselves to others as CFA charterholders. They may state, however, that they were charterholders in the past.

Given the growing popularity of social media, where individuals may anonymously express their opinions, pseudonyms or online profile names created to hide a member's identity should not be tagged with the CFA designation.

Use of the CFA designation by a CFA charterholder is governed by the terms and conditions of the annual Professional Conduct Statement Agreement, entered into between CFA Institute and its membership prior to commencement of use of the CFA designation and reaffirmed annually.

Referring to Candidacy in the CFA Program

Candidates in the CFA Program may refer to their participation in the CFA Program, but such references must clearly state that an individual is a *candidate* in the CFA Program and must not imply that the candidate has achieved any type of partial designation. A person is a candidate in the CFA Program if

- the person's application for registration in the CFA Program has been accepted by CFA Institute, as evidenced by issuance of a notice of acceptance, and the person is enrolled to sit for a specified examination or
- the registered person has sat for a specified examination but exam results have not yet been received.

If an individual is registered for the CFA Program but declines to sit for an exam or otherwise does not meet the definition of a candidate as described in the CFA Institute Bylaws, then that individual is no longer considered an active candidate. Once the person is enrolled to sit for a future examination, his or her CFA Program candidacy resumes.

CFA Program candidates must never state or imply that they have a partial designation as a result of passing one or more levels or cite an expected completion date of any level of the CFA Program. Final award of the charter is subject to meeting the CFA Program requirements and approval by the CFA Institute Board of Governors.

If a candidate passes each level of the exam in consecutive years and wants to state that he or she did so, that is not a violation of Standard VII(B) because it is a statement of fact. If the candidate then goes on to claim or imply superior ability by obtaining the designation in only three years, however, he or she is in violation of Standard VII(B).

Exhibit 3 provides examples of proper and improper references to the CFA designation.

Exhibit 3: Proper and Improper References to the CFA Designation

Proper References	Improper References
"Completion of the CFA Program has enhanced my portfolio management skills."	"CFA charterholders achieve better performance results."

Proper References	Improper References
"John Smith passed all three CFA Program examinations in three consecutive years."	"John Smith is among the elite, having passed all three CFA examinations in three consecutive attempts."
"The CFA designation is globally recognized and attests to a charterholder's success in a rigorous and comprehensive study program in the field of investment management and research analysis."	"As a CFA charterholder, I am the most qualified to manage client investments."
"The credibility that the CFA designation affords and the skills the CFA Program cultivates are key assets for my future career development."	"As a CFA charterholder, Jane White provides the best value in trade execution."
"I enrolled in the CFA Program to obtain the highest set of credentials in the global investment management industry."	"Enrolling as a candidate in the CFA Program ensures one of becoming better at valuing debt securities."
"I passed Level I of the CFA Program."	"CFA, Level II"
"I am a 2010 Level III candidate in the CFA Program."	"CFA, Expected 2011"
"I passed all three levels of the CFA Program and may be eligible for the CFA charter upon completion of the required work experience."	"CFA, Expected 2011" "John Smith, Charter Pending"

63

STANDARD VII(B): RECOMMENDED PROCEDURES

☐ demonstrate a thorough knowledge of the CFA Institute Code of Ethics and Standards of Professional Conduct by applying the Code and Standards to specific situations

Misuse of a member's CFA designation or CFA candidacy or improper reference to it is common by those in a member's or candidate's firm who do not possess knowledge of the requirements of Standard VII(B). As an appropriate step to reduce this risk, members and candidates should disseminate written information about Standard VII(B) and the accompanying guidance to their firm's legal, compliance, public relations, and marketing departments (see www.cfainstitute.org).

For materials that refer to employees' affiliation with CFA Institute, members and candidates should encourage their firms to create templates that are approved by a central authority (such as the compliance department) as being consistent with Standard VII(B). This practice promotes consistency and accuracy in the firm of references to CFA Institute membership, the CFA designation, and CFA candidacy.

STANDARD VII(B): APPLICATION OF THE STANDARD

64

☐ demonstrate a thorough knowledge of the CFA Institute Code of Ethics and Standards of Professional Conduct by applying the Code and Standards to specific situations

☐ recommend practices and procedures designed to prevent violations of the Code of Ethics and Standards of Professional Conduct

Example 1 (Passing Exams in Consecutive Years):

An advertisement for AZ Investment Advisors states that all the firm's principals are CFA charterholders and all passed the three examinations on their first attempt. The advertisement prominently links this fact to the notion that AZ's mutual funds have achieved superior performance.

> *Comment*: AZ may state that all principals passed the three examinations on the first try as long as this statement is true, but it must not be linked to performance or imply superior ability. Implying that (1) CFA charterholders achieve better investment results and (2) those who pass the exams on the first try may be more successful than those who do not violates Standard VII(B).

Example 2 (Right to Use CFA Designation):

Five years after receiving his CFA charter, Louis Vasseur resigns his position as an investment analyst and spends the next two years traveling abroad. Because he is not actively engaged in the investment profession, he does not file a completed Professional Conduct Statement with CFA Institute and does not pay his CFA Institute membership dues. At the conclusion of his travels, Vasseur becomes a self-employed analyst accepting assignments as an independent contractor. Without reinstating his CFA Institute membership by filing his Professional Conduct Statement and paying his dues, he prints business cards that display "CFA" after his name.

> *Comment*: Vasseur has violated Standard VII(B) because his right to use the CFA designation was suspended when he failed to file his Professional Conduct Statement and stopped paying dues. Therefore, he no longer is able to state or imply that he is an active CFA charterholder. When Vasseur files his Professional Conduct Statement, resumes paying CFA Institute dues to activate his membership, and completes the CFA Institute reinstatement procedures, he will be eligible to use the CFA designation.

Example 3 ("Retired" CFA Institute Membership Status):

After a 25-year career, James Simpson retires from his firm. Because he is not actively engaged in the investment profession, he does not file a completed Professional Conduct Statement with CFA Institute and does not pay his CFA Institute membership dues. Simpson designs a plain business card (without a corporate logo) to hand out to friends with his new contact details, and he continues to put "CFA" after his name.

Comment: Simpson has violated Standard VII(B). Because he failed to file his Professional Conduct Statement and ceased paying dues, his membership has been suspended and he has given up the right to use the CFA designation. CFA Institute has procedures, however, for reclassifying a member and charterholder as "retired" and reducing the annual dues. If he wants to obtain retired status, he needs to file the appropriate paperwork with CFA Institute. When Simpson receives his notification from CFA Institute that his membership has been reclassified as retired and he resumes paying reduced dues, his membership will be reactivated and his right to use the CFA designation will be reinstated.

Example 4 (Stating Facts about CFA Designation and Program):

Rhonda Reese has been a CFA charterholder since 2000. In a conversation with a friend who is considering enrolling in the CFA Program, she states that she has learned a great deal from the CFA Program and that many firms require their employees to be CFA charterholders. She would recommend the CFA Program to anyone pursuing a career in investment management.

Comment: Reese's comments comply with Standard VII(B). Her statements refer to facts: The CFA Program enhanced her knowledge, and many firms require the CFA designation for their investment professionals.

Example 5 (Order of Professional and Academic Designations):

Tatiana Prittima has earned both her CFA designation and a PhD in finance. She would like to cite both her accomplishments on her business card but is unsure of the proper method for doing so.

Comment: The order of designations cited on such items as resumes and business cards is a matter of personal preference. Prittima is free to cite the CFA designation either before or after citing her PhD. Multiple designations must be separated by a comma.

Example 6 (Use of Fictitious Name):

Barry Glass is the lead quantitative analyst at CityCenter Hedge Fund. Glass is responsible for the development, maintenance, and enhancement of the proprietary models the fund uses to manage its investors' assets. Glass reads several high-level mathematical publications and blogs to stay informed on current developments. One blog, run by Expert CFA, presents some intriguing research that may benefit one of CityCenter's current models. Glass is under pressure from firm executives to improve the model's predictive abilities, and he incorporates the factors discussed in the online research. The updated output recommends several new investments to the fund's portfolio managers.

Comment: "Expert CFA" has violated Standard VII(B) by using the CFA designation inappropriately. As with any research report, authorship of online comments must include the charterholder's full name along with any reference to the CFA designation.

See also Standard V(A), which Glass has violated for guidance on diligence and reasonable basis.

Practice Problems

389

PRACTICE PROBLEMS

1. Which of the following is a correct statement of a member's or candidate's duty under the Code and Standards?

   A. In the absence of specific applicable law or other regulatory requirements, the Code and Standards govern the member's or candidate's actions.

   B. A member or candidate is required to comply only with applicable local laws, rules, regulations, or customs, even though the Code and Standards may impose a higher degree of responsibility or a higher duty on the member or candidate.

   C. A member or candidate who trades securities in a securities market where no applicable local laws or stock exchange rules regulate the use of material nonpublic information may take investment action based on material nonpublic information.

2. An investment management firm has been hired by ETV Corporation to work on an additional public offering for the company. The firm's brokerage unit now has a "sell" recommendation on ETV, but the head of the investment banking department has asked the head of the brokerage unit to change the recommendation from "sell" to "buy." According to the Standards, the head of the brokerage unit would be permitted to:

   A. Increase the recommendation by no more than one increment (in this case, to a "hold" recommendation).

   B. Place the company on a restricted list and give only factual information about the company.

   C. Assign a new analyst to decide if the stock deserves a higher rating.

3. Ward is scheduled to visit the corporate headquarters of Evans Industries. Ward expects to use the information he obtains there to complete his research report on Evans stock. Ward learns that Evans plans to pay all of Ward's expenses for the trip, including costs of meals, hotel room, and air transportation. Which of the following actions would be the *best* course for Ward to take under the Code and Standards?

   A. Accept the expense-paid trip and write an objective report.

   B. Pay for all travel expenses, including costs of meals and incidental items.

   C. Accept the expense-paid trip but disclose the value of the services accepted in the report.

4. Long has been asked to be the keynote speaker at an upcoming investment conference. The event is being hosted by one of the third-party investment managers currently used by his pension fund. The manager offers to cover all conference and travel costs for Long and make the conference registrations free for three additional members of his investment management team. To ensure that the conference obtains the best speakers, the host firm has arranged for an exclusive golf outing for the day following the conference on a local championship-caliber

course. Which of the following is *least likely* to violate Standard I(B)?

A. Long may accept only the offer to have his conference-related expenses paid by the host firm.

B. Long may accept the offer to have his conference-related expenses paid and may attend the exclusive golf outing at the expense of the hosting firm.

C. Long may accept the entire package of incentives offered to speak at this conference.

The following information relates to questions 5-10

Adam Craw, CFA, is chief executive officer (CEO) of Crawfood, a European private equity firm specializing in food retailers. The retail food industry has been consolidating during the past two years as private equity funds have closed numerous deals and taken many companies private.

Crawfood recently hired Lillian Voser, a CFA Level II candidate, as a controller. On Voser's first day of work, the head of personnel informs her that by signing the employment contract, Voser agrees to comply with the company's code of ethics and compliance manual. She hands Voser copies of the code and compliance manual without further comment. Voser spends the next hour reading both documents. An excerpt from the compliance manual appears in Exhibit 1.

Exhibit 1: Crawfood Company Compliance Manual Excerpts

1. Employees must not accept gifts, benefits, compensation, or consideration that competes with, or might reasonably be expected to create a conflict of interest with their employer's interest unless they obtain written consent from all parties involved.

2. Officers have responsibility for ensuring that their direct reports—that is, employees whom they directly supervise—adhere to applicable laws, rules, and regulations.

3. Employees in possession of material nonpublic information should make reasonable efforts to achieve public dissemination of the information if such actions would not breach a duty.

4. Employees shall not trade or cause others to trade in securities of food retailers that may be potential takeover targets of their employer.

When she enters her new office that afternoon, Voser finds a large gift basket sent by her sister. The card reads "Congratulations on your new position." The basket is filled with expensive high-quality food items from Greenhornfood—a local small, publicly-traded food retailer, which produces many delicatessen products under its own brand name.

During the next two weeks, Voser meets with all of Crawfood's upper management, including the CEO. In his office, Craw praises Voser's efforts to complete the CFA program. "The program is demanding, but it is worthwhile." Craw then explains his investment strategy for choosing Crawfood's acquisition targets. He points to a large map on the wall with multi-colored pins marking Crawfood's previous takeovers. The map shows acquisitions in all the major cities of Germany with one exception—the home of Crawfood headquarters. Craw remarks, "We

Practice Problems

391

are currently in talks for another purchase. Confidentiality prohibits me from discussing it any further, but you will hear more about it soon."

Introduced to Greenhornfood by her sister, Voser quickly becomes a loyal customer. She considers it the best food retailer in the vicinity and she frequently purchases its products.

The following week, the local newspaper features an article about Greenhornfood and its young founders. The article describes the company's loyal and growing customer base as well as its poor quarterly financial results. Voser notes that the stock has steadily declined during the past twelve months. She concludes that the company has an inexperienced management team, but its popular product line and loyal customer base make the company a potential acquisition target. Voser calls her sister and recommends that she purchase Greenhornfood shares because "it would be an attractive acquisition for a larger company." Based on Voser's recommendation, her sister buys €3,000 worth of shares.

During the following two weeks the stock price of Greenhornfood continues to decline. Voser's sister is uncertain of what she should do with her position. She seeks Voser's advice. Voser recommends that her sister wait another few days before making her decision and promises to analyze the situation in the meantime.

While walking by Craw's office the following day, Voser sees a document with Greenhornfood's distinctive logo and overhears the company's name through an open office door. That evening, Voser tells her sister, "with the price decline, the stock is even more attractive." She recommends that her sister increase her position. Based on her recommendation her sister buys an additional €3,000 worth of Greenhornfood shares.

One month later, Crawfood publicly announces the acquisition of Greenhornfood Company at a 20% premium to the previous day's closing price. Following the announcement, Voser's sister boasts about Voser's excellent recommendation and timing to her broker.

Regulatory authorities initiate an investigation into suspicious trading in Greenhornfood shares and options preceding the formal announcement of the acquisition. Craw receives a letter from regulatory authorities stating that he is the subject of a formal investigation into his professional conduct surrounding the acquisition. He learns from the compliance officer that Voser is also under investigation. The compliance officer provides no details and out of respect for Voser's privacy, Craw makes no inquiries.

The situation remains unchanged and the matter is still pending with regulatory authorities several months later when Craw receives his annual Professional Conduct Statement (PCS) from CFA Institute. He reviews the text asking "In the last two years, have you been . . . the subject of . . . any investigation . . . in which your professional conduct, in either a direct or supervisory capacity, was at issue?"

5. Are Excerpts 2 and 3 of Crawfood's compliance procedures consistent with the CFA Institute Standards of Professional Conduct?

   A. Yes.

   B. No, because Excerpt 2 applies only to officers and their direct reports.

   C. No, because Excerpt 3 does not require employees to achieve public dissemination.

6. According to the CFA Institute Standards, must Voser obtain permission from her supervisor before accepting the Greenhornfood gift basket?

   A. No.

   B. Yes, because the value of the basket is higher than €50.

C. Yes, because consent is required by the company's compliance procedures.

7. When making her initial recommendation to purchase Greenhornfood company shares, Voser *most likely* violates the Standard relating to:

   A. loyalty to employer.

   B. integrity of capital markets.

   C. diligence and reasonable basis.

8. When recommending the purchase of additional Greenhornfood company shares, Voser *least likely* violates the Standard relating to:

   A. loyalty to employer.

   B. integrity of capital markets.

   C. diligence and reasonable basis.

9. Does Craw violate any CFA Institute Standards?

   A. No.

   B. Yes, because he passes material nonpublic information to Voser.

   C. Yes, because he does not make reasonable efforts to prevent violations of applicable law.

10. According to the CFA Standards, Craw must disclose to CFA Institute the investigation into:

    A. his conduct.

    B. Voser's conduct.

    C. neither his conduct nor Voser's conduct.

11. Grey recommends the purchase of a mutual fund that invests solely in long-term US Treasury bonds. He makes the following statements to his clients:

    i. "The payment of the bonds is guaranteed by the US government; therefore, the default risk of the bonds is virtually zero."

    ii. "If you invest in the mutual fund, you will earn a 10% rate of return each year for the next several years based on historical performance of the market."

    Did Grey's statements violate the CFA Institute Code and Standards?

    A. Neither statement violated the Code and Standards.

    B. Only statement I violated the Code and Standards.

    C. Only statement II violated the Code and Standards.

12. Michelieu tells a prospective client, "I may not have a long-term track record yet, but I'm sure that you'll be very pleased with my recommendations and service. In the three years that I've been in the business, my equity-oriented clients have averaged a total return of more than 26% a year." The statement is true, but Michelieu only has a few clients, and one of his clients took a large position in a

Practice Problems

penny stock (against Michelieu's advice) and realized a huge gain. This large return caused the average of all of Michelieu's clients to exceed 26% a year. Without this one investment, the average gain would have been 8% a year. Has Michelieu violated the Standards?

A. No, because Michelieu is not promising that he can earn a 26% return in the future.

B. No, because the statement is a true and accurate description of Michelieu's track record.

C. Yes, because the statement misrepresents Michelieu's track record.

13. Anderb, a portfolio manager for XYZ Investment Management Company—a registered investment organization that advises investment firms and private accounts—was promoted to that position three years ago. Bates, her supervisor, is responsible for reviewing Anderb's portfolio account transactions and her required monthly reports of personal stock transactions. Anderb has been using Jonelli, a broker, almost exclusively for brokerage transactions for the portfolio account. For securities in which Jonelli's firm makes a market, Jonelli has been giving Anderb lower prices for personal purchases and higher prices for personal sales than Jonelli gives to Anderb's portfolio accounts and other investors. Anderb has been filing monthly reports with Bates only for those months in which she has no personal transactions, which is about every fourth month. Which of the following is *most likely* to be a violation of the Code and Standards?

A. Anderb failed to disclose to her employer her personal transactions.

B. Anderb owned the same securities as those of her clients.

C. Bates allowed Anderb to use Jonelli as her broker for personal trades.

14. The mosaic theory holds that an analyst:

A. Violates the Code and Standards if the analyst fails to have knowledge of and comply with applicable laws.

B. Can use material public information and nonmaterial nonpublic information in the analyst's analysis.

C. Should use all available and relevant information in support of an investment recommendation.

15. During a round of golf, Rodriguez, chief financial officer of Mega Retail, mentions to Hart, a local investment adviser and long-time personal friend, that Mega is having an exceptional sales quarter. Rodriguez expects the results to be almost 10% above the current estimates. The next day, Hart initiates the purchase of a large stake in the local exchange-traded retail fund for her personal account.

A. Hart violated the Code and Standards by investing in the exchange-traded fund that included Mega Retail.

B. Hart did not violate the Code and Standards because she did not invest directly in securities of Mega Retail.

C. Rodriguez did not violate the Code and Standards because the comments made to Hart were not intended to solicit an investment in Mega Retail.

The following information relates to questions 16-21

Anne Boswin, CFA, is a senior fixed-income analyst at Greenfield Financial Corporation. Boswin develops financial models for predicting changes in bond prices. On the premise that bonds of firms targeted for leveraged buyouts (LBOs) often decline in value, Boswin develops a model to predict which firms are likely to be subject to LBOs.

Boswin works closely with another analyst, Robert Acertado, CFA. Acertado uses Boswin's model frequently to identify potential LBO targets for further research. Using the model and his extensive research skills, Acertado makes timely investment recommendations and develops a strong track record.

Based on this record, Acertado receives an employment offer from the asset management division of Smith & Garner Investments, Inc., a diversified financial services firm. With Boswin's consent, Acertado downloads the model before leaving Greenfield.

At Smith & Garner, Acertado presents the idea of predicting LBO targets as a way to identify bonds that might decline in value and thus be good sell recommendations. After Acertado walks his boss through the model, the supervisor comments, "I like your idea and your model, Robert. I can see that we made the right decision in hiring you."

Because Smith & Garner has both an Investment Banking (IB) and Asset Management (AM) division, Acertado's supervisor reminds him that he should not attempt to contact or engage in conversation with anyone from the Investment Banking division. The supervisor also directs him to eat in the East end of the company cafeteria. "The West end is reserved for the IB folks, and you may laugh at this, but we actually put up a wall between the two ends. If anyone were to accuse us of not having a firewall, we could actually point to it!" Robert's supervisor also tells him, "There should be absolutely no conversation about divisional business while in the hall and elevator that serves as a common access to the cafeteria for both divisions. We are very strict about this."

The following week, Acertado is riding alone in the elevator when it stops on an IB floor. As the doors begin to slide open, Acertado hears a voice whispering, "I am so pleased that we were able to put the financing together for Country Industries. I was concerned because the leverage will go to 80%—higher than our typical deal." As soon as the doors open enough to reveal that the elevator is occupied, all conversation stops.

Late that afternoon, Acertado uses the LBO model to measure the probability of Country Industries receiving an LBO offer. According to the model, the probability is 62%—slightly more than the 60% Acertado generally requires before conducting additional research. It is late in the afternoon and Acertado has little time to research the matter fully before the end of the trading day. He checks his inputs to the model. In the interest of time, Acertado immediately recommends selling Country Industries' senior bonds held in any long-only accounts. He also recommends establishing positions in derivatives contracts that will benefit from a decline in the value of Country Industries' bonds.

The next morning, after the firm has established the derivatives positions he recommended, Acertado calls Boswin. Knowing that his former associate will be preparing Greenfield's monthly newsletter, he tells her, "I ran Country Industries through your model and I think it is likely that they will receive an LBO offer." Acertado explains some of the inputs he used in the model. At the conclusion of the conversation Boswin responds, "You may be right. Country Industries sounds like a possible LBO candidate, and thus, a sell rating on their senior bonds would be in order. If I'm lucky, I can finish researching the issue in time to include the

Practice Problems

recommendation in the upcoming newsletter. Thanks. It was good talking with you, Robert."

After the conversation with Acertado, Boswin quickly runs Country Industries through the model. Based on her inputs, the model calculates that the probability of an LBO is 40%—not enough, in Boswin's opinion, to justify further research. She wonders if there is a discrepancy between her inputs and Acertado's. Pressed for time, Boswin resumes her work on the upcoming newsletter rather than investigating the matter.

Acertado soon begins searching the internet for information on companies that the model predicts have more than a 60% probability of an LBO offer. He scours blogs and company websites looking for signs of a potential offer. He uses evidence of rumored offers in developing sell recommendations on various corporations' bonds.

16. When downloading the model from Greenfield Financial Corporation, does Acertado violate any CFA Institute Standards of Practice and Professional Conduct?

   A. No.

   B. Yes, because he does not have written permission from Boswin.

   C. Yes, because he does not have permission from Greenfield Financial Corporation.

17. When using the model at Smith & Garner, Acertado is *least likely* to violate the Standard relating to:

   A. misrepresentation.

   B. loyalty to employer.

   C. material nonpublic information.

18. When making the recommendation regarding Country Industries, does Acertado violate any CFA Institute Standards?

   A. No.

   B. Yes, relating to diligence and reasonable basis.

   C. Yes, relating to material nonpublic information.

19. In his phone conversation with Boswin, Acertado *least likely* violates the CFA Institute Standard relating to:

   A. suitability.

   B. integrity of capital markets.

   C. preservation of confidentiality.

20. When analyzing the probability of an LBO of Country Industries, does Boswin violate any CFA Institute Standards?

   A. No.

   B. Yes, relating to independence and objectivity.

   C. Yes, relating to diligence and reasonable basis.

21. When searching blogs, does Acertado violate any CFA Institute Standards?

    A. No.

    B. Yes, because he misuses company resources.

    C. Yes, because he seeks inside information on the blogs.

22. An investment banking department of a brokerage firm often receives material nonpublic information that could have considerable value if used in advising the firm's brokerage clients. In order to conform to the Code and Standards, which one of the following is the best policy for the brokerage firm?

    A. Permanently prohibit both "buy" and "sell" recommendations of the stocks of clients of the investment banking department.

    B. Establish physical and informational barriers within the firm to prevent the exchange of information between the investment banking and brokerage operations.

    C. Monitor the exchange of information between the investment banking department and the brokerage operation.

23. Andrews, a private wealth manager, is conducting interviews for a new research analyst for his firm. One of the candidates is Wright, an analyst with a local investment bank. During the interview, while Wright is describing his analytical skills, he mentions a current merger in which his firm is acting as the adviser. Andrews has heard rumors of a possible merger between the two companies, but no releases have been made by the companies concerned. Which of the following actions by Andrews is *least likely* a violation of the Code and Standards?

    A. Waiting until the next day before trading on the information to allow time for it to become public.

    B. Notifying all investment managers in his firm of the new information so none of their clients are disadvantaged.

    C. Placing the securities mentioned as part of the merger on the firm's restricted trading list.

24. Pietro, president of Local Bank, has hired the bank's market maker, Vogt, to seek a merger partner. Local is currently listed on a stock exchange and has not reported that it is seeking strategic alternatives. Vogt has discussed the possibility of a merger with several firms, but they have all decided to wait until after the next period's financial data are available. The potential buyers believe the results will be worse than the results of prior periods and will allow them to pay less for Local Bank.

    Pietro wants to increase the likelihood of structuring a merger deal quickly. Which of the following actions would *most likely* be a violation of the Code and Standards?

    A. Pietro could instruct Local Bank to issue a press release announcing that it has retained Vogt to find a merger partner.

    B. Pietro could place a buy order for 2,000 shares (or four times the average weekly volume) through Vogt for his personal account.

Practice Problems 397

    C. After confirming with Local's chief financial officer, Pietro could instruct Local to issue a press release reaffirming the firm's prior announced earnings guidance for the full fiscal year.

25. Which statement about a manager's use of client brokerage commissions violates the Code and Standards?

    A. A client may direct a manager to use that client's brokerage commissions to purchase goods and services for that client.

    B. Client brokerage commissions should be used to benefit the client and should be commensurate with the value of the brokerage and research services received.

    C. Client brokerage commissions may be directed to pay for the investment manager's operating expenses.

26. One of the discretionary accounts managed by Farnsworth is the Jones Corporation employee profit-sharing plan. Jones, the company president, recently asked Farnsworth to vote the shares in the profit-sharing plan in favor of the slate of directors nominated by Jones Corporation and against the directors sponsored by a dissident stockholder group. Farnsworth does not want to lose this account because he directs all the account's trades to a brokerage firm that provides Farnsworth with useful information about tax-free investments. Although this information is not of value in managing the Jones Corporation account, it does help in managing several other accounts. The brokerage firm providing this information also offers the lowest commissions for trades and provides best execution. Farnsworth investigates the director issue, concludes that the management-nominated slate is better for the long-run performance of the company than the dissident group's slate, and votes accordingly. Farnsworth:

    A. Violated the Standards in voting the shares in the manner requested by Jones but not in directing trades to the brokerage firm.

    B. Did not violate the Standards in voting the shares in the manner requested by Jones or in directing trades to the brokerage firm.

    C. Violated the Standards in directing trades to the brokerage firm but not in voting the shares as requested by Jones.

27. Stewart has been hired by Goodner Industries, Inc., to manage its pension fund. Stewart's duty of loyalty, prudence, and care is owed to:

    A. The management of Goodner.

    B. The participants and beneficiaries of Goodner's pension plan.

    C. The shareholders of Goodner.

28. Carter works for Invest Today, a local asset management firm. A broker that provides Carter with proprietary research through client brokerage arrangements is offering a new trading service. The broker is offering low-fee, execution-only trades to complement its traditional full-service, execution-and-research trades. To entice Carter and other asset managers to send additional business its way, the broker will apply the commissions paid on the new service toward satisfying the brokerage commitment of the prior full-service arrangements. Carter has always been satisfied with the execution provided on the full-service trades, and the new low-fee trades are comparable to the fees of other brokers currently used for the

accounts that prohibit soft dollar arrangements.

A. Carter can trade for his accounts that prohibit soft dollar arrangements under the new low-fee trading scheme.

B. Carter cannot use the new trading scheme because the commissions are prohibited by the soft dollar restrictions of the accounts.

C. Carter should trade only through the new low-fee scheme and should increase his trading volume to meet his required commission commitment.

29. Stafford is a portfolio manager for a specialized real estate mutual fund. Her firm clearly describes in the fund's prospectus its soft dollar policies. Stafford decides that entering the CFA Program will enhance her investment decision-making skill and decides to use the fund's soft dollar account to pay the registration and exam fees for the CFA Program. Which of the following statements is *most likely* correct?

A. Stafford did not violate the Code and Standards because the prospectus informed investors of the fund's soft dollar policies.

B. Stafford violated the Code and Standards because improving her investment skills is not a reasonable use of the soft dollar account.

C. Stafford violated the Code and Standards because the CFA Program does not meet the definition of research allowed to be purchased with brokerage commissions.

The following information relates to questions 30-35

Samuel Telline, CFA, is a portfolio manager at Aiklin Investments with discretionary authority over all of his accounts. One of his clients, Alan Caper, Chief Executive Officer (CEO) of Ellipse Manufacturing, invites Telline to lunch.

At the restaurant, the CEO reveals the reason for the lunch. "As you know Reinhold Partners has made an unsolicited cash offer for all outstanding shares of Ellipse Manufacturing. Reinhold has made it clear that I will not be CEO if they are successful. I can assure you that our shareholders will be better off in the long term if I'm in charge." Caper then shows Telline his projections for a new plan designed to boost both sales and operating margins.

"I know that your firm is the trustee for our firm's Employee Stock Ownership Plan (ESOP). I hope that the trustee will vote in the best interest of our shareholders—and that would be a vote against the takeover offer."

After looking through Caper's business plans, Telline says, "This plan looks good. I will recommend that the trustee vote against the offer."

Caper responds, "I remember my friend Karen Leighton telling me that the Leighton Family's Trust is managed by your firm. Perhaps the trustee could vote those shares against the acquisition as well. Karen Leighton is a close friend. I am sure that she would agree."

Telline responds, "The Family Trust is no longer managed by Aiklin." He adds, "I understand that the Trust is very conservatively managed. I doubt it that it would have holdings in Ellipse Manufacturing." Telline does not mention that although the Family Trust has changed investment managers, Karen Leighton remains an important client at Aiklin with significant personal holdings in Ellipse.

Practice Problems

399

After lunch, Telline meets with Sydney Brown, CFA, trustee of the Ellipse ESOP. He shows her Caper's plan for improvements. "I think the plan is a good one and Caper is one of the firm's most profitable accounts. We don't want to lose him." Brown agrees to analyze the plan. After thoroughly analyzing both the plan and the takeover offer, Brown concludes that the takeover offer is best for the shareholders in the ESOP and votes the plan's shares in favor of the takeover offer.

A few months later the acquisition of Ellipse by Reinhold Partners is completed. Caper again meets Telline for lunch. "I received a generous severance package and I'm counting on you to manage my money well for me. While we are on the subject, I would like to be more aggressive with my portfolio. With my severance package, I can take additional risk." Telline and Caper discuss his current financial situation, risk tolerance, and financial objectives throughout lunch. Telline agrees to adjust Caper's investment policy statement (IPS) to reflect his greater appetite for risk and his increased wealth.

Back at the office, Telline realizes that with the severance package, Caper is now his wealthiest client. He also realizes that Caper's increased appetite for risk gives him a risk profile similar to that of another client. He pulls a copy of the other client's investment policy statement (IPS) and reviews it quickly before realizing that the two clients have very different tax situations. Telline quickly revises Caper's IPS to reflect the changes in his financial situation. He uses the other client's IPS as a reference when revising the section relating to Caper's risk tolerance. He then files the revised IPS in Caper's file.

The following week, an Aiklin analyst issues a buy recommendation on a small technology company with a promising software product. Telline reads the report carefully and concludes it would be suitable under Caper's new IPS. Telline places an order for 10,000 shares in Caper's account and then calls Caper to discuss the stock in more detail. Telline does not purchase the stock for any other clients. Although the one client has the same risk profile as Caper, that client does not have cash available in his account and Telline determines that selling existing holdings does not make sense.

In a subsequent telephone conversation, Caper expresses his lingering anger over the takeover. "You didn't do enough to persuade Aiklin's clients to vote against the takeover. Maybe I should look for an investment manager who is more loyal." Telline tries to calm Caper but is unsuccessful. In an attempt to change the topic of conversation, Telline states, "The firm was just notified of our allocation of a long-awaited IPO. Your account should receive a significant allocation. I would hate to see you lose out by moving your account." Caper seems mollified and concludes the phone call, "I look forward to a long-term relationship with you and your firm."

Aiklin distributes a copy of its firm policies regarding IPO allocations to all clients annually. According to the policy, Aiklin allocates IPO shares to each investment manager and each manager has responsibility for allocating shares to accounts for which the IPO is suitable. The statement also discloses that Aiklin offers different levels of service for different fees.

After carefully reviewing the proposed IPO and his client accounts, Telline determines that the IPO is suitable for 11 clients including Caper. Because the deal is oversubscribed, he receives only half of the shares he expected. Telline directs 50% of his allocation to Caper's account and divides the remaining 50% between the other ten accounts, each with a value equal to half of Caper's account.

30. When discussing the Leighton Family Trust, does Telline violate any CFA Institute Standards of Professional Conduct?

   A. No.

   B. Yes, relating to duties to clients.

C. Yes, relating to misrepresentation.

31. When deciding how to vote the ESOP shares, does Brown violate any CFA Institute Standards?

    A. No.

    B. Yes, relating to loyalty, prudence, and care.

    C. Yes, relating to diligence and reasonable basis.

32. The Standard *least likely* to provide guidance for Telline when working with the clients' investment policy statements would be the Standard relating to:

    A. suitability.

    B. fair dealing.

    C. loyalty, prudence, and care.

33. Does Telline violate any CFA Institute Standards when he places the buy order for shares in the technology company for Caper's account?

    A. No.

    B. Yes, relating to fair dealing.

    C. Yes, relating to diligence and reasonable basis.

34. Is Aiklin's policy with respect to IPO allocations consistent with required and recommended CFA Institute Standards?

    A. Yes.

    B. No, because the IPO policy disadvantages certain clients.

    C. No, because the different levels of service disadvantage certain clients.

35. Does Telline violate any CFA Institute Standards in his allocation of IPO shares to Caper's account?

    A. No.

    B. Yes, because the IPO is not suitable for Caper.

    C. Yes, because he does not treat all his clients fairly.

36. Smith, a research analyst with a brokerage firm, decides to change his recommendation for the common stock of Green Company, Inc., from a "buy" to a "sell." He mails this change in investment advice to all the firm's clients on Wednesday. The day after the mailing, a client calls with a buy order for 500 shares of Green Company. In this circumstance, Smith should:

    A. Accept the order.

    B. Advise the customer of the change in recommendation before accepting the order.

    C. Not accept the order because it is contrary to the firm's recommendation.

37. Which one of the following actions will help to ensure the fair treatment of bro-

Practice Problems

kerage firm clients when a new investment recommendation is made?

    A. Informing all people in the firm in advance that a recommendation is to be disseminated.

    B. Distributing recommendations to institutional clients prior to individual accounts.

    C. Minimizing the time between the decision and the dissemination of a recommendation.

38. Brown works for an investment counseling firm. Green, a new client of the firm, is meeting with Brown for the first time. Green used another counseling firm for financial advice for years, but she has switched her account to Brown's firm. After spending a few minutes getting acquainted, Brown explains to Green that she has discovered a highly undervalued stock that offers large potential gains. She recommends that Green purchase the stock. Brown has committed a violation of the Standards. What should she have done differently?

    A. Brown should have determined Green's needs, objectives, and tolerance for risk before making a recommendation of any type of security.

    B. Brown should have thoroughly explained the characteristics of the company to Green, including the characteristics of the industry in which the company operates.

    C. Brown should have explained her qualifications, including her education, training, and experience and the meaning of the CFA designation.

39. ABC Investment Management acquires a new, very large account with two concentrated positions. The firm's current policy is to add new accounts for the purpose of performance calculation after the first full month of management. Cupp is responsible for calculating the firm's performance returns. Before the end of the initial month, Cupp notices that one of the significant holdings of the new accounts is acquired by another company, causing the value of the investment to double. Because of this holding, Cupp decides to account for the new portfolio as of the date of transfer, thereby allowing ABC Investment to reap the positive impact of that month's portfolio return.

    A. Cupp did not violate the Code and Standards because the GIPS standards allow composites to be updated on the date of large external cash flows.

    B. Cupp did not violate the Code and Standards because companies are allowed to determine when to incorporate new accounts into their composite calculation.

    C. Cupp violated the Code and Standards because the inclusion of the new account produces an inaccurate calculation of the monthly results according to the firm's stated policies.

40. Paper was recently terminated as one of a team of five managers of an equity fund. The fund had two value-focused managers and terminated one of them to reduce costs. In a letter sent to prospective employers, Paper presents, with written permission of the firm, the performance history of the fund to demonstrate his past success.

    A. Paper did not violate the Code and Standards.

B. Paper violated the Code and Standards by claiming the performance of the entire fund as his own.

C. Paper violated the Code and Standards by including the historical results of his prior employer.

The following information relates to questions 41-45

Erik Brecksen, CFA, a portfolio manager at Apfelbaum Kapital, recently recruited Hans Grohl, a CFA candidate and recent MBA graduate from a top university with excellent quantitative analysis skills. Apfelbaum Kapital stresses "top-down" fundamental analysis and uses a team approach to investment management. The firm's investment professionals, all of whom are CFA charterholders or candidates, attend weekly investment committee meetings. At the meetings, analysts responsible for different industrial sectors present their research and recommendations. Following each presentation, the investment committee, consisting of senior portfolio managers, questions the analyst about the recommendation. If the majority of the committee agrees with the recommendation, the recommendation is approved and the stock is placed on a restricted list while the firm executes the necessary trades.

Apfelbaum considers its research proprietary. It is intended for the sole use of its investment professionals and is not distributed outside the firm. The names of all the investment personnel associated with the sector or investment class are listed on each research report regardless of their actual level of contribution to the report.

On Grohl's first day of work, Brecksen assigns him responsibility for a company that Brecksen covered previously. He provides Grohl with his past research including all of his files and reports. Brecksen instructs Grohl to report back when he has finished his research and is ready to submit his own research report on the company.

Grohl reads Brecksen's old reports before studying the financial statements of the company and its competitors. Taking advantage of his quantitative analysis skills, Grohl then conducts a detailed multi-factor analysis. Afterward, he produces a written buy recommendation using Brecksen's old research reports as a guide for format and submits a draft to Brecksen for review.

Brecksen reviews the work and indicates that he is not familiar with multi-factor analysis. He tells Grohl that he agrees with the buy recommendation, but instructs Grohl to omit the multi-factor analysis from the report. Grohl attempts to defend his research methodology, but is interrupted when Brecksen accepts a phone call. Grohl follows Brecksen's instructions and removes all mention of the multi-factor analysis from the final report. Brecksen presents the completed report at the weekly meeting with both his and Grohl's names listed on the document. After Brecksen's initial presentation, the committee turns to Grohl and asks about his research. Grohl takes the opportunity to mention the multi-factor analysis. Satisfied, the committee votes in favor of the recommendation and congratulates Grohl on his work.

Ottie Zardt, CFA, has worked as a real estate analyst for Apfelbaum for the past 18 months. A new independent rating service has determined that Zardt's recommendations have resulted in an excess return of 12% versus the industry's return of 2.7% for the past twelve months. After learning about the rating service, Zardt immediately updates the promotional material he is preparing for distribution at an upcoming industry conference. He includes a reference to the rating

Practice Problems

403

service and quotes its returns results and other information. Before distributing the material at the conference, he adds a footnote stating "Past performance is no guarantee of future success."

41. When preparing the initial draft for Brecksen's review, does Grohl violate any CFA Standards?

    A. No.

    B. Yes, because he used Brecksen's research reports without permission.

    C. Yes, because he did not use reasonable judgment in identifying which factors were important to the analysis.

42. When instructing Grohl to eliminate the multi-factor analysis from the research report, does Brecksen violate any CFA Standards?

    A. No.

    B. Yes, relating to record retention.

    C. Yes, relating to diligence and reasonable basis.

43. When removing the multi-factor analysis from his research report, does Grohl violate any CFA Standards?

    A. No.

    B. Yes, because he no longer has a reasonable basis for his recommendation.

    C. Yes, because he is required to make full and fair disclosure of all relevant information.

44. When listing their names on the research report, do Brecksen and Grohl violate any CFA Standards?

    A. No.

    B. Yes, because Brecksen misrepresents his authorship.

    C. Yes, because Grohl should dissociate from the report.

45. When distributing the material at the industry conference, does Zardt violate any CFA Standards?

    A. No.

    B. Yes, because Zardt does not verify the accuracy of the information.

    C. Yes, because analysts cannot claim performance or promote the accuracy of their recommendations.

46. Bronson provides investment advice to the board of trustees of a private university endowment fund. The trustees have provided Bronson with the fund's financial information, including planned expenditures. Bronson receives a phone call on Friday afternoon from Murdock, a prominent alumnus, requesting that Bronson fax him comprehensive financial information about the fund. According to Murdock, he has a potential contributor but needs the information that day to close the deal and cannot contact any of the trustees. Based on the CFA Institute

Standards, Bronson should:

A. Send Murdock the information because disclosure would benefit the client.

B. Not send Murdock the information to preserve confidentiality.

C. Send Murdock the information, provided Bronson promptly notifies the trustees.

47. Townsend was recently appointed to the board of directors of a youth golf program that is the local chapter of a national not-for-profit organization. The program is beginning a new fund-raising campaign to expand the number of annual scholarships it provides. Townsend believes many of her clients make annual donations to charity. The next week in her regular newsletter to all clients, she includes a small section discussing the fund-raising campaign and her position on the organization's board.

A. Townsend did not violate the Code and Standards.

B. Townsend violated the Code and Standards by soliciting donations from her clients through the newsletter.

C. Townsend violated the Code and Standards by not getting approval of the organization before soliciting her clients.

48. Which of the following statements is *correct* under the Code and Standards?

A. CFA Institute members and candidates are prohibited from undertaking independent practice in competition with their employer.

B. Written consent from the employer is necessary to permit independent practice that could result in compensation or other benefits in competition with a member's or candidate's employer.

C. Members and candidates are prohibited from making arrangements or preparations to go into a competitive business before terminating their relationship with their employer.

49. A former hedge fund manager, Jackman, has decided to launch a new private wealth management firm. From his prior experiences, he believes the new firm needs to achieve US$1 million in assets under management in the first year. Jackman offers a $10,000 incentive to any adviser who joins his firm with the minimum of $200,000 in committed investments. Jackman places notice of the opening on several industry web portals and career search sites. Which of the following is *correct* according to the Code and Standards?

A. A member or candidate is eligible for the new position and incentive if he or she can arrange for enough current clients to switch to the new firm and if the member or candidate discloses the incentive fee.

B. A member or candidate may not accept employment with the new firm because Jackman's incentive offer violates the Code and Standards.

C. A member or candidate is not eligible for the new position unless he or she is currently unemployed because soliciting the clients of the member's or candidate's current employer is prohibited.

50. Jurgen is a portfolio manager. One of her firm's clients has told Jurgen that he will compensate her beyond the compensation provided by her firm on the basis of

Practice Problems

405

the capital appreciation of his portfolio each year. Jurgen should:

A. Turn down the additional compensation because it will result in conflicts with the interests of other clients' accounts.

B. Turn down the additional compensation because it will create undue pressure on her to achieve strong short-term performance.

C. Obtain permission from her employer prior to accepting the compensation arrangement.

51. Willier is the research analyst responsible for following Company X. All the information he has accumulated and documented suggests that the outlook for the company's new products is poor, so the stock should be rated a weak "hold." During lunch, however, Willier overhears a financial analyst from another firm whom he respects offer opinions that conflict with Willier's forecasts and expectations. Upon returning to his office, Willier releases a strong "buy" recommendation to the public. Willier:

A. Violated the Standards by failing to distinguish between facts and opinions in his recommendation.

B. Violated the Standards because he did not have a reasonable and adequate basis for his recommendation.

C. Was in full compliance with the Standards.

52. Scott works for a regional brokerage firm. He estimates that Walkton Industries will increase its dividend by US$1.50 a share during the next year. He realizes that this increase is contingent on pending legislation that would, if enacted, give Walkton a substantial tax break. The US representative for Walkton's home district has told Scott that, although she is lobbying hard for the bill and prospects for its passage are favorable, concern of the US Congress over the federal deficit could cause the tax bill to be voted down. Walkton Industries has not made any statements about a change in dividend policy. Scott writes in his research report, "We expect Walkton's stock price to rise by at least US$8.00 a share by the end of the year because the dividend will increase by US$1.50 a share. Investors buying the stock at the current time should expect to realize a total return of at least 15% on the stock." According to the Standards:

A. Scott violated the Standards because he used material inside information.

B. Scott violated the Standards because he failed to separate opinion from fact.

C. Scott violated the Standards by basing his research on uncertain predictions of future government action.

53. Cannan has been working from home on weekends and occasionally saves correspondence with clients and completed work on her home computer. Because of worsening market conditions, Cannan is one of several employees released by her firm. While Cannan is looking for a new job, she uses the files she saved at home to request letters of recommendation from former clients. She also provides to prospective clients some of the reports as examples of her abilities.

A. Cannan violated the Code and Standards because she did not receive permission from her former employer to keep or use the files after her employment ended.

B. Cannan did not violate the Code and Standards because the files were created and saved on her own time and computer.

C. Cannan violated the Code and Standards because she is prohibited from saving files on her home computer.

54. Jamison is a junior research analyst with Howard & Howard, a brokerage and investment banking firm. Howard & Howard's mergers and acquisitions department has represented the Britland Company in all of its acquisitions for the past 20 years. Two of Howard & Howard's senior officers are directors of various Britland subsidiaries. Jamison has been asked to write a research report on Britland. What is the best course of action for her to follow?

A. Jamison may write the report but must refrain from expressing any opinions because of the special relationships between the two companies.

B. Jamison should not write the report because the two Howard & Howard officers serve as directors for subsidiaries of Britland.

C. Jamison may write the report if she discloses the special relationships with the company in the report.

55. Smith is a financial analyst with XYZ Brokerage Firm. She is preparing a purchase recommendation on JNI Corporation. Which of the following situations is *most likely* to represent a conflict of interest for Smith that would have to be disclosed?

A. Smith frequently purchases items produced by JNI.

B. XYZ holds for its own account a substantial common stock position in JNI.

C. Smith's brother-in-law is a supplier to JNI.

56. Which of the following statements clearly *conflicts* with the recommended procedures for compliance presented in the CFA Institute *Standards of Practice Handbook*?

A. Firms should disclose to clients the personal investing policies and procedures established for their employees.

B. Prior approval must be obtained for the personal investment transactions of all employees.

C. For confidentiality reasons, personal transactions and holdings should not be reported to employers unless mandated by regulatory organizations.

57. Rose, a portfolio manager for a local investment advisory firm, is planning to sell a portion of his personal investment portfolio to cover the costs of his child's academic tuition. Rose wants to sell a portion of his holdings in Household Products, but his firm recently upgraded the stock to "strong buy." Which of the following describes Rose's options under the Code and Standards?

A. Based on his firm's "buy" recommendation, Rose cannot sell the shares because he would be improperly prospering from the inflated recommendation.

B. Rose is free to sell his personal holdings once his firm is properly informed of his intentions.

Practice Problems 407

    C. Rose can sell his personal holdings but only when a client of the firm places an order to buy shares of Household.

58. Which of the following statements is a stated purpose of disclosure in Standard VI(C)—Referral Fees?

    A. Disclosure will allow the client to request discounted service fees.

    B. Disclosure will help the client evaluate any possible partiality shown in the recommendation of services.

    C. Disclosure means advising a prospective client about the referral arrangement once a formal client relationship has been established.

59. Park is very frustrated after taking her Level II exam. While she was studying for the exam, to supplement the curriculum provided, she ordered and used study material from a third-party provider. Park believes the additional material focused her attention on specific topic areas that were not tested while ignoring other areas. She posts the following statement on the provider's discussion board: "I am very dissatisfied with your firm's CFA Program Level II material. I found the exam extremely difficult and myself unprepared for specific questions after using your product. How could your service provide such limited instructional resources on the analysis of inventories and taxes when the exam had multiple questions about them? I will not recommend your products to other candidates."

    A. Park violated the Code and Standards by purchasing third-party review material.

    B. Park violated the Code and Standards by providing her opinion on the difficulty of the exam.

    C. Park violated the Code and Standards by providing specific information on topics tested on the exam.

60. Albert and Tye, who recently started their own investment advisory business, have registered to take the Level III CFA examination. Albert's business card reads, "Judy Albert, CFA Level II." Tye has not put anything about the CFA designation on his business card, but promotional material that he designed for the business describes the CFA requirements and indicates that Tye participates in the CFA Program and has completed Levels I and II. According to the Standards:

    A. Albert has violated the Standards, but Tye has not.

    B. Tye has violated the Standards, but Albert has not.

    C. Both Albert and Tye have violated the Standards.

61. Quinn sat for the Level III CFA exam this past weekend. He updates his resume with the following statement: "In finishing the CFA Program, I improved my skills related to researching investments and managing portfolios. I will be eligible for the CFA charter upon completion of the required work experience."

    A. Quinn violated the Code and Standards by claiming he improved his skills through the CFA Program.

    B. Quinn violated the Code and Standards by incorrectly stating that he is eligible for the CFA charter.

    C. Quinn did not violate the Code and Standards with his resume update.

SOLUTIONS

1. The correct answer is A because this question relates to Standard I(A)—Knowledge of the Law—specifically, global application of the Code and Standards. Members and candidates who practice in multiple jurisdictions may be subject to various securities laws and regulations. If applicable law is more strict than the requirements of the Code and Standards, members and candidates must adhere to applicable law; otherwise, members and candidates must adhere to the Code and Standards. Therefore, answer A is correct. Answer B is incorrect because members and candidates must adhere to the higher standard set by the Code and Standards if local applicable law is less strict. Answer C is incorrect because when no applicable law exists, members and candidates are required to adhere to the Code and Standards, and the Code and Standards prohibit the use of material nonpublic information.

2. The correct answer is B. This question relates to Standard I(B)—Independence and Objectivity. When asked to change a recommendation on a company stock to gain business for the firm, the head of the brokerage unit must refuse in order to maintain his independence and objectivity in making recommendations. He must not yield to pressure by the firm's investment banking department. To avoid the appearance of a conflict of interest, the firm should discontinue issuing recommendations about the company. Answer A is incorrect; changing the recommendation in any manner that is contrary to the analyst's opinion violates the duty to maintain independence and objectivity. Answer C is incorrect because merely assigning a new analyst to decide whether the stock deserves a higher rating will not address the conflict of interest.

3. The correct answer is B. The best course of action under Standard I(B)—Independence and Objectivity is to avoid a conflict of interest whenever possible. Therefore, for Ward to pay for all his expenses is the correct answer. Answer C details a course of action in which the conflict would be disclosed, but the solution is not as appropriate as avoiding the conflict of interest. Answer A would not be the best course because it would not remove the appearance of a conflict of interest; even though the report would not be affected by the reimbursement of expenses, it could appear to be.

4. Answer A is correct. Standard I(B)—Independence and Objectivity emphasizes the need for members and candidates to maintain their independence and objectivity. Best practices dictate that firms adopt a strict policy not to accept compensation for travel arrangements. At times, however, accepting paid travel would not compromise one's independence and objectivity. Answers B and C are incorrect because the added benefits—free conference admission for additional staff members and an exclusive golf retreat for the speaker—could be viewed as inducements related to the firm's working arrangements and not solely related to the speaking engagement. Should Long wish to bring other team members or participate in the golf outing, he or his firm should be responsible for the associated fees.

5. B is correct. Excerpt 2 is inconsistent with CFA Standards because it addresses only officers and only their direct reports, that is, employees whom they directly supervise. Standard IV (C) states that "any investment professionals who have employees subject to their control or influence" exercise supervisory responsibility. Excerpt 3 is consistent with CFA Standards. It is based on a quote from the *Standards of Practice Handbook* stating that "if a member or candidate determines that information is material, the member . . . should make reasonable

Solutions 409

efforts to achieve public dissemination." Members are not required to achieve public dissemination and those bound by a duty of loyalty or a duty to preserve confidentiality would refrain from doing so because it would breach their duty.

6. A is correct. According to Standard I(B)–Independence and Objectivity, members must use reasonable care and judgment to achieve and maintain independence and objectivity in their professional activities. Although it was sent to Voser's office, the gift basket is a private gift from Voser's sister and not likely to affect Voser's professional activities. According to Excerpt 4 of the Crawfood compliance manual and Standard IV(B)–Additional Compensation Arrangements, employees must obtain permission from their employer before accepting gifts, compensation, or other benefits that compete with, or might create a conflict of interest with, the employer's interests. The gift basket does not create a conflict or compete with the employer's interests.

7. A is correct. Voser most likely violated the Standard relating to loyalty to employer, Standard IV(A). While Voser used public information to develop the recommendation to purchase Greenhornfood shares, the company compliance guide states that she should not trade or cause others to trade in securities of companies that may be potential takeover targets. Voser's recommendation caused her sister to trade in Greenhornfood, violating the company's compliance policies, and possibly harming her employer in its attempt to acquire Greenhornfood.

   By advising others to invest in a food retailer that she considered an attractive acquisition target, Voser deprived her employer of the advantage of her skills and abilities and may have caused harm to her employer. Voser could have recommended Greenhornfood to Craw rather than her sister as an acquisition target. Although the sister's trade in Greenhornfood was small, a large trade might have moved the stock price and caused harm to Crawfood in terms of additional cost.

8. C is correct. Voser least likely violated the Standard relating to diligence and reasonable basis. Voser initially applied the mosaic theory and had a reasonable basis for the trade as required by Standard V(A). Eventually, she came into possession of material nonpublic information (corporate logo on a document, overheard conversation). According to Standard II(A), once in possession of material nonpublic information, she is prohibited from acting or causing others to act. Voser also violated her duty of loyalty to her employer, Standard IV(A), by encouraging others to trade in Greenhornfood and possibly harming Crawfood's attempts to acquire the smaller company at an attractive price.

9. C is correct. Craw did not adequately fulfill his responsibilities as a supervisor. As stated in the *Standards of Practice Handbook*, members and candidates with supervisory responsibility also must understand what constitutes an adequate compliance system for their firms and make reasonable efforts to see that appropriate compliance procedures are established, documented, communicated to covered personnel, and followed. "Adequate" procedures are those designed to meet industry standards, regulatory requirements, the requirements of the Code and Standards, and the circumstances of the firm. Once compliance procedures are established, the supervisor must also make reasonable efforts to ensure that the procedures are monitored and enforced. According to Standard IV(C)–Responsibilities of Supervisors, adequate compliance procedures require that once a violation is discovered, Craw conduct a thorough investigation to determine the scope of wrongdoing.

10. A is correct. As stated on page ix of the *Standards of Practice Handbook*, "Members and candidates must self disclose on the annual Professional Conduct Statement all matters that question their professional conduct, such as involvement in civil litigation, a criminal investigation, or being the subject of a written com-

plaint." Standard VII(A)–Conduct as Participants in CFA Institute Programs prohibits conduct that compromises the reputation of the CFA designation including misrepresenting information on the Professional Conduct Statement. Members are encouraged but not required to report violations of others. At a minimum, Craw should remind Voser of her duty to report the investigation.

11. The correct answer is C. This question involves Standard I(C)–Misrepresentation. Statement I is a factual statement that discloses to clients and prospects accurate information about the terms of the investment instrument. Statement II, which guarantees a specific rate of return for a mutual fund, is an opinion stated as a fact and, therefore, violates Standard I(C). If statement II were rephrased to include a qualifying statement, such as "in my opinion, investors may earn . . . ," it would not be in violation of the Standards.

12. The correct answer is C. This question relates to Standard I(C)–Misrepresentation. Although Michelieu's statement about the total return of his clients' accounts on average may be technically true, it is misleading because the majority of the gain resulted from one client's large position taken against Michelieu's advice. Therefore, this statement misrepresents the investment performance the member is responsible for. He has not taken steps to present a fair, accurate, and complete presentation of performance. Answer B is thus incorrect. Answer A is incorrect because although Michelieu is not guaranteeing future results, his words are still a misrepresentation of his performance history.

13. The correct answer is A. This question involves three of the Standards. Anderb, the portfolio manager, has been obtaining more favorable prices for her personal securities transactions than she gets for her clients, which is a breach of Standard III(A)–Loyalty, Prudence, and Care. In addition, she violated Standard I(D)–Misconduct by failing to adhere to company policy and by hiding her personal transactions from her firm. Anderb's supervisor, Bates, violated Standard IV(C)–Responsibilities of Supervisors; although the company had requirements for reporting personal trading, Bates failed to adequately enforce those requirements. Answer B does not represent a violation because Standard VI(B)–Priority of Transactions requires that personal trading in a security be conducted after the trading in that security of clients and the employer. The Code and Standards do not prohibit owning such investments, although firms may establish policies that limit the investment opportunities of members and candidates. Answer C does not represent a violation because the Code and Standards do not contain a prohibition against employees using the same broker for their personal accounts that they use for their client accounts. This arrangement should be disclosed to the employer so that the employer may determine whether a conflict of interest exists.

14. The correct answer is B. This question deals with Standard II(A)–Material Nonpublic Information. The mosaic theory states that an analyst may use material public information and nonmaterial nonpublic information in creating a larger picture than shown by any individual piece of information and the conclusions the analyst reaches become material only after the pieces are assembled. Answers A and C are accurate statements relating to the Code and Standards but do not describe the mosaic theory.

15. Answer A is correct. Hart's decision to invest in the retail fund appears directly correlated with Rodriguez's statement about the successful quarter of Mega Retail and thus violates Standard II(A)–Material Nonpublic Information. Rodriguez's information would be considered material because it would influence the share price of Mega Retail and probably influence the price of the entire exchange-traded retail fund. Thus, answer B is incorrect. Answer C is also incor-

Solutions 411

rect because Rodriguez shared information that was both material and nonpublic. Company officers regularly have such knowledge about their firms, which is not a violation. The sharing of such information, however, even in a conversation between friends, does violate Standard II(A).

16. C is correct. Boswin, as an employee, developed the model on behalf of Greenfield. Therefore, Greenfield, not Boswin, is the owner of the model. Acertado violates Standard IV(A) Duties to Employers: Loyalty when he downloads the model without proper written permission from Greenfield Financial. Acertado is misappropriating employer assets.

17. C is correct. Acertado is least likely to violate Standard II(A) regarding Material Nonpublic Information when using the model at Smith and Garner. Acertado likely violated Standard IV(A), Loyalty, when he used the model. The Standard prohibits members who leave an employer from taking records or files—such as the model—without the written permission of the employer. Acertado also likely violated Standard I(C)–Misrepresentation when he failed to correct his supervisor's impression that the investment idea and the model were Acertado's creation.

18. C is correct. Acertado violates Standard II(A)–Material Nonpublic Information. He has a reasonable belief that the conversation that he overhears is from a reliable source and would have a material impact on security prices. According to the CFA Standards, he must not act, nor cause others to act on the information. Acertado does not violate the Standard relating to Diligence and Reasonable Basis because he bases the recommendation on a reliable model and checks his inputs prior to making the recommendation.

19. A is correct. Acertado least likely violates Standard III(C), which relates to suitability during his phone conversation with Boswin. According to the Standard, members in an advisory relationship with a client must determine an investment's suitability within the context of the client's portfolio. The Standard also requires that members make reasonable inquiries into a client or prospective client's investment experience; risk and return objectives; and financial constraints prior to making investment recommendations. Boswin is neither a client nor a prospective client, thus Acertado is not bound by the Standard of Suitability during their conversation. Acertado is, however, in jeopardy of violating other Standards—specifically those relating to Integrity of Capital Markets and Preservation of Confidentiality by revealing material nonpublic information about a Smith & Garner client. According to Standard II(A), Acertado, who is in possession of material nonpublic information, must not act, nor cause others to act on the information. According to Standard III(E), members must keep information about current, former, and prospective clients confidential.

20. A is correct. Boswin uses her usual process in researching Country Industries. She is not in possession of material nonpublic information and she maintains her objectivity. Her use of the model provides a reasonable basis for the decision not to pursue additional research or make an investment recommendation regarding Country Industries.

21. A is correct. Blogs and company websites are in the public domain and thus do not constitute inside information. Acertado's use of blog sites to supplement his current research process is acceptable.

22. The correct answer is B. The best policy to prevent violation of Standard II(A)–Material Nonpublic Information is the establishment of firewalls in a firm to prevent exchange of insider information. The physical and informational barrier of a firewall between the investment banking department and the brokerage

operation prevents the investment banking department from providing information to analysts on the brokerage side who may be writing recommendations on a company stock. Prohibiting recommendations of the stock of companies that are clients of the investment banking department is an alternative, but answer A states that this prohibition would be permanent, which is not the best answer. Once an offering is complete and the material nonpublic information obtained by the investment banking department becomes public, resuming publishing recommendations on the stock is not a violation of the Code and Standards because the information of the investment banking department no longer gives the brokerage operation an advantage in writing the report. Answer C is incorrect because no exchange of information should be occurring between the investment banking department and the brokerage operation, so monitoring of such exchanges is not an effective compliance procedure for preventing the use of material nonpublic information.

23. Answer C is correct. The guidance to Standard II(A)–Material Nonpublic Information recommends adding securities to the firm's restricted list when the firm has or may have material nonpublic information. By adding these securities to this list, Andrews would uphold this standard. Because waiting until the next day will not ensure that news of the merger is made public, answer A is incorrect. Negotiations may take much longer between the two companies, and the merger may never happen. Andrews must wait until the information is disseminated to the market before he trades on that information. Answer B is incorrect because Andrews should not disclose the information to other managers; no trading is allowed on material nonpublic information.

24. Answer B is correct. Through placing a personal purchase order that is significantly greater than the average volume, Pietro is violating Standard IIB–Market Manipulation. He is attempting to manipulate an increase in the share price and thus bring a buyer to the negotiating table. The news of a possible merger and confirmation of the firm's earnings guidance may also have positive effects on the price of Local Bank, but Pietro's actions in instructing the release of the information does not represent a violation through market manipulation. Announcements of this nature are common and practical to keep investors informed. Thus, answers A and C are incorrect.

25. The correct answer is C. This question involves Standard III(A)–Loyalty, Prudence, and Care and the specific topic of soft dollars or soft commissions. Answer C is the correct choice because client brokerage commissions may not be directed to pay for the investment manager's operating expenses. Answer B describes how members and candidates should determine how to use brokerage commissions—that is, if the use is in the best interests of clients and is commensurate with the value of the services provided. Answer A describes a practice that is commonly referred to as "directed brokerage." Because brokerage is an asset of the client and is used to benefit the client, not the manager, such practice does not violate a duty of loyalty to the client. Members and candidates are obligated in all situations to disclose to clients their practices in the use of client brokerage commissions.

26. The correct answer is B. This question relates to Standard III(A)–Loyalty, Prudence, and Care—specifically, a member's or candidate's responsibility for voting proxies and the use of client brokerage. According to the facts stated in the question, Farnsworth did not violate Standard III(A). Although the company president asked Farnsworth to vote the shares of the Jones Corporation profit-sharing plan a certain way, Farnsworth investigated the issue and concluded, independently, the best way to vote. Therefore, even though his decision coincided with the wishes of the company president, Farnsworth is not in violation

Solutions 413

of his responsibility to be loyal and to provide care to his clients. In this case, the participants and the beneficiaries of the profit-sharing plan are the clients, not the company's management. Had Farnsworth not investigated the issue or had he yielded to the president's wishes and voted for a slate of directors that he had determined was not in the best interest of the company, Farnsworth would have violated his responsibilities to the beneficiaries of the plan. In addition, because the brokerage firm provides the lowest commissions and best execution for securities transactions, Farnsworth has met his obligations to the client in using this brokerage firm. It does not matter that the brokerage firm also provides research information that is not useful for the account generating the commission because Farnsworth is not paying extra money of the client's for that information.

27. The correct answer is B. Under Standard III(A)–Loyalty, Prudence, and Care, members and candidates who manage a company's pension fund owe these duties to the participants and beneficiaries of the pension plan, not the management of the company or the company's shareholders.

28. Answer A is correct. The question relates to Standard III(A)–Loyalty, Prudence, and Care. Carter believes the broker offers effective execution at a fee that is comparable with those of other brokers, so he is free to use the broker for all accounts. Answer B is incorrect because the accounts that prohibit soft dollar arrangements do not want to fund the purchase of research by Carter. The new trading scheme does not incur additional commissions from clients, so it would not go against the prohibitions. Answer C is incorrect because Carter should not incur unnecessary or excessive "churning" of the portfolios (excessive trading) for the purpose of meeting the brokerage commitments of soft dollar arrangements.

29. Answer C is correct. According to Standard III(A)–Loyalty, Prudence, and Care, the CFA Program would be considered a personal or firm expense and should not be paid for with the fund's brokerage commissions. Soft dollar accounts should be used only to purchase research services that directly assist the investment manager in the investment decision-making process, not to assist the management of the firm or to further education. Thus, answer A is incorrect. Answer B is incorrect because the reasonableness of how the money is used is not an issue; the issue is that educational expense is not research.

30. B is correct. Telline has a duty to preserve the confidentiality of current, former, and prospective clients. Telline violates Standard III(E)–Preservation of Confidentiality when he reveals information about the Leighton Family Trust.

31. A is correct. Brown conducts an independent and careful analysis of the plans' benefits for shareholders as well as the takeover offer. In doing so she puts the client's interests ahead of the firm's. Brown's actions are consistent with Standard III(A)–Loyalty, Prudence, and Care; Standard V(A)–Diligence and Reasonable Basis; and Standard III(B)–Fair Dealing.

32. B is correct. Telline is not likely to receive appropriate guidance on developing or revising investment policy statements from the Standard relating to Fair Dealing. Standard III(B) provides members with guidance on treating clients fairly when making investment recommendations, providing investment analysis, or taking investment action. Telline could obtain guidance from the Standards relating to Loyalty, Prudence, and Care and Suitability. Both Standard III(A) and (C) provide guidance for members in determining client objectives and the suitability of investments.

33. A is correct. Telline is careful to consider the investment's suitability for Caper's account. Telline's actions are consistent with CFA Institute Standards III(A)–

Loyalty, Prudence, and Care and III(B)–Fair Dealing. Telline determines that the other client does not have the cash available in his account and selling existing holdings does not make sense.

34. B is correct. The firm violates Standard III(B)–Fair Dealing. Under Aiklin's policy, some clients for whom an IPO is suitable may not receive their pro-rata share of the issue. CFA Standards recommend that firms allocate IPOs on a pro-rata basis to clients, not to portfolio managers.

35. C is correct. Telline violates Standard III(B)–Fair Dealing by over-allocating shares to Caper. Telline carefully reviews both the proposed IPO and his client accounts to determine suitability. He fails to allocate the IPO shares on a pro-rata basis to all clients for whom the investment is suitable.

36. The correct answer is B. This question involves Standard III(B)–Fair Dealing. Smith disseminated a change in the stock recommendation to his clients but then received a request contrary to that recommendation from a client who probably had not yet received the recommendation. Prior to executing the order, Smith should take additional steps to ensure that the customer has received the change of recommendation. Answer A is incorrect because the client placed the order prior to receiving the recommendation and, therefore, does not have the benefit of Smith's most recent recommendation. Answer C is also incorrect; simply because the client request is contrary to the firm's recommendation does not mean a member can override a direct request by a client. After Smith contacts the client to ensure that the client has received the changed recommendation, if the client still wants to place a buy order for the shares, Smith is obligated to comply with the client's directive.

37. The correct answer is C. This question, which relates to Standard III(B)–Fair Dealing, tests the knowledge of the procedures that will assist members and candidates in treating clients fairly when making investment recommendations. The step listed in C will help ensure the fair treatment of clients. Answer A may have negative effects on the fair treatment of clients. The more people who know about a pending change, the greater the chance that someone will inform some clients before the information's release. The firm should establish policies that limit the number of people who are aware in advance that a recommendation is to be disseminated. Answer B, distributing recommendations to institutional clients before distributing them to individual accounts, discriminates among clients on the basis of size and class of assets and is a violation of Standard III(B).

38. The correct answer is A. In this question, Brown is providing investment recommendations before making inquiries about the client's financial situation, investment experience, or investment objectives. Brown is thus violating Standard III(C)–Suitability. Answers B and C provide examples of information members and candidates should discuss with their clients at the outset of the relationship, but these answers do not constitute a complete list of those factors. Answer A is the best answer.

39. Answer C is correct. Cupp violated Standard III(D)–Performance Presentations when he deviated from the firm's stated policies solely to capture the gain from the holding being acquired. Answer A is incorrect because the firm does not claim GIPS compliance and the GIPS standards require external cash flows to be treated in a consistent manner with the firm's documented policies. Answer B is incorrect because the firm does not state that it is updating its composite policies. If such a change were to occur, all cash flows for the month would have to be reviewed to ensure their consistent treatment under the new policy.

Solutions 415

40. Answer B is correct. Paper has violated Standard III(D)–Performance Presentation by not disclosing that he was part of a team of managers that achieved the results shown. If he had also included the return of the portion he directly managed, he would not have violated the standard. Thus, answer A is incorrect. Answer C is incorrect because Paper received written permission from his prior employer to include the results.

41. A is correct. Grohl exercised diligence, independence, and thoroughness in analyzing the company and its competitors. Brecksen provided his research reports for Grohl's use and using the reports as a guide was appropriate. Standard V(A) requires that members distinguish between fact and opinion in communicating investment recommendations to clients. The Standard does not apply to investment recommendations communicated to supervisors or internal investment committees.

42. A is correct. Brecksen does not consider the multi-factor analysis a critical component of the analysis or the resulting investment recommendation and thus, under Standards V(A) and (C), is not required to maintain a record of the analysis within the completed report.

    Apfelbaum uses traditional "top-down" fundamental analysis in the investment process. The report followed the traditional format of previous reports on the same company. It contained a complete fundamental analysis and recommendation—indicating diligence and reasonable basis. The report also contained a multi-factor analysis—which is a quantitative analysis tool. If quantitative analysis were the basis of the investment recommendation, it would constitute a change in the general investment principles used by the firm. According to Standard V(B)–Communications with Clients and Prospective Clients, Brecksen and Grohl would be required to promptly disclose those changes to clients and prospective clients.

43. A is correct. Removing the multi-factor analysis from the research report does not constitute a violation. Grohl diligently prepared the internal document according to the firm's traditional format with a complete fundamental analysis and recommendation—indicating diligence and a reasonable basis for his recommendation. It would be wise for Grohl to retain records of the multi-factor analysis but he need not retain the analysis in the research report to comply with Standards V(A)–Diligence and Reasonable Basis or V(C)–Record Retention.

44. A is correct. According to Standard V(A)–Diligence and Reasonable Basis, research report conclusions or recommendations may represent the consensus of a group and not necessarily the views of the individual members listed. If the member believes that the consensus opinion has a reasonable basis, then he need not dissociate from the report.

45. B is correct. Zardt violated the Standard relating to Performance Presentation because he did not verify the accuracy of the return information before its distribution. According to Standard III(D), analysts may promote the success or accuracy of their recommendations, but they must make reasonable efforts to ensure that the information is fair, accurate, and complete. In addition to providing attribution, Zardt should take steps to ensure the accuracy of the data prior to distributing the material.

46. The correct answer is B. This question relates to Standard III(A)–Loyalty, Prudence, and Care and Standard III(E)–Preservation of Confidentiality. In this case, the member manages funds of a private endowment. Clients, who are, in this case, the trustees of the fund, must place some trust in members and candidates. Bronson cannot disclose confidential financial information to anyone without

the permission of the fund, regardless of whether the disclosure may benefit the fund. Therefore, answer A is incorrect. Answer C is incorrect because Bronson must notify the fund and obtain the fund's permission before publicizing the information.

47. Answer A is correct. Townsend has not provided any information about her clients to the leaders or managers of the golf program; thus, she has not violated Standard III(E)–Preservation of Confidentiality. Providing contact information about her clients for a direct-mail solicitation would have been a violation. Answer B is incorrect because the notice in the newsletter does not violate Standard III(E). Answer C is incorrect because the golf program's fund-raising campaign had already begun, so discussing the opportunity to donate was appropriate.

48. The correct answer is B. Under Standard IV(A)–Loyalty, members and candidates may undertake independent practice that may result in compensation or other benefit in competition with their employer as long as they obtain consent from their employer. Answer C is not consistent with the Standards because the Standards allow members and candidates to make arrangements or preparations to go into competitive business as long as those arrangements do not interfere with their duty to their current employer. Answer A is not consistent with the Standards because the Standards do not include a complete prohibition against undertaking independent practice.

49. Answer C is correct. Standard IV(A)–Loyalty discusses activities permissible to members and candidates when they are leaving their current employer; soliciting clients is strictly prohibited. Thus, answer A is inconsistent with the Code and Standards even with the required disclosure. Answer B is incorrect because the offer does not directly violate the Code and Standards. There may be out-of-work members and candidates who can arrange the necessary commitments without violating the Code and Standards.

50. The correct answer is C. This question involves Standard IV(B)–Additional Compensation Arrangements. The arrangement described in the question—whereby Jurgen would be compensated beyond the compensation provided by her firm, on the basis of an account's performance—is not a violation of the Standards as long as Jurgen discloses the arrangement in writing to her employer and obtains permission from her employer prior to entering into the arrangement. Answers A and B are incorrect; although the private compensation arrangement could conflict with the interests of other clients and lead to short-term performance pressures, members and candidates may enter into such agreements as long as they have disclosed the arrangements to their employer and obtained permission for the arrangement from their employer.

51. The correct answer is B. This question relates to Standard V(A)–Diligence and Reasonable Basis. The opinion of another financial analyst is not an adequate basis for Willier's action in changing the recommendation. Answer C is thus incorrect. So is answer A because, although it is true that members and candidates must distinguish between facts and opinions in recommendations, the question does not illustrate a violation of that nature. If the opinion overheard by Willier had sparked him to conduct additional research and investigation that justified a change of opinion, then a changed recommendation would be appropriate.

52. The correct answer is B. This question relates to Standard V(B)–Communication with Clients and Prospective Clients. Scott has issued a research report stating that he expects the price of Walkton Industries stock to rise by US$8 a share "because the dividend will increase" by US$1.50 per share. He has made this statement knowing that the dividend will increase only if Congress enacts certain

Solutions 417

legislation, an uncertain prospect. By stating that the dividend will increase, Scott failed to separate fact from opinion.

The information regarding passage of legislation is not material nonpublic information because it is conjecture, and the question does not state whether the US representative gave Scott her opinion on the passage of the legislation in confidence. She could have been offering this opinion to anyone who asked. Therefore, statement A is incorrect. It may be acceptable to base a recommendation, in part, on an expectation of future events, even though they may be uncertain. Therefore, answer C is incorrect.

53. Answer A is correct. According to Standard V(C)–Record Retention, Cannan needed the permission of her employer to maintain the files at home after her employment ended. Without that permission, she should have deleted the files. All files created as part of a member's or candidate's professional activity are the property of the firm, even those created outside normal work hours. Thus, answer B is incorrect. Answer C is incorrect because the Code and Standards do not prohibit using one's personal computer to complete work for one's employer.

54. The correct answer is C. This question involves Standard VI(A)–Disclosure of Conflicts. The question establishes a conflict of interest in which an analyst, Jamison, is asked to write a research report on a company that is a client of the analyst's employer. In addition, two directors of the company are senior officers of Jamison's employer. Both facts establish that there are conflicts of interest that must be disclosed by Jamison in her research report. Answer B is incorrect because an analyst is not prevented from writing a report simply because of the special relationship the analyst's employer has with the company as long as that relationship is disclosed. Answer A is incorrect because whether or not Jamison expresses any opinions in the report is irrelevant to her duty to disclose a conflict of interest. Not expressing opinions does not relieve the analyst of the responsibility to disclose the special relationships between the two companies.

55. The correct answer is B. This question involves Standard VI(A)–Disclosure of Conflicts—specifically, the holdings of an analyst's employer in company stock. Answers A and C do not describe conflicts of interest that Smith would have to disclose. Answer A describes the use of a firm's products, which would not be a required disclosure. In answer C, the relationship between the analyst and the company through a relative is so tangential that it does not create a conflict of interest necessitating disclosure.

56. The correct answer is C. This question asks about compliance procedures relating to personal investments of members and candidates. The statement in answer C clearly conflicts with the recommended procedures in the *Standards of Practice Handbook*. Employers should compare personal transactions of employees with those of clients on a regular basis regardless of the existence of a requirement by any regulatory organization. Such comparisons ensure that employees' personal trades do not conflict with their duty to their clients, and the comparisons can be conducted in a confidential manner. The statement in answer A does not conflict with the procedures in the *Handbook*. Disclosure of such policies will give full information to clients regarding potential conflicts of interest on the part of those entrusted to manage their money. Answer B is incorrect because firms are encouraged to establish policies whereby employees clear their personal holdings and transactions with their employers.

57. The correct answer is B. Standard VI(B)–Priority of Transactions does not limit transactions of company employees that differ from current recommendations as long as the sale does not disadvantage current clients. Thus, answer A is incorrect. Answer C is incorrect because the Standard does not require the matching

of personal and client trades.

58. The correct answer is B. Answer B gives one of the two primary reasons listed in the *Handbook* for disclosing referral fees to clients under Standard VI(C)– Referral Fees. (The other is to allow clients and employers to evaluate the full cost of the services.) Answer A is incorrect because Standard VI(C) does not require members or candidates to discount their fees when they receive referral fees. Answer C is inconsistent with Standard VI(C) because disclosure of referral fees, to be effective, should be made to prospective clients before entering into a formal client relationship with them.

59. Answer C is correct. Standard VII(A)–Conduct as Participants in CFA Institute Programs prohibits providing information to candidates or the public that is considered confidential to the CFA Program. In revealing that questions related to the analysis of inventories and analysis of taxes were on the exam, Park has violated this standard. Answer B is incorrect because the guidance for the standard explicitly acknowledges that members and candidates are allowed to offer their opinions about the CFA Program. Answer A is incorrect because candidates are not prohibited from using outside resources.

60. The correct answer is A. Standard VII(B)–Reference to CFA Institute, the CFA Designation, and the CFA Program is the subject of this question. The reference on Albert's business card implies that there is a "CFA Level II" designation; Tye merely indicates in promotional material that he is participating in the CFA Program and has completed Levels I and II. Candidates may not imply that there is some sort of partial designation earned after passing a level of the CFA exam. Therefore, Albert has violated Standard VII(B). Candidates may communicate that they are participating in the CFA Program, however, and may state the levels that they have completed. Therefore, Tye has not violated Standard VII(B).

61. Answer B is correct. According to Standard VII(B)–Reference to CFA Institute, the CFA Designation, and the CFA Program, Quinn cannot claim to have finished the CFA Program or be eligible for the CFA charter until he officially learns that he has passed the Level III exam. Until the results for the most recent exam are released, those who sat for the exam should continue to refer to themselves as "candidates." Thus, answer C is incorrect. Answer A is incorrect because members and candidates may discuss areas of practice in which they believe the CFA Program improved their personal skills.

LEARNING MODULE

3

Application of the Code and Standards: Level II

LEARNING OUTCOMES

Mastery	The candidate should be able to:
☐	evaluate practices, policies, and conduct relative to the CFA Institute Code of Ethics and Standards of Professional Conduct
☐	explain how the practices, policies, and conduct do or do not violate the CFA Institute Code of Ethics and Standards of Professional Conduct

INTRODUCTION

1

This reading presents cases to illustrate how the CFA Institute Code of Ethics and Standards of Professional Conduct (Code and Standards) can be applied in situations requiring professional and ethical judgement. Exhibit 1 presents a useful framework to help guide individuals in their ethical decision-making process and application of the Code and Standards. By identifying where the Code and Standards might be relevant and considering actions and consequences within this framework, individuals can make more ethically sound decisions.

Although the framework's components do not need to be addressed in the sequence shown, a review of the outcome should conclude the process. This review provides insights for improved decision making in the future.

Exhibit 1: A Framework for Ethical Decision Making

- Identify: Relevant facts, stakeholders and duties owed, ethical principles, conflicts of interest
- Consider: Situational influences, additional guidance, alternative actions
- Decide and act
- Reflect: Was the outcome as anticipated? Why or why not?

This reading presents a number of scenarios involving individuals in private and institutional asset management. The first five cases focus on identifying whether violations of the Code and Standards occurred, with discussion and rationale as to

SERENGETI ADVISORY SERVICES

- [ ] evaluate practices, policies, and conduct relative to the CFA Institute Code of Ethics and Standards of Professional Conduct
- [ ] explain how the practices, policies, and conduct do or do not violate the CFA Institute Code of Ethics and Standards of Professional Conduct

Serengeti Advisory Services (Serengeti) is an equity research firm based in Tanzania.[1] It was founded five years ago by three CFA charterholders: Bashar, Shah, and Kariuki. Serengeti analysts conduct investment research on listed African companies and sell the research to institutional asset managers on an annual subscription basis. Their clients are predominantly asset managers based in North America and Europe. Each month, subscribers receive two or three company and/or industry research reports. In her role(s) as CEO and Head of Research, Bashar has recently started a premium subscription service. For an additional fee, clients receive six additional research reports of their choosing per year. Because of the cost of the premium service, Bashar offers it only to clients that she believes can afford it. (Question 1)

Serengeti's research analysts provide investment recommendations for small- to mid-cap African companies. One of the companies included in Serengeti's most recent list of recommendations is Gbeho Telecommunications. Unknown to the researchers, Gbeho was founded by Bashar's father-in-law and is majority owned by Bashar's husband's family. Serengeti's research report does not include mention of Bashar's connection to Gbeho. (Question 2)

For companies not covered by Serengeti, Bashar has created an "approved list" of broker/dealers from across the continent whose research she believes meets Serengeti's standards. Bashar tells her clients, "We partner with these broker/dealers to provide research on companies not covered by our firm. In addition, these relationships provide Serengeti's analysts with insights and information from a wide variety of independent sources that they may use in their own research. Some of the procedures I have implemented to ensure proper use of third-party research include the following:

- **Procedure 1**: When a research report, ours or theirs, cites specific quotations as attributable to 'leading analysts' and 'leading experts,' I require the analyst who wrote the report to name the specific references.

- **Procedure 2**: When a research report contains statistical estimates of forecasts prepared by others (such as economists) and identifies the source, I require the analyst who wrote the report to remove any qualifying statements or caveats that may have been used.

---

1 **Serengeti Advisory Services:** Renée K. Blasky, CFA, CIPM, and Michael G. McMillan, PhD, CFA. *Ethics Cases.* © 2020 CFA Institute. All rights reserved. Consistent with the 11th Edition of the *Standards of Practice Handbook.*

Serengeti Advisory Services

- **Procedure 3**: When a research report contains charts and graphs prepared by others, I require the analyst who wrote the report to cite their sources." (Question 3)

To be on Serengeti's approved list, broker/dealers must undergo a stringent due diligence process carried out by Bashar's team and comply with Procedures 1–3. If the firm passes the initial due diligence, it goes through a more formal process, ending with approval by Serengeti's management committee. Thereafter, Serengeti conducts a follow-up due diligence process annually to ensure continuing compliance.

Over the years, Bashar has established the following referral arrangement with the firms on the approved list: Whenever Serengeti's analysts prepare a research report using information sourced from an approved broker/dealer, Bashar encourages the firm's clients to trade through that broker/dealer. Bashar believes this referral arrangement, which she discloses to clients and prospective clients, provides additional incentive for broker/dealers to share insights and information with her analysts at no cost. Because of Serengeti's large client base, broker/dealers seek to be placed on the firm's "approved list." (Question 4).

Bashar discusses this referral arrangement during a phone conversation with Jon Grant, CFA, of Grant Asset Management, one of Serengeti's largest clients.

> *Grant:* I have found the research partnerships that Serengeti has established with broker/dealers to be very beneficial. The due diligence that you conduct on the broker/dealers on your approved list saves me from investigating these firms on my own. As a result, I always follow the analysts' investment recommendations and execute my clients' trades through the broker/dealer that produced the research report or whose information was used in your research. I noticed that Olatunji Financial, one of the largest broker/dealers in Nigeria, is not on your approved list. Why is that?

> *Bashar:* Thank you so much for the compliment and your support. I am glad that Serengeti can provide this service, and I know the broker/dealers also appreciate your business. I have heard that Olatunji Financial conducts outstanding research on Nigerian-listed companies, but we have not had an opportunity to work with them. (Question 5)

A few days later, Bashar receives an email from Amope Olatunji, CFA, president and CEO of Olatunji Financial Services (OFS). In the email, Olatunji states, "Jon Grant has told me about the great equity research that your firm produces. I would like OFS to be added to Serengeti's approved list. To this end, OFS would like to invite you and two of your colleagues to our upcoming West Africa Investment Forum that we host at our headquarters in Lagos, Nigeria. We will pay all of your expenses related to attending the forum, including air travel and overnight hotel accommodations."

Bashar knows that attending this forum would be beneficial for Serengeti. First, it would give her an opportunity to meet and interview executives of publicly listed companies who are attending or whose offices are located in Lagos. Second, it would give Kariuki, the head of business development, the chance to meet with prospective clients. Third, it would give Shah, the chief Compliance Officer, an opportunity to start the due diligence process on OFS and follow up with the other approved Nigerian broker/dealers in the city. During a meeting with Kariuki and Shah to discuss how to proceed with Olatunji's invitation, Bashar states, "As I see it, we have three possible options:

Option 1	We allow OFS to pay for all of our expenses.
Option 2	We allow OFS to pay for our air travel and hotel accommodations, and we pay for our meals and entertainment.

| Option 3 | We allow OFS to pay for the forum's meals and entertainment, and we pay for our air travel and hotel accommodations." (Question 6) |

At the forum, Bashar, Shah, and Kariuki separate to talk with attendees. When Kariuki walks over to the recycling bin to dispose of her water bottle, she notices a document on top of the bin. Picking up the document, she realizes it is a listing of OFS clients with contact numbers, email addresses, and average trading volumes over the past three years. After taking a photo of the document with her phone, she places it back in the bin and proceeds to seek out those clients with the highest trading volumes. (Question 7)

The next morning, Bashar, Shah, and Olatunji meet to discuss the possibility of OFS being added to Serengeti's approved list. The following are excerpts from their meeting:

> *Olatunji:* Bashar, I propose you open a discretionary personal account with OFS. I will use the cash that you deposit into the account to purchase a "model portfolio" based on the Nigerian equities our analysts are recommending. Any time our analysts change their recommendations or issue new ones, I will execute trades in your account when we do it for our other discretionary clients. I will also send you an instant message before I make the trade just to let you know, and then I will call you afterward to discuss the trade in more detail. With this arrangement, I can prove to you how well our analysts' recommendations perform, and you will be able to participate directly.

> *Bashar:* That's a good idea. Could you send me portfolio performance data monthly as you do with your other clients? Please be aware that I will not disclose this model portfolio to Serengeti's clients until I see how well your analysts' recommendations perform. In the meantime, Shah will continue to conduct due diligence on OFS to determine whether it should be added to our approved list of broker/dealers. (Question 8).

The next day, Bashar opens a discretionary personal account with OFS. Within a few days, Olatunji is able to build the model portfolio in Bashar's account despite liquidity issues in the market. Shortly thereafter, Olatunji calls Bashar.

> *Olatunji:* I have good news for you. At the end of next week, our team of analysts will be issuing a strong buy recommendation on Swann Bank (SWNB), a commercial bank that is headquartered in Lagos. Because its stock is thinly traded, I have already started building a position in SWNB in your portfolio. Three days before the research report is issued, I have instructed our traders to simultaneously buy and sell shares of SWNB to increase its liquidity in the market so it will be easier for our clients to purchase it for their portfolios. (Questions 9, 10, 11)

> *Bashar:* Thank you for the information and update.

Later that same day, after Olatunji establishes a position in SWNB in Bashar's portfolio, Bashar calls Grant to inform him about Olatunji's upcoming recommendation. (Question 12)

Case Questions

1. Does Bashar *most likely* violate the CFA Institute Code and Standards with regard to the premium subscription service?

   A. Yes.

Serengeti Advisory Services

   B. No, because she offers it only to clients who can afford it.

   C. No, because clients must pay an additional fee for this service.

    A is correct. Bashar violates Standard III(B): Fair Dealing because she offers the premium subscription service only to clients she believes can afford it. According to Standard III(B), "Members and Candidates must deal fairly and objectively with all clients when providing investment analysis, making investment recommendations, taking investment action, or engaging in other professional activities." According to the guidance for Standard III(B), "Members and Candidates may differentiate their services to clients, but different levels of service must not disadvantage or negatively affect clients. In addition, the different service levels should be disclosed to clients and prospective clients and should be available to everyone (i.e., different service levels should not be offered selectively)."

    B is incorrect. Bashar offers the premium service only to clients who she believes can afford it and does not make the service available to all clients. According to the guidance for Standard III(B), the premium subscription "should be disclosed to clients and prospective clients and should be available to everyone (i.e., different service levels should not be offered selectively)." Bashar's view on which clients can afford the premium service is irrelevant.

    C is incorrect. Although clients pay an additional fee for the premium subscription service, Bashar offers this service only to clients she believes can afford it. According to the guidance for Standard III(B), "Members and Candidates may provide more personal, specialized, or in-depth service to clients who are willing to pay for premium services through higher management fees or higher levels of brokerage. Members and Candidates may differentiate their services to clients, but different levels of service must not advantage or negatively affect clients. In addition, different service levels should be disclosed to clients and prospective clients and should be available to everyone (i.e., different service levels should not be offered selectively)."

2. By allowing Serengeti to publish a research report and recommendation on Gbeho Telecommunications, did Bashar *most likely* violate the CFA Institute Code and Standards?

   A. No, because Bashar's relationship to Gbeho was not significant.

   B. No, because Serengeti researchers were not aware of Bashar's connection to Gbeho, and therefore, their research was independent and objective.

   C. Yes.

    C is correct. Bashar violated Standard VI(C): Disclosure of Conflicts by allowing Serengeti to publish research on Gbeho Telecommunications without disclosing in the report that her family had a personal financial interest in the company. The disclosure should be prominent and communicate the relevant information effectively, in plain language.

    Bashar should have informed the Serengeti researchers about her husband's family's ownership of the company and instructed the research team to disclose the conflict of interest in the report. Bashar's family's ownership is a potential conflict of interest that could lead clients to question the independence and objectivity of Serengeti's research. Given her family's ownership, Bashar could be viewed as having undue influence on the decision to cover Gbeho and to publish a favorable research recommendation on the company.

A is incorrect. The ownership of Gbeho by her husband's family creates a significant interest for Bashar in the company that should have been clearly disclosed in Serengeti's research report.

B is incorrect. The fact that the researchers were not aware of Bashar's connection to Gbeho raises a question as to their due diligence process in conducting their research on Gbeho. Their lack of awareness of any conflict does not remove, or eliminate, the fact that a perceived conflict of interest exists, given the facts. Bashar's conflict of interest with Gbeho is considered significant and should have been prominently disclosed in Serengeti's research report.

3. Which of Bashar's procedures regarding the use of third-party research *mostly likely* violates the CFA Institute Code and Standards?

   A. Procedure 1

   B. Procedure 2

   C. Procedure 3

   B is correct. Bashar violated Standard I(C): Misrepresentation by asking the analyst who wrote the report to remove qualifying statements or caveats from reports that include the presentation of statistical estimates of forecasts prepared by others. According to the guidance for Standard I(C), when presenting statistical estimates of forecasts prepared by others, the source should be identified along with the qualifying statements or caveats that might have been included.

   A is incorrect. According to the guidance for Standard I(C), to avoid plagiarism, Bashar does need to ensure that when reports cite specific quotations, the specific references are named rather than attributing them generally to "leading analysts" and "investment experts." The guidance further states that "Members and Candidates should disclose whether the research being presented to clients comes from another source—from either within or outside the Member's or Candidate's firm. This allows clients to understand who has the expertise for a research report and whether the work is being done by the analyst, other members of the firm, or an outside party."

   C is incorrect. According to the guidance for Standard I(C), to avoid plagiarism, Bashar does need to ensure that when reports use charts or graphs prepared by others, the sources are cited.

4. Does Bashar's referral arrangement with the broker/dealers on the approved list *most likely* violate the CFA Institute Code and Standards?

   A. No.

   B. Yes, because the broker/dealers might not provide best price and execution.

   C. Yes, because she is placing Serengeti's interests before those of her clients.

Serengeti Advisory Services

A is correct. Nothing indicates that Bashar's referral of clients to the broker/dealer producing the research report or whose information was used by Serengeti is a violation of the CFA Institute Code and Standards. Bashar discloses to clients the broker/dealer responsible for the report or information and suggests that clients trade through that broker/dealer. According to Standard VI(C): Referral Fees, "Members and Candidates must disclose to their employer, clients, and prospective clients, as appropriate, any compensation, consideration, or benefit received from or paid to others for the recommendation of products or services." No quid pro quo benefit is being given to Serengeti or to the broker/dealers. In this case, Bashar is merely suggesting to the firm's clients that they trade through a particular broker/dealer because of the research or other information that the firm provided. The fact that Bashar thinks these suggestions provide additional incentive for broker/dealers to share insights and information with her analysts at no cost is irrelevant. The asset manager client is the one who makes the final decision as to where to direct its trades. Therefore, Bashar has not violated Standard VI(C): Referral Fees.

B is incorrect. It is not Bashar's responsibility to determine whether the broker/dealer that she is referring her asset manager clients to provides best price and best execution. Instead, it is the duty of the asset managers to seek best price and best execution. Policies related to soft commissions as well as to best price and best execution relate to asset managers that have discretion over brokers executing transactions. Therefore, Bashar has not violated Standard III(A): Loyalty, Prudence, and Care.

C is incorrect. The referral arrangement does not place the interests of Serengeti above those of its clients. Bashar only suggests to her clients that they trade through the broker/dealer that provided the research report or other information to Serengeti. This action is not a violation of Standard III(A): Loyalty, Prudence, and Care.

5. With regard to Grant and Bashar's phone conversation about Serengeti's research partnerships, who *most likely* violated the CFA Institute Code and Standards?

    A. Grant

    B. Bashar

    C. Both Bashar and Grant

    A is correct. Grant violated Standard III(A): Loyalty, Prudence, and Care by relying solely on Bashar's suggestions about which broker/dealer to use to execute his clients' trades rather than seeking the broker/dealer that provides best price and best execution. Standard III(A) states, "Members and Candidates have a duty of loyalty to their clients and must act with reasonable care and exercise prudent judgment. Members and Candidates must act for the benefit of their clients and place their clients' interests before their employer's or their own interests." Grant has an obligation to deliver best price and best execution for every trade, which might entail splitting orders among several brokers, if necessary to achieve full execution.

    B is incorrect. Bashar did not violate the CFA Institute Code and Standards during the phone conversation with Grant about the research partnerships. She simply encouraged Grant to use the broker/dealers who produced the research report or whose information was used. According to the guidance for Standard III(A): Loyalty, Prudence, and Care, Grant is "obligated to seek 'best price' and 'best execution' and be assured by the client that the goods or services purchased from the brokerage will benefit the account beneficiaries. 'Best execution' refers to a trading process that seeks to maximize the value of the client's portfolio within the client's stated investment objectives and constraints."

C is incorrect. Only Grant violated the CFA Institute Code and Standards. Grant violated Standard III(A) by relying solely on Bashar's recommendation of a broker/dealer to execute his clients' trades instead of ensuring that the broker/dealer provides best price and best execution. Standard III(A) states, "Members and Candidates have a duty of loyalty to their clients and must act with reasonable care and exercise prudent judgment." Grant has an obligation to deliver best price and best execution for client trades, which might entail splitting orders among several brokers for full execution. Bashar does not violate the CFA Institute Code and Standards during the phone conversation with Grant because she discloses the referral arrangement that Serengeti has with the broker/dealers on its approved list.

6. To avoid violating the CFA Institute Code and Standards, which of Bashar's responses to Olatunji's forum invitation would be *most appropriate*?

   A. Option 1

   B. Option 2

   C. Option 3

   C is correct. To prevent violating Standard I(B): Independence and Objectivity, Bashar's, Kariuki's, and Shah's air travel and overnight hotel accommodations should be paid for by Serengeti. Under Standard I(B), it would be permissible for OFS to pay for meals and entertainment provided at the forum. This action would not likely jeopardize their independence and objectivity when determining whether to add OFS to Serengeti's approved list of broker/dealers. Standard I(B) states, "Members and Candidates must use reasonable care and judgment to achieve and maintain independence and objectivity in their professional activities. Members and Candidates must not offer, solicit, or accept any gift, benefit, compensation, or consideration that reasonably could be expected to compromise their own or another's independence and objectivity." According to the guidance for Standard I(B), "To avoid the appearance of compromising their independence and objectivity, best practice dictates that Members and Candidates always use commercial transportation at their expense or at the expense of their firm rather than accept paid travel arrangements from an outside company."

   A is incorrect. Allowing OFS to pay for all of their expenses could reasonably be expected to compromise the independence and objectivity of Bashar, Shah, and Kariuki when evaluating whether OFS should be included on Serengeti's approved list. Standard I(B): Independence and Objectivity states, "Members and Candidates must use reasonable care and judgment to achieve and maintain independence and objectivity in their professional activities. Members and Candidates must not offer, solicit, or accept any gift, benefit, compensation, or consideration that reasonably could be expected to compromise their own or another's independence and objectivity." According to the guidance for Standard I(B), "To avoid the appearance of compromising their independence and objectivity, best practice dictates

Serengeti Advisory Services 427

that Members and Candidates always use commercial transportation at their expense or at the expense of their firm rather than accept paid travel arrangements from an outside company."

B is incorrect. Allowing OFS to pay for their air travel and overnight hotel accommodations could reasonably be expected to compromise their independence and objectivity when evaluating whether OFS should be included on Serengeti's approved list. Standard I(B): Independence and Objectivity requires "Members and Candidates . . . [to] use reasonable care and judgment to achieve and maintain independence and objectivity in their professional activities. Members and Candidates must not offer, solicit, or accept any gift, benefit, compensation, or consideration that reasonably could be expected to compromise their own or another's independence and objectivity." Travel and accommodations are the largest costs associated with attending the event. According to the guidance for Standard I(B), "To avoid the appearance of compromising their independence and objectivity, best practice dictates that Members and Candidates always use commercial transportation at their expense or at the expense of their firm rather than accept paid travel arrangements from an outside company."

7. Did Kariuki *most likely* violate the CFA Institute Code and Standards by seeking out OFS clients on the list with the highest trading volumes at the forum?

   A. No.

   B. Yes, with regard to Standard I(D): Misconduct.

   C. Yes, with regard to Standard II(A): Material Nonpublic Information.

   B is correct. Kariuki violated Standard I(D): Misconduct by using OFS's confidential and proprietary information that she found on top of the recycling bin. Standard I(D) states, "Members and Candidates must not engage in any professional conduct involving dishonesty, fraud, or deceit or commit any act that reflects adversely on their professional reputation, integrity, or competence." Kariuki is effectively misappropriating confidential information that she knows does not belong to her and is not meant for public consumption, which is a form of dishonesty. The circumstances of her acquiring the information and the misconduct of the person who carelessly handled the information does not mitigate Kariuki's improper behavior in using the information after it is discovered. The person responsible for disposing of this confidential list likely violated Standard III(E): Preservation of Confidentiality by not ensuring the safe disposal of the list so it would not be found by others who did not have permission to access the information.

   A is incorrect. Kariuki violated Standard I(D): Misconduct by using OFS's confidential and proprietary information that she found on top of the recycling bin. Standard I(D) states that "Members and Candidates must not engage in any professional conduct involving dishonesty, fraud, or deceit or commit any act that reflects adversely on their professional reputation, integrity, or competence." The person responsible for disposing of this confidential list likely violated Standard III(E): Preservation of Confidentiality by not ensuring the safe disposal of the list so it would not be found by others who did not have permission to access the information.

C is incorrect. Kariuki did not violate Standard II(A): Material Nonpublic Information because the confidential nonpublic information that she obtains would not have an impact on the price of a security or affect investment decision making. Instead, it is a list of OFS clients, their contact numbers, email addresses, and trading volumes. According to the guidance for Standard II(A), "Information is 'material' if its disclosure would probably have an impact on the price of a security or if reasonable investors would want to know the information before making an investment decision. In other words, information is material if it would significantly alter the total mix of information currently available about a security in such a way that the price of the security would be affected."

8. With respect to the creation and management of the model portfolio, have Bashar or Olatunji *most likely* violated the CFA Institute Code and Standards?

   A. Only Olatunji violated the CFA Institute Code and Standards.

   B. Both Bashar and Olatunji violated the CFA Institute Code and Standards.

   C. Neither Bashar nor Olatunji violated the CFA Institute Code and Standards.

   C is correct. Neither Bashar nor Olatunji violated the CFA Institute Code and Standards.

   - Bashar: It is not a violation of the CFA Institute Code and Standards for her to open a discretionary account at OFS and allow Olatunji to create and manage a model portfolio using his analysts' recommendations. It is also not a violation for her to not disclose this information to Serengeti's clients. These actions will not compromise her independence or objectivity [Standard I(B)] or create a conflict of interest [Standard VI(A)].
   - Olatunji: It is not a violation for him to create and manage Bashar's model portfolio using his analysts' recommendations. Olatunji is not violating Standard III(B): Fair Dealing because he is executing trades in Bashar's account at the same time he executes trades in other client accounts. In addition, he is not violating Standard III(B) by instant messaging Bashar before he executes a trade in her account, by calling her afterward to provide more detail on the trade, or by providing her with monthly performance reports on her portfolio. Nothing indicates that these actions are any different from what Olatunji would do for any other client if they requested the same treatment.

   A is incorrect. Olatunji did not violate the CFA Institute Code and Standards. It is not a violation for him to create and manage a portfolio model for Bashar based on his analysts' recommendations. Olatunji is not violating Standard III(B): Fair Dealing because he is executing trades in Bashar's account at the same time he executes trades in other client accounts. In addition, he is not violating Standard III(B) by instant messaging Bashar before he executes a trade in her account, by calling her afterward to provide more details on the recommendation, or by providing her with monthly performance reports on her portfolio. Nothing indicates that these actions are any different from what Olatunji would do for any other client if they requested the same treatment.

Serengeti Advisory Services   **429**

B is incorrect. Neither Bashar nor Olatunji violated the CFA Institute Code and Standards.

- Bashar: It is not a violation for her to open a discretionary account at OFS and allow Olatunji to create and manage a model portfolio using his analysts' recommendations. In addition, it is not a violation for her to not disclose this information to Serengeti's clients. These actions will not compromise her independence or objectivity [Standard I(B)] or create a conflict of interest [Standard VI(A)].

- Olatunji: It is not a violation for him to create and manage Bashar's model portfolio using his analysts' recommendations. Olatunji is not violating Standard III(B): Fair Dealing because he is executing trades in Bashar's account at the same time he executes trades in other client accounts. In addition, he is not violating Standard III(B) by instant messaging Bashar before he executes a trade in her account, by calling her afterward to provide more details on the trade, or by providing her with monthly performance reports on her portfolio. Nothing indicates that these actions are any different from what Olatunji would do for any other client if they requested the same treatment.

9. In telling Bashar about the upcoming recommendation on SWNB, Olatunji is *most likely* violating the CFA Institute Standard of Professional Conduct on:

   A. Fair Dealing.

   B. Preservation of Confidentiality.

   C. Communication with Clients and Prospective Clients.

   A is correct. Olatunji violated Standard III(B): Fair Dealing by telling Bashar about the strong buy recommendation on SWNB before the research report is disseminated to all clients. According to the guidance for Standard III(B), the standard "addresses the manner in which investment recommendations or changes in prior recommendations are disseminated to clients. Each Member or Candidate is obligated to ensure that information is disseminated in such a way that all clients have a fair opportunity to act on every recommendation."

   B is incorrect. Standard III(E): Preservation of Confidentiality addresses keeping information about current, former, and prospective clients confidential. According to the guidance for Standard III(E), the standard "requires that Members and Candidates preserve the confidentiality of information communicated to them by their clients, prospective clients, and former clients." Olatunji violated Standard III(B): Fair Dealing by telling Bashar about the strong buy recommendation before the research report is disseminated to all clients. Olatunji would need to communicate the strong buy recommendation to all clients at approximately the same time to meet Standard III(B).

   C is incorrect. According to the guidance for Standard V(B): Communication with Clients and Prospective Clients, the standard "addresses Member and Candidate conduct with respect to communicating with clients. Developing and maintaining clear, frequent, and thorough communication practices is critical to providing high-quality financial services to clients." Olatunji violated Standard III(B): Fair Dealing by telling Bashar about the strong buy recommendation before the research report was disseminated to all clients.

10. In building a position in SWNB in Bashar's portfolio, who *most likely* violated the CFA Institute Code and Standards?

A. Only Olatunji

B. Only Bashar

C. Both Bashar and Olatunji

C is correct. Both Olatunji and Bashar violated the CFA Institute Code and Standards.

- Olatunji violated Standard III(B): Fair Dealing by purchasing shares of SWNB in Bashar's model portfolio before the recommendation was disseminated to other clients. According to the guidance for Standard III(B), the standard "addresses the manner in which investment recommendations or changes to prior recommendations are disseminated to clients. Each Member or Candidate is obligated to ensure that the information is disseminated in such a manner that all clients have a fair opportunity to act on every recommendation." If Olatunji had disseminated the strong buy recommendation on SWNB to all clients at approximately the same time he disseminated it to Bashar, he would not be in violation of Standard III(B).

- Bashar violated Standard I(A): Knowledge of the Law. Bashar knows that Olatunji is building a position in SWNB in her portfolio before the research report on SWNB is issued. According to the guidance for Standard I(A), "Members and Candidates are responsible for violations in which they *knowingly* participate or assist." The guidance for Standard I(A) states that "if a Member or Candidate has reasonable grounds to believe that imminent or ongoing client or employer activities are illegal or unethical, the Member or Candidate must dissociate, or separate, from the activity." As head of Serengeti, Bashar needed to advise Olatunji that she rejects the advance purchase of SWNB, requiring an unwinding of the trade, and then communicate Olatunji's violations to the appropriate regulators.

A is incorrect. Bashar also violated the CFA Institute Standards of Professional Conduct. Bashar violated Standard I(A): Knowledge of the Law because she should know that Olatunji violated the Code and Standards by selectively disclosing the strong buy recommendation on SWNB to her and building a position in it before the report is issued to all clients. According to the guidance for Standard I(A), "Members and Candidates are responsible for violations in which they *knowingly* participate or assist." The guidance for Standard I(A) states that "if a Member or Candidate has reasonable grounds to believe that imminent or ongoing client or employer activities are illegal or unethical, the Member or Candidate must dissociate, or separate, from the activity."

B is incorrect. Olatunji also violated the CFA Institute Standards of Professional Conduct. Olatunji violated Standard III(B): Fair Dealing by purchasing shares of SWNB in Bashar's model portfolio before the recommendation was disseminated to other clients. According to the guidance for

Serengeti Advisory Services

Standard III(B), the standard "addresses the manner in which investment recommendations or changes to prior recommendations are disseminated to clients. Each Member or Candidate is obligated to ensure that the information is disseminated in such a manner that all clients have a fair opportunity to act on every recommendation."

11. In his instructions to his traders, Olatunji *most likely* violated all the following CFA Institute Standards of Professional Conduct *except*:

   A. Market Manipulation.

   B. Priority of Transactions.

   C. Responsibilities of Supervisors.

   B is correct. Olatunji did not violate Standard VI(B): Priority of Transactions. According to Standard VI(B), "Investment transactions for clients and employers must have priority over investment transactions in which a Member or Candidate is the beneficial owner." According to the guidance for the standard, it "is designed to prevent any potential conflict of interest or the appearance of a conflict of interest with respect to personal transactions." In this scenario, Olatunji did not trade for himself, beneficially or otherwise.

   A is incorrect. Olatunji violated Standard II(B): Market Manipulation. By instructing his traders to simultaneously buy and sell shares of SWNB a few days before the research report was issued, Olatunji engaged in transaction-based manipulation. Olatunji asked his traders to engage in "wash trading," which is the simultaneous buying and selling of SWNB to create misleading and artificial activity in SWNB's stock.

   C is incorrect. By instructing his traders to simultaneously buy and sell shares of SWNB (called "wash trading," which creates misleading and artificial activity in the stock) just before the research report was issued, Olatunji violated Standard II(B): Market Manipulation as well as Standard IV(C): Responsibilities of Supervisors. According to Standard IV(C), as the traders' supervisor, Olatunji "must make reasonable efforts to ensure that anyone subject to their supervision or authority complies with applicable laws, rules, regulations, and the Code and Standards."

12. By informing Grant about the recommendation on SWNB, Bashar *most likely* violated all the following CFA Institute Standards of Professional Conduct *except*:

   A. Fair Dealing.

   B. Priority of Transactions.

   C. Preservation of Confidentiality.

   C is correct. Bashar did not violate Standard III(E): Preservation of Confidentiality, which addresses keeping information about current, former, and prospective clients confidential. According to the guidance for Standard III(E), the standard "requires that Members and Candidates preserve the confidentiality of information communicated to them by their clients, prospective clients, and former clients." Bashar violated Standard III(B):

Fair Dealing by telling Grant about the strong buy recommendation before telling her other clients. In addition, Bashar violated Standard V(B): Priority of Transactions.

A is incorrect. Bashar told Grant about the new recommendation before telling her other clients; therefore, Bashar violated Standard III(B): Fair Dealing. According to the guidance for Standard III(B), the standard "addresses the manner in which investment recommendations or changes in prior recommendations are disseminated to clients. Each Member or Candidate is obligated to ensure that information is disseminated in such a manner that all clients have a fair opportunity to act on every recommendation."

B is incorrect. By waiting until the position in SWNB was established in her portfolio before telling Grant about the upcoming recommendation, Bashar violated Standard VI(B): Priority of Transactions. According to this standard, "Investment transactions for clients and employers must have priority over investment transactions in which a Member or Candidate is the beneficial owner."

3 BANCO LIBERTAD

☐ evaluate practices, policies, and conduct relative to the CFA Institute Code of Ethics and Standards of Professional Conduct

☐ explain how the practices, policies, and conduct do or do not violate the CFA Institute Code of Ethics and Standards of Professional Conduct

Banco Libertad (BL) is a private bank based in the country of Urutina.[2] Founded in 1957, BL provides investment management, securities research, real estate financing, and wealth management services to high-net-worth individuals.

Sofia Maduro, CFA, is the managing director of BL's investment management division. Prior to joining BL 15 months ago, she spent 20 years as a portfolio manager for a global wealth management firm that has a large operation in Urutina. This morning, Maduro is meeting with two of the portfolio managers she supervises: Julio Ortiz, CFA, and Guadalupe Sanchez, CFA. Ortiz and Sanchez work as a team at BL's headquarters in Urutina, managing approximately USD5.2 billion in assets. All of Ortiz's clients reside in either Urutina or Chiladour, and all of Sanchez's clients reside in either Urutina or Panaguay. For compliance purposes, applicable law for them is that of the country where their clients reside.

Urutina ranks first among countries in the region based on its economic growth (GDP), prosperity, innovation, and infrastructure. It has fair and transparent capital markets and no personal income taxes.

Chiladour is a neighboring country with a developing and rapidly modernizing economy. Because it has a nascent capital market, its wealthy citizens prefer to invest their money in Urutina.

---

2 **Banco Libertad:** Barbara Mainzer, CFA, and Michael G. McMillan, PhD, CFA. *Ethics Cases.* © 2019 CFA Institute. All rights reserved. Consistent with the 11th Edition of the *Standards of Practice Handbook.*

Banco Libertad   **433**

Panaguay shares a border with Urutina. It is a politically unstable country with an emerging economy that is highly dependent on commodities, such as petroleum and agricultural products. It has established capital markets with strict securities laws and regulations, but as result of the political instability, its wealthy citizens prefer to invest their money in Urutina.

Exhibit 2 summarizes each portfolio manager's client jurisdictions. Exhibit 3 contains a comparison of the securities regulations and laws in each country as well as BL's policies.

Exhibit 2: Client Jurisdictions

	Urutina	Chiladour	Panaguay
J. Ortiz	Y	Y	
G. Sanchez	Y		Y

Exhibit 3: Securities Laws and Regulations and BL Policies

	Urutina	Chiladour	Panaguay	BL Policies
Use of social media to post investment information (performance reports, investment opinions, and recommendations)	Allowed	Allowed	Prohibited	No policy
Use of instant messaging for trade executions and confirmations	Prohibited	Allowed	Allowed	No policy
Disclosure of personal or confidential information to law enforcement officials	Allowed	Prohibited	Prohibited	No policy
Insider trading	Prohibited	Prohibited	Prohibited	Prohibited
Referral fees	No disclosure required	No disclosure required	No disclosure required	No disclosure required

After Maduro welcomes the two portfolio managers to her office and they are comfortably seated, the following conversation takes place.

> *Maduro*: Thank you for taking the time out of your busy schedules to meet with me. It must be difficult to manage the portfolios of clients who live in different countries and in different time zones. I want to commend both of you on your use of technology to communicate with your clients. Your use of social media to post investment recommendations, performance reports, and investment opinions has set a great example for other managers at BL.

> *Ortiz*: Thank you for the compliment and for allowing Guadalupe and I to use instant messaging (IM) platforms to manage our clients' portfolios. Now, all our clients have to do is IM us whenever they want to buy and sell securities, and we, in turn, IM them with their trade confirmations once the transactions are complete.

Maduro: On a more serious note, it has been brought to my attention that law enforcement officials from the governments of Chiladour and Panaguay have contacted both of you requesting confidential information on your clients. What are you doing about these inquiries?

Ortiz: I have a client who is the former Minister of Finance in Chiladour. Since establishing his own financial consulting business five years ago, he has deposited more than USD5 million with BL. Now he is under investigation for allegedly embezzling from the Chiladour Treasury. In response to the inquiry into his personal finances, I have given law enforcement officials from Chiladour all of the information they requested on this client.

Sanchez: I have a client who is a general in the Panaguay Army. His grandfather founded the country's second-largest petroleum processing facility. When the general opened his account last summer, he deposited approximately USD35 million and told me that he had inherited the money from his grandfather, who had recently passed away. According to law enforcement officials in Panaguay, this money allegedly came from bribes the general received from directing military contracts to specific corporations. Like Ortiz, I was so disgusted by the client's behavior that I gave the law enforcement officials all of the information they requested on this client. (Questions 1, 2, 3)

Maduro: Thank you for doing this. It is important that BL maintain good relations with law enforcement officials throughout the region. Speaking of good relations, I noticed that many of your clients have been referred by law firms in Chiladour and Panaguay. Do you have any referral arrangements with these firms?

Ortiz and Sanchez: Our referral arrangements are very informal, which is why we do not bother disclosing them to clients. Every year we purchase tickets for the principals of these firms to attend CONMEBOL Copa América, the men's international football tournament. In addition, we always take them out to dinner whenever we travel to Chiladour and Panaguay to meet with our clients or when the principals come to Urutina to meet with their clients. (Question 4)

Maduro: Do you have any other arrangements that I am not aware of?

Ortiz and Sanchez: Now that you mention it, yes, we do. We have special arrangements with two of our largest clients, Juan Fabre and Caroline Zeissl. After our securities analysts post changes to their research recommendations on the BL client website, we immediately call these two to discuss these changes in detail and any impact on their portfolios. Clients can sign up for email or text alerts to notify them when analyst recommendations change, but we feel calling Fabre and Zeissl personally is important because of their asset size. In addition, whenever Fabre and Zeissl are interested in participating in an IPO, we invite them to the company roadshow presentations organized by the investment bank underwriting the issue. Because of capacity constraints, we cannot invite our other clients who are interested in these IPOs to the presentations, so we do not disclose the roadshow opportunity to them. Whether or not they receive an invitation, we make IPO opportunities available to all our clients for whom the investment is suitable. (Questions 5, 6)

Ortiz: I have known and worked with Fabre and his family for about 15 years. In any year that his portfolio outperforms its benchmark, he allows my family and I to use his beach house in Jamaica for a week of our choosing. This arrangement is acknowledged in writing by the client and

Banco Libertad

435

documented as part of the client's investment policy statement (IPS). Three months ago, my family and I used his beach house because, for the first time since he made the offer, his portfolio outperformed its benchmark this past year.

Sanchez: I have known and worked with Zeissl and her family for about 10 years. The Zeissl family owns the Aneka, a luxury hotel and spa in the Bahamas. She has said that in any year that her portfolio outperforms its benchmark, my family and I can spend a week at the Aneka without charge. As Julio described, this arrangement is documented with the client. Her portfolio also outperformed its benchmark this past year, so my family and I spent a week at the Aneka this past summer.

Maduro: Not having reviewed your client files, I was unaware of these arrangements, so thank you for telling me about them. I do have another meeting shortly, so let's end for today. (Question 7)

Case Questions

1. Have Ortiz and/or Sanchez violated the CFA Institute Code and Standards in their use of social media?

   A. Neither has violated the Code and Standards.

   B. Only Sanchez has violated the Code and Standards.

   C. Both Ortiz and Sanchez have violated the Code and Standards.

   B is correct. Sanchez has violated Standard I(A): Professionalism, Knowledge of the Law. According to the guidance for Standard I(A): "Members and Candidates who practice in multiple jurisdictions may be subject to varied securities laws and regulations. If applicable law is stricter than the requirements of the Code and Standards, Members and Candidates must adhere to applicable law; otherwise they must adhere to the Code and Standards." In this case, applicable law is determined by where the clients reside, which for Sanchez is Urutina and Panaguay. Applicable law in Panaguay is stricter than the Code and Standards because it prohibits the use of social media to post investment information (Exhibit 3), so Sanchez must follow the law in Panaguay. Sanchez is allowed to use social media in Urutina because applicable law is similar to the Code and Standards, which does not prohibit the use of social media in this way.

   A is incorrect. Sanchez has violated Standard I(A) because using social media to post investment information is prohibited in Panaguay, where applicable law is stricter than the Code and Standards.

   C is incorrect. The use of social media to post investment information is allowed in Chiladour and Urutina, and Ortiz has not violated the Code and Standards. Applicable laws in these countries are similar to the Code and Standards, which does not prohibit the use of social media in this way. Sanchez has violated Standard I(A) because using social media to post investment information is prohibited in Panaguay.

2. Has Maduro violated the CFA Institute Code and Standards by allowing Ortiz and Sanchez to use social media to post investment information?

   A. No.

B. Yes, by allowing Sanchez to use social media.

C. Yes, by allowing both Ortiz and Sanchez to use social media.

B is correct. Maduro has allowed, and in doing so approved of, Sanchez's use of social media with her clients in Panaguay, despite its use for posting investment information being prohibited in Panaguay, where the applicable law is stricter than the Code and Standards. According to Standard IV(C): Duties to Employers, Responsibilities of Supervisors, "Members and Candidates must make reasonable efforts to ensure that anyone subject to their supervision or authority complies with the applicable laws, rules, regulations, and the Code and Standards."

In this instance, in her supervisory capacity and knowing that Sanchez invests on behalf of her clients in Panaguay, Maduro must ensure, through appropriate education, support, and training, that Sanchez is aware of and complies with applicable Panaguayan laws and regulations.

A is incorrect. Maduro has allowed, and in doing so approved of, Sanchez's use of social media with her clients in Panaguay, where it is prohibited for posting investment information (i.e., applicable law is stricter than the Code and Standards).

C is incorrect. Maduro has allowed, and in doing so approved of, Sanchez's use of social media with her clients in Panaguay, where it is prohibited for posting investment information (i.e., applicable law is stricter than the Code and Standards).

3. Have Ortiz and Sanchez violated the CFA Institute Code and Standards by using IM and disclosing information on their clients to law enforcement officials?

A. Yes, both are violations.

B. It was only a violation to use IM.

C. It was only a violation to disclose information on their clients to law enforcement officials.

A is correct. Ortiz and Sanchez violated Standard I(A): Professionalism, Knowledge of the Law because they have used IM to communicate with their clients in Urutina, where doing so is prohibited. According to the vignette, applicable law is that of the country where the clients reside. Both Ortiz and Sanchez have clients in Urutina, which prohibits the use of IM to communicate investment information. Because applicable law in Urutina is stricter than the Code and Standards (which allows the use of IM), Ortiz and Sanchez must follow applicable law. In addition, the disclosure of personal or confidential information is prohibited in Chiladour and Panaguay. Applicable law in these countries is stricter than the Code and Standards, which requires members and candidates to disclose client information when requested by law enforcement. In disclosing the confidential information, Ortiz and Sanchez violated applicable law, and in doing so, violated Standard I(A): Professionalism, Knowledge of the Law. Guidance for this Standard states, "Members and Candidates who practice in multiple jurisdictions may be subject to varied securities laws and regulations. If applicable law is stricter than the requirements of the Code and Standard, Members and Candidates must adhere to applicable law; otherwise they must adhere to the Code and Standards."

Banco Libertad 437

B is incorrect. Ortiz and Sanchez violated the Code and Standards by using IM to communicate with their clients and by disclosing information on their clients to law enforcement officials. Both are violations of applicable law and therefore violations of the Code and Standards.

C is incorrect. Ortiz and Sanchez violated the Code and Standards by disclosing information on their clients to law enforcement officials and by using IM to communicate with their clients. Both are violations of applicable law and therefore violations of the Code and Standards.

4. Have Ortiz and Sanchez violated the CFA Institute Code and Standards in their referral arrangement with lawyers in Chiladour and Panaguay?

   A. Yes.

   B. No, because they disclosed the arrangement to Maduro.

   C. No, because disclosure is not required in Urutina, Chiladour, or Panaguay.

   A is correct. Ortiz and Sanchez have violated Standard VI(C): Conflicts of Interest, Referral Fees by not disclosing to BL, clients, and prospective clients the benefit they receive and pay to the lawyers who recommend clients to them. According to Standard VI(C), "Members and Candidates must disclose to their employer, clients, and prospective clients, as appropriate, any compensation, consideration, or benefit received from or paid to others for the recommendation of products or services."

   They have also violated Standard I(A): Professionalism, Knowledge of the Law. In this case, Ortiz and Sanchez must follow the Code and Standards because these are stricter than applicable country laws. Guidance for Standard I(A) states, "Members and Candidates who practice in multiple jurisdictions may be subject to varied securities laws and regulations. If applicable law is stricter than the requirements of the Code and Standard, Members and Candidates must adhere to applicable law; otherwise they must adhere to the Code and Standards."

   B is incorrect. Although Ortiz and Sanchez disclosed the fee arrangement to Maduro, they disclosed it after the fact, and they have not disclosed the arrangement to clients and prospective clients.

   C is incorrect. Although disclosure is not required in Urutina, Chiladour, or Panaguay, Ortiz and Sanchez must follow the stricter of "applicable laws, rules, and regulations." In this case, the Code and Standards are stricter than applicable law because they require disclosure of referral arrangements.

5. Do Ortiz and Sanchez violate the CFA Institute Code and Standards by calling Fabre and Zeissl to discuss changes in research recommendations made by BL's analysts?

   A. No.

   B. Yes, because they are not dealing with their other clients fairly.

   C. Yes, because they are not treating their other clients with loyalty, prudence, and care.

A is correct. Ortiz and Sanchez have not violated the Code and Standards. Ortiz and Sanchez call these clients immediately after BL analysts post changes to their research recommendations on the BL client website (i.e., the changes have been publicly posted or made publicly accessible). Because Fabre and Zeissl are the portfolio managers' largest clients, they receive additional personal service because they presumably pay higher fees than other clients or have a large amount of assets under management with the firm. Guidance for Standard III(B): Duties to Clients, Fair Dealing states, "Each Member or Candidate is obligated to ensure that information is disseminated in such a manner that all clients have a fair opportunity to act on every recommendation."

B is incorrect. Ortiz and Sanchez call Fabre and Zeissl after the changes in recommendations have been posted on BL's website (i.e., the changes have been publicly posted or made publicly accessible). Therefore, they are not treating their other clients unfairly but rather are calling their largest clients to discuss the changes in more detail.

C is incorrect. By calling Fabre and Zeissl, their largest clients, after the analysts post their recommendation changes on BL's website (i.e., the changes have been publicly posted or made publicly accessible), Ortiz and Sanchez are acting for the benefit of their clients and placing their clients' interests before BL's or their own interests.

6. Have Ortiz and Sanchez violated the CFA Institute Code and Standards by inviting Fabre and Zeissl to IPO roadshow presentations?

   A. No.

   B. Yes, because they do not invite other clients to the roadshow.

   C. Yes, because they do not disclose this opportunity to other clients.

   A is correct. Inviting clients to the IPO roadshow is not a violation of the Code and Standards. Fabre and Zeissl are their largest clients, and in addition, being invited to the IPO roadshow does not disadvantage other clients who are interested in the IPO. Therefore, they have not violated Standard III(B): Duties to Clients, Fair Dealing. The guidance for Standard III(B) states, "Members and Candidates may differentiate their services to clients, but different levels of service must not disadvantage or negatively affect clients." Attendance at the roadshow does not give Fabre and Zeissl any special advantage or priority over other clients in IPO participation.

   B is incorrect. Not inviting to the roadshow other clients who are interested in the IPO does not disadvantage those clients.

   C is incorrect. Ortiz and Sanchez are not obligated to disclose this opportunity to their other clients because it does not disadvantage those clients.

7. Have Ortiz and Sanchez violated the CFA Institute Code and Standards in not disclosing their respective arrangements with Fabre and Zeissl?

   A. Yes.

   B. No, because Ortiz and Sanchez have documented the arrangements in the clients' IPS.

   C. No, because these types of client arrangements do not have to be disclosed.

QuantHouse 439

A is correct. By not disclosing the arrangements to BL (Maduro) and obtaining written consent, Ortiz and Sanchez are violating Standard IV(B): Duties to Employers, Additional Compensation Arrangements because the arrangements could result in them being partial to Fabre's and Zeissl's accounts at the expense of their other clients'. Standard IV(B) states, "Members and Candidates must not accept gifts, benefits, compensation, or consideration that competes with or might reasonably be expected to create a conflict of interest with their employer's interest unless they obtain written consent from all parties involved."

B is incorrect. Although Ortiz and Sanchez obtained written acknowledgement from Fabre and Zeissl at the time each client made their offer, and included it as part of the IPS, they did not obtain their employer's written consent for the arrangement.

C is incorrect. According to Standard IV(B): Duties to Employers, Additional Compensation Arrangements, members and candidates are required to disclose these types of arrangements to their employer and obtain written consent from all parties. Ortiz and Sanchez did not disclose the arrangements to Maduro until after the arrangements had been accepted and used. In addition, they had only written consent from their clients.

QUANTHOUSE

4

☐ evaluate practices, policies, and conduct relative to the CFA Institute Code of Ethics and Standards of Professional Conduct

☐ explain how the practices, policies, and conduct do or do not violate the CFA Institute Code of Ethics and Standards of Professional Conduct

QuantHouse (QH) is a global investment firm that pioneered the use of quantitative techniques to implement investment strategies.[3] Three years ago, the firm hired Daniel Singh, PhD, CFA, a well-known finance professor. Singh created the Artificial Trading Model (ATM), a comprehensive model that captures and processes a substantial amount of publicly available information (company financial data, news, and industry information) and then makes investment decisions largely without human interaction. The ATM has three components: an Alpha Model, a Risk Model, and an Optimizer. The Alpha Model evaluates public companies based on their earnings and valuation. The Risk Model identifies stock-specific risk and common factor risks (industry specific, country specific, and stock fundamental risks). The Optimizer takes the output from the Alpha and Risk Models, balances them against one other, and recommends an optimal client portfolio based on the client's chosen benchmark.

Singh uses the ATM exclusively for QH's institutional clients and does not mention it when talking with his high-net-worth individual clients. Singh and his team of programmers update the Alpha and Risk components of the ATM on a quarterly basis.

---

3 **QuantHouse:** Asjeet S. Lamba, PhD, CFA, and Michael G. McMillan, PhD, CFA. *Ethics Cases.* © 2018 CFA Institute. All rights reserved. Consistent with the 11th Edition of the *Standards of Practice Handbook.*

On an annual basis, consistent with QH's guidelines for all computer-based models, Singh reviews the Optimizer component and conducts extensive scenario tests with the overall model. (Questions 1, 2)

Recently, some of QH's institutional clients have been voicing concerns about their portfolios' underperformance. In particular, they have expressed dissatisfaction with the overexposure to certain industries in their portfolios, an element that is partly controlled by the ATM's ability to manage risk. In response to these complaints, QH's director of research and Singh's supervisor, Charlotte Ringfield, CFA, asks Singh to review the model. After doing so, Singh finds that the Optimizer is incorrectly reading the Risk Model's assessment of common risk factors and, as a result, is not weighting them appropriately.

Singh then meets with his team of analysts who helped create the model to determine the source of the error. They find that some of the Risk Model components are sending information to the Optimizer in decimal form while other components are sending information in percentages. This improper scaling has resulted in the Optimizer giving inappropriate weights to some of the common risk factors. After discovering the source of the error, Singh and his team meet with Ringfield to present their findings. Singh advocates that the error be fixed as soon as possible, but Ringfield disagrees and tells him to correct the error when the Risk Model is updated at the end of the quarter. She also asks Singh to temporarily disable the common risk factors in the Risk Model until the model is updated. Ringfield then asks Singh and his team not to mention the error to others and reminds them that they signed confidentiality and nondisclosure agreements when they were hired. She goes on to say that she and the investment committee will handle all disclosures to clients and senior management once the model is updated at the end of the quarter. (Questions 3, 4)

Two weeks later, after a very turbulent period in the financial markets, more clients complain about their portfolios' underperformance. Ringfield tells the portfolio managers about the error. When clients inquire about their portfolio's performance, Ringfield attributes the performance to market volatility and the functioning of the model's common risk factors. (Question 5)

Disturbed by the behavior of his colleagues and superiors, who have not yet revealed the error to clients, Singh decides to leave QH. He interviews with QH's largest competitor, Algos-R-Us (ARU). During his interview with ARU's hiring committee, Singh shows them a proprietary model that he has been developing for the past two years in his spare time (nights and weekends). His new model, which he calls StockStar, is based on years of academic research at his university, and Singh considers it his life's work. In addition to backtesting the model, Singh has used StockStar to manage his personal portfolio and the portfolios of his family to generate actual performance results. Impressed by Singh and his model, the hiring committee not only offers him a job but also offers to pay him a special licensing fee for the use of his StockStar model. Singh accepts the offer and returns to QH to tender his resignation. (Question 6)

On his first day at ARU, Singh presents the following information to the marketing department about the StockStar model's performance. This information will be incorporated into a new marketing brochure that will be mailed to current and prospective clients.

StockStar Model Performance: Actual and Backtested Returns*

	Model's Performance (%)	Benchmark Return (%)	Excess Return (%)
Backtested returns			
2012	10.5	6.5	4.0

QuantHouse

	Model's Performance (%)	Benchmark Return (%)	Excess Return (%)
2013	−2.5	−6.0	3.5
2014	20.3	25.0	−4.7
2015	0.5	−6.8	7.3
Actual returns			
2016	8.5	2.2	6.3
2017	12.0	−0.5	12.5

The benchmark return is based on the S&P/ASX 200 Index. Note that past performance does not guarantee future results.

In the brochure, Singh states the following: "This model has been used to manage real portfolios over the past two years and has outperformed its benchmark in both years. In backtests, the model has outperformed its benchmark in three out of four years." (Question 7)

Case Questions

1. Does Singh violate the CFA Institute Code and Standards by using the ATM exclusively for QH's institutional clients?

   A. No.

   B. Yes, because the model might be suitable for some non-institutional clients.

   C. Yes, because he must at least mention the model when talking to high-net-worth individuals.

   > A is correct. It is not a violation of Standard III(B): Duties to Clients, Fair Dealing to use different investment models when working with different types of clients. The ATM might be suitable only for institutional clients because of the size of their portfolios, among other factors. Standard III(B) requires members and candidates to treat all clients fairly when disseminating investment recommendations, when making material changes to prior investment recommendations, and when taking investment action with regard to general purchases, new issues, or secondary offerings. Each client has unique needs, investment criteria, and investment objectives, so not all investment opportunities are suitable for all clients.
   >
   > B is incorrect. It is not a violation of the Code and Standards to use different investment models when working with different types of clients, because some models might be suitable only for specific clients. No information in the case indicates that the model is suitable for clients other than institutional investors.
   >
   > C is incorrect. There is no duty under the Code and Standards to disclose all available investment models when working with different types of clients, because some models might be suitable only for specific clients. No information in the case indicates that the model is suitable for clients other than institutional investors.

2. Prior to the performance concerns voiced by QH's institutional clients, did Singh violate the CFA Institute Code and Standards in the updating of the

ATM's components?

A. Yes.

B. No, because he updates the model's Alpha and Risk components on a quarterly basis.

C. No, because he followed the firm's guidelines and annually reviews the Optimizer and conducts scenario testing on the overall model.

A is correct. Singh violated Standard V(A): Investment Analysis, Recommendations, and Actions, Diligence and Reasonable Basis. Members and candidates must understand the statistical significance of the model results they recommend and must be able to explain these results to clients. Singh did not take adequate care to ensure that the model was being thoroughly reviewed with appropriate frequency. Although the Alpha and Risk components are updated quarterly, he reviews the Optimizer, which links the two prior components, and the overall model itself on only an annual basis. Singh should have tested each of the model's components and their combined interactions with the same quarterly frequency.

B is incorrect. Although Singh updates the Alpha and Risk components quarterly, he reviews the Optimizer, which links these two components, and the overall model itself on only an annual basis. He should review all components as well as the overall model with the same frequency.

C is incorrect. Singh should review all components as well as the overall model on the timeframe that is appropriate (quarterly here) and that at a minimum conforms to the firm's guidelines.

3. According to the CFA Institute Code and Standards, what is the next action (from those below) that Singh should take following his conversation with Ringfield about the model error?

A. Dissociate from the firm

B. Contact the firm's clients

C. Contact senior management

C is correct. Singh should contact senior management before dissociating himself from QH or contacting QH clients. Upon discovery of the error, Singh should try to fix the model immediately. By not fixing the model immediately, Singh is harming QH clients. In not gaining Ringfield's approval to fix the error immediately, the next action Singh should take is to contact Ringfield's boss or senior management to make them aware of the situation.

According to the guidance for Standard I(A): Professionalism, Knowledge of the Law, "If a Member or Candidate has reasonable grounds to believe that imminent or ongoing client or employer activities are illegal or unethical, the Member or Candidate must dissociate, or separate, from the activity. In extreme cases, dissociation may require a member or candidate to leave his or her employment. Members and Candidates may take the following intermediate steps to dissociate from ethical violations of others when direct discussions with the person or persons committing the violation are unsuccessful. The first step should be to attempt to stop the behavior by bringing it to

QuantHouse

the attention of the employer through a supervisor or the firm's compliance department. If this attempt is unsuccessful, then Members and Candidates have a responsibility to step away and dissociate from the activity."

A is incorrect. Dissociating from the firm is the final step in the process. The guidance for Standard I(A) establishes next steps as follows: "The first step should be to attempt to stop the behavior by bringing it to the attention of the employer through a supervisor or the firm's compliance department. If this attempt is unsuccessful, then Members and Candidates have a responsibility to step away and dissociate from the activity."

B is incorrect. Contacting the firm's clients directly is not a permitted intermediate step under Standard I(A).

4. Did Singh violate the CFA Institute Code and Standards by not immediately fixing the error in the ATM?

   A. Yes.

   B. No, because the error will be fixed next quarter.

   C. No, because Singh disabled the common risk factors in the Risk Model as ordered by Ringfield.

   A is correct. By not fixing the error in the ATM immediately, Singh is violating Standard III(A): Duties to Clients, Loyalty, Prudence, and Care. Members and candidates have a duty of loyalty to their clients and must act with reasonable care and exercise prudent judgement. By not immediately fixing the error in the model, Singh is not acting for the benefit of clients, nor is he placing client interests before his employer's or his own interests.

   B is incorrect. The error should have been fixed immediately. According to the guidance for Standard III(A), "Investment actions must be carried out for the sole benefit of the client and in a manner the Member or Candidate believes, given the known facts and circumstances, to be in the best interest of the client." Fixing the error in the model immediately was in the best interest of the clients.

   C is incorrect. Disabling the common risk factors in the Risk Model did not address the underlying error. The error should have been fixed immediately regardless of Ringfield's order. According to the guidance for Standard III(A), "Investment actions must be carried out for the sole benefit of the client and in a manner the Member or Candidate believes, given the known facts and circumstances, to be in the best interest of the client." Fixing the error in the model immediately was in the best interests of the clients.

5. Did Ringfield violate the CFA Institute Code and Standards when talking with clients about their portfolios' underperformance?

   A. Yes.

   B. No, because the market was turbulent.

   C. No, because the model's common risk factors were to blame.

   A is correct. When talking with clients about their portfolios' underperformance, Ringfield was in violation of Standard I(C): Professionalism, Misrepresentation. Members and candidates must not knowingly make any misrepresentations relating to investment analysis, recommendations, actions, or other professional activities. By attributing the underperformance of client portfolios to market volatility, she is not telling them the real reason for the underperformance. In addition, the common risk factors have been disabled, so they are not functioning as intended for the model.

B is incorrect. The reason for the underperformance of client portfolios is the error in the model, not market turbulence. Ringfield violated Standard I(C) regarding misrepresentations relating to investment analysis, recommendations, actions, or other professional activities.

C is incorrect. The reason for the underperformance of client portfolios is the error in the model, not the model's common risk factors. Ringfield violated Standard I(C) regarding misrepresentations relating to investment analysis, recommendations, actions, or other professional activities.

6. Did Singh violate the CFA Institute Code and Standards with respect to his duties to his employer, QH, in developing his StockStar model?

   A. No.

   B. Yes, because the model was developed while he was working at QH.

   C. Yes, because he invests his personal and family portfolios using the model.

   A is correct. Singh is not in violation of the CFA Institute Code and Standards, Standard IV(A): Duties to Employers, Loyalty. In this case, Singh developed the StockStar model in his spare time (on nights and weekends) and used the model to manage only his personal and family portfolios. In addition, he has not been compensated for the model.

   B is incorrect. It is not a violation of Standard IV(A): Duties to Employers, Loyalty to develop a model in his spare time.

   C is incorrect. It is not a violation of Standard IV(A): Duties to Employers, Loyalty, to use his personal and family portfolios to test or invest in the model.

7. In the table that Singh provides to the marketing department, does he violate the CFA Institute Code and Standards?

   A. No, because he presented the performance information in the manner required by the CFA Institute Code and Standards.

   B. Yes, because he should have included only the actual performance results of the model.

   C. Yes, because he should have disclosed that he used his personal and family portfolios to generate actual results.

   A is correct. Singh has not violated Standard III(D): Duties to Clients, Performance Presentation because he has presented both the actual and backtested performance of the model and clearly distinguished between the two. He has also noted that past performance does not guarantee future results.

B is incorrect. Standard III(D): Duties to Clients, Performance Presentation encourages full disclosure of investment performance data. Both actual and simulated performance measures are allowed as long as they are clearly disclosed. Singh fully explained the performance results being reported, stating that results are simulated (backtested) when model results are used and indicating that the actual and backtested results are gross of fees.

C is incorrect. Standard III(D): Duties to Clients, Performance Presentation does not prohibit showing past performance of funds managed as long as appropriate disclosures are made, including the person's role in generating that performance. Singh fully explained the performance results being reported, stating that results are simulated (back tested) when model results are used and indicating that the actual and backtested results are gross of fees.

JR AND ASSOCIATES

5

- [ ] evaluate practices, policies, and conduct relative to the CFA Institute Code of Ethics and Standards of Professional Conduct
- [ ] explain how the practices, policies, and conduct do or do not violate the CFA Institute Code of Ethics and Standards of Professional Conduct

Jacobs, Riccio, and Associates (JRA) is a global investment advisory firm that primarily provides high-net-worth individuals and their families with personalized wealth management solutions such as wealth planning, retirement planning, investment management, and trust and fiduciary services.[4] In addition, the firm has a small number of institutional clients. JRA employs 25 investment advisers and portfolio managers.

Benjamin Jacobs, CFA, and Andrew Riccio, CFA, founded JRA 10 years ago. Prior to establishing the firm, Jacobs worked as a lawyer for Brightman Partners, a large and prestigious law firm that specializes in real estate, family law, and estate planning. Riccio worked as a Certified Public Accountant for Earnest & Olds (E&O), a multinational professional services firm that specializes in providing tax, consulting, and advisory services to corporations and individuals. Kathy Parker, CFA, joined the firm as the third senior partner two years after it was founded. Previously, she had worked for the Frontline Group, a broker/dealer. JRA acquires most of its clients through referral arrangements put in place by the three senior partners.

Jacobs has a fee-sharing arrangement with his former colleagues at Brightman Partners (BP) when they refer clients to JRA. The annual investment fee stated in JRA's marketing brochure is higher than the fee most of its clients pay because Jacobs offers a discount on the investment fee to clients who are referred by BP lawyers. This discount encourages the BP lawyers to market JRA's services to their clients. In return, JRA shares a portion of the clients' annual investment advisory fee with the referring lawyer. The lawyers at BP disclose this fee-sharing arrangement with the clients that

---

4 **JR and Associates:** Marcus Allan Ingram, PhD, CFA, and Michael G. McMillan, PhD, CFA. *Ethics Cases.* © 2018 CFA Institute. All rights reserved. Consistent with the 11th Edition of the *Standards of Practice Handbook.*

they refer to JRA. JRA discloses all of this information in the supplemental policies sent to new clients once they have signed JRA's investment management agreement. (Questions 1, 2)

Riccio offers a similar fee discount and sharing arrangement to accountants at his previous firm, E&O, who refer their clients to JRA. Over time, however, Riccio has observed that many of JRA's clients are reluctant to tell their investment adviser about securities and real estate holdings that are managed at other firms. As a result, the adviser does not have a complete understanding of the client's overall financial position. To assist JRA advisers in developing more-realistic and accurate IPS, the accountants at E&O provide a copy of their referred client's tax returns to the client's JRA adviser after they open an account at JRA. This step allows JRA advisers to "know their client" better and provides greater transparency into their client's financial condition. In return, JRA advisers provide their clients' quarterly account statements to their E&O accountants to help with their tax planning and year-end tax preparation. Client approval is not needed for this information sharing because clients sign confidentiality statements directly with their E&O accountants and JRA advisers, and because they often view their investment adviser and their accountant as a team. (Question 3)

Kathy Parker has a somewhat different referral arrangement in place with the Frontline Group. Frontline's brokerage unit refers all of its small institutional clients (pension plans, profit-sharing plans, and endowments) that are looking for investment management to JRA. In return, all the trading from these accounts continues to be executed through Frontline's broker/dealer. Because Frontline continues to provide "best price and best execution" to these clients, Parker believes no additional client disclosures are necessary because client trading is unaffected. (Question 4)

Since starting JRA, Jacobs and Riccio have developed a close relationship with Tim Carroll, an independent consultant they met at a networking event. Carroll is hired by pension funds to solicit and review proposals from investment advisers who wish to manage a portion of the pension fund's assets. Over the years, Carroll has been instrumental in JRA's success by referring several of his pension fund clients to the firm because of the firm's outstanding performance record and superior client service. To thank Carroll for all of his hard work on JRA's behalf (regardless of whether Carroll's pension fund clients actually hire JRA), Jacobs and Riccio each make sizable annual donations to Carroll's Children's Charity, a non-profit organization Carroll created to benefit orphans. Because these donations are made annually, they are not disclosed to the pension funds referred by Carroll who become JRA clients. (Question 5)

Recently, JRA hired Mufid Othan, an investment adviser and CFA charterholder who previously worked at JRA's largest competitor, Sack International. To attract Othan and his large "book of clients," JRA offered him USD500 for each client he "brought over" from Sack. While at Sack, Othan was allowed to connect with all of his clients through his personal social media platforms. This not only enabled him to build an electronic database containing the names, addresses, phone numbers, and email addresses of all his clients but also helped him to provide superior client service by "following" his clients' personal and professional lives. When Othan tendered his resignation from Sack, he was immediately escorted out of the building. Othan spent the following weekend contacting all of his clients via social media to tell them about his resignation and to encourage them to join him at JRA. He did not disclose to them, however, that he was being paid USD500 for each client he brought over from Sack. (Questions 6, 7)

A few weeks after beginning work at JRA, Othan hired Zane Ode, a recent college graduate, who recently found out she had passed Level III of the CFA Program examination. After hearing the good news about her success with Level III, Ode posted the following comments in a CFA candidate chatroom:

Comment 1	"I can't believe I passed the exam; the ethics questions were super hard."
Comment 2	"Wow, I scored above the Minimum Performance Score (MPS) on derivatives. I still don't know what answer was right for the two-part contango–backwardation question."
Comment 3	"The graders must have been quite lenient in grading my answers to the constructed response questions."

Ode now has three and a half years of experience in the investment industry. Nevertheless, Othan has already made a habit of introducing her to current and prospective clients as the firm's "newest CFA," and Ode has said nothing to correct him. (Questions 8, 9)

Case Questions

1. Does Jacobs violate the CFA Institute Code and Standards by offering his referral clients a lower investment advisory fee than the one quoted in JRA's marketing brochure?

   A. No.

   B. Yes, because JRA is misrepresenting its fees.

   C. Yes, because JRA is not dealing with its clients fairly.

   A is correct. Jacobs is not in violation of the CFA Institute Code and Standards. According to Standard III(B): Duties to Clients, Fair Dealing, members and candidates may provide more personal, specialized, or in-depth service to clients who are willing to pay for premium services through higher management fees or higher levels of brokerage. The term "fair" implies that the member or candidate must take care not to discriminate against any clients when disseminating investment recommendations or taking investment action.

   B is incorrect. JRA is not misrepresenting its fees because some of its clients are paying the fees that are disclosed in its marketing brochure. In addition, the advertised fees represent the highest fees that clients would pay.

   C is incorrect. Standard III(B): Duties to Clients, Fair Dealing focuses on investment recommendations and taking investment action. The case provides no evidence that non-referred clients are being discriminated against or that referred clients are receiving preferential treatment, with respect to the dissemination of investment recommendations or the taking of investment action. Referred clients are simply receiving discounted fees.

2. Does Jacobs violate the CFA Institute Code and Standards in his disclosure of referral arrangements to his clients?

   A. Yes.

   B. No, because the lawyers disclose to their clients the discount that JRA offers.

   C. No, because the discount and the fee-sharing arrangement are fully disclosed to individuals once they become clients.

A is correct. Jacobs is in violation of Standard VI(C): Conflicts of Interest, Referral Fees, which states, "Members and Candidates must disclose to their employer, clients, and prospective clients, as appropriate, any compensation, consideration, or benefit received from or paid to others for the recommendation of products or services." The guidance for Standard VI(C) states, "Appropriate disclosure means that Members and Candidates must advise the client or prospective client, before entry into any formal agreement for services, of any benefit given or received from the recommendation of any services provided by the Member or Candidate." In this case, the disclosure in the supplemental policies does not occur until after the individual has signed JRA's investment management agreement and is already a client, which is too late.

B is incorrect. The case facts state that BP lawyers disclose the fee-sharing arrangement to the clients they refer to JRA. The case facts do not state whether the lawyers disclose the discount offered by JRA. The behavior of the BP lawyers, however, is not covered by the Code and Standards. Disclosures, or lack thereof, by BP lawyers do nothing to mitigate JRA's duties and responsibilities.

C is incorrect. The discount is disclosed in the supplemental policies sent to new clients after they sign JRA's investment management agreement. According to Standard VI(C), disclosure must occur before the client enters into a formal agreement.

3. Do JRA advisers violate the CFA Institute Code and Standards by sharing client information with the accountants at E&O?

   A. Yes.

   B. No, because the client views representatives from both firms as a team.

   C. No, because the client has signed confidentiality agreements with both firms.

   A is correct. JRA advisers have violated the confidentiality of their clients by not obtaining client approval (written approval is recommended) in advance of sharing their information between the firms. According to Standard III(E): Duties to Clients, Preservation of Confidentiality, members and candidates are required to preserve the confidentiality of information communicated to them by their clients, prospective clients, and former clients. This standard is applicable when (1) the member or candidate receives information because of his or her special ability to conduct a portion of the client's business or personal affairs and (2) the member or candidate receives information that arises from or is relevant to that portion of the client's business that is the subject of the special or confidential relationship.

   B is incorrect. Although the client has signed confidentiality agreements with both firms, the client has not signed an agreement allowing the sharing of information between the firms.

   C is incorrect. Although the client might view representatives from both firms as a team, neither team has received client approval in advance of sharing the client's information. As a practical matter, if JRA advisers request information from prospective clients regarding other investment

JR and Associates

income and assets and the prospect denies existence of such assets, the adviser is under no obligation to perform additional due diligence to ascertain the existence of other assets.

4. Has Parker violated the CFA Institute Code and Standards in her referral arrangement with Frontline Group?

A. Yes.

B. No, because Frontline Group continues to provide "best price" and "best execution."

C. No, because nothing has changed—all client trades are still executed by Frontline.

A is correct. By not disclosing the referral arrangement to clients who were referred to her by Frontline Group, Parker has violated Standard VI(C): Conflicts of Interest, Referral Fees, which states, "Members and Candidates must disclose to their employer, clients, and prospective clients, as appropriate, any compensation, consideration, or benefit received from or paid to others for the recommendation of products or services." The guidance for Standard VI(C) states, "Appropriate disclosure means that Members and Candidates must advise the client or prospective client, before entry into any formal agreement for services, of any benefit given or received from the recommendation of any services provided by the Member or Candidate." In this case, there is no evidence to suggest Parker disclosed her referral arrangement with Frontline Group to prospective clients. By not doing so, Parker violated Standard VI(C).

B is incorrect. Regardless of whether Frontline provides "best price" and "best execution" or whether the execution of client trades remains unchanged by Frontline, Parker must still disclose the referral arrangement to her clients.

C is incorrect. Parker must still disclose the referral arrangement to her clients, regardless of the fact that all client trades continue to be executed by Frontline.

5. Did Jacobs and Riccio violate the CFA Institute Code and Standards by making annual donations to Carroll's Children's Charity?

A. No.

B. Yes, because these donations create a conflict of interest.

C. Yes, because these donations represent additional compensation to Carroll.

B is correct. The donations made by Jacobs and Riccio give Carroll an incentive to refer potential clients to JRA and at the very least give the perception that Carroll's objectivity and independence have been compromised. Jacobs and Riccio are in violation of Standard I(B): Professionalism, Independence and Objectivity, which states, "Members and Candidates must use reasonable care and judgement to achieve and maintain independence and objectivity in their professional activities. Members and Candidates must not offer, solicit, or accept any gift, benefit, compensation, or consideration that reasonably could be expected to compromise their own or another's independence and objectivity."

A is incorrect. As already noted, donations made by Jacobs and Riccio give Carroll an incentive to refer potential clients to JRA. This at the very least gives the perception that Carroll's objectivity and independence have been compromised, so Jacobs and Riccio are in violation of the Code and Standards, specifically Standard I(B): Professionalism, Independence and Objectivity.

C is incorrect. The donations were made to Carroll's charity and do not represent additional compensation to Carroll. Additional compensation is defined in Standard IV(B): Duties to Employers, Additional Compensation Arrangements as "gifts, benefits, or compensation, or consideration that competes with or might reasonably be expected to create a conflict of interest with their employer's interest." An additional compensation arrangement is one that creates a conflict of interest between the member or candidate and their employer.

6. Did Othan violate the CFA Institute Code and Standards by contacting his Sack International clients via social media after leaving Sack?

   A. No.

   B. Yes, because he is using confidential client information.

   C. Yes, because the client information he is using belongs to Sack.

   A is correct. Othan is not in violation of the CFA Institute Code and Standards. According to the guidance for Standard IV(A): Duties to Employers, Loyalty, "Members and Candidates should understand and abide by all applicable firm policies and regulations as to the acceptable use of social media platforms to interact with clients and prospective clients. This is especially important when a Member or Candidate is planning to leave an employer." In this case, Sack allowed Othan to use his personal social media platforms to connect with clients. In addition, he did not contact his former clients via social media to inform them about his departure until after he resigned from Sack.

   B is incorrect. Contacting his clients via social media after leaving Sack does not require Othan to use confidential client information.

   C is incorrect. Othan used his personal social media platforms to connect with clients. These platforms are not the property of Sack.

7. Did Othan violate the CFA Institute Code and Standards by not disclosing to clients that he was receiving USD500 for each client that he brought over to JRA from Sack?

   A. No.

   B. Yes, because this is a referral fee.

   C. Yes, because this is additional compensation.

   A is correct. Othan is not in violation of the CFA Institute Code and Standards. The USD500 does not have to be disclosed to clients because it is not a referral fee or additional compensation, and it does not create a conflict of interest with his employer, clients, or prospective clients.

JR and Associates

B is incorrect. According to Standard VI(C): Conflicts of Interest, Referral Fees, referral fees are "any compensation, consideration, or benefit received from or paid to others for the recommendation of products or services." The USD500 Othan received from JRA for each client he brought over from Sack is not a referral fee because the USD500 is being paid by the employer (JRA) to the employee (Othan) for services provided. This amount is compensation paid by the firm, not a fee charged to clients.

C is incorrect. Additional compensation is defined in Standard IV(B): Duties to Employers, Additional Compensation Arrangements as "gifts, benefits, or compensation, or consideration that competes with or might reasonably be expected to create a conflict of interest with their employer's interest." The USD500 is not additional compensation, and there is no conflict with the employer's interests. Although the disclosure of all bonus arrangements might add clarity, the Code and Standards do not require members and candidates to disclose how they are compensated.

8. Which of the comments Ode posted in the CFA candidate chatroom violated the CFA Institute Code and Standards?

   A. Comment 1

   B. Comment 2

   C. Comment 3

   B is correct. Ode's comment 2 violated Standard VII(A): Responsibilities as a CFA Institute Member or CFA Candidate, Conduct as Participants in CFA Institute Programs, whose guidance states: "CFA Institute program rules, regulations, and policies prohibit Candidates from disclosing confidential material gained during the exam process." Examples of information that cannot be disclosed by candidates sitting for an exam include but are not limited to the following:

   - Specific detail of questions appearing on the exam (contango–backwardation)
   - Broad topical areas and formulas tested or not tested on the exam (derivatives)

   In this case, Ode disclosed specific details of questions appearing on the exam.

   A is incorrect. In saying that the ethics questions were super hard, Ode did not disclose confidential information gained during the exam process.

   C is incorrect. In saying that the graders must have been quite lenient in grading her answers to the constructed response questions, Ode did not disclose confidential information gained during the exam process.

9. Did Othan violate the CFA Institute Code and Standards in his description of Ode?

   A. Yes.

   B. No, because Ode will be a CFA charterholder in another six months.

C. No, because Ode has successfully completed all three levels of the CFA Program.

A is correct. Othan is in violation of the CFA Institute Code and Standards. Ode is not yet a CFA charterholder, and in referencing her as the firm's "newest CFA," Othan is misrepresenting Ode. The guidance for Standard VII(B): Responsibilities as a CFA Institute Member or CFA Candidate, Reference to CFA Institute, the CFA Designation, and the CFA Program states that "'CFA Charterholders' are those individuals who have earned the right to use the CFA designation granted by CFA Institute. These people have satisfied certain requirements, including completion of the CFA Program, and required years of acceptable work experience." The recommended procedures for Ode's compliance with Standard VII(B) include educating others in the firm, including re-educating Othan, about her status.

B is incorrect. To be a CFA charterholder, Ode needs to have completed the required four years of work experience.

C is incorrect. The fact that she has completed all three levels of the CFA Program does not make Ode a CFA charterholder. To be a CFA charterholder, she must also have the required four years of work experience.

6   MAGADI ASSET MANAGEMENT

☐   evaluate practices, policies, and conduct relative to the CFA Institute Code of Ethics and Standards of Professional Conduct

☐   explain how the practices, policies, and conduct do or do not violate the CFA Institute Code of Ethics and Standards of Professional Conduct

Magadi Asset Management (Magadi) is a global investment management firm based in Nairobi, Kenya. Magadi manages dedicated equity, fixed income, and real estate funds, as well as other alternative investment vehicles.[5] The firm's clients include pension schemes, sovereign wealth funds, and high-net-worth individuals. Frederick Omondi, CFA, is Magadi's president and chief investment officer. Under Omondi, the CFA Code of Ethics and Standards of Professional Conduct has been adopted as the firm's Code of Conduct for Magadi's employees.

Last year, Omondi established a proprietary trading desk at Magadi. The role of the proprietary traders is to actively trade African securities for the firm's benefit. Proprietary traders do not execute orders for Magadi's institutional or retail clients; these orders are handled by traders on the main trading desk. To increase cooperation among traders and encourage the sharing of best execution practices, both trading desks are located on the same floor at Magadi's headquarters. This proximity has allowed proprietary traders to hear customer order flow and also see customer order

---

5 **Magadi Asset Management:** Renée K. Blasky, CFA, CIPM, and Michael G. McMillan, PhD, CFA. *Ethics Cases.* © 2018 CFA Institute. All rights reserved. Consistent with the 11th Edition of the *Standards of Practice Handbook.*

Magadi Asset Management

information on the computer screens of the main traders. To encourage collaboration between the two trading desks, Omondi offers bonuses to proprietary traders who provide trading ideas to the main traders for the benefit of their clientele.

To allay client concerns about potential front-running, Omondi has told clients that information concerning their orders and business affairs is kept confidential. He further explains that the firm has instituted a firm-wide policy that expressly states the following: "Employees may not discuss the business affairs of any client with any other person, except on a strict need-to-know basis. Trade orders made by the proprietary traders that may be similar to client orders must be executed after the clients' orders have been fully executed by the main dealing desk traders." (Questions 1, 2)

Omondi's biggest business success this year was a large mandate from a sovereign wealth fund to invest in Magadi's managed funds. To secure the mandate win, Omondi hired, as a "sub-adviser" to the managed funds, a business development agent with contacts at the highest level within the government responsible for the sovereign wealth fund. Despite having very limited experience as a financial consultant, the agent had a number of close relationships with senior managers at the sovereign wealth fund because of his connections to the government officials responsible for the fund. The payments made by Omondi, through the sub-adviser, included a "deal fee" and other expenses that facilitated the governmental support of the sovereign wealth fund investment. Omondi did not require the agent to provide details regarding its activities or the specific expenses covered by the fee. The agent's expenses are charged to Omondi's managed funds. As a thank you for being awarded the mandate, Omondi made donations to the favorite charities of the sovereign wealth fund's top management, as he had promised during the due diligence process. (Question 3)

Three years ago, Magadi launched the Pan Africa Frontier Fund (PAFF), a non-listed equity unit trust with an investment mandate that prohibits the use of leverage. The mandate requires the following:

- 80% of the companies in the portfolio to be traded on at least one of the 17 securities exchanges operating within Africa;
- the portfolio be invested in a minimum of eight countries at all times;
- no more than 30% of the portfolio's value can be invested in any single country;
- no more than 10% of the portfolio's value can be invested in cash and cash equivalents; and
- no single security can account for more than 15% of the portfolio's value.

Since its launch, the PAFF has significantly underperformed its peers and has had several quarters of negative returns. As a result, it ranks in the bottom performance quadrant relative to its peers.

Omondi recently hired Bukenya Kirabo, CFA, to take over management of the PAFF. Kirabo was hired to improve the PAFF's performance and move the fund to the top performance quadrant in rankings based on his extensive experience with and knowledge of African equities, as well as his reputation as an astute investment manager. Kirabo has more than two decades of experience analyzing and investing in public companies across Africa. After graduating from a top local university, he moved to London, where he worked for a global asset management firm. Five years ago, Kirabo was transferred to the firm's regional office in Africa to manage one of the firm's local funds. During the past five years, Kirabo has generated average annual returns of 23%. Since returning to Africa, Kirabo has witnessed notable improvements in African securities markets, particularly in the area of settlement risk. Many local markets remain relatively illiquid, however, and most public companies in Africa are under-researched compared with other emerging markets. As a result, systematic risk is considerably higher in African markets than in other emerging markets.

Three months after being hired at Magadi, Kirabo meets with Omondi to review the PAFF's most recent quarterly performance. During the meeting, he states, "The PAFF's solid performance this quarter is a result of three changes I made:

Change 1: Because of strong cash inflows into the PAFF, I have increased the maximum level of cash and cash equivalents to 15% of the portfolio. Given the illiquid nature of many markets in which we are investing, I believe it is more prudent, and less risky, to take sufficient time to find attractive investment opportunities and build position holdings.

Change 2: I have increased the portfolio's geographic diversification from 11 countries (stock exchanges) to 13. Securities traded on 13 different African stock exchanges (up from 11 previously) are now represented in the portfolio. This higher level of diversification has improved the portfolio's Sharpe and information ratios.

Change 3: To increase accountability for the PAFF's performance, I am now making all buy and sell decisions for the PAFF. Previously, when the team of analysts was making the investment decisions, it was difficult to attribute an individual's contribution to fund performance."

Kirabo next meets with the marketing department to discuss the PAFF's new sales campaign. During the meeting, he states, "Please include all of the mandate changes I have made in the PAFF in the new brochure that will be distributed to prospective clients. You can also include the five-year investment performance I achieved while managing a fund at my previous employer. Please do not state where the performance was earned, however, because my previous employer is a direct competitor of Magadi. Finally, because the mandate changes are relatively trivial, there is no need to inform existing clients." (Questions 4, 5, 6)

The PAFF currently owns 9% of the common stock of Mtume, a mining company listed on the Botswana Stock Exchange. Kirabo has been reducing the fund's holdings in Mtume because of the company's declining revenues and profits. This morning, Kirabo speaks with Olivia Moroka, Mtume's chief financial officer. During their conversation, Moroka tells Kirabo, "You might want to stop selling your shares of Mtume because our board of directors just received a very attractive all-cash offer of BWP500 million (Botswana pula) to purchase one of our mining subsidiaries. Although nothing is definite, the board will be meeting next week to vote on the offer."

After getting off the phone with Moroka, Kirabo calls the Magadi analyst who follows Mtume and tells her about his conversation. The analyst then incorporates the expected subsidiary sales price into her financial model of Mtume. The output from her revised model indicates that the sale proceeds will significantly enhance Mtume's credit standing and its ability to reinstitute shareholder cash distributions on an earlier-than-expected schedule and in larger-than-expected amounts. When the analyst tells Kirabo about her findings, Kirabo immediately calls the proprietary and main traders to tell them to start buying "any and all" shares of Mtume. He then calls Omondi and tells him about his conversation with Moroka. After Omondi gets off the phone with Kirabo, Omondi calls his broker and purchases shares in Mtume for his personal account and the family accounts that he controls. (Questions 7, 8)

Case Questions

1. By allowing customer order information to be known to the traders on the proprietary desk, did traders on the main trading desk most likely violate the CFA Institute Code and Standards?

    A. Yes.

Magadi Asset Management

455

B. No, because this information was not shared outside of the firm.

C. No, because proprietary traders were not allowed to act on this information until after client orders were executed.

A is correct. Traders on the main trading desk are in violation of Standard III(E): Duties to Clients, Preservation of Confidentiality. This standard requires members and candidates to preserve the confidentiality of information communicated to them by their clients, prospective clients, and former clients. The sharing of office space such that the proprietary traders can see the screens of the main traders is inappropriate because it allows confidential client information to be disclosed to individuals (proprietary traders) who did not need to know the information. To avoid sharing confidential information and violating firm policy, the main traders should have taken necessary action to ensure the client information was not advertently or inadvertently shared with the proprietary desk traders.

B is incorrect. Although the information was not shared externally, the main traders still allowed its disclosure to individuals who did not meet the "need to know" requirement and, in doing so, violated Standard III(E).

C is incorrect. Whether or not the proprietary traders acted on the information is irrelevant in this case. Traders on the main trading desk needed to take the necessary action to prevent the disclosure of confidential information and in not doing so, they violated Standard III(E).

2. Did Omondi most likely violate the CFA Institute Code and Standards in supervising the employees in the two trading desks?

A. Yes.

B. No, because he implemented a policy to prevent front-running.

C. No, because he encouraged collaboration between the two departments.

A is correct. Omondi was in violation of Standard IV(C): Duties to Employers, Responsibilities of Supervisors. Members and candidates must promote actions by all employees under their supervision and authority to comply with applicable laws, rules, regulations, firm policies and the Code and Standards. Omondi failed to establish effective policies and procedures reasonably designed to prevent traders on the proprietary dealing desk from obtaining confidential customer information. Although the proprietary traders did not have direct access to the computer system used by the main traders to execute customer orders, by being co-located on the same floor, the proprietary traders could still view customer order information on the main traders' computer screens and hear them discuss customer orders. Omondi could have located one set of traders in a separate space or on a different floor with security access restrictions. Omondi would also likely be in violation of Standard I(C): Professionalism, Misrepresentation because his representation to customers was incorrect—that is, client information was made available to other employees outside of those operating on a "need-to-know" basis.

B is incorrect. Although Omondi announced a policy to mitigate front-running, the policy was ineffective and, as implemented, did not prevent or address the sharing of confidential client information (orders) to individuals who did not need to know this information (proprietary traders).

C is also incorrect. Encouraging collaboration between the two trading desks does not address the fact that the proprietary traders could see and hear confidential information about client orders from the main trading desk. Omondi failed to establish sufficient policies and procedures to ensure compliance with the Code and Standards as well as firm policy for the traders under his supervision.

3. Omondi most likely violated the CFA Institute Code and Standards when dealing with the sovereign wealth fund's top managers:

   A. only by making charitable donations.

   B. only by hiring a sub-adviser because of his high-level government contacts.

   C. by both A and B.

   C is correct. Omondi was in violation of Standard I(B): Professionalism, Independence and Objectivity. The guidance for Standard I(B) states, "When working to earn a new investment allocation, Members and Candidates should not offer gifts, contributions, or other compensation to influence the decision of the hiring representative. The offering of these items with the intent to impair another person's independence and objectivity would not comply with Standard I(B). Such prohibited actions may include offering donations to a charitable organization."

   To better serve clients, investment professionals may delegate to third parties work that requires particular specialization, knowledge, or expertise. For instance, an investment adviser may hire sub-advisers to handle a particular strategy or investment style outside the scope of the adviser's ability or experience. A global adviser may hire a sub-adviser to manage an asset allocation invested in a particular country or region, and the payments to the sub-adviser would be legitimate investment expenses that could properly be passed on to investors in the fund. The facts of this case, however, clearly show that Omondi is not hiring a true sub-adviser but instead paying locally connected officials to secure access for the sovereign wealth fund's investment. The "sub-adviser" has limited financial experience but is close to the government officials, and the "deal fees" are not supported by any documentation that details legitimate investment expenses. The "sub-advising expenses" charged by Omondi to the fund could, in all likelihood, be funding corrupt transactions and bribes through local intermediaries. This practice violates multiple standards, including I(A): Knowledge of the Law (because the conduct would violate any type of anti-bribery laws); I(C): Misrepresentation (improperly labeling the expenditures as investment fees); V(A): Diligence and Reasonable Basis (no reasonable and adequate basis for the "investment" action); and V(C): Record Retention (no appropriate records to support the action).

4. According to the CFA Institute Code and Standards, which of the changes in the PAFF does Kirabo *not* have to disclose?

   A. Change 1

   B. Change 2

   C. Change 3

Magadi Asset Management 457

B is correct. Change 2 is not required to be disclosed because, by increasing the country exposure to 13 nations, Kirabo is still within the 80% stated mandate. The investment process has not fundamentally changed. Changes 1 and 3 are modifications to the investment process that, according to Standard V(B): Investment Analysis, Recommendations, and Actions, Communication with Clients and Prospective Clients, must be disclosed. According to Standard V(B), members and candidates must disclose to clients and prospective clients the basic format and general principles of the investment processes they use to analyze investments, select securities, and construct portfolios, and they must promptly disclose any changes that might materially affect those processes.

A is incorrect. Change 1 is a change in the fund's mandate because the maximum amount of cash that the fund can hold has been increased to 15% from 10%.

C is incorrect. Change 3 is a change to the investment process, because all purchase and sell decisions are now being made by Kirabo instead of the team of analysts.

5. Does Kirabo most likely violate the CFA Institute Code and Standards by including his prior performance in the PAFF marketing brochure?

   A. No.

   B. Yes, because the brochure should have stated the name of the firm where he earned the prior performance.

   C. Yes, because the marketing brochure should not show fund performance earned at a prior firm as part of his performance track record.

   B is correct. Kirabo was in violation of Standard III(D): Duties to Clients, Performance Presentation. Standard III(D) does not prohibit showing past performance of funds managed at a prior firm, as long as showing that record is accompanied by appropriate disclosures about where the performance took place and the person's specific role in achieving that performance. Kirabo does not disclose the name of the prior firm or that he alone managed the fund and was solely responsible for its performance. Consequently, he is in violation of Standard III(D): Performance Presentation. Kirabo would also be required to receive permission in writing from his previous employer to take his performance records with him when he left the firm because the performance record is an asset of the firm, not of the individual employee. If he did not receive prior written permission, he would also be in violation of Standard IV(A): Duties to Employers, Loyalty, which requires members and candidates to protect their employers' interests, even when leaving the firm.

   C is incorrect. There is no prohibition on including past investment performance under Standard III(D) so long as disclosures clearly indicate it was earned at a previous entity and what role the manager played in achieving that performance.

6. According to the CFA Institute Code and Standards, whom must Kirabo most likely inform of the material changes related to the PAFF?

   A. Current clients only

458   **Learning Module 3**   **Application of the Code and Standards: Level II**

B. Prospective clients only

C. Current and prospective clients

C is correct. According to Standard V(B): Investment Analysis, Recommendations, and Actions, Communication with Clients and Prospective Clients, Kirabo must disclose to current and prospective clients both the fund mandate change and the change in the investment process.

7. Did Kirabo most likely violate the CFA Institute Code and Standards by purchasing additional shares of Mtume?

A. Yes.

B. No, because the information that Kirabo learned from Moroka was not definite.

C. No, because his decision was based on the output from the analyst's revised model.

A is correct. Kirabo was in violation of Standard II(A): Integrity of Capital Markets, Material Nonpublic Information. Members and candidates who possess material nonpublic information that could affect an investment's value must not act or cause others to act on the information. Information is "material" if its disclosure would probably affect the price of a security or if reasonable investors would want to know the information before making an investment decision. In addition to the substance and specificity of the information, the source or relative reliability of the information also determines materiality. In this case, factual information from a corporate insider regarding the purchase of a subsidiary is likely to be material. Although the offer is not definite or officially accepted by the board, its source, substance, and specificity are enough to make the information material. The output from the analyst's revised model was affected by the insider information.

B is incorrect. Information does not have to be definite to trigger the violation; it needs only be considered both material and nonpublic. In this case, factual information from a corporate insider regarding the purchase of a subsidiary is both nonpublic and material. Trading on this information violates Standard II(A).

C is incorrect. The output from the analyst's revised model was affected by the insider information. Thus, his decision was based on material, nonpublic information, which violates Standard II(A): Material Nonpublic Information.

8. Did Omondi most likely violate the CFA Institute Code and Standards by purchasing shares for his personal and family accounts?

A. Yes.

B. No, because the information is not definite.

C. No, because the board has not voted on the offer.

A is correct. Omondi violated Standard II(A): Integrity of Capital Markets, Material Nonpublic Information. Members and candidates who possess material nonpublic information that could affect an investment's value must not act or cause others to act on the information. Information is "material" if its disclosure would probably affect the price of a security or if reasonable investors would want to know the information before making an investment decision. In addition to the substance and specificity of the information, the source or relative reliability of the information also determines materiality. In this case, factual information from a corporate insider regarding the purchase of a subsidiary is likely to be considered material. Although the offer is not definite or officially accepted by the board, its source, substance, and specificity are enough to make the information material. By purchasing shares informed by material nonpublic information, Omondi violated Standard II(A).

B is incorrect. Information does not have to be definite to trigger the violation; it needs only be considered both material and nonpublic. In this case, factual information from a corporate insider regarding the purchase of a subsidiary is both nonpublic and material. Trading on this information violates Standard II(A).

C is incorrect. There is no requirement that the information must be about something that has actually occurred, such as the action having been taken. Under Standard II(A), "Information is considered material if its disclosure would probably have an impact on the price of a security or if reasonable investors would want to know the information before making an investment decision." Both statements are true here. Thus, the information is material and also nonpublic, so trading on this information violates Standard II(A): Material Nonpublic Information.

SYYARK

7

- [ ] evaluate practices, policies, and conduct relative to the CFA Institute Code of Ethics and Standards of Professional Conduct
- [ ] explain how the practices, policies, and conduct do or do not violate the CFA Institute Code of Ethics and Standards of Professional Conduct

Syyark, CFA, is a private client adviser for Gueoe Bank, a small private bank.[6] In his role, Syyark constructs and manages globally diversified fixed-income and equity portfolios for his clients based on the clients' respective investment objectives, risk tolerance, and time horizon. As part of his service, Syyark periodically reviews client assets held outside the bank and makes recommendations for those assets. Clients have often followed Syyark's advice. In providing this service, Syyark has been able to cultivate stronger relationships and build his client assets under management at the bank.

Syyark has been following developments in digital currencies, also known as cryptocurrencies, for some time. When the national securities regulator announced, some months ago, its decision to regulate cryptocurrencies as securities and began issuing guidance on cryptocurrency best practices, Syyark concluded it was time to

---

6 **Syyark:** David B. Stevens, CIMC, CFA. *Ethics Cases.* © 2017 CFA Institute. All rights reserved. Consistent with the 11th Edition of the *Standards of Practice Handbook.*

consider digital currencies for himself and his clients. Intrigued by the rapid appreciation in value many cryptocurrencies have exhibited, he believes cryptocurrencies might offer clients the potential for higher returns as well as diversification benefits.

Syyark spends two weekends researching the top cryptocurrencies. All are digital currencies created to facilitate different types of secure transactions over the internet. He learns that cryptocurrencies are "held" in online wallets set up by individual account holders and that individuals might earn additional cryptocurrency tokens by helping administer the cryptocurrency network through an activity called "mining." Syyark has read that it is difficult for later entrants to a cryptocurrency network to make money through mining because competitive pressure tends to raise the required level of capital investment over time, so he decides to focus his efforts and research on the newer cryptocurrencies.

After considering several of the newer cryptocurrencies, Syyark decides the best opportunity is with a digital currency called Meerine. To limit his risk of being wrong on the cryptocurrency's potential, Syyark decides to give a buy recommendation to only a few of his smallest clients. He recommends a 1% position in Meerine to these clients. Each of these clients establishes an online wallet to hold his cryptocurrency tokens and buys the recommended position in Meerine.

As Syyark monitors Meerine's price over the next month, he learns more about its trading patterns and its acceptance in the marketplace. Although Meerine's price exhibits significant volatility, Syyark feels optimistic about its potential. From his research, he knows there might also be an opportunity in mining Meerine's currency. Mining would involve using his own computing resources to help process Meerine's digital transactions, but in return, he could earn additional Meerine tokens for his Meerine account.

To learn how to do this, Syyark attends a local cryptocurrency conference and numerous workshops on mining. Syyark believes mining Meerine's currency will give him a better understanding of cryptocurrencies and the technology supporting Meerine; this understanding, in turn, will help him make better cryptocurrency investment recommendations for his clients.

After mining Meerine's currency by running the mining software as a background process on his home computer for several months, Syyark believes he is competent in his understanding of cryptocurrencies and their underlying technology. Mining has also provided him with a way to augment his salary from Gueoe Bank by adding Meerine tokens to his digital account. During this time, Meerine's price has continued to rise strongly. Syyark decides to recommend a 3% Meerine position for all clients.

In his client review meetings, Syyark highlights Meerine's cryptocurrency as an exciting opportunity. He illustrates the low correlation of cryptocurrencies with traditional assets and shows the strong performance of Meerine since his initial 1% buy recommendation. He shares with clients that he is mining the currency for Meerine and discusses his new 3% buy recommendation with each client. His clients, knowing little about cryptocurrencies, have few questions and no objections. Syyark is pleased and feels his recommendation has been well received.

Because Meerine is a newer cryptocurrency, its daily trading volume is low, and it will take his clients several days to establish their positions. As a miner, Syyark receives a steady flow of Meerine tokens into his digital wallet from his mining activities. He offers his larger clients the opportunity to buy Meerine tokens directly from him so that they do not miss out on any potential appreciation of Meerine while trying to establish their positions.

Identify violations or possible violations of the Code and Standards by Syyark. For each identified violation, state what actions Syyark should have taken and make a short policy statement a firm could use to guide employees to help prevent similar violations in the future.

This case highlights ethical challenges individuals might face during their careers as markets evolve and innovative financial products are introduced. The violations or potential violations of the Code and Standards in this case relate to a member's duties to clients; duties to employer; duties regarding investment analysis, recommendations, and actions; and duty to disclose conflicts of interest to the employer and clients.

Duties to Clients

Standard III(B): Duties to Clients, Fair Dealing states that members and candidates must treat all clients fairly when taking investment action with regard to general purchases, new issues, or secondary offerings. Syyark's offer to directly fill orders for his largest clients without making the same offer to all his clients is a breach of Standard III(B).

Standard III(B) does not state that all clients must be treated "equally." Members and candidates may differentiate their services to clients, but different levels of service must not disadvantage or negatively affect clients. When making investments in new offerings, however, members and candidates should distribute the issues to all customers for whom the investments are appropriate in a fair and equitable manner.

In this instance, Syyark has clearly violated Standard III(B). Syyark's offer to fill allocations from his Meerine account for only his largest clients puts his other clients at an economic disadvantage. Syyark has a duty to all his clients to provide fair and impartial access to Meerine tokens.

Actions Required

Because Syyark knows that the market for Meerine tokens is limited, he should either (1) offer each of his clients the opportunity to buy Meerine tokens directly from him, collect their orders, and then allocate his available tokens to each client in proportion to their planned investment or (2) not offer to sell any of his tokens to his clients.

Policy Statement for a Firm

"All client accounts participating in a new issue or security with limited liquidity will be executed as a block trade and shall receive the same execution price. All trade allocations to client accounts shall be made on a pro rata basis prior to or immediately following part or all of a block trade."

Standard III(C): Suitability obligates members and candidates who are in an investment advisory relationship with clients to consider carefully the needs, circumstances, and objectives of the clients when determining the appropriateness and suitability of a given investment. In judging the suitability of a potential investment, the member or candidate should review many aspects of the client's knowledge, experience related to investing, and financial situation. These aspects include, but are not limited to, the risk profile of the investment as compared with the constraints of the client, the impact of the investment on the diversity of the portfolio, and whether the client has the means or net worth to assume the associated risk. Although the national securities regulator is now regulating cryptocurrencies, they are still more suitable for speculation than as an investment, given that no clear consensus exists for determining future expected value for cryptocurrencies.

Although Syyark has considered the potential risk reduction benefits of diversification, his recommendation that all his clients buy a 3% position in Meerine without specific regard to suitability regarding client circumstances or whether this investment is consistent with each client's written objectives, mandates, or constraints is a clear violation of Standard III(C). An additional violation of this standard is Syyark's decision to initially recommend the Meerine investment only for his smallest accounts.

Rather than being determined by his clients' investment objectives, including risk tolerance, his decision is driven by the desire to limit his personal and Gueoe Bank's risk of being wrong in his recommendation.

Actions Required

Although Syyark is clearly excited about the possible benefits of cryptocurrencies, he needs to properly assess each client's circumstances and determine on the basis of her risk tolerance, goals, and objectives whether the client should invest in Meerine and, if so, what the appropriate level of exposure is for that client.

Policy Statement for a Firm

"When making any investment recommendations to clients, investment advisers must carefully consider the impact the proposed change will have on portfolio diversification, how the investment's risk parameters align with the client's assessed risk tolerance, and whether the proposed investment fits within the overall investment strategy, taking into account the client's time horizon, return objectives, and constraints, as well as the type and nature of the client."

Duties to Employers

Standard IV(B): Additional Compensation Arrangements requires members and candidates to obtain permission from their employer before accepting compensation or other benefits from third parties for any services that might create a conflict with their employer's interest.

Syyark has begun mining Meerine for additional cryptocurrency compensation. Doing so creates a conflict of interest with Gueoe Bank, because mining Meerine's cryptocurrency involves activities that compete with Gueoe's services. Mining involves verifying transactions that occur outside of traditional banking channels. As part of normal operations, banks facilitate transactions through credit cards and checking accounts. In mining, Syyark is supporting a service that is competitive with the bank, which creates a conflict. Earning outside compensation is not itself a violation of the Code and Standards, but Syyark should disclose it to his employer for the consideration of conflicts.

Actions Required

Syyark needs to disclose to his supervisor or the compliance department at Gueoe Bank his intention to mine Meerine and the potential earnings expected from this activity. He will need to receive written consent from Gueoe before beginning any mining activity.

Policy Statement for a Firm

"Employees must disclose any external employment or compensation arrangement to the firm and receive express written permission before undertaking any such arrangement. Failure to comply is a violation of company policy and is subject to disciplinary procedures up to and including termination."

Investment Analysis, Recommendations, and Actions

Under Standard V(A): Diligence and Reasonable Basis, members and candidates must exercise diligence, independence, and thoroughness in making investment recommendations. Although Syyark had done some research before recommending that clients buy cryptocurrency, he was still in the learning process when he made the buy recommendation to his smallest clients; therefore, he is in violation of Standard V(A).

Standard V(A) does not require perfect knowledge but does require diligence and thoroughness from members and candidates in gathering as much information and knowledge as possible to inform their professional judgement before making an investment recommendation in order to have a reasonable and adequate basis for making the recommendation.

Actions Required

Syyark should develop a written evaluation of cryptocurrencies and Meerine in particular, detailing the background information and decision framework that support his investment recommendation for cryptocurrencies and Meerine. Syyark's report should consider risks as well as benefits.

Policy Statement for a Firm

"Purchases or recommendations to purchase are limited to securities on the 'Approved for Investment Purchase List' (Approved List). Securities can be added to the Approved List after review and approval by the Investment Committee. A written research report detailing risks and opportunities is required for evaluation by the Investment Committee. The report should also note whether the security is considered speculative or non-speculative."

Conflicts of Interest

Under Standard VI(A): Disclosure of Conflicts, members and candidates must make full and fair disclosure of all matters that could reasonably be expected to impair their independence and objectivity. Members and candidates must maintain their objectivity when rendering investment advice. Requiring members and candidates to disclose all matters that reasonably could be expected to impair the member's or candidate's objectivity allows clients to judge an adviser's motives and possible biases for themselves.

Syyark's mining of Meerine and his recommendation that clients invest in Meerine is a conflict because he is advocating that his clients buy an investment with limited liquidity in which he has a personal holding. His clients' purchases would likely cause Meerine's price to rise, thereby directly benefiting Syyark's position. His lack of full disclosure is a violation of Standard VI(A). Furthermore, his decision to sell some of his own cryptocurrency directly to his clients is a conflict that needs to be disclosed to all his clients who are considering his recommendation to buy Meerine, as well as to his employer, Gueoe Bank. Although he reveals his mining activity in client meetings held after his recommendation of a 3% position in Meerine for all clients, clients should be given an alternative cryptocurrency to invest in to avoid the direct conflict. Also, the information he shares in the client meetings does not fully disclose his conflicted position, because his clients have limited knowledge of cryptocurrencies and might not understand the conflict of Syyark's mining activities and his investment recommendation to buy Meerine.

Because Syyark's clients have a limited knowledge of cryptocurrencies, his duty to disclose his conflict of interest is of paramount importance so that his clients can fully evaluate his recommendation.

Actions Required

Syyark should clearly disclose to his clients and Gueoe Bank his conflict of interest in mining Meerine and recommending Meerine for purchase to his clients. Because cryptocurrencies are relatively unfamiliar to most of his clients, he will need to make sure his clients fully understand his conflict. Before recommending Meerine to clients, Syyark should also determine a suitable alternative cryptocurrency from those he researched for those clients who are uncomfortable with the conflict of interest.

Policy Statement for a Firm

"Employees shall not use their position, directly or indirectly, for private gain or financial benefit, to advance personal interests, or to obtain favors or benefits for themselves, their families, or any other person. Effective conflict management requires all employees to identify and disclose to the company's Compliance Officer all actual or potential conflicts of interest as they become aware of them. Because it is impossible to describe every conflict of interest, all employees are required to exercise sound judgment, seek advice when appropriate, escalate concerns, obtain review of certain activities as required by this policy and other applicable business and jurisdiction-specific policies and procedures, and adhere to the highest ethical standards."

8   AGARWAY

☐   evaluate practices, policies, and conduct relative to the CFA Institute Code of Ethics and Standards of Professional Conduct

☐   explain how the practices, policies, and conduct do or do not violate the CFA Institute Code of Ethics and Standards of Professional Conduct

Agarway, CFA, has recently joined CrowdWisdom as vice president, and he is in charge of due diligence.[7] Agarway is the ninth employee of CrowdWisdom, a young venture capital company that matches investors with startup companies in need of capital. His position at the online company is a newly created one. As head of the due diligence function, Agarway's role is to identify suitable companies for CrowdWisdom to offer to potential investors. Agarway is the only CFA charterholder on the team, which includes two co-founders, Craig Miller and Stephane Etienne. Both Miller and Etienne have substantial experience and strong networks from working at other industry startup companies.

Since its startup four years ago, CrowdWisdom has grown rapidly, funding 50 startup companies with almost USD10 million from investors through its online matching platform. CrowdWisdom's business model markets to a wide range of startup companies seeking public capital. Startups in need of funds submit a listing application to CrowdWisdom. Application approval by CrowdWisdom's due diligence function allows companies to list on the platform for a fee, thereby becoming visible to platform investors as possible investments. Investors on the CrowdWisdom platform include both sophisticated and unsophisticated investors. Owing to a successful business model, Agarway is receiving an unprecedented number of applications from startups wishing to list on the company's platform.

The company's business plan calls for aggressive growth to maintain market share and secure CrowdWisdom's next round of funding. The founders' mandate is to list 100 companies on the CrowdWisdom platform in the next 18 months. In the longer term, the founders hope to do an IPO of CrowdWisdom's stock.

---

7 **Agarway:** Cynthia Harrington, CFA. *Ethics Cases.* © 2017 CFA Institute. All rights reserved. Consistent with the 11th edition of the *Standards of Practice Handbook.*

CrowdWisdom's early success has resulted in part from Miller's and Etienne's work in attracting platform investors who are willing to capitalize young startup companies. Leveraging their collective network, the founders created a large database of potential platform investors shortly after CrowdWisdom was created. As investors began investing on the platform, the founders pioneered an "Investor Club" whose members were the most active in providing capital through the CrowdWisdom platform. Investor Club members receive access to market intelligence research in addition to the research on CrowdWisdom -listed companies that Agarway prepares and posts on the firm's website.

To keep the database growing, Miller asks Agarway to consider companies whose customers appear to be a strong fit from a potential future investor standpoint. Agarway has experience marketing equity investments to customers of platform companies and knows that many companies have successfully raised funds by soliciting their own customers to become investors. Agarway also knows that CrowdWisdom's policies must comply with rules governing marketing over the internet, which include opt-in/opt-out preferences, age of person(s) marketed to, and required disclosures.

During the next two months, Agarway reviews the presentation materials for more than 100 companies that want to list on the CrowdWisdom platform. Agarway uses a process of due diligence he developed over several years, most recently as head of research for his previous employer, FunderWise, a lesser-known crowdfunding platform.

Agarway's due diligence process consists of a two-step process he developed through trial and error at FunderWise. First, he reviews materials provided by companies to screen out those with a potential market for their product or service of less than USD1 billion and those with perceived product or service viability concerns. Together, these criteria typically screen out 75% of applicant companies. Second, Agarway investigates the remaining companies by closely reviewing audited financial statements and interviewing company executives and customers. He is confident in his process and has personally invested in several FunderWise-listed companies using this approach.

After considerable time and effort investigating the companies that made it past the first screen, Agarway's additional research leads him to reject almost all the remaining companies. The rejected companies appear to have issues with improper revenue recognition, questionable user claims, and regulatory litigation.

Of the few remaining applications, Agarway believes one of the most promising is that of a company called Deko, an information technology startup. Deko has impressive founders, attractive prospects, and a unique product. Additionally, Deko seems to have an enviable customer base that CrowdWisdom could approach for future investor funding activity. Deko is unique in that most of its users are preteens and teenagers who love Deko's software, which allows them to create digital collections of their possessions and then share these collections with their friends online. The company's strategy is to market its crowdfunded shares through email communications to the young users. The email contains an announcement on the company's crowdfunding offer and states the offer is available to adults over the age of 18. Companies with loyal users who often bring in friends and family have proven to be among the more successful at equity crowdfunding campaigns.

To help Deko succeed, Agarway creates social media accounts to promote the company. He pays social media "influencers" with significant followers in Deko's user demographic to regularly post positive comments about Deko's product. Agarway, through his own posts and those of his paid promoters, indicates that more enhanced features and capabilities for Deko's product could be released any day now and that a large technology company sees Deko as a possible acquisition target. Although Agarway has no knowledge or information that these developments will happen, he believes they are certainly possible.

During this time, Agarway is asked to take on additional responsibilities. His days and evenings include speaking with founders of listed companies, answering investor questions, and working with attorneys to finalize listing transactions for new companies.

Several months later, after the founders present at two global startup conferences, Agarway's stack of applications for review grows to 300 companies. To meet CrowdWisdom's aggressive growth goals, Miller and Etienne suggest to Agarway that he target an application acceptance rate of 10%. They suggest Agarway research at least one-half of the applying companies in his second-stage process to meet the 10% acceptance rate.

Agarway patiently explains his process and his challenge in finding time to review applicants. In response, the founders suggest he find ways to reduce the time spent on each application. Miller and Etienne also recommend the acceptance of two companies whose founders Miller and Etienne met at the recent conferences.

Several activities in the case are or could be in violation of the Code and Standards. Identify violations or possible violations, state what actions Agarway and the firm should take to correct the violations, and make a short policy statement a firm could use to guide employees to help prevent similar violations from occurring in the future.

This case highlights challenges individuals might face during their careers when working for younger firms whose core business might not be traditional financial services or investment management, or when working for firms where they might be the only CFA charterholder or one of just a few CFA charterholders employed.

Professionalism

Standard I(A): Knowledge of the Law requires candidates and members to understand the applicable laws and regulations of the countries and jurisdictions where they engage in professional activities. Agarway should review the global rules governing online marketing to Deko's teen and preteen customers. The company strategy of offering equity to users' parents (or other adults in the household) through communications to its teen and preteen user base might put CrowdWisdom and Agarway at risk because in many countries, collecting information on such individuals over the internet without first obtaining parental permission is illegal. Unless Agarway can confirm that Deko is in compliance with this requirement, the use of CrowdWisdom's platform to solicit preteens could be against the law. Because Deko has cleared Agarway's due diligence process, if Deko were to be added to CrowdWisdom's platform, CrowdWisdom and Deko could be at risk for prosecution.

Actions Required

Although Agarway does not need to know the laws in every jurisdiction, he does need to stay informed about relevant legal limitations. Agarway and CrowdWisdom should establish a procedure whereby employees are regularly informed about changes in applicable laws and regulations. CrowdWisdom should also have legal counsel available to review planned additions to the platform to ensure that the company's strategy is not in conflict with relevant law.

Policy Statement for a Firm

"When determining whether a company should be included on the platform, careful consideration must be taken to determine whether the company's business strategy violates laws related to marketing and solicitation, particularly if the strategy targets minors or vulnerable adults (those with physical or mental disabilities). If the strategy targets minors or vulnerable adults, legal counsel will be consulted before listing the company on the platform."

Standard I(B): Independence and Objectivity obligates members and candidates to use reasonable care and judgment to achieve and maintain independence and objectivity in their professional activities. Pressure by CrowdWisdom's founders to modify Agarway's due diligence process to increase the number of listing approvals and shorten the review timeframe is likely to put Agarway's independence and objectivity at risk.

Actions Required

Agarway and CrowdWisdom's senior leaders need to create and document a company-approved due diligence process, which will likely blend Agarway's past work with input from CrowdWisdom's founders. As a CFA charterholder, Agarway will need to be comfortable that the process has a reasonable basis and can be applied objectively.

Policy Statement for a Firm

"The selection of companies for inclusion on the platform will comply with the due diligence process approved by the firm's Board as detailed in the Selection Due Diligence Memorandum approved on 25 January 20XX."

II. Integrity of Capital Markets

Standard II(B): Market Manipulation prohibits members and candidates from distorting prices or artificially inflating trading volume with the intent to mislead participants. Such conduct includes disseminating false or misleading information about a security to induce trading by others to affect the security price. Agarway appears to be engaging in this type of information-based market manipulation by sharing positive, unfounded information about Deko, and paying others to do so, with the intent to increase Deko's share price.

Actions required

While Agarway and CrowdWisdom might take steps to promote Deko, they must do so based only on factual information and objective research that does not attempt to manipulate the price or misrepresent the value of Deko securities. CrowdWisdom should adopt written policies that strictly govern public statements made by their employees about companies on their platform and clearly state in writing the internal process employees must comply with before making such statements.

Policy Statement for a Firm

"Employees of the firm are prohibited from making any public statements about companies listed on the firm's investment platform without first clearing those statements with the Compliance Officer to receive approval. Under no circumstances are employees to knowingly make, or cause others to make, any false, misleading, or speculative statements to clients or the investing public regarding companies listed, or under consideration for listing, on the firm's platform. Employees will not engage in any activity with the intent to mislead securities markets or distort the prices or trading volume of any security."

Conflicts of Interest

Standard VI(A): Disclosure of Conflicts requires members and candidates to make full and fair disclosure of all matters that could reasonably be expected to impair their independence and objectivity. Identifying and managing conflicts is a reality of working in the investment industry, where conflicts are often present. When a conflict cannot be reasonably avoided, clear and complete disclosure of its existence is necessary. Some possible conflicts of interest exist in this scenario: CrowdWisdom's Investor Club's selective access to additional market intelligence research and Agarway's personal investment in several companies that could be competitors of firms he is evaluating for the platform or future additions to the CrowdWisdom platform. Conflicts of interest might be inevitable and must be disclosed in a timely manner so that all parties involved can understand the circumstances and potential effects.

Actions Required

CrowdWisdom's Investor Club, which provides select investors with preferential access to additional market intelligence research, needs to be disclosed so that all investors can understand and evaluate the circumstances, the possible impact, and the potential disadvantage they might be placed at relative to Investor Club members.

In his personal portfolio, Agarway has invested in companies that could be competitors of firms he is reviewing in his due diligence work. His personal investments need to be disclosed to both his supervisor and CrowdWisdom's Compliance Officer. Additionally, if these firms also list on the CrowdWisdom platform, Agarway's personal investments would need to be disclosed to CrowdWisdom's users so that they can evaluate the independence and objectivity of each company's inclusion on the platform.

Policy Statement for a Firm

"Employees of the firm must disclose all personal investment holdings to the company's Compliance Officer, and that disclosure must be updated quarterly for public stocks and when invested for private holdings. All employee investments in companies that raise funds through the firm must be approved in advance by the Compliance Officer—or in the case of the founders, by the Board—before the transactions' closing and must be communicated to the firm's clients."

Glossary

Abnormal earnings See *residual income*.

Abnormal return The amount by which a security's actual return differs from its expected return, given the security's risk and the market's return.

Absolute convergence The idea that developing countries, regardless of their particular characteristics, will eventually catch up with the developed countries and match them in per capita output.

Absolute valuation model A model that specifies an asset's intrinsic value.

Absolute version of PPP An extension of the law of one price whereby the prices of goods and services will not differ internationally once exchange rates are considered.

Accounting estimates Estimates used in calculating the value of assets or liabilities and in the amount of revenue and expense to allocate to a period. Examples of accounting estimates include, among others, the useful lives of depreciable assets, the salvage value of depreciable assets, product returns, warranty costs, and the amount of uncollectible receivables.

Accumulated benefit obligation The actuarial present value of benefits (whether vested or non-vested) attributed, generally by the pension benefit formula, to employee service rendered before a specified date and based on employee service and compensation (if applicable) before that date. The accumulated benefit obligation differs from the projected benefit obligation in that it includes no assumption about future compensation levels.

Accuracy The percentage of correctly predicted classes out of total predictions. It is an overall performance metric in classification problems.

Acquisition When one company, the acquirer, purchases from the seller most or all of another company's (the target) shares to gain control of either an entire company, a segment of another company, or a specific group of assets in exchange for cash, stock, or the assumption of liabilities, alone or in combination. Once an acquisition is complete, the acquirer and target merge into a single entity and consolidate management, operations, and resources.

Activation function A functional part of a neural network's node that transforms the total net input received into the final output of the node. The activation function operates like a light dimmer switch that decreases or increases the strength of the input.

Active factor risk The contribution to active risk squared resulting from the portfolio's different-than-benchmark exposures relative to factors specified in the risk model.

Active return The return on a portfolio minus the return on the portfolio's benchmark.

Active risk The standard deviation of active returns.

Active risk squared The variance of active returns; active risk raised to the second power.

Active share A measure of how similar a portfolio is to its benchmark. A manager who precisely replicates the benchmark will have an active share of zero; a manager with no holdings in common with the benchmark will have an active share of one.

Active specific risk The contribution to active risk squared resulting from the portfolio's active weights on individual assets as those weights interact with assets' residual risk.

Adjusted funds from operations (AFFO) Funds from operations adjusted to remove any non-cash rent reported under straight-line rent accounting and to subtract maintenance-type capital expenditures and leasing costs, including leasing agents' commissions and tenants' improvement allowances.

Adjusted present value As an approach to valuing a company, the sum of the value of the company, assuming no use of debt, and the net present value of any effects of debt on company value.

Adjusted R^2 Goodness-of-fit measure that adjusts the coefficient of determination, R^2, for the number of independent variables in the model.

Administrative regulations or administrative law Rules issued by government agencies or other regulators.

Advanced set An arrangement in which the reference interest rate is set at the time the money is deposited.

Advanced settled An arrangement in which a forward rate agreement (FRA) expires and settles at the same time, at the FRA expiration date.

Agency issues Conflicts of interest that arise when the agent in an agency relationship has goals and incentives that differ from the principal to whom the agent owes a fiduciary duty. Also called *agency problems* or *principal–agent problems*.

Agglomerative clustering A bottom-up hierarchical clustering method that begins with each observation being treated as its own cluster. The algorithm finds the two closest clusters, based on some measure of distance (similarity), and combines them into one new larger cluster. This process is repeated iteratively until all observations are clumped into a single large cluster.

Akaike's information criterion (AIC) A statistic used to compare sets of independent variables for explaining a dependent variable. It is preferred for finding the model that is best suited for prediction.

Allowance for loan losses A balance sheet account; it is a contra asset account to loans.

Alpha The return on an asset in excess of the asset's required rate of return; the risk-adjusted return.

American Depositary Receipt A negotiable certificate issued by a depositary bank that represents ownership in a non-US company's deposited equity (i.e., equity held in custody by the depositary bank in the company's home market).

Analysis of variance (ANOVA) The analysis that breaks the total variability of a dataset (such as observations on the dependent variable in a regression) into components representing different sources of variation.

Application programming interface (API) A set of well-defined methods of communication between various software components and typically used for accessing external data.

Arbitrage 1) The simultaneous purchase of an undervalued asset or portfolio and sale of an overvalued but equivalent asset or portfolio, in order to obtain a riskless profit on the price differential. Taking advantage of a market inefficiency in a risk-free manner. 2) The condition in a financial market in which equivalent assets or combinations of assets sell for two different prices, creating an opportunity to profit at no risk with no commitment of money. In a well-functioning financial market, few arbitrage opportunities are possible. 3) A risk-free operation that earns an expected positive net profit but requires no net investment of money.

Arbitrage-free models Term structure models that project future interest rate paths that emanate from the existing term structure. Resulting prices are based on a no-arbitrage condition.

Arbitrage-free valuation An approach to valuation that determines security values consistent with the absence of any opportunity to earn riskless profits without any net investment of money.

Arbitrage opportunity An opportunity to conduct an arbitrage; an opportunity to earn an expected positive net profit without risk and with no net investment of money.

Arbitrage portfolio The portfolio that exploits an arbitrage opportunity.

Ask price The price at which a trader will sell a specified quantity of a security. Also called *ask*, *offer price*, or *offer*.

Asset-based approach Approach that values a private company based on the values of the underlying assets of the entity less the value of any related liabilities.

Asset-based valuation An approach to valuing natural resource companies that estimates company value on the basis of the market value of the natural resources the company controls.

At market contract When a forward contract is established, the forward price is negotiated so that the market value of the forward contract on the initiation date is zero.

Authorized participants (APs) A special group of institutional investors who are authorized by the ETF issuer to participate in the creation/redemption process. APs are large broker/dealers, often market makers.

Autocorrelations The correlations of a time series with its own past values.

Autoregressive model (AR) A time series regressed on its own past values in which the independent variable is a lagged value of the dependent variable.

Backtesting The process that approximates the real-life investment process, using historical data, to assess whether an investment strategy would have produced desirable results.

Backward propagation The process of adjusting weights in a neural network, to reduce total error of the network, by moving backward through the network's layers.

Backwardation A condition in the futures markets in which the spot price exceeds the futures price, the forward curve is downward sloping, and the convenience yield is high.

Bag-of-words (BOW) A collection of a distinct set of tokens from all the texts in a sample dataset. BOW does not capture the position or sequence of words present in the text.

Balance sheet restructuring Altering the composition of the balance sheet by either shifting the asset composition, changing the capital structure, or both.

Bankruptcy A declaration provided for by a country's laws that typically involves the establishment of a legal procedure that forces creditors to defer their claims.

Barbell portfolio Fixed-income portfolio that combines short and long maturities.

Base error Model error due to randomness in the data.

Basic earnings per share (EPS) Net earnings available to common shareholders (i.e., net income minus preferred dividends) divided by the weighted average number of common shares outstanding during the period.

Basis The difference between the spot price and the futures price. As the maturity date of the futures contract nears, the basis converges toward zero.

Basis trade A trade based on the pricing of credit in the bond market versus the price of the same credit in the CDS market. To execute a basis trade, go long the "underpriced" credit and short the "overpriced" credit. A profit is realized as the implied credit prices converge.

Bearish flattening Term structure shift in which short-term bond yields rise more than long-term bond yields, resulting in a flatter yield curve.

Benchmark value of the multiple In using the method of comparables, the value of a price multiple for the comparison asset; when we have comparison assets (a group), the mean or median value of the multiple for the group of assets.

Best ask The offer to sell with the lowest ask price. Also called *best offer* or *inside ask*.

Best bid The highest bid in the market.

Best offer The lowest offer (ask price) in the market.

Bias error Describes the degree to which a model fits the training data. Algorithms with erroneous assumptions produce high bias error with poor approximation, causing underfitting and high in-sample error.

Bid price In a price quotation, the price at which the party making the quotation is willing to buy a specified quantity of an asset or security.

Bid–ask spread The ask price minus the bid price.

Bill-and-hold basis Sales on a bill-and-hold basis involve selling products but not delivering those products until a later date.

Blockage factor An illiquidity discount that occurs when an investor sells a large amount of stock relative to its trading volume (assuming it is not large enough to constitute a controlling ownership).

Bond indenture A legal contract specifying the terms of a bond issue.

Bond risk premium The expected excess return of a default-free long-term bond less that of an equivalent short-term bond.

Bond yield plus risk premium (BYPRP) approach An estimate of the cost of common equity that is produced by summing the before-tax cost of debt and a risk premium that captures the additional yield on a company's stock relative to its bonds.

Bonus issue of shares A type of dividend in which a company distributes additional shares of its common stock to shareholders instead of cash.

Book value The net amount shown for an asset or liability on the balance sheet; book value may also refer to the company's excess of total assets over total liabilities. Also called *carrying value*.

Book value of equity Shareholders' equity (total assets minus total liabilities) minus the value of preferred stock; common shareholders' equity.

Book value per share The amount of book value (also called carrying value) of common equity per share of common stock, calculated by dividing the book value of shareholders' equity by the number of shares of common stock outstanding.

Glossary

Bootstrap aggregating (or bagging) A technique whereby the original training dataset is used to generate n new training datasets or bags of data. Each new bag of data is generated by random sampling with replacement from the initial training set.

Bootstrapping The use of a forward substitution process to determine zero-coupon rates by using the par yields and solving for the zero-coupon rates one by one, from the shortest to longest maturities.

Bottom-up approach With respect to forecasting, an approach that usually begins at the level of the individual company or a unit within the company.

Breakup value The value derived using a sum-of-the-parts valuation.

Breusch–Godfrey (BG) test A test used to detect autocorrelated residuals up to a predesignated order of the lagged residuals.

Breusch–Pagan (BP) test A test for the presence of heteroskedasticity in a regression.

Bullet portfolio A fixed-income portfolio concentrated in a single maturity.

Bullish flattening Term structure change in which the yield curve flattens in response to a greater decline in long-term rates than short-term rates.

Bullish steepening Term structure change in which short-term rates fall by more than long-term yields, resulting in a steeper term structure.

Buy-side analysts Analysts who work for investment management firms, trusts, bank trust departments, and similar institutions.

Buyback A transaction in which a company buys back its own shares. Unlike stock dividends and stock splits, share repurchases use corporate cash.

CDS spread A periodic premium paid by the buyer to the seller that serves as a return over a market reference rate required to protect against credit risk.

Callable bond A bond containing an embedded call option that gives the issuer the right to buy the bond back from the investor at specified prices on pre-determined dates.

Canceled shares Shares that were issued, subsequently repurchased by the company, and then retired (cannot be reissued).

Capital asset pricing model (CAPM) A single factor model such that excess returns on a stock are a function of the returns on a market index.

Capital charge The company's total cost of capital in money terms.

Capital deepening An increase in the capital-to-labor ratio.

Capitalization of earnings method In the context of private company valuation, a valuation model based on an assumption of a constant growth rate of free cash flow to the firm or a constant growth rate of free cash flow to equity.

Capitalization rate The divisor in the expression for the value of perpetuity. In the context of real estate, it is the divisor in the direct capitalization method of estimating value. The cap rate equals net operating income divided by value.

Capitalized cash flow method In the context of private company valuation, a valuation model based on an assumption of a constant growth rate of free cash flow to the firm or a constant growth rate of free cash flow to equity. Also called *capitalized cash flow model.*

Capitalized income method In the context of private company valuation, a valuation model based on an assumption of a constant growth rate of free cash flow to the firm or a constant growth rate of free cash flow to equity.

Capped floater Floating-rate bond with a cap provision that prevents the coupon rate from increasing above a specified maximum rate. It protects the issuer against rising interest rates.

Carry arbitrage model A no-arbitrage approach in which the underlying instrument is either bought or sold along with an opposite position in a forward contract.

Carry benefits Benefits that arise from owning certain underlyings; for example, dividends, foreign interest, and bond coupon payments.

Carry costs Costs that arise from owning certain underlyings. They are generally a function of the physical characteristics of the underlying asset and also the interest forgone on the funds tied up in the asset.

Cash available for distribution See *adjusted funds from operations.*

Cash-generating unit The smallest identifiable group of assets that generates cash inflows that are largely independent of the cash inflows of other assets or groups of assets.

Cash settlement A procedure used in certain derivative transactions that specifies that the long and short parties settle the derivative's difference in value between them by making a cash payment.

Catalyst An event or piece of information that causes the marketplace to re-evaluate the prospects of a company.

Ceiling analysis A systematic process of evaluating different components in the pipeline of model building. It helps to understand what part of the pipeline can potentially improve in performance by further tuning.

Centroid The center of a cluster formed using the k-means clustering algorithm.

Chain rule of forecasting A forecasting process in which the next period's value as predicted by the forecasting equation is substituted into the right-hand side of the equation to give a predicted value two periods ahead.

Cheapest-to-deliver The debt instrument that can be purchased and delivered at the lowest cost yet has the same seniority as the reference obligation.

Classification and regression tree A supervised machine learning technique that can be applied to predict either a categorical target variable, producing a classification tree, or a continuous target variable, producing a regression tree. CART is commonly applied to binary classification or regression.

Clean surplus relation The relationship between earnings, dividends, and book value in which ending book value is equal to the beginning book value plus earnings less dividends, apart from ownership transactions.

Club convergence The idea that only rich and middle-income countries sharing a set of favorable attributes (i.e., are members of the "club") will converge to the income level of the richest countries.

Cluster A subset of observations from a dataset such that all the observations within the same cluster are deemed "similar."

Clustering The sorting of observations into groups (clusters) such that observations in the same cluster are more similar to each other than they are to observations in other clusters.

Cobb–Douglas production function A function of the form $Y = K^{\alpha} L^{1-\alpha}$ relating output (Y) to labor (L) and capital (K) inputs.

Coefficient of determination The percentage of the variation of the dependent variable that is explained by the independent variables. Also referred to as the R-squared or R^2.

Cointegrated Describes two time series that have a long-term financial or economic relationship such that they do not diverge from each other without bound in the long run.

Collateral return The component of the total return on a commodity futures position attributable to the yield for the bonds or cash used to maintain the futures position. Also called *collateral yield*.

Collection frequency (CF) The number of times a given word appears in the whole corpus (i.e., collection of sentences) divided by the total number of words in the corpus.

Commercial real estate properties Income-producing real estate properties; properties purchased with the intent to let, lease, or rent (in other words, produce income).

Commodity swap A type of swap involving the exchange of payments over multiple dates as determined by specified reference prices or indexes relating to commodities.

Company fundamental factors Factors related to the company's internal performance, such as factors relating to earnings growth, earnings variability, earnings momentum, and financial leverage.

Company share-related factors Valuation measures and other factors related to share price or the trading characteristics of the shares, such as earnings yield, dividend yield, and book-to-market value.

Comparables Assets used as benchmarks when applying the method of comparables to value an asset. Also called *comps*, *guideline assets*, or *guideline companies*.

Compiled financial statements Financial statements that are not accompanied by an auditor's opinion letter.

Complexity A term referring to the number of features, parameters, or branches in a model and to whether the model is linear or non-linear (non-linear is more complex).

Composite variable A variable that combines two or more variables that are statistically strongly related to each other.

Comprehensive income All changes in equity other than contributions by, and distributions to, owners; income under clean surplus accounting; includes all changes in equity during a period except those resulting from investments by owners and distributions to owners. Comprehensive income equals net income plus other comprehensive income.

Comps Assets used as benchmarks when applying the method of comparables to value an asset.

Concentrated ownership Ownership structure consisting of an individual shareholder or a group (controlling shareholders) with the ability to exercise control over the corporation.

Conditional convergence The idea that convergence of per capita income is conditional on the countries having the same savings rate, population growth rate, and production function.

Conditional heteroskedasticity A condition in which the variance of residuals of a regression are correlated with the value of the independent variables.

Conditional VaR (CVaR) The weighted average of all loss outcomes in the statistical (i.e., return) distribution that exceed the VaR loss. Thus, CVaR is a more comprehensive measure of tail loss than VaR is. Sometimes referred to as the *expected tail loss* or *expected shortfall*.

Confirmation bias A belief perseverance bias in which people tend to look for and notice what confirms their beliefs, to ignore or undervalue what contradicts their beliefs, and to misinterpret information as support for their beliefs.

Confusion matrix A grid used for error analysis in classification problems, it presents values for four evaluation metrics including true positive (TP), false positive (FP), true negative (TN), and false negative (FN).

Conglomerate discount When an issuer is trading at a valuation lower than the sum of its parts, which is generally the result of diseconomies of scale or scope or the result of the capital markets having overlooked the business and its prospects.

Constant dividend payout ratio policy A policy in which a constant percentage of net income is paid out in dividends.

Constant returns to scale The condition that if all inputs into the production process are increased by a given percentage, then output rises by that same percentage.

Contango A condition in the futures markets in which the spot price is lower than the futures price, the forward curve is upward sloping, and there is little or no convenience yield.

Contingent consideration Potential future payments to the seller that are contingent on the achievement of certain agreed-on occurrences.

Continuing earnings Earnings excluding nonrecurring components. Also referred to as *core earnings*, *persistent earnings*, or *underlying earnings*.

Continuing residual income Residual income after the forecast horizon.

Continuing value The analyst's estimate of a stock's value at a particular point in the future.

Control premium An increment or premium to value associated with a controlling ownership interest in a company.

Convergence The tendency for differences in output per capita across countries to diminish over time. In technical analysis, the term describes the case when an indicator moves in the same manner as the security being analyzed.

Conversion period For a convertible bond, the period during which bondholders have the right to convert their bonds into shares.

Conversion price For a convertible bond, the price per share at which the bond can be converted into shares.

Conversion rate (or ratio) For a convertible bond, the number of shares of common stock that a bondholder receives from converting the bond into shares.

Conversion value For a convertible bond, the value of the bond if it is converted at the market price of the shares. Also called *parity value*.

Convertible bond Bond that gives the bondholder the right to exchange the bond for a specified number of common shares in the issuing company.

Convexity A measure of how interest rate sensitivity changes with a change in interest rates.

Cook's distance A metric for identifying influential data points. Also known as Cook's D (D_i).

Core earnings Earnings excluding nonrecurring components. Also referred to as *continuing earnings*, *persistent earnings*, or *underlying earnings*.

Core real estate investment style Investing in high-quality, well-leased, core property types with low leverage (no more than 30% of asset value) in the largest markets with strong, diversified economies. It is a conservative strategy designed to avoid real estate–specific risks, including leasing, development, and speculation in favor of steady returns. Hotel

Glossary

properties are excluded from the core categories because of the higher cash flow volatility resulting from single-night leases and the greater importance of property operations, brand, and marketing.

Corpus   A collection of text data in any form, including list, matrix, or data table forms.

Cost approach   An approach that values a private company based on the values of the underlying assets of the entity less the value of any related liabilities. In the context of real estate, this approach estimates the value of a property based on what it would cost to buy the land and construct a new property on the site that has the same utility or functionality as the property being appraised.

Cost of carry model   A model that relates the forward price of an asset to the spot price by considering the cost of carry (also referred to as future-spot parity model).

Cost of debt   The required return on debt financing to a company, such as when it issues a bond, takes out a bank loan, or leases an asset through a finance lease.

Cost of equity   The return required by equity investors to compensate for both the time value of money and the risk. Also referred to as the required rate of return on common stock or the required return on equity.

Cost restructuring   Actions to reduce costs by improving operational efficiency and profitability, often to raise margins to a historical level or to those of comparable industry peers.

Country risk premium (CRP)   The additional return required by investors to compensate for the risk associated with investing in a foreign country relative to the investor's domestic market.

Country risk rating (CRR)   The rating of a country based on many risk factors, including economic prosperity, political risk, and ESG risk.

Covariance stationary   Describes a time series when its expected value and variance are constant and finite in all periods and when its covariance with itself for a fixed number of periods in the past or future is constant and finite in all periods.

Covered bonds   A senior debt obligation of a financial institution that gives recourse to the originator/issuer and a predetermined underlying collateral pool.

Covered interest rate parity   The relationship among the spot exchange rate, the forward exchange rate, and the interest rates in two currencies that ensures that the return on a hedged (i.e., covered) foreign risk-free investment is the same as the return on a domestic risk-free investment. Also called *interest rate parity*.

Cox-Ingersoll-Ross model   A general equilibrium term structure model that assumes interest rates are mean reverting and interest rate volatility is directly related to the level of interest rates.

Creation basket   The list of securities (and share amounts) the authorized participant (AP) must deliver to the ETF manager in exchange for ETF shares. The creation basket is published each business day.

Creation units   Large blocks of ETF shares transacted between the authorized participant (AP) and the ETF manager that are usually but not always equal to 50,000 shares of the ETF.

Creation/redemption   The process in which ETF shares are created or redeemed by authorized participants transacting with the ETF issuer.

Credit correlation   The correlation of credit (or default) risks of the underlying single-name CDS contained in an index CDS.

Credit curve   The credit spreads for a range of maturities of a company's debt.

Credit default swap   A derivative contract between two parties in which the buyer makes a series of cash payments to the seller and receives a promise of compensation for credit losses resulting from the default.

Credit derivative   A derivative instrument in which the underlying is a measure of the credit quality of a borrower.

Credit event   An event that defines a payout in a credit derivative. Events are usually defined as bankruptcy, failure to pay an obligation, or an involuntary debt restructuring.

Credit protection buyer   One party to a credit default swap; the buyer makes a series of cash payments to the seller and receives a promise of compensation for credit losses resulting from the default.

Credit protection seller   One party to a credit default swap; the seller makes a promise to pay compensation for credit losses resulting from the default.

Credit risk   The risk of loss caused by a counterparty's or debtor's failure to make a promised payment. Also called *default risk*.

Credit spread   The compensation for the risk inherent in a company's debt security.

Credit valuation adjustment   The value of the credit risk of a bond in present value terms.

Cross-validation   A technique for estimating out-of-sample error directly by determining the error in validation samples.

Cumulative preferred stock   Preferred stock that requires that the dividends be paid in full to preferred stock owners for any missed dividends prior to any payment of dividends to common stock owners.

Current exchange rate   For accounting purposes, the spot exchange rate on the balance sheet date.

Current rate method   Approach to translating foreign currency financial statements for consolidation in which all assets and liabilities are translated at the current exchange rate. The current rate method is the prevalent method of translation.

Curvature   One of the three factors (the other two are level and steepness) that empirically explain most of the changes in the shape of the yield curve. A shock to the curvature factor affects mid-maturity interest rates, resulting in the term structure becoming either more or less hump-shaped.

Curve trade   Buying a CDS of one maturity and selling a CDS on the same reference entity with a different maturity.

Customer concentration risk   The risk associated with sales dependent on a few customers.

Cyclical businesses   Businesses with high sensitivity to business- or industry-cycle influences.

Data preparation (cleansing)   The process of examining, identifying, and mitigating (i.e., cleansing) errors in raw data.

Data snooping   The practice of determining a model by extensive searching through a dataset for statistically significant patterns.

Data wrangling (preprocessing)   This task performs transformations and critical processing steps on cleansed data to make the data ready for ML model training (i.e., preprocessing), and includes dealing with outliers, extracting useful variables from existing data points, and scaling the data.

Deep learning   Machine learning using neural networks with many hidden layers.

Deep neural networks Neural networks with many hidden layers—at least 2 but potentially more than 20—that have proven successful across a wide range of artificial intelligence applications.

Default risk See *credit risk*.

Defined benefit pension plans Plans in which the company promises to pay a certain annual amount (defined benefit) to the employee after retirement. The company bears the investment risk of the plan assets.

Defined contribution pension plans Individual accounts to which an employee and typically the employer makes contributions during their working years and expect to draw on the accumulated funds at retirement. The employee bears the investment and inflation risk of the plan assets.

Delay costs Implicit trading costs that arise from the inability to complete desired trades immediately. Also called *slippage*.

Delta The relationship between the option price and the underlying price, which reflects the sensitivity of the price of the option to changes in the price of the underlying. Delta is a good approximation of how an option price will change for a small change in the stock.

Dendrogram A type of tree diagram used for visualizing a hierarchical cluster analysis; it highlights the hierarchical relationships among the clusters.

Depository Trust and Clearinghouse Corporation A US-headquartered entity providing post-trade clearing, settlement, and information services.

Diluted earnings per share (Diluted EPS)Net income, minus preferred dividends, divided by the weighted average number of common shares outstanding considering all dilutive securities (e.g., convertible debt and options); the EPS that would result if all dilutive securities were converted into common shares.

Dilution A reduction in proportional ownership interest as a result of the issuance of new shares.

Dimension reduction A set of techniques for reducing the number of features in a dataset while retaining variation across observations to preserve the information contained in that variation.

Diminishing marginal productivity When each additional unit of an input, keeping the other inputs unchanged, increases output by a smaller increment.

Direct capitalization method In the context of real estate, this method estimates the value of an income-producing property based on the level and quality of its net operating income.

Discount To reduce the value of a future payment in allowance for how far away it is in time; to calculate the present value of some future amount. Also, the amount by which an instrument is priced below its face value.

Discount factor The price equivalent of a zero rate. Also may be stated as the present value of a currency unit on a future date.

Discount for lack of control An amount or percentage deducted from the pro rata share of 100% of the value of an equity interest in a business to reflect the absence of some or all of the powers of control.

Discount for lack of marketability An amount of percentage deducted from the value of an ownership interest to reflect the relative absence of marketability.

Discount function Discount factors for the range of all possible maturities. The spot curve can be derived from the discount function and vice versa.

Discounted abnormal earnings model A model of stock valuation that views intrinsic value of stock as the sum of book value per share plus the present value of the stock's expected future residual income per share.

Discounted cash flow (DCF) method Income approach that values an asset based on estimates of future cash flows discounted to present value by using a discount rate reflective of the risks associated with the cash flows. In the context of real estate, this method estimates the value of an income-producing property based on discounting future projected cash flows.

Discounted cash flow method Income approach that values an asset based on estimates of future cash flows discounted to present value by using a discount rate reflective of the risks associated with the cash flows. In the context of real estate, this method estimates the value of an income-producing property based on discounting future projected cash flows.

Discounted cash flow model A model of intrinsic value that views the value of an asset as the present value of the asset's expected future cash flows.

Dispersed ownership Ownership structure consisting of many shareholders, none of which has the ability to individually exercise control over the corporation.

Divestiture When a seller sells a company, segment of a company, or group of assets to an acquirer. Once complete, control of the target is transferred to the acquirer.

Dividend A distribution paid to shareholders based on the number of shares owned.

Dividend coverage ratio The ratio of net income to dividends.

Dividend discount model (DDM) A present value model of stock value that views the intrinsic value of a stock as present value of the stock's expected future dividends.

Dividend discount model (DDM) The model of the value of stock that is the present value of all future dividends, discounted at the required return on equity.

Dividend displacement of earnings The concept that dividends paid now displace earnings in all future periods.

Dividend imputation tax system A taxation system that effectively assures corporate profits distributed as dividends are taxed just once and at the shareholder's tax rate.

Dividend index point A measure of the quantity of dividends attributable to a particular index.

Dividend payout ratio The ratio of cash dividends paid to earnings for a period.

Dividend policy The strategy a company follows with regard to the amount and timing of dividend payments.

Dividend rate The annualized amount of the most recent dividend.

Dividend recapitalization Restructuring the mix of debt and equity, typically shifting the capital structure from equity to debt through debt-financed share repurchases. The objective is to reduce the issuer's weighted average cost of capital by replacing expensive equity with cheaper debt by purchasing equity from shareholders using newly issued debt.

Dividend yield Annual dividends per share divided by share price.

Divisive clustering A top-down hierarchical clustering method that starts with all observations belonging to a single large cluster. The observations are then divided into two clusters based on some measure of distance (similarity). The algorithm then progressively partitions the intermediate clusters into smaller ones until each cluster contains only one observation.

Glossary

Document frequency (DF) The number of documents (texts) that contain a particular token divided by the total number of documents. It is the simplest feature selection method and often performs well when many thousands of tokens are present.

Document term matrix (DTM) A matrix where each row belongs to a document (or text file), and each column represents a token (or term). The number of rows is equal to the number of documents (or text files) in a sample text dataset. The number of columns is equal to the number of tokens from the BOW built using all the documents in the sample dataset. The cells typically contain the counts of the number of times a token is present in each document.

Dominance An arbitrage opportunity when a financial asset with a risk-free payoff in the future must have a positive price today.

Double taxation system Corporate earnings are taxed twice when paid out as dividends. First, corporate pretax earnings are taxed regardless of whether they will be distributed as dividends or retained at the corporate level. Second, dividends are taxed again at the individual shareholder level.

Downstream A transaction between two related companies, an investor company (or a parent company) and an associate company (or a subsidiary) such that the investor company records a profit on its income statement. An example is a sale of inventory by the investor company to the associate or by a parent to a subsidiary company.

Dual-class shares Shares that grant one share class superior or even sole voting rights, whereas the other share class has inferior or no voting rights.

Due diligence Investigation and analysis in support of an investment action, decision, or recommendation.

Dummy variable An independent variable that takes on a value of either 1 or 0, depending on a specified condition. Also known as an *indicator variable*.

Duration A measure of the approximate sensitivity of a security to a change in interest rates (i.e., a measure of interest rate risk).

Durbin–Watson (DW) test A test for the presence of first-order serial correlation.

Dutch disease A situation in which currency appreciation driven by strong export demand for resources makes other segments of the economy (particularly manufacturing) globally uncompetitive.

ESG integration An ESG investment approach that focuses on systematic consideration of material ESG factors in asset allocation, security selection, and portfolio construction decisions for the purpose of achieving the product's stated investment objectives. Used interchangeably with **ESG investing**.

Earnings surprise The portion of a company's earnings that is unanticipated by investors and, according to the efficient market hypothesis, merits a price adjustment.

Earnings yield EPS divided by price; the reciprocal of the P/E.

Economic profit Equal to accounting profit less the implicit opportunity costs not included in total accounting costs; the difference between total revenue (TR) and total cost (TC). Also called *abnormal profit* or *supernormal profit*.

Economic sectors Large industry groupings.

Economic value added (EVA*) A commercial implementation of the residual income concept; the computation of EVA* is the net operating profit after taxes minus the cost of capital, where these inputs are adjusted for a number of items.

Economies of scale A situation in which average costs per unit of good or service produced fall as volume rises. In reference to mergers, the savings achieved through the consolidation of operations and elimination of duplicate resources.

Edwards–Bell–Ohlson model A model of stock valuation that views intrinsic value of stock as the sum of book value per share plus the present value of the stock's expected future residual income per share.

Effective convexity A *curve convexity* statistic that measures the secondary effect of a change in a benchmark yield curve on a bond's price.

Effective duration Sensitivity of the bond's price to a 100 bps parallel shift of the benchmark yield curve, assuming no change in the bond's credit spread.

Effective spread Two times the difference between the execution price and the midpoint of the market quote at the time an order is entered.

Eigenvalue A measure that gives the proportion of total variance in the initial dataset that is explained by each eigenvector.

Eigenvector A vector that defines new mutually uncorrelated composite variables that are linear combinations of the original features.

Embedded options Contingency provisions found in a bond's indenture or offering circular representing rights that enable their holders to take advantage of interest rate movements. They can be exercised by the issuer, by the bondholder, or automatically depending on the course of interest rates.

Ensemble learning A technique of combining the predictions from a collection of models to achieve a more accurate prediction.

Ensemble method The method of combining multiple learning algorithms, as in ensemble learning.

Enterprise value Total company value (the market value of debt, common equity, and preferred equity) minus the value of cash and investments.

Enterprise value multiple A valuation multiple that relates the total market value of all sources of a company's capital (net of cash) to a measure of fundamental value for the entire company (such as a pre-interest earnings measure).

Equity charge The estimated cost of equity capital in money terms.

Equity investment A company purchasing another company's equity but less than 50% of its shares. The two companies maintain their independence, but the investor company has investment exposure to the investee and, in some cases depending on the size of the investment, can have representation on the investee's board of directors to influence operations.

Equity REITs REITs that own, operate, and/or selectively develop income-producing real estate.

Equity risk premium (ERP) Compensation for bearing market risk.

Equity swap A swap transaction in which at least one cash flow is tied to the return on an equity portfolio position, often an equity index.

Error autocorrelations The autocorrelations of the error term.

Ex ante tracking error A measure of the degree to which the performance of a given investment portfolio might be expected to deviate from its benchmark; also known as *relative VaR*.

Ex ante version of PPP   The hypothesis that expected changes in the spot exchange rate are equal to expected differences in national inflation rates. An extension of relative purchasing power parity to expected future changes in the exchange rate.

Ex-dividend   Trading ex-dividend refers to shares that no longer carry the right to the next dividend payment.

Ex-dividend date   The first date that a share trades without (i.e., "ex") the right to receive the declared dividend for the period.

Excess earnings method   Income approach that estimates the value of all intangible assets of the business by capitalizing future earnings in excess of the estimated return requirements associated with working capital and fixed assets.

Exercise date   The date when employees actually exercise stock options and convert them to stock.

Exercise value   The value of an option if it were exercised. Also sometimes called *intrinsic value*.

Expanded CAPM   An adaptation of the CAPM that adds to the CAPM a premium for small size and company-specific risk.

Expectations approach   A procedure for obtaining the value of an option derived from discounting at the risk-free rate its expected future payoff based on risk neutral probabilities.

Expected exposure   The projected amount of money an investor could lose if an event of default occurs, before factoring in possible recovery.

Expected shortfall   The average loss conditional on exceeding the VaR cutoff; sometimes referred to as *conditional VaR* or *expected tail loss*.

Expected tail loss   See *expected shortfall*.

Exploratory data analysis (EDA)   The preliminary step in data exploration, where graphs, charts, and other visualizations (heat maps and word clouds) as well as quantitative methods (descriptive statistics and central tendency measures) are used to observe and summarize data.

Exposure to foreign exchange risk   The risk of a change in value of an asset or liability denominated in a foreign currency due to a change in exchange rates.

Extendible bond   Bond with an embedded option that gives the bondholder the right to keep the bond for a number of years after maturity, possibly with a different coupon.

Extra dividend   A dividend paid by a company that does not pay dividends on a regular schedule, or a dividend that supplements regular cash dividends with an extra payment.

F1 score   The harmonic mean of precision and recall. F1 score is a more appropriate overall performance metric (than accuracy) when there is unequal class distribution in the dataset and it is necessary to measure the equilibrium of precision and recall.

FX carry trade   An investment strategy that involves taking long positions in high-yield currencies and short positions in low-yield currencies.

Factor   A common or underlying element with which several variables are correlated.

Factor betas   An asset's sensitivity to a particular factor; a measure of the response of return to each unit of increase in a factor, holding all other factors constant.

Factor portfolio   See *pure factor portfolio*.

Factor price   The expected return in excess of the risk-free rate for a portfolio with a sensitivity of 1 to one factor and a sensitivity of 0 to all other factors.

Factor risk premium   The expected return in excess of the risk-free rate for a portfolio with a sensitivity of 1 to one factor and a sensitivity of 0 to all other factors. Also called *factor price*.

Factor risk premiums   The expected return in excess of the risk-free rate for a portfolio with a sensitivity of 1 to one factor and a sensitivity of 0 to all other factors. Also called factor price.

Failure to pay   When a borrower does not make a scheduled payment of principal or interest on any outstanding obligations after a grace period.

Fair market value   The price, expressed in terms of cash equivalents, at which a property (asset) would change hands between a hypothetical willing and able buyer and a hypothetical willing and able seller, acting at "arm's length" in an open and unrestricted market, when neither is under compulsion to buy or sell and when both have reasonable knowledge of the relevant facts. Fair market value is most often used in a tax reporting context in the United States.

Fair value   The amount at which an asset could be exchanged, or a liability settled, between knowledgeable, willing parties in an arm's-length transaction; the price that would be received to sell an asset or paid to transfer a liability in an orderly transaction between market participants.

Fama–French models   Factor models that explain the drivers of returns related to three, four, or five factors.

Feature engineering   A process of creating new features by changing or transforming existing features.

Feature selection   A process whereby only pertinent features from the dataset are selected for model training. Selecting fewer features decreases model complexity and training time.

Features   The independent variables (X's) in a labeled dataset.

Finance (or capital) lease   A lease that is viewed as a financing arrangement.

Financial contagion   A situation in which financial shocks spread from their place of origin to other locales. In essence, a faltering economy infects other, healthier economies.

Financial leverage   The use of fixed sources of capital, such as debt, relative to sources without fixed costs, such as equity.

Financial transaction   A purchase involving a buyer having essentially no material synergies with the target (e.g., the purchase of a private company by a company in an unrelated industry or by a private equity firm would typically be a financial transaction).

First-differencing   A transformation that subtracts the value of the time series in period $t - 1$ from its value in period t.

First-order serial correlation   The correlation of residuals with residuals adjacent in time.

Fitting curve   A curve which shows in- and out-of-sample error rates (E_{in} and E_{out}) on the y-axis plotted against model complexity on the x-axis.

Fixed price tender offer   Offer made by a company to repurchase a specific number of shares at a fixed price that is typically at a premium to the current market price.

Fixed-rate perpetual preferred stock   Nonconvertible, noncallable preferred stock that has a fixed dividend rate and no maturity date.

Flight to quality   During times of market stress, investors sell higher-risk asset classes such as stocks and commodities in favor of default-risk-free government bonds.

Float   Amounts collected as premium and not yet paid out as benefits.

Glossary

Floored floater Floating-rate bond with a floor provision that prevents the coupon rate from decreasing below a specified minimum rate. It protects the investor against declining interest rates.

Flotation cost Fees charged to companies by investment bankers and other costs associated with raising new capital.

Forced conversion For a convertible bond, when the issuer calls the bond and forces bondholders to convert their bonds into shares, which typically happens when the underlying share price increases above the conversion price.

Foreign currency transactions Transactions that are denominated in a currency other than a company's functional currency.

Forward curve A series of forward rates, each having the same time frame.

Forward dividend yield A dividend yield based on the anticipated dividend during the next 12 months.

Forward-looking estimates Estimates based on current and expectations. Also referred to as ex ante estimates.

Forward P/E A P/E calculated on the basis of a forecast of EPS; a stock's current price divided by next year's expected earnings.

Forward price Represents the price agreed upon in a forward contract to be exchanged at the contract's maturity date, T. This price is shown in equations as $F_0(T)$.

Forward pricing model The model that describes the valuation of forward contracts.

Forward propagation The process of adjusting weights in a neural network, to reduce total error of the network, by moving forward through the network's layers.

Forward rate An interest rate determined today for a loan that will be initiated in a future period.

Forward rate agreement An over-the-counter forward contract in which the underlying is an interest rate on a deposit. A forward rate agreement (FRA) calls for one party to make a fixed interest payment and the other to make an interest payment at a rate to be determined at contract expiration.

Forward rate model The forward pricing model expressed in terms of spot and forward interest rates.

Forward rate parity The proposition that the forward exchange rate is an unbiased predictor of the future spot exchange rate.

Forward value The monetary value of an existing forward contract.

Franchising An owner of an asset and associated intellectual property divests the asset and licenses intellectual property to a third-party operator (franchisee) in exchange for royalties. Franchisees operate under the constraints of a franchise agreement.

Franking credit A tax credit received by shareholders for the taxes that a corporation paid on its distributed earnings.

Free cash flow method Income approach that values an asset based on estimates of future cash flows discounted to present value by using a discount rate reflective of the risks associated with the cash flows.

Free cash flow to equity The cash flow available to a company's common shareholders after all operating expenses, interest, and principal payments have been made and necessary investments in working and fixed capital have been made.

Free cash flow to equity model A model of stock valuation that views a stock's intrinsic value as the present value of expected future free cash flows to equity.

Free cash flow to the firm The cash flow available to the company's suppliers of capital after all operating expenses (including taxes) have been paid and necessary investments in working and fixed capital have been made.

Free cash flow to the firm model A model of stock valuation that views the value of a firm as the present value of expected future free cash flows to the firm.

Frequency analysis The process of quantifying how important tokens are in a sentence and in the corpus as a whole. It helps in filtering unnecessary tokens (or features).

Functional currency The currency of the primary economic environment in which an entity operates.

Fundamental factor models A multifactor model in which the factors are attributes of stocks or companies that are important in explaining cross-sectional differences in stock prices.

Fundamentals Economic characteristics of a business, such as profitability, financial strength, and risk.

Funds available for distribution (FAD) See *adjusted funds from operations*.

Funds from operations (FFO) Net income (computed in accordance with generally accepted accounting principles) *plus* (1) gains and losses from sales of properties and (2) depreciation and amortization.

Futures price The pre-agreed price at which a futures contract buyer (seller) agrees to pay (receive) for the underlying at the maturity date of the futures contract.

Futures value The monetary value of an existing futures contract.

Gamma A numerical measure of how sensitive an option's delta (the sensitivity of the derivative's price) is to a change in the value of the underlying.

General linear *F*-test A test statistic used to assess the goodness of fit for an entire regression model, so it tests all independent variables in the model.

Generalize When a model retains its explanatory power when predicting out-of-sample (i.e., using new data).

Global CAPM (GCAPM) A single-factor model with a global index representing the single factor.

Going-concern assumption The assumption that the business will maintain its business activities into the foreseeable future.

Going-concern value A business's value under a going-concern assumption.

Goodwill An intangible asset that represents the excess of the purchase price of an acquired company over the value of the net identifiable assets acquired.

Gordon growth model A DDM that assumes dividends grow at a constant rate into the future.

Grant date The day that stock options are granted to employees.

Green bond Bonds in which the proceeds are designated by issuers to fund a specific project or portfolio of projects that have environmental or climate benefits.

Greenmail The purchase of the accumulated shares of a hostile investor by a company that is targeted for takeover by that investor, usually at a substantial premium over market price.

Greenwashing The risk that a green bond's proceeds are not actually used for a beneficial environmental or climate-related project.

Grid search A method of systematically training a model by using various combinations of hyperparameter values, cross validating each model, and determining which combination of hyperparameter values ensures the best model performance.

Gross domestic product The market value of all final goods and services produced within the economy during a given period (output definition) or, equivalently, the aggregate income earned by all households, all companies, and the government within the economy during a given period (income definition).

Gross lease A lease under which the tenant pays a gross rent to the landlord, who is responsible for all operating costs, utilities, maintenance expenses, and real estate taxes relating to the property.

Ground truth The known outcome (i.e., target variable) of each observation in a labelled dataset.

Growth accounting equation The production function written in the form of growth rates. For the basic Cobb–Douglas production function, it states that the growth rate of output equals the rate of technological change plus α multiplied by the growth rate of capital plus $(1 - \alpha)$ multiplied by the growth rate of labor.

Growth capital expenditures Capital expenditures needed for expansion.

Guideline assets Assets used as benchmarks when applying the method of comparables to value an asset.

Guideline companies Assets used as benchmarks when applying the method of comparables to value an asset.

Guideline public companies Public-company comparables for the company being valued.

Guideline public company method A variation of the market approach; establishes a value estimate based on the observed multiples from trading activity in the shares of public companies viewed as reasonably comparable to the subject private company.

Guideline transactions method A variation of the market approach; establishes a value estimate based on pricing multiples derived from the acquisition of control of entire public or private companies that were acquired.

Harmonic mean A type of weighted mean computed as the reciprocal of the arithmetic average of the reciprocals.

Hazard rate The probability that an event will occur, given that it has not already occurred.

Hedonic index Unlike a repeat-sales index, a hedonic index does not require repeat sales of the same property. It requires only one sale. The way it controls for the fact that different properties are selling each quarter is to include variables in the regression that control for differences in the characteristics of the property, such as size, age, quality of construction, and location.

Heteroskedastic When the variance of the residuals differs across observations in a regression.

Heteroskedasticity The property of having a nonconstant variance; refers to an error term with the property that its variance differs across observations.

Hierarchical clustering An iterative unsupervised learning procedure used for building a hierarchy of clusters.

High-leverage point An observation of an independent variable that has an extreme value and is potentially influential.

Highest and best use The concept that the best use of a vacant site is the use that would result in the highest value for the land. Presumably, the developer that could earn the highest risk-adjusted profit based on time, effort, construction and development cost, leasing, and exit value would be the one to pay the highest price for the land.

Historical exchange rates For accounting purposes, the exchange rates that existed when the assets and liabilities were initially recorded.

Historical scenario analysis A technique for exploring the performance and risk of investment strategies in different structural regimes.

Historical simulation A simulation method that uses past return data and a random number generator that picks observations from the historical series to simulate an asset's future returns.

Historical simulation method The application of historical price changes to the current portfolio.

Historical stress testing The process that tests how investment strategies would perform under some of the most negative (i.e., adverse) combinations of events and scenarios.

Ho–Lee model The first arbitrage-free term structure model. The model is calibrated to market data and uses a binomial lattice approach to generate a distribution of possible future interest rates.

Holdout samples Data samples that are not used to train a model.

Homoskedasticity The property of having a constant variance; refers to an error term that is constant across observations.

Horizontal ownership Companies with mutual business interests (e.g., key customers or suppliers) that have cross-holding share arrangements with each other.

Human capital An implied asset; the net present value of an investor's future expected labor income weighted by the probability of surviving to each future age. Also called *net employment capital*.

Hybrid approach With respect to forecasting, an approach that combines elements of both top-down and bottom-up analyses.

Hyperparameter A parameter whose value must be set by the researcher before learning begins.

iNAVs "Indicated" net asset values are intraday "fair value" estimates of an ETF share based on its creation basket.

ISDA Master Agreement A standard or "master" agreement published by the International Swaps and Derivatives Association. The master agreement establishes the terms for each party involved in the transaction.

I-spreads Shortened form of "interpolated spreads" and a reference to a linearly interpolated yield.

Idiosyncratic risk premium (IRP) The additional return required for bearing company-specific risks.

Illiquidity discount A reduction or discount to value that reflects the lack of depth of trading or liquidity in that asset's market.

Impairment Diminishment in value as a result of carrying (book) value exceeding fair value and/or recoverable value.

Impairment of capital rule A legal restriction that dividends cannot exceed retained earnings.

Implementation shortfall (IS) The difference between the return for a notional or paper portfolio, where all transactions are assumed to take place at the manager's decision price, and the portfolio's actual return, which reflects realized transactions, including all fees and costs.

Implied volatility The standard deviation that causes an option pricing model to give the current option price.

Glossary

In-sample forecast errors The residuals from a fitted time-series model within the sample period used to fit the model.

Income approach A valuation approach that values an asset as the present discounted value of the income expected from it. In the context of real estate, this approach estimates the value of a property based on an expected rate of return. The estimated value is the present value of the expected future income from the property, including proceeds from resale at the end of a typical investment holding period.

Incremental borrowing rate (IBR) The rate of interest that the lessee would have to pay to borrow using a collateralized loan over the same term as a lease.

Incremental VaR (IVaR) A measure of the incremental effect of an asset on the VaR of a portfolio by measuring the difference between the portfolio's VaR while including a specified asset and the portfolio's VaR with that asset eliminated.

Indenture A written contract between a lender and borrower that specifies the terms of the loan, such as interest rate, interest payment schedule, or maturity.

Independent board directors Directors with no material relationship with the company with regard to employment, ownership, or remuneration.

Independent regulators Regulators recognized and granted authority by a government body or agency. They are not government agencies per se and typically do not rely on government funding.

Index CDS A type of credit default swap that involves a combination of borrowers.

Industry risk premium (IP) The additional return that is required to bear industry -specific risk.

Industry shocks Unexpected changes to an industry from regulations or the legal environment, technology, or changes in the growth rate of the industry.

Industry structure An industry's underlying economic and technical characteristics.

Influence plot A visual that shows, for all observations, studentized residuals on the y-axis, leverage on the x-axis, and Cook's D as circles whose size is proportional to the degree of influence of the given observation.

Influential observation An observation in a statistical analysis whose inclusion may significantly alter regression results.

Information gain A metric which quantifies the amount of information that the feature holds about the response. Information gain can be regarded as a form of non-linear correlation between Y and X.

Information ratio (IR) Mean active return divided by active risk; or alpha divided by the standard deviation of diversifiable risk.

Informational frictions Forces that restrict availability, quality, and/or flow of information and its use.

Inside ask See *best ask*.

Inside bid See *best bid*.

Inside spread The spread between the best bid price and the best ask price. Also called the *market bid-ask spread*, *inside bid-ask spread*, or *market spread*.

Insiders Corporate managers and board directors who are also shareholders of a company.

Intangible assets Assets without a physical form, such as patents and trademarks.

Inter-temporal rate of substitution The ratio of the marginal utility of consumption s periods in the future (the numerator) to the marginal utility of consumption today (the denominator).

Interaction term A term that combines two or more variables and represents their joint influence on the dependent variable.

Intercept dummy An indicator variable that allows a single regression model to estimate two lines of best fit, each with differing intercepts, depending on whether the dummy takes a value of 1 or 0.

Interest rate risk The risk that interest rates will rise and therefore the market value of current portfolio holdings will fall so that their current yields to maturity then match comparable instruments in the marketplace.

Interlocking directorates Corporate structure in which individuals serve on the board of directors of multiple corporations.

International CAPM (ICAPM) A two-factor model with a global index and a wealth-weighted currency index.

International Fisher effect The proposition that nominal interest rate differentials across currencies are determined by expected inflation differentials.

Intrinsic value The amount gained (per unit) by an option buyer if an option is exercised at any given point in time. May be referred to as the exercise value of the option.

Inverse price ratio The reciprocal of a price multiple—for example, in the case of a P/E, the "earnings yield" E/P (where P is share price and E is earnings per share).

Investment value The value to a specific buyer, taking account of potential synergies based on the investor's requirements and expectations.

Joint test of hypotheses The test of hypotheses that specify values for two or more independent variables in the hypotheses.

Joint venture Two or more companies form and control a new, separate company to achieve a business objective. Each participant contributes assets, employees, know-how, or other resources to the joint venture company. The participants maintain their independence otherwise and continue to do business apart from the joint venture, but they share in the joint venture's profits or losses.

Judicial law Interpretations of courts.

Justified price multiple The estimated fair value of the price multiple, usually based on forecasted fundamentals or comparables.

Justified (fundamental) P/E The price-to-earnings ratio that is fair, warranted, or justified on the basis of forecasted fundamentals.

K-fold cross-validation A technique in which data (excluding test sample and fresh data) are shuffled randomly and then are divided into k equal sub-samples, with $k - 1$ samples used as training samples and one sample, the kth, used as a validation sample.

K-means A clustering algorithm that repeatedly partitions observations into a fixed number, k, of non-overlapping clusters.

K-nearest neighbor A supervised learning technique that classifies a new observation by finding similarities ("nearness") between this new observation and the existing data.

Kalotay–Williams–Fabozzi (KWF) model An arbitrage-free term structure model that describes the dynamics of the log of the short rate and assumes constant drift, no mean reversion, and constant volatility.

Key rate durations Sensitivity of a bond's price to changes in specific maturities on the benchmark yield curve. Also called *partial durations*.

kth-order autocorrelation The correlation between observations in a time series separated by k periods.

LASSO Least absolute shrinkage and selection operator is a type of penalized regression which involves minimizing the sum of the absolute values of the regression coefficients. LASSO can also be used for regularization in neural networks.

Labeled dataset A dataset that contains matched sets of observed inputs or features (X's) and the associated output or target (Y).

Labor force Everyone of working age (ages 16 to 64) who either is employed or is available for work but not working.

Labor force participation rate The percentage of the working age population that is in the labor force.

Labor productivity The quantity of goods and services (real GDP) that a worker can produce in one hour of work.

Labor productivity growth accounting equation States that potential GDP growth equals the growth rate of the labor input plus the growth rate of labor productivity.

Lack of marketability discount An extra return to investors to compensate for lack of a public market or lack of marketability.

Latency The elapsed time between the occurrence of an event and a subsequent action that depends on that event.

Law of one price A principle that states that if two investments have the same or equivalent future cash flows regardless of what will happen in the future, then these two investments should have the same current price.

Leading dividend yield Forecasted dividends per share over the next year divided by current stock price.

Leading P/E A P/E calculated on the basis of a forecast of EPS; a stock's current price divided by next year's expected earnings.

Learning curve A curve that plots the accuracy rate (= 1 − error rate) in the validation or test samples (i.e., out-of-sample) against the amount of data in the training sample, which is thus useful for describing under- and overfitting as a function of bias and variance errors.

Learning rate A parameter that affects the magnitude of adjustments in the weights in a neural network.

Level One of the three factors (the other two are steepness and curvature) that empirically explain most yield curve shape changes. A shock to the level factor changes the yield for all maturities by an almost identical amount.

Leverage A measure for identifying a potentially influential high-leverage point.

Leveraged buyout (LBO) An acquirer (typically an investment fund specializing in LBOs) uses a significant amount of debt to finance the acquisition of a target and then pursues restructuring actions, with the goal of exiting the target with a sale or public listing.

Libor–OIS spread The difference between Libor and the overnight indexed swap rate.

Likelihood ratio (LR) test A method to assess the fit of logistic regression models and is based on the log-likelihood metric that describes the model's fit to the data.

Limit order book The book or list of limit orders to buy and sell that pertains to a security.

Linear classifier A binary classifier that makes its classification decision based on a linear combination of the features of each data point.

Linear trend A trend in which the dependent variable changes at a constant rate with time.

Liquidating dividend A dividend that is a return of capital rather than a distribution from earnings or retained earnings.

Liquidation value The value of a company if the company were dissolved and its assets sold individually.

Liquidity preference theory A term structure theory that asserts liquidity premiums exist to compensate investors for the added interest rate risk they face when lending long term.

Liquidity premium An extra return that compensates investors for the risk of loss relative to an investment's fair value if the investment needs to be converted to cash quickly.

Local currency The currency of the country where a company is located.

Local expectations theory A term structure theory that contends the return for all bonds over short periods is the risk-free rate.

Log-linear model With reference to time-series models, a model in which the growth rate of the time series as a function of time is constant.

Log odds The natural log of the odds of an event or characteristic happening. Also known as the *logit function*.

Logistic regression (logit) A regression in which the dependent variable uses a logistic transformation of the event probability.

Logistic transformation The log of the probability of an occurrence of an event or characteristic divided by the probability of the event or characteristic not occurring.

Long/short credit trade A credit protection seller with respect to one entity combined with a credit protection buyer with respect to another entity.

Look-ahead bias A bias caused by using information that was unavailable on the test date.

Lookback period The time period used to gather a historical data set.

Loss given default The amount that will be lost if a default occurs.

Macroeconomic factor model A multifactor model in which the factors are surprises in macroeconomic variables that significantly explain equity returns.

Macroeconomic factors Factors related to the economy, such as the inflation rate, industrial production, or economic sector membership.

Maintenance capital expenditures Capital expenditures needed to maintain operations at the current level.

Majority shareholders Shareholders that own more than 50% of a corporation's shares.

Majority-vote classifier A classifier that assigns to a new data point the predicted label with the most votes (i.e., occurrences).

Marginal VaR (MVaR) A measure of the effect of a small change in a position size on portfolio VaR.

Market approach Valuation approach that values an asset based on pricing multiples from sales of assets viewed as similar to the subject asset.

Market conditions Interest rates, inflation rates, and other economic characteristics that comprise the macroeconomic environment.

Market conversion premium per share For a convertible bond, the difference between the market conversion price and the underlying share price, which allows investors to identify the premium or discount payable when buying a convertible bond rather than the underlying common stock.

Glossary

Market conversion premium ratio   For a convertible bond, the market conversion premium per share expressed as a percentage of the current market price of the shares.

Market efficiency   A finance perspective on capital markets that deals with the relationship of price to intrinsic value. The traditional efficient markets formulation asserts that an asset's price is the best available estimate of its intrinsic value. The rational efficient markets formulation asserts that investors should expect to be rewarded for the costs of information gathering and analysis by higher gross returns.

Market fragmentation   Trading the same instrument in multiple venues.

Market impact   The effect of the trade on transaction prices. Also called *price impact*.

Market model   A regression model with the return on a stock as the dependent variable and the returns on a market index as the independent variable.

Market value of invested capital   The market value of debt and equity.

Mature growth rate   The earnings growth rate in a company's mature phase; an earnings growth rate that can be sustained long term.

Maximum drawdown   The worst cumulative loss ever sustained by an asset or portfolio. More specifically, maximum drawdown is the difference between an asset's or a portfolio's maximum cumulative return and its subsequent lowest cumulative return.

Maximum likelihood estimation (MLE)   A method that estimates values for the intercept and slope coefficients in a logistic regression that make the data in the regression sample most likely.

Mean reversion   The tendency of a time series to fall when its level is above its mean and rise when its level is below its mean; a mean-reverting time series tends to return to its long-term mean.

Metadata   Data that describes and gives information about other data.

Method based on forecasted fundamentals   An approach to using price multiples that relates a price multiple to forecasts of fundamentals through a discounted cash flow model.

Method of comparables   An approach to valuation that involves using a price multiple to evaluate whether an asset is relatively fairly valued, relatively undervalued, or relatively overvalued when compared to a benchmark value of the multiple.

Midquote price   The average, or midpoint, of the prevailing bid and ask prices.

Minority interest   The proportion of the ownership of a subsidiary not held by the parent (controlling) company.

Minority shareholders   Particular shareholders or a block of shareholders holding a small proportion of a company's outstanding shares, resulting in a limited ability to exercise control in voting activities.

Mispricing   Any departure of the market price of an asset from the asset's estimated intrinsic value.

Model specification   The set of independent variables included in a model and the model's functional form.

Molodovsky effect   The observation that P/Es tend to be high on depressed EPS at the bottom of a business cycle and tend to be low on unusually high EPS at the top of a business cycle.

Momentum indicators   Valuation indicators that relate either price or a fundamental (such as earnings) to the time series of their own past values (or in some cases to their expected value).

Monetary assets and liabilities   Assets and liabilities with value equal to the amount of currency contracted for, a fixed amount of currency. Examples are cash, accounts receivable, accounts payable, bonds payable, and mortgages payable. Inventory is not a monetary asset. Most liabilities are monetary.

Monetary/non-monetary method   Approach to translating foreign currency financial statements for consolidation in which monetary assets and liabilities are translated at the current exchange rate. Non-monetary assets and liabilities are translated at historical exchange rates (the exchange rates that existed when the assets and liabilities were acquired).

Monetizing   Unwinding a position to either capture a gain or realize a loss.

Monte Carlo simulation   A technique that uses the inverse transformation method for converting a randomly generated uniformly distributed number into a simulated value of a random variable of a desired distribution. Each key decision variable in a Monte Carlo simulation requires an assumed statistical distribution; this assumption facilitates incorporating non-normality, fat tails, and tail dependence as well as solving high-dimensionality problems.

Mortgage   A loan with real estate serving as collateral for the loan.

Multicollinearity   When two or more independent variables are highly correlated with one another or are approximately linearly related.

Multiple linear regression   Modeling and estimation method that uses two or more independent variables to describe the variation of the dependent variable. Also referred to as *multiple regression*.

Mutual information   Measures how much information is contributed by a token to a class of texts. MI will be 0 if the token's distribution in all text classes is the same. MI approaches 1 as the token in any one class tends to occur more often in only that particular class of text.

N-grams   A representation of word sequences. The length of a sequence varies from 1 to n. When one word is used, it is a unigram; a two-word sequence is a bigram; and a 3-word sequence is a trigram; and so on.

n-Period moving average   The average of the current and immediately prior $n - 1$ values of a time series.

NTM P/E   Next 12-month P/E: current market price divided by an estimated next 12-month EPS.

Naked credit default swap   A position where the owner of the CDS does not have a position in the underlying credit.

Name entity recognition   An algorithm that analyzes individual tokens and their surrounding semantics while referring to its dictionary to tag an object class to the token.

Negative serial correlation   A situation in which residuals are negatively related to other residuals.

Nested models   Models in which one regression model has a subset of the independent variables of another regression model.

Net asset balance sheet exposure   When assets translated at the current exchange rate are greater in amount than liabilities translated at the current exchange rate. Assets exposed to translation gains or losses exceed the exposed liabilities.

Net asset value per share (NAVPS)   Net asset value divided by the number of shares outstanding.

Net lease   A lease under which the tenant pays a net rent to the landlord and an additional amount based on the tenant's pro rata share of the operating costs, utilities, maintenance expenses, and real estate taxes relating to the property.

Net liability balance sheet exposure   When liabilities translated at the current exchange rate are greater assets translated at the current exchange rate. Liabilities exposed to translation gains or losses exceed the exposed assets.

Net operating income (NOI)   Gross rental revenue minus operating costs but before deducting depreciation, corporate overhead, and interest expense. In the context of real estate, a measure of the income from the property after deducting operating expenses for such items as property taxes, insurance, maintenance, utilities, repairs, and insurance but before deducting any costs associated with financing and before deducting federal income taxes. It is similar to EBITDA in a financial reporting context.

Net regulatory burden   The private costs of regulation less the private benefits of regulation.

Network externalities   The impact that users of a good, a service, or a technology have on other users of that product; it can be positive (e.g., a critical mass of users makes a product more useful) or negative (e.g., congestion makes the product less useful).

Neural networks   Computer programs based on how our own brains learn and process information.

No-arbitrage approach   A procedure for obtaining the value of an option based on the creation of a portfolio that replicates the payoffs of the option and deriving the option value from the value of the replicating portfolio.

No-growth company   A company without positive expected net present value projects.

No-growth value per share   The value per share of a no-growth company, equal to the expected level amount of earnings divided by the stock's required rate of return.

Non-cash rent   An amount equal to the difference between the average contractual rent over a lease term (the straight-line rent) and the cash rent actually paid during a period. This figure is one of the deductions made from FFO to calculate AFFO.

Non-convergence trap   A situation in which a country remains relatively poor, or even falls further behind, because it fails to implement necessary institutional reforms and/or adopt leading technologies.

Non-monetary assets and liabilities   Assets and liabilities that are not monetary assets and liabilities. Non-monetary assets include inventory, fixed assets, and intangibles, and non-monetary liabilities include deferred revenue.

Non-renewable resources   Finite resources that are depleted once they are consumed; oil and coal are examples.

Non-residential properties   Commercial real estate properties other than multi-family properties, farmland, and timberland.

Nonearning assets   Cash and investments (specifically cash, cash equivalents, and short-term investments).

Normal EPS   The EPS that a business could achieve currently under mid-cyclical conditions. Also called *normalized EPS.*

Normal Q-Q plot   A visual used to compare the distribution of the residuals from a regression to a theoretical normal distribution.

Normalized EPS   The EPS that a business could achieve currently under mid-cyclical conditions. Also called *normal EPS.*

Normalized earnings   The expected level of mid-cycle earnings for a company in the absence of any unusual or temporary factors that affect profitability (either positively or negatively).

Normalized P/E   P/E based on normalized EPS data.

Notional amount   The amount of protection being purchased in a CDS.

Off-the-run   A series of securities or indexes that were issued/created prior to the most recently issued/created series.

Offshoring   Refers to relocating operations from one country to another, mainly to reduce costs through lower labor costs or to achieve economies of scale through centralization, but still maintaining operations within the corporation.

Omitted variable bias   Bias resulting from the omission of an important independent variable from a regression model.

On-the-run   The most recently issued and most actively traded sovereign securities.

One hot encoding   The process by which categorical variables are converted into binary form (0 or 1) for machine reading. It is one of the most common methods for handling categorical features in text data.

One-sided durations   Effective durations when interest rates go up or down, which are better at capturing the interest rate sensitivity of bonds with embedded options that do not react symmetrically to positive and negative changes in interest rates of the same magnitude.

One-tier board   Board structure consisting of a single board of directors, composed of executive (internal) and non-executive (external) directors.

Opportunity cost   Reflects the foregone opportunity of investing in a different asset. It is typically denoted by the risk-free rate of interest, r.

Option-adjusted spread   (OAS) Constant spread that, when added to all the one-period forward rates on the interest rate tree, makes the arbitrage-free value of the bond equal to its market price.

Orderly liquidation value   The estimated gross amount of money that could be realized from the liquidation sale of an asset or assets, given a reasonable amount of time to find a purchaser or purchasers.

Other comprehensive income   Items of comprehensive income that are not reported on the income statement; comprehensive income minus net income.

Other post-employment benefits   Promises by the company to pay benefits in the future, such as life insurance premiums and all or part of health care insurance for its retirees.

Out-of-sample forecast errors   The differences between actual and predicted values of time series outside the sample period used to fit the model.

Outlier   An observation that has an extreme value of the dependent variable and is potentially influential.

Outsourcing   Shifting internal business services to a subcontractor that can offer services at lower costs by scaling to serve many clients.

Overfitting   Situation in which the model has too many independent variables relative to the number of observations in the sample, such that the coefficients on the independent variables represent noise rather than relationships with the dependent variable.

Overnight indexed swap (OIS) rate An interest rate swap in which the periodic floating rate of the swap equals the geometric average of a daily unsecured overnight rate (or overnight index rate).

PEG ratio The P/E-to-growth ratio, calculated as the stock's P/E divided by the expected earnings growth rate.

Pairs trading An approach to trading that uses pairs of closely related stocks, buying the relatively undervalued stock and selling short the relatively overvalued stock.

Par curve A sequence of yields-to-maturity such that each bond is priced at par value. The bonds are assumed to have the same currency, credit risk, liquidity, tax status, and annual yields stated for the same periodicity.

Par swap A swap in which the fixed rate is set so that no money is exchanged at contract initiation.

Parametric method A method of estimating VaR that uses the historical mean, standard deviation, and correlation of security price movements to estimate the portfolio VaR. Generally assumes a normal distribution but can be adapted to non-normal distributions with the addition of skewness and kurtosis. Sometimes called the *variance–covariance method* or the *analytical method*.

Partial regression coefficient Coefficient that describes the effect of a one-unit change in the independent variable on the dependent variable, holding all other independent variables constant. Also known as *partial slope coefficient*.

Parts of speech An algorithm that uses language structure and dictionaries to tag every token in the text with a corresponding part of speech (i.e., noun, verb, adjective, proper noun, etc.).

Payout amount The loss given default times the notional.

Payout policy The principles by which a company distributes cash to common shareholders by means of cash dividends and/or share repurchases.

Payouts Cash dividends and the value of shares repurchased in any given year.

Penalized regression A regression that includes a constraint such that the regression coefficients are chosen to minimize the sum of squared residuals *plus* a penalty term that increases in size with the number of included features.

Pension obligation The present value of future benefits earned by employees for service provided to date.

Perfect capital markets Markets in which, by assumption, there are no taxes, transaction costs, or bankruptcy costs and in which all investors have equal ("symmetric") information.

Perpetuity A perpetual annuity, or a set of never-ending level sequential cash flows, with the first cash flow occurring one period from now.

Persistent earnings Earnings excluding nonrecurring components. Also referred to as *core earnings*, *continuing earnings*, or *underlying earnings*.

Physical settlement Involves actual delivery of the debt instrument in exchange for a payment by the credit protection seller of the notional amount of the contract.

Point-in-time data Data consisting of the exact information available to market participants as of a given point in time. Point-in-time data is used to address look-ahead bias.

Portfolio balance approach A theory of exchange rate determination that emphasizes the portfolio investment decisions of global investors and the requirement that global investors willingly hold all outstanding securities denominated in each currency at prevailing prices and exchange rates.

Positive serial correlation A situation in which residuals are positively related to other residuals.

Potential GDP The maximum amount of output an economy can sustainably produce without inducing an increase in the inflation rate. The output level that corresponds to full employment with consistent wage and price expectations.

Precision In error analysis for classification problems it is ratio of correctly predicted positive classes to all predicted positive classes. Precision is useful in situations where the cost of false positives (FP), or Type I error, is high.

Preferred habitat theory A term structure theory that contends that investors have maturity preferences and require yield incentives before they will buy bonds outside of their preferred maturities.

Premise of value The status of a company in the sense of whether it is assumed to be a going concern or not.

Premium leg The series of payments the credit protection buyer promises to make to the credit protection seller.

Premiums Amounts paid by the purchaser of insurance products.

Present value model A model of intrinsic value that views the value of an asset as the present value of the asset's expected future cash flows.

Present value of growth opportunities The difference between the actual value per share and the no-growth value per share. Also called *value of growth*.

Presentation currency The currency in which financial statement amounts are presented.

Price improvement When trade execution prices are better than quoted prices.

Price momentum A valuation indicator based on past price movement.

Price multiples The ratio of a stock's market price to some measure of value per share.

Price-to-earnings ratio (P/E) The ratio of share price to earnings per share.

Priced risk Risk for which investors demand compensation for bearing (e.g., equity risk, company-specific factors, macroeconomic factors).

Principal components analysis (PCA) An unsupervised ML technique used to transform highly correlated features of data into a few main, uncorrelated composite variables.

Principle of no arbitrage In well-functioning markets, prices will adjust until there are no arbitrage opportunities.

Prior transaction method A variation of the market approach; considers actual transactions in the stock of the subject private company.

Private market value The value derived using a sum-of-the-parts valuation.

Pro forma financial statements Financial statements that include the effect of a corporate restructuring.

Probability of default The likelihood that a borrower defaults or fails to meet its obligation to make full and timely payments of principal and interest.

Probability of survival The probability that a bond issuer will meet its contractual obligations on schedule.

Procedural law The body of law that focuses on the protection and enforcement of the substantive laws.

Projection error The vertical (perpendicular) distance between a data point and a given principal component.

Prospective P/E A P/E calculated on the basis of a forecast of EPS; a stock's current price divided by next year's expected earnings.

Protection leg The contingent payment that the credit protection seller may have to make to the credit protection buyer.

Protection period Period during which a bond's issuer cannot call the bond.

Provision for loan losses An income statement expense account that increases the amount of the allowance for loan losses.

Prudential supervision Regulation and monitoring of the safety and soundness of financial institutions to promote financial stability, reduce system-wide risks, and protect customers of financial institutions.

Pruning A regularization technique used in CART to reduce the size of the classification or regression tree—by pruning, or removing, sections of the tree that provide little classifying power.

Purchasing power gain A gain in value caused by changes in price levels. Monetary liabilities experience purchasing power gains during periods of inflation.

Purchasing power loss A loss in value caused by changes in price levels. Monetary assets experience purchasing power loss during periods of inflation.

Purchasing power parity (PPP) The idea that exchange rates move to equalize the purchasing power of different currencies.

Pure expectations theory A term structure theory that contends the forward rate is an unbiased predictor of the future spot rate. Also called the *unbiased expectations theory*.

Pure factor portfolio A portfolio with sensitivity of 1 to the factor in question and a sensitivity of 0 to all other factors.

Putable bond Bond that includes an embedded put option, which gives the bondholder the right to put back the bonds to the issuer prior to maturity, typically when interest rates have risen and higher-yielding bonds are available.

Qualitative dependent variable A dependent variable that is discrete (binary). Also known as a *categorical dependent variable*.

Quality of earnings analysis The investigation of issues relating to the accuracy of reported accounting results as reflections of economic performance. Quality of earnings analysis is broadly understood to include not only earnings management but also balance sheet management.

Random forest classifier A collection of a large number of decision trees trained via a bagging method.

Random walk A time series in which the value of the series in one period is the value of the series in the previous period plus an unpredictable random error.

Rate implicit in the lease (RIIL) The discount rate that equates the present value of the lease payment with the fair value of the leased asset, considering also the lessor's direct costs and the present value of the leased asset's residual value.

Rational efficient markets formulation See *market efficiency*.

Readme files Text files provided with raw data that contain information related to a data file. They are useful for understanding the data and how they can be interpreted correctly.

Real estate investment trusts (REITs) Tax-advantaged entities (companies or trusts) that own, operate, and—to a limited extent—develop income-producing real estate property.

Real estate operating companies (REOCs) Regular taxable real estate ownership companies that operate in the real estate industry in countries that do not have a tax-advantaged REIT regime in place or that are engage in real estate activities of a kind and to an extent that do not fit in their country's REIT framework.

Real interest rate parity The proposition that real interest rates will converge to the same level across different markets.

Real options Options that relate to investment decisions such as the option to time the start of a project, the option to adjust its scale, or the option to abandon a project that has begun.

Rebalance return A return from rebalancing the component weights of an index.

Recall Also known as *sensitivity*, in error analysis for classification problems it is the ratio of correctly predicted positive classes to all actual positive classes. Recall is useful in situations where the cost of false negatives (FN), or Type II error, is high.

Recency bias The behavioral tendency to place more relevance on recent events.

Reconstitution When dealers recombine appropriate individual zero-coupon securities and reproduce an underlying coupon Treasury.

Recovery rate The percentage of the loss recovered.

Redemption basket The list of securities (and share amounts) the authorized participant (AP) receives when it redeems ETF shares back to the ETF manager. The redemption basket is published each business day.

Reference entity The borrower (debt issuer) covered by a single-name CDS.

Reference obligation A particular debt instrument issued by the borrower that is the designated instrument being covered.

Regime With reference to a time series, the underlying model generating the times series.

Regular expression (regex) A series of texts that contains characters in a particular order. Regex is used to search for patterns of interest in a given text.

Regularization A term that describes methods for reducing statistical variability in high-dimensional data estimation problems.

Regulatory arbitrage Entities identify and use some aspect of regulations that allows them to exploit differences in economic substance and regulatory interpretation or in foreign and domestic regulatory regimes to their (the entities') advantage.

Regulatory burden The costs of regulation for the regulated entity.

Regulatory capture Theory that regulation often arises to enhance the interests of the regulated.

Regulatory competition Regulators may compete to provide a regulatory environment designed to attract certain entities.

Reinforcement learning Machine learning in which a computer learns from interacting with itself or data generated by the same algorithm.

Relative-strength indicators Valuation indicators that compare a stock's performance during a period either to its own past performance or to the performance of some group of stocks.

Relative VaR See *ex ante tracking error*.

Relative valuation models A model that specifies an asset's value relative to the value of another asset.

Relative version of PPP The hypothesis that changes in (nominal) exchange rates over time are equal to national inflation rate differentials.

Renewable resources Resources that can be replenished, such as a forest.

Rental price of capital The cost per unit of time to rent a unit of capital.

Glossary

Reorganization A court-supervised restructuring process available in some jurisdictions for companies facing insolvency from burdensome debt levels. A bankruptcy court assumes control of the company and oversees an orderly negotiation process between the company and its creditors for asset sales, conversion of debt to equity, refinancing, and so on.

Repeat sales index As the name implies, this type of index relies on repeat sales of the same property. In general, the idea supporting this type of index is that because it is the same property that sold twice, the change in value between the two sale dates indicates how market conditions have changed over time.

Replacement cost In the context of real estate, the value of a building assuming it was built today using current construction costs and standards.

Reporting unit For financial reporting under US GAAP, an operating segment or one level below an operating segment (referred to as a component).

Required rate of return on equity The minimum rate of return required by an investor to invest in an asset, given the asset's riskiness. Also known as the required return on equity.

Residential properties Properties that provide housing for individuals or families. Single-family properties may be owner-occupied or rental properties, whereas multi-family properties are rental properties even if the owner or manager occupies one of the units.

Residual autocorrelations The sample autocorrelations of the residuals.

Residual income Earnings for a given period, minus a deduction for common shareholders' opportunity cost in generating the earnings. Also called *economic profit* or *abnormal earnings*.

Residual income method Income approach that estimates the value of all intangible assets of the business by capitalizing future earnings in excess of the estimated return requirements associated with working capital and fixed assets.

Residual income model (RIM) A model of stock valuation that views intrinsic value of stock as the sum of book value per share plus the present value of the stock's expected future residual income per share. Also called *discounted abnormal earnings model* or *Edwards–Bell–Ohlson model*.

Restricted model A regression model with a subset of the complete set of independent variables.

Restructuring Reorganizing the capital structure of a firm.

Return on invested capital A measure of the profitability of a company relative to the amount of capital invested by the equity- and debtholders.

Reverse carry arbitrage A strategy involving the short sale of the underlying and an offsetting opposite position in the derivative.

Reverse stock split A reduction in the number of shares outstanding with a corresponding increase in share price, but no change to the company's underlying fundamentals.

Reverse stress testing A risk management approach in which the user identifies key risk exposures in the portfolio and subjects those exposures to extreme market movements.

Reviewed financial statements A type of non-audited financial statements; typically provide an opinion letter with representations and assurances by the reviewing accountant that are less than those in audited financial statements.

Rho The change in a given derivative instrument for a given small change in the risk-free interest rate, holding everything else constant. Rho measures the sensitivity of the option to the risk-free interest rate.

Risk-based models Models of the return on equity that identify risk factors or drivers and sensitivities of the return to these factors.

Risk budgeting The establishment of objectives for individuals, groups, or divisions of an organization that takes into account the allocation of an acceptable level of risk.

Risk decomposition The process of converting a set of holdings in a portfolio into a set of exposures to risk factors.

Risk factors Variables or characteristics with which individual asset returns are correlated. Sometimes referred to simply as *factors*.

Risk-free rate The minimum rate of return expected on a security that has no default risk.

Risk parity A portfolio allocation scheme that weights stocks or factors based on an equal risk contribution.

Robust standard errors Method for correcting residuals for conditional heteroskedasticity. Also known as *heteroskedasticity-consistent standard errors* or *White-corrected standard errors*.

Roll When an investor moves its investment position from an older series to the most current series.

Roll return The component of the return on a commodity futures contract attributable to rolling long futures positions forward through time. Also called *roll yield*.

Rolling down the yield curve A maturity trading strategy that involves buying bonds with a maturity longer than the intended investment horizon. Also called *riding the yield curve*.

Rolling windows A backtesting method that uses a rolling-window (or walk-forward) framework, rebalances the portfolio after each period, and then tracks performance over time. As new information arrives each period, the investment manager optimizes (revises and tunes) the model and readjusts stock positions.

Root mean squared error (RMSE) The square root of the average squared forecast error; used to compare the out-of-sample forecasting performance of forecasting models.

Sale-leaseback A situation in which a company sells the building it owns and occupies to a real estate investor and the company then signs a long-term lease with the buyer to continue to occupy the building. At the end of the lease, use of the property reverts to the landlord.

Sales comparison approach In the context of real estate, this approach estimates value based on what similar or comparable properties (comparables) transacted for in the current market.

Sales risk The uncertainty regarding the price and number of units sold of a company's products.

Scaled earnings surprise Unexpected earnings divided by the standard deviation of analysts' earnings forecasts.

Scaling The process of adjusting the range of a feature by shifting and changing the scale of the data. Two of the most common ways of scaling are normalization and standardization.

Scatterplot matrix A visualization technique that shows the scatterplots between different sets of variables, often with the histogram for each variable on the diagonal. Also referred to as a *pairs plot*.

Scenario analysis A technique for exploring the performance and risk of investment strategies in different structural regimes.

Schwarz's Bayesian information criterion (BIC or SBC) A statistic used to compare sets of independent variables for explaining a dependent variable. It is preferred for finding the model with the best goodness of fit.

Scree plots A plot that shows the proportion of total variance in the data explained by each principal component.

Screening The application of a set of criteria to reduce a set of potential investments to a smaller set having certain desired characteristics.

Seasonality A characteristic of a time series in which the data experience regular and predictable periodic changes; for example, fan sales are highest during the summer months.

Secured overnight financing rate (SOFR) A daily volume-weighted index of rates on qualified cash borrowings collateralized by US Treasuries that is expected to replace Libor as a floating reference rate for swaps.

Security selection risk See *active specific risk*.

Segmented markets theory A term structure theory that contends yields are solely a function of the supply and demand for funds of a particular maturity.

Self-regulating organizations (SROs) Self-regulating bodies that are given recognition and authority, including enforcement power, by a government body or agency.

Self-regulatory bodies Private, non-governmental organizations that both represent and regulate their members. Some self-regulating organizations are also independent regulators.

Sell-side analysts Analysts who work at brokerages.

Sensitivity analysis Analysis that shows the range of possible outcomes as specific assumptions are changed.

Sentence length The number of characters, including spaces, in a sentence.

Serial correlation A condition found most often in time series in which residuals are correlated across observations. Also known as *autocorrelation*.

Serial-correlation consistent standard errors Method for correcting serial correlation. Also known as *serial correlation and heteroskedasticity adjusted standard errors*, *Newey–West standard errors*, and *robust standard errors*.

Service period For employee stock options, usually the period between the grant date and the vesting date.

Settled in arrears An arrangement in which the interest payment is made (i.e., settlement occurs) at the maturity of the underlying instrument.

Settlement The closing date at which the counterparties of a derivative contract exchange payment for the underlying as required by the contract.

Shadow banking Lending by financial institutions that are not regulated as banks.

Shaping risk The sensitivity of a bond's price to the changing shape of the yield curve.

Share repurchase A transaction in which a company buys back its own shares. Unlike stock dividends and stock splits, share repurchases use corporate cash.

Shareholder activism Strategies used by shareholders to attempt to compel a company to act in a desired manner.

Shareholders' equity Total assets minus total liabilities.

Simulation A technique for exploring how a target variable (e.g. portfolio returns) would perform in a hypothetical environment specified by the user, rather than a historical setting.

Single-name CDS Credit default swap on one specific borrower.

Sinking fund bond A bond that requires the issuer to set aside funds over time to retire the bond issue, thus reducing credit risk.

Size premium (SP) Additional return compensation for bearing the additional risk associated with smaller companies.

Slope dummy An indicator variable that allows a single regression model to estimate two lines of best fit, each with differing slopes, depending on whether the dummy takes a value of 1 or 0.

Soft margin classification An adaptation in the support vector machine algorithm which adds a penalty to the objective function for observations in the training set that are misclassified.

Sovereign yield spread The spread between the yield on a foreign country's sovereign bond and a similar-maturity domestic sovereign bond.

Special dividend A dividend paid by a company that does not pay dividends on a regular schedule, or a dividend that supplements regular cash dividends with an extra payment.

Specific-company risk premium (SCRP) Additional return required by investors for bearing non-diversifiable company-specific risk.

Spin off When a company separates a distinct part of its business into a new, independent company. The term is used to describe both the transaction and the separated component, while the company that conducts the transaction and formerly owned the spin off is known as the parent.

Split-rate tax system In reference to corporate taxes, a split-rate system taxes earnings to be distributed as dividends at a different rate than earnings to be retained. Corporate profits distributed as dividends are taxed at a lower rate than those retained in the business.

Spot curve A sequence of yields-to-maturity on zero-coupon bonds. Sometimes called *zero* or *strip curve* (because coupon payments are "stripped" off the bonds).

Spot price The current price of an asset or security. For commodities, the current price to deliver a physical commodity to a specific location or purchase and transport it away from a designated location.

Spot rate The interest rate that is determined today for a risk-free, single-unit payment at a specified future date.

Spot yield curve The term structure of spot rates for loans made today.

Stabilized NOI In the context of real estate, the expected NOI when a renovation is complete.

Stable dividend policy A policy in which regular dividends are paid that reflect long-run expected earnings. In contrast to a constant dividend payout ratio policy, a stable dividend policy does not reflect short-term volatility in earnings.

Standardized beta With reference to fundamental factor models, the value of the attribute for an asset minus the average value of the attribute across all stocks, divided by the standard deviation of the attribute across all stocks.

Standardized unexpected earnings Unexpected earnings per share divided by the standard deviation of unexpected earnings per share over a specified prior time period.

Statistical factor model A multifactor model in which statistical methods are applied to a set of historical returns to determine portfolios that best explain either historical return covariances or variances.

Statutes Laws enacted by legislative bodies.

Steady-state rate of growth The constant growth rate of output (or output per capita) that can or will be sustained indefinitely once it is reached. Key ratios, such as the capital–output ratio, are constant on the steady-state growth path.

Steepness The difference between long-term and short-term yields that constitutes one of the three factors (the other two are level and curvature) that empirically explain most of the changes in the shape of the yield curve.

Stock dividend A type of dividend in which a company distributes additional shares of its common stock to shareholders instead of cash.

Stop-loss limit Constraint used in risk management that requires a reduction in the size of a portfolio, or its complete liquidation, when a loss of a particular size occurs in a specified period.

Straight bond An underlying option-free bond with a specified issuer, issue date, maturity date, principal amount and repayment structure, coupon rate and payment structure, and currency denomination.

Straight debt Debt with no embedded options.

Straight-line rent The average annual rent under a multi-year lease agreement that contains contractual increases in rent during the life of the lease.

Straight-line rent adjustment See *non-cash rent*.

Straight voting A shareholder voting process in which shareholders receive one vote for each share owned.

Stranded assets Assets that are obsolete or not economically viable.

Strategic transaction A purchase involving a buyer that would benefit from certain synergies associated with owning the target firm.

Stress tests A risk management technique that assesses the portfolio's response to extreme market movements.

Stripping A dealer's ability to separate a bond's individual cash flows and trade them as zero-coupon securities.

Studentized residual A t-distributed statistic that is used to detect outliers.

Substantive law The body of law that focuses on the rights and responsibilities of entities and relationships among entities.

Succession event A change of corporate structure of the reference entity, such as through a merger, a divestiture, a spinoff, or any similar action, in which ultimate responsibility for the debt in question is unclear.

Sum-of-the-parts valuation A valuation that sums the estimated values of each of a company's businesses as if each business were an independent going concern.

Summation operator A functional part of a neural network's node that multiplies each input value received by a weight and sums the weighted values to form the total net input, which is then passed to the activation function.

Supernormal growth Above-average or abnormally high growth rate in earnings per share.

Supervised learning A machine learning approach that makes use of labeled training data.

Support vector machine A linear classifier that determines the hyperplane that optimally separates the observations into two sets of data points.

Survivorship bias The exclusion of poorly performing or defunct companies from an index or database, biasing the index or database toward financially healthy companies.

Sustainable growth rate The rate of dividend (and earnings) growth that can be sustained over time for a given level of return on equity, keeping the capital structure constant and without issuing additional common stock.

Swap curve The term structure of swap rates.

Swap rate The fixed rate to be paid by the fixed-rate payer specified in a swap contract.

Swap rate curve The term structure of swap rates.

Swap spread The difference between the fixed rate on an interest rate swap and the rate on a Treasury note with equivalent maturity; it reflects the general level of credit risk in the market.

Synergies The combination of two companies being more valuable than the sum of the parts. Generally, synergies take the form of lower costs ("cost synergies") or increased revenues ("revenue synergies") through combinations that generate lower costs or higher revenues, respectively.

Systematic risk Risk that affects the entire market or economy; it cannot be avoided and is inherent in the overall market. Systematic risk is also known as non-diversifiable or market risk.

Systemic risk Refers to risks supervisory authorities believe are likely to have broad impact across the financial market infrastructure and affect a wide swath of market participants.

TED spread A measure of perceived credit risk determined as the difference between Libor and the T-bill yield of matching maturity.

Tail risk The risk that losses in extreme events could be greater than would be expected for a portfolio of assets with a normal distribution.

Takeover premium The amount by which the per-share takeover price exceeds the unaffected price expressed as a percentage of the unaffected price. It reflects the amount shareholders require to relinquish their control of the company to the acquirer.

Tangible assets Identifiable, physical assets such as property, plant, and equipment.

Tangible book value per share Common shareholders' equity minus intangible assets reported on the balance sheet, divided by the number of shares outstanding.

Target In machine learning, the dependent variable (Y) in a labeled dataset; the company in a merger or acquisition that is being acquired.

Target capital structure A company's chosen proportions of debt and equity.

Target payout ratio A strategic corporate goal representing the long-term proportion of earnings that the company intends to distribute to shareholders as dividends.

Taxable REIT subsidiaries Subsidiaries that pay income taxes on earnings from non-REIT-qualifying activities like merchant development or third-party property management.

Technical indicators Momentum indicators based on price.

Temporal method A variation of the monetary/non-monetary translation method that requires not only monetary assets and liabilities, but also non-monetary assets and liabilities that are measured at their current value on the balance sheet date to be translated at the current exchange rate. Assets and liabilities are translated at rates consistent with the timing of their measurement value. This method is typically used when the functional currency is other than the local currency.

Term frequency (TF) Ratio of the number of times a given token occurs in all the texts in the dataset to the total number of tokens in the dataset.

Term premium The additional return required by lenders to invest in a bond to maturity net of the expected return from continually reinvesting at the short-term rate over that same time horizon.

Terminal price multiples The price multiple for a stock assumed to hold at a stated future time.

Terminal share price The share price at a particular point in the future.

Terminal value of the stock The analyst's estimate of a stock's value at a particular point in the future. Also called *continuing value of the stock*.

Test sample A data sample that is used to test a model's ability to predict well on new data.

Theta The change in a derivative instrument for a given small change in calendar time, holding everything else constant. Specifically, the theta calculation assumes nothing changes except calendar time. Theta also reflects the rate at which an option's time value decays.

Time series A set of observations on a variable's outcomes in different time periods.

Tobin's q The ratio of the market value of debt and equity to the replacement cost of total assets.

Token The equivalent of a word (or sometimes a character).

Tokenization The process of representing ownership rights to physical assets on a blockchain or distributed ledger.

Top-down approach With respect to forecasting, an approach that usually begins at the level of the overall economy. Forecasts are then made at more narrowly defined levels, such as sector, industry, and market for a specific product.

Total factor productivity (TFP) A multiplicative scale factor that reflects the general level of productivity or technology in the economy. Changes in total factor productivity generate proportional changes in output for any input combination.

Total invested capital The sum of market value of common equity, book value of preferred equity, and face value of debt.

Tracking error The standard deviation of the differences between a portfolio's returns and its benchmark's returns; a synonym of *active risk*. Also called *tracking risk*.

Tracking risk The standard deviation of the differences between a portfolio's returns and its benchmarks returns. Also called *tracking error*.

Trailing dividend yield The reciprocal of current market price divided by the most recent annualized dividend.

Trailing P/E A stock's current market price divided by the most recent four quarters of EPS (or the most recent two semi-annual periods for companies that report interim data semi-annually). Also called *current P/E*.

Training sample A data sample that is used to train a model.

Tranche CDS A type of credit default swap that covers a combination of borrowers but only up to pre-specified levels of losses.

Transaction exposure The risk of a change in value between the transaction date and the settlement date of an asset of liability denominated in a foreign currency.

Treasury shares/stock Shares that were issued and subsequently repurchased by the company.

Trend A long-term pattern of movement in a particular direction.

Triangular arbitrage An arbitrage transaction involving three currencies that attempts to exploit inconsistencies among pairwise exchange rates.

Trimming Also called truncation, it is the process of removing extreme values and outliers from a dataset.

Triple-net leases Leases that require each tenant to pay its share of the following three operating expenses: common area maintenance and repair expenses; property taxes; and building insurance costs. Also known as *NNN leases*.

Two-tier board Board structure consisting of a supervisory board that oversees a management board.

Unbiased expectations theory A term structure theory that contends the forward rate is an unbiased predictor of the future spot rate. Also called the *pure expectations theory*.

Unconditional heteroskedasticity When heteroskedasticity of the error variance is not correlated with the regression's independent variables.

Uncovered interest rate parity The proposition that the expected return on an uncovered (i.e., unhedged) foreign currency (risk-free) investment should equal the return on a comparable domestic currency investment.

Underlying earnings Earnings excluding nonrecurring components. Also referred to as *continuing earnings*, *core earnings*, or *persistent earnings*.

Unexpected earnings The difference between reported EPS and expected EPS. Also referred to as an *earnings surprise*.

Unit root A time series that is not covariance stationary is said to have a unit root.

Unrestricted model A regression model with the complete set of independent variables.

Unsupervised learning A machine learning approach that does not make use of labeled training data.

Upfront payment The difference between the credit spread and the standard rate paid by the protection buyer if the standard rate is insufficient to compensate the protection seller. Also called *upfront premium*.

Upfront premium See *upfront payment*.

Upstream A transaction between two related companies, an investor company (or a parent company) and an associate company (or a subsidiary company) such that the associate company records a profit on its income statement. An example is a sale of inventory by the associate to the investor company or by a subsidiary to a parent company.

Validation sample A data sample that is used to validate and tune a model.

Valuation The process of determining the value of an asset or service either on the basis of variables perceived to be related to future investment returns or on the basis of comparisons with closely similar assets.

Value additivity An arbitrage opportunity when the value of the whole equals the sum of the values of the parts.

Value at risk (VaR) The minimum loss that would be expected a certain percentage of the time over a certain period of time given the assumed market conditions.

Value of growth The difference between the actual value per share and the no-growth value per share.

Variance error Describes how much a model's results change in response to new data from validation and test samples. Unstable models pick up noise and produce high variance error, causing overfitting and high out-of-sample error.

Variance inflation factor (VIF) A statistic that quantifies the degree of multicollinearity in a model.

Glossary

Vasicek model A partial equilibrium term structure model that assumes interest rates are mean reverting and interest rate volatility is constant.

Vega The change in a given derivative instrument for a given small change in volatility, holding everything else constant. A sensitivity measure for options that reflects the effect of volatility.

Venture capital investors Private equity investors in development-stage companies.

Vertical ownership Ownership structure in which a company or group that has a controlling interest in two or more holding companies, which in turn have controlling interests in various operating companies.

Vested benefit obligation The actuarial present value of vested benefits.

Vesting date The date that employees can first exercise stock options.

Visibility The extent to which a company's operations are predictable with substantial confidence.

Voting caps Legal restrictions on the voting rights of large share positions.

Web spidering (scraping or crawling) programs Programs that extract raw content from a source, typically web pages.

Weighted average cost of capital (WACC) A weighted average of the after-tax required rates of return on a company's common stock, preferred stock, and long-term debt, where the weights are the fraction of each source of financing in the company's target capital structure.

Weighted harmonic mean See *harmonic mean.*

Winsorization The process of replacing extreme values and outliers in a dataset with the maximum (for large value outliers) and minimum (for small value outliers) values of data points that are not outliers.

Write-down A reduction in the value of an asset as stated in the balance sheet.

Yield curve factor model A model or a description of yield curve movements that can be considered realistic when compared with historical data.

Zero A bond that does not pay a coupon but is priced at a discount and pays its full face value at maturity.

Zero-coupon bond A bond that does not pay interest during its life. It is issued at a discount to par value and redeemed at par. Also called *pure discount bond.*